W.H. Auden Encyclopedia

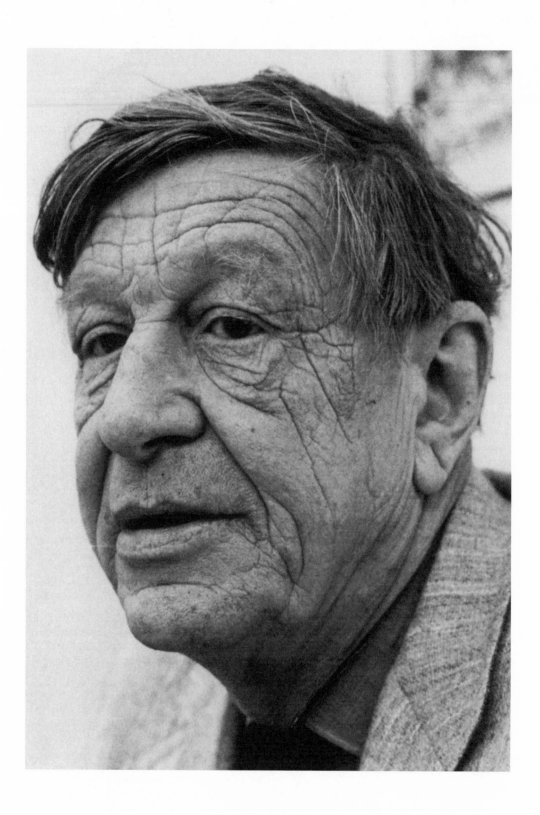

W. H. Auden Encyclopedia

DAVID GARRETT IZZO

McFarland & Company, Inc., Publishers
Jefferson, North Carolina, and London

ALSO BY DAVID GARRETT IZZO

The Writings of Richard Stern:
The Education of an Intellectual Everyman
(McFarland, 2002)

BY DAVID GARRETT IZZO AND LINCOLN KONKLE

Stephen Vincent Benét:
Essays on His Life and Work
(McFarland, 2003)

All excerpts from letters by W.H. Auden were previously published in critical and biographical studies of Auden and are reprinted here with the permission of the estate of W.H. Auden.

The postcard from Auden to Lloyd Frankenberg is reproduced with the permissions of the estate of W.H. Auden.

Frontispiece: W.H. Auden, 1965.

LIBRARY OF CONGRESS CATALOGUING-IN-PUBLICATION DATA

Izzo, David Garrett.
W.H. Auden Encyclopedia / David Garrett Izzo.
p.   cm.
Includes bibliographical references and index.

ISBN 0-7864-1443-X (illustrated case binding : 50# alkaline paper)

1. Auden, W.H. (Wystan Hugh), 1907–1973 — Encyclopedias.   2. Poets, English — 20th century — Biography — Encyclopedias.   3. British — United States — Biography — Encyclopedias.   I. Title.
PR6001.U4Z7518   2004   811'.52 — dc22   2003021127

British Library cataloguing data are available

On the cover: A 1940 photograph of W.H. Auden; *Background images ©2004 PhotoSpin*

Manufactured in the United States of America

McFarland & Company, Inc., Publishers
Box 611, Jefferson, North Carolina 28640
www.mcfarlandpub.com

To Carol Ann Corrody
and Edward Mendelson

Contents

Preface

The plan of this volume is to provide a self-contained reference resource that could introduce Auden to those who know little of him, expand Auden to the reader of literature in general, refresh Auden to teachers of literature, and serve Auden scholars who can quickly be reminded of people, places, poems, essays, plays, libretti, influences, and the myriad details that few — even Auden aficionados — can retain in that overburdened file cabinet called memory. I include myself as one who needs this book even though it is my third on Auden, for when memory is imperfect, I often find myself thumbing through numerous books for help with a name or date, or an influence on a poem or essay. This volume does not replace those books, but it does offer handy facts and summaries that one can supplement, if one so chooses, with the many books by and about Auden that are listed at the end of this volume.

One of the great pleasures of doing this Auden encyclopedia was that I was able to comprehensively indulge my fascination in knowing about his life and work. The process was a puzzle of referencing and cross-referencing over and over, detail after delightful detail. I hope that you will enjoy working out this puzzle as much as I enjoyed making it up.

I have also quoted from other Auden scholars to amplify numerous subjects in which they have demonstrated an especial expertise; indeed, some entries are written entirely by these experts and are included here with their permission and with their bylines: Robert Caserio, Paul Eros, James Young, Rod Jellema, Brian Conniff, Douglas Kerr, Peter Grosvenor, Piotr Gwiazda, Roger Lathbury, James Fisher, Christopher Hopkins, Adrienne Hacker-Daniels, Solveig Robinson, Robert Stanley, and Heather Clark. I also refer particularly to Humphrey Carpenter's biography of Auden and to Edward Mendelson's works on Auden, mainly his *Early Auden* and *Later Auden*. To all, I say thank you; in Mendelson's case, not only do I refer all readers to his books, I also cite him as the exemplar for how a literary executor can honor his trust to an author with dedication, diligence, and responsibility.

Introduction

He grew up in a household in which the scientific inquiries of his father maintained an uneasy truce with the ritualized religion of his mother.—Edward Mendelson

With this remark, Auden's literary executor and the leading Auden scholar has summed up the poet's life and explained the two periods now designated *Early Auden* and *Later Auden* as neatly as the diverging terms science and religion suggest. In the 1930s Auden looked for answers in science, psychology, sociology, politics, and art, but none of his varied and amalgamated means produced the ends he had hoped for—namely, no less than saving the world. (One can say that even in this immersion in the "pragmatic" solutions of the public sphere, he never strayed too far from the truth: that answers were lying dormant in the private sphere if only one could entice the answers to appear.) From 1939 forward he still sought to amalgamate his sources for answers, but he searched through different Christian spiritual theorists including Charles Williams, Søren Kierkegaard, Paul Tillich, and Reinhold Niebuhr.

The answers did appear once, on a summer night in 1933, when the mystical Vision of Agape convinced him that there was a spirit somewhere begging his indulgence that he might stop his running about the public sphere and listen to his private sphere. Yet, Auden's gang tacitly designated him their de facto leader, and he thought he had some leading to do by example. After all, he was the wunderkind poet, the new T.S. Eliot (who discovered him), and the "coming" man. Auden, along with his friends Christopher Isherwood, Stephen Spender, Cecil Day Lewis, Edward Upward, Michael Roberts, Rex Warner, John Lehmann, Louis MacNeice, and many others, became the Auden Generation. Their decade, the 1930s, was world-shaking, and they made their claim not only for their time but also for future generations of angry young men that came after them.

Still, even though the noise and tumult of that decade impelled Auden to be an activist, this wasn't his true nature; and after Auden's arrival in America, he did not change his nature, as many critics would have us believe. He merely reasserted the more contemplative self that had existed before he became the famous poet who believed that there was a public role he was supposed to play. Later, he would ban certain poems from the 1930s from collections, feeling he had not been sincere in writing them but had succumbed to the lure of achieving a political effect. He, however, did not stop writing for effect, but rather chose spiritual and philosophical effects as his aims. A long poem of 1940, "New Year Letter," has over 90 pages of notes giving quotes and sources from his theological reading in Christianity. If anything, in the 1940s Auden was much more of an activist than he had been in the previous decade, except that now he chose to be active in a manner that he felt more suited to embrace — change from within, as he had first encountered it on that summer night. That night was *the* event in Auden's life, and he sought to understand it and, more importantly, re-create it thereafter.

As for that life, the bare facts can be found in the chronology that follows this introduction; yet, of course, the bare facts sketch the surface of the ineffable, which is the inner life of Auden — or anyone, for that matter.

He was the son of a doctor and a nurse, both socially progressive, the father more so (he had added psychoanalysis to his practice by 1907, well before it became fashionable in the 1920s). Auden's mother was more of a religious conservative and did not abide colloquial "low church" manners, preferring the magic and ritual of "high church" mystery. Auden would initially be more like his father, but more enduringly became like his mother, especially after she passed away in 1941.

He went to Oxford, understood he was gay (an identity he would alternately take up enthusiastically, as in his visits to Berlin, or eschew, as in his brief engagement to a nurse), and met Christopher Isherwood, Stephen Spender, and many others who would join him as artists and writers. In 1930 T.S. Eliot, as poetry editor for the firm Faber & Faber,

published Auden's *Poems*, and Auden became the Eliot of the 1930s. He was the tacit leader of the Auden Generation, and writers from Auden country were the new rage. His poetic images and diction were a sharp departure from those of previous poets — or at least the previous poets widely recognized — and Auden's audacious "newness" set him apart. He, Yeats, and Eliot became the long shadows that would stretch over the rest of their century.

The 1930s was the decade of the Great Depression, and of the rise of Communism and Fascism, which were in deadly opposition. Then came Hitler's ascension and the Spanish Civil War. Auden the reluctant activist became engaged with his activist peers but remained cynical about the frailties of human nature that live in the private spheres of those who wear masks in the public sphere. He despised propaganda, even when used for the causes he agreed with — and even though he wrote propaganda, for which he would ever after reproach himself. In the mid to late 1930s Auden would write about his place in the context of English middle-class life — and by extension in English history — in his plays, in *Letters from Iceland* (with "Letter to Lord Byron" as highpoint), in his volume *Look, Stranger!* and in his essays.

In the 1930s he wrote plays alone and plays with Isherwood, and was in demand for essays. Auden read and studied voraciously and his enthusiasms — Gerald Heard, Homer Lane, D.H. Lawrence, George Groddeck, Sigmund Freud, et al., in the 1930s, and the Kierkegaards and Tillichs thereafter — were reflected in his essays as well as his verse; Auden, much like Thornton Wilder, was an artful appropriator (as are all artists, with these two just being more conscious of their sources).

With war inevitable in Europe, and all hopes dashed that the Auden Generation could prevent the war, Auden and Isherwood left for America. Both would espouse spiritual beliefs that featured the mystical approach to divinity where one could intuit and recreate the awe of the Vision of Agape as Auden had felt it in 1933. Isherwood chose the eastern way of Vedanta, Auden the western way of an existential Christianity grounded in Kierkegaard and Paul Tillich. Speaking of "ground," the differences in approaches were not really different. The divine ground of *The Perennial Philosophy*, as set forth by Aldous Huxley in his "Minimum Working Hypothesis," united the mystical aspects of all religions as being derived from the same basic concepts begun with Vedanta. Auden and Isherwood's writing in America would always have either a direct or underlying resonance shaped by their spirituality. The travails of Auden's relationship with Chester Kallman became Auden's impetus for becoming not only a Christian, but one whose chief attribute was a self-sacrificing forgiveness.

W. H. Auden, 1940.

In the 1940s Auden's verse, displaying the zeal of the recently converted, was explicitly religious with four long verse-as-philosophy epics stating his case: "New Year Letter," "For the Time Being," "The Sea and the Mirror," and *The Age of Anxiety*. All explore Auden's philosophical inquiries into his re-conversion to Christianity. They also express his rationalizations for putting up with Kallman.

Some critics like to think Auden was a better poet in the 1930s. One can attribute this faulty canonical dogma to a resentment of his leaving Britain on one hand, and an equal, if not greater resentment for the daring darling of the intellectuals who was now shouting his religion in the face of many of those intellectuals to whom a spirituality based in a relative religious orthodoxy was not sufficiently sophisticated. But there is as much if not more virtuosity in going against popular notions of sophistication or fashion than there is in giving readers and critics what they think they want to hear.

Kallman introduced Auden to the joys of opera, and by the late 1940s they began collaborating on libretti, starting with *The Rake's Progress* (1947). Also by the late 1940s, Auden's zeal, while still sincere, was mellowing into a more personal approach to spirituality with less grandiose enthusiasm shouted from rooftops and more contemplative verse about home, hearth, and Auden's personal relation to his mind, body, and the cosmos with which these are intertwined. The theoretical letter of his Vision of Agape as a world mind concept was now more concerned with the spirit of that vision on *his* mind, *his* body, *his* world.

By the 1960s, Auden was seeing his personal self as connected to a self integral to the correlated sense of an organic whole equal to animals and plants; in this view, humans were not greater than other organisms, and perhaps not even equal to them. His poems became more conversational while tacitly conveying the same intensity of philosophy, with little shouting and much more clever subtlety. Auden wished to amuse, to make us laugh — and think a bit while we are laughing.

The last verse of the mid 1960s to his death in 1973 began to reflect his later views on the nature of language (with which he had always been enormously interested), but now, to Auden, all of those years of manipulating language through verse seemed to have led him to a truism he first learned from Gerald Heard in the early 1930s: Man once did not need language to communicate but could do so instinctively, without words. The more man used language, the more he became separated from this soundless intuition. The truest man is the mystical man, or in the term he and Isherwood coined even before Heard, the Truly Strong Man.

Auden as early as 1933 believed answers came from within. By 1973, he accepted that these answers also came to one in silence just as on that summer night forty years earlier. This is not to say that Auden came to believe that poetry could not speak to others. Rather, he knew that verse could only help one come to those intuitive feelings about spirit that can only be felt, never stated, and in verse perhaps intimated, but never duplicated. The ineffable remains the ineffable — even for a poet of Auden's genius, who came as close as anyone to pushing the door of the glorious ineffable ever so slightly ajar so that one could sense, if not quite see and hear, the light behind the light and the sound behind the sound, which wait on the other side of that door.

Chronology

1907 . . . . Wystan Hugh Auden is born on 21 February in York, England.

1908 . . . . Family moves to Birmingham, where Auden's father, a physician, is appointed school medical officer for the city and a professor of public health at the university.

1915 . . . . Attends St. Edmund's School, where he first meets Christopher Isherwood; attendance continues to 1920.

1920 . . . . Attends Gresham's School until 1925 and begins reading Freud.

1925 . . . . Attends Oxford until 1928.

1928 . . . . In the summer, Oxford classmate and friend Stephen Spender purchases a hand press in order to print forty-five copies of Auden's *Poems*. In August Auden begins a year's stay in Berlin, which will change his life.

1930 . . . . Becomes a schoolmaster at Larchfield Academy in Scotland. In September, the publisher Faber & Faber, under the auspices of T.S. Eliot, publishes *Poems*.

1932 . . . . Faber publishes *The Orators* and Auden begins teaching at the Downs Preparatory School, Colwal, and begins a period of great happiness. He becomes an influence on both pupils and parents in this progressive school.

1933 . . . . On a summer night Auden has the mystical and life-changing experience of *agape*, the transcendental love for all existence. In November his play *The Dance of Death* is published.

1935 . . . . The Auden-Isherwood play *The Dog Beneath the Skin* is published and then produced by the Group Theatre on 15 January 1936. Auden marries German refugee Erika Mann in order to provide her with a British passport. After leaving the Downs School at the end of summer, Auden begins six months with the GPO film unit, working as a writer and assistant director and taking on other tasks as well.

1936 . . . . Auden visits Iceland with Oxford classmate and fellow poet Louis MacNeice. The second Auden-Isherwood play, *The Ascent of F6*, is published and produced by the Group Theatre, 26 February 1937. In October, Auden publishes new verse in *Look, Stranger*. American edition is published in 1937 with the title *On This Island*.

1937 . . . . From January to March, Auden visits Spain during its civil war, supporting the Republican government. In May his poem *Spain* is published with all royalties going for medical aid to the Republicans. In August *Letters from Iceland*, co-written with MacNeice, is published.

1938 . . . . In January Auden and Isherwood go to China to record their impressions of the Sino-Japanese war for their book *Journey to a War*. Auden visits America and decides to move there. In October the third and last play with Isherwood, *On the Frontier*, is published and produced by the Group Theatre in November.

1939 . . . . In January Auden and Isherwood leave for America. Auden lives in New York City; Isherwood goes to Los Angeles. *Journey to a War* is published in March. Auden meets Chester Kallman, who is at first his lover, but will become his lifetime platonic companion.

1940 . . . . *Another Time* is published. In the fall Auden begins teaching for a year at the New School of Social Research in Manhattan. Also in the fall, he returns to the Anglican Church.

1941 . . . . *The Double Man* is published (English title, *New Year Letter*). An operetta, *Paul Bunyan*, libretto by Auden, music by Benjamin Britten, is performed at Columbia University on 5 May. In the fall he begins a year of teaching at the University of Michigan.

1942 . . . . Begins three years of teaching at Swarthmore and adds Bryn Mawr in 1943–45. In the summers he stays in Fire Island, NY.

1944 . . . . *For the Time Being* is published.

1945 . . . . *The Collected Poetry* is published. From April to August, Auden goes to Germany and other parts of Europe as civilian research chief in uniform with a rank of major in the Morale Division of the U.S. Strategic Bombing Survey. He visits England for the first time since he left in 1939.

1946 . . . . In spring Auden teaches at Bennington College in Vermont and becomes an American citizen. In the fall he returns to the New School to teach Shakespeare.

1947 . . . . In spring, at Barnard College, he teaches as an associate in religion. *The Age of Anxiety* is published and wins a Pulitzer Prize.

1948 . . . . Spends springs and summers from 1949 to 1957 in Ischia, Italy. In the fall he teaches at the New School.

1950 . . . . Auden publishes a prose work, *The Enchafèd Flood*, based on his 1949 Page-Barbour Lectures at the University of Virginia.

1951 . . . . *Nones* published. Stravinsky's Opera *The Rake's Progress* is produced in Vienna with a libretto by Auden and Kallman.

1952 . . . . In spring term Auden is a research professor at Smith College.

1955 . . . . *The Shield of Achilles* is published.

1956 . . . . Auden is elected professor of poetry at Oxford for a term of five years. In each year he gives three public lectures. His first, *Making, Knowing and Judging*, is published.

1958 . . . . In the spring he buys and moves into a house in Kirchstetten, Austria, where he will spend every spring and summer until his death.

1960 . . . . *Homage to Clio* is published.

1961 . . . . An opera composed by Hans Werner Henze, *Elegy for Young Lovers*, and with a libretto by Auden and Kallman, is performed in Stuttgart, Germany.

1962 . . . . *The Dyer's Hand* (essays) is published.

1964 . . . . Returns to Iceland. Six months in Germany as an artist-in-residence sponsored by the Ford Foundation.

1965 . . . . *About the House* is published.

1966 . . . . *The Bassarids*, music by Henze, libretto by Auden and Kallman, is performed in Salzburg, Germany. *Collected Shorter Poems 1927–1957* is published.

1968 . . . . *Collected Longer Poems* and *Secondary Worlds* (essays) are published.

1969 . . . . *City Without Walls* is published.

1970 . . . . *A Certain World*, a commonplace anthology with Auden's commentary, is published.

1971 . . . . *Academic Graffiti* is published.

1972 . . . . *Epistle to a Godson* is published. In October, Auden returns to Oxford to live in a cottage at Christ Church.

1973 . . . . *Love's Labour's Lost*, music by Nicholas Nabokov, libretto by Auden and Kallman, is performed in Brussels. Auden dies in his sleep sometime on 28 or 29 September. He is buried in Kirchstetten on 4 October.

1974 . . . . *Thank You Fog* is published

THE ENCYCLOPEDIA

"A.E. Housman" 1938

This is a bitter poem about the artist who withdraws into "savage footnotes" of pedantry and nostalgia, the artist who is unable to continue saying that existence is wrong and needs to be fixed and that poetry is one of the possible correctives. It is a matter of chance whether life distinguishes the "coarse hanged soldier from the don." Auden's poem about A.E. Housman was included in *Another Time* in 1940 and warns against the artist who withdraws ("Deliberately he chose the dry-as-dust") and forsakes his art. Auden challenges Housman's withdrawal from the public sphere; yet, by the time *Another Time* was published, he could be considered to have agreed with him. The poem "The Composer" is a contrast. (*See also* Housman, A.E.)

About the House 1964

Dedicated to Edmund Wilson and Elena Wilson. Published in 1964, this volume of verse included twelve poems comprising "Thanksgiving for a Habitat," referring to Auden's house in Kirchstetten. The "Habitat" poems exalted the cozy nest Auden had found in his house, the first and last house he would own. This is a sequence of blessed domesticity and a celebration, as well as a defense of the Good City even

with its faults. (The City, with a capital "C," and how it works, past and present, was a prevalent theme of Auden's work in America.) Auden said he wished to sound like Horace.

I. "Prologue: The Birth of Architecture" 1962 (for John Bayley, the husband of Iris Murdoch). II. "Thanksgiving for a Habitat" 1964 (for Geoffrey Gorer). III. "The Cave of Making" 1962 (In Memoriam Louis MacNeice). The poet/maker makes poems. This is Auden's rededication to his poetic gift in which he says he would like to be known as a minor Atlantic Goethe. IV. "Down There" 1963 (for Irving Weis), the cellar with allusions to *Richard III*. V. "Up There" 1963 (for Anne Weis), the house. VI. "The Geography of the House" 1964 (for Christopher Isherwood). VII. "Encomium Balnei" 1962 (for Neil Little), the bathroom is beside the kitchen for a supreme achievement in utilitarian humility. Auden imitates William Carlos Williams. A house, as is life, is one of achievement as well as limitations. VIII. "Grub First, Then Ethics" 1958 (for Margaret Gardiner), the title is a quote from Brecht's *Mahogonny*. IX. "For Friends Only" 1964 (for John and Thekla Clark). X. "To-Night at Seven-Thirty" 1963 (for M.F.K. Fisher) Guests and dinner parties. XI. "In the Cave of Nakedness" 1963 (For Louis and Emmie Kronenberger). The bedroom. XII. "The Common Life" 1963 (for Chester Kallman). The living room and the bliss of coupledness. Auden chose Kirchstetten,

11

not England, America, or Ischia to be laid to rest.

"Academic Graffiti" 1952, 1970

("In Memoriam Ogden Nash.") Nash was an American light verse poet. Here, Auden writes a litany of four-line "shorts," each about a person, with drawings by Fillipo Sanjust: Henry Adams, St. Thomas Aquinas, J.S. Bach, Thomas Lowell, Beddoes, Beethoven, "Good Queen Bess," William Blake, Robert Bridges, Robert Browning, Martin Buber, Lord Byron, Shelley, Arthur Hugh Clough, Dante, Hugo De Vries, Dickens, Erasmus, Fulke Greville, Goethe, Rider Haggard, Handel, Thomas Hardy, Haydn, George Herbert, Robert Herrick, Henry James, Kant, Kierkegaard, Karl Kraus, Archbishop Laud, Edward Lear, Joseph Lister, Robert Liston, Luther & Zwingli, Stephane Mallarme, Mary, Queen of Scots, Queen Mary (The Bloody), Marx, Milton, William Henry Monk, Thomas Moore, Cardinal Newman, Nietzsche, Oxbridge philosophers, Louis Pasteur, Alexander Pope, Christina Rosetti, Sir Walter Scott, Stendahl, Adalbert Sifter, Thackeray, Thomas the Rhymer, T.S. Eliot (and indirectly, George Eliot), and Yeats.

Ackerley, J.R.

1896–1967. English author, most notably of *Hindoo Holiday*, and editor; also wrote drama and poetry and two books about his love for his dog. Ackerley was literary editor of *The Listener* 1935–1939, working with the leading writers of his era including Auden. He was a great friend of E.M. Forster who was a friend and role model to Auden and Isherwood, with both extolling him as an exemplar of the Truly Strong Man.

In 1971 Auden reviewed Ackerley's memoir *My Father and Myself* more or less favorably in a review titled "Papa Was a Sly Old Boots." Still, Auden chided Ackerley a bit concerning a lack of sexual explicitness, something Auden himself would have been loath to do: "Trying to read between the lines, I conclude that he [Ackerley] did not belong to either the 'orals' who play Son-and/or mother, nor to the 'anals' who play wife-and/or husband. My guess is at the back of his mind lay a daydream of an innocent Eden where children play 'Doctor,' so that the acts he really preferred were the most 'Brotherly,' Plain-Sewing and Princeton-First year."

"Adam as a Welshman" 1963

In this review of David Jones's long poem *Anathemata*, Auden calls Jones's epic poem the most important of the twentieth century, surpassing even Eliot's *The Waste Land*. Auden writes that this is an epic about two Adams. The mood, he says, is of a Roman Catholic Mass that evokes Adam's personal memories in "Wool Gathering," which obscures the Mass temporarily but heeds its subconscious drive. The priest is the amanuensis of this one-time event. Christ is the second Adam who redeems the first Adam. Each of us is unique in himself, as was Christ, so a man's unique mode of speech (here, Jones's poem) must be uniquely translated by a reader's unique understanding of the reader's inner symbolism. Jones's Adam of the poem is an old man, a Catholic convert, and within him overlap inherited classes as Jones describes in two sections of the poem: "Rite and Foretime" (which sees man as an accumulation of myths and sacred cults) and "Middle Sea and Lear" (which describes the historical creation of a Western European persona rolling into a specific Londoner of Welsh descent using seafaring images and symbols just as the Catholic Mass signifies a quest voyage that repeats the voyage of incarnation). (*See also* "The Enchafèd Flood" for Auden's sea symbolism.) Jones's allusions are subject to the contextual and personal interpretation of the reader so that this poem is a cooperative act of repeated readings to discern the code contained therein. Seeking action, the reader has the potential to become an *aesthetic hero* (*see* Kierkegaard).

"Address to the Beasts" 1973

"Auden closed a catalogue of the differences between his own species and all other animal species by anticipating their joint future" when these differences will no longer be different (Mendelson, *Later Auden*).

"Adolescence" *see The Orators*

AE (George Russell)

1867–1935, Irish author, b. Lurgan, educated in Dublin. An active member of the Irish nationalist movement, he edited the *Irish Homestead* (1904–23) and the *Irish Statesman* (1923–30). He worked for Irish agricultural improvement, and he was also a talented painter and conversationalist. Russell was one of the major writers in the Irish literary renaissance. His poems and plays are noted for their mystical tone and their view of humanity's spiritual nature. AE's being a mystic and follower of Vedanta subsumed his point of view. He became a friend of and influence on Gerald Heard

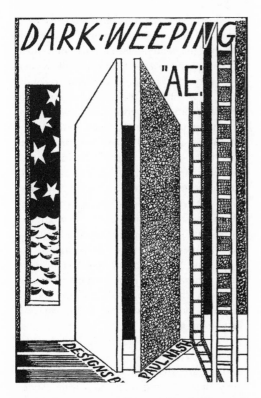

The AE (George Russell) poem "Dark Weeping" 1931.

who became a friend of and a great influence on Auden. Even before meeting Heard in 1929, a teenage Auden was reading Russell's poems with their unabashedly mystical themes. In Auden's last years he was often addressing the same disembodied or natural objects in a manner similar to AE.

Aesthetes and Hearties (Highbrows and Lowbrows)

The distinction between aesthetes (liberal intellectuals such as Auden) and hearties (conservative athletes, aristocrats, and bourgeois upper class) in the British Public Schools can be extended to a more comprehensive dichotomy of the distinction between highbrows and lowbrows in the world at large. Aesthetes equate to highbrows and hearties to lowbrows. In the British public schools that the Auden Generation rebelled against, the lowbrow hearties that constituted the majority regarded highbrow aesthetes with suspicion. This was (is) also the case in the larger world in which exists that amorphous pseudo-person identified as the lowbrow Public by the nineteenth century Christian existential polemicist Søren Kierkegaard. Defining Kierkegaard's construct of the Public enhances an understanding of the Auden Generation's writings of the 1930s.

The differences between the lowbrow Public and the highbrows are often associated with money. Those with more income may have access to a better education and more culture than those with less. However, for Auden, the factor that ultimately determines who becomes a highbrow is not strictly based on money, or social status, or snobbery, or even innate intellectual capacity. What makes highbrows distinct from lowbrows is their intellectual ability combined with a desire for more than just utilitarian knowledge. The lowbrow passively observes while the highbrow actively observes and from these observations he also actively perceives. Auden said that a highbrow is "someone who is not passive to his experience but who tries to organise, explain, and alter it, someone, in fact, who tries to influence history: a man struggling in the water is, for the time being, a highbrow. The decisive factor is the conflict between the person and his environment" ("Reviews," *The English Auden*).

When a person chooses to be a highbrow in order to overcome his environment, this can also entail a challenge to the authority ruling that environment. Throughout history, highbrows in general and artists in particular have been considered threats to authority. Auden also wrote, "Why should the authorities feel that a highbrow artist is important enough to be worth destroying? It can only be because so long as artists exist, making what they please, even if it is not very good, even if very few people appreciate it, they remind the management of something the management does not like to be reminded of, namely that the managed people are people with faces, not anonymous numbers" ("Dyer's Hand," *Anchor Review*). Highbrows are non-conformists. Lowbrows are conformists. This is a natural antipathy. Emerging totalitarian regimes have always targeted intellectuals as potential enemies because intellectuals would question the propaganda that lowbrows accept at face value. "Management" can't afford for highbrows to blow the whistle on them by alerting the lowbrows so it is easier for tyrants to suppress or eliminate highbrows. When the 1930s saw the rise of fascism in Europe, the first in Britain to recognize it for what it was were the highbrows, those former aesthetes who had already experienced a form of fascism in the public schools. As Auden said at the time, "The best reason I have for opposing fascism is that at school I lived in a fascist state" ("The Liberal Fascist").

The British Public Schools would be Auden's and Christopher Isherwood's first adventures away from the safe cocoon of their nurturing homes. At St. Edmund's School they would begin their rebellion against established authority. As one can surmise from Auden, he believed that the distinctions of lowbrow and highbrow are as real as the societal pressures that have produced them. Is there such a disparity? Between particular individuals, there can be; but within the continuum of a collective humanity, not really. All people, as engendered from the original tribe/group, have been subject to the same evolving consciousness. Personal distinctness exists in the one, the single self of the separated ego, but not in the many

of the larger Self within the Divine Ground. (*See* Minimum Working Hypothesis.) This common denominator of human universality, when it is conveyed in colloquial, common speech, can be understood by almost everyone, or at least everyone who chooses to perceive and not just observe. For Auden, this worldview was *the* view, ultimately meaning that there is no real gulf between highbrow and lowbrow.

"After Reading a Child's Guide to Modern Physics" 1961

Do we discover science and use it, or does science discover man and abuse him?

The Age of Anxiety 1947

The Age of Anxiety is a poem that became a catch phrase for the modern dilemma of Everyman and won the Pulitzer Prize for Poetry in 1947.

Søren Kierkegaard's *The Concept of Dread* and Paul Tillich's interpretation of the demonic influence the content and narrative movement of *The Age of Anxiety*— the poem Tillich cited as the perfect expression of the modern condition — in which the familiar social gestures of men and women who meet in a New York bar give way, in the course of a night, to deep associations, psychological projections, and inarticulate fears. The "demonic" would become Auden's preferred term for most any especially dangerous personal excess, as in his essay "Kierkegaard," in which he writes that "the sufferer by fate" is tempted into "demonic defiance" (guilt-ridden and foolish rebellion), and "demonic despair" (guilt-ridden cynicism and depression). Yet his most powerful applications of this particular term involve his efforts to confront, as a Christian poet, the political and social forces most destructive of the human spirit (*see* Christianity).

This long poem's subtitle is *A Baroque Eclogue*. "Baroque," while more often applied to visual arts than literature, can be used to imply an ornate and sumptuous style. Auden defined "Baroque" as the "counterreformation's theatrical use of *matter* against the abstract and *earnest* thinking of the reformers" (in lecture notes from a Swarthmore seminar). An "eclogue" refers to a dialogue and/or soliloquy that conveys ideas a poet wishes to express more colloquially — even if this is a heightened colloquialism. These dialogues and soliloquies take place in a Manhattan bar so there is a contrast of poetic elevation and, perhaps, the quintessential forum for "worldliness." *The Age of Anxiety* was written 1944–1946 with the end of World War II in sight and the transition to "peace" near. Auden no doubt also incorporated the angst of the many years before the war started and the collective anxiety of waiting for it to start, during which he engaged in an activism he later disavowed. Auden opens with a prose "Prologue": "When the historical process breaks down and armies organize with their embossed debates the ensuing void which they can never consecrate, when necessity is associated with horror and freedom with boredom, then it looks good to the bar business."

So begins this ironic epic, which will feature Pastoral imagery (shepherds and flock symbology), as well as references to Old Norse and Old English literature that incorporate saga inferences of mock-heroic and Baroque conflict. This may be a bar, but it is a bar on a border-frontier adjoined with some metaphysical state of being where ideas hang in the ether and emerge from the poem's speakers.

This epic is a sympathetic satire on how humans try to escape from guilt-induced anxiety — now the prevalent modern condition that finds no relief in the religious phenomenon as a viable means of finding calm in the face of a persistent guilt that modernity seems to require, guilt intensified by the failure of traditional beliefs. Is this an insoluble dilemma? The poem's protagonists "pastorally" and "baroquely" share and exchange the roles of shepherd and flock so that they all can have their say ornately and sumptuously.

The scene begins in a Manhattan bar, continues in a taxi ride, and ends in Rosetta's apartment on "All Hallow's Eve" (Halloween), the aura of which assumes that these speeches will be otherworldly. Each character is a soul in purgatory dreaming of escape. The overriding genre is The Quest Saga. The metaphorical grail sought by the searchers is to reclaim an in-

The Age of Anxiety, **cover of first edition.**

nocence of a childhood Eden long lost to the horrors of a world that allowed World War II and its atrocities to happen. An Eden where the Vision of Eros (pure love) can make Eros and Logos (love and reason) one entity so that love becomes law. Each character is a facet of a whole with his/her own symbology and each represents Jung's four archetypal faculties — Intuition, Thought, Feeling, and Sensation.

Malin is a guide and commentator, a closet Christian as *ethical hero* (*see* Kierkegaard, Søren). (Malin is based on Auden's friend John Thompson.) *Rosetta* is Jewish (*see* Jaffee, Rhoda), and the only character that changes in the course of the evening's quest; she is a sharper protagonist in how she affects the others. *Quant* is the nihilist and represents a despair of weakness, which is seemingly callous but is a surface cynicism that is actually a thin veil barely hiding an underlying fear and timidity. *Emble* is the youth that seeks a vocation at sea (the navy) and also seeks something to believe in. In seeking action he has the potential to become an *aesthetic hero* (*see* Kierkegaard, Søren).

Edward Mendelson notes in *Later Auden*: "When Auden began *The Age of Anxiety* in July 1944, he had in mind the same themes of theatricality and murder that pervaded 'The Sea and the Mirror' (1944), but his new long poem seemed to have ideas of its own. By the time he finished it early in 1947, it had proved to be less about isolating guilt and about an almost instinctive wish for a shared community we can imagine but never achieve."

Life is a hurricane. Man most often gets caught up in the spin and can't see or think clearly; if only he could get to the calm center and then become calm himself. If he could, then he would become a witness, not an object flung about, and thus it would be easier to see through his guilt and anxiety. That this is easier said than done, yet nonetheless worth striving for, is Auden's purpose in *The Age of Anxiety*. Mendelson also notes some nods to Joyce's *Finnegan's Wake* in Rosetta's last speech as Auden had read Campbell and Robinson's *A Skeleton Key to Finnegans Wake* in 1944. Auden was also reading Arnold Toynbee's six volume *A Study of History* and takes ancient names from the text and drops them into the poem to signify the no-beginning, no-end circularity. See also Auden's "The Guilty Vicarage: Notes on the Detective Story by an Addict," written in 1948 which has similar ideas as *The Age of Anxiety*.

Dedicated to John Betjeman, Auden's Oxford classmate and friend who, in his own style, also wrote eclogues as "the most famous exponent of Victorian ornament and extravagance" (Mendelson, *Later Auden*) for whose volume *Slick but not Streamlined* Auden wrote an introduction in the same year of 1947.

Composer Leonard Bernstein wrote a symphony of the same title inspired by the poem, and Jerome Robbins created a ballet using Bernstein's music. — with BRIAN CONNIFF

Alfred 1936

Dedicated to Therese Giehse, whom Auden met through Erika Mann. Auden helped Giehse get a British passport by having her marry a friend of E.M. Forster's, John Simpson. Auden wrote *Alfred* as a cabaret sketch for Giehse and it first appeared in *New Writing* in 1936, was reprinted in *New Letters in America* in 1937, and was, as *The Dark Valley*, written for radio in America. *Alfred* is now in *The Complete Works of W.H. Auden: Plays* (ed. Mendelson).

"The Aliens" 1970

Auden here talks about the empathy that humans can have for animals and plants — sometimes more than with each other — while they all have an antipathy to insects. Phrases from Milton are scattered throughout.

"The Almighty Dollar" 1962

In this essay, Auden considers that Europeans do not associate wealth with personal merit or poverty with personal failure, while Americans do to their endless suffering.

America

Perhaps no day has acquired more significance, among readers of W.H. Auden's poetry, than January 26, 1939. By most ways of looking at it, through the combined lenses of literature and history, it appears to have been a day of desolation, even despair. In New York City, as Humphrey Carpenter notes in *W.H. Auden*, it was the coldest day of the winter, with snow falling and blocks of ice floating in the Hudson River. For the rest of his life, Christopher Isherwood would remember standing in that snow. Standing on the shore, Isherwood paused, just as one might expect, to look at "the made-in-France Giantess with her liberty torch" (*Christopher and His Kind*). The "nervous New World" seemed determined to flaunt its "rude steel nudity." "We're Americans here," she told him, "and we keep at it, twenty-four hours a day, *being* Americans.... Don't you come snooting us with your European traditions — we know the mess they've got you into. Do things our way or take the next boat back — back to your Europe that's falling apart at the seams" (*CK*). Even the Statue of Liberty herself "seemed to threaten, not welcome, the newcomer" (*CK*). This atmosphere must have seemed all the more forbidding when, early in the afternoon, the news arrived that Franco's forces had captured Barcelona, effectively ending the Spanish Civil War and, many observers assumed, hastening Great Britain's inevitable entry into a widening struggle against fascism in the heart of Europe.

That morning, Isherwood and Auden set out to begin their new lives in this "nervous New World." For decades since then, Auden's critics, biographers and assorted literary observers have recorded the moment of emigration with accounts that are sometimes adulatory, sometime bitter, but always highly dramatic. The British novelist Michael Nelson would recall a former student, soon to be killed in the war, weeping when he heard the news. The American poet Guy Davenport would see Auden's arrival as a heroic attempt "to ensure that he was among humanity at its worst in this century" (Quoted in Davenport-Hines, *Auden*). For its part, the British literary establishment, like the British Parliament, would be quick and savage in its condemnation. More than thirty years later, reading his morning paper, novelist Anthony Powell would spot Auden's obituary. "No more Auden," he would joyfully proclaim "I'm delighted that shit is gone.... It should have happened years ago ... scuttling off to America in 1939 with his boyfriend like a ... like a..." at which point he became too excited to finish his sentence (Quoted in Davenport-Hines, *Auden*). (Despite these attacks, and Auden's supposed de-activism, "he worked with an organization that found American homes for British children sent abroad to escape the war, and told his mother to use money in his English bank account for war relief" [Mendelson *Later Auden*]. Indeed, homes were found in Texas for the children of Storm Jameson's sister Dorothy — nicknamed Dodo as Auden had been — just before Dorothy was killed in the London Blitz.)

These reactions to Auden's arrival on the shores of America were not merely hero worship, on the one hand, or merely reactionary politics and homophobia on the other. In the literary politics of the time, played out against the backdrop of the European crisis, this otherwise minor event could be treated as though it were momentous, even historic. As Richard Davenport-Hines has written, for much of the English-speaking world, Auden's change of residence would become the most visible sign of an irreversible transformation in national identity and cultural authority:

> It was hard for some English to forgive Auden for settling in the USA on the eve of war because that war so firmly settled Britain's pretensions to cultural and political hegemony of the English-speaking world. Those who considered him to be a military deserter were often those who resented Britain's eclipse as a world power after 1945, and were most reluctant to admit that the greatest English-language novelists and poets in the 1950s were not British-born or British-resident [*Auden*].

As Auden himself had put it so compellingly in his poetry of the early 1930s, the "old life" had just about come to an end, at least in a literary sense. Now, he was discovering that he could dramatize this moment of transformation more powerfully by moving to New York, and reinventing himself, than by staying in Europe and continuing, as he had done for more than a decade, to prophesy a vaguely political apocalypse.

At the same time, the rather excessive reactions of Auden's large audience show how firmly his reputation had been established, by the time he was 31 years old, as the engaged, engaging, prophetic, outrageous, innovative, infuriating, camp young poet of the British left. It was a cultural construction of the poet's role so persuasive that he would never be able to escape it, particularly in England. For the vast majority of his readers, anything Auden wrote after crossing the Great Divide of January 26, 1939, would have to be anticlimactic.

In America, Auden would lose Christopher Isherwood to California and Vedanta. One could speculate that Auden's escape to America was contingent on Isherwood staying with him in New York, and that Isherwood's second escape set up Auden to seek solace by getting serious with Chester Kallman. (This is not to say that Auden needed Isherwood as a lover, but he certainly thought he would keep him as best friend.) The Kallman euphoria lasted until Kallman's infidelities. Auden remained in love with him platonically as per the Vision of Eros, the same vision he would have viewed Isherwood with had Isherwood not gone west. Auden needed a haven to calm his fury over Kallman and this became his return to Christianity via Kierkegaard, Paul Tillich, Reinhold Niebuhr, and other influences. His life and work in America would be shaped by his forming a hybrid of Auden's Christianity and Auden's Mysticism.

See also Berlin, Isaiah — BRIAN CONNIFF

"The American Scene" *see James, Henry*

"Amor Loci" 1965

This poem is a recollection of Auden's childhood visions of "Dame Kind" when he loved his Pennine landscape. The old feeling contrasts to current loneliness.

Ancestral Curse and Family Ghosts

"The tyranny of the dead," wrote Auden. "One cannot react against them."

The Auden Generation seemed haunted by the past. In particular Auden and Isherwood rebelled against the Others, or, in line with the title of Isherwood's first novel, *All the Conspirators*, the "old men" who had caused the events leading to World War I and its aftermath that damaged the psyches of the Auden Generation. Auden used the terms "ancestral curse" and "ghosts" in his poems with the cryptic intent of signifying the teachers at the old school, preachers, politicians, and the poshocracy, that is, the British upper middle and upper classes they represented. Included were the widowed mothers, such as Isherwood's, and the guilt they subjected their bound sons to.

Anderson, Hedli

The second wife of Louis MacNeice and a cabaret singer for whom Auden would write lyrics for songs, including at least one composed by Benjamin Britten, "Calypso."

"Anger" 1962

In this essay, Auden explains that in the book *Seven Deadly Sins* (ed. Ian Fleming, creator of James Bond and brother of Peter Fleming), anger is caused by pride as a flip side of innocence, a perverted reaction to a threat either real or imagined. The anger inhibits fear, the more natural emotion, as a defense mechanism against fear. Anger's only virtue is when it is a motivation to overcome sloth; otherwise, it is either futile or unnecessary. The British middle and upper classes repress anger.

Auden then considers his own types of anger: A) a situation not to my liking, B) one I can't change, C) or a situation where no one else is responsible but my own foolishness. Then he talks about types of anger in general.

A Change of nature: we cannot be angry at others who act according to their nature even if it is not our nature, but we can react to a malicious choice to inflict hurt, and aggression can be verbal, needing no victim present.

Self-importance: we wish to hurt others and make them suffer, and as we do we wish to release our anger of impotence and resentment. Auden gives an example of anger at another who plays at helplessness that allows either ill treatment by others or is a way to get pity from others in order to manipulate them. (Could this be the Kallman-Auden relationship? If so, who plays whom?) Since anger is based on pride or resentment, punishment just leads to more blows to pride and more resentment. With public exposure added then shame makes matters worse.

Righteous anger: Anger of authorities whose wish to punish stems not from the act done, but from the fact that they, the authorities, forbid it and perhaps wish to have done it themselves. Righteous anger diverts energy from common good, but in peace there is no one to hate, no target for the release of righteous anger, which is very much tied to the ego. Theological definitions are by necessity analogical, with hell the equal of imposed law; this doesn't work because imposed law depends on detection and punishment — not spiritual enlightenment from within.

Church's hell: God is an omniscient cop not only aware of every sin committed but every sin we will commit; but what if, for 70 years, God does nothing and lets humans get away with sin; then, suddenly, God decides to get even.

Souls in hell: The above scenario is not Christian. God created the world and is not about to be brought in to fix it. "If His love could ever be coercive and effect the human will then his failure to exercise it from the first moment would make him directly responsible for all evil and suffering in the world. He does not punish us; we punish ourselves by denying His grace." Man insists on suffering because his ego cannot bear the pain of facing reality and a diminution of self-importance, which a cure (the abnegation of the willful ego) would involve. If there are any souls in hell, they have not been sent but insisted on going.

"Another Time" 1939

A new vision of time as that which has neither past nor present nor future but exists in the eternal now of mystical time that unifies both time and consciousness. At around this "time" Isherwood was learning the same mystical concept of time as an eternal now but from a Vedantic rather than a Christian perspective.

Another Time 1940

In 1940 Auden's third volume of strictly poems (in the interim he had published the prose-verse hybrids *Letters From Iceland* and *Journey to a War*) appeared in America (Random House) and five months later in England (Faber & Faber). This was the first book published after Auden's Arrival in America. The book is transitional as it contains the last poems Auden wrote in England (1937-38 and the title refers to this life), and the first written in America (1939). A revised version of "Spain" appears and seems a response to George Orwell's criticism of the original 1937 version. The poems written in America begin to refute Auden's role

Another Time, cover of first edition.

in the "low dishonest decade" of the 1930s, and to promote his search for a new way of seeing the world that would start with Kierkegaard and his re-conversion to a particular brand of what could be called Auden's Christianity. The poems are topical and discursive and are concerned with man's relation to time and history and man's temptation to escape into a past that shackles, or into a future that is fantasy, both as escapes from living in the now. Here is an eclectic humanism celebrating secular saints and substitute gods: Yeats, Freud, et al. There are also escapes into religion and romantic love, which are, as per Auden, no help if selfishly motivated. One must learn real love and unlearn hatred. Auden returns to Christianity, but not as a rebuke of previous years, but rather as a fulfillment of earlier beliefs that he shouldn't have forsaken.

In addition to the revised version of "Spain," other notable poems included are "Lay Your Sleeping Head," "Musée des Beaux Arts," "A.E. Housman," "The Unknown Citizen," "In Memory of W.B. Yeats," "In Memory of Ernst

Toller," "In Memory of Sigmund Freud," "As I Walked Out One Evening," and, along with "Spain," another of the best poems Auden wished he had never written, "September 1, 1939," which, in the aftermath of attacks on the U.S. on September 11, 2001, has been seen widely as a reflection of that terrible day. The book is dedicated to Chester Kallman, whom Auden met in America. They became lovers and Auden enjoyed an intensely happy, though brief, period with him, until he discovered Kallman's infidelity. The dedication and some of the American poems reflect the good rather than the ugly that would come later. The poem that accompanies the dedication testifies to Auden's knowledge that contentment would only come from an "abnegation of the will" (as in *The Ascent of F6*). Until "I will" is "overthrown," that is, the egotistical "I" is removed to be replaced by "I love," then true love will not be found — or as Auden's Christianity would soon see it, the "I will" will not see the Vision of Eros that leads to the Vision of Agape.

Ansen, Alan *see The Table Talk of W.H. Auden*

"Archaeology" 1973

This poem was Auden's last published. In it he considers how one can understand the unknowable by learning from the past, but not the past as recorded. Rather, one must see the past as containing secret meanings, which a metaphorical archaeologist must unearth.

Archives and Papers

The majority of Auden's archives and papers are housed in the Berg Collection of the New York Public Library. A smaller collection of papers from the British years is housed at the University of Texas.

Arendt, Hannah

1906–75, German-American political theorist. Arendt immigrated (1941) to the United States. Her book *Origins of Totalitarianism* (1951) examined totalitarianism, Nazism and Communism. Her work explored "the banality of evil."

Auden befriended Arendt in New York City in 1958 after he read her work. He admired *The Human Condition*, as it seemed to substantiate his own ideas about alienation and vocation, public, and private worlds, and the correlation between speech and responsibility. Auden proposed marriage to Arendt, but as a partnership of friends so Auden could stave off feelings of loneliness. She declined.

Ariel *see The Sea and the Mirror*; also de la Mare, Walter; Frost, Robert

Arnold, Matthew

1822–88, English poet and critic. Arnold was professor of poetry at Oxford from 1857 to 1867. From 1851 to 1886, he served as inspector of schools. He was an advocate of humanism. Arnold began his literary career as a poet, but by 1867 he gave up writing poetry altogether. Instead, Arnold wrote essays for culture and against middle-class materialism.

Arnold began his literary career as a poet, publishing his first volume of poetry in 1849. Dissatisfied with his earliest work, he withdrew his first two volumes of poems, and by 1867 he gave up writing poetry altogether. The Preface to his 1853 *Poems* outlines his poetic theory and marks the beginning of his critical career to which he would devote the greater part of his attention from 1857 on. In *Essays in Criticism* (1865), *Culture and Anarchy* (1869), and other works, Arnold prescribed culture as the antidote to the narrow-minded, materialistic impulses of the Victorian middle class.

Arnold's attacks on English society appealed to Auden, as (to a lesser degree) did Arnold's suggestion that culture might serve as a substitute for religion. But at the same time, Auden felt that Arnold — like Yeats and Rimbaud — had violated his gift for verse when he traded sincerity for polemics. Auden's 1939 elegy "Matthew Arnold," written after "In Memory of W.B. Yeats," suggests, according to Mendelson (also quoting Auden), that Arnold "chose to write essays of 'clear denunciation' instead of poems of praise, and 'thrust his gift in prison till it died.' Auden insisted that the gift survived the poet, yet, in the end, the poet held the gift's life or death in his own power" (*Later Auden*).

"As He Is" 1937

This is a poem about history and another Auden reaction to his having written "Spain." He feels isolation from natural objects, an entrapment in the past, faithlessness in love, and more distance from politics. He sees that one must encounter grief, however reluctantly, in order to learn how to cope with it.

"As I Walked Out One Evening" 1937

This poem was written after the bitter aftermath of the Spanish Civil War and was Auden's response to the anger he felt after the war. Love's ephemeral effusions are countered by the implications of the clock that chimes for the time that is running out toward the start of a new war. Which is reality, the ephemeral or the clock? One can heed the warnings, but one still can choose his path, particularly if one does not give in to pride that will taint judgment. As for that ephemeral love, whether it will last cannot be blamed on the world but only on the lovers, and Auden knows that his homosexuality ("crooked heart") is not the excuse for his isolation, it is himself. (*See also* "A Bride in the 30s"; "As He Is.")

"As It Seemed to Us" 1964

A review of the autobiographies of Evelyn Waugh and Virginia Woolf turns into Auden's autobiography via the method of comparing himself to Waugh and Woolf.

"Ascension Day 1964" 1964

The poem contemplates Christ's last appearance on earth before ascending to heaven. This withdrawal also refers to Auden's from Kallman, who had decided to spend half the year on his own roving in Athens.

The Ascent of F6 see Plays with Isherwood

Ashberry, John

1927– . Auden selected Ashberry as the 1957 winner of the Yale Series of Younger Poets for his volume *Some Trees*. In Auden's foreword to this book he considered the difficulty of finding poetic subjects meriting a poet's attention and then creating verse that is equal to the subjects. He also considered the role of a poet in the modern world as compared to the classical world when "real" meant sacred and numinous.

"At the End of the Quest, Victory" *see History*

"At the Grave of Henry James" *see* James, Henry

"Atlantis" 1941

This is a love poem to Kallman as a series of warnings to a person on a quest for Atlantis, or the Just City, or the City of God, or that place in the heart and mind that is pure. Auden was in part inspired after reading C.P. Cavafy's poem "Ithaca."

"Aubade" 1972

This poem reflects both Auden's ideas and those he admired in Rosenstock-Huessy's essays. Rosenstock-Huessy wrote that there is "an *a prori* that presupposes a power in man to establish relations with his neighbor that transcend their private interests." Indeed, in Auden's last years he valued the ability to hear and to listen carefully, not only to fellow humans, but to the universe and all its constituents — animal, mineral, and vegetable.

The Auden Generation

Many of the British writers between the wars (1919–1939) indicted the failed liberalism that led to World War I. They also believed that the punitive Treaty of Versailles that ended the first war would lead to a second. The 1920s emphasized the residual shock of the war with a cynical nihilism as represented by T.S. Eliot's *The Waste Land* in 1922 and the novels of Aldous Huxley. Huxley summed up the 1920s by portraying the seemingly purposeless frivolity of the middle and upper classes that actually masked pervasive despair. Eliot and Huxley were adults during the war and fully understood the events that caused it, the horror of the war itself, and the debilitating consequences that followed it. The immediately succeeding writers of the 1930s, though only some ten to fifteen years younger and exemplified by Auden, Christopher Isherwood, and Stephen Spender, were distanced from the causes of the war but became the inheritors of the war's effects. Rather than being cynical nihilists as were the 1920s' writers, they became cynical idealists who rejected their predecessors and wished to create a socialist world inspired by the public experiment of the Soviet Union and the private experiments discovered through Freud and psychoanalysis.

Identified as the Auden Generation (most notably by Samuel Hynes in his book of the same name), Isherwood, Auden, and Spender were aided and abetted by Edward Upward, Cecil Day Lewis, Rex Warner, William Plomer, John Lehman, Geoffrey Grigson, Louis MacNeice, and Michael Roberts, among others. In the 1930s they contributed to a redefining of the male hero (and anti-hero) by moving him toward his more contemporary configuration: the sensitive man. Auden's generation witnessed a precipitous end to pre-war traditions. This new world was confronted by an unknown future that would be either a socialist utopia, a fascist tragedy, or both. From that era's uncertain perspective to this era's uncertain perspective, the anti-hero's changing face has been a progress of different masks.

The anti-hero's evolutionary process began after World War I when writers such as Huxley blamed the war's causes on the "old men" in high places. These writers also recognized the paranoia of the middle and upper classes who feared that the Bolsheviks would take over Britain and redistribute their bourgeois wealth. In the 1920s the bitter war heroes such as the martyred poet Wilfred Owen, and the dis-engaged cynics depicted by Huxley and Eliot, became magnets for the youthful intelligentsia who would become fervently engaged activists in the next decade. In the late 1920s, Auden, Isherwood, and Upward began their consideration of the anti-hero as the person who makes the heroic trek that actually only proves he is weak, until he finds the inner peace that is truly strong. In the 1930s the Auden generation developed the "mythified" dichotomy of the Truly Strong and Truly Weak Man.

Although the Strong Man and Weak Man could be distinct individual personas, more often the Strong Man and Weak Man represented conflicting aspects within the same person. Auden's generation developed this mythos by emphasizing the conflicts of divided minds that anticipated the future of literary characterization ushered in by Auden's *Age of Anxiety* after World War II.

Before publishing *Lions and Shadows* in 1938 Isherwood's writing of the previous ten years implicitly portrayed the Truly Strong and Truly Weak theme. The autobiographical *Lions and Shadows*, however, explicitly traces "an education in the Twenties" shared by many in the Auden-Isherwood generation, one which endured the guilt of not having been in the war. Consequently, they were unable to prove themselves as had the noble dead war heroes including Isherwood's father. (Auden's father, a doctor, served and while he was not home for four years he did not fight.) These martyred fathers, husbands, brothers, uncles, sons, cousins, and friends were eulogized endlessly and a constant source to Isherwood and his peers of a latent, or not-so latent, guilt by comparison. This contrast engendered psychological insecurity that was magnified by widowed, possessive mothers who were intent on dominating their sons. Isherwood and Edward Upward, as Cambridge undergraduates from 1925 to 1928, agonized over these insecurities and transformed them into their Mortmere fantasies. These short stories were outrageous, yet deadpan satires of the middle and upper classes of which they were members. Mortmere signified an Us against Them mentality. To Isherwood and Upward, "Them," or "The Others," meant the "Poshocracy" who had caused the war in order to protect and preserve the British traditions and class divisions that had given them disproportionate advantages. Upward, who became a Communist in the 1930s, was the perfect accomplice to Isherwood who said of him: "His natural hatred of all established authority impressed me and I felt that it [would be] a weakness in myself not to share it." They categorized this antagonism as one requiring Tests that would prove they were just as capable as the noble dead had been. For example, Isherwood purchased an unneeded motorcycle in order to emulate T.E. Lawrence. The goal of these tests was to make the journey over a metaphorical Northwest Passage within the mind and over the border/frontier of the old world and to a new world of promise. Initially, for Auden, this new world meant Berlin in 1929 before Hitler took power. Similar pseudo-heroic posturing of the 1920s was soon to be trivialized by the harsher realities of the next decade: propaganda emerging to its full power, Stalinism, and the travesty of the Spanish Civil War. For the Auden generation this world of the 1930s was one of pervasive paranoia with shadowy deals and betrayals thought to be standard operating procedure. By *Lions and Shadows* in 1938, Isherwood was quite clear that the unconscious, symptomatic acts he described concerning school life in the 1920s now had a more consciously recognizable context in the 1930s. The "Test" was now understood to have been a symptom caused by the much more profound thematic dichotomy of The Truly Weak or Truly Strong Man.

The Truly Weak Man (exemplified by T.E. Lawrence) suffered from a compulsion to prove

himself by seeking, confronting, and passing tests of rebellious derring-do. It did not matter whether the tests were actual or imagined. Conversely, the Truly Strong Man was pure-in-heart, which was Auden's term co-opted from psychologist Homer Lane. In *Lions and Shadows* Isherwood defines the Truly Strong Man in the terms "spoken of by the homicidal paranoiac whose statement is quoted by [the German psychologist] Bleuler: 'the signs of the truly strong are repose and good-will ... the strong individuals are those who without any fuss do their duty. These have neither the time nor the occasion to throw themselves into a pose and try to be something great.'" Isherwood adds, "In other words, the Test exists only for the Truly Weak Man: no matter whether he passes it or whether he fails, he cannot alter his essential nature." The Truly Weak Man can pass individual tests, but he can never truly be satisfied because the underlying subconscious needs that are motivating the tests are not really being assuaged.

The Truly Weak Man must try to decipher the psychological compulsions that push him to prove himself so that he can aspire to overcome them and become Truly Strong instead. In the interim his bifurcated self struggles to reconcile these conflicting urges, resulting in a duality of a private face and a public face. There is a confusion of his public and private spheres, inner and outer personas, real and fantasy worlds. Consequently, no real distinction exists, only an ambiguous blurring of inner and outer, public and private, Truly Weak and Truly Strong.

As regards the dissemination of the Truly Weak and Truly Strong mythos, Isherwood, who was three years older than Auden and five years older than Spender, befriended them in the late 1920s and his influence became apparent as they incorporated his (and Upward's) themes into their own work. However, Auden in 1930, and Spender, in 1933, would achieve celebrity ahead of Isherwood. Nonetheless, with Auden as a medium Isherwood's themes of the Truly Weak and Truly Strong Man, us against them, and the divided mind became the staging area for those who gave homage to Auden as the *de facto* leader of his generation. Britain's Angry Young Men of the 1930s emulated Isherwood by emulating Auden. This like-minded group signified their mutual admiration through artistic imitation and by dedicating their poems, plays, and prose to each other.

As the decade progressed the satiric tone that was highlighted in the writings of the early 1930s gave way to more alarmist poetry, prose, and essays that were warnings concerning the advance of fascism. The principal theme portrayed within these warnings was the conflict of the Truly Weak Man and the Truly Strong Man who battle with public and private personas. This duality was summarized succinctly by Auden in 1932 with his dedication of *The Orators* to Stephen Spender:

> Private faces in public places
> Are wiser and nicer
> Than public faces in private places.

If one feels comfortable enough to wear his private face in public, showing his true self without resorting to masks and posturing, then one is pure-in-heart and Truly Strong. Easier said than done, and the Auden Generation knew this was a path to seek, rather than a destination assured. The hero's worthiness comes from the search, and the sincere search is the goal in itself.

As writers reaching adulthood during the period between the wars the Auden Generation were witnesses to the most turbulent era of world-changing events in the history of man, particularly in the West. The world order underwent drastic revisions that affected every aspect of people's lives. These revisions derived from the negative reverberations that began in the 1800s with the shift from small-town agrarianism to the industrialized metropolis. City living for the large majority with little or no money was a stultifying, ultimately Dickensian existence and one where the class-conscious divisions of the rich and not so rich that had been somewhat sublimated in the farm milieu, were more apparent — and volatile. By the early 1900s, the problems of city life that had begun in the 1800s still remained, but with even more intensity. The watershed which became the breaking point for these problems was World War I.

After the collective trauma of the war to end all wars, and the equally collective despair about the world that had allowed it to happen, many among the not so rich blamed the upper classes for the war and grew more intolerant of acquiescing to the old class divisions. The working class, now out of the sunshine and sweating in factories or mines, demanded better conditions and struggled against violent opposition to organize themselves. The psychic damage of the war affected more than just the working class, and was responded to by the Freudian revolution which asserted that the world inside the mind was as much or more important than the world outside it, and that if one could better understand and change his or her mind, one might better understand and change the world. And if all the answers were not in the mind, there was a possible solution in the pseudo–Marxist/Communist revolution of the USSR. The rise of the great experiment of Soviet Union in the 1920s was first seen as the secular New Jerusalem by the workers/socialists of the world and their compatriots among artists and intellectuals. During the 1930s, however, their hopes were betrayed, as Stalin's totalitarian version of the USSR proved to be little better than the rabid fascism of Hitler, Mussolini, and Franco that would lead to World War II.

During this tumultuous era the Auden Generation felt compelled to respond to these events, to become socially responsible and actively *engagé* in trying to address them. It was "in" for the artist/man of letters to have and express points of view about the news of the world. Auden and his peers certainly had opinions and did not hesitate to share them through their art and essays. One reward of reading these writers comparatively is that, as writers from the same era, influenced by the same events, they have world views on many issues that match philosophically. The fact that they could do so with a sardonic wink never obscured the intended message.

When the 1930s ended with the start of World War II, the angry young men bitterly realized that they had not changed the world for the better, but that the world had defeated them. In the struggle just to save it, they knew that they could only hope to change themselves individually. During the war the need for single-minded heroes outweighed the reality of the divided personality that the Auden Generation had nurtured. Consequently, the conflicted anti-hero would temporarily step aside. He would reassert himself permanently after the war when the conflict of public and private, inner and outer, weak and strong, became not just an intellectual's dilemma, but the generalized modus operandi for the post-war era. Hereafter, the anti-hero was Everyman whose thoughts and actions were symptoms of his (or her) quest for a reconciliation of a bifurcated self into one Self, pure in heart and Truly Strong. The Quest to find the Truly Strong Man in life and art became Auden's quest in America.

The Auden Generation "Mother" *see* Plays with Isherwood (*The Ascent of F6*); Ancestral Curse and Family Ghosts; Lawrence, D.H.)

Audience

"The ideal audience the poet imagines," Auden wrote in *Squares and Oblongs*, "consists of the beautiful who go to bed with him, the powerful who invite him to dinner and tell him secrets of state, and his fellow-poets." Regarding audience tastes, he wrote in "Nursery Library" (*A Certain World*): "As readers, we remain in the nursery stage so long as we cannot distinguish between taste and judgment, so long, that is, as the only possible verdicts we can pass on a book are two: this I like; this I don't like. For an adult reader, the possible verdicts are five: I can see this is good and I like it; I can see this is good but I don't like it; I can see this is good and, through perseverance, I shall come to like it; I can see this is trash but I like it; I can see this is trash and I don't like it."

Auden the poet knew that poems were written to be read and heard. While he didn't worry much, if at all, over who read him specifically, he cared a great deal about the interplay of the artist and audience in general, and he wrote essays that gave his views on this relationship.

"What people want to appreciate in art is its function as harmless white magic that intimates and arouses awe, and no artist, whether he wants to or not, as far as an audience is concerned," said Auden, "can prevent his work being used as magic, for that is what all of us, highbrow and lowbrow alike, secretly want art to be" ("The Poet of the Encirclement"). And, more specifically, what is it about poetry those audiences "secretly want"? Auden's answer: "What the child, and the child-in-the-adult, most enjoys in poetry … is the manipulation [the magic] of language for its own sake, the sound and rhythm of words" ("Walter de la Mare").

And what do we secretly want from a particular poem? "We want a poem," Auden said, "to be a beautiful object, a verbal Garden of Eden which by its formal perfection, keeps alive in us the hope that there exists a state of joy without evil or suffering which it can be our destiny to attain. At the same time, we look to a poem for some kind of illumination about our present wandering condition, since, without self-insight and knowledge of the world, we must err blindly" ("Walter de la Mare").

Who will be the readers of these poems? Can a poet write for any and every possible person who might happen to read a certain poem? Can he determine who will possibly even see his poem? A poet, unless he reacts to the lowest common denominator of potential readership, cannot write something for everyone. The poet's best course is the one Polonius prescribed: "To thine own self be true." A sincere poet (or novelist, or essayist, or dramatist) should write as play, for self-satisfaction, which he hopes will also please others. But if the poet writes to fit what will, so to speak, sell, he may please an audience, but not himself; in effect, play is no longer play, but work.

For example, Auden, when asked if he thought about whom he was writing for, said: "No, I just try to put the thing out and hope somebody will read it. Someone says: 'Whom do you write for?' I reply: 'Do you read me?' If they say, 'Yes,' I say, 'Do you like it?' If they say, 'No,' then I say, 'I don't write for you'" ("Interview with W.H. Auden," *Writers at Work: Paris Review Interviews, Fourth Series*).

Auden wrote to please his own aesthetic

needs. His audience found Auden; Auden did not look for his audience. He did believe that it would be easier for an audience to find him if he wrote, as per Yeats via Maud Gonne, the thoughts of the wise man in the speech of the common people. Auden believed that poetry in the era prior to his own had become a medium for the highbrow few, which he believed was not poetry's original intention, and he wished to disprove that the common man would not appreciate poetry if it were presented in a more colloquial manner.

The fact that Auden felt a need to defend poetry indicates the actuality of resistance to it, particularly among the working class and their mistaken association of it as an emblem of the upper class. Auden, left-leaning, was to follow the socialist bent of the 1930s which called for a "proletarian" literature using common speech that included images from the urban-industrial landscape that workers lived in. Many authors of Auden's generation tried, with varying degrees of success, to depict this world. Still, resistance to poetry persisted. Auden wrote, "The low-brow says: 'I don't like poetry. It requires too much effort to understand and I'm afraid that if I learnt exactly what I felt, it would make me most uncomfortable.' He is in the wrong, of course..." ("Squares and Oblongs").

Moreover, Auden believed that after the Industrial Revolution, the population was divided into two main groups: employers and workers with little leisure, and a smaller group who were shareholders (a *rentier* class) who did no work and had leisure but no responsibilities and thus needed diversions. To accommodate each group, Auden said, "literature has tended ... to divide into two streams, one providing the first with a compensation and escape, the second with a religion and a drug" (Introduction to *The Poet's Tongue*).

In order to appeal to a wider audience, poets must give readers not just the "eternal verities" suspended somewhere in a gossamer haze, but please them with some down-to-earth, "gossipy" news included, too.

In order to deflect the hostility to highbrows Auden made the search for a common denominator the subject of a 1937 essay, "In Defense of Gossip." In it, Auden combined his view of the inclusiveness of poetic subject matter with a view concerning the force behind the creation of poetry. Auden writes: 'Gossip is the art form of the man and woman in the street, and the proper subject for gossip, as for all art, is the behaviour of mankind" ("In Defense of Gossip").

This essay suggests that the source of both art and gossip is ordinary curiosity about life around us, curiosity shared by all. Hence this is a defense of poetry as well as a defense of gossip, and ideally it should convince the man in the street that reading poetry provides enjoyment and satisfaction, just as one enjoys the tabloid gossip pages or the *Police Gazette*. In real life, a "gossip" session, besides being about people telling what they themselves and others are doing, is also a vehicle to talk about one's self in comparison to those "others." When the artist "gossips," he does best when he arouses sympathy.

A ready can feel sympathy only when a writer provides recognizable characters and circumstances for the reader to identify with. Writes Auden: "When we read a book, it is as if we were with a person" ("Writing," *An Outline for Boys and Girls and Their Parents*).

A poet is obliged to consider intuitively the four basic tenets of his craft that will help insure in his successful intervention or connection with potential readers:

1) To convey the "thoughts of the wise man in the speech of the common people."
2) To "see with the eyes of children" and bring a freshness of insight that seems to have been rendered with a seemingly effortless naturalness (rather than sounding in any way artificial).
3) To tell the truth, to the best of his ability as he sees it, but not to compromise his inner truth or sincerity by manipulating the message and pandering to what he thinks readers want to hear in order to get their approval. The poet's goal is for readers to hear what he really thinks.
4) To spread some relevant news that also intimates associations as if they've been transmitted from the muse of inspiration directly to the writing hand in a trance. (The hard work is supposed to be a secret.)

Consequently, the poet's art seeks a balance between recalled emotions and the choice of language to evoke those memories for a reader. A poem is not about what we know, but how we feel about what we know. The key to this balancing act of emotive evocation is to strive for telling the news with a pleasing aesthetic framework. A poem's beauty is a symbolic evocation of the natural world as derived from memories of immediate experience and recorded for posterity.

"August 1968" 1968

This poem is a reaction to the Soviet Union's march into Czechoslovakia.

"Augustus to Augustine" 1944

A review of Charles Norris Cochrane's *Christianity and Classical Culture: A Study of Thought and Action from Augustus to Augustine*.

"Authority in America" *see* Marx, Karl

"Authors Take Sides on the Spanish Civil War" 1937

The success with which British intellectuals were mobilized was revealed in the measure of support for the Spanish Republic taken by the *Left Review* (1934–1938). This journal was edited by Communist Party members but, in keeping with the spirit of the Popular Front, opened its pages to non–Communist left sympathizers, including Auden. The writer Nancy Cunard conducted a survey of prominent British writers on the Spanish situation. The results were published in *Authors Take Sides on the Spanish War* (1937). Out of 149 responses, 127 names appeared for the Republic, including Auden's. Only sixteen declared themselves to be neutral, though these included some extremely influential figures, such as Eliot, Pound, H.G. Wells, and Vita Sackville-West, wife of Nigel Nicholson. Eliot felt that "it is best that at least a few men of letters should remain isolated, and take no part in these collective activities" (Cunningham, *Spanish Front* 56). The handful of respondents declaring themselves for the Nationalists included Evelyn Waugh, who wrote, "If I were a Spaniard I should be fighting for General Franco" (Cunningham, *Spanish Front* 57). Others who may have been expected to offer a view did not reply to the questionnaire, one being Graham Greene. Another was George Orwell, who actually fought in Spain and angrily dismissed the survey, which he later described as "bloody rot" (letter to Stephen Spender, 2 April 1938; *Collected Essays* Vol. 1.)—PETER GROSVENOR

Autism

Auden considered that individuals have an aspect of their inner selves that on occasion chooses to be autistic, that is, to make a retreat of some kind into an inner world of their own devising. As a child he chose an inner world of mines and mining; later, he chose art as his inner world.

Those who are autistic seem to have chosen a permanent escape from the primary world into some Secondary World of their own creation. Auden was fascinated by the research on autism, particularly of Dr. Bruno Bettelheim (1903–1990), who wrote on how autistic children used language, with Auden commenting: "For anybody interested in language, the linguistic behavior of autistic children is of the greatest interest and significance." Bettelheim observed: "…the autistic child creates a language to fit his emotional experience of the world. Far from not knowing how to use language correctly, there is a spontaneous decision to create a language which will match how he experiences things" ("Children, Autistic," *A Certain World*). Consequently, language evolves from experience of a world, even if that world is autistically separated from everyone else's. Auden was very interested in the work of Bettelheim and others as concerned the autistic as he recognized in himself a need to escape into his own Secondary Worlds.

"Autumn Song" *see* **"Twelve Songs"**

Awe *see* **Mysticism**

Bachardy, Don

1934– , American portrait painter, devoted companion of Christopher Isherwood from 1953 to Isherwood's death in 1986. Auden must have observed the strong compatibility and mutual support between Bachardy and Isherwood that Auden had always longed for but never found. He hoped for it from Chester Kallman but was disappointed. (*See also A Meeting by the River.*)

Bahktin *see* **"Epistle to a God son" (1968)**

"Balaam and His Ass" 1954

According to this essay in the social and historical roles of master and servant there is a tacit contract. In these roles man discloses himself to himself. (Self-disclosure is dialogue; self-concealment is soliloquy.) The servant knows and judges his master, but a master may never know his servant unless the master wishes to. In the inner life of the artist the dialogue of art is between the master and servant imperatives with the artist alternating both roles. In the artist, the master, servant, slave, actor, witness and judge exist all in one. Love given freely gives self-esteem; love taken for granted is boredom; unrequited love is delightful suffering. Slaves to time (an ordained schedule repeated over and over) suffer from the hubris of attempting to control fate. Auden was a slave to time, and this essay was self-criticism.

Barfield, Owen

1898–1997, British lawyer, author and theological philosopher. Auden's poem "Friday's Child," was influenced by Barfield's *Saving the Appearances* (1957). Auden respected Barfield's previous books on language and wrote a preface to a reissue of Barfield's *History in English Words*. In "Friday's Child" and other poems Auden saw Barfield's ideas in *Saving the Appearances* as giving clarity to some spiritual and literary concerns. (*See also* Mysticism.)

Barnard College

In 1947 Auden taught a class here, "The Quest in Modern Literature."

Barth, Karl

1886–1968, Swiss Protestant theologian who taught in Germany until 1935 when Hitler had him deported to Switzerland. Barth argued that people must listen for God with an attitude of awe, trust, and obedience.

Auden first knew of Barth in 1933. In 1934, he noted Barth's insistence on Grace, which Auden had felt during "A Summer Night" in 1933. After Auden's arrival in America, he would study Barth, Kierkegaard, Niebuhr, Tillich, and Barfield, among others, in his quest for what would be his own unique formulation of Christianity. Auden found Barth's quest for Grace a worthy goal but was not so sure of Barth's equal insistence on an orthodox view of Original Sin. (*See also* Camus, Albert.)

The Bassarids 1963

In writing this libretto, Auden and Kallman worked again with composer Hans Werner Henze, for whom they previously created the libretto for his *Elegy for Young Lovers* (1960). Auden wished to do something grand, like Wagner, and suggested an adaptation of Euripides' *The Bacchae*. The Bassarids refers to both men and women, and not just women as followers of Dionysus. "In adapting the myth Auden and Kallman elaborated the psychology of the existing characters, added new ones, and gave all of them costumes taken from historical eras that best represented their separate points of view. Tiresias, who adjusts his religion to policy and fashion, appears as an Anglican archdeacon; Dionysus makes his apotheosis in the style of Beau Brummel.... In some of these details, and many other ways, the libretto draws on [Auden's friend] E. R. Dodds's commentary to his Oxford edition of the play.... *The Bassarids* gives special emphasis to Euripides' portrayal of the arbitrary injustice of the Gods, and the final confrontation of Cadmus and Agave with Dionysus, with the great laments that follow, is the summit of Auden's art as a librettist" (Mendelson, *W.H. Auden, Libretti and Other Dramatic Writings*). *The Bassarids* was first performed on 6 August 1966 in Germany.

Baudelaire, Charles

1821–1867. French poet and critic, first symbolist poet. The only volume of his poems published during his lifetime, *Les Fleurs du Mal* (1857), was considered obscene. Later, the volume became an influence on many poets. Baudelaire's work was moody and rebellious, with an intense religious mysticism, and depicted inner despair and the duality of nature and beauty with decadence. He admired Poe (about whom Auden would write an introduction for a Poe anthology), whose works he translated and brought to the attention of the French public.

Auden's best friend, Isherwood translated *Journaux Intimes* in 1930, a job attained for him by Auden's influence. Auden told the publisher that Isherwood was an expert in French — not quite. Isherwood admits that in the 1930 version there a few "howlers" that he corrects for the 1947 edition that has an introduction by Auden. The 1930 edition's introduction is by T.S. Eliot who discovered and published Auden, which gave Auden the ability to get work for his friends.

Eliot said of Baudelaire: "Baudelaire was in some ways far in advance of the point of view of his own time, and yet was very much of it.... He had a great part in forming the generation of poets after him."

Moreover, Baudelaire's rebelliousness against middle-class stagnancy became an inspiration. In Isherwood's autobiography of his

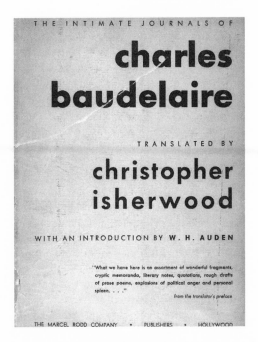

Charles Baudelaire

school days, *Lions and Shadows*, he writes about discovering Baudelaire through his friend and classmate Allen Chalmers (Edward Upward), who told Isherwood, "It's the very greatest ... I shall never forget the first time I ... you see he exposes once and for all, the tremendous sham ... the thing we never realized at school...." To which Isherwood replied: "Chalmers set me on fire.... I had to buy my first copy of Baudelaire before the book stores closed." Baudelaire's secret life of the mind — certainly not included in the public school curriculum — encouraged Isherwood and Upward to live in their own secret world and later write weird stories about a mad town called Mortmere that satirized British middle-class life. Isherwood shared this excitement with Auden who would cite Baudelaire as one of many influences on his own Mortmereish prose work *The Orators*. Auden would say in his 1947 introduction to the revised version of *Journaux Intimes*, "Few of the entries in Baudelaire's *Intimate Journals* are concerned with the art of poetry; most of them are reflections on subjects which concern all men at all times, love, religion, politics, etc; at the same time they are reflections of a poet living in Paris in the middle of the nineteenth century.... They require, therefore — and this is a great part of their fascination — to be read in four different ways at once: as the observations of a human spirit irrespective of time or place but as distinguished from men with other gifts or professions.... Random jottings as they are, most of the entries revolve around one central preoccupation of Baudelaire's, namely: what makes a man a hero, i.e. an individual: or, conversely, what makes him a churl...."

Later, Auden would amplify this distinction into two questions borrowed from Robert Frost: "Who Am I? Whom ought I to become?" Auden believed that individuals should — consciously or unconsciously — ask themselves these questions when they formed impressions from reading, listening, or viewing art.

In his 1944 introduction to a selection of Tennyson Auden compared the two: "Baudelaire was right in seeing that art is beyond good and evil, and Tennyson was a fool to try and write poetry which would teach the ideal."

From the very first days of his career Auden would see as a major theme the Duality within an individual's life of the mind. Baudelaire was one of his original motivations for doing so as well as being a model for the role of artist as critic, a function Auden pursued voluminously.

Beaton, Cecil

1904–1980, English photographer, theatre designer, author, and another expatriate Briton in America in the late 1930s. Photographed both Auden and Isherwood.

Bell, Julian

1908–1937, English poet, nephew of Virginia Woolf, and the best friend of John Lehmann. He died 18 July 1937 during the Spanish Civil War. He had been a month in Spain and had led an English ambulance.

Bennington College

Auden taught a class here in the spring of 1946.

Bergson, Henri *see* "Criticism in a Mass Society"

Berlin

For Auden his first, yearlong visit to Berlin from 1928 to 1929 would be a life-changing revelation as it would also be for his best friends Christopher Isherwood and Stephen Spender.

At the end of World War I Germany was obliged to accept the harsh peace terms of the Versailles Treaty that demanded exorbitant and economy-crippling reparations to be paid to the victors.

A democratic and more centralized federal constitution was adopted at Weimar in 1919, and Germany became known as the Weimar Republic. A middle-of-the-road government suppressed attempts by the radical left and by the extreme right to seize power. However, the economic crisis of the postwar years, marked by mass unemployment and rampant currency inflation, strengthened the extremist parties and wiped out a large portion of the middle class. Assassinations were symptomatic of the terrorist tactics adopted by the extreme nationalists, many of whom later joined the National Socialist (Nazi) party of Adolf Hitler or the Nationalist (monarchist) party.

The election (1925) of Hindenburg as president seemed a nationalist victory, but Hindenburg cooperated with coalitions drawn mainly from the Social Democrats, the Catholic Center party, and the conservative German People's Party to fulfill moderate programs. This helped stabilize the currency, and there was an easing of the terms of the Treaty of Versailles with regard to reparation payments.

But soon afterward the world economic depression brought about mass unemployment and business failure, and political and social tensions mounted. The Nazi and Communist parties gained strength in the Reichstag but failed in their efforts to mold parliamentary majorities. Government came to a standstill.

Auden and Isherwood's friend John Lehmann recalls the aura of Hitler's new authority: "I noticed something I had not foreseen, an element puzzling and deeply disturbing, that had been left out of the reporters' reckonings of Right versus Left, reactionary capitalism versus the working-class movement, and so on. All over the city, especially in the middle-class residential and shopping districts, huge pictures of Hitler were displayed in the fading light in windows illuminated by devout candles. The crude likenesses of the Man of Germany's Destiny, row upon row above us, were like altars dedicated to some primitive, irrational demon cult" (*The Whispering Gallery*).

Rather than accept the alternative of a military dictatorship, in January 1933, Hindenburg made Hitler chancellor. In the elections of March 1933, Hitler played upon the electorate's fear of the Communists and Jews to win a bare majority of seats for the National Socialists and the Nationalists. On March 23, the Enabling Act, opposed only by the Social Democrats and the disbarred Communist Party, gave Hitler full dictatorial powers.

The key to this context is the depression of 1929 that turned Germany into a poverty-stricken country of desperation. In Berlin one of the new and thriving forms of employment was male and female prostitution in the streets and more so in the nightlife of straight and gay bars. This became an industry that attracted people from the rest of Europe and America. There were also the remnants of a very ambitious artistic and intellectual milieu that offered its own attractions.

Norman Page notes, "If, during his first few months in Berlin, Auden was overwhelmed by the unprecedented freedoms now placed at his disposal, what is really extraordinary is the speed with which he passed from the immaturity of his initial responses to an articulated self-awareness and self-knowledge.... Studying his laconic but penetrating analyses, it is easy to forget that this was a young man of barely twenty-two who had only just stepped off the class-driven conveyor belt of public school and ancient university" (*Auden and Isherwood: The Berlin Years*).

After Auden returned from his first visit to Berlin, Christopher Isherwood wrote in *Christopher and His Kind*, "He was full of stories from Berlin, that astonishingly vicious yet fundamentally so respectable city, where even the night-life has a cosy domestic quality and where

the films were the most interesting in Europe." The nightlife meant bars with "boys"—something he could not say in *Lions and Shadows* (1938), but would later make up for in *Christopher and His Kind* (1976). In addition to the discovery of Berlin itself, Auden had met John Layard (Barnard in *Lions and Shadows*) a disciple of the psychologist Homer Lane who gave Auden a new vocabulary that amounted to a rationale for their unrepressed desires that had been very repressed in England. *Isherwood*: "In Weston [Auden] Layard had found an intelligent listener who became, overnight, an enthusiastic disciple" (*Lions and Shadows*). Isherwood continues that according to Auden's interpretation of Layard's interpretation of Lane, "Every disease, Lane had taught, is itself a cure—if we know how to take it. There is only one sin: disobedience to the inner law of our own nature. The results of this disobedience show themselves in crime or disease; but the disobedience is never, in the first place, our own fault—it is the fault of those who teach us, as children, to control God (our desires) instead of giving him room to grow.... Conventional education ... inverts the whole natural system in childhood, turning the child into a spurious adult. So that later, when the child grows up physically into a man, he is bound to try to regain his childhood—by means which, to the outside world, appear ever more and more unreasonable.... Diseases are therefore only warning symptoms of the sickness of the soul" (*LS*).

For two relatively recent adolescents, Lane's references to childhood sounded wonderful; and for two homosexuals who felt constrained in Britain, Lane, plus Berlin, sounded even better. Isherwood writes that Auden's "whole vocabulary ... was renovated ... he was reproving me for harbouring a 'death-Wish'.... 'You've got to drop all that ... You must be pure in heart.'" Isherwood then defines the term as per Auden: "The pure-in-heart man became our new ideal. He was essentially free and easy, generous with his money and his belongings, without worries or inhibitions.... He was a wonderful listener, but he never 'sympathized' with your troubles; and the only advice he ever gave was in the form of parables—stories about other people which you could apply to your own problems.... He was entirely without fear"

(*LS*). The pure-in-heart man is Truly Strong. The pure-in-heart man who is "essentially free and generous" became the role model of the 1930s as the Auden gang would freely and generously support each other's art, help each other get published, and generally act upon altruistic inclinations. (Auden in the late 1930s married — on paper only — Thomas Mann's daughter Erika so she could flee Germany and stay in Britain.)

The influence of the Lane-Auden-Isherwood connection was profound for the coming decade: (1) The persona of The Truly Strong Man now had an enhanced status, having been given the official sanction by a great authority — Lane; (2) the concept of parable-art, which both Isherwood and Auden had already enacted in their stories and poems, was now also sanctioned. Private spheres could become parables to explain public chaos. These two themes became integral aspects of the Isherwood-Auden schema, and would be widely imitated in the 1930s and after. As for Isherwood there could only be one place for him to find redemption for his feeling of being a "misfit." This was Berlin: "You want to commit the unforgivable sin, to shock Mummy and Daddy and Nanny, to smash the nursery clock, to be a really naughty little boy.... If you stick to your safe London nursery-life, you never *will* grow up. You'll die a time-shrivelled Peter Pan. At present, you're exactly seven years old.... I told my family [who were] patient but bewildered as ever, [and they] agreed sadly..." (*LS*).

By family, Isherwood really meant his mother, Kathleen. By "unforgivable sin," the Isherwood of 1938 wasn't being specific.

In 1976 he would rectify this lack of specificity in *Christopher and His Kind*. He goes back in time to this section in *Lions and Shadows* and gives the real lowdown: "[Layard] had introduced Wystan to Lane's revolutionary teachings, thus inspiring him to use them as a frame of reference for his poems.... 'Publish each healer.... It is time for the destruction of error ... prohibit sharply the rehearsed response.... Harrow the house of the dead.... The game is up for you and the others.... Love ... needs death ... death of the old gang [the past of The Others].... New styles of architecture, a change of heart.'" These were all terms that made their way into Auden's 1930 *Poems*, which would make him the avatar of his generation. Then Isherwood puts matters on a more viscerally personal level by reiterating the Lane philosophy, particularly about freeing one's inner desires: "Life-shaking words! When Christopher heard them ... they justified a change in his own life which he had been longing but not quite daring to make. Now he burned to put them into practice, to unchain his desires and hurl reason and sanity into prison. However, when *Lions and Shadows* suggests that Christopher's chief motive for going to Berlin was that he wanted to meet Layard, it is avoiding the truth ... that wasn't why he was in such a hurry ... it was Berlin itself he was hungry to meet; the Berlin Wystan had promised him. To Christopher [and Auden], Berlin meant Boys" (*CK*). And more specifically, working class boys as explained by Isherwood:

"At school, Christopher had fallen in love with many boys and had been yearningly romantic about them. At college he had managed to get into bed with one. This was due entirely to the initiative of his partner, who, when Christopher became scared and started to raise objections, locked the door, and sat firmly on Christopher's lap. I am still grateful to him.... Other experiences followed, all of them enjoyable but none entirely satisfying. This was because Christopher was suffering from an inhibition, then not unusual among upper-class homosexuals; he couldn't relax sexually with a member of his own class or nation." So began an egalitarian notion of solidarity with the working class in the most tangible way possible. Auden wrote the poem "This Loved One" for "Bubi" (baby), one of Isherwood's first "boys" in Berlin.

Auden wrote his poems and Isherwood wrote his *Berlin Stories*, although these would not be published until 1935 (*Mr. Norris Changes Trains*), 1937 (Sally Bowles), and 1938 (*Goodbye to Berlin*), all of which would become the basis for John van Druten's 1951 play *I Am a Camera*, which in turn became the enormously successful and still running 1967 musical *Cabaret*. Isherwood stayed in Berlin the longest, from 1929 to 1933, and witnessed Hitler's rise to power and dictatorship. Auden made return visits. Among the many who visited also were

Stephen Spender, Edward Upward, John Lehman, Aaron Copland, Paul Bowles, William Plomer, Gerald Hamilton (Mr. Norris), and Harold Nicolson.

Norman Page writes of this period, "When Auden, in the last line of one of the best known of his early poems (written, incidentally, in the first month of his stay in Berlin), expressed a wish for 'New styles of architecture, a change of heart' ["Sir, No Man's Enemy"] he may have had only the Bauhaus specifically in mind but was surely not speaking only of architecture. The line expresses the mood of a whole generation for whom Berlin seemed to offer the promise of artistic and social tolerance. The tragedy ... is that the heyday passed so quickly — was indeed, already under serious threat, though many of those with whom it is concerned came to recognize this grim reality only with the passing of time."

Berlin, Sir Isaiah

1909–97, English political scientist, b. Latvia (then in Russia). He was educated at Oxford, where he became a fellow (1932) and a professor of social and political theory (1957–67). He was also president of Wolfson College (1966–75). His works include *Karl Marx* (3d ed. 1963), *Four Essays on Liberty* (1969), *Personal Impressions* (1980), and the essay collection *The Proper Study of Mankind* (1997). He was knighted in 1957.

Berlin recalled the fuss made when Auden, Christopher Isherwood, Aldous Huxley, Gerald Heard, and others emigrated from Britain in the late 1930s for America. Some Britons called them cowards. Isherwood noted the British criticism in his *Diaries* (Volume 1, 1996) by writing down this doggerel verse he had heard was "going around London":

"The literary erstwhile Left-well-wisher would" Seek vainly now for Auden and for Isherwood: The dog beneath the skin has had the brains To save it, Norris-like by changing trains."

The sarcasm is increased by the references to the Auden-Isherwood play *The Dog Beneath Skin* and Isherwood's novel, *Mr. Norris Changes Trains,* in which Norris is an amoral scoundrel. Isaiah Berlin, also a friend of Aldous Huxley,

did not agree with the Auden-Isherwood critics. Auden, very much interested in theories of history, appreciated Berlin's views on history. Auden dedicated "Lakes" in "Bucolics" to Berlin. (*See also* America.)

Bernstein, Leonard

1918–90, American composer, conductor, and pianist, perhaps best known for his score to the Broadway musical *West Side Story.* Bernstein was a great admirer of Auden, and the poet's *The Age of Anxiety* became the theme of his second symphony. Auden was not a fan of the symphony and even less so of the ballet by Jerome Robbins using Bernstein's music.

Beside the Seaside see Grierson, John

Betjeman, John

1906–84, English poet, b. London. His verse was marked by satire of the present and nostalgic feelings for the Victorian past. His published collections include *Mt. Zion* (1933*), Continental Dew* (1937), *Old Lights for New Chancels* (1940), *Slick but Not Streamlined* (1947) with an introduction by Auden, *A Few Late Chrysanthemums* (1954), *High and Low* (1966), *Collected Poems* (1971), *Metro-Land* (1977), *and Church Poems (*1981). He also published numerous architectural studies, including *Ghastly Good Taste or a Depressing Story of the Rise and Fall of English Architecture* (1933, rev. ed. 1971) and *A Pictorial History of English Architecture* (1972). Knighted in 1969, he was Poet Laureate of England from 1972 until 1984.

Auden first met John Betjeman when they were students at Oxford in 1926. They may or may not have had a single sexual encounter. Auden was "amused by Betjeman's taste for High Anglicanism and Victorian Gothic, all of which (said Auden) exactly harmonized with his own childhood memories of provincial gaslit towns, seaside lodgings, harmoniums, and High Mass. Their enthusiasm for these things was so similar that Auden once suggested facetiously that he had actually created Betjeman out of his own substance. 'I can never make up my mind,' he said, 'whether Mr. Betjeman was born after the flesh or whether he was magically conceived by myself...'" (Carpenter, *W.H. Auden*). Auden long retained his fondness for Betjeman and his predilections. In 1947 Auden used his influence to publish Betjeman's *Slick But Not Streamlined*, for which Auden selected the verse and wrote an introduction. (He hated the title that the publisher chose after they rejected Auden's choice: *Betjeman's Bust*.) Auden notes facetiously in the introduction: "It is difficult to write seriously about a man who one has sung hymns with or judiciously about a poet whose work makes one violently jealous."

Bettelheim, Bruno *see* Autism

"Between Adventure" *see* Poems

Billy Budd *see* The Enchafed Flood

Blake, Nicholas *see* Day Lewis, Cecil

Blake, William

1757–1827, English poet and artist, b. London. While thought of as English romantic, Blake was unique in a style that depicted the human condition, a quality that appealed to Auden.

Blake attended drawing school and worked in his youth as an apprentice to an engraver. He also attended the Royal Academy, but he rebelled against the school's stifling atmosphere — a rebellion Auden identified with and left to establish his own engraving business.

In his lifetime Blake saw only one of his works — his first book, *Poetical Sketches* (1783), published conventionally. The rest of his major poetry he engraved and published himself,

using a method of his own creation in which text and illustration were engraved on the same plate. These publications were largely unsuccessful in Blake's lifetime; not until long after his death did he achieve critical acclaim.

In *Songs of Innocence* (1789) and *Songs of Experience* (1794) the world is seen from a child's eyes: There are beauty and pain and cruelty inflicted by people rather than by fate. As parables of adult life and Duality, the *Songs* would be a great influence on Auden.

Blake's Prophetic Books include *The Book of Thel* (1789), *The Marriage of Heaven and Hell* (c. 1790), *The French Revolution* (1791), *America* (1793), *Europe* (1794), *The Book of Urizon* (1794), *The Book of Los* (1795), *Milton* (1804–8), and *Jerusalem* (1804–20). Blake's mysticism was a fusing of reality and imagination, in which the spiritual was an expression of the human.

Blake would become a factor in Auden's mind and art very early. "Auden revered Blake" according to his literary executor Edward Mendelson (*Later Auden*). Blake's take on Duality is first enunciated in his *Songs of Innocence* (1789) and *Songs of Experience* (1794), which, while told from a child's view, are hardly childish, and within the nursery tableau are quite a harsh indictment of the terrible passage (or quest) that every individual must negotiate in a path to maturity and responsibility, which, of course, some never achieve. *Songs of Innocence* see the world before an individual's corruption by experience of the world. *Songs of Experience* are seen from the post-corruption view. Auden also enjoyed Blake's mystical visions with their fairytale qualities — and Auden, as Blake, understood that fairytales, quests, and saga stories are not really for children. Blake, though considered a Romantic, had more of an underlying cynicism than other romantics (Keats, Shelley) that underscored the reality within every fantasy and did not overglorify life and art. Byron was another cynic with tongue in cheek and was also favored by Auden who emulated his style in a very sharp *Letter to Lord Byron* (1937). Still, when Auden returned to Christianity in 1940, the mystical aspects in Blake appealed to him most.

In an early poem (c. 1929) Auden refers to a Blake title, "The Questioner Who Sits So

Sly," to imply the need for questors who are not gullible or, as Blake would have it, not innocent but experienced. In a 1930 poem Auden listed Blake as one of the seers who went unappreciated along with T.E. Lawrence and Homer Lane.

In a 1935 essay Auden noted that "the whole of Freud's teaching" about internal conflicts could be found in *The Marriage of Heaven and Hell.*

In 1936, while Auden was working for John Grierson and the GPO Film Unit, Auden began a script that would have included a poem by Blake, but the documentary was never made.

In 1937's *Letter to Lord Byron* Auden alludes to Blake's *Marriage of Heaven and Hell* as "a nice idea of Blake's, but won't take place, alas," signifying that Auden's own experiences had matured him into more of a skepticism than an acceptance of human frailty.

In his introduction to *The Oxford Book of Light Verse* (1938), Auden writes in a footnote that while Blake's "Auguries of Innocence" "may not exactly be 'light verse,' they are written in a popular style and remind readers that in general, as with Blake, 'light verse' can be very serious."

Auden's book of Mandarin *pensées, The Prolific and the Devourer* (1939), takes its title from ideas in Blake's *Marriage of Heaven and Hell* and is another journey from Innocence to Experience. For Auden, the Prolific are the makers and artists, the Devourers, consumers and politicians. (These terms also owe much to C.G. Jung whom Auden was fascinated with at this time and for the next decade.) Indeed he said to E.R. Dodds while writing *The Prolific and the Devourer* that "It is just a new *Marriage of Heaven and Hell* that I am doing" (Carpenter *W.H. Auden*).

In the verse commentary to the sonnet sequence "In Time of War" (1938), published in *Journey to a War* (1939), Auden refers to Blake's lines concerning "gratified desire."

In 1939 Auden often quoted Blake's line from *The Marriage of Heaven and Hell* "everything that lives is holy," using it at the end of "I Believe" and in *The Prolific and the Devourer,* and a variation of it in the poem "Pascal."

In 1940 when Auden first met his lifetime companion Chester Kallman, he gave Kallman an inscribed volume of Blake, a measure of Auden's affection for both Kallman *and* Blake. Moreover, Auden hoped that with Kallman, he would have a similar relationship as Blake had with his wife. Concurrently, Auden wrote his long poem "New Year Letter" and in it asserts that artists should give order to our perceptions of the world. Among the "orderers" he venerates are Blake, Voltaire, Hardy, Rilke, and Dryden with the last's style imitated.

When Auden moved into his East Village Manhattan apartment at 77 St. Mark's Place in 1954, he hung an original Blake watercolor on the wall.

Blake remained an enormous influence for Auden for the remainder of his life and career. In Auden's "Commonplace Book," *A Certain World* (1970), published just three years before his passing, Blake's wisdom is quoted in sections titled "Imagination, "Nature, and "The Lord's Prayer."

Blunt, Anthony

1907–83, English art historian. In 1964 he confessed to membership in a Soviet spy ring that included Donald MacLean, Guy Burgess, and Kim Philby. As a result, Blunt was stripped of his knighthood. His writings include *François Mansart and the Origins of French Classical Architecture* (1941); *The Drawings of Poussin* (with Walter Friedlaender, 3 vol., 1939–53); *Art and Architecture in France, 1500–1700* (1953); *The Art of William Blake* (1959); *The Paintings of Nicolas Poussin* (1968); *Picasso's Guernica* (1968); and *Sicilian Baroque* (1968).

Blunt was a great friend of Auden's Oxford classmate, friend, and fellow poet Louis MacNeice as well as with another Auden-Isherwood friend Guy Burgess. In 1936 Auden stayed a short period with Blunt at Cambridge. Blunt was an actively fervent Marxist. (How fervent is noted above.) While together, they likely discussed their strong mutual interest in William Blake, and Blunt may have encouraged Auden to take a more active role in the Spanish Civil War, which Auden would shortly do by going to Spain.

Later Blunt would visit Auden in Ischia.

Bogan, Louise

1897–1970, American poet and critic, b. Livermore, Maine. She spent much of her life in New York City and was the poetry editor for the *New Yorker* magazine for many years. In 1964 she co-translated with Elizabeth Mayer Goethe's *Elective Affinities*, and in 1971 she co-translated again with Mayer a version of Goethe's *The Sorrows of Young Werther and Novella* for which Auden translated poems and wrote an introduction.

After Auden's arrival in America he befriended Bogan, who published Auden in *The New Yorker*. In 1942 Auden wrote to her about how a poet feels looking at past poems: "Now and then I look through books and is my face red. One of the troubles of our time is that we are all, I think, precocious as personalities and backwards as characters. Looking at old work I keep finding ideas which one had no business to see already at that age, and a style of treatment which one ought to have outgrown."

In 1942 Auden wrote a laudatory review of a book of poems by Bogan. The review also served as a self-critical depiction of Auden himself in similar terms to his letter above. The review includes autobiographical data, and since he was a man who said he would never write an autobiography per se, this is one of his indirect efforts, as are *Letter to Lord Byron* and *A Certain World*.

Bogardus, Edgar

1928–1958, poet, critic, he worked as managing editor of the *Kenyon Review*. Bogardus wrote poems that were skeptical and satirical about love and sex. His book *Various Jangling Keys* was selected by Auden for the Yale Younger Poets Series in 1953. He died in his home in 1958, at the age of 30, as a result of carbon monoxide poisoning, *Kenyon Review* published his collection *Last Poems* (1960).

"The Bond and the Free" 1935

This is a review of four books concerning university life, prison reform and the "Means Test." *Auden*: "Every sensible person knows that the means test and the prison are as those books describe them and that the social system under which they are possible is grotesque." Auden discusses Communism (*see also* Marxism) in relation to the above, but Communism is not the answer, nor is liberalism. Everyone also knows that 1) violence is bad, and that 2) greed prevents sharing. Auden sees Communism as a possible, if not perfect answer, as it rejects self-interest.

Bonhoeffer, Dietrich *see* "Friday's Child"

"The Book of Talbot" 1933

This is a review of Violet Clifton's book *The Book of Talbot*, and both Clifton and Auden extol the traditional virtues of a "life of a husband written by a wife that loved him," with love being the cause of all good. The book gives a "a sense of glory which is the privilege of great art to give."

The review was written shortly after Auden's poem "A Summer Night" described his Vision of Agape which influenced this review and his life thereafter. Auden always looked for married happiness in others and sought it for himself with gender not an issue.

Border-Frontier

The battle between the past and the present sets up the divisive demilitarized-zone of the Auden-Isherwood "frontier," a theme that would become a pivotal concept in the 1930s. Mendelson writes, "The war that peace occasionally interrupts is a civil war between broken fragments of a whole. Its forces are mutually opposed efforts toward wholeness made by different halves of a divided city or a divided self. This civil war, as Auden wrote to Isherwood in a verse letter in April 1929, was 'our study and our interest'" (*Early Auden*).

In the war against The Others; the border to be crossed was to reform an old life into a new; the Northwest Passage would be surmounted to reach the frontier, which was represented by Berlin and the revelations found there. The Border-Frontier imagery would be a strong element in Auden's poems and plays, with the last of the three plays with Isherwood titled *On the Frontier* (1938). Edward Upward, a mutual friend of Auden and Isherwood would write a 1937 novel, *Journey to the Border*, and other members of the Auden Generation would also directly or indirectly refer to similar imagery.

Bowles, Paul and Jane

Paul Bowles, 1910–99, American writer and composer, b. New York City. He studied in Paris with Virgil Thomson and Aaron Copland, and the three met Isherwood on a visit to Berlin in 1931, which was likely conveyed to Auden in the letters he received from Isherwood. Isherwood appropriated Bowles's name for his most famous character "Sally Bowles" (based on Jean Ross). During the early 1940s Paul and his wife Jane, also a writer, lived with W.H. Auden in a house in Brooklyn owned by George Davis (later knocked down for the subsequent construction of the Brooklyn-Queens Expressway). Other guests in Chez Davis with Auden were Erika and Golo Mann, Carson McCullers, Benjamin Britten, Peter Pears, Louis MacNeice, and Gypsy Rose Lee. Auden was reputed to have been unofficial house manager, keeping things in order.

Bowles composed (1930s–1940s) a number of modernist operas, ballets, song cycles, and orchestral and chamber pieces. From 1947 on he lived in Tangier, Morocco. His fiction often traces the corruption of innocence and the psychic disintegration of civilized man in a savagely primitive environment.

His wife was Jane Auer Bowles, 1917–73, American writer, b. New York City. Her works often treat the conflict between the weak and the strong.

Bowra, Maurice

1898–1971, English classical scholar, b. China. Associated with Oxford University throughout his adult life. He was knighted in 1951. Bowra is particularly known for his studies of ancient Greek poetry and culture.

He was a Wadham College don during Auden's student days at Oxford and his set included John Betjeman and Brian Howard, a set that Auden wished, but failed to be included in. When, in 1955, Enid Starkie of Oxford asked Auden to consider her nomination of him for professor of poetry at Oxford, Bowra, who was an old "enemy" of Auden's friend and another Oxford don E.R. Dodds, supported Harold Nicolson over Auden. Auden won the vote and entered into his post in 1956.

"Brand Versus Peer" 1960

This essay was first published as the introduction to the 1960 edition of *Brand* by Ibsen., tr. Michael Meyer. (Auden would write about Brand Versus Peer Gynt again in a 1962 essay, "The Genius and the Apostle," with Kierkegaard as the frame of reference in both essays.) The plays are of dramatic verse dominated by a single character. Auden notes that Ibsen's surface polemics in these plays concern Ibsen's rage at Norway for not aiding Denmark against Prussia. The contrasting heroes in the plays indicate Ibsen's subcontext, as each character complements and also critiques the other. Brand will not compromise; he is all or nothing (what Norway should be). Peer sees the devil as a viper and believes that man should retreat from evil; this is a satire of Norway as it was, but should not be. For Auden, moral approval and disapproval and personal liking and disliking in real life are not the same, while in art they are; in art lovable equals good, detestable equals bad. Yet, Brand is unlikable despite his courage and his pitiable fate because he seems unreal. Peer, though a selfish scoundrel, is lovable in the manner of Falstaff, as he is described in Auden's essay "The Prince's Dog."

Peer is a genius with a gift and ego that seek reward. It is easy to depict a man of active will. Brand is an apostle who cannot be truly manifested in art. He has a calling from God and seeks not to be rewarded, but to hear God's command; he is not enamored with "I" but with "Thou." He is known by his converts but never for his inner truth, which can't be tested except by negation. (If he flees, he fails.) An apostle is impossible to depict, as his existence is an accident. Ibsen's *Peer Gynt* poses the different problem of depicting poetic genius, which Ibsen does; his success in doing so for *Peer Gynt* illuminates his failure to do so in *Brand*.

A poet is a maker of the timeless; a doer's deed is finite. Art cannot reveal the nature of the maker as a deed will of the doer. The maker, the poet, requires no others — directly — in order to create. Drama can depict deeds but not creativity (making). A poet's life can be depicted but not his intellectual process of making art. A person is what he does in terms of deeds, but a poet is not necessarily what he makes in terms of art. Ibsen solves this problem by having Peer act out "roles" without ever fulfilling them; that is, he does not actually do the deeds required of the roles. Play-acting stands in for making.

The poet is a dreamer-madman with his dreams ruled by wish and desire. The dreaming ego fulfills the self's waking need. The ego is a victim of the self; it cannot say, "I'm dreaming." The madman's self is victim of an ego that says, "I'm Napoleon," and the self cannot say, "I'm a liar." Both dreamer and madman are in earnest, not play-acting. Conversely, the poet-actor pretends for fun and asserts freedom by playful lying, but he *knows* he is lying (*see* Play and Work). For Ibsen as poet, Peer had an isolated childhood cut off by his father's drunkenness; his mother was his playmate and imaginative stimulant for fantasy. When she dies, Solveig becomes the muse and mother and a timeless platonic love (as Auden tried to imagine Chester Kallman was).

Peer Gynt is a parable. If *Brand* were parabolic like Don Quixote, the play would be better, but the direct, didactic, and too real portrait is weak; his loveless selfish mother is discouraging, not inspiring. Because of his mother's idol, which is her greed, her son's calling, which is God, may be his defiance of her rather than a true calling; consequently, his is a false apostleship of self-inflicted pain that may engender pity, but not sympathy. An apostle and marriage are incompatible because the wife — in his case, Brand's wife Agnes — cannot deal with answering to both man and God indivisibly, without depriving her of her own personality. Brand

chooses to let his son die so he can remain a priest, and he later accuses Agnes of idolatry in her grief for her son. His intransigence becomes his God, and thus he is not a true apostle, but an idolater. Ibsen tried to do the impossible — portray an apostle by his actions, which, by the fact that they are Brand's actions and not God's, defeats the intent. Brand chooses the tragic instead of being chosen by a divine will, which is the true apostle's fate. *Brand* teaches the audience by being an example of what not to do, which is to misconstrue God's love, as most of us do.

Brave New World see Huxley, Aldous; Plays with Isherwood (*The Dog Beneath the Skin*)

Brecht, Bertolt

1898–1956. German playwright, poet and director. Few mid–twentieth century dramatists can claim as pervasive an influence on late twentieth century theatre and drama as Brecht, both in pioneering new stage techniques and in the use of the theatre as a political forum. From his earliest dramatic works, written around World War I, to the innovative staging of his own mature works at the Berliner Ensemble in the decade following the end of World War II, Brecht perfected the epic theatre style as an approach that suited the Marxist views of his progressive plays. His earliest dramas reject the illusionism of the numerous productions of Max Reinhardt, as well as the guarded idealism inherent in German expressionism, which depicted the horrors of World War I and frightening new technologies. Brecht instead rejected traditional values in works like *Drums in the Night* (1922), that depicts a young soldier who deserts the army to return to the arms of his lover. Other early Brecht plays include *Baal* (1923), *In the Jungle of Cities* (1923), and *Man Equals Man* (1926), all of which explore the impact of bourgeois values on man's striving for fulfillment. Full use of epic theatre, particularly the alienation technique, are fully seen in Brecht's *Edward II* (1924), adapted from Christopher Marlowe's play. Brecht's fame was assured with *The Threepenny Opera* (1928), loosely based on John Gay's *The Beggar's Opera* and featuring original music by Kurt Weill. Brecht and Weill teamed again for *Mahagonny* (1929), *He Who Said Yes and He Who Said No* (1930), and *The Seven Deadly Sins* (1933). Brecht's interest in Marxism led him to sharpen the ideological focus of his plays in this era. Following *The Threepenny Opera*, Brecht composed a series of Lehrstücke, or "teaching plays," emphasizing issues of class-consciousness. At the rise of the Nazis in 1933, Brecht left Germany for Denmark, where he wrote *Round Heads and Pointed Heads* (1936), adapted from William Shakespeare's *Measure for Measure*, along with two anti-fascists plays in a naturalistic style, *Señora Carrar's Rifles* (1937) and *Fear and Misery of the Third Reich* (1938; called *The Private Life of the Master Race* when performed in the U.S.). Brecht moved to Finland in 1941 prior to traveling through the Soviet Union and on to the United States. From the mid 1930s through the end of World War II, Brecht wrote his greatest plays in the epic theatre style, including *Mother Courage and Her Children* (1941), *Life of Galileo* (1943), *The Good Person of Setzuan* (1943), *The Caucasian Chalk Circle* (1948), and *Mr. Puntila and His Man Matti* (1948). Brecht was called to testify before the House Un-American Activities Committee during the days of the Communist witch-hunt following World War II, and he left the United States permanently shortly after his appearance. He settled in East Berlin, founding the Berliner Ensemble, a collective dedicated to performing his work until his death in 1956.

Auden's first verifiable knowledge of the works of Bertolt Brecht was in 1929. While visiting in Berlin, Auden had seen Brecht's *The Threepenny Opera* (1928), featuring Kurt Weill's music. In his seminal *The Theatre of Bertolt Brecht*, John Willett stresses the influence of Brecht's *Hauspostille* poems, *Mahagonny* (1929), and *The Threepenny Opera* on Auden's poetry and theatrical works. Auden's poem, "1929," written around the time of his Berlin trip, reflects, as Edward Callan writes, Auden's "first-hand acquaintance with protest verse recited in the cabarets, for which Bertolt Brecht had shown the way with his 'The Legend of the Dead Soldier' in 1922." George T. Wright, in

assessing the significance of German writers and artists on Auden's development, lists Brecht centrally along with Rilke, Kafka, Freud, Marx, Kierkegaard, the German Protestant tradition, and German popular songs. Monroe K. Spears underscores the Brechtian influence on Auden's first operatic adaptation, *Paul Bunyan* (1941), with music by Benjamin Britten, first performed on May 5, 1941, at Columbia University. More importantly, it seems clear that the Auden and Christopher Isherwood dramatic collaborations of the 1930s, *The Dog Beneath the Skin* (1936), *The Ascent of F6* (1937), and *On the Frontier* (1938), owe a significant debt to German expressionism and the epic theatre style pioneered by Erwin Piscator and employed most effectively by Brecht in his plays beginning in the 1920s. Eric Bentley has called the Auden plays imitations of Brecht, but Richard Hoggart writes that epic theatre was a too limiting style for the "scope" Auden's mind required. Auden and Isherwood both denied any significant knowledge of Brecht's achievement at the time they collaborated on their plays. It is most likely that the epic theatre style was in the intellectual air during these years, leading writers and artists like Brecht, Auden, and Isherwood to recognize the worth of the epic approach in presenting their socially conscious brand of experimental drama. Norman Page, in *Auden and Isherwood: The Berlin Years*, writes appreciatively of the most significant Auden-Isherwood collaboration, *The Dog Beneath the Skin*, stressing that their "rejection of traditional forms and modes, and the collaborative nature of their art," led them to create "pastiches of ballads, cabaret songs or graffiti drawn zestfully on popular sources in defiance of traditional hierarchies of the 'serious' and the 'light,'" inspired, in part, by Weill and Brecht. In describing the connections between Auden and Brecht, Eric Bentley writes that "Brecht is not a pure folk poet but also the parodist of folk poetry, a sarcastic mind, superficially anti-literary, fundamentally lyrical, tough, angular, righteously indignant, all that W.H. Auden in his satiric days tried to be. But Auden's wit was always that of a clever and rather priggish undergraduate, and since a poet cannot be perpetually precocious, one guessed that he would take to religion" (*Brecht Commentaries*). The

Auden-Isherwood dramatic collaborations were staged by London's Group Theatre, which had also staged Auden's solo dramatic experiments. In London in 1934, Brecht attended Group Theatre performances of Eliot's *Sweeney Agonistes* and Auden's *The Dance of Death*, which John Fuegi describes as "clearly epic" in the Brechtian tradition. Brecht also met Auden and Isherwood again in London in 1936. Auden admired Brecht as a writer and artist, but described him as a distasteful human being. In a June 12, 1942, entry to his journal, Brecht wrote of reading the poetry of Eliot and Auden, finding that both offered "veritable poetic prophecy," but otherwise condemned them with faint praise and seemed to feel, as he did of many of his contemporaries, that they had somehow sold out to commercial and popular considerations as well as to the demands of a culture Brecht found corrupt. However, none of this prevented some minor Brecht-Auden collaborations. In early 1943, Brecht, working on his adaptation of John Webster's *The Duchess of Malfi* with poet H. R. Hayes, went to Auden without the knowledge of Hayes in hopes of persuading Auden to assist on the English-language version of the adaptation. Auden agreed and, in due course, Hayes was dropped from the project. *The Duchess of Malfi*, which Brecht had planned as a vehicle for German actress Elisabeth Bergner, was produced on Broadway in October 1946 for a modest run at the Barrymore Theatre. At about this time, Brecht urged Auden to complete an English translation of his *The Caucasian Chalk Circle*, a project Auden worked on with James and Tania Stern (Act V of the translation was published in the *Kenyon Review*, Vol. VIII, No. 2, Spring 1946, pp. 188–202) in 1944–45. Auden did not find working with Brecht a positive experience. John Fuegi, in his *Brecht & Co.*, quotes British publisher Charles Monteith, who claimed that Auden said "that of the literary men he had known only three struck him as positively evil: Robert Frost, Yeats and Brecht!" because they lacked generosity and were unsupportive of the young. On finishing the adaptation of *The Duchess of Malfi* in April 1946, Auden delivered it and ended his relationship with Brecht. Direct influences of Brecht's work can be found in Auden's ballads,

"Miss Gee," "James Honeyman," "Victor," and "Sue," all described by John Fuller as "Brechtian" in tone. Fuller also identifies Brecht-inspired elements in Auden's 1947 poem "In Schrafft's," as well as "On Installing an American Kitchen in Lower Austria" (1958), with Fuller noting that there is "a distinction to be made here between the good-naturedly Epicurean solidarity of Auden, and the Marxist accusations of Brecht" inherent in Brecht's epigraph "Grub First, Then Ethics" that inspired Auden's poem. In collaboration with Chester Kallman, Auden also translated Brecht's *The Seven Deadly Sins*, which was successfully produced in 1959 (and published in the *Tulane Drama Review* in the Autumn 1961 issue), and *Mahagonny*. Spears stressed that Auden's "debt to Brecht in the ballads and some of the songs in the 1930s is plain, and the plays all follow the Brechtian model in many respects." Late in his life, Auden contributed songs for a National Theatre of Great Britain production of Brecht's masterwork *Mother Courage and Her Children*.

"A Bride in the 30s" 1934

Auden's poem about the conflict between straight love and "crooked" (homosexual) love starts with a youth's emergence into adult sex with its dangers of choice as he lies with his lover of the moment. He thinks of the outer world to block out this reality. The magic of the vision of Eros (romance) obscures the reality that always lurks nearby. Does one choose private or public spheres? What compromises must be made? The ghosts of childhood influence all adult choices. These stanzas of childhood's effect are didactic preparation for the choices of adulthood. Don't let "ghosts" make the choices for you. Do not listen to ghosts; do not settle for lust. Choose love not money. There is a language of learning and one for love; is one "crooked" or "straight as a dove?" The last line refers back to the lesson of a "A Summer Night."

British Public Schools

In Christopher Isherwood's first novel, *All*

the Conspirators, his protagonist remembers his days in public school:

> For the first day or two, the new boys hung about the passages, keeping together.... A baize notice board in the passage.... Any boy found ragging or fooling in the lavatories will be severely dealt with....
>
> Garvel got lammed for using a senior's bat.... They talked and quarelled among themselves.... Let's rebel.... We're going to chuck you out into that gorse-bush.... Please sir, I want to go home.
>
> MY DARLING MOTHER,
>
> I am quite certain that I shall always loathe and detest this place. Do please come and take me away as soon as you possibly can. I *hate* it.

A dominant theme that emerges from the recollections of the Auden Generation is the pervasive hatred of their experiences in preparatory and public schools. They didn't recall so much that they were being prepared for life by the schools because they received a classical education, but that they were being prepared for their lives as the class-conscious protectors and saviors of the British Empire. Although empire-saving as an end may not seem so deleterious, it was the means to this end that the future intellectuals and artists reacted against so strongly. They considered the public school to be anti-intellectual, anti-working class, anti-egalitarian, and concerned only with the preservation of the moneyed classes against everyone else. As Auden said of these schools in a 1934 essay, "The mass production of gentlemen is their *raison d'etre,* and one can hardly suggest that they should adopt principles which would destroy them. The fact remains that the public school boy's attitude to the working-class and to the not-quite-quite has altered very little since the [the first World] war ... their lives and needs remain as remote to him as those of another species. [This is] true of the staff as well ... a master was sacked for taking part in left-wing politics outside the school .... which seems to me a shameful thing ("The Liberal Fascist").

It was indeed a shame. Any hint of nonconformity by students was, for the most part, stunted by the great majority of the teachers.

The masters discouraged progressive ideas that students may have learned from their parents. More precisely, while Isherwood and Auden were encouraged by their parents in endeavors that encouraged independent thinking, the school's masters wanted dependent thinking instead. Auden recalled, "a master once caught me writing poetry in prep.... He said, 'you shouldn't waste your sweetness on the desert air like this Auden'; today I cannot think of him without wishing him evil" ("The Liberal Fascist"). This remark was first written in 1934, but Auden's anger lasted into his old age, as he would repeat it decades later.

The subliminally psychological intent of the prep and public schools was that the maintaining of the old order would be preserved within the school and inculcated in the students. While the Auden Generation protested against the perpetuation of traditions that they saw as anachronistic failures, they were in the minority. The great majority of their fellow students had no objections concerning how they were being developed. They would have approved of the preservation of their status as class-conscious "gentlemen." The Auden Generation were the "aesthetes" who were in opposition to the "hearties."

The hearties were the anti-intellectual athletes and game-players of both a physical and psychological nature. The games that they played were amongst themselves and even more so against the aesthetes and lower grades. They were expected by the school to demand obedient conformity and were given the power to use or abuse corporal punishment in order to get it. Conformity meant adherence to a school's rules of conduct. In themselves these rules were not unreasonable; however, students were encouraged on their "honor" to tell on each other when rules were violated. Auden remembers this honor system as ultimately dishonorable:

> I feel compelled to say that I believe no more potent engine for turning [students] into neurotic innocents, for perpetuating those very faults of character which it was intended to cure, was ever devised. Everyone knows that the only emotion that is fully developed in a boy of fourteen is the emotion of loyalty and honour. By appealing to it, you can do

almost anything you choose, you can suppress the expression of all those emotions, particularly the sexual, which are still undeveloped; like a modern dictator you can defeat almost any opposition from other parts of the psyche, but if you do, if you deny these other emotions their expression and development ... they will not only never grow up, but they will go backward ... like all things that are shut up.

[This] meant that [at school] the whole of our moral life was based on fear, not to mention the temptation it offered to the natural informer, and fear is not a healthy basis. It makes one furtive and dishonest, unadventurous. The best reason I have for opposing fascism is that at school I lived in a fascist state ["The Liberal Fascist"].

This "fascist state" in the public school, besides engendering antipathy for the aesthetes, also inspired a counterattack that evolved into an art form. Christopher Isherwood wrote in *Lions and Shadows*, "Gradually, in the most utter secrecy, I began to evolve a cult of the public-school system." What evolved was the pseudo-war of Auden, Isherwood, Upward, Spender and their aesthete peers versus snobbism, hypocrisy, and the hearties. Isherwood understood that while the de facto fascism of the public school was superficially a source of humor, it was also, subliminally, a nefarious danger: "It is so very easy, in the mature calm of a library, to sneer at all this homosexual romanticism [herein meant an all-boys school]. But the rulers of Fascist states do not sneer — they profoundly understand and make use of just these phantasies and longings. I wonder how, at this period, I should have reacted to the preaching of an English Fascist leader clever enough to serve up his 'message' in a suitably disguised and palatable form? He would have converted me inside half an hour — provided always that Chalmers [Upward] hadn't been there to interfere" (*Lions and Shadows*).

In time, the "cult of the public school system" was satirized (sometimes with painful reality) by the Auden Generation in Isherwood and Upward's Mortmere Stories, Isherwood's "Gems of Belgium Architecture," Auden's *Paid on Both Sides* and *The Orators*, and other works emulating these works.

Britten, Benjamin

1913–76, English composer. *The Young Person's Guide to the Orchestra* (1946), written for a film, is based on a theme by Purcell. His many song cycles and choral works *include A Boy Was Born* (1933); *A Ceremony of Carols* (1942); and *War Requiem* (1962), based on the war poems of Wilfred Owen. His operas include *Paul Bunyan*, with libretto by Auden in 1941, *Peter Grimes* (1945), *The Rape of Lucretia* (1946), *The Turn of the Screw* (1954), *A Midsummer Night's Dream* (1960), and *Death in Venice* (1973).

Auden met Britten when both were with John Grierson and the GPO Film Unit. Auden then connected Britten with Rupert Doone and the Group Theatre. Britten scored the music for the Auden-Isherwood plays *The Ascent of F6* (1937), and *On the Frontier* (1938). Britten and his lifetime companion and librettist, Peter Pears, landed in America shortly after Auden and Isherwood in 1939, although Britten and Pears returned to England in 1942.

Britten was six years younger than Auden and did not have quite the confidence that Auden exuded, which included Auden's stark bluntness that both amazed and charmed Britten. Auden encouraged Britten as an artist and as a homosexual (though not as partners, although Auden apparently tried). Britten set some Auden poems to music, including "The Creatures," "Night Covers Up the Rigid Land," and "Our Hunting Fathers" as well as Auden's section of the GPO documentary film *Night Mail* and BBC radio programs *Up the Garden Path* and *Hadrian's Wall*.

Auden and Britten collaborated on the opera of *Paul Bunyan*. This work signifies Auden's commitment to America as he deliberately chose an American subject for his collaboration with Britten. Auden researched for *Paul Bunyan* at the New York Public Library, which now houses his papers. Since its first performance in 1941, *Paul Bunyan* has had the reputation of an interesting failure. Even after its 1970s revival, it was treated as a curiosity rather than a work worthy of consideration on its own merits.

Brodsky, Joseph

1940–1996. Russian-American poet, b. Leningrad (St. Petersburg). A disciple of Anna

Akhmatova, he began writing poetry in 1955. He was denounced by the state (for "decadence and modernism," among other charges) in 1963 and was exiled by Soviet authorities in 1972. Brodsky immigrated to the United States, where he became a citizen and taught at several colleges. His poetry often treats themes of loss and exile. In the summer of 1972 Auden helped raise money to bring Brodsky to America.

In 1974 his *Selected Poems* was published, translated by George L. Kline and with a Foreword by Auden who died just prior to publication and to whom the book is dedicated. Auden wrote: "Mr. Brodsky is not an easy poet, but even a cursory reading will reveal that, like Van Gogh, and Virginia Woolf, he has an extraordinary capacity to envision material objects as sacramental signs, messengers from the unseen." Here, Auden manifests his pronounced emphasis on art as a form of Mysticism that finds the sacred within the profane.

The recipient of a MacArthur Award (1981), a National Book Award (1986), and many other honors, he won the 1987 Nobel Prize for Literature. Brodsky was Poet Laureate of the United States from 1991 to 1992.

"Brothers & Others" 1962

In Shakespeare's England, writes Auden in this essay, wealth was in land rather than capital. A change of wealth from land to capital changes one's conception of time. Land is static, representing stability, hierarchy, and reverence for the past. Capital is unpredictable, representing instability, hierarchy changes, and reverence for the future. Auden sees *The Merchant of Venice* as a transition of the landed past to a capitalist future, and finds it an "unpleasant play," a pseudo-fairytale with both malice and love (love thy neighbor, loan to thy enemy). Dante and Shakespeare both use usury as metaphor for the dichotomy of a love relationship (similar to the master-servant metaphor in Auden's essay "*Balaam and His Ass*"), and this relationship correlates to the rise of mercantilism.

The Brown Book of Nazi Terror

A central event of 1933 was the publication of *The Brown Book of Nazi Terror*. Without byline, the book was a chronological list of crimes during the Nazis' rise to power and after. German Communist Willi Munsterberg was tacitly credited with putting it together. Since the Nazis had avowed their intention to destroy Communism, the Communists countered with this effort that was translated into twenty-three languages and sold 600,000 copies throughout Europe and America. Even up to the day before *The Brown Book* became widespread news, the British still pretended that Hitler was just another buffoon like Mussolini and both were someone else's local problem. Yes, one had heard things, but one imagined these were rag press exaggerations promulgated by the Communist Party. However, the book's introduction by the esteemed Lord Marley attested to the veracity of the facts, and the facts defied — if not credence — decency.

Samuel Hynes writes in *The Auden Generation*: "If *The Brown Book* was a true history of existence in what had been a civilized European country, then it compelled any ordinary reader to alter and extend his sense of reality, of what was possible to men in the twentieth century. If it was true — and no one questioned the essential accuracy of the reporting — then reality meant something other, and worse, than men had thought and human beings were capable of greater evil than liberalism had allowed for. *The Brown Book* did not create this change — the Nazis did that — but it helped force a recognition of the change upon western consciousness."

The Auden Generation was duly warned and would react as artists and essayists against Hitler's fascism.

"Brussels in Winter" 1938

This poem concerns the general threat of a coming war and the relation of this feeling to the urban desolation of city life where one thinks there is security to be found in a collective misery. Here, Auden secretly marries public and private spheres as being intertwined, not separate as in previous poems. Private must accommodate public in order to find peace in either. The use of sexual metaphor is a first intimation of Auden's later sense of a personal responsibility to improve the imperfect city into the Great Good Place, the City of God, or a secular Eden.

"Bubi" *see* Berlin; *Poems* ("This Loved One")

"Bucolics" 1952–1953

This is Auden's commune with nature and a logical follow-up to "In Praise of Limestone." When Auden edited *The Portable Greek Reader* in 1947 he reread the Greek bucolic poets. His "Bucolics" were written as an interlude to Auden's "Horae Canonicae," that Mendelson says "expand on the chance rhyme *will* and *kill*," while "'Bucolics' expand on *face* and *place*" (*Later Auden*).

"Winds": For Alexis Leger (St-John Perse). The arbitrariness of both weather and fate, poetry as ceremonial praise, wind as the breath of God. Mendelson observes in *Later Auden* that this poem — between the lines — is also about breaking wind; that is, farting.

"Woods": For Nicolas Nabokov. Not savage but stable and solid, but still prone to quick destruction. "This great society is going to smash" is inspired by a line in Rosenstock-Huessy's *The Christian Future*.

"Mountains": For Hedwig Petzold. Exceptional yet isolated; unsociable and monstrous; lovers love them, the ordinary don't; mountains require "nerve."

"Streams": *For Elizabeth Drew. Streams are more in tune with the psychic landscape that is dominated by the exhaling flow of mild water. Streams represent a prelapsarian, dreamy Eden. This Eden is of a liberal inclination.

"Islands": Mendelson: "Among the many who seek refuge on islands are old saints looking for a solitude where" women will not "'Threaten their [Vision of] agape.'" Islands for Auden are places to escape to or from but they are never neutral or permanent "refuges." (See also *Look, Stranger.*)

"Plains": For Wendell Johnson. Plains are a horror of uniformity and dead-level evil that remind Auden of loneliness.

"Lakes": *For Isaiah Berlin. Lakes are cozier than oceans and rivers. Berlin and Auden shared liberal views, but the coziness of these lakes, according to Mendelson, reflects Auden's ideas that Berlin's liberalism was a bit too "comfy" (*Later Auden*).

*Mendelson: "Yet the wishes of water … are the poem's analogy for a real personal love that sees splendor in the names and places where lovelessness sees only numbers and masses…. Water weeps over a named beloved cat in the quatrain epitaph "'In Memoriam L.K.A.,' written in October 1953 … the waters [are] off Ischia where Auden and Kallman buried their cats at sea" (*Later Auden*).

Burgess, Guy

1910–1963, British diplomat and spy for the Soviet Union. He became a Communist at Cambridge. With the BBC in the 1930s, he joined the British Foreign Service in the 1940s. In 1951, Burgess was warned by Louis MacNeice's friend Anthony Blunt that the service feared he was a double agent. He then defected to Moscow. Burgess was gay and had been friendly with Auden, Isherwood, and Spender in the early 1930s. "Just before [his] flight [he] had tried … to reach Auden by phone at Stephen Spender's house in London…. But after Spender told the story to the press … was shadowed for weeks by reporters and police" (Mendelson, *Later Auden*).

Burrow, Trigant

1875–1950, British psychoanalyst, a very early advocate of group therapy. Auden read Burrow's *The Social Basis of Consciousness* (1927), and this influenced Part II of "1929" (see *Poems* 1930). Burrow echoed Homer Lane in believing that instinct should not be repressed.

Byron, Lord George Gordon

1788–1824, Auden drew inspiration and lessons from Byron's rebellious life and art. His first volume was *Fugitive Pieces* (1806). This was followed *by Hours of Idleness* (1807), which was attacked by the *Edinburgh Review*. Byron replied with *English Bards and Scotch Reviewers* (1809), a satire in heroic couplets, which brought him fame. In 1811 he finished Cantos I and II of the melancholy *Childe Harold* (1812). Byron was romantically linked with a number of women, but his sexuality is a matter of debate today; there is some evidence that he had several homosexual relationships.

In April 1816 Byron departed England forever. He stayed for some time in Switzerland with the poet Perry Bysche Shelley, writing Canto III of *Childe Harold* (1816) and The *Prisoner of Chillon* (1816). Byron settled in Venice (1817), where he produced Canto IV of *Childe Harold* (1818), *Beppo* (1818), and *Mazeppa* (1819) and began *Don Juan*. Byron worked the cause of Greek independence from the Turks in 1824, but caught a fever and died the same year. Ranked with Shelley and Keats as one of the great Romantic poets, Byron became famous throughout Europe as the embodiment of romanticism, the Byronic anti-hero.

Byron's daringly rebellious (and possibly bisexual or homosexual) life and varied verse appealed to Auden, who chose to write a *Letter to Lord Byron* and did so imitating the mock-heroic style, saying that Byron was the "master of the airy manner." Auden became famous in his early twenties, as did Byron. In Auden's introduction to *The Oxford Book of Light Verse*, he writes that light verse means "poetry written for performance, to be spoken or sung before an audience, poetry intended to be read, but having for its subject matter the everyday social life of its period or the experiences of the poet as an ordinary human being," as in the poems of Chaucer, Pope, and Byron.

In the Auden-Isherwood play *The Ascent of F6*, the depiction of Ransom's ascent up the mountain come from Byron's *Manfred*. In 1938 Auden included selections from Byron, along with Pope, in his *Oxford Book of Light Verse*. Auden wrote of Byron for the anthology *Fifteen Poets* (1938 but not published until 1941). By 1941 Auden understood that Byron in particular and others in general had isolating burdens of their own and that these might be shared through art.

In a 1941 essay called "Byron" (published in *Fifteen Poets*, editor unknown), Auden wrote, "No egoist can become a mature writer until he has learnt to recognize and to accept, a little ruefully, perhaps, his egoism. When Byron had ceased to identify his moral sense with himself and had discovered how to extract Byronic Satanism from his lonely hero and to turn it into the Byronic irony which illuminated the whole setting, when he realized that he was a little ridiculous, but also not as odd as he had imagined, he became a great poet. For Byron is not really odd like Wordsworth; his experiences were those of the ordinary.... He fashioned a style of poetry which for speed, wit, and moral seriousness combined with a lack of pulpit pomposity is unique, and a lesson to all young would-be writers who are conscious of similar temptations and defects." As Auden often did in his essays, he was also writing about himself.

In 1962, Auden's essay "Don Juan" focused on Byron's work of that name. When one is in the mood for it, Auden said, it's perfect, but only then, the mood being distaste for everything. Satire tries to overturn contradictions; comedy accepts them as fated. *Don Juan* is comedy. What is the difference between a giggle and laugh: one giggles at sacred intruding on profane; one laughs only at profane. Don Juan's name conjures up a pure rake, such as Byron's image; Byron's character is not so much seducer as seduced, and he is capable of love. Don Juan is about Byron in his own self-defense.

A third essay on Byron was Auden's 1966 Introduction to *Byron, Selected Poetry and Prose*. Auden wrote that one should read Byron's prose to see him without his poetic mask and the prose shows that his best work, *Beppo*, *Vision of Judgement*, and *Don Juan*, are closest to his true voice. Byron while linked to the Romantics was an anti–Romantic voicing realism over transcendentalism, choosing to be vulgarly honest; that is, to give the thoughts of the wise man in the speech of the common people (Auden via Yeats via Lady Gregory). His skills were limited and realism fit them. He is authentic rather than trying to fit an "image" as Shelley did. Byron was mainly melancholic with spurts of manic energy that became poetry of a sardonic humor that accepted human nature bemusedly as a humorist, not a satirist, and without being judgmental. Comic style allowed for punchy effect and digressions of self-explanation. *Don Juan* is heavy but not gloomy. He is charming and adaptable, successful without effort, passive rather than promiscuous, and capable of love, and as such, is Byron's daydream aspiration, and a defense of his own life. He attacks the rant and cant of The Others, as did Auden's generation.

Cadbury, George

1839–1922, English manufacturer and social reformer. In 1861, Cadbury and his brother Richard assumed control of their father's Birmingham cocoa and chocolate factory. Interested in housing problems, the brothers moved (1880) the plant to Bournville and laid out a garden village. The successful venture influenced European model housing and garden city projects. Agitation for national old-age pensions and insurance was financed by Cadbury, who also worked to eliminate harsh labor conditions. Cadbury founded the Downs School where Auden taught in the mid 1930s, and his years there may have been the happiest of his life.

Calder-Marshall, Arthur

1908–1992. British writer and editor, he was at Oxford with Stephen Spender and remained a friend. His novel *Dead Centre* (1935) shred the British public schools. Auden and Isherwood listed him as a coming writer in a 1939 article for *Vogue*.

Camus, Albert

1913–60, French writer, philosopher, b. Algiers. He believed that man's condition is absurd, which identified him with the existentialists. The characters in his novels and plays, while aware of the vacuity of the human condition, assert their humanity by going against their circumstances. Camus was awarded the 1957 Nobel Prize for Literature.

Camus exerted a great influence on post–World War II thought. Auden's relation to Camus is that Auden disagreed with him enough to provoke written reactions. If man's condition is absurd then there is no value to free will and conscious choice, the central forces driving Auden's Christianity. In a 1954 review Auden asked why Camus should "defeat himself by accepting the Hegelian-Marxian use of History that robs it of all meaning, since for them all historical events are natural events? To believe in freedom and reality of the person means to believe in an order of unique (though analogous) events which occur, neither necessarily nor arbitrarily, but voluntarily, according to motive and provocation and for which, therefore, the actor is responsible (since history is something man *makes*, it is meaningless to talk of obeying it)" ("Fog in the Mediterranean," *The Christian Scholar*, December 1954).

Mendelson adds, "In writing about Christianity, Camus adopts the views of its nineteenth century opponents instead of performing the more useful task of identifying the heresies that conflict Christianity now (Auden had written earlier about the Barthian heresy of an absolutely distant God" (*Later Auden*). Auden would not accept either that history was arbitrary or that God was unapproachable, which he had long disbelieved since "A Summer Night" in 1933 after which he began moving towards his own version of Auden's Mysticism.

The Canterbury Pilgrims 1956

This collection edited by cleric James A. Pike contains 23 essays by prominent people who returned to the Anglican Communion, including Auden. Pike writes that Auden summarized his essay by saying, "The way in is sometimes the way 'round." Auden refers to Kierkegaard, Charles Williams, and gives the fullest account of his Christian commitment.

Auden begins: "The Christian doctrine of a personal God implies that the relation of every human being to Him is unique and historical, so that any individual who discusses the Faith is compelled to begin with autobiography." Auden relates his religious upbringing and that "At thirteen I was confirmed." He claims a falling away shortly after, but more so as to external observance. He would argue with his friend Robert Medley, when they were in public school after Medley disparaged Christianity; and as late as the mid 1930s, John Duguid, Auden's student at the Downs School, recalls Auden joining his students at mass and singing the hymns. In his essay Auden sees that the contemporary church faces the problem of having to relate to a modern constituency, but he rejects updating the liturgy away from Latin. "Whatever drawbacks it may have, a liturgy in a dead language, like Latin, which the average worshipper does not understand or to which, at least, he has no personal relation, has one great advantage over a vernacular liturgy: it cannot strike him as comic," and by its heightened ritualistic presentation, can evoke mystical feelings of transcendence. Auden asserts that some of his 1930s enthusiasms — "the 'kerygmas' of Blake, of Lawrence, of Freud, of Marx" — could have only resulted from their own rejections of conventional Christianity. That is, they enacted the internal process of the "Destructive Element," which is the tearing down of unbelief to make way for new belief, and that Auden's reaction to these views was to reverse the process by tearing down their beliefs and re-building his Christian beliefs. With World War II, he observes that fascists and Communists believed that killing one part of society — each other — was the wave of the future. Then Auden met Charles Williams, whose presence made Auden feel sanctity. This motivated him to read Kierkegaard: "I was forced to know in person what it is like to feel oneself the prey of demonic powers, in both the Greek and the Christian sense, stripped of self-control and self-respect, behaving like a ham actor in a Strindberg play." As "ham actor," Auden refers to his rage over Chester Kallman's infidelity, a rage that terrified him and motivated him to seek "self-control" and "self-respect" in Christianity. He credits Kierkegaard for "making Christianity sound bohemian," and, thus, more appealing.

"As a spirit, a conscious person endowed with free will, every man, has, through faith and grace, a unique, 'existential' relation to God, and few since St. Augustine have described this relation more profoundly than Kierkegaard. But every man has a second relation to God which is neither unique nor existential: as a creature composed of matter, as a biological organism, every man is related by necessity to the God who created the universe and saw that it was good, for the laws of nature to which, whether he likes it or not, he must conform are of divine origin."

"Divine origin" here is similar to the *Divine Ground* of Aldous Huxley's Minimum Working Hypothesis. Huxley also said, relating to Auden's inference of divine interconnectedness: "Any given event in any part of the universe has as its determining conditions all previous and contemporary events in all parts of the universe."

"Canzone" 1942

This poem employs Dante's stanzas as in his own *canzone* (songs) from *La Vita Nuova* (the new life) with the five end words repeated throughout the five twelve-line stanzas. The poem's theme is about the defeat of the individual when he tries to exert possession and control over another. Auden meant his own will in trying to possess and control Chester Kallman, for which Auden berates himself.

Carnival *see* "Epistle to a God son"

Carpenter, Edward

1844–1929, English author. Ordained a minister in 1869, he became a Fabian socialist in 1874 and rejected religion. Among his works on social reform are *Towards Democracy* (1883–1902), revealing the influence of his friend Walt Whitman; *England's Ideal* (1887); *Civilization: Its Cause and Cure* (1889); and *Love's Coming of Age* (1896), which considers relations between the sexes.

Edward Carpenter can be considered one of Auden's influences as a gay man as Carpenter was a great propounder of shamanism for English homosexual cultures. In *Intermediate*

Types Among Primitive Folk (1914) Carpenter's shaman is the prophet or priest of all cultural advance, including an advance upon hetero-sexuality. (Carpenter associates the latter with arrested development.) Carpenter's shaman is at once a priest of love and an ascetic, for his vision of Eros inspires those sublimations — for example, religion and art — that build civiliza-tion. Both homosexuality and art in Carpenter are the vehicles of *humanity's* conquest of au-tonomy. But the Carpenter shaman-priest is no heresiarch. What the shaman advances towards is democracy, Carpenter's greatest passion, with which Carpenter believed homosexuality had an innate affinity. He discovered this affinity partly through an experience he recounts in an afterword to poems he wrote in the 1880s about democracy. The experience was of an inward autonomous place or space, "transcending the ordinary bounds of personality" and suggesting individuality to be an illusion. Carpenter un-derstood the experience as a political vision, for the transcendence of personality spoke of a common mystery of being, which is shared by all without distinction or discrimination, and which hence guarantees our universal equal-ity.—ROBERT L. CASERIO (See also *Letters from Iceland.*)

The vision described by Carpenter is much like Auden's "A Summer Night " Vision of Agape. (*See* Mysticism.)

Carritt, Gabriel

1910–1999, Oxford 1927–1931. Auden fell in love with Carritt and wrote poems for him, but Carritt did not respond other than with friendship. Some of Auden's verse in *Poems* (1930), about the difficulty of finding love and the vulnerability that one hides behind a pub-lic mask that disguises inner feelings, relates to Carritt. In *W.H. Auden: A Tribute* (1975), edited by Stephen Spender, Carritt and Rex Warner recall Auden at Oxford.

Carroll, Lewis

1832–98, Pseud. of Charles Lutwidge Dodgson, English writer, mathematician, and amateur photographer. Educated at Oxford, where he remained for the rest of his life as a deacon. Carroll is the author of the children's books *Alice's Adventures in Wonderland* (1865) and its sequel, *Through the Looking Glass* (1872). He developed these stories from tales he told to the children of H.G. Liddell, one of whom was named Alice. His characters — the Mad Hatter, the March Hare, the White Rab-bit, the Red Queen, and the White Queen — have become familiar figures. He also wrote hu-morous verses; the most popular is *The Hunting of the Snark* (1876). In 1856 he took up pho-tography and his photographs of children are still regarded highly today.

That Auden admired Carroll is clear in Auden's anthology *A Certain World: A Com-monplace Book*, where he has a subject titled "Nursery Library, My," in which he lists the books that he considered crucial to his or any-one's nursery library. On the list: "Lewis Car-roll — the two *Alice* books." Also in *A Certain World*, under "Logic," he has Carroll's "Four Logical Exercises," in which Carroll anticipates the weird analytical questions that appear on the GRE exam that prove, rather than disprove, that this type of puzzle is really illogical. Humphrey Carpenter writes of the section of Auden's madcap *The Orators* titled "Journal of an Airman," that, "the second part of *The Or-ators* is a piece of verbal anarchy; but its juxta-position of diary entries, quasi-scientific obser-vations complete with diagrams, plans for absurd military operations, and lists and cata-logues of every kind, produces an effect that re-sembles not so much true surrealism as the more extreme nonsense of Lewis Carroll" (*W.H. Auden*).

In 1962 Auden wrote an essay about Car-roll for the *New York Times Magazine*, "Today's Wonder World Needs Alice" (reprinted as "Lewis Carroll" in *Forewords and Afterwords*).

Cats

Auden loved cats, giving them free rein including permission to walk on the dinner table, to the dismay of some dinner guests. There is a lovely photo (George Csnerna) of Auden holding a cat that is the cover of *The*

Table Talk of W.H. Auden. (*See also* "Bucolics" about Auden's cat Lucinda.)

The Caucasian Chalk Circle see Brecht, Bertolt

Caudwell, Christopher

Christopher Caudwell was the pseudonym for Christopher St. John-Sprigg (1907–1937). As St. John-Sprigg, he wrote weird and satiric detective novels that were evocative of Auden's *The Orators*. One was titled *Death of an Airman* (1935) that was inspired by the "Journal of an Airman" in *The Orators*. As Christopher Caudwell he was a committed Marxist who was killed in the Spanish Civil War. His philosophical Marxist study *Illusion and Reality* was published after his death in 1937 and is considered a crucial Marxist literary text.

In 1937 Auden read *Illusion and Reality* to review for *New Verse*. He also wrote the poem "Spain" poem about the Spanish Civil War. These two pieces of work proved to be closely interrelated.

Cavafy, C.P.

1863–1933, Greek poet. Although he published little, he is one of the foremost modern Greek poets. He was critical of Christian and nationalistic morality and was one of the first to write openly about homosexuality. Among his best-known poems are "The City" and "Waiting for the Barbarians." His poem "Ithaca" influenced Auden's poem "Atlantis."

E.M. Forster first brought Cavafy's poetry to the attention of British readers in the late 1920s when Forster encouraged the initial poems of Cavafy's to be translated into English. Auden read these poems around 1931. Thirty years later, in 1961, Auden wrote an introduction to *The Complete Poems of Cavafy*. "Ever since I was first introduced to his poetry … C.P. Cavafy has remained an influence on my own writing; that is to say, I can think of poems which, if Cavafy were unknown to me, I should

have written quite differently or perhaps not written at all." Auden continues that he believed that for the most part poetry is not readily translatable from one language into another without a large loss of the metaphorical implications of the original. But Cavafy is an exception. This is because of "Cavafy's imagery, for simile and metaphor are devices he never uses; whether he is speaking of a scene, and event, or an emotion, every line of his is plain factual description without any ornamentation whatsoever."

What also appealed to Auden was that "Cavafy was a homosexual, and his erotic poems make no attempt to conceal the fact. Poems made by human beings are no more exempt from moral judgment than acts done by human beings, but the moral criterion is not the same. One duty of a poem, among others, is to bear witness to the truth. A moral witness is one who gives true testimony to the best of his ability in order that the court (or the reader) shall be in a better position to judge the case justly…. As a witness, Cavafy is exceptionally honest." For Auden sincerity should be the artist's first and paramount virtue.

Cavalcanti, Alberto see Grierson, John

"The Cave of Making" see About the House

Cerf, Bennett

1898–1971. Founder of Random House publishers and also the Modern Library. First American publisher of Auden, Spender, Isherwood, and Day Lewis. (*See also* Pound, Ezra.)

A Certain World 1970

In Auden's introduction to *A Certain World: A Commonplace Book*, he said he would be loath to write an official autobiography (or for anyone else to write a biography), and that

A Certain World, **cover of first edition.**

his selections for the anthology were as close as anyone would get. In the foreword he writes: "I realize this sort of compilation is a sort of auto-biography…. Here then is a map of my planet. Certain features are, deliberately or necessarily missing…. Then, much as we should all like to, none of us can preserve our personal planet as an unsullied Eden. According to our time and place, unpleasant facts from the world we all have in common keep intruding, matters about which either we are compelled, against our will, to think or feel it is our duty to think, though in such matters, nobody can tell another what his duty is. The bulk of this book will, I hope, make pleasant reading, but there are some entries which will, I trust, disturb a reader as much as they disturb me. I have tried to keep my own reflections (unsigned entries) to a minimum, and let others, more learned, intelligent, imaginative, and witty than I, speak for me."

The last sentence is graciously polite, but Auden was not immodest and his comments, while proportionately short, are just as pointed and opinionated as he claims they aren't. Indeed, this is a "personal map" of his ideas and attitudes, which are the much more important autobiography of an individual than his details: i.e., date and place of birth, what he did in 1939. Speaking of 1939, after Auden's arrival in America, his biographers and literary critics have made much of his avowed apolitical announcements in both life and art that were a refutation of his 1930s activism and that in America he would "de-activate" himself as an opinion maker for public consumption. This was never true. Auden remained just as interested and just as active in regard to new situations and new ideas and gave his opinions through his verse and essays. Much has been made of his disavowal of activism; yet, there was really very little difference in his actions after 1939 compared with before. Other than going to Spain briefly during the Spanish civil War, Auden spent most of the 1930s letting his pen do the talking just as he would continue to do in America.

A Certain World, by Auden's choices of what to include, is a socio-political statement. There are delightful diversions such as the entries by Lewis Carroll, and "Anagrams," in which Wystan Hugh Auden becomes "Why shun a nude tag," and there are entries such as "Camps, Concentration" that are reminders of what happens when attention is not paid. His choices do much to explain his sympathies, which were as they had always been, before and after America, that of a liberal humanist.

The structure and method of *A Certain World* has much in common with Aldous Huxley's 1932 commonplace anthology, *Texts and Pretexts*, which indeed, Auden refers to in his own anthology. Huxley and Auden had a great deal in common intellectually, and as Huxley was thirteen years older than Auden, and a vastly influential literary figure in the 1920s, as was T.S. Eliot, Auden took some cues from him, directly, and indirectly.

Preceding many of the categories in the book are comments by Auden, which are briefly herein summarized. *Aging*: One never believes it. *Algebra*: W=F 2/L (love of world equals fear of God/love of God). *Baroque*: preening power and glory/Camp. *Baths, Cold*: Boarding school torture of sick minds. *Behaviorism*: WHA disagrees with it as theory. *Belief*: man cannot separate experience from his interpretation of it. We believe from others before we doubt, doubt before we deny. *Bishops*: If WHA was one he would be politically liberal, theologically conservative. *Black*: (as in African-American) John Howard Griffin. *Castration complex*: a "pleasing fictional fear." *Choir Boys*: WHA's first interest in words with cadence. *Engaged*: Poems that are activist but not for WHA who says a poet is not a reformer. *Conception*: Immaculate. *Conscience*: Freud and society. *Cultures, Two*: literature and science. *Double Entendre*: caused by changes in historical meaning. *Dreams*: release from insanity, but usually boring. *Drinking Songs*: false bonhomie. *Eating*: significance of (church) mass — learning is assimilation. *Education, Classical*: WHA deplores lack of it. *Enchantment*: self-deception that fades and our cynical disillusion seeks to recapture it by force; Christ did not enchant. *Faces of Children*: masks not yet formed (and hardened). *Forgiveness*: is Christian. *Friday*: good. *God*: free will — His faith in us is more difficult than our faith in Him; "God is love" is hard for children to understand; God is meditation, then work. *Hell*: law and language of spiritual law and sin. *History, political*: should be studied by young. *Inverted commas*: bad poetry. *Liturgy*: WHA disagrees with the reform of mass from Latin to English. *Love, romantic*: source of misery because nothing can live up to it — for language of love, Auden prefers comic to coarse or whiny/pathetic. *Machines*: loss of individual skill. *Madness*: poets and language. *Marriage*: a good one is much more interesting than romance. *Middle Class*: the phrase is not as pejorative as Bourgeois; the middle class is the source of progress. *Mnemonics*: poetry. *Napoleon*: not a nice person. *Nature*: science and theology. *Neighbor*: love of, commanded by God. *Nursery Library*: WHA's childhood books. *Penis Rivalry*: men, weapons, war. *Pleasure*: becomes addiction from the evil one (devil). *Prayer*: to pay attention to others than one's self — in art, in work, all is prayer, and this should be taught to children. *Saints*: sanctity is the state about which theology has nothing to say. *Sins*: allowing the "I" to prevent the "We" is the primal sin. *Songs*: poetry. *Tyranny*: belief that politics is scientific produces tyrannies; systems require authority, which can become corrupt. *Verse*: words with accents. *War*: once heroic, now just ugly. *Writing*: *See* Writing, Auden on. (*See also* Secondary Worlds.)

"A Change of Air" 1961

This poem was written while Auden and Elizabeth Mayer were translating Goethe's *Italian Journey* and is Auden's final farewell to Ischia. It is also about "the dissociation of a person's private and public aspects, the 'you' who is the inner ego and 'your name' who is the outer self" (Mendelson *Later Auden*). The Kenyon Review (Winter 1964), chose to have a "symposium" on the poem with remarks by fellow poets George Elliot, Karl Shapiro, and Stephen Spender, to which Auden responded (later reprinted in *The Contemporary Poet as Artist and Critic*, 1964, ed. Ostroff).

"A Change of Place" *see* Poems

The Changing Face of England *see* Collett, Anthony

The Chase 1934

This was Auden's second Group Theatre play for the (*The Dance of Death* was the first). Three distinct plots are spoken in part by two supernatural Witnesses (as in the poem "The Witnesses"). Auden wrote to Naomi Mitchison, "The epic has turned in [to] drama and much of the choral narration in *The Chase* comes directly from the poem." "From *The Fronny* Auden took Alan Norman's pursuit of the missing heir Sir Francis Crewe. From *The Enemies of a Bishop* he took the plot of an escape from a reformatory and the theme of troubles at a lead mine. But in *The Chase* the mine's troubles are political, as they were not in the earlier play.... Auden felt dissatisfied with the play as soon as he finished it" (Mendelson, *The Complete Works: Plays*).

Auden sent it to Isherwood, who devised a new scenario. They retitled the play *Where is Francis?* and worked together to produce their first of three plays in collaboration, *The Dog Beneath the Skin*. (*See* Plays with Isherwood.)

Chesterton, Gilbert Keith

1874–1936, English author. A conservative, Chesterton converted to Roman Catholicism in

1922. He wrote studies of Browning (1903) and Dickens (1906); several novels including *The Napoleon of Notting Hill* (1904) and *The Man Who Was Thursday* (1908); a series of mysteries featuring Father Brown as detective, which Auden, the mystery fan, read; many poems, collected in 1927; and essays, collected in *Tremendous Trifles* (1909), *Come to Think of It* (1930), and other volumes. The editor of *G.K.'s Weekly,* an organ of the Distributist League, which advocated the small-holding system, Chesterton also was an artist, illustrating books by Hillarie Belloc, his friend and collaborator.

For Auden, Chesterton's "reactionary" Catholicism only emphasized his evasive relations to Jews. Auden would rebut Chesterton. "The disingenuousness of [Chesterton's] argument is revealed in the quiet shift from the term *nation* to the term *race*. It is always permissible to criticize a nation (including Israel), a religion (including Orthodox Judaism), or a culture, because these are the creations of human thought and will: a nation, a religion, a culture, can always reform themselves if they so choose. A man's ethnic heritage, on the other hand, is not in his power to alter. If it were true, and there is no evidence whatsoever to suppose that it is, that certain moral defects or virtues are racially inherited, they could not become subject for moral judgment by others" ("G.K. Chesterton's Non-Fictional Prose").

"The Chimeras" *see* Kassner, Rudolph

"A Choice of de la Mare's Verse" *see* de la Mare, Walter

Christianity

In 1938 when Isherwood was blasting religion, Auden told him, "Careful, careful, my dear — if you keep going on like that, you'll have *such* a conversion, one of these days" (*Christopher and His Kind*). Auden did not know that in just a year that conversion would happen to both of them.

There has always been much talk of Auden's "conversion" to Christianity after he arrived in America. More emphasis should be placed on this as a "re-conversion" as the younger Auden — before Oxford — was quite devout and even by the mid thirties he was accompanying his preparatory school students to church where he sang in the choir. Then in Spain during the Spanish Civil War he was gravely dismayed at the burning of churches and the mistreatment of priests. Hence, his arrival in America was not followed by a sudden return to the church but a reaffirmation for an Auden whose spirituality had really never left him.

His pious mother raised the pre–Oxford Auden, and her son was also dutifully pious. His school friend Robert Medley recalls offending Auden when Medley disparaged Christianity. Auden, both pre- and post–Oxford, loved to sing in choirs (see "The Student and the Master" in Izzo, *W.H. Auden: A Legacy*), and bang out hymns on the piano. Consequently, Auden's "conversion" to Christianity in America was really a re-conversion.

Auden's re-conversion dramatically shaped the direction of his American poetry, which became the contextual reflections of the mirror in which Auden gazed at his own unique brand of mystical Christianity; it was his verse that looked back at him. Of course, at the heart of these literary developments was Auden's decision to return to the Anglican Communion in which he had been raised. His biographers and critics have generally agreed that his move to America occurred near the mid-point of a period in which Auden was profoundly questioning what he himself described as "laws" — "call them for convenience divine laws" (*The Prolific and the Devourer*).

In fact, Auden scholars have reached a high degree of consensus on the most salient moments in this biographical narrative. Auden's journey to the Spanish Civil War early in 1937, from which he returned, in a few weeks, largely disillusioned with his prospects for uniting his poetry with the causes of leftist politics; his meeting later that year in Oxford with Charles Williams, who impressed him, he would later claim, in a way that made him aware for the first time of the "presence of personal sanctity";

a night in Manhattan in 1939 when he was watching a film on the Nazi invasion of Poland and, as Poles appeared on the screen, heard members of the audience shout "Kill them!"—an experience that led him to react "against the denial of every humanistic value" by going "back to the Church."

Auden assumed that his religious belief required that he commit himself to a "vocation"; and so, if he were going to continue as a writer, he would need to understand this practice, day by day, as a religious activity. In this respect and others, his understanding of Christianity was similar to that of Søren Kierkegaard, the theologian for whom his affinities would eventually be most apparent and enduring. Like Kierkegaard, Auden did not see himself *as a Christian* so much as he saw himself as a person striving *to become a Christian*. And he had to undertake this struggle in a time and a place, like Kierkegaard's "Christendom," in which such a task was likely to be unpredictable, isolating, and anxiety-ridden. Late in his life, in one of his two major essays on Kierkegaard, Auden still described his own situation in the terms he had established in the first few years after his move to America:

"Today, in our part of the world, society could not care less what one believes; to be a Christian is regarded by the majority as a rather silly but quite harmless eccentricity, like being a Baconian or a flat-earth man. But there are large areas elsewhere where Christianity is taken seriously, where a Christian is debarred from all but the lowliest jobs and may even lose his life. What would Kierkegaard say to all this?" ("Knight of Doleful Countenance").

He has come to believe that "Kierkegaard speaks with absolute authority" on the one problem that has plagued him since he arrived in America, and that would continue to plague him until the end of his life: "No person of talent who has read him can fail to realize that the talented man, even more than the millionaire, is the rich man for whom it is so difficult to enter the Kingdom of Heaven" ("Knight...").

Just as Auden struggled in his "private life" to come to terms with the question of how to use his own talent — or, as he more often put it, his "gift" — to become a Christian poet, in a modern world in which such a feat had not

been accomplished in any way that seemed to him sufficient, in the early 1940s the problem of becoming a Christian emerged as the most compelling and productive theme of his poetry. For a period of just about five years, from Auden's Arrival in America until his completion of *The Sea and the Mirror* around the start of 1944, Auden would succeed brilliantly in his efforts to give poetic expression to this theme, writing much of his most powerful poetry and demonstrating some of the vast possibilities of a contemporary Christian poetics.

In other words, the central point about the "later Auden" is that the development of his poetry throughout this period can best be explained as a result of his deliberate attempt to reinvent himself as a Christian poet. Auden articulated his struggle for faith, especially its relationship to his poetic gift, through a rich and sometimes idiosyncratic encounter with modern theology.

The "New World" of America began to play as significant a role in his poetry of the early 1940s as the more recognized British setting of the Auden Generation had played in his poetry of the early 1930s. The nexus around Union Theological Seminary, where Reinhold Niebuhr was on the faculty, and the New School for Social Research (both in NYC), where Auden sometimes lectured, was an especially challenging and exciting scene, most of all for a poet with Auden's concerns and interests. They considered it their moral and professional obligation to oppose nationalism and the rise of fascism, and the escalating European war invested even their most intellectual debates with a heightened sense of human and historical consequence.

In fact, as far as the ongoing development of Auden's poetry is concerned, an argument might be made that he could not have been in a better place. Contrary to popular belief—which Auden himself did much to encourage, along the lines of that notorious phrase "poetry makes nothing happen"—Auden found, in New York, a place in which poetry could matter a great deal. At the same time, however, this vital intellectual "scene" would force him to arrive at a new understanding of the *kind* of poetry that would matter, at this particular historical moment, and the *way* it would matter.

His vaguely political notions of the early 1930s, for which he had already become famous, could no longer go unexamined.

Even as Auden found in his New World a chance to reformulate his enduring moral preoccupations in light of religious practice and modern theology, and despite his recent disavowal of British partisan politics, his new understanding of the poet's vocation, much like his earlier one, was largely a response to the fascist threat to European culture and common humanity. In particular, Auden's attraction to the Christian realism and neo-orthodox theology of Reinhold Niebuhr and Paul Tillich was a logical response — and a distinctly nonescapist response — to the heightened sense of the human capacity for evil that he, like many other European intellectuals of his day, had developed largely by witnessing the rise of fascism.

Of all the European émigrés Auden met in his early years in New York, the one who would eventually have the most profound influence on his poetry was Paul Tillich.

In the early 1930s, while Tillich was struggling with the fascist assault on German universities, his fate was already being played out, more than he knew, in New York City. As the suspensions of German scholars began, Columbia University formed a committee to arrange for the employment of those who could be brought to the United States. A list of "deposed professors" was circulated. Henry Sloane Coffin, president of Union Theological Seminary, attended the committee's initial meeting and, seeing Tillich's name on the list, began negotiations to provide him with a position. Reinhold Niebuhr, who with his brother had translated Tillich's *The Religious Situation,* joined in the effort, and before long he played a crucial role by gathering information and convincing Tillich to leave Germany. A few year's later, when Auden entered the Niebuhrs' circle, Reinhold would also bring Tillich's writing to the poet. In particular, the Niebuhrs loaned Auden a copy of *The Interpretation of History.*

To the Niebuhrs, he quickly reported that he found Tillich's work "exciting."

Enter Tillich. Before long a number of Tillich's "special terms" — including the Abyss,

the Void, the Demonic, and *Kairos* (*see* "Kairos and Logos") — "began to appear" in Auden's writing. Especially in times of crisis, Auden was increasingly inclined to turn to Tillich's category of "the demonic." Eventually, "the demonic" would become his preferred term for most any especially dangerous personal excess, as in his essay "Kierkegaard," in which he writes that "the sufferer by fate" is tempted into "demonic defiance" and "demonic despair." Yet his most powerful applications of this particular term involve his efforts to confront, as a Christian poet, the political and social forces most destructive of the human spirit.

Tillich devotes the second part of *The Interpretation of History* to the "demonic."

Tillich shared with many of the artistic and literary modernists of his time — Picasso, Stravinsky, Joyce, and Eliot, to mention a few — a sense that traditional language and subjects needed to be revived through formal innovation and methodological complexity, and he shared their tenuous hope that such approaches might provide order and clarity. At the same time, like Auden in particular, Tillich had eagerly appropriated central ideas, language, and metaphors from modernism's intellectual precursors of the late nineteenth and early twentieth centuries, especially Marx, Freud, and, increasingly through the 1930s, Nietzsche. This powerfully ambivalent approach to modernity, which had made Auden's poetry so compelling for the English writers who began their careers between the two world wars — including Graham Greene, Cecil Day Lewis, Stephen Spender, and George Orwell — now made Tillich's theology just as compelling for Auden.

Tillich's treatment of the demonic in *The Interpretation of History* is one of his most extensive and richly suggestive. He refers to it as "the unity of form-creating and form-destroying strength"; the separation in existence of "form of being and inexhaustibility of being ... the relatively independent eruption of the 'abyss' in things"; "the actual uprising of the abyss against the form"; "the reign of a superindividual, sacred form which supports life, which at the same time contains the force of destruction in such a way that the destructive power is essentially connected with its creative power"; "the perversion of the creative"; and so on. Later in his career, especially in his *Systematic Theology*, Tillich would more often identify the demonic as a danger, and a potentially destructive force, in the religious life itself. But in *The Interpretation of History*, his view is more expansive; his primary interest is to demonstrate that the demonic can be a useful conceptual tool for the interpretation of (among other things) visual art, the history of religion, individual personality, mysticism, spirituality, sin, myth, history, and oppressive social and political organization. By approaching the topic in this multidisciplinary, prismatic way, the demonic seems to be everywhere, and artists and intellectuals must summon all available resources to discern it and oppose it.

He consistently characterizes the demonic as the inflation of a finite quality, perhaps an individual personality trait that is presumed to be more than merely human, or an aspect of social organization that it is treated as more than a historical product. As Tillich succinctly puts it in *The Protestant Era*, the demonic is "an absolute claim made for a relative reality." Or, to use the terms he would prefer in the *Systematic Theology*, it is "the elevation of something conditional to unconditional significance."

Because of this "relative" or "conditional" quality, the demonic is never found in a pure form. Its destructive power is always merged, inextricably, with creative or productive energy. On a political or historical level, Tillich writes — with his own recent experiences clearly in mind — the demonic can be found when the "national impulses of the bourgeois era," which contain at their best "the strength to offer resistance to the technical economization of the whole of Occidental existence," develop into "the last great demonry of the present," imperialistic nationalism.

By the same token, in *The Interpretation of History* Tillich suggests that the demonic can be a driving force of social conservatism or social progress. Yet even in its more apparently progressive forms, its promise is deceptive and dangerous: it devalues human life in the temporal world by obscuring its relationship to the eternal. In a language that anticipates the "Christian Realism" with which he would later be associated — a language highly attractive for a writer like Auden who was so deeply influenced by modernist poetics — Tillich's discussion of the demonic often amounts to a deep suspicion of "revolutionary" or "utopian" social schemes. Even a seemingly innocuous concept like "progress" must be treated with suspicion: it is often merely another name for "revolutionary Utopianism that has become tame," and as such it "devaluates every moment of history in favor of the ideal that lies in infinity instead of in eternity."

When applied to art, Tillich believes, developments of the 1920s and 1930s in the study of religion, art history and, most of all, "the new psychology of the subconscious," provide modern intellectuals with the means of recognizing the "destructive elements" so often disguised by creative energy. In this way, Tillich arrives at an idea of artistic form that accounts for the modernism of his own favorite example, Picasso's *Guernica*. At the same time, he anticipates some of the more striking features of Auden's later Christian poetics, especially its method of imbedding destructive energy in the various guises of modern sophistication.

Within a very short period — roughly two years — Tillich's theology of culture would complement, in Auden's poetics, Kierkegaard's critique of aesthetics and Niebuhr's more distinctly moral and political version of Christian Realism. Auden certainly would have understood that, in Tillich's system, the poet could have a powerful social role. Throughout his first year and a half or so in America, Auden recorded the constant vicissitudes of his own search for faith in letters, diaries, poems, essays, reviews — on just about every scrap of paper, it seems, that came his way. For a while, Auden experimented with various moral and religious propositions, until he finally set out to work toward a more systematic understanding of his religious commitment. Most notably, in the summer and fall of 1939 — that is, the midpoint between his move to America and his meeting with the Niebuhrs — he recorded many of the nuances of his search for faith in a series of prose meditations called *The Prolific and the Devourer*, that is informed, in part, by the idea of the demonic.

In one of his essays on Kierkegaard, Auden dealt with the twin temptations of "demonic defiance" and "demonic despair":

For, while ultimately the Christian message is the good news: "Glory to God in the highest and on earth peace, good-will towards men —" "Come unto me all that travail and are heavy laden and I will refresh you"; it is proximately to man's self-love the worst possible news —"Take up thy cross and follow me" ("Kierkegaard").

This acceptance of suffering only makes sense if one believes that one's suffering is an inescapable consequence of bearing the cross — that is, as Auden suggests with the final line break of "In Memory of Ernst Toller," that "existence is believing." Even though the language of "In Memory of Ernst Toller" is never specifically religious, the poem concludes with a powerful statement of one of the central concerns of Auden's later career: his growing need for a community of faith, his city of God — the "we" of the poem's closing lines — to confront the demonic forces, the "powers we pretend to understand," that will live our lives if we let them.

Throughout his early years in America, Auden's poetry would consider the presence of the demonic in one complex manifestation after another. Tillich's concept of the demonic informs Caliban's speech in *The Sea and the Mirror*, in which primitive energy and anarchic impulse are nearly — but not quite — concealed by the refined prose of Henry James. The same concept influences the narrative movement of *The Age of Anxiety*, and, in another very different setting, of the most powerful of Auden's later lyric poems, "The Shield of Achilles."

Auden's fullest and most effective depiction of the demonic is found in his most explicitly Christian poem, *For the Time Being*— and in the guise of a cultivated, thoroughly modern man.

For Auden's part, by the time he wrote *For the Time Being*, he had come to understand his vocation as a poet much as Tillich had imagined the social role of the creative artist: to counteract Toller's "demonic despair" and Herod's "demonic defiance." That was why, for Auden, to become a Christian poet was not to abandon social responsibility, and it was not to surrender to forces beyond his control. Rather, to become a Christian poet was to perform an

essential act designed to protect the creative mind and the innocent life from the demonic forces that seemed to dominate his troubled historical moment. His "conversion" was an effort to resist the forces that he — and Tillich, and Toller, and so many in the community of exiles he discovered in the "nervous New World"—found trying to live every life.— BRIAN CONNIFF

(*See also The Canterbury Pilgrims*; Camus, Albert; Kierkegaard, Søren; Mysticism; Barfield, Owen; Barth, Karl; Toller, Ernst; "In Memory of Ernst Toller" 1939; Rosenstock-Huessy, Eugen.)

"Christianity & Art" 1962

Auden believed that Christianity and art never quite match up. He wrote in this essay that to try and express Christianity as art becomes static because of its limiting single-mindedness. Devotional poems, drama, etc., attempt to secularize what should be intuitive knowledge, which can only be known by faith alone; hence, a knowledge found only in each individual's inner vision. Conversely, art, by design, appeals to a universal vision.

Ciceronian Rhetoric

Cicero (106 B.C.E.–43 B.C.E., Marcus Tullius Cicero), a great Roman rhetorician, lawyer and statesman. His greatest works are considered to be *De Oratore* (55 B.C.E.), *Brutus* (46 B.C.E.) and *Orator* (46 B.C.E.). His *De Inventione* (84 B.C.E.) serves an important role in illuminating the rhetorical dimensions of Auden's *The Orators*. In *De Inventione*, Cicero articulates his concerns regarding the relationship between wisdom and eloquence, and that eloquence unaccompanied by the imperative of "moral duty," can be a vitiating influence on society and the lives of those therein.

In 1966, Auden wrote an essay entitled "The Fall of Rome" which was originally commissioned by *Life* magazine, but ultimately rejected for publication. It appeared for the first time in "In Solitude for Company': W.H. Auden After 1940," and in it Auden expresses his obloquy toward classical Rome, which includes the statement, "One reason why I like Italy and the Italians so much is that, aside from their unfortunate addiction to rhetoric, I cannot imagine a people less like the Romans of antiquity."

Notwithstanding Auden's expressed and unapologetic disdain for rhetoric and its Roman progenitors, *The Orators*, in particular, generates compelling parallels between Britain of the 1930s and its classical counterpart of the Roman Republic; between the oratorical practices of Britain and those of the Roman Republic (at once both important and impotent), and the Ciceronian conflation of the canons of invention *(invention)* and style *(elocutio),* allowing for the metaphor as a mode of proof within the canon of invention — a modern conceptualization of the metaphorical construct with roots in classical rhetorical theory.

Looking at *The Orators* through this prism allows for militating against the notion that the poetic-rhetorical devices devolve into "infractions" of sorts, which ultimately impede the communication. And given the presumed diminished communicative status, one could too easily and erroneously conclude that Auden is perspicacious without perspicuity, engaging a density of idiom which obfuscates meaning and compromises any semblance of connection with audience. Auden's unique challenges as a poet are rhetorical challenges: Who is his public who is his audience and what is his attitude toward his subject? As David Daiches discusses in light of Auden's first volume *Poems:* "On the whole, these poems give the impression of a man of genuine poetic gifts and possessing to a quite uncanny extent the power to do new things with words, who is not quite sure what he wants to say, and who is even less decided about whom he wants to speak to. The latter problem, we feel, is the more urgent: once he finds his audience — either a real or an ideal audience; it does not matter which, for the problem is simply to give consistency to his symbolism and coherence to his attitude — he will be able to speak more clearly."

In *W.H. Auden: A Commentary*, John Fuller sees in *The Orators* "the Ciceronian political ideal [as] mirrored in the British educational and diplomatic system." Fuller sees parallels between Book I and *De Oratore*, between Book II and *Brutus* and between Book III and *Orator.*

The subject and style of Book I of *The Orators*, influenced by Cicero's *De Inventione* and *De Oratore*, engage speechmaking, as having a beginning, a middle and an end. Monroe Spears argues for a double irony in "Address for a Prize-Day," with the movement from irony and absurdity to seriousness and back to absurdity and irony. Spears sees the Part II of Book I as a search for a savior, while Fuller sees "Argument" about an "elusive leader," and the Part III "statement," as a "display of prophetic fatalism." In Part IV, "Letter to a Wound," the public rhetoric gives way to a more private rhetoric, realized in the epistolary mode. Book I is a genuine instantiation of Auden's ambivalence about language. And although Cicero espoused that language and concomitant speech are the cachet of a civilized people and a civilized society, they were equally aware of its deficiencies and exploitations in the hands (the mouths) of the morally corrupt.

Book II, "Journal of an Airman," embodies tenets of Cicero's *Brutus*, in which, according to Spears, Auden shows man "dedicated to the overthrow of the society represented by the orator-initiates of the first book."

In Book III entitled "Odes," Auden harks back to a fundamental Ciceronian question: what constitutes an ideal orator? Like "Odes," and *The Orators* as a whole, the *Orator* is an apologia on behalf of Cicero's career.

Neal Wood explains that for Cicero, speech is a divine faculty, and bereft of it, one is left without human reason, with an inextricable relationship between *ratio* and *oratorio.* Wood suggests that Cicero's entire life "can be said to have been dedicated to remedying what he takes to be the widespread malady afflicting his countrymen which he holds responsible for the serious troubles besetting the late Roman Republic." At the conclusion of *The Orators*, the scales seem to tip on the side of pessimism, with a distorted and perverted eloquence winning out over wisdom. But in the end, for Auden, as it was for Cicero, our only hope for *humanitas* resides in our ability to communicate, and achieving that proper balance between wisdom and eloquence.—ADRIENNE HACKER-DANIELS

"City Without Walls" 1967

This poem is an attack on urban alienation and alienation in general that starts out stark but then retreats from its own harshness: "'My,' I blustered, 'How moral we're getting.'"

City Without Walls 1969

Contained poems written by Auden from 1965 to 1968.

"A Civilized Voice" see Pope, Alexander

Clark, Thekla

Befriended Auden and Chester Kallman starting in 1951 during summers when the pair lived on the Italian island of Ischia. In 1996 she published the memoir *Wystan and Chester*, which is a very insightful look at the Auden-Kallman relationship. She records Auden's belief that homosexuality was wrong. In fact, Auden proposed to Clark in 1952. She declined. Clark has raised many refugee children, an activity that Auden no doubt would praise as Christian generosity, and has published a book of her experiences.

Clifton, Violet see The Book of Talbot

Coal Face see Grierson, John

Cochran, Charles Norris see For the Time Being

Cocteau, Jean

1889–1963, French writer, surrealist visual artist and filmmaker. A leader of the French avant-garde in the 1920s, his first success was *Les Enfants Terribles* (1929), a novel that he made into a film in 1950. Among his plays are *Orphée* (1926) and *La Machine Infernale* (1934, translated 1936), in which the Orpheus and Oedipus myths are adapted to modern circumstances. His films include *The Blood of a Poet* (1933), *Beauty and the Beast* (1946), and *Orphée* (1949), and *The Knights of the Round Table*, translated by Auden in 1963 (*The Infernal Machine and Other Plays*). He is also responsible for ballets, sketches, monologues, drawings, and the text (written with Stravinsky) for the opera-oratorio *Oedipus Rex* (1927). Before Rupert Doone led the Group Theatre he was a protégé of Cocteau and this influence can be seen in Auden's plays done for the Group.

Coghill, Nevill

1899–1980, one of Auden's tutors at Oxford with whom he remained a lifelong friend. "...he put me so at ease that I felt I could say anything to him, however silly, whether about literature or my personal life, without fear of being laughed at or scorned" (quoted in Carpenter, *W.H. Auden*). In 1966 upon Coghill's retirement Auden and John Lawlor compiled the book *To Nevill Coghill from Friends*, which included Auden's poem "To Professor Nevill Coghill upon his retirement in A.D. 1966."

Coldstream, William

1908–1987. Coldstream was a realist painter whom Auden met in the autumn of 1925 during Auden's first term at Christ Church College, Oxford. In mid June of 1937, after both were working with John Grierson and the GPO Film Unit, Coldstream began his likeness of Auden. Auden briefly became Coldstream's lodger in 1936 where he endeared himself to the painter and his wife Nancy. In *Letters from Iceland*, one verse letter is from "W.H. Auden to William Coldstream, Esq." On 12 January 1937 Coldstream saw Auden off at Victoria Station en route to the Spanish Civil War. Mendelson notes in *Later Auden* that Auden had a crush on Coldstream but nothing came of it. Coldstream became a very respected artist.

THE COLLECTED POETRY OF W.H. AUDEN

RANDOM HOUSE · NEW YORK

Collected Poetry of W.H. Auden, cover of 1945 first edition.

The Collected Poetry of W.H. Auden 1945

Auden suggested to Bennett Cerf at Random House that he would like to collect his work up to this point because he felt that his future work would be very different and wished to have the volume mark this distinction. Cerf at first resisted but the book went on to sell very well. Auden arranged the poems alphabetically so they would not be interpreted as his personal biography or history. By 1965 he changed his mind and put his poems in chronological order.

Collett, Anthony

Author of *The Changing Face of England* (1930), a book that the early Auden borrowed words and phrases from copiously for his own work. Mendelson notes that the geographic montage in the opening chorus of the 1935 play *The Dog Beneath the Skin* (praised by Auden critics for its imagination) is all Collett. Auden also took from Collett words and phrases for a birthday poem to Isherwood in 1935 and that

year included more in "Look, Stranger." In 1948 Collett's line "a network of caves and conduits" became a "secret system of caves and conduits" in the poem "In Praise of Limestone," and another phrase of Collett's is in the poem "Deftly, Admiral."

Collingwood, R.G.

1889–1943, English philosopher and historian, Collingwood's 1940 book *An Essay on Metaphysics* had an impact on Auden, particularly as Collingwood had written an insightful review of *The Ascent of F6*. "Collingwood argued that metaphysics was not the study of the absolute itself, as philosophy assumed it to be, but the study of 'absolute presuppositions,' the unverifiable (but not always unexampled) assumptions about the universe that in every society underlie the sum of available knowledge.... Its aims are to discover the absolute presuppositions of earlier cultures and our own, and to understand the processes through which these presuppositions change over time" (Mendelson, *Later Auden*). Aldous Huxley and Gerald Heard, the latter a large influence on Auden in the early 1930s, already had formulated similar notions. Huxley's novel *Grey Eminence*, written in 1939–1940, which is a forum to discuss mysticism, included this thought: "Any given event in any part of the universe has as its determining conditions all previous and contemporary events in all parts of the universe." In 1944 Huxley published *The Perennial Philosophy*, an anthology of metaphysical/mystical quotations that display "absolute presuppositions" signifying the underlying unity of spiritual thought, which includes Huxley's Minimum Working Hypothesis, the four basic principles of timeless and universal mysticism.

Auden needed to counter Hitler's onslaught, which seemed to obfuscate any sense of morality, with a belief that nihilistic history is distinct from the principles of an intuitive goodness and that as Heard postulated years before, man's acts are not the true history of man but that man's consciousness, his intuition as it evolved, is the true history. Force may obscure truth by silencing it, but the truth exists nonetheless.

"The Common Life" see About the House

Communism see Marxism

"Compline" see Horae Canonicae

"The Composer" 1938

This poem was written for Benjamin Britten and is a companion to the poem Auden wrote for Christopher Isherwood, "The Novelist." Here, life is reconciled through praise for art and beauty, which serves as a metaphoric communion between man and spirit. This is the true activism rather than political activism. This theme is a counterpoint to the poem "A.E. Housman."

"Concerning the Unpredictable" see Carnival; Eiseley, Loren; "Epistle to a Godson" (1968)

Connolly, Cyril

1903–74, English critic and editor, b. Coventry, England. He was educated at Oxford and began his career as a journalist. He founded *Horizon* (1939–49), a literary magazine with Stephen Spender. He was a long-time book reviewer for *The New Statesman* and London's *Sunday Times*. Among his works are *Rock Pool* (1935), a satirical novel; *Enemies of Promise* (1938), an autobiography; *The Unquiet Grave* (1944), a mix of commentaries, quotations, and aphorisms; *The Condemned Playground* (1945) and *Previous Convictions* (1964), collections of literary essays; and *The Modern Movement: 100 Key Books From England, France, and America, 1880–1950* (1965).

While friendly with Auden and Isherwood he still wrote publicly that they should have returned from America to Britain at the outbreak of World War II. His first wife, Jean Connolly,

shows up as "Ruthie" in Isherwood's *Down There on a Visit*. In 1937 Auden borrowed a tail-coat from Connolly to receive an award at Buckingham Palace. (*See* Masefield, John.) In 1939 Auden reviewed Connolly's non-fiction *Enemies of Promise*, a combination autobiography-commentary of Connolly's life and of the 1930s. After Auden met Chester Kallman, Connolly, as did many others who observed his relationship to Auden, thought him a parasite. Auden did not speak to him for a while but since this was a general opinion, Auden would have precluded speaking with a great many people if he had enforced his bans.

"A Consciousness of Reality" see Woolf, Virginia

"Consider" see Poems

Conversations with Auden 1981

Ed. Howard Griffin, 1915–1975. In 1946, Griffin, an admirer of Auden the poet, inquired of Auden if he could assist him and Auden agreed but insisted that Griffin be paid just as he had done for another assistant Alan Ansen. And just like Ansen, Griffin made notes of his chats with Auden and in 1981 these were published as *Conversations with Auden* (ed. by Donald Allen), much like Ansen's *The Table Talk of W.H. Auden* in 1991. Griffin grew up on Westbury, Long Island, in affluence. He briefly attended Columbia, and published a book of poems, *Cry Cadence*, in 1947. *Conversations with Auden* began as separate pieces published in a number of literary magazines, *Accent* (1949, 1952), *Hudson Review* (1951), *Partisan Review* (1953), *Semi-colon* (1953), and in an anthology, *The Avon Book of Modern Writing* (1953). The conversations display Auden's wit and volubility. The range and diversity over just 113 pages is startling.

Cornford, John

1915–1936, poet/martyr of the Spanish Civil War. While still in school, Cornford said of Auden's *Poems* (1930), "Whatever its ultimate value, it is already of the greatest historical and literary importance" (quoted in Stansky, *Journey to the Frontier* [1966]). Prior to the Spanish Civil War Cornford's teacher John Stowe sent Auden one of his student's poems, and Auden, already well-known, wrote to Cornford. "Real poetry originates in the guts and only flowers in the head. But one is always trying to reverse the process and works one's guts from one's head. Just when the Daemon is going to speak, the Prig clasps his hand over his mouth and edits it" (quoted in Carpenter, *W.H. Auden*). Auden's choice of the word "Daemon" is intriguing, as the concept of Christian theologian Paul Tillich's *"demonic"* would dominate Auden's thought in America.

Cosy Corner

The boy bar in Berlin first enjoyed by Auden and then shared with Isherwood, Spender, and Lehman.

"The Council" 1940

This poem was written at a time when Auden was searching for "absolutes"—in Kierkegaard, Collingwood, and others—that countered the present nihilism of war. The poem is a parable derived from the sixteenth century Council of Trent, which, according to Auden, was where the true meaning of "Agape and Eros [was] finally defined." Defined, yes, but adopted by humanity—not quite.

Craft, Robert

1924– Musical critic and author. Stravinsky's amanuensis and colleague until the composer's death. Chronicled Stravinsky's life and work, including the opera *The Rake's Progress* with libretto by Auden and Chester Kallman. Craft's first meeting with the composer occurred on the day the Auden-Kallman libretto for *The Rake's Progress* arrived, just in time for Craft to prove useful in matters pertaining to the English language. Until his arrival the language of daily life in the Stravinsky household had been almost exclusively Russian. (In a memoir Craft would write, "Wystan Auden's devotion to Chester Kallman was ... the real subject of the libretto [the fidelity of true love]" (quoted in Carpenter, *W.H. Auden*).

"The Creatures" 1935

This poem was written for a song cycle to music by Benjamin Britten. The theme comes from Shiller's essay *Uber naïve und sentimentalische Dichtung*, which says of nature's wonders: "They are what we were; they are what we should once again become."

Criterion

The very influential literary magazine edited by T.S. Eliot for Faber & Faber. Eliot endorsed Auden and published *Paid on Both Sides* in the *Criterion*, February 1930, and later for Faber published Auden's first book, *Poems*, October 1930, which also reprinted *Paid on Both Sides*.

"Criticism in a Mass Society" 1941

(In *The Intent of the Critic*, ed. Stauffer.) This essay was much influenced by Auden's experiences in the 1930s, including Henri Bergson's ideas of open and closed societies in the book *The Two Sources of Morality and Religion* (1932). The essay was also augmented by Auden's more recent readings of Kierkegaard's ideas on media and the public.

Why do the majority prefer opinions imposed by the few over discovering knowledge on their own? The degree of acceptance of imposed opinions depends on the degree of openness in a society. The more open the society, the less discerning is the public in questioning truth, which the public takes for granted. In a closed society, there is a general mistrust of imposed opinion by a public that would prefer real knowledge because this public knows that real knowledge is hard to come by.

Art meets internal needs; science meets external needs. In an open society, more art is tolerated, as opinion is free; in a closed society art is less tolerated because the "managers" of the closed society do not want the masses hearing opinions that fill their internal void, particularly if these opinions might stir them to action. In an open society the artist is unlimited; in a closed society the artist is controlled or eliminated. An open society encourages innovation; a closed society encourages stagnation.

The critic, much like the artist, is subject to his society, with latitude of opinion in an open society, a rigidity of opinion in a closed society. When the critic is in an open society, he can explain the individuation of art by comparison to others and find the universality in the art that can be shared. When the critic is in a closed society, his opinions must conform to the will of the state; he must describe art that is pleasing to the state, and his description must also please the state. Art that is not pleasing to the state is forbidden. Hence, in a closed society the critic is restrained in the choices of what he can criticize and of what he says in his criticism. In the past man was a person activated by the group's activities, and his own activities were subject to his group's approval or disapproval because all the members of the group knew each other. In the present man is a member of Kierkegaard's anonymous Public, a mass unknown to each other, and there is no group to exert moral authority, only the mass media to evoke a mass response through collective subjectivity. In the open society, the artist, while still dealing with a public, is more capable of reaching that public through the greater accessibility of a more open media. In a closed society, the artist works only if his message satisfies the state, and critics work only if they applaud the artist that works for the state, as these are the only artists that they are allowed to comment on; the other artists are gone, or are hiding underground, or are dead, and reach a very few.

In terms of Auden's Christianity, man is either "fallen" with a bias to evil, or man is good but corrupted by society. Auden leans towards the first view of man as fallen, but a critic must account for both views consciously or subconsciously. The open artist and open critic who share in their community seek unity within the anonymous public's isolation.

In the Renaissance the pedant substituted for the priest of the Middle Ages. The Romantics eschewed both peasant and priest to study nature. Artists then bifurcated into realists or surrealists in order to mediate an understanding of the ineffable and incommunicable human mysteries. In the psychoanalytic age artists are also psychologists as they are as subjective and as isolated as their audience; they sometimes subordinate artistic interpretation to political views (i.e. the Auden Generation in the 1930s). The critic does the same, looking for politics in the art. This leads to propaganda even if with good intentions, which leads to false beliefs and false poetics (*see* "Spain").

Eliot's *The Waste Land* tears down belief by believing in nothing so that readers are forced to consider what beliefs should come to exist in place of this nihilism (see the destructive element in *Plays with Isherwood, The Ascent of F6* and also *Stephen Spender*). The true critic in an open society will interpret the artist and help the audience to think for themselves rather than tell them what to think. In a democracy there is a choice to believe and succeed; not to believe is a failure of individuals. In Fascism, the state knows best; individual belief is not allowed. A democratic critic should learn to overcome prejudice and judge impartially to see the underlying unity in art. He should explain his own origins, be willing to accept original sin and fallibility, and offer himself in service to the just community. A Fascist critic says what he is forced to say to support the state.

Crossman, Richard

1907–1974. Richard Crossman was a leader in the British Labour Party, serving in the Cabinet from 1964 until 1970. In 1934 Auden contributed an essay, "The Group Movement and the Middle Class," to the Crossman-edited *Oxford and the Group Movement*. After World War II Crossman would edit another book with a more substantial impact. *The God that Failed* contained essays by former Communists, including Crossman, who now realized that Stalin's Communism was not what they had once believed in and disavowed it. Writers included André Gide, Arthur Koestler, and Stephen Spender.

"A Curse" *see* **Thank You Fog**

Curtiss, Mina

1896–1985. Writer and Lincoln Kirstein's sister and benefactor of the arts and artists. Also companion to poet Alexis Leger (St.-John Perse) whom Auden knew and admired.

She did not like Chester Kallman, which led to a temporary freeze in her relation to Auden.

"D.H. Lawrence" *see* Lawrence, D.H.

"Dame Kind" 1959

Dame Kind, AKA Mother Nature, is roughly equivalent to the appetitive goddesses Artemis/Aphrodite who rule over sex; yet, this is still a defense of Dame Kind's earthly part in human life, and although she might not be perfect, "She *is* our Mum."

The Dance of Death 1933

Auden's play, according to the announcer's opening statement, is "a picture of the decline of a class, of how its members dream of a new life, but secretly desire the old, for there is death inside them. We show you that death as a dancer." While this play was influenced by the Berlin nightlife, its themes are still dominated by those of *The Orators*. The announcer says: "Comrades … We must have revolution." A chorus agrees. Later, the announcer says: "Revolutionary worker / I get what you mean. / But what you're needing / 'S a revolution within." Written a year after *The Orators*, in which the airman had also concluded that change must come from within, Auden was still straddling the fence of political activism or metaphysical

The Dance of Death, cover of first edition.

activism. When the Dancer appears, the Announcer says he is "known simply as Pilot. His ambition is no less than to reach the very heart of reality." After various farcical machinations and allusions to different groups seeking to exert their influence on him, the Dancer dies. Karl Marx then appears stating: "The instruments of production have been too much for him. He is liquidated." The play ends and it is unclear if Marx and Communism are supposed to be part of the solution or part of the problem. (In the 1940s Auden would say the last lines were "nihilistic leg-pull.") Auden did not believe the answer rested in politics alone. Auden had learned from an intense personal experience on "A Summer Night" that occurred during the writing of this play that change would need, indeed, to come from within and work its way out from there to the rest of the world. (*See* Mysticism.)

The play was produced by Rupert Doone and the Group Theatre early in 1934. In the play's program, under the title "I Want the Theatre to Be…." Auden gave his view (with a nod to Brecht) that "drama began as the act of a whole community. Ideally there would be no spectators. In practice every member of the audience should feel like an understudy.... The subject of the drama ... is the commonly known, the universally familiar stories of the society or generation in which it is written. The audience, like the child listening to the fairy tale, ought to know what is going to happen next.... Similarly the drama is not suited to the analysis of character, which is the province of the novel. Dramatic characters are simplified, easily recognisable and over life-size.... Drama in fact deals with the general and universal, not with the particular and local." The Group Theatre would also produce Auden's plays with Isherwood.

"Danse Macabre" 1937

The title indicates that life is a morbid dance. This poem was written just before Auden left to visit the Spanish Civil War, which must have engendered nervous anxiety in the author. The "voice" of the poem is that of a mad dictator and Auden had certainly witnessed the rise of Hitler in Berlin. The dictator is caught up in the spin of history and both history and the dictator are trapped in random madness. His only possible and ultimately "macabre" solution is to get rid of the devil behind all of the madness by eliminating the devils' motivation, which is the human race, and then all will return to a natural state, that is, pre-human, pre-corruption.

Dante

1265–1321, Italian poet, b. Florence. Dante was the author of the *Divine Comedy*. It tells of the poet's journey through Hell, Purgatory, and Heaven, and is divided accordingly into three parts. Dante is guided by Vergil through Hell and Purgatory, and then by Beatrice, whom the poem exalts, through Heaven.

Auden's early poem "The Questioner Who Sits So Sly" (1929) features the diseased and perverted of Dante's *Purgatorio*. In Auden's poem "Happy New Year" (c. 1932, uncollected, except for a portion called "The Watchers"), "Vergil" guides Auden in the guise of Gerald Heard, and Heard does the same in the poem

"In the year of My Youth" (c. 1932), where Auden calls Vergil-Heard "Sampson." At this time Auden was quite taken up with Heard's theories of an evolving consciousness. In Auden's *The Orators*, as in Dante's Purgatory, Auden lists crimes against love. In the Isherwood-Auden play *The Ascent of F6*, Michael Ransom's opening monologue is addressed to Dante, and Auden then quotes from Canto XXVI of the Inferno to foreshadow the play's events. In the later 1930s Auden met Charles Williams, a lay theologian whose book *The Descent of the Dove* became very instrumental in Auden's Christianity. Dante influenced Williams' views. In Auden's 1942 poem "Canzone," he imitates Dante's *canzone* from *la vita nuova*.

"The Dark Valley" 1940

This half-hour radio play was written for a CBS series, the *Columbia Workshop*. Auden had just finished "New Year Letter," and this play resonates with the overflow of that poem's emotion. The play derived from a 1936 vignette called "Alfred" that Auden subtitled "The Psychological Reactions of the Woman who Killed the Goose that laid the Golden Egg." The monologue is of an old woman, and a stage direction from the original 1936 version says she has something about her that "reminds us of certain prominent European figures." Mendelson writes that "her monologue does not entirely reassure the goose whom she prepares to slaughter in the final moments" and one infers that the European figures are Hitler and Mussolini, et al. The radio version "intermittently adopts the alliterative *Beowulf* metre that Auden had used early in his career to evoke a world pervaded by violence [i.e. *Paid on Both Sides*].... Like 'New Year Letter' the play looks back to betrayed heroes" (*Later Auden*). Almost unknown, this was one of Auden's favorite efforts.

"The Dark Years" 1940

This poem was originally the epilogue of "New Year Letter." It is in the form of a prayer with Auden searching for some absolute that will counter the horrors of the present war. The last stanza takes all of its words from the opening chapter of the Gospel According to John.

Davis, George

American editor and writer who first met Auden and Isherwood in London in 1937. He became editor of *Harper's Bazaar* and published an article about China by them and later showed them New York after their first visit there for nine days in 1938 (after which they decided to return to America permanently). Davis rented a house at 15 Middagh Street in Brooklyn where Auden lived from October 1940 with Davis, Golo Mann, Carson McCullers, Gypsy Rose Lee, Louis MacNeice, Benjamin Britten, Peter Pears, and Paul and Jane Bowles. Davis would later marry Bertolt Brecht's former wife Lotte Lenya.

Day, Dorothy

1897–1980. Dorothy Day began her adult life as a Communist seeking religious truth and ended it as a Catholic influenced by Communist ideals. She anticipated liberation theology by some thirty-five years. She began and ran until the end of her life a shelter for the homeless and indigent in the Lower East Side of Manhattan. Her life became the subject of a television film.

While Communism and religion may seem mismatched, how good a match are capitalism and religion? Day answered, "The scandal of businesslike priests, of collective wealth, the lack of a sense of responsibility for the poor, the worker…. There was plenty of charity but too little justice." Day's view of Christian charity matched Auden's.

In 1956 Auden lived at 77 St. Marks Place near Day's shelter. According to Carpenter in *W.H. Auden*, "he handed over a check to Catholic social worker Dorothy Day, who needed the money to pay a court fine imposed because a hostel for derelicts she was running transgressed New York fire regulations. Auden went up to her as she came out of court, looking so scruffy that she mistook him for a derelict himself, and he

Revolution in Writing by C. Day Lewis, first edition.

muttered 'here's two-fifty.' Miss Day assumed that he meant $2.50, and thanked him briefly. After he had gone, she discovered the cheque was for the full amount of the fine, $250, which was perhaps worth over $1000 in 1956. Auden would later say he met only two saints, Day and Charles Williams."

Day Lewis, Cecil

1904–72, English author, poet, b. Ireland. He became Auden's friend at Oxford, and introduced Auden to Rex Warner. After graduation he taught at various schools before devoting himself to writing in 1935. Lewis was a member of the Communist party from 1935 to 1938, and concern for social issues mark his early work. Besides poetry, C. Day Lewis is noted for the collection of essays *A Hope for Poetry* (1934); for a verse translation of Vergil's *Aeneid* (1952); and for detective stories written under the pseudonym Nicholas Blake. In his first detective novel as Blake, *A Question of Proof*, the sleuth is named Nigel Strangeways, and he is based on Auden. From 1967 to 1972 he was poet laureate of Great Britain.

In his 1960 autobiography Day Lewis said of Auden's verse, which he had read when they were classmates at Oxford: "the vigor of the language, the exciting novelty of the images and ideas embodied in these early poems, and the delighted sense they gave me of a poetry which, so to say, knew its own mind—all this proved so infectious that my own verse became for a time pastiche-Auden" (*The Buried Day*). In October 1929, the Hogarth Press published *Transitional Poem*, a title entirely apt not only for Day Lewis, but for his generation to announce its coming and declare that the passive, cynical nihilism of Eliot and Huxley's 1920s' decade would give way to an active, yet still cynical iconoclasm of the 1930s. Day Lewis, whose first two books of verse, *Beechen Vigil*, 1925, and *Country Comets*, 1927, were pastorally Georgian and influenced by the light verse of Humbert Wolfe, kept his traditional pre–Auden technique in *Transitional Poem*, but loaded it with post–Auden influences, many of which were those of Isherwood and Auden in philosophical collaboration.

Transitional Poem is about the psychology of the transitions in a maturing human mind. This single mind, by extension, represents the corresponding maturity of the collective Oxfordian Group mind or the *world mind* of Vedanta. Day Lewis did not know Vedanta directly, but was interpreting it indirectly from the influence of W.B. Yeats who was also an influence on Auden. The Yeats connection is noted by Samuel Hynes in commenting on *Transitional Poem*: "More fundamental to the structure are oppositions: mind/body, ideal/real, infinite/finite, love/fear, eternity/time. Day Lewis's use of these terms echoes Yeats very closely, indeed the whole sequence is heavy with Yeatsian borrowings, and it is not surprising that Day Lewis used Yeats's word for such oppositions: 'antinomies'" (*The Auden Generation*). Yeats based much of his own cosmology on Vedic cosmology and augmented it with Neo-Celtic nuances. (In 1938, Yeats would render a translation of The *Upanishads*.) The "antinomies" in *Transitional Poem* that echo Yeats are based on the Vedantic reconciliation of opposites, which create the energy that allows the world mind to progress, although in a time frame of eons, not single lifetimes. (In Vedanta, each single lifetime is integral to, and co-existent with, all past, present, and future lifetimes.) Day Lewis takes a particular mind, or "private sphere," and in his four transitions of that mind aims to demonstrate how the single mind merges into the universal mind in order to overcome "public chaos." At the end of the poem the transitions are defined in endnotes that emulate Eliot's notes for *The Waste Land*: "The central theme of this poem is the single mind. The poem is divided into four parts, which essentially represent four phases of personal experience in the pursuit of single-mindedness: it will be seen that a transition is intended from one part to the next such as implies a certain spiritual progress and a consequent shifting of aspect." Day Lewis then categorizes the four aspects: "(1) metaphysical, (2) ethical, (3) psychological, (4) an attempt to relate the poetic impulse with the experience as a whole."

Transitional Poem is a young man's poem, full of imitative energy and even though it would be eclipsed a year later by Auden's arrival, it is still a worthy poem. Its value was recognized on publication, which was concurrent with the Stock Market crash of 1929 that was the symbolic arrival of the 1930s. This poem, with its Isherwood-Auden schema that Day Lewis had copied from Auden directly, introduced themes for the coming decade: the divided mind, the mind's metaphysical progress, the rejection of tradition for new ways of thinking that could cope with new types of crises, and the poet as an activist who is pure in heart and Truly Strong. Hynes has more than capably detailed how Day Lewis incorporated these themes and their derivation from the Auden-Isherwood influence. The psychological transitions in the poem are, as Hynes said, "a conventional young man's statement of the transition from adolescence to manhood." The young man is both one man and Everyman, or at least every poet. As Everyman, he attempts the Northwest Passage of The Truly Weak who attempts to learn how to become Truly Strong.

The allusions to Auden are both explicit and tacit. Explicitly, Day Lewis refers to the "tow-haired Poet" and uses an Auden epigram to open Part IV, in which Day Lewis makes a closing statement about finding a new world:

"There are going to be some changes made to-day." Day Lewis refers to the "Hawk-faced man," Rex Warner, a mutual friend whom Auden calls by name in *Paid on Both Sides*. He also refers to the "rag and bone man," Yeats. Tacitly, Day Lewis evokes the Auden who, influenced by Lane, said life's lessons should be taught as parables. *Day Lewis:* "I became lord of / Light's interplay — stoker of an old parable." He also echoes Auden's aloof cypher-witness that is on the outside looking in. *Auden:* "As the hawk sees it or the helmeted airman." *Day Lewis:* "As arrogant as the hawk as he mounts the morning." Then there is Auden on the conflicting duality in man's nature. *Auden:* "While the divided face has no grace." *Day Lewis:* "The mind against its own forked speculation." Then the Auden (plus Isherwood) who tries to break from the past: *Auden:* "But their ancestral curse." *Day Lewis:* "the ancestral curse." Finally, the Auden influence is again explicitly credited:

> Last the tow-haired poet, never done
> With cutting and planing some new gnomic
>   prop
> To jack his all too stable universe up: —
> Conduct's Old Dobbin, thought's
>   chameleon.
> Single mind copes with split intelligence,
> Breeding a piebald strain of truth and
>   nonsense,

With the last line, Day Lewis tempers the previous praise as if to say he knows enough to separate the wheat from the chaff. Nonetheless, *Transitional Poem* wouldn't have been an early clarion for the 1930s without the influence of Auden and Isherwood. Ultimately, the message of *Transitional Poem* is that the Truly Weak Everyman can heal his divided mind by rejecting the past to move forward as a single-minded Truly Strong Man who is carefree, generous, and an active iconoclast. Day Lewis became one of the artistic leaders of the next decade. He was the first in the 1930s to take his cues from Auden and Isherwood.

Day Lewis's next long poem, *From Feathers to Iron*, was published in 1932 and was more personal. This work was also about a man in transition. The man passes from the single man of *Transitional Poem* to make new transitions as a sensitive lover, husband, and father. In this poem, the "I" of Day Lewis also becomes a "we." The poem is traditionally pastoral in style while being dominated by Auden-country images as embellishments and homage. The poet celebrates the man's new family life but also hints at the growing public apprehension that has begun to encroach on private spheres. The poem makes clear that to respond to these contemporary issues, the poet must use contemporary terms to deal with a New World of action, politics, and propaganda. The title of the poem comes from preceding epigrams by Auden (feathers) and Keats (iron). That Day Lewis would pair them was homage enough. In the poem, the man's observations are keenly sensitive, often didactically so. He is aware of the divided mind, but more in others as he himself is now more single-minded to match his new family responsibilities: "negative's made positive.... / positives change to negative." In stanza VIII, there is an alternation of male and female voices designated by "He" and "She" that signify equality. This stanza concludes with the unity of a last verse, "Both," in which they speak together as one entity.

In stanza XIII, the man knows that his private world is not separated from the whole world and that he, even "when in love's air," shares that same air with "absolute dictators" who "close a door between the closest hearts." Later he speaks to his unborn child (as Auden spoke to the just-born child of their mutual friend Rex Warner in an ode from *The Orators*). He hopes the child can learn how to "be metal to bore through / The impermeable clay" of life's tribulations. For his life, his wife, and his child, love is all: "Faith may move mountains; but love's twice as strong." The Epilogue of *From Feathers to Iron* is a "Letter to W.H. Auden" of whom, Day Lewis says, he has written "on heaven a new signature."

The year 1933 saw publication of Day Lewis's third long poem, *The Magnetic Mountain*, which is an homage to *The Orators*. This poem reflects the new literary activism and it is a statement by Day Lewis that poetry and revolution are compatible. In it, the mountain, compelling in its magnetic attraction, is the symbol of a new life calling to the sensitive man. The poem is evocative of *The Orators* in that it satirizes the sick members of a sick society in a non-realistic narrative that carries within it a more serious moral message.

A young man journeys to leave his sick country and exhorts others to go with him: "Then I'll hit the trail for that promising land/ … with Wystan and Rex my friend" (*MM* 111). During the journey Day Lewis acknowledges public turmoil and the conflicts of dead life against new, us against them, evil against good. The Truly Strong Man appears in a stanza that begins, "Let us now praise famous men / Not your earth-shakers, not the dynamiters" (*MM* 117). This line recollects Spender's poem that begins: "I think continually of those who are truly great" that is also a tribute to the Truly Strong. Day Lewis intended a similar message to that of *The Orators*, but while *The Orators* was an obscure parable, *The Magnetic Mountain* is didactic propaganda.

After the 1930s Day Lewis did not include that decade's work in later collections; consequently, one must refer to first editions for the lines quoted above. (See, however, Izzo, *Christopher Isherwood, His Era, His Gang, and the Legacy of the Truly Strong Man*, 2001, for details.)

Just as Cecil Day Lewis was published before Auden, he also discovered just before Auden that verse does not makes one's living; hence, again before Auden, he became a school master. Unlike Auden, he was not quite so fond of it. In addition to verse, he wrote polemics that earned him much attention, especially after Michael Roberts in *New Signatures* said the new poets were not just poets but also iconoclastic activists. Two essays in particular, "A Hope for Poetry" and "Revolution in Writing," developed Roberts' argument more precisely, and Cecil's left bent made him a very appealing figure of the new poetic sensibility. None of this, however, paid well. He considered a more commercial form of writing and this he undertook as Nicholas Blake, mystery writer.

Mysteries and eccentric detectives were presently the escapist rage. Sherlock Holmes remained a stalwart, as did Agatha Christie's Hercule Poirot, Bulldog Drummond, Sayers' Lord Peter Wimsey, Charteris's Simon Templar (The Saint), and numerous others. To these, Day Lewis, as Blake, would add Nigel Strangeways. "Blake" was presently at work on his first

effort, *A Question of Proof*, in which one may recognize that Strangeways seems to be taken from the author's acquaintances, one of them a little bit and another rather much.

The murder mystery takes place at a prep school. One of the masters was a chum of Nigel's at Oxford and describes him to another.

Could not stick two years of the place [Oxford], the spectacle of so many quite decent youths being got at and ruined for life was too much for him. Heard that at Cambridge their hearties were still heartier and the intelligentsia even less intelligent, so he decided to dispense with further education. So he answered all of his examinations in limericks — very good answers, I believe — he's a first-rate brain, but it alienated the dons, they have no taste for modern poetry, and he got sent down. Travelled about for a bit learning languages. Then settled down to investigate crime; said it was the only career left which offered scope to good manners and scientific curiosity. He's been very successful; made pots of money…. A Nordic type. He's rather faddy, by the way; his protective mechanism developed them, I dare say. But you must have water perpetually on the boil; he drinks tea at all hours of the day. And he can't sleep unless he has enormous weight on his bed. If you don't give him enough blankets for three, you'll find that he has torn the carpets up or the curtains down.

"The Decoys" 1931

This poem concerns the necessity not to be taken in by The Others and is a contrast with the poem "Have a Good Time."

de la Mare, Walter

1873–1956, English poet and novelist who wrote of the fantastic. Included among his books of poetry are *Songs of Childhood* (1902), *The Listeners* (1912), *Peacock Pie* (1913), *Poems for Children* (1930), and *The Fleeting and Other Poems* (1933). His fiction includes *Henry Brocken* (1904), *The Return* (1910), *Memoirs of a*

Midget (1921), and *On the Edge* (1930), and a collection of bizarre tales.

For Auden, de la Mare was an early favorite along with AE (George Russell). De la Mare also edited the poetry anthology. *Come Hither* (1923), which introduced Auden to a number of poets including Robert Frost, who had an impact on Auden. Another appeal of *Come Hither* was that de la Mare mixed in the serious with the light and humorous, and Auden thereafter believed that he should do so as well. Indeed when Auden and John Garrett edited their own anthology for children, *The Poet's Tongue* (1935), many selections came from *Come Hither*. No doubt, the fact that de la Mare was, by many accounts, particularly in author Storm Jameson's autobiography *Journey from the North*, a kind, generous, and gentle man, was not a small influence on Auden as well. Auden would select and introduce *A Choice of de la Mare's Verse* in 1963.

In that introductory essay, Auden supplies two very important definitions to his idea of how poetry works. The idea of Eden and the idea that Ariel and Prospero exist in every poet with one perhaps more dominant than the other depending on the individual poet. (*See also* "The Sea and the Mirror.") *Auden*: "We expect a poem to tell us some home truth, however minor, and as we know, most home truths are neither pretty nor pleasant. One might say that in every poet, there dwells an Ariel, who sings, and a Prospero, who comprehends, but in any particular poem, sometimes even in a whole work of a particular poet, one of the partners plays a greater role than the other. Thus Campion, one of de la Mare's favorite poets, is an example of an Ariel-dominated poet in whose work verbal beauty is *almost* everything, and what is said matters very little. In Wordsworth's *The Prelude*, on the other hand, Prospero dominates and Ariel contributes very little; it might almost have been written in prose.... Though the role of Prospero in de la Mare's poetry is much greater than one may realize on a first reading, it would not be unfair, I think, to call him an Ariel-dominated poet. Certainly, his most obvious virtues, those which no reader can fail to see immediately, are verbal and formal, the delicacy of his metrical fingering and the graceful architecture of his stanzas." (*See also* Audience.)

Delia, or A Masque of Night 1953

Published in *Botthege Oscure*, 1953, the Auden-Kallman libretto *Delia, or a Masque of Night,* which Stravinsky rejected, has not since found a composer. The theme is suggested from George Peele's play *The Old Wives' Tale.*

The Demonic *see* Christianity; Tillich, Paul

de Rougemont, Denis

1906–1985, Swiss writer of French expression, partisan of the personal philosophy of E. Mounier. He founded, in Geneva, the European Center of the Culture (1950). His book *Love in the Western World* (1938) defended a political union founded on the respect of cultural diversity. Auden read this book and factored it into his introductions for the series *Poets of the English Language.*

The Descent of the Dove *see* Williams, Charles

Destructive Element *see* Plays with Isherwood; Spender, Ste phen

"Detective Story" 1936

Auden loved detective stories, and this poem was written shortly after C. Day Lewis, as Nicholas Blake, wrote his first mystery novel, *A Question of Proof,* in which there is a detective named Nigel Strangeways who is Auden in all of his idiosyncratic charm. This poem traces a life as if a detective looking for clues.

"Dichtung und Wahrheit" 1959

(The title is from Goethe's autobiography, and means poetry and truth.) Subtitled "An

Unwritten Poem," and called "An Interlude" in the collection *Homage to Clio*, it is in fact, in prose over a number of pages and fifty paragraphs, short and long, an exploration of the relation of poetry/truth to the "real" world. The poet, as the exponent of purified language (*see* Mallarmé, Stéphane), which is the distinctive human characteristic, seeks to turn particular words into universal intimations, and, thus, purify these words. Nonetheless, words can only intimate, never duplicate reality, so that a love poem that is true to the actual situation cannot be written and, instead, ironically, involves the Vision of Dame Kind (of beautiful nature that inspires transcendent feelings) as the tone that will actually preside over a meeting of lovers rather than any words that they say; the poet's words intimate that tone. (*See* "Dame Kind.") This prose exposition is a lesson on the nature of language that Auden gave much theoretical thought to throughout his life, particularly the discrepancy in the I-You relationship where the "I" and the "You" use inadequate words to convey feelings that are much more complex. (*See also* Language.)

Dickey, William *see* Yale Series of Younger Poets

Dickinson, Emily

1830–86, American poet, b. Amherst, Mass. She is one of the most original poets in American literature. Her lyrics are metaphysical intimations of transcendental mysticism. She was virtually unknown as a poet during her lifetime, which was spent largely, and reclusively at home. After her death in 1886, her sister Lavinia Dickinson discovered over 1,000 poems in her sister's bureau.

Auden was introduced to Dickinson at Oxford and attempted a poem in her manner, which likely appealed for its dense brevity and clipped diction where a great deal is inferred. Auden's verse that would be published in 1930, *Poems*, is also clipped, dense, and seemed obscure except to the initiated such as Isherwood, Spender, Day Lewis, and a few others. Dickinson was among Auden's early influences up until 1926 along

with Thomas Hardy, Edward Thomas, A.E. Housman, and Robert Frost. Then he went into his T.S. Eliot phase.

Emily Dickinson

"Dingley Dell & Fleet" 1962

In this essay, Auden observes that mythopoetic characters live in any reader's milieu. Sherlock Holmes is one because he is not *too* specific as a real person; he is more of a superhero. Anna Karenina isn't mythopoetic because Tolstoy's greater talent has more specificity but less universality. The greatest writers have characters of both myth and specificity; Dickens' Pickwick is one. This distinction extends to how one seeks utopia. In the quest for utopian good, one can seek Eden and revive the past in the manner of generalized good, or one can seek a New Jerusalem to create a future of a more specified good. In *Eden* the evil must leave; in *New Jerusalem*, evil is not allowed in. Dickens is an Eden Man and Christian-oriented. Pickwick lives in a shame culture. He has no shame because he plays it safe, but he reads of others who aren't safe; it is vicarious and a secret pleasure, hence he feels no guilt.

Dodds, A.E.

D. 1973, wife of E.R. Dodds. She and her husband befriended Auden throughout Auden's life, often being his confidants in person or through letters. She assisted on the completion of Auden's *The Oxford Book of Light Verse*, checking copy and making selections.

Dodds, E.R.

1893–1979, professor of Greek at Birmingham who first met Auden's father, then Auden. Dodds was also very friendly with Louis MacNeice, and often Auden and MacNeice would visit Dodds together. By 1938, Dodds was teaching at Oxford. Auden dedicated *The Oxford Book of Light Verse* to Dodds. Dodds thought the book should have been dedicated to Mrs. Dodds (above) who assisted in its completion.

Dodo Minor

Christopher Isherwood wrote in *Lions and Shadows*: "At my preparatory school [St. Edmund's], during the last two years of the War, there had been a boy named Hugh Weston [Auden] ... nicknamed 'Dodo Minor' because of the solemn and somewhat birdlike appearance of his bespectacled elder brother.... His father was a doctor: Weston had discovered, very early in life, the key to the bookcase which contained anatomical manuals with coloured German plates. To several of us ... he confided the first naughty stupendous breath-taking hints about the facts of sex.... With his hinted forbidden knowledge and stock of mispronounced scientific words, portentously uttered, he enjoyed among us, his semi-savage credulous school fellows the status of a kind of witch-doctor.... Just before Christmas, 1925, a mutual acquaintance brought him to tea. I found him very little changed."

The Dog Beneath the Skin see Plays with Isherwood

"Doggerel by a Senior Citizen" 1969

Auden, who in his youth refuted and rebelled against "family ghosts" (tradition), now agrees with them.

"Don Juan" *see* Byron, Lord George Gordon

Don Quixote

The character created by Cervantes 1547–1616, Spanish novelist, dramatist, and poet, author of *Don Quixote de la Mancha*. *Don Quixote* as a novel considers two conflicting views toward the world: idealistic illusion and bitter reality. Quixote the character is a country gentleman who has read too many chivalric romances. He and the peasant Sancho Panza, who serves as his squire, set forth on a series of adventures aggrandized in Quixote's mind. The illusory idealism of Don Quixote and the more realistic pragmatism of Sancho are in opposition.

Auden once confessed — truthfully or not — that he never finished *Don Quixote* and that he believed no one else had either; yet, the character had a profound effect on him. The duality of illusion and reality, the sense of an eternal quest, and the single-minded honor of Quixote, who, in fact, is quite mad, seemed, to Auden, to reflect the conflicted modern world where the alienating effects of the urban-industrial life created many Quixotes but without the safety net of a rural, simple life that offered some protection, even to a madman. Auden often lectured on Quixote (see also *The Enchafèd Flood*). In 1963, he was asked to write lyrics for a planned stage musical the *Man of La Mancha*. He and Chester Kallman did so but the lyrics were not used. The musical (with lyrics by Joe Darion) went on to be a great success — its song "The Impossible Dream" became a standard, and a summation of the Quixote mystique. For Auden Don Quixote is an indirect apostle as — in his mind, if not in actuality — a Kierkegaardian Knight of Faith manqué who is really more of a Knight-errant. He reads books, goes mad, becomes what he reads, never succeeds, yet never despairs as his madness defines the effort to be noble as the goal, with actual success secondary. Quixote is a prisoner of romance and, in a manner of speaking, so was Auden.

Donne, John

1572–1631, English poet and divine. He is considered the greatest of the metaphysical poets. Reared a Roman Catholic, Donne was educated at Oxford and Cambridge. Donne's court career was ruined by the discovery of his marriage in 1601 to Anne More, and he was imprisoned for a short time, after which his poetry became more serious. *An Anatomy of the World* (1611) and *Of the Progress of the Soul* reveal that his faith in the medieval order of things had been disrupted by the political, scientific, and philosophic doubt of the times. He wrote prose and polemics on religious and moral subjects. Donne yielded to the wishes of King James I and took orders in 1615. Two years later his wife died. The tone of his poetry deepened even more after her death. After his ordination, Donne wrote more religious works.

All of Donne's verse shows passion and reason. His love poetry treats the breadth of the experience of loving, emphasizing, in such poems as "The Ecstasie," the root of spiritual love in physical love. The devotional poems and sermons reveal a deep concern with death, decay, damnation and the possibility of the soul's transcendent union with God.

Donne was rediscovered by twentieth century critics, and his work has had a profound influence on a number of poets including W.B. Yeats, T.S. Eliot, and Auden.

For Auden, early and late, Donne had lessons as both poet and man. The early Auden appreciated Donne's seeking spiritual love in human form. Later Auden would see this as the Vision of Eros that becomes the Vision of Agape. Donne's marrying secretly and his jail time for doing so gave Donne a rebel's air in the name of love that also appealed to Auden. Auden's 1940 poem "In Sickness and in Health" is a long rhymed essay on theology and marriage

that Mendelson considers to be a "blatant" imitation of Donne. Consequently, in the year that Auden was becoming committed to his reconversion to Christianity, Donne's life and work seemed an example for emulation. Mendelson adds, "[The poem] ends in an updated version of Donne's 'The Litanie,' a poem Auden was urging on his friends." (At this time Chester Kallman was the object of Auden's hope for a happy marriage.) Auden thought so much of "The Litanie" that he quotes a favorite passage from it in his notes to "New Year Letter" in *The Double Man*, his Swarthmore lecture of 1950, and in the Viking Book of Aphorisms co-edited with Louis Kronenberger, 1962. Still, Auden did not agree with Donne wholeheartedly. In his essay "Christianity and Art," he writes, "Poems, like many of Donne's and [Gerard Manley] Hopkins', which express a poet's personal feelings of religious devotion or penitence, make me uneasy.… Is there not something a little odd, to say the least, about making an admirable public object out of one's feelings of guilt and penitence before God?" Indeed, while he admired Donne, he preferred George Herbert's poetic approach to God.

Doone, Rupert

1903–1966, Pseudonym of Reginald Woodfield. Founder of the Group Theatre; English theatrical producer, dancer, and choreographer. The Group Theatre was a left-tilted experimental theatre that produced Auden's *The Dance of Death* in 1934 and then the three Auden-Isherwood plays, *The Dog Beneath the Skin* (1935), *The Ascent of F6* (1937), and *On the Frontier* (1938). Doone was working class with artistic aspirations. He went to Paris in the 1920s where he worked as a dancer and met Jean Cocteau and Diaghilev. Cocteau was a dramatist read by Auden, and later Auden would translate Cocteau's play *The Knights of the Round Table.*

The Double Man 1940

Dedicated to Elizabeth Mayer, this volume contains the long poems "New Year Letter" and

"The Quest." Ninety pages of notes, a first for Auden, follow "New Year Letter" and these notes are his declaration of a changed life in America and as a re-converted Christian. The notes are an invaluable source in seeing the early, and intense, stages of Auden's Christianity. He refers to or quotes (and sometimes often) Tolstoy, Gorki, E.M. Forster, Chekhov, D.H. Lawrence, Hitler, Henry James, Margaret Meade, Kierkegaard, Kafka, Rimbaud, Rilke, Shakespeare, Kipling, Cyril Connolly, Nietzsche, the Gospels, Milton, Wolfgang Kohler, Pascal, Baudelaire, Yeats, Blake, Flaubert, Jung, Boethius, Spinoza, Wagner, T.S. Eliot, George Groddeck, Paul Tillich, Goethe, Horace, Voltaire, Dante, Vachel Lindsay, Henry Adams, C.S. Lewis, Whitman, Thomas Mann, A.N. Whitehead, Christopher Smart, Chaucer, Donne, William Langland (*Piers Ploughman*).

"Dover" 1937

"Dover" was written after Auden had visited Spain during the Spanish Civil War, but before he and Isherwood made their Journey to a War in China. Auden came to realize that the idea of the border/frontier as a crisis point in earlier poems had now become a mere exercise, a ritual of the mind that was becoming inadequate as a metaphor as compared to real frontiers and real wars such as in Spain. In reality frontiers make nothing happen in the mind; only the mind can act, wherever it is.

"Down There" *see About the House*

Downs School

The Downs School, located in the lush Malverns, was a progressive school founded by George Cadbury. Auden's time there as teacher was perhaps the happiest of his life. The headmaster, Geoffrey Hoyland — to whom Auden dedicated "A Summer Night" — was a liberal and pursued innovative teaching methods. Auden created the school's literary magazine,

The *Badger* (after the school's symbol that represented "We build"), and had a large part in school theatricals. His students adored him.

Drew, Elizabeth

1887–1965, Anglo-U.S. author, critic, became acquainted with Auden. She wrote *The Literature of Gossip* (1964), that must have appealed to Auden who said the poet must be a mixture of "spy and gossip." One of Auden's "Bucolics" is dedicated to her.

Dryden, John

1631–1700, English poet, dramatist, and critic. Graduated from Cambridge, 1654. He first came to public notice with his *Heroic Stanzas* (1659), commemorating the death of Oliver Cromwell. His long poem on the Dutch War, *Annus Mirabilis*, appeared in 1667. The following year he became poet laureate. He had a long and varied career as a dramatist with *All for Love* (1677) a retelling of Shakespeare's *Antony and Cleopatra*, and the comedy *Marriage à la Mode* (1672). His political satire *Absalom and Achitophel* appeared in two parts (1681, 1682). It was followed by *Religio Laici* (1682), a poetical exposition of the Protestant layman's creed. In 1687, however, Dryden announced his conversion to Roman Catholicism.

Auden at Oxford appreciated both Dryden and Pope — more or less didacticists — who were then "out" while Donne, Dickinson, and the metaphysics were "in" and Auden appreciated these poets as well. He said in 1973 in his introduction of *A Choice of Dryden's Verse*, that Dryden was "pre-eminent in English as the poet of Common Sense ... the ideal poet to read when one is weary, as I often am, of poetry with a capital P." In Auden's 1940 "New Year Letter" Dryden's style is imitated in respect of its didactic and, as necessary, satirical clarity, and Dryden is included in a tribunal of Auden's masters that includes, among others, Blake, Voltaire, Hardy, and Rilke. Also in 1940 Auden wrote the libretto for Britten's *Paul Bunyan* and took some inspiration from Dryden's libretto for *King Arthur*. Auden considered

Dryden to be a "professional" poet in Auden's Introduction to *Poets of the English* language, Vol. III.

Duality

During the 1930s Auden sought by numerous means to justify, to his own satisfaction, the idea that duality of mind and body existed, in large part so that his homosexual pleasures should not be disrupted by the guilt in his mind over being gay. Early avatars of this form of duality were John Layard, Homer Lane, D.H. Lawrence, and George Groddeck. By 1939, Auden had changed his mind, defining what he called the only two philosophies of life, one false and one true. He believed dualism was a false philosophy that the body ruled over the intellect, sometimes with terrible results, such as the twisted philosophies of Adolf Hitler.

The Duchess of Malfi see Brecht, Bertolt

"The Duet" 1947

This poem contrasts a rich but "sad" lady with a "scrunty beggar" and their whining is not appealing. "Auden's insistence that the beggar's 'scrannel-music making' was the true voice of praise was his means of renouncing the Miltonic claims he had made in his elegy for Yeats. 'Scrannel' was the dismissive adjective in 'Lycidas' for songs that were lean, flashy, grating, and false. He was renouncing old errors without finding plausible truths to put in their place" (Mendelson, *Later Auden*).

"The Dyer's Hand" 1956

This was an essay published in the *Anchor Review*, derived from three BBC radio broadcasts in 1955, and not to be confused with Auden's 1962 essay collection with the same title.

What is the poetic subject? For the poet who is egotistical and fated to poetry, mankind is the poetic subject. For a historian, life is not fated, but chosen — as shown by the past as lessons for the present and future. The poet deals with inner man and the themes of universality and posterity. Both the poet and the historian know all men are not alike, but a poet divides them into those who do and those who do not fulfill their destiny.

Theological Question: each historian can believe differently, but all believe in something. This belief is the true voice that art cannot dictate but only reflect. Modern poetry (from A.D. 500) requires a reader's active and creative partnership as interpreter. Poetry affirms being and becoming and defeats the enemies of being and becoming, which are the accidental and fantastic. Man is an amphibian of adaptable body and mind versatility.

Dynamo: The dynamo is the scientist who measures a world that is recurrent, bound by law, inevitable, and identified by numbers and exactitude, so that all being is the same, that is, measurable, and all beings are replaceable. Freedom is the consciousness of necessity.

Virgin: The virgin is the artist (as opposed to the dynamo, or scientist) who is concerned with reflecting a historical happenstance that is unique, and related by analogy, rather than law. The artist identifies these happenstances through metaphorical representation, and to the artist all beings are irreplaceable. Necessity is the consciousness of freedom.

Science and art, as well as the scientist and the artist, balance so that each prevents the hubris of the other. A pseudo-artist becomes incapable of recognizing beauty; a pseudo-scientist becomes incapable of recognizing truth.

For the dynamo (scientist) the world consists of pluralities, crowds, societies, and communities. A *crowd* is indiscriminately together without purpose. A *society* is a defined unity, finite, and collectively purposeful in that it loves itself chauvinistically.

For the virgin (artist) a community is joined by a common love of something other than themselves. Love becomes a goal. Science and art are both spiritual activities originating from different perspectives. The scientist seeks ordering of the physical universe to make sense of it; the artist seeks ordering of the historical universe for the same reason but also to form a community from its lessons. Poets were once respected, trained craftsmen nurtured for their magic to transform minds. This is no longer the case, nor desirable. The poet now records and amplifies the history of either outstanding ideas or significant events; these ideas and events may be either noteworthy to everyone immediately, or noteworthy to only certain people. The poet seeks to transform events into a community embodied in a verbal society that like the physical universe of the scientist has laws and structures (prosody and syntax). The nature of the final order of a poem is the outcome of a dialectical struggle between the events poets wish to embody and the verbal system. When events dominate, the accurate evocation restricts style because *fancy* is precluded.

A poet, writes Auden, can work in two ways: 1) thinking of the community he desires, he will work backward to find a system to embody it; or 2) within a certain system, he will find a community to fit his system in. In practice, he does both.

Regarding verbal societies and the limitations of language, Auden notes that language attempts to civilize divergences, but since language is always misdirection, the progress of civilized thought is always imperfect.

Poets follow three absolute presuppositions/dogma. 1) A historical world of unique events and persons exists and its existence is good. 2) It is a fallen world of unfreedom and disorder—it's good that it exists, though its way is evil. 3) This world is still redeemable, and the lack of freedom and disorder of the past can be reconciled. Every poem is an analogue of the possible paradise, Eden—but not an imitation of that state, which is impossible to reproduce as art. Art can only intimate; it can never become what it describes.

Poetry in the present age is a continuation of the modern age of poetry begun with Yeats through Eliot, in which poets are colonizers rather than explorers, and they are still coping with the problems of the industrial age. Technology gives us access to previous ages, changing the meaning of tradition, which is no longer a handing down of knowledge but a knowledge of both the past and present as one continuous era that is now merging into the next era. In this present, originality in art is no longer a

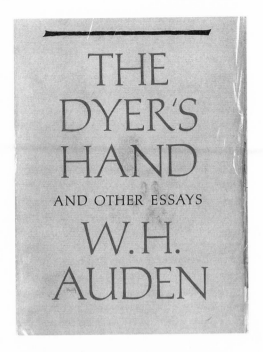

The Dyer's Hand, cover of first edition.

slight modification of its immediate precursor but an obligation to know *all* of the past so that the treatment of the present is an all-encompassing sensibility. Will a poet's poetry hold up to the future shock of the next generation? This question tempts poets to follow ephemeral changes in order to stay current, but they will betray themselves with insincerity. Today's poet can only truly know his own inner life or attempt to depict another's inner life; his hero doesn't rule, but resists rule to keep his integrity, and this is the anti-hero.

Finally, Auden writes of highbrow and Lowbrow poets: a highbrow poet always has a small cult following; a lowbrow poet just produces consumable entertainment for the mass. Propaganda is the use of black magic on the public to get them to follow and believe. The state encourages lowbrows either as direct propagandists or as pabulum purveyors. The state attacks highbrows who encourage individualism.

The Dyer's Hand 1962

Essay collection that takes its title from a line of Shakespeare, and that Auden had used twice before, the second time for a 1956 essay in the *Anchor Review* (see above).

"Easy Knowledge" *see* *Poems*

Eberhart, Richard

1904–1996, American poet, b. Austin, Minn., grad. Dartmouth (1926) and Cambridge (1929).

Eberhart attended Cambridge University and was one of the poets included in the crucial poetry anthology of 1932, *New Signatures*, edited by Michael Roberts, that was the unofficial, but, by its effect, the collected coming of the Auden Generation. Eberhart did not know Auden until Auden's arrival in America in 1939, about which he wrote, "Auden's coming to America may prove to be as significant as Eliot leaving it." When Auden arrived in New York, he mentioned an interest in teaching. Eberhart, teaching at St. Marks School in Southborough, Massachusetts, convinced the school to invite Auden for a four-week guest teaching post. Eberhart, just as Glenway Wescott in comparing Auden to Vachel Lindsay, found Auden to be prodigiously enthusiastic and energetic.

Eberhart also noticed that Auden gave himself a little help with the amphetamine Benzedrine.

Eden *see* Audience; Mysticism

"Education Today and Tomorrow" 1939

This essay, written with T.C. Worsley, asserts that a small undifferentiated economy and community make education easier as roles are defined and both vocation and social integration are clear. Conversely, a complex and diverse economy and society ask: "What do we teach to whom?" In the Victorian era of a post-industrial revolution a systemized, universal education was needed to produce followers and

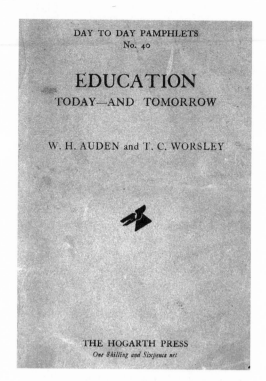

DAY TO DAY PAMPHLETS
No. 40

EDUCATION
TODAY—AND TOMORROW

W. H. AUDEN and T. C. WORSLEY

THE HOGARTH PRESS
One Shilling and Sixpence net

Education, first edition.

leaders through organized games and a military setting. Universal education also produces a minority of nonconforming rebels. Democracy offers equality in theory, but the "Haves" still have advantages, and they allow only a small number of the lower classes to join them (as long as that small number conforms). Ultimately, education can make people good only to the extent that a society is good. People will behave as their society does with the influence of the society's education system because state schools imitate society for good or ill. Private or progressive schools for aesthetes (artists and intellectuals) do not have the obligation to encourage the survival skills of courage and cunning needed by the hearties. D.H. Lawrence advocated anti-idealism and fascism (unintentionally), as he attacked liberal ideas as lip service; fascists co-opted his views and distorted them.

Auden elaborates his educational theory: 1) man fell (from grace) when he became self-conscious (Adam eating the apple from the tree of knowledge); 2) the mind and body hate each other; 3) idealism is the adherence to an instinctive life, but self-consciousness corrupts life and leads to 4) conflicted "ninnies"; 5) every individual is unique and cannot be systemized; 6) very few people are suited to the introspective contemplation needed for the progress of consciousness; 7) the aim of education should be to help people realize their deepest instinctive needs.

Also, 1) education should reject book learning to teach crafts and trades (craft includes art); 2) schools should train body and spirit with sports; 3) schools should select the mind-trainees very carefully. Number two seems rather disingenuous as Auden hated sports, although when he was a teacher at the Downs school he attempted to participate in the sports, if rather clumsily, according to a former student, John Duguid.

"Edward Lear" *see* Lear, Edward

Eiseley, Loren

1907–1977, b. in Lincoln, Nebraska, sociologist and anthropologist. Eiseley was known for his examination of human evolution, *The Immense Journey* (1946), that combined science and humanism. From 1969 to 1977, Eiseley published many volumes of personal essays and poetry. Just like Oliver Sacks, Eiseley was a scientist who could talk contemplatively about his work and not just measure it. He and Auden both had a childhood fascination with caves. Auden would review *The Unexpected Universe* ("Concerning the Unpredictable"), in which he would explain his meaning of Carnival. Auden befriended Eiseley in the 1960s.

Ekelöf, Gunnar

1907–68, Swedish poet. Ekelöf's lifelong interest in mysticism was evident in his first book, *Late Arrival on Earth* (1932, tr. 1967), a collection of surrealist poems. Later works involved the conflict between mystical experience and reason and the subjective experience of time. In 1971 Auden and Leif Sjoberg translated a selection of Ekelöf's poems. This duo

would do the same for another Swedish poet in 1973, Pär Lagerkvist. Ekelöf's interest in mysticism likely found resonance with Auden's mysticism, and even in the last two years of his life, Auden was still deeply interested in Norse literature, a passion that started with Old Norse epics when he was a child.

The Elder Edda 1969

Dedicated to J.R.R. Tolkien, *The Elder Edda* is the Icelandic saga co-translated by Auden and Paul Taylor. It is a compilation from about A.D. 1200 of earlier Icelandic poems on cosmology, mythology, and the stories of Norse heroes. Together with the *Prose or Younger Edda*, it is the main resource for knowledge of Scandinavian mythology. (*See also* Old Norse and Old English Literature.)

Elegy for Young Lovers 1961

Hans Werner Henze met Auden and Chester Kallman on the Italian island Ischia in 1953. In 1957 he asked them to write a libretto for *Elegy for Young Lovers*. It would be a small chamber opera without chorus. Henze left the choice of subject and evocation to Auden and Kallman. The protagonist, Gregor Mittenhofer, "embodies the romantic myth of the artist-genius who stands above ordinary moral standards and obligations.... Mittenhofer is a great artist who is also a monster, one who can knowingly bring about the death of young lovers for the sake of the elegy he will write about them.... The theme combines the egoism of the artist with Auden's earlier theme in *The Ascent of F6*, where the climber sacrifices himself and his friends to his neurotic wish for power" (Mendelson, *Libretti*). Auden and Kallman said they were trying for something akin to the Japanese Noh plays. Mendelson sees the influence of W.B. Yeats. Auden injects a bit of reality concerning Mittenhofer and his patroness Carolina who is Caroline Newton, and the trio of Mittenhofer's mistress and her love as that of Auden, Kallman's, and Kallman's lover(s). The first performance was at the Glyndebourne Festival Opera on 13 July 1961.

T.S. Eliot

Eliot, T.S.

1888–1965, born Thomas Stearns Eliot, American-British poet and critic, b. St. Louis, Mo. One of the most important literary figures of the twentieth century, he won the 1948 Nobel Prize in Literature. He studied at Harvard, the Sorbonne, and Oxford, established residence in London in 1914 and became a British subject in 1927. After working as a teacher and a bank clerk, he began a publishing career, working as assistant editor of the *Egoist* (1917–19) and editing his own quarterly, the *Criterion* (1922–39). In 1925 he was employed by the publishing house of Faber and Faber, and eventually became one of its directors. His first marriage, to Vivien Haigh-Wood, in 1915, was troubled, and ended with their separation in 1933. ("Auden had the experience, some time in the early 1930s, of being invited to dinner by Eliot and his first wife Vivien, of whose strangeness he was made aware on arrival: 'I told Mrs. that I was glad to be there and she said: 'Well Tom's not glad.'" (Craft, *W.H. Auden: A Tribute*) He was then married to Valerie Fletcher in 1957, a union that was more successful.

Eliot's early verse — *Prufrock and Other Observations* (1917), *Poems* (1920), and *The Waste Land* (1922) — deal with the pain of modern life.

The Waste Land, whose published version reflects the astute editing by Eliot's friend Ezra Pound, brought him immediate notoriety. His complex early poems made use of such literary devices as myths, religious symbolism, and literary allusion. In his later poetry, especially *Ash Wednesday* (1930) and the *Four Quartets* (1935–42), Eliot sought spirituality for human salvation. He accepted religious faith as a solution to the human dilemma and converted to Anglo-Catholicism in 1927.

Eliot was a prominent critic; his later criticism supports Christianity. Eliot's plays tried to revitalize verse drama and usually featured the same themes that his poetry did. They include *Murder in the Cathedral* (1935), dealing with the final hours of Thomas à Becket; *The Family Reunion* (1939); *The Cocktail Party* (1950); *The Confidential Clerk* (1954); and *The Elder Statesman* (1959).

Eliot's influence on twentieth century poetry cannot be overstated. After *The Waste Land* all of serious English language poetry was a reaction to Eliot whether for or against; one could not write without knowing that one would now be compared to Eliot. This impact was no less for Auden. Isherwood writes in *Lions and Shadows* that when Auden's tastes moved away from Thomas Hardy and Edward Thomas to T.S. Eliot and *The Waste Land*, their conversations now required Eliot-like allusions: "quotations and misquotations were allowed, together with bits of foreign languages, proper names and private jokes." Isherwood and Auden indulged in what they called "*The Waste Land* game" and played with a private nomenclature that suited their mutual artistic interests. Both were looking for a new way of writing that was to be more objective and austere.

Eliot's impact on Auden was not just philosophical. It would be Eliot who would discover and publish Auden. First, with the verse play *Paid on Both Sides* in the *Criterion* (February 1930), and then by having Faber & Faber publish *Poems* (October 1930), after which Auden was the "coming man" of 1930 as Eliot had been the "coming man" of 1922. (Eliot did not love Auden's verse at first sight. Auden originally submitted poems while still an undergraduate in 1927, but Eliot rejected them. However, he encouraged Auden to keep sending him more, which Auden took positively, and rightly so. Auden stayed with Faber and Faber as the British publisher for his entire career although he almost once bolted to Hogarth with *The Double Man* in 1940 to repay a favor to John Lehman. Eliot reminded him that he couldn't as provided in his contract with Faber.)

The 1930s Auden admired Eliot and was grateful to him but was not quite so keen on Eliot's conservative views and Anglo-Catholicism. After Auden's arrival in America and his conversion to Christianity, there was more sympathy with Eliot while not whole-hearted agreement on both theological and philosophical perspectives. Eliot's theology did not include Auden's Christian rebels Kierkegaard, Paul Tillich, and others of a more liberal view of Christianity.

Tom Driberg introduced Auden to Eliot's poetry in 1926. Auden told his Oxford tutor Nevill Coghill, "I have torn up all my poems … because they were no good. You ought to read Eliot…. I now see the way I want to write" (quoted in Carpenter, *W.H. Auden*), after which came Auden's Eliot imitations. Moreover, Auden read Eliot's 1919 essay "Tradition and the Individual Talent" and he began to take on a new vision of what poetry should be. Now Auden wished to be objective and clinical, even surgical in paring words from the body of language and reconstructing them in spare and cryptic constructions. Emotion was out. "Modernity" was in; a move from pastoral and green to industrial and gray enter Auden's choices of city and machine images for his poems. Auden was precocious enough to understand that one could not continue in Eliot's style without being criticized, but that he could take Eliot's views and apply them to his own style.

After Eliot published Auden, as poetry editor for Faber & Faber he would see through all of Auden's volumes, including the plays. Eliot deserves much credit for encouraging Auden's work, which in its views, was not like his own views. That he would, in 1932, publish *The Orators,* Auden's most difficult and anarchic work, both in style and content, is to have had trust and faith in Auden's ability and his future.

In 1933, after Auden's "A Summer Night" Vision of Agape, he asked Eliot if he could review Violet Clifton's *The Book of Talbot.* He did and this is a very important book and review in terms of Auden's vision as man and poet.

In 1935 Auden included Eliot in the anthology *The Poet's Tongue.* In 1935, despite initial objections, Eliot agreed to let Auden and his best friend Isherwood co-author their first play in collaboration, *The Dog Beneath the Skin.* In 1936 Rupert Doone and the Group Theatre revived Auden's 1933 play *The Dance of Death* on a double bill with Eliot's *Sweeney Agonistes.* In 1937 Eliot chose the title for Auden's volume *Look Stranger* while Auden was in Iceland. Auden was not pleased and had the American edition called *On This Island.*

In America Auden made up a game called "purgatory mates" and paired Eliot with Whitman (as well as Tolstoy with Oscar Wilde). In 1944 Simeon's speech in Auden's *For the Time Being* echoes Eliot's *Four Quartets.* Eliot had dinner with Auden in New York in 1947 and around this time Eliot was concerned that Auden's poetic technique was not up to par with his spiritual development.

When Eliot died in 1965 Auden said that Eliot would never lose his place as an artist. His feelings are summed up in a remark in a letter to Louise Bogan: "I shall never be as great and good a man if I live to be a hundred."

An Elizabethan Song Book see New York Pro Musica

Empson, William

1906–84, English critic and poet. Attended Cambridge with American poet Richard Eberhart. His *Seven Types of Ambiguity* (1930), studied the meanings of poetry. It was followed by *Some Versions of Pastoral* (1935) and *The Structure of Complex Words* (1951). In *Milton's God* (1961) Empson attacked Puritanism. His poetry — *Poems* (1935) and *The Gathering Storm* (1940) — is considered witty and metaphysical. For many years Empson appeared on the BBC as did George Orwell and they became friends. A collected edition of his poems appeared in 1955. Empson was knighted in 1979. When

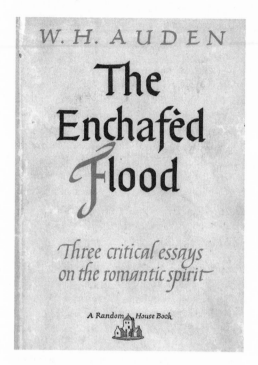

W. H. A U D E N

The Enchafèd Flood

Three critical essays on the romantic spirit

A Random House Book

The Enchafèd Flood, **cover of first edition.**

Auden and Isherwood went to China for their *Journey to a War*, Empson, already there, met them in Hong Kong. Carpenter writes in *W.H. Auden* that later, Auden "lent some money to William Empson, who was returning to England from the Far East via the U.S.A. and had been robbed. Empson recalled of Auden's kindness: 'When you consider that all money from England was frozen, and he was certain that I could not repay him, his behavior should be recognized as noble.'" Empson did pay him back.

In 1955 when Empson's *Collected Poems* appeared Auden wrote a poem, "One Circumlocution." "The subject [of the poem] ... is the way in which every work of art is a riddle — the solution of which can be named only outside of art, or perhaps not at all. Auden derived the poem's cryptic, riddling wit from William Empson..." (Mendelson, *Later Auden*). In 1971 Auden wrote the poem "A Toast for William Empson" to introduce a book of essays titled *William Empson the Man and his Work*. One line reads "if I could manage *Just a Smack at Empson*," which is Eberhart's line from his own poem about Empson.

The Enchafèd Flood 1949

Essays derived from lectures given at the University of Virginia. Auden said he wanted the lectures to be as difficult as reading Heidegger, whom he admired. They are, but they also represent an intense decade in which Auden studied and formulated his Christianity, and these essays represent many of his formulations.

Part I is titled "The Sea and the Desert: Romanticism and the Sea," Auden writes that in Wordsworth's dream in his *Prelude* (V 56-139) are these symbols: desert and sea, a stone of abstract geometry and a seashell whose echo inspires a dreamer. These represent alternative routes to salvation for a dual-natured hero.

The sea was in a primordial flux prior to God's initiative to create the earth and became all sea again after God's wrath by flood. Humanity is, in microcosm, a proverbial *ship of fools*; the mariners are to be pitied and they are a metaphor for a society in danger. A metaphorical Edenic *garden* represents society in peace; a metaphorical *voyage* is interpreted as a crossing of the psychological ocean that separates humanity. *Shakespeare's sea* as a metaphorical symbol is the bridge between the classical and romantic interpretations of human nature: In Shakespeare's early plays there is a contrast of the tempest vs. the idyllic. In his later plays the sea or island is a purgatory for involuntary learning by his characters. After Shakespeare, there is a transition to the *Romantic period* where voluntary voyages are a passage for honorable men to seek their true condition. *The desert* that lies outside the city represents barrenness, literally and figuratively. The desert is a place of outcasts, whose exile is either forced upon them or self-imposed; those in the latter group will learn about God or prepare for God. The desert is a place of punishment (exiles) or purge (seekers of truth). It sits between cities and is the testing place for both the exiles and seekers. It may even have been a former city needing to be redeemed and rebuilt.

Part II is titled "Freedom and Solitude: The Romantic Sea and Desert," As Auden explains, both sea and desert are in flux and outside the normal community. They are free from both evil and responsibility. Upon the sea, on the ship of fools, is tumult, below the sea is calm. The sea and the desert are both free but lonely, and both sea and desert engender a longing for home.

Differences: In the desert is a void; the sea signifies a future life and potential inner growth. *The oasis* (in the desert) and *the happy island* (in the sea) represent the "happy place" where all is innocence with no conflicts over natural desire; in the oasis and the happy island there is natural beauty in both reality and metaphor. *The level desert* symbolizes how democracy destroys the heroic individual with obliteration by absorbing him into the crowd or the anonymous public that eviscerates his individualism. Blind followers deserve no credit, mercy, or absolution. *The mechanized desert* symbolizes industrialization and alienated human robots. To sever oneself from the crowd or the machine is to be an *isolato*. *Moby Dick*'s Ishmael and the ship of fools on the *Pequod* are a community of isolatoes linked by the kinship of flight they all make from the conformist, stagnating city.

Opposite modes of truth: as in Wordsworth's dream from *The Prelude*, the Stone represents science, the desert, and an escape into abstraction, and the shell represents poetry and the sea. Auden, with *Moby Dick* and the *Pequod* as his symbol, asks: Is an individual exalted (Ishmael, Queequeg) or damned (Ahab, Pip)?

The desert's escape mode is an escape into abstraction; the shell, representing poetry, is worth more than the desert. The stone represents divine unity; the shell represents a divine multiplicity of people and ideas that are combined as the means to building a true city, but this energy, if used wrongly, can also prevent the building of a true city or destroy one already inhabited. Ultimately, it is man's choice: the stone's unity, or the shell's multiplicity. The stone's unity gives up some individuality for the sake of the whole, while the Shell's individualistic multiplicity can be either creative or destructive, depending on which individuals take control and what they do with their authority. A *polemical romanticism* divides the body from the mind, as in Newton's cosmology, and then man becomes an object to be controlled by the powerful. The *poet* must overcome Newtonian tradition and its hold on society. He must convey that the rational universe is a result of a benignly abstracted God, and that the good city is founded in reason, commonsense, and good taste, as represented by the influence of priests and seers, teachers and artists who see God as good, if not necessarily personally involved. Conversely, Newton's cosmology renders God as not only impersonal but indifferent, as a God who does not give or take — or care. This is inimical to Auden's Christianity, which seeks the differentiation of good and evil and believes that man has the free will to choose between them. Auden believed that one of his heroes, William Blake, and the Romantics in general decry depersonalization as the outcome of a too-objective secularism and autocratic authority that applied dry and impersonal Newtonian reasoning to society. Auden then analyzes a post-romantic, Herman Melville, as a responder to the romantics through literature.

Moby Dick and Billy Budd: Captain Ahab defied reason to his death, but reason cannot save Billy Budd. Queequeg, the supposed savage, is actually a saint who does not reason but rather intuits the spirit, which is a better way to interact with life than is reasoned objectivism.

Politics and individualism: Romantics replaced the man of reason with the poet. *Romantic aesthetic theory* deified nature, and the Romantic artist crowns the kingdom of "within" anew using his individual imagination as the guide to the inner life of the spirit. He is decipherer, translator, and transcender of subject and object so that they merge into an indivisible mystical unity.

Romantic use of Symbol: *Moby Dick* best examines the relation of subjective to objective experience. The whaling ship becomes a synecdoche (a particular case metaphorically made into everyone's case); all men are enveloped in the transcendent consciousness of whale lines. Ahab hates that inscrutable "thing" which he cannot understand but feels is behind his enemy, the whale.

The ship as mankind: The artist's problem is to decide, as society grows more complex, how he fits society into a microcosm without loose ends. For Auden, the ship is as good a device as any, since it 1) contains all ages, 2) has a hierarchy, 3) has societal function and individual functions (and passive passengers), 4) is a venue for both societal and community interaction, and 5) is self-sustained as decreed by God (hence mutiny is blasphemy), and by *civitas* (society) (hence mutiny is civil rebellion).

The ship vs. the city represents the search for possibility and the escape from necessity (necessity means obligation, responsibility and memory. It also represents a search for necessity and certainty to escape from uncertainty.)

Ishmael and *Don Quixote* are compared: the hero is an exceptional individual reflecting his age; he has authority over the average individual. Heroes are of three types: aesthetic, ethical, and religious (terms from Kierkegaard). The *aesthetic hero* has gifts from nature or God, superior beauty and brains, and can be or do what others can't; by his gifts this hero will lead and command admiration. The danger for the aesthetic hero is that hubris may convince him that his gifts are self-created, not given, and that this attitude will cause envy in others. The *ethical hero* knows universal truth. This hero knows more than the group (society), and he can teach what the group needs to learn. His danger is that he might become too protective of his knowledge, causing jealousy within the group. The *religious hero* has an absolute passion for God and hopes he can engender this same passion within the group. The danger for this hero is that temptation can lead to his fall from grace, which would cause disillusionment in the group.

Auden writes, too, of the *romantic hero*, considering first Ishmael: he is first born and has superior powers; he has a grievance for a wrong not of his own doing; he dislikes an "establishment" that mocks him; he is an outcast in the wilderness, he consorts with other outcasts, some of whom, however, may become future leaders; he develops his skills in solitude; he relishes his outcast role and quasi-martyrdom as a sign of his superiority.

Next Auden considers Don Quixote: he is poor; he is not really a knight; he has a mild crush on a fictitious damsel; he reads chivalrous books that provoke his madness; he is eccentric. Don Quixote becomes insane, thinking he is a knight-errant, and in his obsession he acts out the ultimate religious hero of absolute passion. He is plausible until he recovers his sanity and dies.

Ishmael and *Don Quixote compared*: Both

are *isolatoes*—Ishmael escapes from society, Quixote escapes in it. Both are unhappy: Ishmael for himself, and Quixote for the world. They are unsuccessful in love: Ishmael unrequited, Quixote unproven. Both consort in "low" company: Ishmael descends to them; Quixote raises them up. Both are brave and tough: Ishmael is brave as a form of self-esteem, while Quixote's bravery is taken for granted. Both are wanderers: Ishmael by default, Quixote by design. Ishmael has gifts, but lacks self-esteem to lead or share; Quixote has no gifts, but acts (unsuccessfully) as if he did. Ishmael is pejoratively self-conscience, while Quixote is ignorantly self-forgetful.

The *heroic action* of the classical Renaissance existed only by social recognition. The romantic hero (anti-hero) is made heroic by his unhappy striving for heroism despite acting in solitude. His suffering, not his happiness, lead to his joy and redemption.

The Grievance: The classic hero builds on tradition and conformity; he acts out revenge as a duty to the past. The romantic hero is a nonconformist; he is proud of his "mad" ancestry, which in itself is a grievance towards the society that rejects him; he acts out of revenge as a cry for trying to find a place in the future.

Ishmael's rejection of hypocritical Christian society is aided by Queequeg's acts of intuitive spirituality. *Father Mapple's Sermon* acts as a frame of moral precepts by which to judge Ahab and the other characters in *Moby Dick*. The *story of Jonah* is a voyage of repentance through suffering, which becomes a version of ethical truth where one can "obey God by disobeying him," that is, undo the societal image of God in order to intuitively find the real self and the God within.

The voyage of the *Pequod* is Ishmael's (and the reader's); the rest of the crew has a common motive in their community, which is to earn a living. *Fours squires* are non-white—one is from the South Sea, one is an American Indian, one an African Negro, one Asiatic. They serve as contrasts to Starbuck, Stubb, and Flask, who are white. Queequeg, the supposed savage, is an unconscious (pure) Christian; Fedullah is anti–Christian. Queequeg obeys God without disobeying himself.

The three mates represent spiritual sloth:

Starbuck is a cautious authority who fears God. He is aware of the danger to Ahab's soul but is compelled by duty to obey Ahab, which means he is disobeying God. *Stubb* fears suffering; his bluster is to reassure himself. He laughs at himself ironically, and knows of the depths of wisdom, but seldom dives into that wisdom. He senses mysteries, but fears them; he seeks to hide his fear, and his pipe is a comforting mother (infantile feeding). He is a back-slapper and everyone's buddy, but he really knows no one. Stubb allows Pip's madness through his ignorance of Pip as a real person. *Flask* denies suffering exists. He is the least sympathetic, as he often acts out childish cruelty. He trivializes fear because he is actually very afraid. *Pip* is a foolish innocent, incapable of coping; he is Ahab's anti-type. Flask envies Pip's humility. Pip envies Flask's power; if they were combined, they'd be saved.

Ahab represents the Bible, and he exists in an ivory-tower unreality in which he worships a false idol (revenge) in order to express his anger at God for allowing Moby Dick to bite off his leg. He is a symbol of defiant despair and has a hatred for existence. The scar on his face came before he lost his leg, and the lost leg is a castration symbol. Ahab is an aesthetic hero whose false pride demands that he present a false face to the world. This false face declares: *I will not be average.* Ahab is fate's lieutenant and when he ascetically — and symbolically — discards his pipe, he becomes a slave of revenge; conversely, Stubb clutches at his pipe for the security of a surrogate mother. Ahab destroys the ship's quadrant, which eyes heaven and symbolizes the science and reason that is his enemy — for if he acted reasonably, he would have to disavow his cause for hate.

Billy Budd is a religious hero. Claggart is a religious devil. Auden declares that it is hard to write of a Christ-like figure such as Billy, for several reasons: he is sinless, yet still human, which is unlikely in the real world; he fails in his conflict with the worldly law; his failure only proves him capable of suffering, and does not represent an act of faith; his suffering is both willed (for he does not resist his fate) and unwilled (for he has done nothing wrong). For Melville, innocence and sinlessness are identical, and knowledge of the law is the same as knowledge of sin. If Budd knows what the laws are and still breaks a law, however

unintentionally, then he understands what his fate will be. In this way Budd is compared to Adam before the serpent's temptation.

An artist, says Auden, is like Don Quixote. The romantic artist, just like the romantic hero, records through his characters his own journey into consciousness. Auden writes, "It is not madness we need to flee, but prostitution." It is better to be mad and be independent while seeking to find the true place than to knowingly give allegiance to a false city. (*See also* "The Sea and the Mirror.")

"Encomium Balnei" *see About the House*

Encounter see Spender, Stephen; Connolly, Cyril

"An Encounter" 1970

This poem takes a meeting between Pope Leo and Attila the Hun and imagines what might have been said to cause Attila to end his siege of Rome.

The Enemies of a Bishop see Plays with Isherwood

The Entertainment of the Senses 1973

This libretto was the last Auden-Kallman collaboration, requested by composer John Gardner to be a contemporary antimasque inserted into the James Shirley's seventeenth century masque *Cupid and Death*. The duo wrote about five apes as being the five senses with each lambasting the onslaught on the senses in the twentieth century.

"The Epigoni" 1955

This poem concerns the collapse of classicism and the changing role of the poet in the modern world. In the early 1930s Auden rejected the past; older, he now accepts the useful lessons of the past.

"Epistle to a Godson" 1968

The godson is the son of Stephen Spender; the title is from an Isherwood Mortmere story. Auden read Mikhail Bakhtin's *Rabelais and his World*, and this poem was the first written afterwards. Auden considers what he might write that would help and encourage the young as they begin their quest through life as all people do. Bakhtin's Rabelais lived for *Carnival* in the sense of a tactful politesse that encouraged laughter as a means of harmonious discourse. "Carnival is the realm of laughter, the true belly laughter, as Auden called it, 'not to be confused with the superior titter of the intellect.' It is a realm that 'celebrates the unity of our human race as mortal creatures, who must come into this world and depart from it without our consent, who must eat, drink, defecate, belch, and break wind in order to live, and procreate" (Mendelson, *Later Auden*, and Auden "Concerning the Unpredictable" that is an essay about his friend Dr. Loren Eiseley, in which Auden writes about his meaning of Carnival).

Epistle to a Godson 1972

Poems from 1969 to 1972. The title is from one of Isherwood's Mortmere stories. The godson is Auden's, the son of Stephen Spender.

Essays

Even though the poets of the 1930s never formed an organization or held a single meeting, they were joined together by their private responses to the public chaos. Since the public events were known to all, and in that sense shared, their responses were similar in the "news" aspect while being distinct in each poet's style and personality. Art reflects the temper of its period even when the art does not necessarily directly comment on the period itself. Poetry is the symbolic and symptomatic response of how one feels about what one knows;

it does not, if it is good parable-art, describe the known, but reacts to it.

Essays, conversely, are not consciously symbolic and usually not meant to be parables. (The fact that essays can be both symbolic and parables unconsciously is certainly true. That the essay can be a medium for satiric parable is evidenced by, among many possible examples, Swift's "A Modest Proposal," and William Golding's "Thinking as a Hobby." George Orwell's "Shooting an Elephant" may not be a satire, but it is certainly a parable.) Essays give the writer an opportunity to express what he knows and how he feels about what he knows. The artists of the 1930s took advantage of the opportunity. The writer-as-essayist wrote on many issues.

From 1930 forward Auden as artist and essayist was the exemplar that his peers looked to for direction. Here are excerpts from essays Auden wrote from 1930 to 1934 that intimate or directly state aspects of the Isherwood-Auden schema:

Duality is one of our oldest concepts; it appears and reappears in every religion, metaphysic, and code of ethics" [1930, "Review of *Instinct and Intuition: A Study in Mental Duality*, by George Binney Dibblee"].

At some time or other in human history ... man became self-conscious; he began to feel, I am I, and you are not I; we are shut inside ourselves and apart from each other.

The urge to write, like the urge to speak, came from man's growing sense of personal loneliness, of the need for group communication.... The writer is like a schoolboy who carves his initials on a desk [or into a park bench as in "Letter to Wound" in *The Orators*]; he wishes to live forever.... When we read a book it is as if we were with a person [1932, "Writing," *An Outline for Boys and Girls and Their Parents*].

Before a man wants to understand, he wants to command or obey instinctively, to live with others in a relation of power [1932, "Private Pleasure"].

Don't think you can behave as you like at a liberal school — a little recalcitrance, yes that is amusing. But a will of your own! Make no mistake about that [1932, "Private Pleasure"].

The trouble is … that man's nature is dual, and that each part of him has its own conception of justice and morality. In his passionate nature man wants lordship, to love in a relation of power to others, to obey and to command, to strut and to swagger. He desires mystery and glory. In his cerebral nature he cares for none of these things. He wants to know and be gentle; he feels his other passionate nature is frightening and cruel [1932, "Problems of Education"].

Auden tacitly suggests the differences between the Truly Weak and Truly Strong Man; the former "swaggers" while the latter has sensitive virtues. In an essay two years later, Auden would lay out his meaning explicitly for his generation.

For Auden, to be Truly Strong is to be sensitive and a highbrow.

What is a highbrow? Someone who is not passive to his experience but who tries to organize, explain and alter it, someone in fact, who tries to influence history [1933, "VII"].

Auden also considered the true basis upon which a highbrow succeeds:

[*The Book of Talbot*] shows more clearly than anything I have read for a long time that the first criterion of success in any human activity, the necessary preliminary, whether to scientific discovery or to artistic vision, is intensity of attention or, less pompously, love [1933, "Review of *The Book of Talbot*, by Violet Clifton"].

The highbrow and sensitive Truly Strong Man acts from love; conversely the Truly Weak Man acts from fear.

Auden's gang admired his art and essays and took him very seriously as an ideologue. If Auden talked about a reasonable and sensitive Truly Strong Man of action, this had an impact. However, the call for action was responded to first; the call to be Truly Strong and the understanding of what this meant would take a little more time. Auden was the star of his peer group.

However, dualism became a primary concern for Auden in the 1930s. By 1939, in a lecture at the University of North Carolina at Chapel Hill, he had decided that a dualism that divided body/mind was false, and a philosophy that integrated mind/body as well as the mind itself was correct.

Auden would write essays and book reviews for the rest of his career as they, indeed, paid, and allowed him to express new ideas as new subjects consumed his interest. In certain cases, the essays resulted from lectures he gave at various universities.

In this volume essays are listed with the years they were written as, for Auden, his essays enormously correlate to what he was reading and absorbing by at the time. In the 1930s his influences included Homer Lane, Freud, Marxism, among others. In the 1940s his influences were Kierkegaard, Charles Williams, Paul Tillich, and other writers of existential Christianity to which Auden added Carl Jung and his vision of universal archetypes. These influences entered Auden's essays, and then his poems, which makes his essays a guide to his poetry. No matter what Auden was writing about, his personal vision becomes the important focus of an essay. (Mendelson notes in *Early Auden* that "for a few months in 1939–40 his book reviews in the liberal weeklies amounted to bulletins on his emotional state and his rediscovery of religion.") Hence, if he is writing about Byron, one learns as much or more about Auden as Byron. Every essay contained herein is summarized from Auden's vision, which always was the focus of his essays, more so than the ostensible subject of an essay. He wrote, for example, in the opening sentence of a book review, "If the business of a reviewer is to describe the contents of the books he reviews and to appraise their value, this is not going to be a review" ("The Bond and the Free"). One must always understand that an Auden essay is about Auden, with the subject of the essay an excuse for giving his views.

"Eulogy" 1965

For Nevill Coghill's retirement.

"The Exiles" 1930

This poem is an extended metaphor for the doomed bourgeois who are consigned to insanity now or later.

"Eyes Look into the Well" 1940

This poem feigns a sweet lyric that belies the brutal world that signifies the year it was written. A similar 1940 poem is "Lady Weeping at the Crossroads."

Faber & Faber

Auden's British publisher.

"Fabian Figaro" *see* Shaw, George Bernard

"Fairground" 1966

An aging Auden now wishes to avoid the light and noise of the fairground, which is also the light and noise of life itself.

"The Fall of Rome" 1947

This poem is dedicated to Cyril Connolly and compares Rome's fall to a present bankrupt secularism where faith is shallow or nonexistent.

Family

Auden, Bernard—brother, 1900–1978. The oldest brother but not so intellectually inclined as the two younger boys. Wystan Auden was close to John, but not to Bernard, who migrated to Canada and had little contact with his family.

Auden, Constance Rosalie (Bicknell)—mother, 1869–1941. One of the first women to earn a university degree in Britain, she met her husband while learning to become a missionary nurse. Both were Anglo-Catholic; she was devout and passed this on to her children. "She reserved her fiercest anger for the Low Church Bishop Barnes of Birmingham, a mathematician and scientist who tried to suppress the High Church ceremonies she favored. 'My first

religious memories,' Auden wrote later, 'are of exciting magical rites'" (Mendelson, *Later Auden*).

Auden's mother provided him with both pride and fear: Even as an adult, and after she passed away, he would consider how to deal with a situation based on whether he thought Mother would approve.

Auden, George Augustus—father, 1872–1957. Son of a clergyman, he became a physician. He was editor and writer for the *Historical and Scientific Survey of York and District*, to which he contributed the chapter on prehistory and archaeology. In 1908 George Auden was appointed by the city of Birmingham as first School Medical Officer, and he was also Professor of Public Health at Birmingham University. He was an early advocate of psychoanalytic theory and technique. "Auden's father was also deeply learned in classical and Northern Literature and archaeology, and published scholarly essays on fields as varied as madness in Greek tragedy, Norse antiquities, mathematical prodigies, and the psychology of juvenile delinquency. He transmitted to his son a lifetime love for Norse sagas, folktales, and myths" (Mendelson, *Later Auden*).

Auden, John Bicknell—1903–1991, was a geologist and Auden's older brother, the second of the three sons. He attended St. Edmund's School (Wystan followed him there where he was called Dodo Minor as John had been called Dodo), Marlborough, and Cambridge, studying geology. In 1926 he joined the Geological Survey of India, later became the head of the survey, and remained with it until he retired in the 1950s. In 1960 he began ten years' work with the Land and Water Sources Division of the Food and Agricultural Organization in Rome, and then retired to London. His first marriage ended in divorce. In 1940 he married Sheila Bonnergee; their two daughters are Dr. Rita Auden and Anita Auden Money. John Auden was a founding member of The W.H. Auden Society. John and Wystan Auden were united by close emotional ties and shared intellectual interests. John's passion for geology found an echo in Wystan's childhood fascination with lead mines. Wystan's early poems seem to have prompted John to write poetry of his own. John's mountaineering gave Auden the idea for the play *The Ascent of F6* (*see* Plays with Isherwood), that he dedicated to John. Wystan reconverted to Anglicanism at around the same time that John converted to Catholicism. Wystan and John saw each other infrequently after John left England for India, but their meetings were significant. In 1965 Auden published an epithalamium for the marriage of John and Sheila's daughter Rita.

"Family Ghosts" *see Poems*

"Few and Simple" 1944

This poem declares Auden's continuing love for Chester Kallman in spite of the difficulties this love entailed.

Firbank, Ronald

1886–1926, English author. Firbank lived the life of a leisured aesthete. His novels, which have appealed to a small but appreciative audience, include *Vainglory* (1915), *Valmouth* (1919), and *Concerning the Eccentricities of Cardinal Pirelli* (1926). His books are satiric, and with strange characters. His writings have had an influence on the novels of such writers as Evelyn Waugh, Ivy Compton-Burnett, and Aldous Huxley.

In August 1947, for a carnival on Fire Island, Auden posed as a bishop a propos Firbank's cardinal. In Auden's essay "Notes on the Comic," his reference point is Firbank.

Fire Island

Southeast of New York City, Fire Island is a retreat of the city's residents. Fire Island has long been noted for its varied communities, including resorts favored by gay vacationers. Auden and James and Tania Stern shared a tar shack there called Bective Poplars in the late 1940s.

"First Things First" 1957

This poem "is an impressive example of Auden's ability simultaneously to conduct a complex argument about language and write a love poem whose emotional subtleties make it different from any other.... "'First Things First' treats the problem of writing poetry in the era of subjective uniqueness as exactly parallel to the problem of writing a love poem to an irrevocably absent beloved" (Mendelson, *Later Auden*). Mendelson also observes that the poem's last line — "Thousands have lived without love, not one without water" — is a rebuttal to the line in "September 1 1939," "We must love one another or die."

Fleming, Peter

1907–1971, British writer, particularly of travel books, brother of Ian Fleming, creator of James Bond (*see* "Anger" 1962 Essay). Auden and Isherwood met Fleming in China (see *Journey to a War*) and he was the seasoned English explorer and war correspondent (that they weren't), a real professional and already author of two travel books about China and one on Brazil, with which he had made his name at the age of twenty-four.

The narrative of *One's Company* shows him a gentleman adventurer, modest but resourceful and well informed, and full of the traveler's *savoir-faire* that Auden and Isherwood portray themselves as lacking. Fleming always knows exactly where he is, in relation both to his material and to his readers. He had traveled longer and further in China, including at least two visits to Peking, though he was cool enough to forego a description of the capital — "You will be spared the pen-picture which you had good reason to dread," he told his readers suavely. *Noblesse oblige*. He was an Etonian and well connected. Auden and Isherwood make much of an interview they secured with Mme. Chiang Kai-shek, who rather overawed them ("certainly a great heroic figure") (*Journey*). But Fleming had interviewed the Generalissimo himself, *and* the emperor Pu Yi, on his first journey to China, in which he had also made the first visit by a foreigner to the anti-Communist front: at the end of the journey he and his companion Gerald Yorke were debriefed by the British authorities in Hong Kong and, later, in Shanghai. "We had become — or at any rate we had no difficulty in passing ourselves off as — the Greatest Living Authorities on a subject." And in the journey from Peking to Kashmir, for all the self-deprecation with which it is described in *News from Tartary*, Fleming had undergone hardships beyond the dreams of riding-booted Isherwood and carpet-slippered Auden. Here was a real traveler, with an authority he had earned for himself. (The metaphor of the real traveler's *earned* authority is not a casual one. Being a tourist, by contrast, was something to feel rather ashamed of, like having an unearned income; in *Letters from Iceland* Auden says that the tourist always looks with the eye of a *rentier*.) As writer and gentleman adventurer, Fleming occupies an intertextual niche in the travels of Auden and Isherwood in China similar to that assigned to Byron in the equally belated travels of Auden and MacNeice in Iceland.

So when their paths cross for a few days in *Journey to a War*, Isherwood and Auden defer to Fleming's travel expertise, and half-mockingly entitle him the Chief. Their initial reaction of anti–Etonianism and professional jealousy quickly gives way to admiration. As a traveler, he is tried and tested. They recognize him as a strong precursor; they would follow him anywhere. "Laughing and perspiring we scrambled uphill; the Fleming Legend accompanying us like a distorted shadow" (*Journey*). They amuse themselves by improvising passages from an imaginary travel book called *With Fleming to the Front* (*Journey*). The formula of the title is that of many historical adventure stories by G.A. Henty, often about boys whose path crosses that of some hero of imperial destiny — *With Wolfe in Canada, With Kitchener in the Soudan, With the Allies to Pekin*, etc. — DOUGLAS KERR

"For Friends Only" *see About the House*

For the Time Being 1944

Dedicated: "In memoriam, Constance Rosalie Auden, 1870–1941." Constance Rosalie

For the Time Being, **cover of first edition.**

Auden was Auden's mother, who had the greatest impact on his religious life.

Auden's fullest and most effective depiction of Paul Tillich's term demonic is found in his most explicitly Christian poem — and in the guise of a cultivated, thoroughly modern man. When he finally appears near the end of *For the Time Being*, Herod is a model civic administrator. He presides over the Rational City where there is no visible sign of disorder, no crime. The coastal highway "goes straight up over the mountains." The price of soft drinks and sandwiches is reasonable. After twenty years of work, he can boast that there are children in his province "who have never seen a louse, shopkeepers who have never handled a counterfeit coin, women of forty who have never hidden in a ditch except for fun." Now, he can look down condescendingly at those who live in the outlying regions, where many still believe in witches and a good bookstore still cannot turn a decent profit. Considering all he has accomplished, he tells himself that, perhaps, after all, "nothing could be more innocent than the birth of an artisan's son."

Still, there is something about this particular child that makes him anxious. After all, despite his efforts, Herod must admit that the empire is only "a tiny patch of light compared with those immense areas of barbaric night that surround it on all sides"—where superstition reigns, "where the best cuts of meat are preserved for the dead," and even within "the little civilized patch" he has cultivated with such devotion, there arises a "wild prayer of longing" against which even the most carefully calculated legislation remains helpless. On this level, which he does not understand, the anonymous Kierkegaardian Public simply refuses to be reasonable. He knows that the time has come when he can no longer rely on the "Poetic Compromise," all the "lovely fairy tales in which Zeus, disguising himself as a swan or a bull or a shower of rain or what-have-you, lay with some beautiful woman and begot a hero." The Public senses that, behind such myths of origins, there must be a "real human excellence that is a reproach to its own baseness." If he is not careful, Herod fears, this peculiar need to worship "will be driven into totally unsocial channels where no education can reach it." Beneath his appearance of self-assurance, he suspects that the Rational Law, which has had such a difficult time of it all along, might prove to be helpless when confronted with Prophecy and Revelation. So, with impeccable logic, he orders the massacre of the innocents.

Of course, Herod claims he has no choice. For all his faith in progress, he understands, as Tillich would, that "the appearance of the New Being overcomes the ultimate power of the demonic 'structures of destruction'" (Tillich, *Systematic Theology*). But Herod does not realize that he has drawn his power from the same surrender of humanity that led Ernst Toller to his destruction—what Auden called, elsewhere, the "abdication of the free-willing and individual before the collective and daemonic." Just as much as the suicidal playwright, Herod is being lived by demonic powers; but rather than succumbing to "demonic despair," he chooses to act out of "demonic defiance."

For Auden's part, by the time he wrote *For the Time Being*, he had come to understand his vocation as a poet much as Tillich had imagined the social role of the creative artist: to counteract Toller's "demonic despair" and Herod's "demonic defiance." That was why, for Auden, to become a Christian poet was not to abandon social responsibility, and it was not to surrender to forces beyond his control. Rather, to become a Christian poet was to perform an essential act designed to protect the creative mind and the innocent life from the demonic forces that seemed to dominate his troubled historical moment. His "conversion" (really reconversion) was an effort to resist the forces that he—and Tillich, and Toller, and so many in the community of exiles he discovered in the "nervous New World"—found trying to live every life.—Brian Conniff

In *For the Time Being* Christianity negates the differences between the exceptional man and the average man as both are equal in the eyes of God, thus dispelling the cult of an elite in favor of priest/seers. Each man is a unique incarnation. Christmas is a central event that reminds man of his incarnation after Christ. Auden's re-conversion to Christianity is no longer transitional but fully declared and influenced by Kierkegaard, Paul Tillich, Charles Williams, Reinhold Niebuhr, R.G. Collingwood, Charles Norris Cochran and others.

"In retelling the Christmas story in contemporary terms, Auden adopted the content, vocabulary, and rhetorical technique of a historical study published in 1940, *Christianity and Classical Culture*, by Charles Norris Cochrane. This book is a massive elaboration on an argument that had briefly been sketched by Cochrane's teacher Collingwood in *An Essay on Metaphysics*, to the effect that the early patristic writers had solved the metaphysical problems that had baffled classical philosophy, and that the world was converted to Christianity because Christian thought was more coherent and accurate..." (Mendelson, *Later Auden*). Auden reviewed the book and wrote, " I have read the book many times, and my conviction of its importance to the understanding not only of the epoch with which it is concerned, but also of our own, has increased with each rereading."

This long poem is in five sections: *Advent*: There is a historical sense of exhaustion and despair on the eve of Christ (although no different than contemporary despair). Man without Christ in his heart prepares for Christmas without understanding his true nature. A *Semi-Chorus* describes the loss of hope for a secular savior. *Narrator:* something new is coming, which is not referential to the past and alters the relation of time to reality (mystics' eternal now *is* reality) and will also alter man's role in reality.

Recitative: considers the paradoxical nature of religious truth.

Chorus (Greek style): lists man's temptations and difficulties.

Annunciation: intuition for feelings and sensations, thoughts which were once unified (*see* Heard, Gerald) became disparate after the Fall, and these fragmented thoughts are now distractions (seven deadly sins) and temptations in the garden of Eden.

The Temptation of St. Joseph: he is the average man seeking faith despite appearances.

Narrator: on relations between the sexes, and on how faith abolishes distinction between the usual and the exceptional.

Semi-Chorus: prayer for types of sinners, offers redemption for the "average way." *Summons:* human wisdom vs. Christian revelation.

Magi: reveals inadequacy of classical philosophy.

Fugal Chorus: reveals the inadequacy of political philosophy. Parallel of "year one (birth of Christ)," and 1941, is explicit.

Wise Men: thought breaks down into prose/confusion, the scientist, philosopher, and sociologist, (those who can help) follow the star.

The Vision of the Shepherds: is about the modern poor who keep the world going and deserve better.

At the Manger: maternal care, anxiety for the child (all children) fear of death wish vs. regression to banality, love wins over all.

Meditation of Simeon: philosophical meaning of incarnation; Christ: I am, thou art; we are all as one. One hears echoes of Eliot's *Four Quartets* here as allusive homage.

Hermes: Christian intellectual.

Herod and the massacre of the Innocents— the liberal but secular intellectual who learns that faith is needed too.

Apollo: the bureaucratic manager.

Soldiers: the ultimate solution of brutality in a secular world.

The poem ends with "*The Flight into Egypt*" as the Chorus recites "He [Christ] is the Way."

(*See also* Christianity; "In Memory of Ernst Toller"; Tillich, Paul.)

Forewords & Afterwords 1973

Dedicated to Hannah Arendt. Collection of essays. As the title indicates, the essays were forewords and book reviews.

Forster, E.M.

1879–1970, born Edward Morgan Forster, English novelist. Forster's fiction is in the manner of wholly truthful art and deals with the repression in the British middle and upper classes. His first novel, *Where Angels Fear to Tread*, appeared in 1905 and was quickly followed by *The Longest Journey* (1907), *A Room with a View* (1908), and *Howard's End* (1910). His last novel, *A Passage to India* (1924), deals with the relations between a group of British colonials and native Indians. Forster's short stories are collected in *The Celestial Omnibus* (1911) and *The Eternal Moment* (1928). After 1928 he turned his attention more to essays and literary criticism, and wrote *Abinger Harvest* (1936) and *Two Cheers for Democracy* (1951). *Aspects of the Novel* (1927) is Forster's most significant critical work. In 1971, *Maurice*, a novel he had written in 1913–14, was published posthumously by Christopher Isherwood, whom Forster had designated to do so. A homosexual, Forster did not publish it during his lifetime because of its sympathetic treatment of homosexuality. The story of a young man's self-awakening, *Maurice* follows a familiar Forster theme: the difficulty of human connection. His unpublished short stories and essays were published posthumously in *Albergo Empedocle and Other Writings* (1972). His style is direct and unsentimental.

Auden's friend Christopher Isherwood records in *Lions and Shadows* of Edward Upward's discovery of Forster's style while they were at Cambridge. "Forster's the only one who understands what the modern novel ought to be ... our frightful mistake was that we believed in tragedy: the point is, tragedy's quite impossible nowadays.... We ought to aim at being essentially comic writers.... The whole of Forster's technique is based on the tea-table: instead of trying to screw all his scenes up to the highest possible pitch, he tones them down until they sound like mother's-meeting gossip.... In fact, there's actually *less* emphasis laid on the big scenes than on the unimportant ones: that's what's so utterly terrific. It's the completely new kind of accentuation — like a person talking a different language."

Moreover Forster became Isherwood's role model for the Truly Strong Man as recounted in *Down There on a Visit*: "Well, my England is E.M. [Forster]; the antiheroic hero, with his straggly straw mustache, his light, gay, baby blue eyes and his elderly stoop. Instead of a folded umbrella or a brown uniform, his emblems are his tweed cap (which is too small for him) and the odd-shaped brown paper parcels in which he carries his belongings from country to town and back again. While the others tell their followers to be ready to die, he advises us to live as if we were immortal. And he really does this himself, although he is as anxious and afraid as any of us, and never for an instant pretends not to be. He and his books and what they stand for are all that is truly worth saving from Hitler; and the vast majority of people on this island aren't even aware that he exists.... What a tonic for me it was, having lunch with E.M. today! He says he's afraid of going mad, of suddenly turning and running away from the people in the street. But actually, he's the last person who'd ever go mad; he's far saner than anyone else I know. And immensely, superhumanly strong. He's strong because he doesn't try to be a stiff-lipped stoic like the rest of us, and so he'll never crack. He's absolutely flexible. He lives by love, not by will."

Auden shared Isherwood's respect for Forster. *Journey to a War* is dedicated to Forster with a sonnet to him, praising him for "insisting the inner life can pay." In a 1939 collection of essays by individuals asked to give their personal philosophies, *I Believe*, Auden contributed, as did Forster.

Forster placed the highest value on interpersonal relationships and kindness: If two persons could relate, then two by two, group to group, city to city, nation to nation, then the whole of humanity could be transformed. And it would be at the "tea-table," as stated by Upward, where the two by two would begin. Auden would write in an essay on James Joyce: "Christianity would introduce the tea-table into literature." Thus, he indirectly credited Forster with the Christian intention of loving thy neighbor as thyself. (*See also* "September 1 1939.")

"Forty Years On" 1968

In this poem, just as in "Caliban to the Audience," Auden plays himself in the guise of Shakespeare. An elderly Autocylus remembers the days of *The Winter's Tale*, days that Auden is comparing to his century. Echoing "Prologue at Sixty," the poem welcomes death but with a gentle humor: "To dispense with solemnity is to accept one's comic humanity."

Fox, Orlan

1939–1987. In 1965–66 Fox lived with Auden. Auden had known Fox since 1959, and they were occasionally lovers but mainly friends. By this time Auden had gotten used to being alone, and eventually Fox left amicably. Through Fox Auden met the neurologist Oliver Sacks.

Frankenburg, Lloyd

1907–1975, American poet and critic for the now defunct *New York Herald Tribune*. In 1940 Frankenburg gave Auden's *The Double Man* a very good review. Auden sent Frankenburg a postcard with the return address of "7 Middagh Street, Brooklyn Heights."

Dear Mr. Frankenburg, It was nice of you to send me your review, particularly as it was such a generous one. I didn't see it in the *Tribune* (being a *Times* reader) but I know what editors are. Yours very sincerely, W.H. Auden" (Izzo Collection). The Middagh St. address was the house in which various people lived, including, Carson McCullers, Paul and Jane Bowles, Erika and Golo Mann, Benjamin Britten, Peter Pears, and Louis MacNeice.

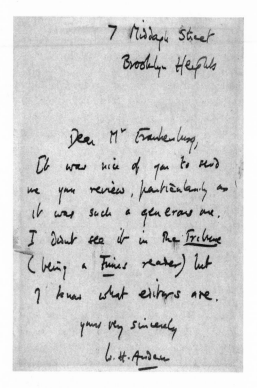

7 Middagh Street
Brooklyn Heights

Dear Mr Frankenburg,

It was nice of you to send
me your review, particularly as
it was such a generous one.
I don't see it in the *Tribune*
(being a *Times* reader) but
I know what editors are.

yours very sincerely

W. H. Auden

Postcard from Auden to Mr. Frankenburg (1940).

Fremantle, Anne

Theologically inclined writer, she edited *The Protestant Mystics* (1962), to which Auden contributed an introduction. This introduction describes Auden's "A Summer Night" Vision of Agape, which is very important in understanding Auden's life and art after 1933. (See *Mysticism.*)

Freud, Sigmund

1856–1939, b. Austria, the first modern psychoanalyst. Freud's influence on modern life, let alone Auden, is profound. With the Nazi occupation of Austria, Freud fled (1938) to England, where he died the following year. Isherwood recalled in *Lions and Shadows* that when he met Auden again when Auden was at Oxford after they had first met at St. Edmund's School, that Auden was quite absorbed with psychoanalysis and its terminology. Auden, in fact, psychoanalyzed all of his friends —

whether they wanted his services or not. Auden's father, the doctor, a progressive man, had employed psychoanalysis in his work, and his son followed this example. At Oxford, Auden had numerous poetic influences while sociologically, Freud and Marx were his early guides, although Freud was not embraced in total. In a 1929 Journal entry Auden wrote under the heading "*Pleasure.* "The error of Freud and most psychologists is making pleasure a negative thing, progress towards a state of rest. This is only one half of pleasure and the least most important half. Creative pleasure is like pain, an increase in tension. What does the psychologist make of contemplation and joy? The essence of creation is doing things for no reason, it is pointless. [See *Play and Work.*] Possessive pleasure is always rational. Freud you see really believes that pleasure is immoral, i.e. happiness is displeasing to God…. If you believe this of course the death wish becomes the most important emotion, and 'reinstatement of an earlier condition' [from Freud's *Beyond the Pleasure Principle*]. Entropy is another name for despair."

Mendelson adds, "man's strivings for entropic peace amount to the despair of the death wish. 'Creative Pleasure' has nothing to do with personal or sexual peace; it is the making of a poem, an act that increases tension and division. To enjoy life, make a poem out of it…. Freud saw a basic opposition between Eros [love/sex/pleasure] and Thanatos [death/death wish], between the two great organic impulses toward sex and death. For Auden this opposition was false" (*Early Auden*).

Auden's journal continued: "The question is what do we mean by sex. The union or the fission of sex cells, i.e. love or hate. Freud makes sex the first and places it in opposition to the death wish. It seems to me jolly similar…. The real 'life-wish' is the desire for separation, from family, from one's literary predecessors."

Hence, the Auden Generation's "life-wish" was to reject the past, and remake the world in their own way. Mendelson interprets this rejection to be of Freud as well, but just as Freud's disciples broke from him only after learning from him, so did Auden. Freud was the impetus for Auden to learn psychoanalysis, and even though Auden wrote that "The trouble with

Freud is that he accepts conventional morality as if it were the only one," by reacting to Freud's conservatism he was finding his own psychological interpretations of Freud, in which he sought to give "pleasure" a positive and affirming voice. Auden would shape his views more in line with George Groddeck, Homer Lane, Gerald Heard, and later Jung; yet, they, as Auden, had shaped their views after the model created by Freud from which they extrapolated and adapted.

In 1935 Auden's essay "Psychology and Art Today" would explicate Freud, and in 1939, his poem "In Memory of Sigmund Freud" would honor him. In the essay, Auden strongly asserts the influence of Freud. Artists gain power over objects by representing them in order to relieve isolation and neurosis. In past eras, the patronage of artists proved art had value to society. An artist seeks control and power, mainly over himself. Auden does not agree with Freud in total but concurs that 1) no artist is disinterested, that is, impartial, and 2) the artist has a highbrow self-consciousness. Auden lists familial situations that encourage artists: 1) parents who dote on children, if not each other; 2) an only child; 3) the youngest child (as was Auden). Art is symptomatic of childhood neuroses (but art is not the cause of the public's perception of the artist's egghead image with spectacles and myopia); the causes of art are the neuroses and here Auden expresses the influence of Homer Lane via John Layard.

Psychosomatic illnesses are means of escape in five possible ways: 1) as a sham of being dead or an idiot; 2) as fantasy or schizophrenia; 3) as panic attacks or criminality; 4) as a means of evoking pity by being (acting) as if ill or an invalid; 5) as a way to talk about one's illness through the mediums of either art or science.

Art is a wish vicariously fulfilled; fantasy is a dream denied. A dream represents an unresolved conflict; art is a conflict resolved (even if only temporarily). Poetic craftsmanship is art, as an inspiration (possessed artist), and art as a craft (artist as maker) are comparable. Art is work, and only rarely psychically spontaneous. The artist's work is a conscious element as is psychoanalysis, and like psychoanalysis both are a process of re-living a situation: 1) the artist deals in his time with his own conflicts, fantasies,

and interests. 2) He takes data from the outer world and makes it subject to his unique inner interpretation. 3) The artistic medium is applied to a new situation where the associations intimated in the art are always greater than the individual artist or his audience.

Auden considers what would be Freudian Literature: a chart divides the Christian era into 3 periods. Freud's period is third, and began with Nietzsche (although, according to Auden, all of Freud's teaching is in Blake's *Heaven and Hell*), and is Freud's reaction to the Romantic era; 1) sexual pleasure drives everything. 2) The ability to reason is mainly for rationalization. 3) All people are equal until parents help or hurt them. 4) The Good Life is to be able to do as you like, such as being an artist. 5) The cure for all ills is promiscuity (satisfaction of sexual desire) or autobiography (art, journals, diaries).

Implications of Freud: 1) Life's driving force is the libido-driven instinct. 2) Sex is a creative activity leading to art. 3) The mind is the best aphrodisiac. 4) Man is unique, his inner development of evolving consciousness still unfinished (*see* Heard, Gerald). 5) An ego-driven self-consciousness is the break in that inner development, and evil and sin are its consequences. 6) The fall resulted from man's divided consciousness that took the place of Heard's "unified consciousness," and this divided consciousness is divided into a) a conscious mind of ideas and ideals, b) an impersonal unconsciousness that derives power but not understanding, or c) a personal unconsciousness that forgets society's morality. 7) The nineteenth century doctrine of "working out the beast" in man is false; man's instincts are really meek, and sociable; his hostility is a learned faculty. 8) Man's egoistic conscious mind and this egoistic mind's choices inhibit the development of a "unified consciousness" by demanding a "my way or the highway" mentality. 9) All evil or sin is acted on with the purposive attempt to cure inhibitions. 10) All change, for good or ill, results from sexual tension sublimated as activity. 11) One's morality depends on his past and present relations with parents. 12) All disease or sin comes from guilt. 13) The cure is the relief of guilt through understanding and forgiveness. 14) Art can't tell people what to do but only show them what to do because the psychology of art teaches by parable and allegory. 15) Psychology opposes generalizations because individual perceptions cause conflict. 16) Marx asserts that failure comes from poverty or that man is affected from the outside in; this conflicts with Freud, who asserts that failure comes from the mind or that man is affected from inside out.

Auden's conclusion: Artists provide society with what it needs in two forms: 1) escape, with art as a stress reliever; 2) parable art that teaches as a pain reliever.

Auden's youthful views on Freud would evolve over time.

"Friday's Child" 1959

(In memory of Dietrich Bonhoeffer, martyred at Flossenburg, April 9, 1945.) This poem, inspired by both Bonhoeffer and Owen Barfield, is a meditation on how dreadfully complete man's freedom is since the Good Friday of Resurrection, on which day man was eternally bestowed with the freedom to choose for good or ill. Bonhoeffer was a pastor active in the resistance and was killed by the Nazis. His posthumous *Letters and Papers from Prison* (1948) was read by Auden and motivated this poem.

"The Frivolous & the Earnest" 1962

This essay holds that Greek polytheism is frivolous: the Greek gods don't take themselves or humans seriously. Auden's Christianity is earnest, but allows frivolity.

"From Anne to Victoria" *see* Pope, Alexander

The Fronny 1930

This play was an unpublished version of what would later become the Auden-Isherwood play *The Dog Beneath the Skin* (see *Plays with*

Isherwood). The title derived from Auden and Isherwood's Berlin friend Francis Turville-Petre whom the boys in the Berlin bars called, "Der Franni." He is the basis for the lost heir Sir Francis Crewe in the early and later versions of the play.

Frost, Robert

1874–1963, American poet, b. San Francisco. In 1912 he went to England, where he received his first recognition, then returned to the United States and settled in New Hampshire. His poems often have metaphysical significance, and are concerned with human tragedies and fears, and his reactions to the complexities of life. Frost was awarded the Pulitzer Prize for poetry in 1924, 1931, 1937, and 1943.

Frost was one of Auden's earliest influences whom he first read in Walter de la Mare's verse anthology *Come Hither* while a student at Oxford. In 1957 Auden returned to Oxford and lectured on Frost. Auden's 1950 poem "Their Lonely Betters," in the last line, deliberately alludes to Frost's "Stopping by Woods on a Snowy Evening." Mendelson writes of Auden's later work: "Auden had perfected a technique of writing about the darkest possible subjects in a tone that deceived real or imaginary enemies into thinking him too mild and avuncular to bother contending with. He apparently learned his tactics from Robert Frost, whose combination of folksy diction and bleak content was a cunning version of pastoral that Auden greatly admired, and he had quickly set to work studying the lessons of this master" (*Later Auden*). While Auden admired Frost as a poet, he was less admiring of Frost as a person, a view shared by others as well. Nonetheless, Auden did write an essay praising Frost the artist, from which Auden borrowed an idea from Frost that was to be an important aspect of Auden's later philosophy, Who Am I? Whom Ought I to Become?

In the 1962 essay "Robert Frost," Auden wrote, "Art arises out of our desire for both beauty and truth and our knowledge that they are not identical." Art is an escape from our strict historicity, with beauty an enlightening elucidation that mirrors time but does not objectify it. Truth is a rivalry of Ariel and Prospero

(Beauty vs. moralism). Some poems are technically adroit, but ephemerally vague; others (Frost) are both adroit and humanly identifiable and moving. Ariel leaves a visceral impression, but asks no questions; when Ariel can't write, he doesn't: When Prospero can't write, he shouldn't, but sometimes does. Frost is a Prospero-dominant poet. *Frost*: "a poem begins in delight; ends in wisdom, simple profundity, authenticity, auditory chastity, subdued passions." *Auden*: Any poems that aim at wisdom should tacitly make a reader ask: "Who am I? Whom ought I to become?" A writer's intent is universal; readers' answers are particular. Frost *is* New England: a favorite image is the abandoned house as a symbol of heroic struggle. Nature is a challenging maker of strong hearts, quiet courage. Cautious and cunning, the salt of the earth coexists with the cream of the city. *RF*: "I would have written of me on my stone: 'I had a lover's quarrel with the world.'"

Fuller, John

In 1970 Fuller published *A Reader's Guide to W.H. Auden* about which Mendelson notes in *Early Auden,* "Like everyone else who writes about Auden I am deeply indebted to the scholarship and intelligence of this pioneering book."

"Funeral Blues" *see* "Twelve Songs"

Gardiner, Margaret

A friend of John Layard and of Auden's in Berlin, 1928–29, she warned Auden of Layard's suicidal impulse to which Auden did not take heed until Layard showed up at his door with a bullet wound in his head. She was of a leftist inclination as was Auden at this time but both were more concerned with helping their friends than active political action. In 1929 Auden asked her if she knew of any teaching posts. Her friend's sister needed a tutor for her son, and he returned to England to tutor Peter Benenson,

whose father, Colonel Solomon, in a wheelchair from World War I wounds, would end up in a poem that begins "Will You Turn a Deaf Ear." Gardiner also returned to England and visited Auden when he was teaching at Larchfield Academy, a post gotten for him through C. Day Lewis. Auden told her a teacher ought to be a clown in order to get the boys' attention and keep discipline. Auden maintained a correspondence with Gardiner although there was a hiatus from 1939 until 1951 when she visited him at Ischia, Italy, where she remarked at how much his face had aged. Later she would also visit Auden at Kirschstetten, Austria, and in New York, and they remained friends until Auden died in 1973.

"Gare du Midi" 1938

Behind the noisy leaders and agitators are the quiet contributors, the ones who really change the world for the better and who are Truly Strong because they act without self-interest or a need for vainglorious attention. This is another post–"Spain" rebuke of Auden's noisier activism of the previous years.

Garrett, John

Co-edited with Auden the 1935 anthology *The Poet's Tongue*, meant as verse for children (of all ages).

"The Garrison" 1969

An older Auden considers his internal fortress that "We, Chester and the choir we sort with" must build for protection.

Gay Consciousness *see Letters from Iceland*

Generosity

When Auden returned from Berlin in 1929 he had embraced the credo of the pure in heart man who acted selflessly on behalf of others. Auden lived up to this credo throughout his life. He helped friends to pursue their art, and gave money away without any need for recognition (see Empson, William). Mendelson notes: "In the 1950s when a friend told him about two Austrian boys in their early teens who could not afford to stay in school, Auden, who had not met them, paid their fees; afterward, he paid for the university educations of two war-orphaned young men.... He continued to do this, with different beneficiaries from different countries..." (*Later Auden*). Auden preferred to live modestly in order to help others. Aldous Huxley did the same.

"A Genius and a Gentleman" 1972

This essay is a review of *Letters of Giuseppe Verdi*, edited by Charles Osborne, who would later do an Auden biography.

"The Genius and the Apostle" 1962

Auden's second essay on Brand Versus Peer Gynt (see "Brand Versus Peer"), it covers ground similar to the first.

"The Geography of the House" *see About the House*

"George MacDonald" 1954

Auden's introduction to *The Visionary Novels of George MacDonald*, ed. Anne Fremantle, which praises MacDonald's fairytales written with a Christian perspective.

MacDonald (1824–1905) was a Scottish preacher and teacher as well as an author of thirty novels, numerous fairy tales, poetry, essays, and sermons. MacDonald's writing was largely influenced by the German and English Romantics. Through his visionary theology, MacDonald has made his greatest contributions

in the realms of fantasy and children's literature. His fairy tales for children and his two fantasies for adults are his best literary achievements. George MacDonald's *Phantastes* is recognized as a classic of adult fantasy writing. Authors who have been influenced by MacDonald include Auden, C.S. Lewis, G.K. Chesterton, and Madeleine L'Engle.

Ghosts *see* Ancestral Curse and Family Ghosts

Gide, André

1869–1951, French writer. He established his reputation with *The Immoralist* (1902, tr. 1930), a partly autobiographical work of a young man in search of self-fulfillment. In this and other novels, including *Strait Is the Gate* (1909, tr. 1924), *Lafcadio's Adventures* (1914, tr. 1927), and *The Counterfeiters* (1926, tr. 1927), Gide features individuals exploring and learning about their own natures, which may be at conflict with society. Gide was raised a Protestant, but became a leader of French liberal thought and was one of the founders (1909) of the influential *Nouvelle Revue Française*. He was controversial for his defense of homosexuality, his support of Communism, and his subsequent disapproval of Stalin's Russia after a visit to the Soviet Union in 1937. Later, in *The God That Failed*, Gide gave up Communism entirely. His writings include plays, stories, essays, and a libretto for Stravinsky's opera *Persephone*—with whom Auden-Kallman would also do a libretto for *The Rake's Progress*. In 1947 he was awarded the Nobel Prize in Literature.

Auden was influenced by Gide through John Layard whom Auden met in Berlin in 1929. Layard was a disciple of Homer Lane and Gide had similar ideas in that humans should not restrain natural desires as this only leads to repression, then physical and psychological illness. For Gide, as an outspoken homosexual, France was a bit more liberal than England, and he appealed to Auden with some authority as a member of the Homintern. Consequently, when

André Gide

André Gide's *Return from the U.S.S.R.*, cover of first U.S. edition.

Gide made a trip to the Soviet Union in 1936, arriving with great enthusiasm as a theoretical Communist, he departed greatly disappointed. In *Letter to Lord Byron* (1937), Auden mentions Gide with admiration. In 1937 Gide published *Return from the USSR* and this recorded what he saw as theory having been replaced by authoritarianism and propaganda. The book, from such a respected source, was a major blow to leftist intellectuals in Europe and America who thought that the Soviet Union was the model for a future without the corruption and inequities of capitalism. Gide was attacked by diehards on the left who said he should have kept quiet. Of this, Auden told Stephen Spender, "exigence is never an excuse for not telling the truth." Spender later wrote: "This conversation remains in my mind as a turning point in our attitudes towards politics during the thirties" (Spender "The Thirties and After"). (*See also* Perse, St.-John.)

Gift

For Auden "The gift was the special form taken by larger and more mysterious forces when they made themselves incarnate in the artist. These demonic, unnamable powers had made shadowy appearances in Auden's work since the 1930s, but until he broke away from England he never imagined them to be in his own keeping" (Mendelson, *Later Auden*). After Auden's arrival in America, the nature of the Gift and his judgments as to which poets did or didn't obey the call of the Gift became a major theme of his art and essays. The poem "In Memory of William Butler Yeats" is an early and crucial example, along with the companion essay, "The Public vs. W.B. Yeats." Shakespeare made the best use of his gift; Milton, Yeats, Matthew Arnold, Tennyson, among others, did sometimes, but not always.

Ginsberg, Allen

1926–97, American poet, b. Paterson, N.J., grad. Columbia, 1949. A member of the beat generation, Ginsberg is best known for *Howl* (1956), a long poem attacking American values of the 1950s. The beat poets of the 1950s who rebelled against that static, conservative decade were comparable to the Auden Generation poets who rebelled against the 1920s. The poets of the 1950s began their momentum earlier in the 1940s. In 1945 Auden began to be sought out by undergraduate poets from the city's universities. These included Ginsberg, John Hollander, Louis Simpson, Daniel Hoffman, and others.

"Glad" 1965

This poem is to a "Hugerl," a young man with whom Auden had sexual relations until he married, after which they were still friends.

"The Globe" 1962

Essay on Shakespeare, whose Everyman, as Auden describes him, is an allegorical figure in two ways: 1) what he feels results from action and is subjective, 2) when he observes others he becomes a recorder of outcomes, but he cannot know what the others' motives are that produced the outcomes. Shakespeare synthesized both viewpoints, and he did so with the influence of mystery plays; he considered 1) the significance of time, 2) the significance of choice, and 3) the significance of suffering. In Shakespeare's tragedies, suffering becomes despair. In the comedies, suffering leads to love.

Shakespeare's audiences, unlike the classic Greek audiences, are not just spectators, but participants, viewing history as parable; the tragedies feature "noble sinners" masking their deeds in poetic pleas for the understanding, if not the forgiveness, of their crimes. Comedies are a release from life through commiseration with the actors in the comedy, who are as fallible as the members of the audience. In both tragedy and comedy, the inner life supersedes the status or class of the characters so that, at least on stage, there is greater equality. Later, the Ibsen and Shaw "revolt" returned to Shakespeare as the master, as Shakespeare's ambivalence towards his characters is his greatness.

Goethe, Johann Wolfgang von

1749–1832, German poet, dramatist, novelist, and scientist, b. Frankfurt. Goethe describes his happy, sheltered childhood in his autobiography, *Dichtung und Wahrheit* (1811–33). Auden would write his own "Dicthung und Wahrheit" as a prose poem. Two of the lasting influences on Goethe's youth were J.J. Rousseau and Spinoza, who appealed to his mystic and poetic feeling for nature. It was during this time that Goethe began his study of animals and plants and his work in biological morphology (which the later Auden would also take up) that would occupy him for the rest of his life.

The epistolary novel *The Sorrows of Young Werther* (1774), was written on the verge of suicide following a case of unrequited love. *Werther* brought him immediate fame and was widely translated. A trip to Italy (1786–88) fired his enthusiasm for the classical ideal, recorded in *Italian Journey* (1816). Also written under the classical influence was the historical drama *Egmont* (1788), well known for Beethoven's *Egmont Overture*. His novel *Elective Affinities* (1809) is one of his most important, as is the Wilhelm Meister series. The novel *The Apprenticeship of Wilhelm Meister* (1796) became the prototype of the German *Bildungsroman*, or novel of character development. In *Faust*, Goethe refashioned the traditional Faust legend. His main deviation from the original is the salvation of Faust.

Westöstlicher Diwan (1819), a collection of Goethe's lyric poetry, was inspired by Marianne von Willemer, who figures as Suleika in the cycle. The Diwan introduces Eastern elements derived from Goethe's reading of the Persian poet Hafiz.

Goethe's opinions are recorded not only in his own writings but also in conversations recorded by his secretary J.P. Eckermann. His views can also be seen in correspondence with the composer Zelter and others, including Schiller, Byron, Carlyle, and Manzoni. Goethe's influence on the subsequent history of literature cannot be overemphasized.

Since Auden learned German in Berlin and developed it thereafter he could read Goethe in the original. Goethe was among Auden's "secular gods" as Spears called them along with Blake, Tolstoy, Wagner, Yeats, Freud, Voltaire, Edward Lear, Pascal, Rimbaud, Melville, and others. Auden would write introductions for Goethe's *Italian Journey* (which he also co-translated with Elizabeth Mayer), *The Sorrows of Young Werther and Novella,* and *Elective Affinities.* He believed Goethe to be the chief representative of his age, just as Dante and Shakespeare were to theirs. Mendelson in *Later Auden* writes, "*New Year Letter* is Auden's Faust." In Auden's *For the Time Being* in the section called "The Annunciation," the diameter quatrains are "Faustian," and "The Sea and the Mirror" also refers to Faust and a sense of illusion when one looks at oneself. Goethe makes numerous appearances in the Auden-Kronenberger *Viking Book of Aphorisms* and in Auden's commonplace anthology *A Certain World.*

Auden considered *Italian Journey* to be a quest by Goethe, and this appealed to him as he co-translated it. And despite noticing Goethe's occasional pompous and hypocritical moments Auden wrote, "One is forced to admit in the end that he was a great poet and a great man." Carpenter, in *W.H. Auden*, adds, "Auden liked to think of Goethe not as 'Great Mr. G' but as 'Dear Mr. G'; and Goethe came, too, to be an image of what he hoped to achieve himself in this period of his life. 'I should like,' he said, to become, if possible, a minor Atlantic Goethe.' His interest in Goethe is reflected in two poems.... 'A Change of Air' ... deals with the way a physical journey may relate to a spiritual quest.... The second ... is really a collection of prose aphorisms ... 'Dichtung und Warheit' (poetry and truth)." In one of Auden's last poems, "A Thanksgiving," he includes Goethe among the literary figures who still inspired him. Auden's "Natural Linguistics" is also an homage to Goethe.

In 1964, Auden reviewed an edition of Goethe's *Elective Affinities*, translated by Auden's friends Elizabeth Mayer and Louise Bogan. In this review, Auden writes that most novelists start with details and evolve these into themes, ideas, and messages. Conversely, Goethe begins with an agenda and fits his novel into it. He evades the danger of having mouthpieces instead of characters. The title of his novel signifies a scientific experiment of separation vs. attachment with a minimum of characters: Edouard is a rich, middle-aged landowner; the Captain, who must work for his living; Edouard's wife, Charlotte; their daugh-

ter; Ottillie, an orphan of Charlotte's friend. As Goethe places these characters in opposition, an experiment unfolds.

Edouard behaves petulantly; to Auden he is "unauthentic." Ottillie behaves masochistically and slavishly. Much turmoil ensues. For Goethe love is not our sole interest. Love and other behaviors are learned through societal influence. Man is the maker who seeks posterity through artifacts and art. Goethe's characters *make* life and love, with nature always as the backdrop revealing both permanence and cycles — as do birthdays, which Edouard abhors for their reference to his mortality. This is a psychological novel forecasting Freud and psychosomatic illnesses.

In 1970, Auden wrote an introduction for *The Sorrows of Young Werther and Novella,* prose tr. by Elizabeth Mayer and Louise Bogan; poems tr. by Auden. Auden wrote that Goethe's unhappy love is only a spur of other ideas, which are similar but not autobiographical. Goethe, who was the first artist-as-celebrity with his conscious and unconscious motives at odds, approved of Werther as hero and wrote of him as therapy as did Byron for *Childe Harold* in which Byron escaped gloom by writing as a comic poet. *Werther* is tragic love in the portrait of an egotist. *Auden:* "If Goethe wanted us to admire Werther why did he not include the story of a servant in love with the widowed mistress with whom Werther identifies?" If Goethe wished us to side with Werther in the Werther-Lotte-Albert triangle, he would have made Albert coarse, but rather he is a good man. Lotte sees Werther as a platonic brother; her weakness is in not admitting disagreeable notions that are apparent. Werther escapes the triangle by becoming a civil servant (as did Goethe) to a count who invites him to a dinner of snobs against whom he reacts, which is his vanity reacting when he should have understood his role and accepted it. *Auden:* "To earn respect he should either defer graciously or deliberately flaunt [*sic*] convention to enjoy the shock...." Werther resigns and returns to Lotte and disaster.

Novella is an example of a German idyll with man and nature in harmony and is a postscript to Goethe's epic poem "Herman and Dorothea." An idyll is more realistic than a pastoral and, like comedy, ends happily while being serious. There are two locations: town/market/good society, and an old castle as a ruin overwhelmed by forest.

This is a parable of untamed nature vs. *techne*—human craft. Man must respect nature, not attempt to enslave nature, while nature needs man's help to realize its potential. The prince and his court need to learn "reverence for life" and nature, and they will.

Auden also wrote an introduction for the edition of Goethe's *Italian Journey* (1962), which he co-translated with Elizabeth Mayer, and "Mr. G" (1967) was a review of *Goethe: Conversations and Encounters*, ed. and tr. by D. Luke, R. Pick.

"The Good Life" 1935

This essay should be considered as a companion to Auden's essay in the same year, "Psychology and Art Today" (*see* under Sigmund Freud). Man's desires cannot be fulfilled, so he devises his theories in order to seek relief from these desires. Do we modify our desires (through religion and psychology) or modify the environment (through science and politics)? What are desires, why do we have them, and how do we deal with them? What fails in our environment and how do we fix it? Whether one thinks in terms of desires or in terms of one's relation to the environment, one can react as a either stoic, or a fascist, or a defeatist. The upper class is losing ground, while the lower class seeks vengeance. Conflicts derive from each class having illusions of what represents good vs. bad (from Nietzsche). One realizes how life ought to be but isn't.

Politics of the Gospels: Do we choose God or Caesar? Jesus' politics are unclear, as his teaching was as a God/man who was indifferent to politics; he was anti-class and anti-prejudice by example. If one ignores class and prejudice, they will fade away. The heart will govern the inner spirit and change man over time. Economic inequality is caused by greed — the inner heart cannot know greed once it listens to the inner spirit. A change of heart will be sudden, sincerely felt, moral and not political, and signify a new universe purged of evil; man has politicized society for his own purposes. Christianity accepts an environment as it is, but seeks to change man's role in it.

Our desire is to be one with God, but we confuse that desire with earthly pseudo-gods (nationalism, fascism, communism) that we chase instead of the life of the spirit. Jesus' means of realization is non-moralistic and dogmatic — simply love God and thy neighbor and the Good Life will come. "Neighbor" means *all* are equal. The psychology of this realization principally concerns the nature of evil and seeks to understand what prevents people from being good. *The libido* is one factor — an unconscious and creative driving force perceived as limited to individual consciousness. Another factor is *self consciousness* (the development of egotism), which marked man's break from the rest of the organic world; evil is derived from the mind's conflict over the knowledge of sex with the sex drive mistakenly thought of as evil. The Fall, while representing the beast — that is, man's temptation for sex — is not inherent in man but created by him; however, the Fall was inevitable and not a conscious choice. The Fall denies original sin so that man can choose his destiny, that is, choose between good and evil. Man must choose good over evil in order to be saved. *Primitive impulses* (i.e., sex) were once thought of as instinctive but now cornered by societal mores; society has put shackles on what was once thought to be good before the mind was corrupted by the ego's rationalizing. But what can be loved can be cured; the barriers to love are ignorance and fear, which must be overcome by self-confession (self-knowledge), compassion, and psychology. Christianity is pacifistic; one cannot be forced to it. Truth comes in its own time as self-conversion. The mistake of liberalism was that it thought discussion alone could bring freedom, when only the shared experience of love unifies. Psychology is a rationalist movement, which does not deny free will except in a Christian sense: man has fallen and is in bondage to evil; this is the same as the man who is neurotic and in bondage to impulses from which he can be freed only by his inner self-discovery that leads to his being able to make choices without conflict. Communism, Christianity, and Psychology are all equal in the sense of allowing man to make free choices.

The church was pure until aligned with the state. Revelation became dogmatic as taught by clerics rather than as self-inspired discovery by each individual. Dogmatic religion then became a form of societal coercion without sincerity, a pagan pacifier for the mass, truly Christian only for the few who sought self-inspiration. The political mind demonstrates that no politician can be truly liberal, as his theories are vitiated by 1) the confusion of what the state is with what it ought to be; 2) the incorrect assumption that there is a community of collective will among the constituency; 3) the creation of false analogies to enforce the state's will through propaganda.

Psychology and Religion: Psychology asserts that religion is only a transference and a sublimation of unconscious needs. A Christian retorts that these impulses — i.e., parental relations — are symbols of a divine relation, not vice versa.

Communism and Psychology: Both unmask hidden conflicts; both see conflicts as inevitable in order to find truth; both see that thought and knowledge are determined by a conflict of an instinctive, self-inspired inner awareness vs. a limited awareness as propagandized by the state and society. The drive of communism is to solve the hunger of the masses; the drive for psychology is to find love, family, and freedom through exposing individual conflict, with psychologists trying to fit individuals into an unjust society. Conversely, communists would change society into a more just world that would remove the conflicts that cause the psychological problems.

Communism on religion: Communists say that religion is the opiate of people and pawn of the state.

Communism as pseudo-religion: Christianity says communism is anti–Christian, and this is true; Christianity will also say that communists use violence to make changes and that these changes deny individuality and destroy the family unit.

Ultimately, both communism and Christianity become dogmatic vehicles through propaganda. Neither is effective if its constituents follow blindly rather than seeking inner truth on their own.

Auden's views are here inspired by much youthful precocity and these views would modify over time.

"Goodbye to Mezzogiorno" 1958

Dedicated to Carlo Izzo, Auden's Italian translator, who would also translate this poem that is a lighthearted commentary on Italy's, or at least the island of Ischia's, "national" characteristics.

Gossip *see* "In Defense of Gossip"

GPO Film Unit *see* Grierson, John

Graves, Robert

1895–1985, English poet, novelist, and critic. He gained fame with *Good-bye to All That* (1929), a book on his war experiences. Graves considered himself primarily a poet but was best known for his novels of Roman history, *I, Claudius* (1934) and *Claudius the God* (1934) (that became a popular televised drama series in the mid 1970s), as well as fictionalized accounts of history and legend such as *King Jesus* (1946) and *Homer's Daughter* (1955). Graves's studies of the mythological and psychological sources of poetry are *The White Goddess* (1947), *Greek Myths* (2 vol., 1955), and *Hebrew Myths* (1963). Other works of criticism include *The Common Asphodel* (1949), *Poetic Craft and Principle* (1967), *On Poetry: Collected Talks and Essays* (1969), and translations of *The Golden Ass of Apuleius* and the *Iliad*. Graves was a good friend to poet Laura Riding who was an early influence on Auden. From 1961 until 1966 he was professor of poetry at Oxford and in fact succeeded Auden who voted for Graves to be his successor. This, despite Graves having given a lecture six years earlier at Cambridge that railed against Auden and his contemporaries. Auden in an essay, "The Poet as Professor," explained this role, while appearing to endorse Graves. Yet, he still took an indirect shot at Graves by saying, "There is only one topic upon which no poet is ever worth listening to, his contemporaries; it is highly unlikely that he has read most of them." Still, Auden also wrote that Graves was "one of the very few poets whose volumes I have always bought as soon as they appeared" (Spears, *Disenchanted Island*).

"A Great Democrat: Voltaire" *see* **Voltaire**

Great Depression

In world history, the economic crisis precipitated by the U.S. stock market crash of 1929. The Great Depression was unprecedented in its length and in the poverty and tragedy it inflicted on society. The boom of the 1920s was unevenly distributed in the American economy with the result that the nation's productive capacity was greater than its capacity to consume. In addition, the tariff and war-debt policies of the Republican administrations of the 1920s had cut down the foreign market for American goods. Finally, easy-money policies led to an inordinate expansion of credit and installment buying and speculation in the stock market. The American depression produced severe effects abroad, especially in Europe, where many countries had not fully recovered from the aftermath of World War I; in Germany, the economic disaster and resulting social dislocation contributed to the rise of Adolf Hitler (see Berlin). During the 1920s, labor, after the Soviet revolution, increasingly saw socialism or communism as an answer to the gap between haves and have-nots. When the Depression hit, the workers became much more vocal in their bitterness, and artists and intellectuals supported them. The Auden Generation in England blamed the Depression on the Others in high places and the outworn traditions that enforced class divisions. The artist and intellectual of the 1930s could not help but react to the Depression as it affected every aspect of society, and led to fascism, which was a reaction against socialism/Communism. Many artists and intellectuals supported socialism or Communism, and were the early alarmists over fascism. (*See also* The Auden Generation; Marx, Karl.)

"The Greatest of the Monsters" *see* Wagner, Richard

"Greatness Finding Itself" 1960

A review of Erickson's *Young Man Luther*.

Greenberg, Noah *see* New York Pro Musica

Greene, Graham

1904–91, English novelist and playwright, distant cousin of Christopher Isherwood. His novels are parables of the lost seeking salvation. He converted to Roman Catholicism and was concerned with the moral problems of humans in relation to God. He wrote film scripts, including the mystery melodrama *The Third Man* (1950). Greene attended Oxford, and his last year overlapped with Auden's first, though it appears they did not socialize. In 1932 Greene reviewed Auden's *The Orators*, saying in the *Oxford Magazine*, "The subject of the book is certainly political, though it is hard to tell whether the author's sympathies are Communist or Fascist." (Years later, Auden would admit that he wasn't sure himself.) By 1938 Greene would say Auden was the best living poet. After Auden's arrival in America and a re-conversion to Auden's Christianity, Auden took more interest in Greene's Christianity. In 1949 Auden gave a talk on Greene's *The Ministry of Fear*, which became Auden's take on both Greene's novel and his own view on love and pity.

Gresham's School

Auden's preparatory school.

Grierson, John

1898–1972, b. Scotland, Grierson became a pioneer of documentary film after he produced the *Drifters* (1929), about the herring fishing fleets. Grierson took a Ph.D. at Glasgow University. In World War I he served on a minesweeper. He went to the U.S. to study the effects of the media on public opinion, a theme that Auden would elaborate on throughout his career. Grierson first used the word documentary in 1925, and on his return to Britain two years later he promoted the idea of a government-funded organization to make educational and propaganda films. In 1929 he made *Drifters*; it was a novelty to viewers who were accustomed to movies that were filmed entirely in the studio. His film unit, with a group of innovative directors, moved to the General Post Office (GPO), where it was to produce groundbreaking work, notably the documentary *Night Mail*, with a script by Auden. Grierson moved to Canada just before World War II, and as Canadian film commissioner, established the National Film Board of Canada. In 1945 he went to the U.S. where he formed the World Today, a company for producing films to promote international understanding. He was subsequently appointed director of mass media at UNESCO. He is probably best known as the host of *This Wonderful World*, which featured a selection of documentary films from around the world.

Auden inquired, through Basil Wright — an Oxford classmate, friend of C. Day Lewis, and a director for Grierson — about working for the GPO in June 1935 and Grierson responded quickly, hiring Auden full time and giving him the task of writing commentaries for two documentaries in progress: *Night Mail*, about the delivery of night mail to Scotland, and *Coal Face*, about miners in the north of England. (George Orwell would, nearly concurrently, write his prose documentary about these miners, *The Road to Wigan Pier*.) It was this very idea, that of presenting the lives of working people, that attracted Auden to the GPO. Wright traveled to the Downs School to meet Auden and brought Benjamin Britten, a novice composer, with him who would be working with Auden. Later Auden would also reacquaint himself with artist William Coldstream at the GPO. Auden worked mainly with Alberto Cavalcanti, a Brazilian who had made films in France.

For *Coal Face* Britten composed music for Auden's "O Lurcher-loving Collier," and Auden scripted recitations for actors as miners. The thrust of the film was to show the terrible conditions and dangers miners endure. *Coal Face* was released in late 1935 and it was an experiment that did not win over reviewers or the public. *Night Mail* would do better. It followed the "postal special" train from London to Glasgow, but also wove in the soon-to-be-recipients of this mail. An Auden poem would be the

means to do so with Britten's music. *Night Mail* became the GPO's best commercial success with reviews noting Auden and Britten's work. Auden, however, began to lose his enthusiasm for the GPO. He had roomed with Wright and they didn't get along so he then lodged with William and Nancy Coldstream. Coldstream was also not quite so keen over his job. Auden, in making *Night Mail*, had been treated, as just another laborer, which, while Auden was not a dilettante by any means, did not seem to have any respect for his role as screenwriter and esteemed poet. Moreover, after *Coal Face* and *Night Mail*, he sat around with little to do, no doubt begrudging that he had left the Downs for the GPO at half the salary. The unit began but did not finish a project on African slaves in the West Indies for which Auden would have included a poem by William Blake, an Auden favorite. Finally after six months, Auden resigned.

Here are his other projects at the GPO.

Beside the Seaside, 1935 documentary: The film, released in 1935, was about the British seaside as commissioned by the Travel and Industrial Association. "Auden's name is not listed on the credits, but in a lecture ... Auden briefly described the film.... The commentary on the soundtrack may have been revised from a lost earlier version that included the poem 'Look, stranger, at this island now'; the soundtrack includes phrases from the poem" (Mendelson, *Collected Works: Plays* in which soundtrack text is reprinted).

The Londoners, 1939 film: Basil Wright and John Grierson produced this film for the jubilee of the London County Council. Auden is given credit for "Sections of Commentary" (reprinted in *Collected Works: Plays*).

Negroes, 1935: "This film was conceived by Auden, Benjamin Britten, and Basil Wright in 1935. Auden wrote a commentary but the film was not made. However, Auden did adapt the final chorus for the play *The Ascent of F6* (reprinted in *Collected Works: Plays*).

The Way to the Sea, 1936: Paul Rotha for the Southern Railway produced this film with music by Britten and an "End Commentary" by Auden. "The film celebrated the electrification of the railway from London to Southampton. Auden and Britten worked on their verse and music for the final third of the film.... The tone ... was a deliberate send-up of the portentous manner of British documentaries of the period" (Mendelson, *Collected Works: Plays*).

Griffin, Howard *see Conversations with Auden*

Griffin, John Howard

1920–1980, writer, b. Dallas, Texas, best remembered for *Black Like Me* (1961). Griffin assumed the identity of a black man and visited several racially segregated states during a six-week period of 1959. His book became a best seller.

Mendelson (*Later Auden*) writes, "Auden understood the brutal truth of unjust exclusion from the safety of civil peace and the inextricably double truth of the excluded victim's innocence and blood." Auden's friend Thekla Clark called 1961 "the *Black Like Me* year" because of Auden's unrelenting insistence, during that time, that all his friends read the book. In 1970, Auden chose to include passages from *Black Like Me* in *A Certain World*, and he noted: "In my opinion, the most heroic living white American is Mr. John Howard Griffin." Mendelson says Griffin's heroism lay in his "voluntary acceptance of suffering and humiliations"—sufferings that might be compared to those of Christ. Later in the 1960s, when organizing lecture and reading tours, Auden always stipulated that he was not to be booked in colleges or communities that were racially segregated.

Also, Mendelson notes, it was in 1961 that Auden "began to discuss racial injustice in print." (*See also* "The Poet and the City.")

Grigson, Geoffrey *see New Verse*

"Grimm and Andersen" 1952

Essay written for the Modern Library's *Tales of Grimm and Andersen*. See Izzo in

"Auden on Fairytales, Quests, and Sagas," in *W.H. Auden: A Legacy* (2002).

Groddeck, George

1866–1934. Groddeck was a psychologist whose work was introduced to Auden by John Layard in Berlin (c. 1928). Groddeck, who had similar ideas to Homer Lane and was thought to have been the only rival to Freud that Freud was influenced by, "believed that the deepest element of human personality is the 'It', a mysterious force which rules both body and mind. Auden himself once paraphrased this doctrine of Groddeck's in a poem: 'We are lived by powers we pretend to understand ["In Memory of Ernst Toller"].' Groddeck held that diseases are caused by this 'It', for other than physical reasons. For example, constipation (he alleged) is an indication that the sufferer is a miser by nature, a hoarder of things. Tonsillitis shows an unwillingness to swallow, a desire to guard against outside influences.... Sickness is ... evidence of some self-deception in the sufferer and can only be eradicated not by medical treatment but by the elimination of this deceit from the personality" (Carpenter, *W.H. Auden*). Auden admired Groddeck, Lane, and Layard in large part because they also seemed to infer that the only way to confront one's desires was by fulfilling them. This seemed to sanction Auden's homosexuality.

"The Group Movement and the Middle Class" 1934

The idea of a "group" derived as a reaction to the mass impersonalization of modern society that needed to be redressed by getting people to know each other once again. Alienation would be reduced, spirit would increase, leading to renewed faith and cooperation. In an introduction for the 1934 book *Oxford and the Group Movement*, R.H.S. Crossman—a friend of Auden's—explains that the Group Movement in Britain began at Oxford but should now reach the greater world society. Crossman compares the Group Movement to other movements that also wish to change society (he intimates, but does not name, fascism and Communism), but writes that their approach is of the opposite formulation. Indeed, fascists and Communists would collectivize society into a massive subordination to a totalitarian world state. Auden contributed an essay, "The Group Movement and the Middle Class." In that essay, Auden observed that as soon as any religious movement acquires any appreciable number of members, it becomes a force that politicians need to consider and perhaps control.

As soon as a movement becomes an organization, it requires money "and those who supply it will expect special considerations." Auden ponders the unlikely success of attempting to separate "the things of God and the things of Caesar," which has not purified religion but served only "its rationalization in the interests of material wishes.... Today the light which has been shed by Freud and Marx on the motivation of thought makes it criminal to be uncritical, and no movement, secular or religious, which is afraid to examine dispassionately and to acknowledge openly what self-interest would make it want to believe, is worthy of anything but contempt."

For Auden the idea of a cooperative tribe or group was much inspired by Gerald Heard and the work of Wolfgang Kohler as described by Heard. (*See also* Heard, Gerald.)

Group Theatre

1933–1954. Private experimental theatre company. Founded in 1933 with the goal of producing original experimental non-commercial plays along with occasional revivals of earlier experimental dramas, the Group Theatre (not to be confused with the New York–based Group Theatre of the 1930s which provided a platform for the plays of Clifford Odets, among others, and Stanislavsky-based naturalistic acting styles), based primarily in London's Westminster Theatre, staged an impressive array of works, from a modern-dress presentation of William Shakespeare's *Timon of Athens* to new plays by T.S. Eliot (*Sweeney Agonistes*; 1935), Jean Giono (*Sowers of the Hills*; 1935), Stephen Spender (*Trial of a Judge*; 1938), and the poetic

dramas of W.H. Auden and Christopher Isherwood, including *The Dog Beneath the Skin* (1936), *The Ascent of F6* (1937), and *On the Frontier* (1938). Another contributor was Louis MacNeice. Most of these productions were directed by one of the Group Theatre's founders, choreographer Rupert Doone. Along with co-founders Ormerod Greenwood and Tyrone Guthrie, Doone dedicated the company to the performance of poetic drama constructed on the socialist principles of the Workers' Theatre Movement. The Group's characteristic style involved the use of minimal scenic elements and props, although some classical theatre elements, like masks, were occasionally employed. Benjamin Britten contributed original music for some of the productions, John Masefield and E.M. Forster lectured for the Group Theatre, and numerous artists and literary figures were significantly inspired by the Group's experiments and theories. The productivity of the Group was curtailed by the outbreak of World War II, but it reformed briefly in 1950 with a notable staging of Jean-Paul Sartre's *Les Mouches* under the title *The Flies*. The Group continued to occasionally present work before finally shutting down in 1954.

The Group Theatre's interest in and experimentation with verse drama was an obvious attraction to Auden as an environment in which he could explore the dramatic medium, while also promoting his socio-political views which, at the time, were closely aligned to the socialist underpinnings of the Group Theatre. The Group, drawing some of its concepts from the turn-of-the-century theories of Edward Gordon Craig, whose *The Art of the Theatre* (1905) had both inspired and outraged theatrical practitioners around the world, was devoted to the progress of British drama through techniques similar to German expressionism and epic theatre. The dramatic techniques and Marxist politics of Bertolt Brecht seem to have influenced the Group, but Rupert Doone, the Group's guiding force, had never heard of Brecht at all prior to Brecht's attendance at the Group's production of Auden's *The Dance of Death* in late 1934. In 1965, Auden himself recalled that the influence of German expressionist drama on his plays and the work of the Group was purely accidental. He claimed that medieval mystery and miracle play cycles were the greater influence on his dramatic output (Auden had, in fact, adapted the medieval mystery play *The Deluge* to accompany the first performance of *The Dance of Death*). In a Group Theatre program, Auden stressed the importance of the actor when he wrote that "Drama is essentially an art of the body. The basic of acting is acrobatic, dancing and all forms of physical skill." It is difficult to imagine that a writer as serious as Auden could ever equate the actors' art with his own, but it is certain that Auden's solo contributions, along with his collaborations with Isherwood, powerfully aided the Group Theatre's mission of promoting verse drama and, more significantly, the value of a politicized form of expressionistic drama that is unmistakably similar to that of Brecht and the German expressionists. The Auden-Isherwood plays, which include their first pre–Group Theatre drama, *The Enemies of a Bishop* or *Die When I Say* (1929), a morality play in four acts, inspired Auden to write a "dramatic and psychological manifesto," revised by Isherwood, which seems to have been planned as a preface for the play. This manifesto, much of which paralleled the goals of the Group Theatre, proposes that "Dramatic action is ritual" while stressing the importance of realistic art. From 1932 until its disbanding in 1939 (the same year Auden and Isherwood left England to report on the Chinese-Japanese War), Auden and Isherwood were involved with the Group. Auden also supplied plays, among these, *The Dance of Death,* as well as other solo efforts including *Paid on Both Sides* (1928), *The Chase* (1934), several documentary films, a cabaret entertainment (*Alfred* [1936]), and a radio play (*Hadrian's Wall* [1937]). Most scholars and critics regard the 1936 Auden-Isherwood play, *The Dog Beneath the Skin* or *Where Is Francis?*, their outstanding stage collaboration and one of the Group's most important (and characteristic) productions. The Auden-Isherwood association with the Group Theatre continued with the moderately successful play *The Ascent of F6* (1937), and a failed production of *On the Frontier* (1938). Doone, and his producing partner Robert Medley, felt that Auden lacked knowledge in the creation of dramatic form despite his skill at creating theatrical scenes. In his own works, Auden explores the textures of human experience, binding him to Isherwood who similarly pursues the same goal with different tools. Most critics stress that the Auden-Isherwood plays produced by the Group Theatre only partly succeed. More experimental than assured dramaturgy, these works are most interesting in the extent to which each depicts the desire of the authors to break free from the conventions of early twentieth century British drama, which, in turn, was a major goal of the Group Theatre.

"Grub First, Then Ethics" *see* *About the House*

"The Guilty Vicarage" 1948

Auden loved mysteries and detective stories. This essay, subtitled "Notes on the Detective Story by an Addict," is an analysis of the detective mystery genre as a form of White Magic rather than pure art with its purpose being to indulge the fantasy of escape from guilt. It has similar ideas as Auden's long poem *The Age of Anxiety*, published the year before. The detective story is a formula for the dialectic of innocence/guilt. Detectives choose to find reality (truth/innocence): murderers choose concealment (lies/guilt).

Sherlock Holmes: duty to self and to escape boredom; *Inspector French*: duty to society; *Father Brown* (*see also* Chesterton, G.K.): compassion for guilty/duty to God. *The reader*: vicarious heroics and/or guilt, the solution of the mystery is a return to Eden.

Guinness, Sir Alec

1914–2000, English actor. After his stage debut in 1934, in 1937 Guinness played Michael Ransom in Auden and Isherwood's play *The Ascent of F6*, directed by Rupert Doone at the Group theatre. Then Guinness performed with John Gielgud's company and at the Old Vic. He was an actor of enormous versatility and range on stage and in film, winning an Academy Award for best actor, 1956, for *The Bridge on the River Kwai*.

Hadrian's Wall 1937

Written during the autumn of 1937 with music by Benjamin Britten as a broadcast for BBC radio. The program was arranged by John Pudney, whom Auden had known at Gresham's School in 1925. The full title was *Hadrian's Wall from Caesar to the National Trust*. The wall ran through lead-mine country and thus recalled to Auden his childhood fascination with mines and mining. He also thought, as he wrote in the BBC's *Radio Times*, the wall "stood as symbol for a certain imperialistic conception of life, for military discipline and an international order; in opposition to the Celtic and Germanic tribal loyalties which overwhelmed it…. The front of history now lies elsewhere, but the same issues of order versus liberty … still remain." The script was of prose and verse, concluding: "That man is born a savage, there needs no other proof than the Roman Wall…. Whoever deprives an unoffending man of his right, is a barbarian." No doubt Auden was referring to Hitler.

"Half Way" *see Poems*

Hammarskjöld, Dag

1905–61, Swedish statesman, secretary-general of the United Nations 1953–61. Hammarskjöld increased the influence of the United Nations and the image of the secretary-general. He was on a mission to the Congo when his plane crashed in Northern Rhodesia (now Zambia). In 1961 Hammarskjöld was posthumously awarded that year's Nobel Peace Prize.

Auden met Hammarskjöld through Lincoln Kirstein and found him very well read in poetry. After just a few more meetings Auden considered him "one of the two most selfless people I have ever met." (Introduction to *Markings*. Auden did not name the other, but this could have been Dorothy Day.) After Hammarskjöld died, a notebook of his pensées

was published in Sweden. Auden asked to do a translation. Leif Sjoberg translated literally and then Auden reworked it into poetic prose.

"Hands" 1959

Each human being is unique, a New Adam. Each hand is unique, and each hand writing words even more so.

Hardy, Thomas

1840–1928, English novelist and poet, b. near Dorchester. Hardy, a stonemason's son, could not afford to pursue a scholarly career as he wished (this would replay in his novel *Jude the Obscure*), and learned architecture from John Hicks while also writing. After the appearance of *Far from the Madding Crowd* (1874), he wrote exclusively. His major works are *The Return of the Native* (1878), *The Mayor of Casterbridge* (1886), *Tess of the D'Urbervilles* (1891), and *Jude the Obscure* (1896).

After age 58, Hardy published many volumes of poetry.

Hardy was one of the earliest poetic influences for Auden, who first read him in Walter de la Mare's anthology *Come Hither* in 1923. Auden said, "I was fortunate indeed in finding the only poet who wrote of my world…. For more than a year I read no one else" (*Southern Review summer* 1940). Hardy appealed to a public school aesthete who was more or less separated from the hearties, as Hardy was far from an optimist and his world bore a greater resemblance to Auden's own experiences. Hardy's poems did not see love as romantic but as dangerous and sad, which Auden's life also reflected. Auden also thought that Hardy resembled his father. Auden's juvenilia poems are imitation Hardy in subject, style, and stark landscapes. "The Old Colliery," about a coal mine was certainly recalled when Auden scripted the miners' documentary *Coal Face* (*see* Grierson, John*)*. The images of rusted machinery in desolate, barren, farms in his *Poems* (1930), are also Hardy-esque. Auden would use images of hawks or helmeted airmen looking down from a great height detachedly observing a troubled world and this was also from Hardy, particularly the opening of his novel *The Return of the Native*. In Auden's 1940 "New Year Letter" Hardy is one of the masters Auden credits with his development. In 1973, Auden's last year, he credits Hardy again in his poem "A Thanksgiving."

In an essay, Auden wrote, "I cannot write objectively about Thomas Hardy because I was once in love with him.... Hardy was my poetical father and if I seldom read him now, it is, perhaps, because our relationship is so assured as no longer to need being made conscious" ("A Literary Transference" 1940).

"Have a Good Time" 1931

"Have a Good Time" is a contrast to the poem "The Decoys," which warns about being fooled by The Others. "Have a Good Time" refers to a "flying trickster" who is John Layard, a major influence on Auden, and then a disappointment. The flying trickster was from observations Layard made of South Sea primitives in an anthropology paper. The poem sends off its protagonist into the country, given a map by unnamed supporters. He is encouraged to have a good time in a place that is described more in detail than in previous poems and this place is a more tangible, less vaguely symbolic, point of reference, a place worth being in and returning to, which is in contrast to earlier poems that were more about frontiers and danger. There is still warning here but also hope.

"A Healthy Spot" 1944

This poem was written about Auden's observations of the people at Swarthmore when he taught there. He noticed "happy" marriages of unhappy people.

Heard, Gerald

1889–1971. Heard's influence on Auden's mysticism was early, profound, and enduring. Henry Fitzgerald Heard was an anthropologist/ scientific journalist/mystic who met Aldous Huxley in 1929 and remained one of his closest, lifelong friends, coming to America with him in 1937. Before leaving England, he also befriended Auden in 1929. Heard expounded theories of man's destiny being to reclaim the unified consciousness with the eternal reality which man had lost asserting his individual ego and separateness. Heard was a key influence on Huxley, Auden, and later Christopher Isherwood; many of his ideas are evident in the work of all three, and he introduced the latter to Vedanta (and Swami Prabhavananda) which changed Isherwood's life.

Auden was first introduced to Gerald Heard by Naomi Mitchison in 1929, and from their first meeting Auden regarded Heard as a sort of guru. Auden openly admits his respect for Heard in a poetic fragment (first published by Lucy McDiarmid in 1978) entitled "In the Year of My Youth...." Harold Nicolson notes the subject of the uncompleted poem in his diary entry of 4 August 1933: "The idea," Nicolson writes, "is Heard as Virgil guiding him through modern life" (*Diaries*). Heard was a ubiquitous and popular figure in the 1930s. Aldous Huxley, for example, would be enabled to embrace both pacifism and mysticism under his guidance; Christopher Isherwood would be introduced to Vedanta by him; William Somerset Maugham incorporated Heard's thought into the mystically inclined Larry Darrell in *The Razor's Edge*. Heard was well known for hosting a radio program of new scientific advances and ideas entitled *This Surprising World*.

Heard was most famous for his vision of a utopian future made possible by advances in psychology. Heard argued that psychology could demonstrate an underlying subconscious bond between all individuals, a corporate mind that enabled us to be sociable. By applying psychological thought to history, Heard constructed what he called an "outline of the evolution of consciousness" in his 1929 book *The Ascent of Humanity*. (Heard argued that our earliest pre-historic ancestors were not self-interested, but rather possessed of a tribal sense which precluded "any consciousness of individual separateness" from the group. As Heard writes, the "first human unit is the group, not the individual" [*Ascent*].)

Heard called this tribal sense "co-consciousness," a level of consciousness below self-awareness in which each individual constituent was only part of a larger whole. However, at some point in history, this "co-consciousness" dissolved. In his 1932 essay "The History of Ideas, or How We Got Separate" (published alongside Auden's "Writing" essay in Naomi Mitchison's *An Outline for Boys and Girls and Their Parents*), Heard asserts that Palaeolithic humans, who "did not think of themselves as self-conscious, separate individuals," could scarcely help but feel a unity with all life.

However, growing human knowledge brought about an evolutionary advance in our consciousness. Such advances were only possible by what Heard called a "power of separating," the power to regard the world objectively. Despite the material benefits afforded by this new-found power to dissect and study, it ultimately brought about the dissolution of our original sense of unity. It was at the moment when individuals became conscious of their detachment from the world that the tribal "co-consciousness" vanished.

Heard would write that, psychically, "we are divided against ourselves" (*Substance*) by a "threshold," or a "'limen' ... that now divides the subconscious and conscious mind so completely that the conscious mind can generally have no direct knowledge of the subconscious" ("Religion").

Heard felt it was imperative to break down the bulkhead between the subconscious and conscious mind if we were to enjoy a true sense of community with others. Despite being isolated by the conscious mind, the subconscious mind is "still the source of all human energy" (*Substance*). This blind, innate social power of our ancestors somehow percolates through our conscious minds, and is visible in our perpetual attempts to find unity with one another through love or friendship.

In 1932, Heard wrote a four-part series in *Time and Tide* entitled *Religion and the Problems of a Modern Society*, in which he discusses how religious experience had worked to alleviate the sudden isolation felt by our first self-conscious ancestors. "Religious communion" enabled each individual to feel a "direct sense of the union with their community and through

it with eternal life" ("Religion"). United "in a like minded group," Heard believed that the limen in our consciousness could be surmounted, enabling "the individual ... to recover his symbiotic relationship with his fellows." Heard is essentially describing the vision of agape in which the individual participant experiences a life that is "supra-personal and unlimited," achieving what Heard calls "at-one-ment" ("Religion") with his or her community.

However, once religion became "infected with the very thing it exists to cure — Individualism" ("Religion"), it only served to further their isolation by stressing personal salvation instead of promoting group unity. With the failure of religion, Heard sought a new means of uniting our divided consciousness.

He wrote about developing a "deliberate technique" to tap the subconscious "social and greater self" (*Source*), or a "psychic hygiene" ("Religion"), which would enable each individual to "re-mend the fissure in his own psyche and so see himself and his community, it and Life, and Life and the universe as one" (*Source*). Our earliest self-conscious ancestors were able to cross over that limen quite easily, having been recently "condensed" out of a natural co-consciousness. However, Heard asserted that, "in a self-conscious age," any attempt "to explore the subconscious, cross the limen, and make the vital contact that exists beyond the individual self-consciousness" had to be made "deliberately, self-consciously" (*Source*). The first step in Heard's solution was to recognize that individualism was not the correct paradigm for human relations.

Beyond co-consciousness and self-consciousness awaited what Heard called "superconsciousness" (*Ascent*), a state in which we would be simultaneously self-aware and aware of our subconscious extra-individuality. Heard proposed a combination of psychological analysis and mystical experience as a means to achieve this transition. By means of psychological analysis, Heard believed we could understand and apprehend the deep-seated forces which motivated us. By meditation, Heard argued, our subconscious "social habits" could be raised from the depths of the subconscious mind and into the conscious mind. Heard believed that group meditation was essential to breaking down the barrier both in our minds and between each other.

While Heard believed the experience of communion could be "obtained by any group of like-minded people," he also remarks "the dozen seems to be the number which gives best results. Heard envisioned a society in which group meditation would reassure individuals of their greater supra-personal unity before they returned to their daily lives. Having been reassured of their unity with all life, individuals could then return to a larger community, confident in their role as part of a larger whole.

In his early poetry, Auden gives much consideration to the existence of an almost insurmountable barrier dividing our sub-conscious social instincts from our self-conscious rational mind. Auden's 1928 poem "The Secret Agent" deals overtly with the question of crossing this border into potentially hostile territory and tapping the pent-up energy it contains. According to Edward Mendelson, the "frontier" motif in Auden's poetry began in 1927. Auden's "frontier," Mendelson explains, represents "a watershed or divide isolating the mind from the cycles of unconscious nature" (*Early Auden*). The poem reads well as a statement about the divide between the conscious and subconscious mind. However, Mendelson remarks, the border in "The Secret Agent" presents a new possibility, that of "using a barrier to produce energy rather than restrict it" (*Early Auden*).

The secret agent emblematizes the relationship between the conscious and subconscious; all communication is covert, and our conscious mind sees only glimpses of the strange world beyond. The speaker reflects that there is "easy power" ("Secret") to be had at this border, remarking that it is a "fine site for a dam." A dam is a liminal space, which would control, rather than restrict, communication between two realms. The image of the dam fits neatly within Heard's and Auden's belief in bridging the gap between the subconscious and conscious mind.

In his 1932 fragment "In the Year of My Youth…" (uncollected, but see Mendelson, *Early Auden*), Auden borrows heavily from Heard's 1932 book *The Social Substance of Religion* in order to discuss the social implications of this psychic rift. The speaker of the poem,

led through modern London by his friend Sampson (a model of Heard), observes men and women who live like automatons, working but without purpose or satisfaction. Sampson attributes this to a division between motivation and "executive" power.

Auden also borrows the word "executive" from *The Social Substance of Religion*. Heard uses the word to describe the rational, conscious mind, which sees only what it can use. The outer side of our nature is unstable because it changes and grows as we learn and develop. Heard goes on to say that our inner nature is "unadapting, unalterable"; "the subconscious," he writes, "is completely resistant to change in its circumstances, and remains unaltered by the outward economic modification of its environment." By "denying [the subconscious mind] those expressions natural to it," our condition is one of "profound distress"; while advancing outwardly, we have no inner conception of what it is we work towards. Unaware of the potential for real unity that exists within us, we work to further isolate ourselves from one another by listening to the demands of the "surface mind." The problem for both Heard and Auden was that the subconscious mind, the realm of "desire" which ultimately governs our social behavior, was isolated and ignored, while the conscious mind, the world of "data," was made invincible. Auden, who describes the subconscious mind as "possessing no argument but the absolute veto," is simply reworking Heard's conception of the subconscious, "possessed of an absolute veto but shut off with equal absoluteness from the argument" (*Substance*).

Auden's "Writing" shows how closely his conception of the subconscious social self resembles Heard's. For example, Auden's discussion of prehistoric "co-consciousness" and of the birth of individualism are identical to Heard's. Auden writes about the "continuously present group life" ("Writing") of our pre-individual ancestors that preceded language, and, like Heard, Auden posited that this "continuously present" group sense was akin to a kind of telepathy.

Auden's familiarity with Heard's *Ascent* is further supported by his argument for the dissolution of this co-consciousness and the birth of self-consciousness. "At sometime or other in human history," writes Auden, "man became self conscious, he began to feel, I am I, and You are Not I; we are shut inside ourselves and apart from each other." Self-consciousness, as in Heard's scheme, meant that each individual constituent of a society became aware of him or herself as an individual entity first, and a part of the group second; Auden describes this initial state of self awareness, in which each constituent of a society perceived itself as "an individual thing, different from other things, but without meaning except in its connection with other things." Ultimately, Auden argues, individual autonomy supplanted this feeling of unity entirely. As Auden writes, "a part begins to work not only as if it were a whole (which it is) but as if there were no larger wholes." "The more this feeling grew," argues Auden, there was an increasingly greater need "to bridge over the gulf, to recover the sense of being as much part of life as the cells in his body are part of him." Auden suggests that the more fundamental development of language was developed by self-conscious individuals as a means to recover the lost sense of co-consciousness. The origin of language, argues Auden, goes back to the noises of excitement made during intensely social activities enjoyed by a co-conscious group. Before the loss of our co-conscious unity, Auden writes, when early humans were "doing things together in a group, such [as] hunting; when feeling was strongest, ... the group had made noises, grunts, howls, grimaces." "If he made the noise," Auden asks, "could he not recover the feeling?" By using language, individuals attempted to "bridge" the rift between the individual self and a larger whole. Auden describes language as "a tunnel under which the currents of feeling can pass unseen." Izzo, in his *W.H. Auden and Aldous Huxley: On Language*, explains Auden's conception of the duality of language, which exists in the "individual mind *in part*" but also within "a collective unconscious that unites each individual — a world mind."

Language is a bridge between the two, the act of communication briefly connecting our individual mind to a greater whole. Language not only proves the existence of this subconscious social mind, but also presents a means by which self-conscious individuals can access it.

In the early 1930s, Auden began to look seriously for a means of uniting these two realms more concretely. The solution he suggested owes much to Gerald Heard's theories on group meditation and agape. In his 1934 essay "The Group Movement and the Middle Classes," Auden discusses the potential for "a group of very moderate size, probably not larger than twelve" in which it would be possible for an individual to "lose himself, for his death instincts to be neutralised in the same way as those of the separate cells of the metazoan neutralise each other in the body." Auden's cellular imagery is a recapitulation of his argument in "Writing" that early individuals sought some means to "recover the sense of being as much a part of life as the cells in his body are a part of him." Auden's reflection that group activities can suspend the individual's "death instinct" is identical to Heard's description of group meditation.

Auden's 1933 poem "A Summer's Night," and his later commentary on the experience of vision of agape in his introduction to *The Protestant Mystics*, shows the influence of Heard on his thoughts on meditation. In "A Summer's Night," the speaker of the poem, sitting "equal with colleagues in a ring," finds himself possessed of a feeling of unity between them. The image of the ring appears in Heard's *Social Substance to Religion* in reference to early Christian agape. Heard believed that a "small group of about a dozen" had come together regularly and "formed an inward-looking group — perhaps a ring" (*Substance*). So assembled, Heard argued, early Christians merged in a common "psychic field" (*Substance*) which reassured them of their bond to one another. Writing his introduction for *The Protestant Mystics* in 1963, Auden would describe how on that summer night in 1933 he had "quite suddenly and unexpectedly" found himself "invaded by a power" which made it possible for him to know "what it means to love one's neighbour as oneself." Auden had successfully stepped outside himself into the larger life, and transcended his fear of individual death; as he writes in "A Summer's Night," at the height of his experience "Fear gave his watch no look" and "Death put down his book." The individual's sense of self-preservation and fear of death vanish with this experience of a greater eternal life of which he or she is a part. This experience, however, he knows to be fleeting; "I also knew that the power would, of course, withdraw sooner or later and that, when it did, my greeds and self-regard would return." However, the memory of the experience stayed with him, and it was "more difficult for [him] to deceive [him] self" when he behaved greedily or selfishly towards others. Like Heard, Auden believed the vision of Agape would provide individuals with an intense feeling of their place within a larger whole. And although that experience would fade, the memory of it would remind them that their individual autonomy is illusory. The self-regarding instinct would return, as Auden admits, but the memory of the experience would make it impossible to believe in the insolubility of the individual, and reaffirm communal ties.

For the rest of Auden's career as a poet and also as a philosopher via his essays, the impetus of Heard's early influence that conditioned a search for consciousness in Auden would remain, steadfastly, the dominating concern of Auden's life and art.—PAUL EROS (*See also* Language; Mitchison, Naomi.)

"Heavy Date" 1939

This poem was written after Auden met Chester Kallman and celebrates how love transforms the mundane into the wonderful when the lovers' shared feelings heighten awareness.

Heidegger, Martin

1889–1976, German philosopher who developed existential phenomenology. He studied Roman Catholic theology and was a student of Edmund Husserl, the founder of phenomenology. Besides Husserl, Heidegger was influenced by the Danish philosopher Søren Kierkegaard, and by the German philosopher Friedrich Nietzsche. In his most important work, *Being and Time* (1927), Heidegger considered the philosophical question "What is it, to be?"

Auden's poem "One Circumlocution," about a work of art as a riddle, is influenced by Heidegger whom Auden mentioned in a review as early as 1942. Heidegger's interest in Kierkegaard also drew Auden to him. Mendelson

notes that Auden's phrase "the nothing who nothings" in *The Age of Anxiety* is from Heidegger. Auden's Heidegger-inspired lectures, collectively titled *The Enchafèd Flood*, were a long rumination on the nature of man's being, with the examples coming from *Moby Dick*, *Billy Budd*, and *Don Quixote*.

"Hell" 1939

This is another poem written in the latter half of 1939 in which Auden was concerned with the construct of time. It is frustrating to dream about the future or be haunted by the past, "and so much easier to be" in the eternal now of the mystic.

"Henry James and the Artist in America" *see* James, Henry

Henze, Hans Werner

1926–, German composer. His early works were influenced by Stravinsky, Hindemith, and Bartók. Henze's leftist politics of the 1960s and 1970s are manifested in works such as the *Essay on Pigs* for baritone and chamber orchestra (1969) and the oratorio *The Raft of the Frigate Medusa* (1968). He has also written eight symphonies (1947–93), concertos for various instruments and several operas. Among the latter are *Elegy for Young Lovers* (1961) and *The Bassarids* (1965), both to texts by Auden and Chester Kallman, *The Young Lord* (1965), and *English Cat* (1983).

Herbert, George

1593–1633, an English metaphysical poet. In 1630 he was ordained an Anglican priest and made rector at Bemerton. Herbert's devotional poems are straightforward and reverent. All unpublished at his death, they were left by Herbert to his friend Nicholas Ferrar, who had them published as *The Temple* (1633). The twentieth century revival of interest in the metaphysical poets rediscovered Herbert.

Of the metaphysicals Auden preferred Herbert to Donne after reading both at Oxford. His appreciation lasted as in Auden's last year he edited and introduced a selection of Herbert for Penguin's "Poet to Poet" series. Auden asserts in the introduction that while wishing to meet very few of the poets he has read, he would have liked to meet Herbert who Auden believed "must have been an exceptionally good man, and exceptionally nice as well." Herbert was a poet of divine devotion and the rare one who could do so simply without either grandiose floridity or self-flagellation as seen sometimes in Donne and Hopkins. (Aldous Huxley admired him for the same reason, see his *Literature and Science*—which is another Auden-Huxley correlation.) Auden thought that poems about God should bring attention to God, more so than the writer. In this Auden cited Herbert as one who understood this and for whom "My own sympathy is unbounded."

"Herman Melville" 1940

Dedicated to Lincoln Kirstein, this poem looks at the nature of evil and the dilemma of the spurned artist. Melville wrote *Moby Dick* about the compulsive obsession of Ahab's for that terrible Whale, which to him was the epitome of evil that, to Auden, had emasculated him. The whale did no such thing, nor is it evil. "Evil is unspectacular and always human." (Here Auden refers to Melville's more subdued account of evil in *Billy Budd*.) Moreover, the contemporary "failure" of Moby Dick drove Melville into a thirty-year refusal to write again and instead, restrain his gift of art in the role of a bureaucrat. Melville after this self-imposed exile realizes that he has given in to a perverse form of vanity, and sits down to write *Billy Budd* as atonement. (See also *The Enchafèd Flood*.)

Heroes and Hero-Worship *see* Lawrence, D.H.; *The Orators*; Plays with Isherwood (*The Ascent of F6*)

"Hic & Ille" 1956

In this essay, the curse of Narcissus (vanity/self-indulgence) is contained in Auden's aphorisms on sight, sound, illusion, and self-image. Man's life is a mirror: psychoanalysts interpret "the distorted" individual's mirror; politicians manipulate the collective mirror of the anonymous Kierkegaardian public. Self-interpretation is inherently distorted by the ego. Public martyrdom is boring unless it is converted into aphorisms that teach. Panic is solitary; joy is communal. Relationships are a form of barter. (*See also* "Balaam and his Ass.")

"The Hidden Law" 1941

Spiritual consciousness of a greater unity is veiled only by ignorance.

Highbrows and Lowbrows *see* Aesthetes and Hearties

History

Auden was absorbed with the nature of what the term "history" meant. In the 1930s, he read Marx less for what Communism was than for how Communism would come to be as a historical process. Gerald Heard told him history was not about what man did outside of himself, as these actions were mere symptoms of the true history that was the inner evolution of evolving consciousness. While Heard's consciousness was collective, Auden learned about individual consciousness from Freud and other psychoanalysts. In the 1940s Auden's Christianity turned history into that which led up to and then followed Christ. In the 1950s, history became more pointedly inevitable, with types of events repeated as lessons from which we do or do not learn. After this, history became more benign as aging and the prospect of death rendered moot much of the previous decade's arguments.

In a 1956 essay Auden wrote, as regards history: "Life, as I experience it, in my own person is primarily a continuous succession of choices between alternatives, made for short-term or long-term purpose; the actions I take … are less significant to me than the conflicts of motives, temptations, doubts in which they originate, [in which time] is not of a cyclical motion outside myself but of an irreversible history of unique moments which are made by my decisions…. Life is fleeting and full of sorrow and no words can prevent the brave and the beautiful from dying or annihilate grief. What poetry can do is transform the real world into an imaginary one which is godlike in its permanence and beauty, providing a picture of life which is worthy of imitation…. Art cannot teach…. It can only hold a mirror in which each person sees his face reflected…. The way for each person is unique" ("At the End of the Quest, Victory").

"The History of Science" 1955

Fairytale about a brother who rejects advice, seeks a goal, does not find it, then blunders into another, more wonderful goal; hence, role of error, unpredictability, wrong-headedness, can have a place in progress.

"The History of Truth" 1958

Contrasts past of lasting objects and truth to the present of disposable products and anti-truth.

Hitler *see* Berlin

Hockney, David

1937– , English painter. Moving from a distorted, semiexpressionist form of pop art, Hockney developed a personal realistic style, producing images with wit. Hockney is also known for his photographs, his photomontages, and his stage sets for ballets and operas. His subjects include still lifes, portraits, and aspects of homosexual life.

Hockney drew the old Auden in 1969. Carpenter writers: "…the sitting was not a great success. Hockney brought two other people with him … and this annoyed Auden, who be-

haved in a grumpy fashion. 'He gave me the impression,' said Hockney, 'of being rather like the headmaster of an English school'" (*W.H. Auden*).

Hoffman, Daniel

1923– . B. in New York city, he has published nine books of poetry including *An Armada of Thirty Whales* (1954), which was chosen by W.H. Auden for the Yale Series of Younger Poets. He is also the author of seven volumes of criticism.

Hogarth Press

The Hogarth Press, founded in 1917 by Leonard and Virginia Woolf, originally intended as a hobby for its founders, emerged as a commercial publishing enterprise following the success in 1919 of Virginia's *Kew Gardens*. The Hogarth Press is associated with the literary reputation and influence of its owners. The Woolfs published new and experimental works by relatively unknown writers, such as Auden, Katherine Mansfield, T.S. Eliot, Clive Bell, C. Day Lewis, Robert Graves, E.M. Forster, Christopher Isherwood, John Maynard Keynes, William Plomer, Vita Sackville-West, and the Woolfs. They published the first English translations of contemporary foreign works, and brought Freud and the papers of the International Psycho-Analytical Institute to the English reading public. In addition, through a number of series covering topics that ranged from literature and poetry to politics and economics, the press provided the general reading public with affordable booklets by well-known writers and critics of the day, including Auden and Worsley (*Education Today and Tomorrow* [1938]), Eliot, C. Day Lewis, Keynes, Roger Fry, Gertrude Stein, Robinson Jeffers, and H.G. Wells. The press also printed many artists, photographers, illustrators and designers including John Banting, Vanessa Bell (Virginia's sister and the mother of Julian Bell), Dora Carrington, Roger Fry, Duncan Grant, and E. McKnight Kauffer.

The Hogarth Press was owned and operated

by Leonard and Virginia from its inception to the end of 1938, when Virginia relinquished her interest as a partner in the business. In 1939, John Lehman, who had served as an assistant at the press, filled the partnership vacated by Virginia, and he and Leonard Woolf managed the press until 1946, when Lehman terminated his partnership, and Leonard sold Lehmann's share to the directors of Chatto & Windus. Between 1917 and 1946, the Hogarth Press published 525 titles.

Hollander, John

1929– , b. New York City. He has written seventeen volumes of poetry and seven books of criticism. *A Crackling of Thorns* (1958) was chosen by Auden for the Yale Series of Younger Poets.

"Homage to Clio" 1955

Theme is of modern era's massive volume in everything that denies subtlety and that contrasts with earlier era of Clio, the muse of man's time and history along with Artemis/Aphrodite who govern plants/animals. The poem celebrates the virtue of silence (as in contemplation), and unique humans and moments of chosen goodness that are much preferred to a neutral nature that seems indifferent. The theme of a past having more virtue than the present can also be seen in "The History of Science," "The History of Truth," and "Makers of History." One may note the difference between the mid 1950s Auden and the Auden of 1930 when that earlier Auden rejected the past as an enemy; now he wants readers to learn from the past.

Homage to Clio 1960

Volume containing poems written from 1955 to 1960. Dedicated to Mr. and Mrs. E.R. and A.E. Dodds.

Homer

Mendelson writes in *Early Auden* that the British Auden was concerned with determining what the role of poetry was: public activism or private expression. "Homer knew the distinction…. In *The Odyssey* he tells of the poets … who compose their songs at the command of their listeners. It never occurs to them to sing for the sake of singing." In *The Odyssey*, poets serve utilitarian and public needs. Conversely, in *The Iliad*, Homer's Achilles sings alone for himself to hear. Homer's literary heirs are all poets whose first law is the law of their genius, seers who live in voluntary or psychological exile, at home only in their art. The later Auden became the second poet after the early Auden decided that public service was not the poet's avocation. For Auden Homer was the realist of Wholly-Truthful Art and also a factor in Auden's poem "Musée des Beaux Arts," in which, despite witnessing tragedy, the world goes about its business and life goes on with the mundane and the tragic in tandem.

In Auden's introduction to *The Portable Greek Reader* (1948), in which there are excerpts from Homer, he notes: "The Homeric hero has the military virtues of courage, resourcefulness, magnanimity in victory, and dignity in defeat to an exceptional degree. His heroism is manifested in exceptional deeds that can be judged by others…. He is not a tragic figure, i.e. he does not suffer more than others, but his death has exceptional pathos—the great warrior comes to the same end as the lowest churl." On one hand, the Homeric hero is somewhat like a pure-in-heart man, but he is also subject to the reality that any man endures. For "Happy New Year" (1932, uncollected but quoted in *Early Auden*, Mendelson), Auden refers to the "tamer of horses," a Homeric phrase. In "The Shield of Achilles," 1952, Auden refers to chapter 18 of *The Iliad*.

Homintern

Homintern, adapted from the 1930s term "Comintern" meaning Communist International, means Homosexual International.

Hopkins, Gerard Manley

1844–89, English poet, educated at Oxford. Hopkins entered the Roman Catholic

Church in 1866, and the Jesuit novitiate in 1868, and was ordained in 1877. His *Poems,* edited by his friend and poet Robert Bridges, did not appear in print until 1918. Hopkins' poetry tried to approximate the rhythm of everyday speech with a new meter called "sprung rhythm."

The young Auden was greatly interested in Hopkins' sprung rhythm and colloquialism as well as his intensity (although an older Auden would say such floridity in religious themes was unbecoming and that simplicity, such as one finds in George Herbert's religious verse, was better). The early Auden was a convert to the thought of Homer Lane, John Layard, George Groddeck, and Freud, among others, and his "conversion" was as dramatic as Hopkins' devotion, but with a different focus. The second "Ode" at the end of *The Orators* (1932) is a take-off on Hopkins' style. By this time, Auden thought that Hopkins was something of an indulgence and a bit subversive, saying to John Lehmann, "Hopkins ought to be kept on a special shelf like a dirty book, and only allowed to readers who won't be ruined by him" (*The Whispering Gallery*).

Horace

(65 B.C.–8 B.C. Quintus Horatius Flaccus), Latin lyric poet. His first book of *Satires* appeared in 35 B.C., the *Epodes* c. 30 B.C., the second book of *Satires* in 29 B.C., three books of *Odes* c. 24 B.C., and the first book of *Epistles* c. 20 B.C. The fourth book of *Odes,* the second book of *Epistles,* a hymn (the *Carmen Saeculare*), and the *Ars Poetica,* or *Epistle to the Pisos,* appeared c. 13 B.C. He gives a picture of contemporary Roman society and represents especially the spirit of the Augustan age of Rome — a time of peace, when the arts were cultivated earnestly without pretense. He had much influence on European poetry.

In *Early Auden* Mendelson refers to a later Auden as "Horatian," that is, a statesman and "poet of civilization." But even in the late 1930s Auden employed Horatian stanzas to infer that one must be more circumspect about one's life and art, rather than flushed with immediate and sometimes pretentious (anti–Horatian), but, per-

haps, not truly sincere emotion. (*See* "Spain.") "In Praise of Limestone" (1948), is a Horatian Ode. In 1968 Auden's poem "The Horatians" "ends in the quietly self-satisfied credo of the Horatians, who have learned from the long-dead Horace to say of themselves, in effect, to be proud but from a sober perspective" (*Later Auden*).

Horae Canonicae 1949–1954

The title for this seven-part poem is Latin for canonical hours, in which duties and offices are set relating to the hours of the crucifixion. Auden sought to see them as a structure for everyday life. Auden considered punctuality a virtue that one could best assert by having a schedule to be punctual about. *Auden*: "Not to know the time of day is to be governed, like animals and children, by the immediate mood of the self. To know the time of day, to structure the passage of time, is to submit the self to the ego, which takes purposive decision with a view to attaining some future good; it signifies that a person is conscious of a vocation, of the kind of person he intends to become" ("Notes on the Comic," *Thought,* spring 1952; this passage left out when reprinted in *The Dyer's Hand*).

The order of the seven parts is not the same as the order in which they were written from 1949 to 1954. Clearly Auden thought a great deal over this poem and how to approach its writing.

"Prime 1949": The spirit in the boy wakes and assumes its human nature, which is to enter history. Over and over, in replication of the First Adam or Eve, the spirit sees anew that paradise is lost and that the human task is to begin again the slow, eon by eon, task of regaining it.

"Terce 1953": Domesticated man is both within and apart from his transformative duties that make every day Good Friday.

"Sext 1954": Celebrates vocation, and the sense of forgetfulness in work that makes civilization possible, but presents the paradox that it is also the source of guilt as in both respects man goes beyond nature with his capacity for both achievement and also sin, which make him uniquely human.

"Nones 1950": Crucifixion has taken place

and we, the crowd, try to evade responsibility, even though innocence is now lost and evil cannot be ignored. It is 3 A.M. and one escapes into dream but also nightmares. "Nones" ends with the contrast of human guilt and nature's ambivalence.

"Vespers 1954": The poet, through his art, seeks a new Eden (Arcadia), or is it a New Jerusalem (Utopia)? Is the New City based on faith or on secular and civic virtue? He is not sure. What they have in common is that both are united in guilt.

"Compline 1954": In sleep there is both a meditation and mediation upon guilt and forgiveness.

"Lauds 1952": At dawn, after the meditation/mediation, one awakes renewed with compassion for others and strives for the creation of the just community. (See also "One Circumlocution.")

Horan, Robert

1922– , Auden's choice as Yale Younger Poet of 1948 for the volume *A Beginning*. Auden met him through Lincoln Kirstein, as Horan also wrote on dance.

Horizon see Spender, Stephen

"A Household" 1948

In this poem the idea of a "household" is from Cochrane's *Christianity and Classical Culture*, but here becomes Auden's melancholy inner household. For Auden in general the psyche's inner household compares to St. Augustine's spiritual household. (*See also* "Port and Nuts with the Eliots.")

Housman, A.E.

1859–1936, poet and classical scholar. Born in Staffordshire, next to the county of Shropshire that his first collection of poetry made famous, Alfred Edward Housman was the first of seven children. His father's inability to

handle a modest income resulted in Housman's early career at Oxford being marked by poverty, which did not, however, prevent him from focusing his mental energies and showing promise as a classical scholar. At Oxford Housman met the only person he ever loved deeply, Moses Jackson. Jackson's inability to reciprocate Housman's affection was the central feature of Housman's emotional life and the motivation from which both his lyric poetry and classical scholarship sprang.

After graduating with less than top honors from Oxford, perhaps because of emotional upset, Housman worked in the Patent Office in London and on his own pursued classical scholarship. In 1892 his scholarly publications enabled him to secure a position as professor of Latin at the University College in London. Jackson, with whom Housman remained in close contact, subsequently departed for India and married. In a flood of sustained creativity and anguish, Housman wrote most of the poems in his first book, *A Shropshire Lad* (1896). He continued his classical scholarship by working on a definitive edition of the obscure Latin poet Manilius.

A Shropshire Lad proved one of the most enduring collections of late Victorian verse. Its pessimism and lyric beauty gave it wide appeal, and although Housman wrote a few poems in the next decades, most of his work was focused on Manilius and his academic career. He moved to Cambridge University in 1911.

In early 1921, Housman learned that Jackson was mortally ill with cancer. His grief occasioned another spurt of poetry; *Last Poems* appeared in 1922 shortly before Jackson's death. For the rest of his life Housman worked on Manilius, finishing a definitive, five-volume edition in 1932. A savage, witty reviewer of the scholarly efforts of others, Housman continued teaching at Cambridge until his death in 1936. Later that year, his brother Laurence Housman, also a poet, brought out a third collection of verse, *More Poems* culled from Housman's papers.

Auden saw Housman as a minor poet, which he defined as one who "never risks failure." Almost no poem of Housman's, Auden reports in his lecture on *Troilus and Cressida*, "fails to come off." The consistent plangency of

Housman's poetry Auden identified with the crisis of adolescence and its unhappiness. If Housman's adolescent crises were like Auden's, this similarity may make one suspect the cruelty of Auden's 1938 sonnet on the Cambridge don as more defensive than condign. Characterized as one who channeled his interests into non-emotional matters and deliberately locked up his feelings, Housman "put the money of his feelings on/The uncritical relations of the dead."

Housman seems to have been a constant presence for Auden throughout his career, for as late as 1971, in "A Shock," Auden quotes him, and it is impossible to read the passage in *The Dyer's Hand* where "an exquisite minor work can make a master feel thoroughly ashamed of himself" as anything other than a tacit reproach by a minor writer to one who knew himself as a major one. —ROGER LATHBURY (*See also* "A.E. Housman"; "Jehovah Housman and Satan Housman")

Aldous Huxley

"How to Be Masters of the Machine" 1933

A near duplicate of part of an essay by Aldous Huxley in *Do What You Will*, 1929 ("Spinoza's Worm"). Machines lead to leisure, which leads to thinking, which leads to anxiety and fear. There are machines to distract us and to produce luxury items as more distractions that make one wretched and spoiled.

Howard, Brian

1905–1958, British poet born of American parents. Anti-fascist and in the RAF during World War II. Met Auden at Oxford. His lifestyle of drink, drugs, and vagabondage became a model for characters by Evelyn Waugh — Ambrose Silk in *Put Out More Flags*, and Anthony Blanche in *Brideshead Revisited*. He died of a drug overdose.

Hoyland, Geoffrey

Auden's headmaster at the Downs School where Auden taught in the mid 1930s. Auden admired Hoyland's progressive methods and dedicated a "A Summer Night" to him.

Huxley, Aldous

1894–1963, English author, grandson of Thomas Henry Huxley and great nephew of Matthew Arnold on his mother's side. He came to the United States in the late 1930s and lived in California. He wrote critical essays and symbolist poetry, but then wrote novels and short stories that satirize bourgeois decadence. *Brave New World* (1932) is his most famous work. It was followed *by Eyeless in Gaza* (1936), *After Many a Summer Dies the Swan* (1939), *Ape and Essence* (1948), *The Devils of Loudon* (1952), *The Genius and the Goddess* (1955), and *Island* (1962). His later writings —fiction and non-fiction — show his interest in mysticism and Eastern philosophy.

Huxley was *the man* in British Literature in the 1920s, much more so than Eliot was, although Eliot's reputation has fared better since then. His influence was enormous directly or indirectly in the U.K. and U.S. Undergraduates made sure to read him in the 1920s and while Auden would later pretend antipathy to Huxley for his Eastern mysticism (and no doubt also blamed Huxley and Gerald Heard for luring Isherwood to California to believe in it as well), Auden also knew of Huxley, as did anyone with any interest in literature at the time. Isherwood was Auden's mentor in the late 1920s and in a Mortmere story that Auden certainly read, "Prefatory Epistle to my Godson on the Study of History" (in 1972, Auden published *Epistle to a Godson,* a volume of poems dedicated to Stephen Spender's son Philip), a Mr. Starn proclaims, sounding Huxley-esque, that "man is the sole and supreme irrelevance. He is without method, without order, without proportion. His childish passions, enthusiasms, beliefs are unsightly protuberances in the surface of the Universal Curve ... how perfect would be the evolutions of nature in a world unpeopled." Starn also warns his godson to be skeptical of the New Testament saying, in a footnote: "I refer to this exploded forgery with all due reference to Professor Pillard, who has, by the Historical Method, clearly proved that it is the work of Mr. Aldous Huxley." Huxley in the 1920s was a marked man by The Others who considered him the most cynical of the post-war cynics.

Huxley would quote Kierkegaard in his 1932 commonplace anthology, *Texts and Pretexts,* in the section "Memory." That Auden had read Huxley's collection is evidenced by his reference to it in *The Dyer's Hand* and by his also later using the same quotation. Thus, Huxley knew of Kierkegaard years before Auden embraced him. Huxley quoted Goethe, and the same quote shows up in Auden. A number of Auden's essays in the 1930s seem inspired by Huxley directly — for example, Auden's "How To Be Masters of the Machine" (1932), sounds like pages in Huxley's *Do What You Will* in the essay "Spinoza's Worm." That Huxley and Auden bear great similarity as essayists throughout their careers is also clear. In the Auden-Isherwood play *The Dog Beneath the Skin*, Huxley's *Brave New World* is described (*see* Plays with Isherwood). Indirect influences on Auden came from sources closely associated with Huxley, including D.H. Lawrence and Gerald Heard. Huxley and Auden had read and commented on Lawrence's *Fantasia on the Unconscious* specifically, and other works in general. (Huxley's friendship with Lawrence was such

that Aldous and his wife Maria joined Frieda Lawrence to be the only people with her husband upon his death.)

In 1947 Huxley turned down Stravinsky's request to write a libretto for him. Instead Huxley recommended Auden. The result was *The Rake's Progress.*

After World War I, the general response of the highbrows who sought to change the conditions that had led to the war were the bywords decentralization, simplicity, reality. Lowbrows were content to forget the war and retreat into the secondary worlds of the cinema and escapist fiction that emphasized style over substance. Among the highbrows, however, there was a call for substance over style. In the 1920s Huxley wrote copiously on the need for simplicity and reality in literature (and life) with essays such as "The Subject Matter of Poetry" and "Tragedy and the Whole Truth." He made two assertions: 1) everything and anything between the mundane and the magnificent could and should be suitable subject matter for literature if the artist writes about it as sincere truth; 2) the artist's striving for reality in art was not new but a mode that was as old as classical antiquity: Writing in 1923, Huxley said,

[Writers today] are at liberty to do what Homer did — to write freely about the immediately moving facts of everyday life. Where Homer wrote of horses and tamers of horses [we] write of trains, automobiles, and the various species of ... bohunks who control the horse-power. Much too much stress has been laid on the newness of the new poetry; its newness is simply a return from the jeweled exquisiteness of the eighteen-nineties to the facts and feelings of ordinary life. There is nothing intrinsically novel or surprising in the introduction into poetry of machinery and industrialism, of labour unrest and modern psychology: these things belong to us, they affect us daily as enjoying and suffering beings; they are part of our lives, just as the kings, the warriors, the horses and chariots, the picturesque mythology were part of Homer's life.... The critics who would have us believe that there is something essentially unpoetical about a bohunk (whatever a bohunk may be) and something essentially poetical about Sir Lancelot of the Lake are, of course, simply negligible. [In "Subject matter of Poetry." The poet who used "bohunk" was Carl Sandburg.]

Writing in 1933, Auden agreed. "The test of a poet is the frequency and diversity of the occasions we remember his poetry. Memorable speech then. About what? Birth, death, the Beatific vision, the abysses of hatred and fear.... Yes, all of these, but not these only. Everything that we remember no matter how trivial: the mark on the wall, the joke at luncheon, word games, these, like the dance of a stoat or the raven's gamble, are equally the subject of poetry. We shall do poetry a great disservice if we confine it only to the major experiences of life" ("Poets, Poetry, and Taste"). Auden would also say, "...a moment in which the characters are emotionally relaxed may be just as significant as one in which they are emotionally stirred" ("Dyer's Hand," *Anchor Review*). This idea reflects the "tea-tabling" technique that Edward Upward admired in Forster. To "tea-table" was to reveal important and even emotional information without necessarily doing so in a traditionally histrionic tragic scene. Jane Austen had mastered tea-tabling a century earlier, particularly in *Emma*. Isherwood himself alludes to tea-tabling in a Mortmere story when a character says: "You know, I think the trouble with all you literary johnnies is that you're always looking for mysteries in the most ordinary everyday things" ("Christmas in the Country").

Of the "ordinary, everyday things," Huxley writes that the commonplace and the tragic can be combined:

What are the values of Wholly Truthful art? *Wholly-Truthful* art overflows the limits of tragedy and shows us, if only by hints and implications, what happened before the tragic story began, what will happen after it is over, what is happening simultaneously elsewhere (and "elsewhere" includes all those parts of the minds and bodies of the protagonists not immediately engaged in the tragic struggle). Tragedy is an isolated eddy on the surface of a vast river that flows majestically, irresistibly, around, beneath, and to either side of it. Wholly Truthful art contrives to imply the existence of the entire river as well as the eddy.... Consequently, Wholly Truthful art

produces in us an effect quite different from that produced by tragedy. Our mood when we have read a Wholly-Truthful book is never one of heroic exultation; it is one of resignation, of acceptance. (Acceptance can also be heroic.) The catharsis of tragedy is violent and apocalyptic; but the milder catharsis of Wholly Truthful literature is more lasting. There is no reason why the two kinds of literature should not exist simultaneously.... The human spirit has need of both ["Tragedy and the Whole Truth"].

Hynes, Samuel

Author of the landmark study *The Auden Generation* (1971) from which the rest of us got started.

"I Am Not a Camera" 1969

This poem affectionately counters Isherwood's opening line "I am a camera," from *Goodbye to Berlin* (1939), and takes its epigraph from Rosenstock-Huessy: "Photographed life is always either trivial or already sterilized."

"I Believe" 1939

Auden contributed this essay to a book of the same title with numerous Britons contributing their beliefs, including a very telling, poignant and subsequently famous essay by E.M Forster, an Auden-Isherwood role model.

Auden's essay is a precursor to *The Prolific and the Devourer*: I) goodness is easier to recognize than define; goodness derives from the happiness of satisfactory vocation. Goodness is 1) natural (equilibrium with environment; "bad environment is the chief cause of badness in individuals") 2) moral (social progress defined by new choices.) II) obstacles to goodness: natural evil (limits to freedom in struggle to survive) and moral evil (limits perpetrated by selfishness); III) history is the way in which life deals with environment/organisms; one either adapts or relocates; only man has continued his evolution after his biological development finished (A Gerald Heard theory). "Freedom is consciousness of necessity" (from Kierkegaard), and it means that man knows what is required and what isn't even if he doesn't always make the best choices. IV) man was divinely "chosen" by his "foetalized" nature (Heard); he is continually reborn and adapts to changing need. V) man thinks about stimuli and makes choices; other life forms only react. VI) man's social — he cannot exist otherwise; he is born neither free nor good. VII) societies/culture vary — just as man varies to fit in. VIII) Societal acculturation through collective subjectivity of the public is man's greatest influence as it works on each individual's need for approval by conformity (or, conversely, he seeks attention by rebellious non-conformity). IX) Marx: social contract is not with the whole but with those who control production; theories of human rights result from social strain; that is, as reactions to oppression. X) class does not determine abilities, only natural gifts determine ability. XI) survival of the (physically) fittest is bogus theory disproved by Heard's theory of foetalization, in which man, while physically weaker, has thrived. XII) industrialization inhibits naturally good life and encourages morally bad one. 1) society is good insofar as: A) there is the widest choice of suitable vocations, B) develops new vocations for new needs. 2) no society can be absolutely good unless it is static — without change at all. 3) societal development depends on how far we think bad influences are due to preventable causes. 4) Society is fairly optimistic about change even in face of great evidence to the contrary. 5) what inhibits man from mere progress can be fixed by providing: A) material needs equitably, the lack of which in the present world is a moral evil, B) equal education, the lack of which is also an inequitable moral evil, C) suitable vocations — "only jobs worthy of respect are being a creative artist, craftsman, scientist, doctor, teacher, farmer: most work is degrading," D) better psychological conditions, which otherwise create dissatisfaction, unhappiness, stagnant lives of repression with only negative outlets; man wants to gain/give approval, but obstacles persist in stagnant society due to lack of community; thus a need for industrial decentralization and a halt to social injustice/inequality to form a just community (Aldous Huxley's *Ends and*

Means, with a plan for such a societal revitalization appeared two years before).

Society is formed from individual wills working in association, but they do not do so equally: 1) some want power; some are indifferent. 2) a minority rules majority with varying consent by that majority. 3) democracy assumes right of revolution by vote, but reality is that class, power, money, and location render power to influence inequitably. 4) legislation is a form of coercion limiting freedom for the many because of acts of the few; laws should be restricted to preventing acts in isolation (murder, etc.), not to impose morality. 5) everyone should have equal right to accept or reject in order to reach a consensus — but societal inequalities prevent this — intolerance is evil. 6) it's up to each of us to redress oppression and reassert freedom.

"I Want the Theatre to Be…" *see The Dance of Death*

"The 'I' Without a Self" *see Kafka, Franz*

Icelandic Literature *see* Old Norse and Old English Literature

"The Icon and the Portrait" 1940

Auden reviewed two cartoon books by James Thurber and William Steig, which he turned into this essay about the contemporary opposition between "iconography and portraiture, the symbolic and the unique, the God and the mortal."

"Impressions of Valencia" 1937

Auden offered only one dispatch from Spain — an article entitled "Impressions of Valencia" — which appeared 30 January 1937. The article was something of a disappointment to its readers, as many were unsettled by its flippant tone and its detailing of trivia, such as the stimulant the war had provided to poster artists. But the piece must be judged to be unequivocally pro–Republican in its insistence that "a revolution is really taking place, not an odd shuffle or two in cabinet appointments," and in its mockery of the right-wing caricature of Spain as a "bloodthirsty and unshaven Anarchy." It also conveys Auden's internalization of the Republican morale at that early stage of the Civil War, in its assertion that "General Franco has already lost two professional armies and is in the process of losing a third" (Cunningham, *Spanish Civil War Verse*).

"Impressions of Valencia" was written within a couple of weeks of Auden's arrival in Spain, and therefore makes no mention of the factors that would later cause him anxiety. There were two such factors, namely Communist culpability in the internecine conflicts on the Spanish left, and the evidence of anti-clericalism on the part of the Republican government. In private correspondence in 1962, Auden wrote, "I did not wish to talk about Spain when I returned because I was upset by many things I saw or heard about. Some of them were described better than I could ever have done by George Orwell in *Homage to Catalonia*. Others were what I learned about the treatment of priests" (letter quoted in Osborne).

This wording implies that political and religious factors contributed equally to Auden's Spanish dilemma. Orwell's civil war memoir was a damning indictment of the Moscow-directed Spanish Communists for their domination of the Republican government, and for their brutal purge of the anarchists and Trotskyists, despite the military value of their front-line units at the opening of the war. In fact, Orwell's account of the Soviet Union's manipulation of the Spanish situation for Stalinist goals was so uncongenial to the British left that the Left Book Club actually turned down *Homage to Catalonia* for publication. There is good reason to believe that Auden and Orwell had reached similar conclusions about the political unviability of the Republican coalition.

Auden writes that man needs "freedom to choose for himself and to organize his life, freedom not to depend for good fortune on a clever or outrageous piece of overcharging or a wind

fall of drunken charity. War is too real to think life should be left to a game of chance." This essay is a prelude to "I Believe."—PETER GROSVENOR

"In Defense of Gossip" 1937

In this essay — another appeal for "selling" poetry to the masses (*see also* "Poets, Poetry, and Taste") — Auden asserts that verse, no differently than fiction or journalism, is at its most appealing when it takes a little gossip and then extrapolates grandly. (*See also* Audience.)

"In Memory of Ernst Toller" *see* Toller, Ernst

"In Memory of Sigmund Freud" *see* Freud, Sigmund

"In Memory of W.B. Yeats" *see* Yeats, W.B.

"In Praise of Limestone" 1948

An ode as per Horace, written during Auden's first summer in Ischia, Italy, it measures his pleasure in the Mediterranean warmth in terms of a bodily inner glow, as he records his limestone surroundings — that remind him of his childhood in England — and the glory of the simple lives of the natives who do not trouble themselves with Emerson's "eternal verities" but just live. For Auden, this bucolic Eden is how man is meant to live as Kierkegaard's Knight of Faith, removed from urban-industrial alienation. This poem is a prelude to "Bucolics." (*See also* "Goodbye to Mezzogiorno"; "The Platonic Blow.")

"In Schrafft's" 1947

This poem is about a middle-aged woman who smiles in a coffee shop as she contemplates how it is "worth kneeling to" a God sometimes.

"In Sickness and in Health" 1940

The poem is dedicated to Maurice and Gwen Mandelbaum who were friends of Auden. Maurice taught philosophy at Swarthmore where Auden also taught. The influence from Kierkegaard and his *Either/Or* as well as Paul Tillich are perhaps the strongest here in Auden's poems; it also takes cues from John Donne's "The Litanie." The title, taken from the marriage vow, is meant as praise for the Mandelbaums, but Auden was also well aware that in the face of Chester Kallman's infidelity, the term could also be a cross to bear — a metaphor intended as regards the poet's very recent re-conversion to Auden's Christianity. The poem considers the death of, and perversion of, love in our time. True love is not easy; it is work and devotion in the face of obstacles; Auden cites Tristan and Isolde as examples. Auden refers to the "phallus and the sword," thus equating sex, politics, and power. If the Vision of Eros arises between two lovers, and it arouses the Vision of Agape for these two, then two by two, group to group, the one and the many, selfishness will fall away.

"In the Cave of Nakedness" *see About the House*

"In the Year of My Youth..." *see Heard, Gerald; Pope, Alexander*

"In Time of War" *see Journey to a War*

Innes, Michael *see* Stewart, J.I.M.

"Insignificant Elephants" 1966

Auden wrote this after reading *The Penguin Dictionary of Saints*, which caused him to eschew his old fantasies about saints as "bosh," and that sanctity came from within, not from without.

Ischia

Ischia is a volcanic island in the Campania region of Southern Italy, in the Tyrrhenian Sea between the Gulf of Gaeta and the Bay of Naples. Known as the Emerald Isle, it is a health resort and a tourist center, celebrated for its warm mineral springs and for its scenery. Ischia, the main town, has an imposing fifteenth century castle, constructed on foundations built by the Greeks in the fifteenth century B.C. Auden spent his summers here from 1948 to 1957 and its landscape, history and bucolic charms meant a great deal to him. In Ischia his "poetry almost immediately found a new more conversational tone of voice and a new theme of civil comforts and obligations" (Mendelson, *Later Auden*).

"Ischia" 1948

This poem was written during Auden's first summer on this Mediterranean isle, and he praises Ischia's restorative powers. He compared the landscape to the Pennines of his English youth. (*See also* "In Praise of Limestone," "Bucolics," and "Goodbye to Mezzogiorno.")

Isherwood, Christopher

1904–1986, British-American author. After his unsuccessful first novel, *All the Conspirators* (1928), Isherwood lived in Berlin for four years and his experiences gave him the material for the novels *Mr. Norris Changes Trains* (1935, American title *The Last of Mr. Norris*) and *Goodbye to Berlin* (1939; reissued together as *The Berlin Stories*, 1946); John Van Druten's play *I Am a Camera* (1951) and the Broadway musical *Cabaret* (1966) were based on these books. The Berlin novels, which describe the Nazis rise to power, depict Isherwood's distress over the idea of an intellectual in a tyrannical society.

The best friend of W.H. Auden, Isherwood collaborated with him on the dramas *The Dog Beneath the Skin* (1935), *The Ascent of F6*

(1936), and *On the Frontier* (1938); (*see* Plays with Isherwood), as well as on *Journey to a War* (1939), a "travel" book on China. In 1938 he also published his autobiography, *Lions and Shadows*, which tells in detail of his friendship with Auden and others. Isherwood immigrated (1939) to the United States, becoming a citizen (1946). During the 1940s his interests turned to Hinduism, or rather Vedanta; see his *My Guru and His Disciple* (1980), and he co-translated with his guru Swami Prabhavananda *The Bhagavad-Gita*, *The Crest Jewel of Discrimination*, and *How to Know God*. Among his later works are *Prater Violet* (1945), *The World in the Evening* (1954), *Down There on a Visit* (1962), *A Single Man* (1964), and Auden's favorite Isherwood novel, *Meeting by the River* (1967), and a study of his parents, *Kathleen and Frank* (1971). Isherwood was an early advocate of declaring one's homosexuality, a subject discussed in his memoir, *Christopher and His Kind* (1976).

The importance of Christopher Isherwood to early Auden and his generation is impossible to overstate. Auden was in the driver's seat, but Isherwood gave directions.

It is curious that before I knew Isherwood and before I had a read a word by him, I had been so convinced by his legend.... Auden seemed to us the highest peak within the range of our humble vision from Oxford; for Auden there was another peak, namely Isherwood ... he was the Critic in whom Auden had absolute trust. If Isherwood disliked a poem, Auden would destroy it without demur. After I saw Isherwood ... he simplified all the problems which entangled me, merely by describing his own life and his own attitudes....— Stephen Spender, *World Within World*

It was part of the romantic mythology in which Stephen [Spender] delighted to cloak his contemporaries, to present himself as a learner at the feet of Auden, the great prophet, but to suggest that behind both of them stood an even greater Socratic prophet, cool in the centre of the stormy drama of remote Berlin: Christopher Isherwood.— John Lehmann, The *Whispering Gallery*

Who is that funny-looking man so squat with a top-heavy head...
A brilliant young novelist?

You don't say — W.H. Auden, written for Isherwood in 1937 [quoted in Finney, *Christopher Isherwood*].

The truth is, we are both only really happy living among lunatics. — Auden to Isherwood 1936

The Angry Young Man of my generation was angry with the Family and its official representatives; he called them hypocrites, he challenged the truth of what they taught. He declared that a Freudian revolution had taken place of which they were trying to remain unaware. He accused them of reactionary dullness, snobbery, complacency, apathy.... — Christopher Isherwood, Introduction, *All the Conspirators* 1957

Spender and Auden always acknowledged their respect for Isherwood as a writer and as an influence. They also considered him the rebellious leader of their iconoclastic trio. Isherwood rebelled against British tradition, and the Auden Generation joined him in their efforts to rescue the British Empire, of which W.H. Auden asked in 1932: "What do you think about England, this country of ours where nobody is well?" (*The Orators*).

Christopher Isherwood became a literary elder brother and symbolic godfather not only to Auden and Spender but also to the Auden Generation who, in emulating Auden, were emulating Isherwood. Their sensitive antiheroes began to represent more realistic dichotomies of the modern conflicted individual who struggles to exist in a hostile world outside and to reconcile this outer threat with the inner, bifurcated self that this threatening outer world engenders in their inner spheres.

When, in 1928, Auden casually told Isherwood that he'd switched from his childhood interest of lead-mining to poetry, Isherwood just as casually asked to see some and "a big envelope full of manuscript arrived, a few days later, by post.... I was touched and flattered to discover, bit by bit, that he [Auden] admired me; looked up to me, indeed, as sort of literary elder brother. My own vanity and inexperience propelled me into this role easily enough" (*Lions and Shadows*). Each spurred the other's imagination. Isherwood said later: "We were always making things up, having fantasy conversations

Christopher Isherwood

to describe the future to each other, telling stories, discussing everything you can imagine,
giving imitations of people, making up paro-
dies of different writers — the way people talk
when they know each other very well" (*Lions
and Shadows*).

As for Isherwood there could only be one
place for him to find redemption from his feeling of being a misfit. This was Berlin, which he
couldn't wait to see after Auden went there first
and reported back to England. The main point
of Auden's report was that in Berlin, one could
find "boys."

In 1938 *Lions and Shadows* looks back and
interprets the neuroses Isherwood did not fully
understand in the 1920s. This was a pattern
and obsession for him, to go back and reexam-
ine his past in order to better understand his
present. In 1938 after a decade of portraying
characters and their symptoms, Isherwood, perhaps in response to the obscurantism that he
and Auden were sometimes accused of, decided
he would share the "secret language" with a
wider audience. Now thirty-four, not twenty-
four, with some success as a writer to fortify his
ego's insecurities, Isherwood was still angry, but

slightly less rebellious and combative. With fascism ever more threatening after the travesty of
the Spanish Civil War, and another, wider war
seemingly inevitable, Isherwood, as did the
other members of his gang, finally had their attention averted from themselves. They had to
face the reality that the fascist oppression of the
British Public School with the hearties and
their paddles antagonizing aesthetes was now
being manifested by "gangs" of fascist armies
with their guns and bombs. In Germany, it was
as if the hearties had achieved the end of their
training and turned into a herd-intoxicated
mass-mob fueled by media-manipulated nationalist propaganda. Compared to this the
tacit school and generational warfare of the
1920s did not become less important, but less
palpably immediate. Isherwood's analysis in
Lions and Shadows is an autobiographical parable comparing the 1920s to the 1930s. In Germany the former schoolchildren of the 1920s
became the Hitler Youth of the 1930s. England
of the 1920s had its own fascist in Sir Oswald
Mosley, and his British Youth were brainwashed
in the Public Schools. The threat of a Mosley
was not to be taken lightly; the highbrows such
as Aldous Huxley, and later Isherwood, were
sounding an alarm. In literature, among others,
Huxley's distant-future *Brave New World*, 1932,
and Storm Jameson's near future *In the Second
Year*, 1936, both about Britain as a fascist state,
were written by two of the 1920s' old guard.
The new guard of the 1930s did the same: there
were Isherwood and Auden's plays, *The Dog Beneath the Skin*, 1935, *The Ascent of F6*, 1937,
and *On the Frontier*, 1938, and also Rex Warner's novel *The Professor*, 1938, which was a
Jameson replay and a brilliant one as her original had been. These works were anti-fascist
parables. For the didactic version of fascists-in-
training, one can turn to *Lions and Shadows* in
which Isherwood describes the atmosphere and
terms that he shared with Auden:

The Watcher in Spanish: As symptoms, Isherwood's compulsive obsessions, fantasies, and
game playing were assertions of autonomy that
Isherwood pursued to counter his feeling of
being otherwise arbitrary and out of control.
Each, in its way, was a secondary world within
which he could pose as the master and feel less
arbitrary by being more controlling. The es-

capism of fantasy is a conceit in that word's sense of being a fanciful whim meant to elevate one's self-esteem. Fantasy is also an attempt, Auden said, "to create a necessary order out of an arbitrary chaos." To seek order is to be followed by trying to maintain it; consequently, while seeking order through fantasy and a secret language, Isherwood and his Cambridge friend Edward Upward sought to guard this order from the temptations or "bribes" of the enemy by setting up an imagined Doppelgänger who symbolized the clan's conscience: "'The Watcher in Spanish' was the latest of our conceits…. He appeared to us in moments when our behavior was particularly insincere; one might be telling a boastful story, or pretending an interest in heraldry, or flattering the wife of a don—and there, suddenly, he would be standing, visible only to ourselves…. His mere presence was a sufficient reminder and warning. Mutely, he reminded us that the 'two sides' continued to exist, that our enemies remained implacable…. he warned us never to betray ourselves by word or deed. He was our familiar, our imaginary mascot, our guardian spirit" (*LS*).

For Isherwood and Upward the "Watcher in Spanish" served as an alter ego that reminded each of the other. (This Watcher would appear as the silent cypher in Auden's early poems.) The silent Watcher affirmed their Anti-Other status against The Others with whom any contact was a dangerous, disloyal flirtation. When Isherwood tried to get Upward to soften his resistance toward the Poshocracy so that they could enjoy the enemy's society together, they had their "first serious quarrel" (*LS*). Upward tested the loyalty of a guilty Isherwood who passed by forsaking society and remaining loyal to the clan of two. This was the first Test in the context of the Truly Strong and Truly Weak Man mythos. Having passed the test, Isherwood thereafter rejected any but the most minimal contact with the poshocracy and solidified his relationship with Upward:

> We were the other's ideal audience; nothing, not the slightest innuendo or the subtlest shade of meaning, was lost between us. A joke which, if I had been speaking five minutes to a stranger, would have taken five minutes to lead up to and elaborate and explain,

could be conveyed to Chalmers by the faintest hint. In fact, there existed between us that semi-telepathic relationship…. Our conversation would have been hardly intelligible to anyone who had happened to overhear it; it was a rigmarole of private slang, deliberate misquotations, bad puns, bits of parody and preparatory school smut:

> "Ashmeade's giving a political tea-party to six puss-dragons from the union."
> "Let's go in and *j'en apelle* it."
> "No good. They'd only namby us off. It'd just be quisb."
> "What are Ashmeade's politics?"
> "He's a lava–Tory" [*LS* 65-6].

This secret code—for example, Upward said "quisb" meant "squirm-making"—was a game that compensated for the rejection they felt from their Auden-Generation Mothers and the society their mothers represented. Isherwood and Upward defended themselves by, in turn, rejecting The Others in what amounted to a face-saving preemptive strike: You're not rejecting us; we're rejecting you and everything about you! This included rejecting The Others' language, which Isherwood and Upward refuted by creating their own language; Auden would do the same in his early verse that Isherwood read and arbitrated on with Auden revising as required. Their new proprietary language renamed things and constructs in the mythopoeic manner of the archetypal Adam who gained dominion over his new and intimidating world by naming what was in it. Metaphorically, each new person—a new Isherwood or new Upward—is a new Adam, one who discovers the world for the first time—over and over again. Isherwood and Upward, as new Adams who were also in a new and intimidating world as represented by Repton and Cambridge, would assert their opposition to the primary world by replacing it with a secondary world created from their secret language. Auden's early poetry was read and arbitrated upon by Isherwood, and Auden would make changes without hesitation. Auden's *The Orators* is directly influenced by the Isherwood-Upward insane stories about the mad—and fictitious—British town of Mortmere. (*See also* The Auden Generation.)

While the Auden-Isherwood collaborations

only took place in the 1930s, Isherwood's influence was to be permanent, and, of course, Isherwood and Auden went to America together. When Isherwood sought spirituality in Eastern Mysticism, Auden did the same with Christian mysticism. The Auden-Isherwood connection influenced Isherwood thirty years later in the play *A Meeting By the River*.

Italian Journey see Goethe, Johann Wolfgang von

Izzo, Carlo

Auden scholar and Auden's Italian translator.

"Jacob and the Angel" 1939

Mendelson calls this review of Walter de la Mare's *Behold, the Dreamer!* a "lurid archetypal parable of the daemon," which Auden wrote after seeing a German film with a German audience in Manhattan; he was appalled at how they cheered the killing of Poles. Mendelson: "The struggle between the worlds of night and day, instinct and reason, [Auden] wrote, was no longer one in which the night world needed to be restored its rights that materialistic rationalism had repressed — which is how he had viewed the matter in his elegy for Freud. We are confronted, he wrote, 'by an ecstatic and morbid abdication of the free-willing and individual before the collective and the daemonic. We have become obscene night-worshippers who, having discovered that we cannot live exactly as we will, deny the possibility of willing anything and are content masochistically *to be lived*, a denial that betrays not only us but our daemon itself'" (*Later Auden*). Auden continued that man in the modern era no longer hid his negative impulses in night and dreams but that these dark aspects were blurring into daytime behavior. The essay was written with the influence of Kierkegaard and Tillich. He wrote this review while he was working on the libretto of *Paul Bunyan*, which

was also a factor in the review's content. (*See also* Toller, Ernst and "In Memory of Ernst Toller" 1939)

Jaffe, Rhoda

1924–1965. Auden met Jaffe in 1944, and in 1946, to the amazement of everyone, began an intimate relationship with her. (She is, in part, Rosetta in *The Age of Anxiety*.) During the mid 1940s Auden questioned his gayness, and, in fact, he sometimes said he believed it was wrong. Auden's Christianity was certainly an impetus for his trying to be straight rather than "crooked" — his term. Jaffe had been a classmate of Chester Kallman's at Brooklyn College. Carpenter: "It is possible that he embarked on the affair because he had now despaired of forming any permanent and satisfactory homosexual relationship, or at least because his relations with Chester were continuing to be difficult — the fact that they had agreed not to have sex together did not prevent Auden being jealous of Chester's love affairs.... Rhoda Jaffe had become, for Auden, something of a substitute for Chester" (*W.H. Auden*). Yet, although he courted Jaffe and was kind to her, by 1947, she ended it, though they remained friends, and he seemed to understand he could not let go of Chester or deny his gayness and the relationship ended as such.

James, Henry

"Without exception ... the characters in Henry James are concerned with moral choices; they may choose evil, but we are left in no doubt about the importance of choosing it."

—Auden, in a lecture on James

1843–1916, American novelist and critic, b. New York City. James was an early exponent of the psychological novel. Stephen Spender would write in *The Destructive Element* that James was the first truly modern novelist. He was the son of Henry James, Sr., a Swedenborgian theologian, and the brother of William James, the philosopher. He went to live in London in 1876 and became a British subject in 1915.

James gave himself to literature, assuming the role of a detached analyst of life. In his early novels, and some of his later work, he contrasts the sophisticated Europeans with upstart Americans. His middle period included *The Bostonians* (1886), *The Princess Casamassima* (1886), and *The Tragic Muse* (1890).

From 1889 to 1895 he tried and failed to succeed as a playwright. He then wrote a series of short novels, including *The Aspern Papers* (1888), *What Maisie Knew* (1897), *The Spoils of Poynton* (1897), *The Turn of the Screw* (1898), and *The Sacred Fount* (1901). His last novels were *The Wings of the Dove* (1902), *The Ambassadors* (1903), and *The Golden Bowl* (1904), in which James depicted psychologically detailed characters in a complex style that Auden would imitate.

James was a favorite of many in the Auden Generation and Auden always said that his prose poem "Caliban to the Audience," his late James imitation from *The Sea and the Mirror*, was his favorite effort in any genre, whether verse, drama, or essay. James makes an important appearance in "New Year Letter" of which Mendelson writes, "Henry James, the American who in Auden's version of literary history first portrayed a world in which all acts that matter are invisible inward ones, begins to rise to the heroic stature he maintained in Auden's thought for the next half decade" (*Later Auden*).

The poem "At the Grave of Henry James" (1941) is another sympathetic parody, as was "Caliban to the Audience," portraying James as a secular saint from whom an artist can learn.

For a new edition of James's essay collection *The American Scene* published in 1946, Auden wrote an introduction in which he notes that Henry James is a writer, not a journalist, which is both his strength and weakness. He is unabashedly subjective. His cantankerous anger is subdued, but not mollified in his acerbic "tourist" writings. Yet, he is not a naturalist as D.H. Lawrence or Marianne Moore, but a "city boy" regarding nature as novelty. He is more comfortable with "things which become persons" whom he addresses as you, while the rough natural environment keeps Americans ever vigilant, thus shaping their character. In America, the absence of a European mind-set of "squire/parson/romanitas" mentality encourages independence. In Europe there is virtue before liberty; in America, liberty before virtue (if not necessarily equality). Rationalizations are required to account for the treatment of blacks and Jews excluded from the country club. The mediocre American is possessed by the present; the mediocre European is possessed by the past. But without mediocrity there'd be no drive to transcend it. Europe vs. America is Rome vs. Monticello. In each case, not all can be saved.

Auden also wrote "Henry James and the Artist in America" a 1948 essay, in which he says that the artist struggles to keep faith with his art in the face of the temptation to be distracted. Those who persevere as Henry James did become examples to the rest with their lives of constant integrity to their work as a guide. By foreigners (Auden as a Briton in America), the work of Americans from 1918 to 1940 is hailed as the best, but it depressingly belies American optimism with a flipside of shady hustlers depicted as heroes (or as anti-heroes), to whom temptation — and succumbing — is natural. The American novelist depicts a lack of will by an act of will — writing. (The artist is the only free being.) "This view should be combatted" by reading James. His characters are concerned with moral choices and readers are clear on the importance of these choices. His characters are human because they choose and are free, which is what captivates readers. Many of his characters are renunciations, which have been confused with passivity — only our age would confuse passion with will, when will can also be exerted quietly. Artists fail because they 1) have no talent, 2) are seduced by allure, 3) or succumb to the devil's subtlest temptation, the desire to do good works through their art. (This was Auden's temptation in the 1930s.) Today too many pseudo-artists seek freedom of choice absent to them elsewhere. James's best work is of group 2, of those who are seduced by the world, a world in which artists, by their calling, must pay a price; moreover, there is art vs. romance/marriage — the honorable choice is not to hurt others by attempting to have art and marriage too, but, as James chose, to be alone.

American business ethos causes a writer to confuse art with profit (Europeans have more of a medieval call of service). James was no exception in his wish for success. Today, group 3 is particularly vulnerable, as "the age of anxiety" requires more of artists in their messianic role to placate the public's idea of the artist as an official magician (or a fraud who in fact deceives them). Today, in the age of alienation, the seekers need new teachers such as a Henry James in order to tear down old beliefs and build up new beliefs to replace them. (*See also* Spender, Sir Stephen)

"James Honeyman" 1937

This poem (to the melody of the song "Stagolee") is a reaction to Auden's visit to the Spanish Civil War and is an absurdist poem on the order of Mortmere and *The Orators*. The speaker is brilliant but blind to the consequences of his own actions. It is a companion to the poems "Miss Gee" and "Victor."

"James Joyce and Richard Wagner" *see* Joyce, James

Jameson, Storm

1891–1986, English novelist and critic, b. Whitby, Yorkshire, graduated from Leeds University in 1912. Margaret Storm Jameson was descended from a shipbuilding family and drew on her knowledge of that business for her first three novels, a family chronicle trilogy reprinted as *The Triumph of Time* (1932). Most of her novels treat ethical and moral problems.

Novelist, feminist, activist, socialist, pacifist, she was particularly well known in the 1930s and was one of the original members of H.R.L. Sheppard's Peace Pledge Union. In her autobiography, Jameson wrote of Auden's attendance at a 1934 meeting of the Writer's Committee of the Anti-War Council. She describes the contrast of Auden with an older, vocal Communist: "I looked [at] the thin tired twisted face of the middle-aged Communist who was there to keep us straight, and W.H. Auden's face, with its extraordinary patina of age [Auden was twenty-seven]. I have never seen so old a young face, it might have been

overhanging a mediaeval cathedral during centuries of frost and sun. He hardly spoke" (*Journey From the North: Autobiography of Storm Jameson*).

"Jehovah Housman and Satan Housman" 1938

In this essay, Auden contemplates the duality of worlds in conflict; one can be happy, but passively incurious (dully insensitive), or sensitive and aware of sadness; the second case desires the first, but not the means to it. A.E. Housman is a classic example of keeping heaven and hell rigidly apart. As Jehovah, he is an aesthete, iconoclastic critic, and virginal don who believes in masters/servants dichotomy, while preferring master role.

As Satan his essence of poetry was the lack of intellectual content that did not accept injustice so lightly. Each Housman had the common ground of death, dead soldiers and dead texts with death the reconciler beyond sex and thought. Can socialism marry Housman's two worlds? Or will it be a Christian world for which neither Housman had much use?

Jesus

Auden's Christianity is based in a good deal of theory and philosophy from Kierkegaard, Tillich, Niebuhr, Heidegger, and others, but Auden's view of Jesus can be summed up from a passage in *The Prolific and the Devourer* that is prefaced by "Thou shalt love thy neighbor as thyself." Auden comments: "Again Jesus based love on the most primitive instinct of all, self-preservation. Those who hate themselves will hate their neighbors or endow them with romantic perfections. The Neo-Romantics like Nietzsche and D.H. Lawrence have misread this text as 'Thou shalt love thy neighbor *more* than thyself,' and based their attack on Christianity upon this misreading…. Jesus never said this, only the churches…. On the contrary, at the last supper, he took eating, the most elementary and solitary act of all, the primary act of self-love, the only thing that … all living creatures must do, irrespective of species, sex, race, or belief— and made it the symbol of universal love." It is in *The Prolific and the Devourer* that Auden gives his fullest account of Jesus and his teachings. (*See also* Christianity.)

Johnson, Wendell

1927–1990, Auden's friend and colleague, b. Kansas City, Missouri. He graduated and then received a Ph.D. from Ohio State University. From 1962 to 1990 he was a professor of English at Hunter College in New York City. His publications include *Sex and Marriage in Victorian Poetry* (1975), and *W.H. Auden* (1990), a recollection. Auden met Johnson in the spring of 1953 when he was a visiting lecturer to Smith College. Johnson donated Auden's letters to him to the Berg Collection of the New York Public Library. The letters contain Auden's literary views in the 1950s, with explications of the meters for his poetry. "Plains" from the "Bucolics" cycle is dedicated to Wendell Johnson, and one of the letters now in the Berg Collection gives insight into the accompanying "Streams."

"Joker in the Pack" 1961

In this essay Auden considers the figure of Iago, who acts while the rest react in a peculiar tragedy unlike the usual Shakespeare tragedy. The hero's fall is neither divine fate nor self-imposed, but 100 percent Iago's doing; Iago gets our "aesthetic" respect for his masterful deceit motivated by pure malice, rather than by any material gain, although villains do enjoy the means to their ends. Iago takes risks and is not strictly jealous, but also insane. He is, superficially, a practical joker, behind which, as often is the case, there is barely latent malice. He is antisocial and even sociopathic.

Auden writes that jokes may be either personal or impersonal. Personal jokes seek to educate or deintoxicate; the initiator enjoys revelatory satisfaction of manipulation of others' weaknesses in order to compensate for his own weaknesses. Without others, the joker (and Iago) are nullities. Othello seeks social acceptance not just as a general who protects the city but

for himself, and he believes Desdemona gives his ego that approval and he is bound to her. Iago plays on this motivation. Desdemona is an immature hero-worshiper who deceived her father in order to marry Othello, which "proves" to Othello she is capable of deceit. Iago experiments on his subjects just to see the results.

Jones, David *see* "Adam as a Welshman"

"Joseph Weinheber" 1965

This poem is about a victim of the Nazis as a reminder that the Nazi mentality still exists.

Journey to a War 1939

From January to July of 1938 Isherwood and Auden went to China to write their collaborative book on the Sino-Japanese war *Journey to a War*. Auden wrote the poems, among his best, Isherwood most of the prose including this self-assessment. "Christopher was in masquerade as a war correspondent. He may have looked the part — correspondents can be a bit absurd — but he must often have betrayed his amateur status by his nervousness. The threat of air raids kept him keyed up, especially when he was on a train. If they were ordered to leave it and take cover, he couldn't restrain himself from hurrying. Wystan never hurried.... Were the two of them ever in serious danger of being killed? Two or three times perhaps" (*Christopher and His Kind*). Isherwood understates his concern. This exposure to real danger lent some reality to his perception of war, one which would further alienate him from the political activism of the preceding years. War was no longer an abstraction to be thought of in slogans and banners:

A pause. Then, far off, the hollow, approaching roar of the bombers, boring their way invisibly through the dark. The dull, punching thud of bombs falling, near the airfield.... The searchlights criss-crossed, plot-

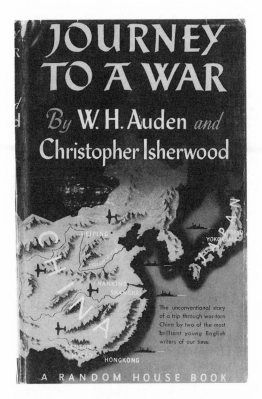

Journey to a War, cover of first edition.

in the opposite bed, Auden slept deeply, with the long, calm snores of the truly strong.

During this period Isherwood was thinking about *Lions and Shadows* where he would define The Truly Weak and Truly Strong Man. *Journey to a War* is dedicated to Isherwood's Truly Strong role model, novelist E. M. Forster.

The air-raid was war at a distance. Isherwood and Auden would get a closer look: "We then went into a Chinese military hospital — actually a square of miserable, windowless huts…. The wounded lay … on straw — three men beneath a single blanket. The orderly told us that they hardly had any dressings or antiseptics, and no proper surgical instruments at all…. In one hut the sweet stench of gas-gangrene from a rotting leg was so violent that I had to step outside to avoid vomiting." Rickshaws transported the wounded and the dead. Later, the war reporters boarded an overnight train for their next destination in China: "I slept uneasily that night — in my trousers and shirt: not wishing to have to leave the train and bolt for cover in my pyjamas. Auden, with his monumental calm, had completely undressed." While on the train a Japanese plane flies over and there is concern for an air attack: "Auden, of course, was certain that nothing would happen. 'I *know* they won't shoot' he kept repeating…." After all was clear: "'You see,' said Auden. 'I told you so … I knew they wouldn't…. Nothing of that sort ever happens to *me*.' 'But it does to *me*,' I objected; 'and if it had this time you'd have been there, too.' 'Ah, but it didn't you see.' 'No, but it might.' 'But it didn't.'" Isherwood concludes: "There is no arguing with the complacency of a mystic. I turned over and went to sleep." The humor relieves the tragic images of the war.

While this *Journey* describes places, faces, and events, Isherwood and Auden the "mystic" were moving away from politics and returning to introspection, which in fact they had never left. The book opens with Auden's sonnet to Forster whose promise — "still the inner life shall pay" — provides the perspective from which both writers proceed to view China at war. Like Forster they insist upon a creed of personal relationships and see China in wartime not as a battleground of political and economic forces,

ting points, like dividers; and suddenly there they were, six of them, flying close together and high up. It was as if a microscope had brought dramatically into focus the bacilli of a fatal disease. They passed, bright, tiny, and deadly, infecting the night. The searchlights followed them right across the sky; guns smashed out; tracer-bullets bounced up towards them, falling hopelessly short, like slow-motion rockets. The concussions made you catch your breath; the watchers around us on the roof exclaimed, softly, breathlessly: "Look! Look! There!" It was as tremendous as Beethoven, but *wrong*— a cosmic offence, an insult to the whole of Nature and the entire earth. I don't know if I was frightened. Something inside me was flapping like a fish. If you looked closely you could see dull red shrapnel-bursts and vicious swarms of red sparks, as the Japanese planes spat back. Over by the aerodrome a great crimson blossom of fire burst from burning hangars. In ten minutes it was all over, and they had gone.

I slept very badly that night, dozing in only five minute snatches until dawn…. Meanwhile, but as a condition of modern man, an image of mankind overtaken once more by the indiscriminately destructive forces of war.

In addition to Auden's opening sonnet in *Journey to a War*, there is his astonishing sonnet sequence "In Time of War," which Mendelson calls: "Auden's most profound and audacious poem of the 1930s, perhaps the greatest English poem of the decade…. The harsh crude textures of its verse, its emotional clarity in the face of disaster, the rigor and inclusiveness of its moral logic, contribute to the poem's extraordinary weight and force…. Each sonnet presents the history of a human type — farmer, poet, scientist — as if it were compressed into a single individual who experiences centuries of change in one lifetime…. Auden's figures are neither villains nor heroes nor larger than life. They are representative men, fallible and complex, as bewildered as everyone is by the outcome of their choices (*Early Auden*).

Auden himself was one of the bewildered men. Yet, his bewilderment is not about confusion that leads to indecision. His bewilderment is more of a mystification at human nature's inexorable consistency. His puzzlement comes not from a misunderstanding of man but from understanding him too well. Hence, his representative figures are timeless; they are of the past, present, and future simultaneously. The puzzle is how little man has changed. The enigma is not about what choices man makes or why he makes them; rather, the puzzle is that man seems to face the same choices and chooses in the same manner — over and over and over. Herein, is the direction of Auden's future art, a direction that would include his return to the Anglican Church. He would augment the Anglican ritual with his own unique blend of Kierkegaardian existentialism and Auden's Mysticism. Life for Auden was now about choice and freedom. The Test was now about how every new Adam and new Eve is faced with choices that are object lessons from which one can choose to turn away from God, and remain Truly Weak, or turn toward God, and aspire to be Truly Strong. Consequently, history is not really about history. The stuff of history is merely put before man in order that he must choose his direction. One chooses consciously or unconsciously. The Bhagavad-Gita

says: "There are some who have actually looked upon the Atman [God], and understood It in all Its wonder. Others can only speak of It as wonderful beyond their understanding."

Auden's photographs in *Journey to a War* comprise a narrative of their own. There are sixty-three of them, the great majority being portraits, most of them head-and-shoulders, almost all of men. Three women are portrayed — a doctor, a beggar, and the photogenic Mme. Chiang. The sequence begins with "United Front," six portraits of leaders including Chiang Kai-shek and Chou En-lai. These people are identified by name, but the rest of the portraits gloss their subjects by rank, function (like missionaries, or doctors) or type, such as "Railway Engineer," "Press Bureau," "Shanghai Businessman"; when names are given it is seemingly as an afterthought, as with "Intellectual (C.C. Yeh)" and even "Special Correspondent."

This pattern continues with the photographs from the "War Zone," which include pictures of the wounded and the dead, allegorized as "The Innocent" and "The Guilty," and even "Train Parasites" (a beggar woman at the carriage window). Even in this most particular and naturalistic of media Auden seems to be drawn towards generalization, allegory and myth. The images are not unmoving but they are subject to an eerie depersonalization. A photograph of cheery children, perhaps refugees, is given Malraux's title *La Condition Humaine*: its subjects are made to stand for something beyond themselves. Towards the end of the sequence (its actual end is a portrait of a young Chinese in uniform, perhaps inevitably entitled "Unknown Soldier"), as if finally surrendering any ambition to render actual particular experience, Auden prints two stills from *Fight to the Last*, a Nationalist propaganda film made at the Hangkow Film Studios. The meaning of propaganda images is public and, if anything, overdetermined. These pictures are at the far end of the epistemological scale from Isherwood's inability to process the story of the officer and the burning book (his inability to "get the picture").

The photographs themselves serve Auden's urge to generalization and the global view. In contrast to Isherwood, not once does Auden speak in the first-person singular in this book.

The generalized vision that enables him to survey from the beginning of evolution to the end of history, and from China to Peru and beyond, also enables and indeed obliges him to see the orient and oriental people as generic, representative, exemplary. For Auden, Chinese experience always stands for something else, as it must as he lifts further and further away from particularity.—DOUGLAS KERR (*See also* Smedley, Agnes; Fleming, Peter.)

"Journey to Iceland" 1936

This poem was written for the "travel" book *Letters from Iceland*, which also has sections penned by Louis MacNeice. While on the trip news reached Auden of the outbreak of the Spanish Civil War and this impacted how and what he wrote about while in Iceland. The traditional "travel" book as light fare was now not an option and an expression of current events, most notably in *Letter to Lord Byron*, that is both history and social study and Auden's study of his own life, became more relevant. This poem begins as a quest epic but is also a rejection of Auden's redeemer fantasies in favor of just wanting to be left alone so that the quest turns into more of a deviating voyage. He is in the land of sagas and epic love that has been inspired by Norse ancestors and his fondness for Old Norse literature; yet, in the wake of the news from Spain, there is now also a feeling that a quest is futile. He refers to sagas but also to the ghosts that haunt the present. He sees an "indigenous figure on horseback" against the backdrop of ancient legends, but realizes that even though he came to Iceland to escape reality and seek fantasy that this place is just as fallible as any other, and that here, his wish for fantasy and escape will go as unfulfilled as anywhere else he has been. (*See* McTurk in Izzo, *W.H. Auden: A Legacy* for a complete explication of this poem including references to Icelandic legend and history.)

Joyce, James

1882–1941, Irish novelist. His novels featured new literary techniques and forms. *Ulysses*,

James Joyce, Ezra Pound, Ford Madox Ford, John Quinn

written between 1914 and 1921, was published in Paris in 1922. Its publication was banned in the United States until 1933. From 1922 to 1939, Joyce worked on *Finnegans Wake* (1939), his most intricate novel.

A Portrait of the Artist as a Young Man is autobiographical, in that it considers the adolescence and youth of Stephen Dedalus, who realizes that to be a true artist he must free himself of the effects of Irish religion, politics, and prejudice. In this it resembles Auden's feelings about England.

For Auden the self-defined voices of Yeats, Pound, and Eliot in poetry were akin to the prose definitions of Joyce, Lawrence, and Woolf. These writers all published new visions between 1920 and 1928, with Joyce's *Ulysses* in 1923. These were the voices Oxford undergraduates were reading and talking about, including Auden. Mendelson in *Early Auden* notes that Auden's early work, poetry and drama sought the "distant ironic perspective" of modern novels, and that Leopold Bloom in *Ulysses* is never let in on the "in" joke that he is Homer Redux. As Joyce bent to his own ends the use of the English language, so did Auden. Auden also wanted to be "epiphanic" with the reader having a personal, parable-induced revelation based on similar circular inferences as in Joyce where one always returns to some central idea, however circuitous the path, or as Mendelson also notes of modernism, "Poetic language had now grown so centripetal that it could swallow up even the encyclopedic language of nineteenth-century realism. In Joyce the fictional patterns in *Ulysses* and the linguistic relations in *Finnegan's Wake* take control over virtually all the data of experience, and subject them impartially to the ordered rigors of mythographic structure" (*Early Auden*). Of the latter Joyce mentions Auden in a footnote. Auden and Isherwood also created a "mythography" out of their experiences in the British Public School system in their earliest efforts, Auden's *Paid on Both Sides* and Isherwood's "Gems of Belgian Architecture." Myth remained an aspect of their work with Auden in the 1940s adapting the foremost systematic myth-explainer, Jung. Joyce's myths chose to shock and get the attention that would then allow him to make a point. Auden wrote that Joyce, in his manner, revealed "to each of us those layers of his soul which are susceptible to the ambiguous and hypnotic Hitlerian cry"; that is, one will learn through Joyce how much of an idiot he is capable of being ("James Joyce and Richard Wagner," *Common Sense*, March 1941). Auden didn't buy into Joyce completely but gave him credit for provoking him, which, he believed, made Joyce a success as a writer. As for *Finnegan's Wake*, Auden had enough respect for it to imitate it somewhat for Rosetta's last speech in *The Age of Anxiety*. Later, his outlines for "Horae Canonicae" look like the chart of correspondence in *Ulysses*. Auden perhaps planned for more extensive Joycean hidden patterns than he ultimately ended up with. Later, when Auden became less enchanted with intellectual puzzles and more with direct simplicity, Joyce fell out of favor as a writer because he was more interested in displaying his ego than in dealing with readers as persons who need to be understood. Auden was thus refuting his own earlier cleverness, no matter how much good he thought he had intended. "New Year Letter," perhaps, with its copious notes in order to explain it, might have seemed a bit much to the elder statesman Auden who, from about 1960 saw Goethe, not an Eliot or any other modernist, as his model for emulation. Nonetheless, Joyce (and others) allowed Auden to tear down old belief in order to build up new belief even if it turned out that this was a return to some of those old beliefs now seen from a new perspective.

Jung, Carl Gustav

1875–1961, Swiss psychiatrist, founder of analytical psychology. He worked with Sigmund Freud for a number of years but came to disagree with the Freud's ideas about sexual trauma. Jung posited two modes of the unconscious—the personal and the archetypes of a collective unconscious. (*See also* Heard, Gerald.) For Jung, a person's fulfillment comes through the harmony of conscious and unconscious, which makes a person whole.

Jung had a profound influence on Auden after Auden's arrival in America. Auden had read Jung—and Freud, and Heard—in the mid 1920s and imagined himself a lay psychoanalyst according to recollections of Isherwood, Spender, and Day Lewis, but Jung's hold was greater, later. Jung became a strong influence on Auden from 1939 to 1949 beginning with his *The Prolific and the Devourer* (1939). While the title comes from William Blake, and the impetus from Blake's *The Marriage of Heaven and Hell*, the fruition of the work resulted when Auden saw Blake's archetypes in Jung's archetypes of the introvert and extrovert (Jung's *Psychological Types*, 1923). For the next ten years Auden put Jung's archetypes into his work. Mendelson: "Jung's mythicizing optimism and his conviction that impersonal archetypes shape personal identities encouraged Auden to retain Marxist determinism without Marxist anger. For the next few years, he peopled his poetic landscape with Jungian figures like the anima and animus, and incorporated phrases from Jung's latest writings into his verse" (*Later Auden*). Jung will "appear" in "September 1 1939"; in a review of Walter de la Mare's *Behold the Dreamer*, in which, as Auden often did, the review became the excuse to write about something else; *Paul Bunyan*, the ultimate American archetype; "New Year Letter" with Elizabeth Mayer as Jung's *solificatio* (an illumination of the unconscious by the anima). Auden would refer to himself as Jung's "thinking-intuitive type" (like Henry James and Paul Valéry), who needed a great deal of information before he could feel anything. *The Age of Anxiety* features Jung's four archetypal faculties: Intuition, Thought, Feeling, and Sensation with a character representing each. By 1948, however—and coinciding with his first summer in Ischia — Auden did not give up on Jung but began to personalize human beings within the archetypes until they were people and not archetypes. Now he saw in threes, not fours; that is, Jung's four gave way to St. Augustine's three, or trinity. As Auden often did, he evolved out of one and into the other.

"The Justice of Dame Kind" 1962

Auden's review of *The Sense of Animals and Men*, by Loris and Margery Milne. (*See also* Dame Kind.)

Kafka, Franz

1883–1924, German language novelist, b. Prague. Kafka is one of the most influential writers of the twentieth century. Most of his works were published after his death. His novels include *The Trial* (1925), *The Castle* (1926, 1998), and *Amerika* (1927). Kafka's work is both real and surreal, and his characters feel guilt, isolation, anxiety, and futility. Auden considered Kafka a healer and truthteller. Kafka's hallucinatory allegories seemed to forecast ahead of their time the effects of an alienated Kierkegaardian public manipulated by totalitarian governments and mass media propaganda. Auden would write an essay about Kafka in 1960.

In the 1960 essay "The 'I' Without a Self," Auden says *Kafka* was a master of parable with faceless characters that we, as readers, become and, in effect, we become "Kafka-esque," the term itself a tribute to a unique vision. Kafka turns the heroic quest upside down. For Kafka, the hero's goal is his own, not a shared one. He knows he will not succeed but is compelled to the denouement without any reward other than knowing the answer that eludes him. The quest is heavy, not heroic or entertaining. For Kafka writing was a form of prayer and nothing was real until his notebook was closed for the day or night.

"Kairos and Logos" 1941

In many of the poems written during 1940, Auden is coming back gradually to Auden's Christianity, but the poems are not explicit in crediting his re-conversion to a specific denomination. Kierkegaard's existential and rebellious Christianity is a factor in the 1940 poems although he is not specifically named. (He does, however, appear in Auden's copious notes to "New Year Letter.") In 1941, Auden moves closer to the church, and some of his poems begin to assert his beliefs more directly. *Kairos* (the right moment for the subjective individual) and *Logos* (a timelessly objective law and logic) must conjoin when the seeker feels that the propitious instant of his sensitive understanding matches with the clarity to know what needs to be understood. At this time Auden was reading Paul Tillich on the concept of Kairos and Logos.

The poem is in four long stanzas. 1) The Romans were obsessed with death and, consequently, with time, as that which will run out; hence, this self-absorption became self-love. They did not have the mystics' view of time as an eternal now. Christ was predestined to love outside of time exemplifying a love with no beginning or end, and he is the vision of agape both as man and spirit. 2) The vision of agape has existed always as has its dwelling place, Auden's metaphorical Eden, into which all are born as innocents — new Adams and Eves who will relive the incarnation and the choices that, after Christ, all must make. Over time the children of God began to take their secret garden for granted and choose badly, but all will still be forgiven.

"One must be passive to receive the truth." One must renounce the assertive ego and with egoless discrimination choose knowledge. One must also be wary of the shadow cast by language upon truth, as language can be either teacher or deceiver depending on its user. One must recognize that even while missing the father (Christ) one must know him as the face of truth.

We are lost but can still be found if we heed the omnipresent signposts; but we will see them only when we have removed the blinders of old knowledge and have reconstituted that old knowledge with a vision of new knowledge won by renunciation of the ego. One must tear down old belief to build up new belief. (*See also* Language; The Public and Propaganda.)

Kallman, Chester

1921–1975. Auden met Kallman in America in 1939 — and initially referred to him in terms in which Dante gushed about Beatrice — and they became lovers briefly, and loving companions until Auden's death in 1973. Auden had hoped for a happy marriage and even wore a wedding ring after they first met and for their honeymoon — Auden's word — in Taos, New Mexico. Kallman was incessantly roving after "rough trade" sex, and from 1963 they lived for six months on and six months off a year in New York, and Kirschstetten. Kallman's "off" periods were spent with lovers, much to Auden's dismay. Indeed, when Auden learned early on of Kallman's infidelities, he sought a re-conversion to Christianity, in part, as balm to his anger.

Carpenter: "When the blow of Chester's unfaithfulness fell on him in July 1941, Auden had tried to understand how such a thing could be consonant with the will of a loving God. Gradually during the following months he came to think of what had happened to him almost as a trial that God had imposed" (*W.H. Auden*). From 1947 all of Auden's libretti were written with Kallman who himself published poetry but not with great success. (Kallman, indeed, introduced Auden to opera and was, in this case, teacher and mentor.)

This relationship was a puzzle to many of Auden's friends who didn't understand his complete devotion and financial support of Kallman who was very willing to allow Auden to have his Christian charity with himself as object. Many of Auden's friends would try to see Auden without Kallman. Cyril Connolly considered Kallman a parasite. Still, Auden may not have as deeply returned to Christianity, which produced a new philosophy and poetry, without having Kallman to give him such a strong reason. By many accounts Kallman was a charming raconteur, and Don Bachardy, Isherwood's companion, recalled that he was "very entertaining." Yet, he did not please everyone. Auden would attribute this to anti–Semitism, but this was unlikely and more the case that Auden's friends like Stephen Spender, himself a quarter Jewish, saw Kallman as a very negative factor in Auden's life. It is well documented that as Auden got older, he was terribly lonely for the half a year he would spend without Kallman. Indeed, his resentment began to surface in his prose.

Most telling is his 1964 introduction to Shakespeare's Sonnets when he describes the mysterious "W.H." to whom the poems were addressed. To those who knew Auden it was no mystery that he was describing Kallman: "The story of the sonnets seems to me to be the story of an agonized struggle by Shakespeare to preserve the glory of the vision he had been granted in a relationship ... with a person who seemed intent by his actions upon covering the vision with dirt.... The impression we get of his friend is one of a young man who was not really very nice, very conscious of his good looks, able to switch on the charm at any moment, but essentially frivolous, cold-hearted, and self-centered, aware, probably, that he had some power over Shakespeare — if he thought about it all, no doubt he gave a cynical explanation — but with no conception of the intensity of feelings he had, unwittingly, aroused.... Did Shakespeare later feel that the anguish at the end was not too great a price to pay for the glory of the initial vision? I hope so and believe so. Anyway poets are tough and profit from the most dreadful experiences."

In 1972 Auden reviewed Kallman's volume of verse, *A Sense of Occasion*, very favorably, which may have done it more harm than good among other critics and writers, as it seemed another biased indulgence by Auden for Kallman.

Auden's Christianity, while very complex and with its own theoretical basis adapted from many sources, was really about convincing himself that he was being a good Christian for putting up with Kallman. His poem "The More Loving One" makes this very clear. (*See also* Jaffe, Rhoda.)

Kassner, Rudolph

Friend of Rainer Rilke and author of *Rilke Zahl und Gesicht* (1919), which influenced Auden in the 1950s as it expressed the duality of personality and impersonality. Auden's poem "The Chimeras" (1950) is about people who have been absorbed into Kierkegaard's anonymous public. Auden quoted from Kassner's *Die Geburt Christi* in *The Dyer's Hand* on the idea that the Christian word was made flesh and that poetry was not needed because the word was now self-sufficient. This idea echoes in all the mystical aspects of religion, as to feel God in the body is an ineffable sensation beyond the possibility of words to describe. All forms of art are attempts to find this feeling indirectly.

Keats, John

1795–1821, English poet, b. London. One of the romantic poets. His first volume of poems appeared in 1817. *Endymion,* a long poem, was published in 1818. The publication of *Lamia, Isabella, The Eve of St. Agnes, and Other Poems* (1820) contains most of his important work. In spite of his brief career, Keats is one of the most important English poets. He was also personally appealing, capable not only of passionate love but also of warm, steadfast friendship. His poetry has an inspiring sense of beauty and joy. Keats's prose philosophy involves not abstract thought but rather absolute receptivity to experience, as indicated by his term "negative capability" — to let the mind be a passageway for all thought.

Auden was never a fan of the Romantic era, which he noted for an excess of personal egoistic emotion. He particularly disliked Shelley. He did like Blake and Byron, but for what he considered their anti–Romantic stances even though they are categorized as Romantics. As for Keats, Auden was not enamored of the poetry, although he believed that Keats had died so young that he would have grown into poetic maturity had he lived. He was more in favor of Keats the person and admired his letters. Since Keats was a major catalyst for the dialectic question of what constitutes truth/beauty, beauty/truth in art ("The Grecian Urn"), which was an Auden preoccupation, Auden gave Keats his due on that count.

Keynes, John Maynard

1883–1946, English economist and monetary expert. His *Economic Consequences of the Peace* (1919) presented his views and won him fame. Keynes criticized the Versailles Treaty for its vindictiveness; specifically the impossibly high reparations levied on the Germans. He foresaw that German economic weakness stemming from the Versailles provisions would involve the whole of Europe in ruin. Keynes's departure from classical concepts of laissez-faire dated from the mid 1920s, when he formulated the Liberal Party's program to promote employment by a program of government spending on public works. Keynes came to believe that such a program would increase national purchasing power as well as foster employment in complementary industries.

The direct connection between Auden and Keynes is that Keynes backed the Group Theatre's production of the Auden-Isherwood play *On the Frontier* in 1938. Keynes had founded the Arts Theatre at Cambridge in 1936, an interest developed from his wife's work as an actress and dancer (Lydia Lopokova.) He more or less funded the enterprise and made up for losses. In 1937 he had seen Auden-Isherwood's play *The Ascent of F6* and admired it, and when Auden sent Keynes the manuscript for *On the Frontier,* he agreed to participate. A second connection between the two can be inferred: in Keynes' economic policies he supported that efforts be made to benefit the working class as being for the good of the whole nation, and no doubt Auden agreed. On a more personal level, Keynes observed that Auden's compulsive nail biting signified something amiss or incomplete in the poet's nature.

Kierkegaard, Søren

1813–55, Danish philosopher and religious thinker. He may be the most important influence on Auden's Christianity. "Life can only be understood backwards; but must be lived forwards." Kierkegaard's aphorism is a remark that Aldous Huxley and Auden quoted — in each case more than once — to illuminate succinctly that knowledge only matters in so far as what a man/maker/artist/poet does with what he learns.

Kierkegaard's intensive inner examination of self and society resulted in many philosophical writings with the theme that "truth" is subjective. Kierkegaard argued that in religion the important thing is not truth as objective fact but rather the individual's relationship to that truth. It is not enough to believe the Christian doctrine; one must also live it. He attacks the metaphysics of Hegel, and the bourgeois complacency of the Danish church. His writings fall into two categories — the aesthetic and the religious. The aesthetic works, which include *Either/Or* (1843), *Philosophical Fragments* (1844), *Stages on Life's Way* (1845), and *The Concluding Unscientific Postscript* (1846), interpret human existence through the eyes of poetically delineated characters. In those works Kierkegaard developed an "existential dialectic" in opposition to the Hegelian dialectic, and described the various stages of existence as the *aesthetic, the ethical, and the religious*. As the individual advances through these stages he becomes increasingly more aware of his relationship to God. This awareness leads to despair as the individual realizes the antithesis between temporal existence and eternal truth. The specifically religious writings include *Works of Love* (1847) and *Training in Christianity* (1850). Kierkegaard also kept an extensive journal that contains many of his deepest insights. He later exerted a tremendous influence upon both contemporary Protestant theology and the philosophic movement known as existentialism. Auden became one of Kierkegaard's foremost exponents beginning in 1940, and in 1952 Auden selected and introduced *The Living Thoughts of Kierkegaard*. (*See also* Christianity.)

Auden was the editor of the 1952 book *Living Thoughts of Kierkegaard*. In his introduction to that work, Auden says that Kierkegaard was an existential preacher of Christian doctrine to *2* groups: inside pulpit and outside of it. Kierkegaard was in a situation of unique tribulation. Isolated and severe, he resembles Pascal. A sufferer can be tempted by demonic (egoistic) defiance (Captain Ahab) or demonic despair (guilt), or asceticism (suffering by design, thinking it will gain one entry to heaven).

Kierkegaard is a polemicist who 1) informs/warns Bourgeois Protestants; 2) warns himself to beware of his own suffering. His existentialism is based on these presuppositions: 1) the existence of terms relating to a timeless and universal ground of knowledge and being

(*see* Minimum Working Hypothesis). 2) the subjective "I exist" is unique within each individual. 3) this "I exist" is private/ incommunicable. 4) but this "I exist" can be merged into a collective consciousness if the "I" removes from its subjective existence all objective consciousness of materiality: A) existence is not self-derived "I can speak of MY feelings, not of my existence. B) freedom of choice can only be subjective. C) one must learn the awareness of being *with* time as in the *eternal now* rather than *in* time as artificial construct. D) anxiety, dread, pride are due to (Christian) wish to be God, which is unknowable objectively.

Kierkegaard's categories of how man lives: 1) *Aesthetic* religion (magnified passions) Greek gods (hero/ king). At best man can only attract or repel gods; gods deal only with the exceptional (heroic) men to whom gods have already decided to have good or bad fortune sent. All art is ritual to attract or repel gods; tragic drama signifies *A)* man's lack of control over his fate (attracting death/weakness); and *B)* power and goodness are not identical. 2) *Ethical* Religion (god of Greek philosophy), God as idea/first cause, a universal with whom man coexists (as priest/seer) beyond finite passions (time). Instead of Aesthetic strength or weakness, ethical hero has knowledge of ignorance, but does not know if virtue can be taught to the ignorant. Will the priest/seer have to fall back on the good will of an Aesthetic hero/king to enforce virtue? 3) *Revealed Religion* (Judeo-Christian). Here god is neither arbitrary (aesthetic) nor objectively willed (ethical) but a revelation (subjective) perceived as God the father. Man's relationship to God is a not a presupposition but a means of communication/relating. Ethical man can *choose* to know or not know, but revealed man *always* knows and even when veiled by ignorance, the truth exhibits itself as guilt or despair (sin). Man can choose knowledge or remain ignorant; moral law defines his choices. Knowledge is upward transcendence toward God; ignorance is downward transcendence away from God.

Christ the Offense: Christ's trial offered Holy Spirit to man as means to accept truth and be forgiven. God/Christ is related to all men/women but gives to each a unique existence capable of choice. Life is neither *Aesthetic* admiration nor *Ethical* appropriation (of truth) but a WAY to be followed with an inclination of the heart. A Christian preaching to a non-believer proposes, 1) that Jesus existed, 2) that to disbelieve in Christ is to despair. This despair sets up the non-believer to be asked why aesthetic paganism (i.e., nationalism) or ethical philosophy (i.e. Academia) don't work. Preaching to believers, one must overcome dogmatic restraints of Christianity as taught collectively rather than revealed individually.

Auden's second essay on Kierkegaard, the 1968 work "A Knight of Doleful Countenance" (title from *Don Quixote*, another Knight of Faith), still has praise for Kierkegaard the philosopher, but Auden also recognizes that the man of the journals had foibles and contradictions, which, in effect, were okay because this meant he was as human as Auden was with his own foibles. Kierkegaard's childhood (father) rendered him severely, but unrealistically, anti-clerical — all are corrupted by church influence (and society's) — he will not recognize that there are good men. His moderate counterpart is Sidney Smith.

Kipling, Rudyard

1865–1936, English author, b. Bombay, India. Kipling was educated in England, then returned to India in 1882 and worked as an editor at a Lahore paper. His early poems were collected in *Departmental Ditties* (1886), *Barrack-Room Ballads* (1892), and other volumes. His first short stories about Anglo-Indian life appeared in *Plain Tales from the Hills* (1888) and *Soldiers Three* (1888). In 1889 he returned to London, where his novel *The Light That Failed* (1890) was published. His idealization of imperialism and characterization of the true Englishman as courageous, conscientious, and self-reliant made him famous (but not with the post World War intellectuals and artists of the 1920s and 1930s including early Auden). In 1892, Kipling married Caroline Balestier, an American, in London. They lived in Vermont for four years, where he wrote *The Jungle Book* (1894), *Second Jungle Book* (1895), *Kim* (1901), *Just So Stories* (1902), and *Captains Courageous* (1897). He returning to England in 1900 and he lived in Sussex, the setting of *Puck of Pook's Hill* (1906).

Other works include *Stalky and Co.* (1899) and his famous poem "If" (1910). He was England's first Nobel Prize winner in literature (1907).

To Auden's generation of the 1930s, tradition accounted for all that was wrong in the world, especially the British world, and Kipling was the chief symbol of that tradition as he glorified the British way of life, including the twin evils of a rabid and rampant nationalism and imperialism. Even as late as 1962 Auden would say, "There are some poets, Kipling, for example, whose relation to language reminds one of a drill sergeant" ("Writing," *The Dyer's Hand*).

In a 1943 review of an Eliot selection of Kipling's verse, Auden, as was his way, used the review to give his views on the nature of poetry as magic. In so doing he takes a smack at Kipling as well: "In so far as he is an artist, no one, not even Kipling, is intentionally a magician" ("The Poet of the Encirclement"). But Kipling *is* a propagandist, although Auden tries to make it seem as if Kipling was so unintentionally. Indeed, Auden may have believed that Kipling was well intentioned but misguided. Kipling makes two appearances in the Auden-Kronenberger *Viking Book of Aphorisms*.

Kirchstetten

Kirchstetten is embedded in the foothills of the Austrian Alps; yet, still only an hour from Vienna. There in 1958 Auden purchased his first and only house and this home is now an Auden Museum. Auden also chose to be buried here. In Kirchstetten Auden enjoyed the cozy security of home and hearth, and his art, while on one hand becoming more avuncular, also, as if in contrast to his snugness, "explored the bleakly modern religion ... that affirmed Christian belief in a world where no divine authority held back the violence and evil inflicted by the nazis — whose strongest supporters, Auden observed, had been Among Auden's Austrian neighbors" (Mendelson, *Later Auden*). (See also *About the House*.)

Kirstein, Lincoln

1907–96, American dance and theater executive and writer, b. Rochester, N.Y. Before

Kirstein became a dance maven, he was co-editor of the influential American literary magazine *The Hound and Horn* (1927–1934). A prominent contributor was Stephen Spender (see his letters in *The Hound and Horn Letters*, ed. Hamovitch). In June 1934, Spender, a champion of Henry James, wrote for a Henry James issue, which played a major role in a revival of James's reputation and work. (Among fellow contributors were Marianne Moore, Edmund Wilson, and Glenway Wescott.) Through Spender, Kirstein would also come to know Auden and Isherwood, particularly after Auden's arrival in America, as he and Wescott, a friend of Kirstein's, were among the first to greet them. Auden also befriended Kirstein's sister Mina Curtiss. Kirstein was cofounder of the American Ballet and the School of the American Ballet in 1934 and of Ballet Caravan in 1936. He is best known for helping to establish the New York City Ballet, and was its general director from 1948 to 1989. With choreographer George Balanchine he encouraged an American style of dance. He wrote many books on dance, as well as essays, a novel (1932), two books of poetry (1965, 1987), and works on modern figurative artists, including Elie Nadelman (1973) and Pavel Tchelitchew (1947, 1994). In the U.S. army during and after World War II (when Auden also served and met Kirstein in Europe), Kirstein was instrumental in recovering for their owners works of art plundered by Nazi officials. In 1961 Kirstein introduced Auden to Dag Hammarskjöld. As a producer he worked with the Shakespeare Memorial Theater at Stratford, Conn., and for many years presented the twelfth century musical drama *The Play of Daniel* (with narrative by Auden) annually at Christmas in New York. In 1964 Auden's essay "Private Poet" was a review of Kirstein's *Rhymes of a Pfc*.

"The Kitchen of Life" 1963

Auden's introduction to M.F.K. Fisher's *The Art of Eating*.

"A Knight of Doleful Countenance" *see* Kierkegaard, Søren

The Knights of the Round Table see Cocteau, Jean

Koestler, Arthur

1905–83, English writer, b. Budapest. Koestler spent his early years in Vienna and Palestine. A Communist journalist in Berlin in the early 1930s, Koestler coined the phrase "We must organize the intellectuals" for the Spanish Civil War, and was subsequently captured by Franco's forces during that war; *Spanish Testament* (1937) relates his experiences. Released in 1937, he edited an anti–Nazi and anti–Soviet French weekly and served in the French Foreign Legion (1939–40). After the German invasion he was interned in a concentration camp, but escaped from France in 1940 and lived thereafter in England. Koestler broke with Communism as a result of the Soviet purge trials of the late 1930s. *Darkness at Noon* (1941), a novel, describes the execution of an old Bolshevik for "deviationist belief in the individual." Other accounts of the evil of Stalinism include *The Yogi and the Commissar* (1945), and an essay in *The God That Failed* (ed. by R.H. Crossman, 1951) that also included one by Stephen Spender. Greatly concerned in later life with euthanasia and the right to die, Koestler and his wife committed a joint suicide in 1983.

Auden met Koestler in Spain on 25 January 1937 and spent the evening with him in the Hotel Victoria drinking. Koestler recalled that they were with a rather cosmopolitan crowd, and that he only met Auden one more time twelve years later and that Auden remembered the evening as oppressive. Koestler was a great friend of George Orwell who would have strong words for Auden's poem "Spain" that Auden took very seriously.

Köhler, Wolfgang

1887–1967, American psychologist, b. Estonia. Köhler earned his Ph.D. from the University of Berlin in 1909. He came to the United States in 1934, and became professor of psychology at Swarthmore College. Köhler is best known for his experiments in problem-solving in apes and the significant influence his writings had on the founding of Gestalt psychology. His writings include *Gestalt Psychology* (1930, rev. ed. 1947) and *The Mentality of Apes* (1925, rev. ed. 1948). Isherwood and Edward Upward read Kohler's *The Mentality of Apes* in the late 1920s and told Auden about it. Auden also learned about this book from Gerald Heard, who used Kohler's work to formulate his own theories, which were very influential to Auden. In *The Orators* (the 1932 first edition) Auden lifts diagrams from Kohler's *Gestalt Psychology*. Kohler became friendly with Auden in the 1940s after both taught at Swarthmore.

Kronenberger, Louis

1904–1980, American writer and critic. Kronenberger and Auden co-edited *The Viking Book of Aphorisms* (1962).

"Lady Weeping at the Crossroads" 1940

This poem feigns sweetness but intimates massive tragedy indicative of the year it was written. The approach is similar to that of another 1940 poem without title with the first line "Eyes Look into the Well."

Lagerkvist, Pär

1891–1974, Swedish poet, dramatist, and novelist. His central concern is the human soul, his main theme the problem of good and evil. He received the 1951 Nobel Prize in Literature. In Auden's last year, 1973, he and Leif Sjöberg translated a book of Lagerkvist's poems.

Lane, Homer

1875–1925, American psychologist, juvenile reformer and healer. In England he started the innovative Little Commonwealth School for juvenile delinquents who were given love, work, and responsibility. He believed that man sought perfection and only needed proper guid-

ance to find it. He thought thwarted desires would remain a drag on consciousness, and only when they were fulfilled would these desires grow out of themselves and end, allowing spiritual advancement. (*See also* Berlin.)

Language

For Auden as well as for Aldous Huxley, who predicted a *Brave New World,* language is the symbolic representation of all man's previous and current knowledge of what he has come to comprehend about himself and his universe. Man learns by evaluating the past and applying his understanding of it to the present and future. It is language, as the principal medium of communication, that makes this possible. The genesis of language is that it perpetually derives itself from the very same necessity that is the mother of invention. Language constantly invents and reinvents itself because human beings need to explain themselves and their experiences. Initially, primitive man created language as a process that was predicated on cause and effect: Something would happen while he was out hunting (the cause) and he would need to describe the effect of it. These initial attempts to create language in order to react to external stimuli started a domino effect of more cause and effect which is still going on in a continuum of perpetual experiencing, interpreting, integrating, translating, recording, and reinterpreting.

Language is the sum total of man's past experiences brought forward to the present, or as Kierkegaard, who was read by both Auden and Huxley, said: "Life is understood backward but must be lived forwards." The words that comprise language have no meanings in and of themselves until a listener/reader correlates them with his or her own unique experiences as they are stored in memory. The mind then processes these words, which are symbols that were originally created to selectively activate stored memories, and puts them into a coherent context. When words are independent of a context, they signify much less than they do put into one. Each individual person's present context as represented by language is the result of what all his progenitors and contemporaries have learned, assimilated, and reflected upon throughout history from the cave man to Einstein. No single person knows all of this knowledge, but people in their multiplicity do. Huxley and Auden should be paired as essayists for it is in their essays that they reveal remarkably similar views about the greater world in general and language in particular.

In order to explain and understand all the potential for good that language can promulgate, one also learns that language has an equal potential for spreading notions that are not so good. Language, to this point, has herein been given credit for the history and evolution of man's knowledge, as without it there would be no history or evolution. Conversely, language must also accept culpability for man's failures. For in addition to the achievements of language in its role as the infinitely malleable medium which allows man to record, teach, and entertain, it is also the infinitely malleable means for the individual ego or collective egos to assert self-serving ends. Language can become a source for misdirection when those who wish to achieve certain personal goals manipulate it. Some of these goals are positive: to record, teach, entertain; some may not be, ranging from goals that might be considered benignly neutral, such as advertising, to goals that can become malignantly activist such as those motivated by individual anger, or the greed of con artists, or the group or state which resorts to propaganda.

It is Huxley and Auden's intent to explain the psychological implications of language and what this means to people as individuals, and more so, *The People* as an amorphous mass toward whom the potent tool of mass media — print, radio, later TV — is directed. This mass, as created by mass media, becomes that anonymous pseudo-person, The Public—which the media can appeal to and arouse with advertising and propaganda, while it and its faceless constituents are absolved of any responsibility for the results. It is also their intent to trace the archetypal poet/artist from his first appearance as ritual historian, storyteller, bard, and initial mythmaker for the tribe/group, to his/her present role as accomplished modern wordsmith.

For Huxley and Auden, the goal is to explain how, through poetry, both the poet and his readers might ask themselves the two paramount questions of individual existence: Who am I? Whom ought I to become? (*See also* Heard, Gerald; Huxley, Aldous; Audience; Writing, Auden on; "Writing.")

Larchfield Academy

Here in 1930 Auden began his first full-time teaching position, replacing C. Day Lewis.

"Last Will and Testament" 1936

This poem, in *Letters from Iceland,* is a collaboration between Auden and Louis MacNeice, which is a satirical Will that names numerous ideas, places, and people that both knew, for tongue-in-cheek inheritances. For example, Auden names Upward and Isherwood his executors to judge his work "good or bad." Among others named are family members, politicians, the scientist Wittgenstein, I.A. Richards, Julian Huxley (Aldous Huxley's brother, the scientist), "an ant, a bee ... and Aldous," Bertrand Russell, H.G. Wells, Rupert Doone and the Group Theatre, poet Hugh McDiarmid, Maurice Bowra, writers Compton Mackenzie and Roy Campbell, Naomi Mitchison, Edith Sitwell, Sir Oswald Mosley (not with praise), James Barrie, George Bernard Shaw, mystic Evelyn Underwood, Stephen Spender, Cecil Day Lewis, William and Nancy Coldstream, John Grierson, Benjamin Britten, Herbert Read, Peter Fleming, Wyndham Lewis, filmmakers Alexander Korda and the "Balcon Boys" (many years later one of the "boys'" daughters, Jill, would marry Day Lewis and produce son Daniel, the actor), Alfred Hitchcock, Berthold Viertel, future spy Anthony Blunt, Mr. and Mrs. E.R. and A.E. Dodds, Robert Medley, Ruthven Todd, John Betjeman, John Andrews, E.M. Forster, Noel Coward, Dylan Thomas, John Maynard Keynes, Brian Howard, Nevill Coghill, Geoffrey Grigson, William Empson, Gerald Heard, Geoffrey Hoyland, John Layard, Robert Graves and Laura Riding, Richard Crossman, Gabriel Carritt, Rex Warner, Leonard and Virginia Woolf, Michael Roberts, and Erika Mann.

"Lauds" *see* *Horae Canonicae*

"Law Like Love" 1939

This poem was written shortly after Auden met Chester Kallman. Both law and love are in the eye of the beholder; if law is arbitrary, how can love be any less so?

Lawrence, D.H.

1885–1930, English author, a primary shaper of twentieth century fiction. David Herbert Lawrence was the son of a Nottingham coal miner, but was devoted to his refined but domineering mother, who insisted upon his education. He became a schoolmaster in a London suburb in 1905. In 1909 some of his poems were published in the *English Review*, edited by Ford Madox Ford, who was also instrumental in the publication of Lawrence's first novel, *The White Peacock* (1911).

Lawrence eloped to the Continent in 1912 with Frieda von Richthofen Weekley, a German noblewoman who was the wife of a Nottingham professor; they were married in 1914. During World War I the couple was forced to remain in England; Lawrence's outspoken opposition to the war and Frieda's German birth aroused suspicion that they were spies. In 1919 they left England, returning only for brief visits. Their nomadic existence was spent variously in Ceylon (now Sri Lanka), Australia, the United States (New Mexico), and Mexico. Lawrence became a great friend of Aldous Huxley who was with him and Frieda when Lawrence died at the age of 45 of tuberculosis, a disease with which he had struggled for years.

Lawrence believed that industrialized Western culture was dehumanizing because it emphasized intellectual attributes to the exclusion of natural or physical instincts. He thought that this culture was in decline and that humanity would evolve into a new awareness of being a part of nature. One aspect of this blood consciousness would be an acceptance of the need for sexual fulfillment. His three novels *Sons and Lovers* (1913), *The Rainbow* (1915), and *Women in Love* (1921) concern the consequences of trying to deny humanity's union with nature.

After World War I, Lawrence began to believe that society needed to be reorganized under one superhuman leader. The novels containing this theme are *Aaron's Rod* (1922), *Kangaroo* (1923), and *The Plumed Serpent* (19-26). Lawrence's novel *Lady Chatterley's Lover* (1928) is the story of an English noblewoman who finds love and sexual fulfillment with her husband's gamekeeper. Because their lovemaking is described in intimate detail (for the 1920s), the novel caused a sensation and was banned in England and the United States until 1959. Lawrence's works include volumes of stories, poems, and essays, plays, travel books, and literary criticism.

Auden's early interest in consciousness was struck by Lawrence's call for less intellectualizing about life and for more natural living — to feel blood first before applying the brain. (*See also* Lane, Homer; Layard, John; Groddeck, George; Freud, Sigmund) Such notions appealed to the cultural left — and, in misguided interpretations, to the fascist right.

For Auden, who was a gay man in a convention-ridden, straight society, living one's natural way and confronting the problem of isolation held enormous appeal. By Auden's own account, as in *Letter to Lord Byron* (1936), "Part came from Lane, and part from D.H. Lawrence."

Before the end of the 1920s, Auden came to see the "life-wish" as the desire for separation from the family, literary predecessors, and conventions, which is to say from the closed systems of the family and of conventionality, including the conventional morality of Freud. At this point, Lawrence remains a touchstone, and one must, Auden holds, lose inhibitions imposed by society, by the tyranny of the dead (*see* Ancestral Curse and Family Ghosts) depicted in his play *Paid on Both Sides* (1928), which contains the additional Lawrentian theme of the negative role of women, chiefly of mothers upon their sons.

While rebellious, Auden remained, like Lawrence, within bourgeois parameters. Auden, who sought — like Lawrence — to approach life scientifically, focused upon the psychology of the individual, even as he diagnosed the whole of English society as sick (in *The Orators*). While in Berlin in 1928–29, Auden's

D.H. Lawrence

lifestyle tempted him to believe human evolution was leading toward a separation of mind and body, in which state the mind will occupy itself with "the incommunicable privacy of abstract thought" while the body may be left to sexual coupling and other physical pleasures.

Auden soon realized that the mind requires more than the Lawrentian separation between thinking and nature; into the 1930s he is still concerned about the individual's separation from society.

Lawrence and Auden lived the middle class, which both found wanting. Yet, the enemy — The Others — even when depicted as the rich, are not condemned for exploitation or for idle consumption, but for their sickness of conformity and their anxiety. For Auden and Lawrence, the unnatural life, bourgeois society, and the burden of the past frustrate the young and the natural.

The female parent is "the Enemy," a giantess, in Auden's *The Orators* (1932), and the perpetuator of a family feud in *Paid on Both Sides*

(1928); both suggest the stereotype of mothers who receive gratification by sacrificing their sons to war. The older generation clings to its ways and its power over the young, even to the latter's destruction. Memory, then, as ingrained cultural influence, is death; for it prevents the young from attaining the balance required to love and live naturally.

The young view contemporary British society as decadent and ill, psychologically. The theme is repeated in *The Orators* when the speaker asks, "What do you think of England, this country of ours where nobody is well?" The monologue continues, depicting categories consistent with the sinners in Dante's *Purgatorio* "...three main groups" of imperfect lovers. Auden's speaker adheres to theories of Homer Lane, who associated various physical symptoms with corresponding personality traits and behaviors, a position consistent with Lawrence's views. Yet, by the time Auden completed *The Orators*, he no longer considered the work an argument *for* Lawrence's ideas but a satirical refutation of some of these ideas, particularly "The cult of the Leader" as he had seen what this could lead to in Hitler's Berlin.

Auden's "Argument" section of *The Orators*, like Lawrence, looks for a leader, a Truly Strong Man who will provide the Way Out, a leader to die for, if need be. "Argument" also remains faithful to Lawrence's division of the psyche into four centers as the speaker prayerfully seeks protection against "the drought that withers the lower centers," i.e., the physical and natural impulses. Returning to the Leader — the masculine singular pronoun capitalized, as in a deity but also suggestive of Der Führer and Il Duce — the monologue in Part III of "Argument" slips into stream of consciousness wherein the Leader disappears.

In the "Statement" section of *The Orators*, Auden seems (in part III) to endorse Lawrence's insistence that the sexes remain segregated because "The nice clean intimacy which we now so admire between the sexes is sterilizing. It makes neuters" and spoils any future "deep, magical sex-life" (Lawrence, *Fantasia*). Auden also remains attached to Lawrence's theories on the opposites which comprise the final paragraph of the section and which — right/left, sun/moon, light/dark — are consistent with

Lawrentian cosmological dualism as well as with W.B. Yeats' antinomies, which he borrowed from the ancient Hindu Vedas. It is, however, in the "Journal of the Airman" that Auden and Lawrence come nearest in *The Orators* as the result of a spiritual relationship suggested in the first ode of Book III.

"Journal of the Airman" implies much and sows considerable confusion. Posed again is the question of leadership, but raised as well is the problem of individual human relationships to the whole of society. The nebulous Enemy is still at work confounding those who seek to balance mind and body, society and the individual. At some junctures Auden approaches Lawrence's apparent disparagement of women: "Self-regard ... like haemophilia is a sex-linked disease. Man is the sufferer, woman the carrier." Further, one cannot evaluate a woman according to her specific attributes, for he says: "Not so fast: wait till you see her son" (*English*). This seems little different from Lawrence's "old serpent-advised Eve" and his "And then, oh, young husband of the next generation, prepare for the daughter's revenge" (Lawrence, *Articles*).

A major concern of the Airman is, again, the problem of the Leader as demonstrated by his strategies and tactics, which resemble military considerations. He decides, as he prepares for his final encounter and envies "the simple life of the gut," that traditional acts of heroism will not effectively resist the enemy, that the only effective resistance lies in "self-destruction, the sacrifice of all resistance, reducing him [the Enemy] to the state of a man trying to walk on a frictionless surface." The odes that compose Book III begin with a dream that associates the death of Lawrence with the narrator's coming out from under morphine following an operation; and, in Ode IV the hero-worship often associated with Lawrence is ridiculed, as are the working class, the upper class, and various named political leaders and groups. "This is the season of the change of heart," the ode proclaims. In the same vein, as *The Orators* nears the end, Ode VI predicts "Our necessary defeat" and that light will "...disarm/Illumine, and not kill" (*English*). The breech with Lawrence would seem to have opened.

Auden's later treatment of Lawrence indicates his growing distance. No longer did

Auden share the enthusiasm of Lawrence for a lofty hero, although some did pose the question of whether the Airman was a Fascist. Auden, however, added the concluding odes as a deliberate postscript to point out that the material preceding them is not to be taken seriously but as satire. In a review of B.H. Liddell Hart's biography of T.E. Lawrence published in the spring of 1934, Auden expresses admiration, not for the man of exceptional deeds and blind action, but for the man like T.E. Lawrence who understood that "...action and reason are inseparable" because they complement each other. This view breaks with D.H. Lawrence's view, echoed by Auden in 1930, that the mind stultifies. Yet, in the next paragraph Auden cites approvingly the view of D.H. Lawrence that the Western conception of romantic love is a poor (and neurotic) substitute for human rootedness in life. If the parting of ways with Lawrence had begun in 1931-32, Auden still kept his predecessor in full view as late as 1934, but would shortly after forsake him altogether.

When Auden wrote the *Letter to Lord Byron* (1936) he seemed to have rejected much of Lawrence, and he said so. Auden makes an early reference to Lawrence that is ambiguous but which implies that Lawrence wrote all that he actually had to say very early, implying perhaps that Lawrence failed to develop after an early stage. In Part II Auden refers to "D.H. Lawrence hocus pocus," and Auden notes that Byron's (Romantic) hero could "...know instinctively what's done, and do it," but that such a natural life has been prevented by industrial capitalism and its "more efficient modes of stealing" (*English*). This surely breaks away from Lawrence — but does it? In the year of his death (1930), Lawrence published a short collection, *Assorted Articles*, of pieces that he had written for periodicals. Among the articles are several which deal with the socio-economic situation of the time, and one, "The State of Funk," in which Lawrence asserts that "...people want to be more decent, more good-hearted than our social system of money and grab allows them to be." Of course, he would not have been Lawrence if he had not followed with the contention that the same holds true of sexual feelings, "only worse" (*Articles*). Nonetheless, significant similarities between Auden and Lawrence remain obvious well into the 1930s.

D.H. Lawrence's influence upon Auden was lasting — even if this later led to a reverse process of conscious refutation. Carlo Izzo, Auden scholar and Italian translator, includes Lawrence among the nine components of "the armature" upon which Auden built his work, and this seems appropriate; for, the chief concerns of Auden — the divisions of mind and body, thought and action, and the individual and society — arose within a context dependent upon Lawrence and remained Auden's focus into middle age although he would address these concerns by looking at new influences — Gerald Heard and Paul Tillich, among others. In 1938 for a Hogarth Press booklet, *Education Today and Tomorrow* (with T.C. Worsley), Auden would finally denounce Lawrence as misguided but dangerously so. Auden nevertheless acknowledges the Lawrentian component well into his long career — after his move to the United States in 1939 and, in a sense, retains it to the end. (See also *The Orators,* Lords of Limit.)

Auden's 1962 essay "D.H. Lawrence" was on Lawrence's poetry: The seer (priest and mystic) and his code (way of living) supersedes the artist and his creations because the artist exalts the code and reacts to the code. There are rare artists (Blake, Lawrence), who are both artist and, in their fashion, also priest-mystic and apostle. A danger for these artists is that their art may be overshadowed by their message. Man is a historical creature, perpetually modifying himself and his environment. Lawrence was a pilgrim in the manner of Whitman and both advocated life worship.

Free verse, says Auden, is the outpouring of the spontaneous "eternal now" of the mystic. However, in the contemporary present, with its advanced ability to record through print and other media and keep the "genuine art" of the past more accessible, that past becomes part of the "eternal now" for successive generations, and today's artist must take it into account in a way that previous generations did not. Lawrence decried affected, trendy nonsense, which is different than passionate nonsense, which is what he considered religion to be. Art, however, unlike history, does not imitate

cyclical life; art is the means to an end for recapturing unique moments. Lawrence, the historical man, represents love, passion, and change; the historical woman is law and stability.

Auden believes that Lawrence violated his own bias against affectation as Lawrence's later poems are stilted by his own efforts to be unstilted. Conversely, Lawrence's earlier works, written in dialect, are more natural.

Auden asserts that formal verse is Catholic (more rigid) while free verse is Protestant (reformist). Although Lawrence admired Whitman and his free verse, the real Whitman seems at odds with his poetic persona. Lawrence, however, wrote down in art exactly what he was in life. Whitman wrote of an extended "I" as being included in the universal "We." Lawrence wrote of an intensive "I" that is unique for each individual.

Lawrence was an island, uncomfortable in both the middle class he grew into and the working class he grew out of. His passion was for conveying passion, not friendship or charity (except to nature). His nature poems have a gentleness not found in his prose. Lawrence as pilgrim never attached himself to any "city" in order to discover any positive stability; hence, his vision is negative.

Lawrence, T.E.

1888–1935, born Thomas Edward Lawrence, British adventurer, soldier, and scholar, known as Lawrence of Arabia. While at Oxford, he went on a walking tour of Syria and in 1911 joined a British Museum archaeological expedition in Mesopotamia. He stayed in the Middle East until 1914, learning Arabic and making exploratory trips and conducting archaeological surveys. Lawrence was assigned to the intelligence section of the British army in Egypt in World War I. In 1916, he joined the Arab forces under Faisal al Husayn (Faisal I) and became a leader in their revolt against Turkish domination. His use of guerilla assaults defeated strong Turkish armies with a small Arab force of only a few thousand. After the war he was a delegate to the Paris Peace Conference, where he sought Arab independence but to no avail.

Lawrence had become something of a legend, but in 1922 he enlisted, under the name of Ross, as a mechanic in the Royal Air Force. Why did he seek anonymity? Did he feel that he had disappointed his Arab friends who wanted independence, or, perhaps, did he believe that he had done all he could for them? Or was it to flee publicity or the emotional trauma brought on by his war experiences? When Lawrence's identity was discovered in 1923, he went into the tank corps. In 1925, he rejoined the air force. He legally adopted the name T.E. Shaw in 1927. (Hence, the character Shawcross in *The Ascent of F6*.)

In Paris in 1919, Lawrence began to write a narrative of his Arabian adventures, but he lost most of the manuscript and had to rewrite the whole without his notes, which he had destroyed. The result was the celebrated *Seven Pillars of Wisdom*, which was privately printed and circulated in 1926 although not published commercially until 1935. An abridged version, *Revolt in the Desert*, appeared in 1927. *The Mint*, an account of his life in the Royal Air Force, written under the pseudonym J.H. Ross (Shawcross again), was published in 1955.

For the Auden Generation, T.E. Lawrence was a major figure of both historical and allegorical importance. For Auden and Isherwood and other homosexuals, Lawrence was one of them and one who refuted that a gay man could not be brave and heroic. The mystery of Lawrence's quest for anonymity was no small matter as it seemed to signify the purpose of a sensitive, pure in heart man who is Truly Strong, a major component of Auden's world view at this time. In 1934 Auden wrote: "To me [T.E.] Lawrence's life is an allegory of the transformation of the Truly Weak Man into the Truly Strong Man, an answer to the question 'How shall the self-conscious man be saved?'" and the moral seems to be this, "'self-consciousness is an asset, in fact the only friend of our progress....' But a misinterpretation of absorption [self-consciousness] is one of the great heresies of our generation. To interpret it as blind action without consideration of meaning or ends, as an escape ... that is indeed to become the Truly Weak Man, to enlist in the great Fascist retreat.... Action and reason are inseparable; it is only in action that reason can

realise itself, and only through reason that action can become free. [Lenin] and Lawrence ... exemplify ... a synthesis of feeling and reason, act and thought." (1934)

Is this Auden's call to action? It is as close as he would get at this point in time. In this review of the Lawrence biography by B.H. Liddell Hart, Auden said that he believed in action, but only if that action was tempered by the calm reason that signifies a Truly Strong Man who is pure-in-heart, a man must be aware of his true Self so that his private and public faces are the same. When reason makes action free — that is, when the actions are derived not from an ego-bound self, but an egoless Self — the contemplative man does not withdraw, but goes among the people, or as Auden said: "Consciousness necessitates more action not less." In 1937 Auden and Isherwood would exemplify Lawrence as the character Michael Ransom in the play *The Ascent of F6*. While the other Lawrence, D.H., made a strong impact on Auden who became flushed with him for a brief period up until 1932, T.E. Lawrence had a more lasting significance. (See also *Letters from Iceland*.)

Layard, John

1891–1975, British anthropologist and Jungian psychoanalyst. After a nervous breakdown he saw American psychologist Homer Lane and became patient and follower. When Lane died he saw Jung. He met Auden in Berlin in 1928 and taught him about Lane. Auden became enraptured with the idea that he need not thwart his desires but should pursue them and become pure-in-heart and Truly Strong. (Layard would be mentioned in a version of *Paid on Both Sides*.) Layard had a brief affair with Auden and Auden's Berlin friend Gerhart Meyer that led him to a botched suicide attempt after which he went to Auden for help. (Auden's description to Isherwood is depicted twice, in both Isherwood's *The Memorial* and *Lions and Shadows* where Layard is "Barnard.") Concerning The *Orators* Auden wrote in a letter: "The genesis ... was a paper written by an anthropologist friend of mine about ritual epilepsy among the Trob[r]iand Islanders [in the South Pacific], linking it up with the flying powers of witches, sexual abnormalities, etc." Layard referred to the witches as "Flying Tricksters." In the paper the rite of becoming a trickster is initiated by a maternal uncle to his nephew and in *The Orators* this is Isherwood's Uncle Henry. Layard's influence then waned and Auden would even refer to "loony Layard" in an ode for *The Orators*. Later, Auden was more tolerant, particularly as both he and Layard returned to the Anglican Church. Layard later married and had a son while continuing to work and write. (*See also* "Have a Good Time.")

"Leap Before You Look" 1940

At this very early period of Auden's Christianity he was still strongly influenced by Kierkegaard's existential Christian philosophy in which one is faced with the terrible freedom of *choice*—hence the poem's title. In general, one would rather follow than think; one would prefer to be a member of a media-influenced Kierkegaardian public and allow opinions to be formed without one's own clear and studied judgment. Yet, as Christ chose the cross, one must also choose to be responsible for his own judgments. Choice is not easy; ignoring the need for reasoned choice is worse, leading to the voice of dictators.

Lear, Edward

1812–88, English humorist and artist. At 19 he was employed as a draftsman by the London Zoological Society; the paintings of birds that he produced for *The Family of the Psittacidae* (1832) were among the first color plates of animals ever published in Great Britain. Lear is best known for his illustrated limericks and nonsense verse, which were collected in *A Book of Nonsense* (1846), *Nonsense Songs* (1871), *Laughable Lyrics* (1877), and others. He wrote several illustrated journals of his travels through southern Europe.

Lear was an Auden favorite, which Auden's 1939 poem "Edward Lear" makes clear. The poem is a contrast to poems about "A.E. Housman" and "Rimbaud," and praises Lear as

a poet who obeyed his poetic gifts instead of his vanity. He went from being a lonely voyager to a beacon, from fear to recognition and acceptance of who he was: a man with a gift to make art.

Leavis, F.R.

1895–1978, Frank Raymond Leavis, writer and critic. His works include *The Great Tradition* (1948), *The Common Pursuit* (1952), *D.H. Lawrence, Novelist* (1955), and *Anna Karenina and Other Essays* (1968). He was cofounder of the influential quarterly *Scrutiny* (to which Auden contributed) and its editor from 1932 until its demise in 1953. From 1936 to 1962, Leavis was at Cambridge. He attacked "mass culture" in his writings on education and society. Leavis supported Auden in the 1930s, although he associated the Auden gang with Communism, which he did not support. And Leavis, in reviewing Auden's play *The Dance of Death* (1933), criticized lines he thought were written to appeal to the proletariat; apparently he did not realize that only a small percentage of his countrymen spoke the Queen's English, and that, indeed, the rest were working-class and spoke dialects, principally cockney. Leavis began to turn against Auden with the volume *Look Stranger* (1936) and this mutual antipathy lasted permanently.

Lee, Gypsy Rose

1914–1970, burlesque star, singer, actress. In 1940–41 Lee lived in the 15 Maddagh Street ménage with Auden, Carson McCullers, George Davis, Paul and Jane Bowles, Erika and Golo Mann, Louis MacNeice, Benjamin Britten and Peter Pears.

"Legend" 1931

Love is on a mythical quest as a companion to a youthful hero who follows the Northwest Passage through treacherous landscapes; the trek is a metaphor for adolescent sexuality. Only through seeking legend can one learn how to love and let love begin, after which one can shed the past and grow. The hero tries to escape through self-created fiction into more self-created fiction and this contradictory effort is a result of Auden's wish for a simple love between two people even if the whole world opposes. And if romance should later fade, one may find a true avatar from the effort to love. Here Auden consciously or unconsciously hints that a vision of Eros may become a more fulfilling vision of agape.

Lehmann, John

1907–1988, British poet, author, editor, autobiographer. He met Auden and Isherwood when he was working for Leonard and Virginia Woolf and their Hogarth Press, which published the new elite of the literary intellectuals from the late 1920s until 1946. Lehman started his own literary publication, *New Writing*, in 1936, and Isherwood persuaded Auden and his circle to contribute. *New Writing* lasted fourteen years and was one of the best and most versatile of literary journals. Lehman was the brother of two distinguished sisters, Rosamund (a novelist) and Beatrix (an actress). After *New Writing*, Lehman became editor of *Penguin New Writing*. In 1955 he wrote *The Whispering Gallery*, his autobiography of the 1930s.

Lenin, Vladimir

1870–1924, Russian revolutionary, the founder of Bolshevism and the major force behind the Soviet revolution of October 1917. In the 1920s and 1930s many artists and intellectuals saw in Lenin's Soviet Union a New Hope for a socialist/Communist world that would see a more equitable treatment of all people and do away with the traditions of bourgeois mentality that hindered progress. Since Lenin died in 1924 he achieved a martyr's status that gave him more credibility than he might have gotten had he lived to lead as merely a man.

In the early 1930s Auden seemed impressed with Lenin as a man rather than as a politician and revolutionary. In a review of a biography of T.E. Lawrence, Auden links the two

and considers both to be pure in heart and Truly Strong. He thought that both had abnegated their willful egos for the greater good. He wrote, "The self must first learn to be indifferent; as Lenin said, 'To go hungry, work illegally and be anonymous.'" (Auden means indifference here as the mystic sees it, which is the ability to be indifferent to the call of one's selfish ego, and by doing so, be able to care more for others.) Once Auden lost his interest in Communism after it became clear that Stalin was no Lenin, he lost interest in Lenin as well.

"The Lesson" 1942

This poem is in three sonnets and is a softer, quieter version of Auden's "Canzone" also in 1942. Both poems are self-rebukes for Auden's wish to possess and control Kallman.

Letter to Lord Byron 1936

The artist in creating art should ask the same question that, according to Auden in *Letter to Lord Byron*, "Both Eros and Apollo ask," which is, do art and life "each intend a synthesis" to bring about the "end/That all self-loving things intend?"

The end Auden refers to is Gerald Heard's unified consciousness, and these lines succinctly highlight the need for order to emerge from the synthesis of the artist's feeling and the scientist's reason, with the scientist recording facts while the artist synthesizes the facts to reflect the tenor of his time. The Vision of Eros as romantic love represents feeling, and Apollo, the Greco-Roman God of music and poetry (feeling), prophecy and medicine (reason) signifies an equitable synthesizing of feeling and reason.

Letter to Lord Byron is a hallmark of Auden's indiscriminatingly allusive poetic method. Auden's poem contains allusions not only to Byron, but also to Pope, Housman, Henry James, Milton, and Shakespeare. The allusions in this poem do exactly what they ought to do: they give the poet a sense of validation from the figures of authority. Exuberant in substance, buoyant in diction, it is perhaps the best longer light-verse poem Auden ever wrote. It offers a commentary on the manners, life, and literature of the late 1930s, discusses the role of an artist in modern society, and gives account of Auden's own poetic influences. Above all, Auden's address to Byron aims at establishing his own reputation as a poet. Auden ostensibly writes his letter to Byron in order to "chat about your poetry or mine" and, despite a consistent tone of self-deprecation, he hopes that Byron will have "all eternity to read it." Auden's epistle to Lord Byron is one-sided; the addressee never answers the younger poet from the "eternity" he inhabits.—PIOTR GWIAZDA

Indeed, Byron does not answer because he would just get in Auden's way. This long poem considers many things, not the least of which was Auden's conflict over whether an artist should be an activist. Rabid oratory, even for a just cause, only reminded him of the British Public School cant and rant. Propaganda of any kind did not suit him. Auden would later say in 1939: " Beware of … the dictator who says 'my people': The writer who says 'my public'" (*The Prolific and Devourer*). Throughout the 1930s Auden couldn't decide if art-as-propaganda should serve a political cause or not. His intuition leaned against it but in writing the plays and in certain prose and poems, particularly *Spain,* Auden became caught up in the activism of his peers. By March 1939 Auden finally made a choice after giving his first and last political speech: "I suddenly found I could really do it, that I could make a fighting demagogic speech and have the audience roaring. And … it is so exciting but so absolutely degrading. I felt just covered with dirt afterwards. It isn't that one shouldn't do any 'social' work but one must do something that is in one's nature to do, and for me that means 'teaching'" (*P and D*). For Auden, this meant teaching through parable-art. Before reaching his conclusion in 1939, Auden wrestled with his dilemma by thinking through his pen. Along with writing the plays with Isherwood, Auden wrote three works that concern his internal conflict: *Letter to Lord Byron*, 1936, *Look! Stranger*, 1936, *Spain*, 1937.

Edward Mendelson writes in *Early Auden*: "*Letter to Lord Byron* is a discursive poem in five parts, urbane, conversational, *au courant*, tolerantly amused by the literary scene, savagely amused by the political one. The poem is splendidly funny, but it has none of the uncontrolled slapstick of *The Orators*. Auden adds a note of comic self-mocking irony whenever the poem gets didactic, but he is more didactic than in anything he wrote before. He claims at the end to have reached only 'the rather tame conclusion / That no man by himself has life's solution.'"

Auden began *Letter to Lord Byron* a few months after completing *The Ascent of F6*. The play, a meditation on man's public and private spheres, was a prelude to Auden's further meditation on his own public and private spheres. According to Mendelson, "it was while writing *The Ascent of F6*, that he realized he must someday leave England" (*EA*). Consequently, *Letter* is a summing up of Auden's life in England as well as Auden's history of English life. This long poem is an homage to Byron and written (more or less) in Byronic style. It is alternately satirically serious and seriously satiric. After the grandiloquently serious *F6*, Auden wished to lighten up and chose Byron's "airy manner" to do so. Obscurantist no longer as in *Poems* and *The Orators*, Auden would be didactic and explain himself clearly, directly, and to great effect. Auden puts himself in the middle of British history — not in a chronological sense, but as the current product incorporating all of that history simultaneously. The product he depicts is a British middle-class intellectual and artist. Auden ruminates on the conflicts derived from being an artist in the modern world. Mendelson considers *Letter* to be three history lessons: 1) the changes in English society; 2) the modern and romantic concept of the hero-artist and his isolation in society; 3) Auden's autobiography of his own art and class. While exploring these three "histories," Auden reiterates the Isherwood-Auden schema of a haunting past and the Truly Weak and Truly Strong Man. He does so with greater compassion, seeing England, not with the hawk's vision of an alienated cypher-witness, but as a citizen among citizens. He does so even though he cannot always agree with or even understand some of his fellow citizens: "You can't change human nature, don't you know!"

Auden also praises the common man who is Truly Strong and wants to be like him: "I am like you," he says, "and you, and you." What he is not like is The Others.

In Part III Auden explains the dilemma of the post-romantic artist who now lives in an age of flux. He is without roots in a time of socio-economic instability. Neither he nor readers, who are among the alienated herd within the Public, have a mutual ground for understanding. The artist cannot be sure of the temper of his times so he cannot be sure about his art. Consequently, the conflict arises of what to say and how to say it. Should the artist transcend propaganda or succumb to it. As he considers his answer, Auden writes: "I'm more intuitive than analytic." He would later rely on intuition, mistrusting the "analytic" as leading one astray, saying: "To me Art's subject is the human clay," and that the background, natural or otherwise, is just something man stands in front of. The background should not take precedence over man's story without which there is no background. An artist, "like a secret agent must keep hidden his passion...." The artist should not preach, but teach through parable. His passion must be hidden behind his parable due to the lowbrow public's mistrust of highbrows that has been inculcated in them by "the management." Didactic artists are easy targets to either use or subvert as necessary. The result may be a time when the independent, iconoclastic highbrow becomes extinct and a child may ask in the future during his history class what was "An intellectual of the middle classes?" Auden understands the pressure to conform saying that for the sake of normality "What murders are committed in thy name." Auden spares the British Public Schools in his *Letter* but only because "I've said my say on public schools elsewhere." He does, however, recall youthful influences, Layard, Lane, D.H. Lawrence and Gerald Heard who taught him to abhor anyone who chose art over "Life and Love and being Pure-inHeart."

Older and wiser, Auden is more bemused about his previous enthusiasms; he doesn't reject them, but tempers them with a greater understanding of life's contingencies. *Letter to Lord Byron* is in itself pragmatic and didactic, but always with tongue in cheek. After the histrionics of *The Ascent of F6*, the *Letter* was also a respite from neo-tragedy.

Letters from Iceland 1936

(Dedicated to Auden's father: George Augustus Auden.) No doubt one of the oddest travel books ever composed as most of it is in verse and less of it is about Iceland. Scholar Robert Caserio considers that the book is in large part Auden's own self-consideration of himself as a gay — or as Auden would say "crooked"— person in the straight world.

Caserio writes: The first problem one wants to address is the always perplexing relation of Auden's published work to his homosexuality. Auden at times does outrightly own that relation, even though until recently critics have overlooked the fact and the impact of his avowals. And when they do not overlook the fact, critics too frequently take Auden's comment in 1947 to Alan Ansen — "It's wrong to be queer"— as Auden's summary credo, rather than as a temporary speculation, or a passing remark, or a sign of the poet's negative capability. Still, there is also undoubted reticence and self-criticism in Auden's disclosures: far more than current taste and assumptions expect and indeed require. Does the reticence mean that Auden's work suffers from, and even is shaped by, self-censorship and cultural homophobia?

The answer is not simple. It must comprehend the possibility that expressions of homosexuality in Auden's work, or even criticisms and disavowals of it, are shaped by Auden's debate with writers who are, as it were, Auden's gay elders in the practice of loving and writing. What looks to us, from a long distance, as closeting and censorship is really the buried sign of a once-open conversation among gay modernists, and a generational conflict among them too. If Auden doesn't speak up loudly about his homosexuality, or speak loudly for it, the cause might be his aim to speak differently from earlier gay ways of speaking up. The cause also might be an intention to extend a predecessor's reticence, even if Auden's motives are not the same as the predecessor's. Multiple gay personalities and voices — not just Auden's own, but others'— inform his work. In what follows one can suggest that Auden's *Letters from Iceland* (1937), besides being a product of collaboration with his "heter[osexual]" poet friend Louis

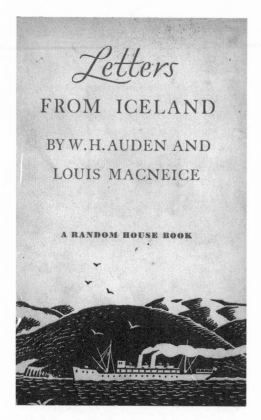

Letters from Iceland, **cover of first U.S. edition.**

defining relation for art. The poem, in spite of its jaunty tone, is intelligible as an act of resignation. Auden resigns himself and his poetry to dependence on everything external: on class ambitions and conflicts; on normality; on the mundane order of things; on "Capitalism in its later phases." And yet *Letter to Lord Byron* addresses one of the conquerors of autonomy. The conquerors, according to the poem, created a Poet's Party, a political independence movement, in the name of the special character, the singularity of art. Is the conquest only a delusion? If so, why is Auden writing to Byron in Byron's style, as if Auden was Byron's double, and Byron was writing to himself?

One must consider that the most important aim of *Letters from Iceland* is to meditate upon, rethink, and even to instance, the relations of art to its own autonomy as well as to its heteronymous contexts. For Auden a poet does yield or resign his independence, but only thanks to art's capacity for discovering a measure of liberty from context, and only thanks as well to the singularity of the poet and the poet's work, which also marks a limit for context. The Iceland of *Letters from Iceland* is no less a real place than the English isle or MacNeice's native Ireland, but it is also an island of letters: a literary place. In Iceland, we need to see, the two poets produce a book on literature's situation, its ground in the world. That ground is admitted to be unreal in the poem called "Journey to Iceland": "This is an island and therefore," Auden writes, "Unreal." "But," MacNeice writes in an answering poem in the collection, "we are not changing ground to escape from facts/But rather to find them." From such lines as these, one gathers that the unreal, which includes art's phantasms, the litter of letters, is not Limbo, and even might save us from death.

If nothing rummaged from the islanded autonomous literary space were to survive the journey home to context, we'd have to resign ourselves to autonomy's defeat. Nevertheless, even if hidden within a historical reality named Iceland, the island is there: a mystery, or an alter ego, out of which or for the sake of which one might shape a speech or a vision that reconciles us to where we are.

But what does Auden suggest the island place of letters has to do with homosexuality?

MacNeice, also originates in, and expresses, Auden's inward conversations, collaborations, and conflicts with two, indeed with three, preceding generations of gay elders. The elders are represented by Edward Carpenter, Frederick Rolfe, W. Somerset Maugham, and T.E. Lawrence. Auden's characteristic reticences and utterances result as much from his relation to these writers as from his alliance with heteronormality.

Within or alongside the problem of Auden's modes of avowing his homosexuality in print arises a second problem, one equally difficult to explore. It is the problem of the autonomy of poetry in relation to the culture in which any poet produces it. In *Letters from Iceland*, a so-called travel book that is a brilliant modernist collage, Auden includes a five-part verse epistle, *Letter to Lord Byron*. In the epistle Auden acknowledges that art is dependent on economic history, and the artist's class situation. *Letter to Lord Byron* concedes context's

If homosexuality's isolated place, *its* autonomy, can not survive a return home, should *its* reconciliation to a censorious context be accepted or tolerated? In Part V of *Letter to Lord Byron* Auden doubts if homosexuality, represented in one of Part V's stanzas by Hugo Wolf's art song about Ganymede, can move us creatively away from that intractably real ground of our contexts: the political state and economic order. "The Great Utopia, free of all complexes, / the Withered State is, at the moment, such / A dream as that of being both the sexes. / I like Wolf's *Goethe-Lieder* very much, / But doubt if *Ganymede*'s appeal will touch / — That marvelous cry with its ascending phrases — / Capitalism in its later phases." Ganymede can help neither the state nor its capitalist underpinnings whither away. And if Auden believes that, doesn't his resignation, coupled with his indirect avowal of homosexuality here, help the State flourish? What has happened to the power whereby a journey to a place of letters, a change of ground from fact to fantasy, can be a finding of new facts, rather than an escape from, or a capitulation to, facts at their old, oppressive worst? Wouldn't directly confrontational speech by Auden about sex and about Auden's homosexual kind wither the state more than Goethe and Hugo Wolf? Art song be damned!

We have to remember, however, that not just Auden is speaking. Directness of statement is limited by the poem's bi-textual voice: the side by sideness of Byron with Auden. A sideways rather than straightforward speech results from intergenerational talk. Besides, there is also intragenerational conversation in progress, since Auden and MacNeice are writing in company. *The company* disperses directness. But it *can* claim *indirectness* as an autonomous, state-withering force. For the authorial comradeship of *Letters from Iceland* serves notice of a straight-gay alliance. The writers seem to know in advance the strong hatred for the so-called Nancy poets which George Orwell, within a year of *Letters from Iceland*, will utter in *The Road to Wigan Pier*. It's MacNeice who contributes to the *Letters* a campy segment, composed of a long-winded epistolary chat by an ex-schoolteacher named Hetty, who writes vacation letters from Iceland to a correspondent named Nancy. The joke is that "Hetty" is code for "heter," as in *heterosexual*, so that the letters are a Hetty-Nancy boy line of communication and friendship.

Auden's reticence, then, is not censorship but resistance to censorship, a mark of autonomy; and the reticence also reflects in part MacNeice's pro-gay third-party contribution to the Auden-Byron pair. Where more than one person is expressing himself, there is bound to be a knotting complication of speech. But there is even more complexity of conversation producing Auden's autonomizing reticence. Neither Auden's collaboration with a member of his own generation of writers, nor his doubling of Byron's ancient generation, matters more to his poetry's character and career than does Auden's implicit conversation with gay modernists in the era preceding his own.

In the letter to Byron, Auden describes his and MacNeice's generation in the following way: "We were the tail, a sort of poor relation / To that debauched, eccentric generation / That … made new glosses on the noun Amor." Thanks to those glosses made by an earlier generation, the 29-year-old Auden doesn't have to gloss over his own Amor. When in the *Letter* he jokingly allegorizes himself as Pure-in-Heart, Auden reports of his personification that "He's gay." The report is complemented by the poem's acknowledgment of Gide as another inspiring influence, and it also is complemented by the poem's imagination that Byron, were he alive, would form a political United Front with Gide. The Gide-Byron coalition makes sense in terms of the poem's evocation of the current social prominence of homosexuality in England. Mother England, Auden says "'looks odd today dressed up in peers / Slums, aspidistras, shooting-sticks, and queers.'" In that last diction there is, to be sure, a satiric or self-satiric aggression. But Auden permits himself a flippancy about homosexuality's established appearance, in order to suggest that homosexual Amor is open to flippancy, and open even to criticism and to contest, not only because of its vulnerable minority, but also because of its now (in 1936) recognized public place. The use of "queer" is part of *Letter to Lord Byron*'s conversational commonplace style. And queer was made conversationally commonplace because of that prior time when an eccentric generation found itself uniquely receptive to the strange variety of modes whereby *Amor vincit omnia*. Since we are told that the *earlier* eccentric generation "grew up with their fathers at the War," we can surmise that *their* fathers — the grandfathers of Auden's era — grew up because of *their* new glosses on Eros no less than because of combat. Auden and his fellows are the tail to at least a pair of generations.

To attend to the effects of generational alliances, differences or conflicts among gay modernists might help us resist the attractive temptation to simplify cultural history. We simplify when we assume that there is a post–Stonewall consciousness superior to its predecessors; and we simplify when we assume that a previous era is characterized by a uniform epistemology of the closet. In the era of that hypothetical epistemology, as Auden's poem attests, something distinctly un-closeted went on. And its having gone on across generations facilitated gay writers' speculations and arguments about what constitutes a queer tradition or about what use one might make of such tradition. —ROBERT CASERIO (*See also* Maugham, W.S.; Carpenter, Edward; Rolfe, Frederick; Lawrence, T.E.)

"The Liberal Fascist" *see* British Public Schools

The Life of an American 1938-39

This scenario, an Auden-Isherwood collaboration, is mostly Isherwood and was never used. The opening reads: "An interesting and cheap four-reeler could be made in which the part of the central character was taken by the camera. The hero sees life through the lens of the camera, so that the audience identifies itself with him. To make this possible the story must be as ordinary and universal as possible. We suggest the life of an average American." In this instance Isherwood's line "I am a camera," from *Goodbye to Berlin*, was to be taken literally.

"Limbo Culture" 1957

This poem is about an imaginary tribe incapable of both an unselfish love or a stultifying

exactness of thought that prevents flexibility, which is in contrast to the contemporary human capacity for both.

Lindsay, Vachel

1879–1931, born Nicholas Vachel Lindsay, American poet, b. Springfield, Ill. Lindsay was one of the first performance artists and an actor when reading his own poems. Volumes of his poetry include *General William Booth Enters into Heaven* (1913), *The Congo* (1914), *The Chinese Nightingale* (1917), and *Collected Poems* (19-38). In his last years, his popularity declined, he was faced with poverty and illness, and he finally committed suicide. In 1935, Thornton Wilder based his novel *Heaven's My Destination* on Lindsay.

Auden in his pre–Oxford, early Oxford days, admired Lindsay's work, which was visceral and meant for the "common man." Lindsay had visited England in 1916 and gave a rousing recital praised by the British press and which even won over the poet William Butler Yeats. In 1922 a British travel writer, Stephen Graham, trekked with Lindsay in the American West, writing *Tramping with a Poet in the Rockies*. ("Tramping" meant hiking/camping/vagabondage.) Auden had read the British "tramper" W.H. Davies, and likely compared the two. In 1939, Glenway Wescott met Auden and compared his enthusiasm to Lindsay's.

"Lines for Elizabeth Mayer" 1964

For Mayer's eightieth birthday. Auden bemoans that she is now in a nursing home.

Lions and Shadows see Isherwood, Christopher; The Auden Generation

"A Literary Transference" *see* Hardy, Thomas

The Londoners see Grierson, John

"Loneliness" 1971

This poem is perhaps Auden's saddest poem as it is addressed to that terrible shadow figure, loneliness, who tortures him until "Chester, my chum, will return" (Chester Kallman).

Look, Stranger 1936

Published in 1936, *Look, Stranger* (American title *On This Island*) was Auden's first collection of poems since the 1932 second printing of his first volume. Included in *Look, Stranger* is "A Summer Night" that was written three years earlier. The dedication is to Erika Mann whom Auden married so she could remain in England after fleeing Germany. This volume's poems have neither *The Ascent of F6*'s histrionics nor, conversely, the satirical airy manner of *Letter to Lord Byron*. These poems are more introspective and meditative. Yet, all three works examine similar themes but from different angles of Auden's perception. The American title *On This Island* is a clue, which Mendelson notes, to the focus of Auden's mid 1930s perspective: "In the early 1930s Auden dreamed of innocent islands. He woke on a guilty one. From the end of 1935 to the end of 1938, whenever he needed an emblem for his separation from responsibility, audience, love, history, all that is real outside the mind's inner chambers, he invoked the solitary island.... The island supplanted the border as Auden's geographical sign of entrapment and enclosure. [Auden] carried his isolation with him" (*Early Auden*).

If an island had become an emblem of isolation, an island could also be a haven for salvation. Just as one sometimes feels alone in a crowd wherever he may be, one can also find a haven wherever he may be. For the mystic, the kingdom of God is within, and all existence is integrally unified if one chooses, as the mystic does, to believe this. The center of the universe for a mystic is wherever he happens to be. This center is a shelter from life's hurricane. The goal is to remain fast to the center and not get caught up in the spin of external reality. Auden's experience on that "Summer Night" had

been some evidence that an island can be a blessing as well as a curse. One escapes from a solitary island, but one can also escape to an enlightened island. The question remains: where is the enlightened island? Auden spared no energy in looking for it. The poems of *Look, Stranger* continue Auden's search.

"A Summer Night" was inspired by Auden's mystical experience and his reading of *The Book of Talbot*, which he believed to be a supreme expression of unconditional love. This book was a statement of romantic love as a manifestation of the Vision of Eros, spiritual love for one person. *The Book of Talbot* was written in the past. For Auden the ghosts and traditions of the past were no longer exclusively evil. The past can also guide a search for love in the present. One must learn to select knowledge from the past with sensitive discrimination. The balance of poems in the volume signifies a shift for Auden away from being an unreserved Anti-Other to having a more tolerant and even appreciative view of at least some of The Others. The 1930s in some ways had been too independent, leaving itself with little to lean on from the past it disclaimed. During the period that many of the poems were written Auden was a teacher (master) at the Downs preparatory school. Geoffrey Hoyland was the school's progressive headmaster and Auden dedicated "A Summer Night" to him. By many accounts Auden's tenure at the Downs was the happiest period of his life in England. John Duguid, a student of Auden's at the Downs, recalled that his teacher was "jolly" and inviting, enjoying his charges a great deal. (See an interview with Duguid in Izzo, *W.H. Auden: A Legacy*.)

As in *Letter to Lord Byron*, the verse in *Look, Stranger* is more of an analysis and less of an attack. The poem "Our Hunting Fathers" asserts that these fathers explained the fable "Of the sadness of the creatures." Auden gives credit to the "fathers" for trying to teach, but their message became distorted by the pressures of public chaos that they reacted to with individual and collective egotism. The result is "sadness" as love was overcome by guilt. This poem follows "A Summer Night" as a contrast. In the former love exists if one seeks it by "an abnegation of the will"; in the latter the will did not abnegate and love has been lost, but it can be found again by overcoming guilt.

Throughout these poems there are islands to escape from and the hint of islands where one might escape to if obstacles are overcome. There is a gulf between the inexorable pull of public chaos and possible peace in the private sphere. Auden considers how the gulf can be bridged. In *Early Auden*, Mendelson cites five possible escape routes: 1) erotic: sexual love leading to the vision of Eros and then agape; 2) redemptive: save mankind by example or direct cure; 3) didactive: teach through parables to unlearn hatred and learn love. 4) world-historical: solutions by determined altruistic forces; 5) escapist: flee to an island refuge of the mind in fantasy.

Before 1933 Auden's obscure anonymity as a cypher-witness revealed to him that taking the Northwest Passage to distant frontiers makes nothing happen within, where real change must begin. People will change one at a time through a change of heart. Only then will civilization follow. Gerald Heard's vision of a unified collective consciousness stated that people could erase ego-generated societal divisions through what Heard called "intentional living." For Heard, to live intentionally began with recognizing that the ego is the enemy to serenity. Heard taught a secular version of what the world's religions had long advocated, particularly the mystical exponents in each case. With all the wrestling in these poems, Auden ultimately rejects the solitary island for an island in the heart; one that is to be found in contemplative silence. Auden's intuition was moving him back toward a mythical version of his childhood High Anglican Christianity that he had never really forsaken. Still, there would be some more wrestling with the public chaos against his private sphere. In 1937 Auden would write *Spain*.

Lord of the Rings *see* Tolkien, J.R.R.

Lords of Limit

The Lords of Limit are in Auden's 19-32 poem "The Watchers" (as well as in his unpublished 1932 poem "A Happy New Year"). These Lords unify the self that Auden had split in his earlier verse and thought. The Lords are the rules by which persons or objects are made, and the parameters for this making are distinct. It is the Lord of Limit in Shakespeare's *The Phoenix and the Turtle* who abhors the idea of the lovers effacing their distinctness by joining together. These Lords are also connected to the Book of Revelation in the interpretation of D.H. Lawrence in *Apocalypse* (1931), where Lawrence writes that they "put a limit on man. They say to him ... thus far and no further."

"The Love Feast" 1948

"The love feast" is the modern secular equivalent of ancient Christian Agape as symbolized in the communion service, and signifies Auden's return for the first time since "A Summer Night" in 1933 to including his body and not just his mind in art; this is a juxtaposition of sacred and profane and asks if present sinners are complacent. Quotes St. Augustine: "Make me chaste, lord, but not yet."

Love's Labour's Lost *see* Nabokov, Nicolas; Shakespeare

Lowbrows *see* Aesthetes and Hearties

"Lullaby" 1937

One of Auden's more remembered love poems that begins, "Lay your sleeping head, my love." It is a respite from the world and Auden's other poems about the troubles in the world. Auden wishes to freeze this moment with his lover and set it apart from external reality as its own distinct reality immune from pain. He has, momentarily, the power of waking over sleeping while his lover sleeps, older over younger, thoughtful over instinctive, and he ruminates over the conflict of flesh over thought.

"A Lullaby" *see Thank You Fog*

Lynes, George Platt

1907–1955, American photographer. Took photos of Auden and Isherwood after their arrival in America in 1939. A Lynes photo of Auden is on the cover of Mendelson's *Later Auden*.

McCullers, Carson

1917–67, American novelist, b. Columbus, Ga., studied at Columbia. A main theme of her work is the individual's alienation in the world. In her first novel, *The Heart Is a Lonely Hunter* (1940), a deaf-mute is at the center of a group of unhappy characters. *The Member of the Wedding* (1946; dramatization, 1950) tells the story of an adolescent girl. In her twenties, McCullers suffered a series of strokes that left her partially paralyzed; during her last years she was confined to a wheelchair.

In the early 1940s McCullers was one of the renters in a house owned by George Davis. Auden, Gypsy Rose Lee, Paul and Jane Bowles, Benjamin Britten and Peter Pears also spent time there. Carpenter: "Another early resident was Carson McCullers, who had recently made a reputation with her novel *The Heart Is a Lonely Hunter*; her marriage had foundered, and she was now falling in love with a succession of women, including Erika Mann, Auden's "paper-only" wife whom he married so she could flee nazi Germany."

MacDonald, George *see* "George MacDonald"

McGinley, Phyllis

1905–1978. McGinley was a light verse poet who celebrated American life but did so with a satirical edge. Auden enjoyed her immensely and wrote a foreword for her collected poems *Times Three* (1961), in which Auden writes on the differences between male and female imagina-

tions, and that the former benefits when influenced by the latter.

Up until *Times Three* McGinley was not taken seriously, but with help from Auden's endorsement the volume won that year's Pulitzer Prize for poetry.

MacNeice, Louis

1907–1963, Northern Irish poet, b. Belfast. It is difficult to categorize MacNeice as either British or Irish; indeed, he straddled both identities from a young age. Though MacNeice was a Protestant, his parents originally hailed from the Catholic west of Ireland and were sympathetic to the cause of Irish Home Rule. Later, when the family moved to Belfast, MacNeice's father — an Anglican rector at the Holy Trinity Church — refused to support Unionist sectarianism. It is little wonder, then, that MacNeice grew up with a sense of dual identity. Educated at Oxford, he nonetheless claimed he felt more at home in Ireland. Yet he admitted he was "hopelessly Anglicized," and characterized himself as "an example of uprootability." Though Ireland became a vacation destination — which is one reason he often writes of it with a foreigner's detachment — his childhood memories of life in his father's Carrickfergus rectory provide the backbone of some of his most penetrating poems. This self-division, somewhere between English and Irish, set MacNeice apart from the thirties poets. Even though he romanticized his Irish connections and enjoyed telling friends he was descended from Connemara peasants, he spent most of his life in England, befriending the major British poets of his time, including Auden, Spender, and Day Lewis.

MacNeice began publishing his poetry at Oxford, where he met Auden, and in 1929 published his first collection, *Blind Fireworks*. The next year he was appointed assistant lecturer in classics at Birmingham University. There he met the professor E.R. Dodds, who would become a lifelong friend and mentor. Encouraged by Dodds, he continued writing, and, in 1932, sent a batch of poems to T.S. Eliot, who had published Auden's *Poems* in 1930. Eliot offered to publish some in *The Criterion*. In 1934, he

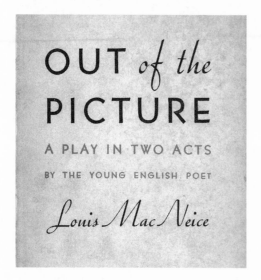

OUT *of the* PICTURE

A PLAY IN TWO ACTS

BY THE YOUNG ENGLISH POET

Louis MacNeice

Out of the Picture, cover of first U.S. edition.

finally accepted MacNeice's *Poems*; thereafter, Faber published almost every collection he wrote. In 1936 MacNeice traveled to Iceland with Auden, where the two collaborated on *Letters from Iceland* (1937). Auden later remembered this journey as one of the happiest times of his life.

In 1939, MacNeice published *Autumn Journal*, an uneasy account of the state of Europe — particularly Britain, Spain, and Ireland — at the end of 1938, interwoven with personal reminiscences from childhood, adolescence, and after. In 1940, he spent a semester teaching at Cornell and, later, stayed as Auden's guest at 7 Middagh Street in New York City. He returned to a bombed-out London that winter, and began writing features for the BBC — a job he would keep for the rest of his life. Though he had attempted to enlist in the British Navy (he was turned down on account of poor eyesight), he supported Auden and Isherwood's move to New York in 1939, feeling strongly that "The expatriates do not need anybody else to act as their ersatz conscience: they have consciences of their own and the last word must be said by their own instinct as artists." Yet his feelings on the matter were perhaps more complicated, as he admitted in a 1941 *Horizon* article, writing, "if I had stayed in America I do not suppose I should have felt morally guilty, though I might have felt instinctively so."

MacNeice continued publishing poetry, plays, and literary criticism until his death in 1963. For years afterward, his reputation waned in Auden's shadow until a group of Northern Irish poets, including Seamus Heaney and Paul Muldoon, began to champion his work. As both outsider and insider, possessor and dispossessed, MacNeice was a model of cultural transience and displacement for these poets, who were raised on the literal and metaphorical frontier between England and Ireland. Due in part to their campaign, MacNeice is no longer viewed as a minor English poet, but a major Irish writer whose work has influenced some of the greatest post-war poetry of the twentieth century.

Auden first met MacNeice at a champagne party at Oxford in 1926. The encounter was brief, but MacNeice was determined to spend more time with the young college poet. Soon after their first meeting, Louis took the initiative and visited Auden in his room at Christ Church, where he found him reading quietly with the blinds down. Though the two would eventually grow close, MacNeice was, at this time, less enthralled by Auden's political ideas than Spender and Day Lewis. He was on the periphery of this clique, and it was not until 1933, after he gave Auden's *Poems* a favorable review, that he and Wystan became good friends.

In 1936, Auden was commissioned by Faber to write a book of "verse-epistles" about Iceland. He immediately invited Louis to join him, and, that summer, the two set sail for Iceland — Auden in June, MacNeice in August. Auden spent most of June in Reykjavik (where he endured endless amounts of dried fish, bad beer, and bland soup) but preferred the countryside, which he toured in July. When MacNeice arrived in August, the two poets spent eight days circumnavigating the ice fields of Langjökull on horseback with a group of boys from the Bryanston School in Britain. Riding single file, the poets shared many quiet moments admiring the glaciers; in the evening, they sometimes shared a tent. MacNeice, Auden wrote, was "the ideal travelling companion, funny, observant, tolerant and good-tempered." After the boys departed for home, Wystan and Louis took a boat north to Patreksjördur, where they were appalled by the carnage they witnessed at a local whaling station. They moved on the next day to Isafjördur, near the Arctic Circle, and lunched in the North Pole café. In early September, they returned to England.

Initially, Auden was unsure how to begin the book, but, after reading about the outbreak of the Spanish Civil War, he decided to write a verse *Letter to Lord Byron*. This letter, he wrote, had "very little to do with Iceland, but will be rather a description of an effect of travelling in distant places which is to make one reflect on one's past and one's culture from the outside." Indeed, the journey north was partly an act of temporary escapism from the political situation at home, as Auden wrote in his foreword to the 1965 edition of *Letters from Iceland*: "Though writing in a 'holiday' spirit, its authors were all the time conscious of a threatening horizon to their picnic — world-wide unemployment, Hitler growing every day more powerful and a world-war more inevitable." It was also a physical manifestation of disillusion and dissent; as Auden writes to Isherwood, "And North means to all: 'Reject!'" By traveling north instead of south, the poets set themselves apart from the Romantics, as Auden intimated in *Letter to Lord Byron*:

The North though was never your cup of tea;
"Moral" you thought it so you kept away.

This rocky, volcanic, cold land invited a tougher kind of writer than did the frescoed courtyards of the Mediterranean — though of course the irony is that Byron ultimately lost his life in the struggle for Greek independence. This is perhaps why Auden chose to address him rather than, say, Shelley — Byron had shown the kind of political commitment Auden (at that time) admired.

In the end, the poets packed *Letters from Iceland* with poems (including "Auden and MacNeice: Their Last Will and Testament"), sketches, prose letters, satire, history, curious photographs, pullout maps, and tourist information. As a result, the work is difficult to categorize — part travel book, part poetry collection, it was, as MacNeice later wrote, "a hodgepodge, thrown together in gaiety." Though the book contains good poems by both authors, particularly Auden's *Letter to Lord Byron*, it is also, as MacNeice's biographer Jon Stallworthy has noted, "somewhat self-indulgent." It was, however, a success — chosen as the Book of the Month by the Book Society and reprinted after selling 8,000 copies.

Looking back on his trip with MacNeice in 1965, Auden wrote, "I have very rarely in my life enjoyed myself so much as I did during those weeks when we were constantly together." He would eventually deliver the eulogy at MacNeice's memorial service in 1963, and address a later poem, "The Cave of Making," to his old friend. — HEATHER CLARK

MacSpaunday

This sobriquet meant MacNeice, Spender, Auden, and Day Lewis and was given to them by the British fascist poet Roy Campbell.

The Magic Flute 1956

"In 1955, [Auden] found an opportunity to expunge what he judged to be a wicked doctrine from a work written two hundred years earlier. He and Kallman, working on a translation of [Mozart's] *The Magic Flute* ... threw out everything in the original libretto that celebrated the triumph of masculine reason over feminine passion. The eighteenth century text, in Auden's view, was an example of history written by the victors" (Mendelson, Later Auden).

This libretto for *The Magic Flute* was as much a reworking of the original libretto as it was a translation. In the introduction to their version of the libretto of Mozart's beloved last opera, Auden and Kallman go to the trouble of explaining why they took such liberties in the translation. They felt themselves obliged to correct some of the idiosyncrasies and sources of confusion inherent in the original libretto. This is particularly true in regard to the Queen of the Night, with whom the audience tends to empathize in the first act (since she is portrayed as the grief-stricken mother wrongfully robbed of her beloved daughter Pamina), and whom the audience regards with a mixture of fascination

The Magic Flute, cover of first U.S. edition.

and horror in the second act, since she astoundingly threatens her daughter with all sorts of unpleasant things if the daughter does not kill Sarastro, the Queen's deadly enemy. It is a known fact that Mozart's original librettists (Schikaneder and Giesecke) shifted their treatment of the Queen of the Night between the first and second acts. As Auden and Kallman write:

> [...] to allow the Night [i.e., the irrational and the unconscious] a creative role is very untypical of the Enlightenment doctrines for which they [the librettists Schikaneder and Giesecke] stood and, had they denied it to the Queen, they would have spared themselves the most obvious criticism which is always brought against them, namely, that without any warning the audience has to switch its sympathies at the end of the First Act [Libretti, 130].

This basic "flaw" in the structure of *The Magic Flute* is one of the features which Auden and Kallman attempted to correct in their version. Although the Queen of the Night is unnamed in the Schikaneder-Giesecke libretto, Auden and Kallman call her Astrafiammante ("flaming star"), a name, moreover, which could well have been suggested by Papageno's reference to her rather early in the first act as "die sternflammende Königin."

It must be made clear from the outset that the translation of Mozart's *Die Zauberflöte* made by Auden and Kallman was more than just a translation: it was, in certain aspects, a reworking and a "clarification" of various points that the two translators regarded as muddled and confused. Mention has already been made of the inconsistencies in the original treatment of the Queen of the Night. But the translators of the libretto also took it upon themselves to re-arrange certain scenes of the second and final act of the opera.

In addition, they also saw fit to add three pieces of poetry that were most definitely not a part of the original. They added a prologue or "proem," as they called it, that consists of nine strophes of four lines apiece; a "metalogue" of considerable length which they positioned between the two acts of the opera and which is supposedly spoken by the singer who plays the role of Sarastro; and an epilogue or, to use their term, a postscript, that contains exactly 12 strophes of 3 lines, all 3 lines of which rhyme throughout each individual strophe. The last word in each of the 3 lines, respectively, of the first strophe are "throne," "own," and "known." Moreover, this postscript is presumably addressed to the two translators by Astrafiammante, the name they arbitrarily assigned to the Queen of the Night. All three of these poems are intentionally humorous, presumably in keeping with the humor that is to be found in some parts, though by no means in all parts, of the opera.—ROBERT STANLEY

"Makers of History" 1955

Kings and warriors who assert self-importance may become myths, but they are forgotten as individuals. The real makers are the artists who are remembered for themselves. See "T the Great" as a companion poem with a more specific example of the formerly great who has become obscure.

"Making, Knowing and Judging" 1956

One of Auden's most self-defining essays, given originally as a lecture at Oxford.

To illustrate the process of "becoming" a poet, one turns to Auden's first Oxford lecture, "Making, Knowing and Judging" (delivered in June of 1956 and subsequently published in *The Dyer's Hand*), whose subject matter is the acquisition of the Censor, or poetic self-consciousness, necessary for poetic development from apprenticeship to mastery, from imitating other poets to imitating oneself. The belief that the process of poetic maturation inevitably culminates in imitation of one's own poetic style indicates that emulation is, at all times, the predominant mode of writing: although its object changes, it can never entirely disappear. The critical stage in this process is the birth of what Auden calls the Censor. Once the Censor is born, it will assist the poet in writing poems that can for once seem real. It will become the poet's first and only audience. But before this intrinsic voice can be acquired, the young poet can only imitate other poets and model his work on those written in the past. He has no right to self-identity. The novice poet "has to pretend to be somebody else; he has to get a literary transference upon some poet in particular."

At this point, Auden indulges in a kind of idealistic speculation about perfect poetry workshops in which young poets could substantially better their skills: "I can imagine a system under which an established poet would take on a small number of apprentices who would begin by changing his blotting paper, advance to typing his manuscripts and end up by ghostwriting poems for him which he was too busy to start or finish. The apprentices might really learn something for, knowing that he would get the blame as well as the credit for their work, the Master would be extremely choosy about his apprentices and do his best to teach them all he knew." Of course this is not what really happens in today's creative writing workshops, but Auden's point is that, in very early stages of their

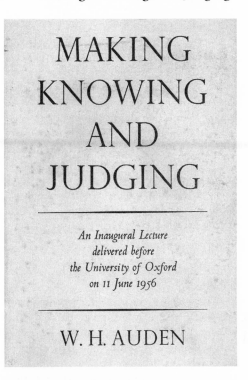

Making, Knowing, and Judging, first edition.

poetic development, the apprentices faithfully copy the style of their master. Since the kind of workshop he imagined in his lecture is also impossible, Auden admits the best form of apprenticeship takes place in a library: "This has its advantages. Though the Master is deaf and dumb and gives neither instruction nor criticism, the apprentice can choose any Master he likes, living or dead, the Master is available at any hour of the day or night, lessons are all for free, and his passionate admiration of his Master will ensure that he work hard to please him."—PIOTR GWIAZDA

In "Making, Knowing and Judging," Auden says that the poet's choices are from sacred objects that the poet turns into symbols, words, and associations for subconscious poetic usage. A poet's company (other poets) should not be so far above him as to be intimidating. Masterpieces should be taken out only for high holidays. A poet writes poetry; a scholar preserves the past. Poetry criticism is based on personal liking; "liking" by a reader of poetry supersedes and is more important than the critical approving of poetry by a critic.

Auden describes four types of critics: Prig — nothing is good enough (compared to his jealous fantasies of what he'd write himself). Critic's Critic — glorifies his critique to the near exclusion of that which is criticized. Romancer — imagines poet's life as his own. Maniac — imagines about everything.

On Judging Poems: What are the technical aspects? What are the writer's moral bases and influences? Man is an analogy-drawing animal who reads and judges by comparing a poem's symbolism to his own inner symbolism. Younger poets must pass the stage of imitating others; the older poet must pass the stage of imitating himself.

Auden then categorizes the sacred and profane in terms that reference both Coleridge and Tolkien.

The sacred is constituted of ascending beings and events that are recognized and activated in the primary imagination. The recognition of these sacred beings and events is intuitively emotive, priming the imagination with a passive awe that initiates the conversion of psychology into dreams. A sacred object just *is*, in a form that is beautiful. The secondary imagination (of the artist) pursues an active choice of forms for imitating sacred objects but never duplicating them, for duplication is impossible; the artistic form chosen is just what the artist wishes it to be, but the artistic form succeeds only if it is appreciated by an audience of one or many.

The profane is created when the sacred beings or events become artistic forms and descend to the material world, after which the former sacred beings, now having taken form through imitation as artistic forms, are no longer sacred and will need to be replaced by new sacred beings and events.

The primary imagination that intuits sacred beings and events inspires the secondary imagination to create homage to these intuited sacred beings and events in the form of artistic beauty. This artistic beauty imitates or evokes the sacred intuitions so that both an artist and an audience can be reminded of the initial awe inspired by the sacred.

The recreation of awe as art is a rite meant to be shared. Poetry is a rite-by-naming. Naming is a rite of symbolic analogy that inspires

awe by using words to evoke sacred feelings. Poetry is analogy; it always uses words to point to inner correlations that are greater than the words themselves. Large changes in a society will alter what that society considers sacred and profane, and these are reflected in artistic expression. A poem reflects the cumulative symbolism in the artist's and the audience's conscious and unconscious collective subjectivity that incorporates both past and present.

The Virgin and the Dynamo: The Dynamo (science) is the natural world and how one survives in it. The Virgin is the historical and artistic world of compassion. Without art there is no notion of the sacred; without science we would worship false gods. Science measures nature; art "metaphorizes" nature. We give faces to what and whom we revere; conversely, it is the faceless (those who are dehumanized) that we revile.

Pluralities: A crowd is anarchic, representing potential hell. A society has norms; a community has norms and also goals. Rival communities can bring each other to disorder.

Man as a soul and body is individual and natural; man as a mind and spirit is a member of a society, which is historical.

A poem is symbiotic; readers are interdependent with the artist, and neither can truly exist without the other. A poem is unique. A poet cumulatively learns about his world and cumulatively reacts to his community through analogy. Every good poem is utopian in that it conveys and intimates a verbal Eden that the artist and his audience wish could become real.

Mallarmé, Stéphane

1842–98, French poet. Mallarmé was one of the first symbolists and believed that poetry was a medium of metaphysical symbols that should transcend the words and evoke in readers a sense of "otherness." The influence of his poetry was particularly felt by Paul Valéry, who was read by Auden.

Mallarmé wrote that the poet's role was "Donner un sens plus pur aux les mots de la tribu" ("To give a purer sense to the words of the tribe"). Auden took this remark very seriously as an implication that the poet took particular words that could be looked up in the dictionary and then gave them universal meaning that transcended book meaning and that could relate to the collective unconscious that resides in any reader. Yet, Auden also saw Mallarmé's phrase as a warning for poets not to become too infatuated with words to the point of losing sight of their purpose in reaching the audience; that is, the words are "beautified" for their own sake, with intended message secondary. The beauty of words should never be more important than the truth of words; beauty should attract readers to the truth that is within the beauty.

"The Malverns" 1933

Written in the fall of 1933, this poem follows Auden's "A Summer Night" experience and his poem describing it. "The Malverns" is a contrast with the love-transcending vision of agape Auden felt in "A Summer Night"; yet the two poems are related as the first took place at the Downs School, which was located in the Malverns. The second seems to indicate that even in the same place one will see the world in a completely different way on different occasions. "The Malverns" does not discount transcendent love but considers the world pragmatically with references to Wilfred Owen and Katherine Mansfield who both died very young. The all-accepting love of "A Summer Night" is now a bit more cynical about the common herd of humanity that will always stand in the way of greater understanding. Ultimately, while the poem appeared in the volume *Look, Stranger* (1937), Auden expressed his dissatisfaction with it by thereafter excluding it from collections.

Man of La Mancha

Auden and Kallman were asked to write lyrics for this musical, but their lyrics were not used. The lyrics were published in Auden's last volume of poems, *Thank You Fog* (1974).

"The Managers" 1948

Contrasts contemporary (1948) secular saviors with those of the "bad old days." The present are managers/bureaucrats that are not motivated by service but the need for approval.

Mandelbaum, Maurice and Gwen *see* "In Sickness and in Health"

Mann, Thomas, and Children (Erika, Klaus, Golo)

Thomas Mann 1875–1955, German novelist and essayist, won the Nobel Prize for Literature in 1929. A writer of intellectual novels, Mann developed themes that searched the inner self and related inner problems caused by changes in European cultural values. Mann became famous with the publication of his first novel, *Buddenbrooks* (1901), that depicts the rise and disintegration of a merchant family. Other works are *Death in Venice* (1925), a novella in which the hero, a great writer, falls prey to an uncontrolled passion, weakens, and eventually dies; *Mario and the Magician* (1930), an allegorical attack on fascism; *The Magic Mountain* (1927); his tetrology *Joseph and His Brothers* (1934–44), a detailed recreation of the biblical story of Joseph; and *Doctor Faustus* (1947), in which Mann used the Faust motif to examine spirituality and sensuality. Mann left Germany in 1933 and later went to America. He became Auden's father-in-law when Auden married Erika Mann.

Erika Mann 1905–1969, German author, actress, Thomas Mann's oldest child. Her stage revues offended the Nazis and she became an enemy of the state; she met Isherwood in 1933 and asked him to marry her so she could get a British passport. Isherwood could not, but he asked Auden if he would. Auden agreed and they married on 15 June 1935. They were and remained friends only, and when she lived briefly in Brooklyn with Auden in 1941 she was the object of Carson McCullers' unrequited affection.

Klaus Mann 1906–49, novelist, essayist, and playwright. He left Germany in 1933 and edited an anti–Nazi journal in Amsterdam. He went to the United States in 1935 and became a citizen in 1943 when he entered the U.S.

Thomas Mann

army. His writings include *André Gide* and *The Crisis in Modern Thought* (1943). With his sister he wrote *Escape to Life* (1939) and *The Other Germany* (tr. 1940).

Golo Mann 1909–1994 was a roomer with Auden at Middagh Street in Brooklyn from March to July 1941. Golo Mann fled from Germany with his family in 1933. Auden first met him at Küsnacht in 1935. Golo Mann's best-known work was *German History in the 19th and 20th Century* (1958).

Auden enjoyed the friendship of the Mann children and respected their father although he was not a great admirer of Thomas Mann's writings in general. He did, however, praise Mann's *Coming Victory* as a definition of democracy and believed that Mann had an intuitive sense of Kierkegaard's ideas. In 1970 Auden, in a review titled "Lame Shadows," reviewed Mann's *Tonio Kruger and Other Stories*, and, in Auden's usual manner, the review is about Mann as well as Auden's views on aesthetics.

Mansfield, Katherine

1888–1923, British author, b. New Zealand. The stories in *Bliss* (1920) and *The Garden Party* (1922) made her famous. Among her later volumes of stories are *The Dove's Nest* (1923) and *Something Childish* (1924; Am. Ed. *The Little Girl*, 1924). Her collected stories were published in 1937. *Novels and Novelists* (1930) is a compilation of critical essays. She married editor and critic John Middleton Murry in 1918. She suffered from tuberculosis during the last five years of her life. Mansfield's stories are straightforward but have deeper meanings found between the lines. Murry edited her poems (1923, new ed. 1930); her letters (1928); and a collection of her unfinished pieces (1940).

The Oxford Auden was much influenced by Mansfield's letters, and said in a letter, "Her remarks about the relation between art and life are true for the most part. One must be clean in mind. I am so conscious of my failure in this, of one's self-conscious satisfaction with one's work. Writing should be like shitting, one's sole feeling that of a natural function properly performed, and I get excited about it" (British Library). Auden mentions "Kathy" in his poem "The Malverns" and Auden quotes from her journals that "To be rooted in life" is his goal.

"Many Happy Returns" 1942

(For John Rettger.) This poem is addressed to a child, as were a number from this period, and "is ostensibly a set of Birthday maxims to the seven-year-old son of a couple that befriended Auden in Ann Arbor [Michigan]. But it was also addressed privately to Kallman a few weeks after his twenty-first birthday, and to Auden himself as a rebuke to his own parental ambitions [towards Kallman]" (Mendelson, *Later Auden*). One line reads, "Tao is a tightrope." Auden had been impressed by a recent reading of Arthur Waley's *The Way and its Power*, a translation of the *Tao Te Ching*. (See also "Mundans et Infans.")

"Marianne Moore" *see* Moore, Marianne

"The Martyr as Dramatic Hero" 1968

In this essay Auden notes that death is the martyr's most significant act. The martyr becomes a sacrificial victim when his death is decided by others. The epic hero chooses to be a martyr in defending his group. The tragic hero seeks an expiation of guilt; this becomes a lesson to the group as he dies for this truth as a martyr, having chosen to be sacrificed for the group, which is his destiny, even though the group may not care, may not even realize his sacrifice, or even scorn him. The archetypal Christian martyr dies alone, forsaken, and humiliated. The Christian dilemma is martyrs who are motivated by the pride of epic glory. Auden then compares two verse plays: T.S. Eliot's *Murder in the Cathedral* has a martyr who is prideful, and Charles Williams' *Thomas Cramer* (Cramer authored the *Book of Common Prayer*) represents Cramer as the archetypal Christian martyr.

Marxism

Marxism changed twentieth century culture significantly; communism and socialism are derived from it, and most modern socialist theories are also based on it. It has also impacted economics, philosophy, and literary history. *The Communist Manifesto* and *Das Kapital* are its principal texts.

Marxism sees dialectical materialism as a force based on economic determinants that find society in a perpetual class struggle. The class that controls economic production rules until it becomes obsolete and is replaced by another. From this continuing process of opposition, a classless society would eventually develop. In the modern capitalist era, the bourgeois is the ruling class in conflict with the workers who actually produce goods but do not control their production. When the workers take control of production then society will start to function on a more equal basis and become classless.

After the Soviet revolution (see The Auden Generation), artists and intellectuals on the left saw this as a solution to the miseries that capitalism created. In the 1930s Auden was left politically and certainly interested in Marxism and Communism, but much more so as intellectual ideas than as a construct that he could act on more directly. He never did join the Communist Party, while C. Day Lewis, Edward Upward, and Stephen Spender (very briefly) did. (And they, along with scores of others would renounce the Soviet Union when it became clear that Stalin was a dictator no different than Hitler.) Auden danced with ideas but, as he would do throughout his life, changed partners frequently. He mentions Marx in *The Dance of Death*, praises Lenin in a 1934 essay (see Essays), and discusses Communism in other 1930s essays, and praises Christopher Caudwell's *Illusion and Reality* as a great Marxist text on art and history, and one which would influence his writing of "Spain"— but his praise always had reservations such as in "The Good Life," and *The Prolific and the Devourer*. Still, even by 1939, when Stalin's tyranny was evident, he made a distinction between Marxist theory and Soviet reality, still giving credit to the former, but denouncing the latter.

Auden: "Looking back, it seems to me that the interest in Marx taken by myself and my friends ... was more psychological than political; we were interested in Marx in the same way we were interested in Freud, as a technique of unmasking middle-class ideologies; ... our great error was not a false admiration for Russia but a snobbish feeling that nothing which happened in a semi-barbarous country which had experienced neither the Renaissance nor the Enlightenment could be of any importance.... Nobody I know who went to Spain during the Civil War who was not a dyed-in-the-wool Stalinist came back with his illusions intact" ("Authority in America" 1955).

In the end, as with anything to do with secular, social or political theories, Auden, for the most part, discounted all and any if there was not first a change in human nature, which, after Auden's arrival in America, would best come through his spiritual awakening to Auden's Christianity.

Masefield, John

1878–1967, English poet. He went to sea as a youth and later spent several years in the United States. In 1897 he returned to England and was on the staff of the *Manchester Guardian*. His first volumes of poetry, *Salt-Water Ballads* (1902), and *Ballads* (1903), earned him the title "Poet of the Sea." It was his realistic, long narrative poems — *The Everlasting Mercy* (1911), *The Widow in the Bye Street* (1912), *Dauber* (1913), and *Reynard the Fox* (1919) — that made him famous. He was also a playwright and novelist. He was poet laureate from 1930 until his death and was awarded the Order of Merit in 1935.

Masefield was the multi-faceted writer Auden also strove to be. Auden and Masefield met during the 1930s and would meet at Oxford on occasion. Their first meeting had been at the Downs School in 1933 when Auden invited the poet laureate to see his students in the miracle play *Deluge*. Masefield told I. A. Richards that Auden was a dynamic man of genius. Masefield knew Charles Williams, poet, novelist, and editor for the Oxford University Press, and may have introduced Auden to Williams who would later have a great impact on Auden. In 1937 Auden "had been named as the winner of the King's Gold Medal for Poetry, an award given to the author of what was judged to be the best first or second volume of verse — in Auden's case *Look Stranger!* The choice of Auden as winner was no doubt largely due to John Masefield, who as poet laureate was chairman of the committee that made the award. Masefield presented Auden to George VI on 23 November 1937 when, wearing a tail-coat borrowed from Cyril Connolly, Auden came to Buckingham Palace to receive the medal. The award annoyed many of Auden's supporters, who saw it as something of a betrayal of the left" (Carpenter, *W.H. Auden*).

Maugham, William Somerset

1874–1965, English author, b. Paris. Maugham wrote with a cynical and ironic wit. He first achieved fame as a dramatist before writing novels and short stories. His novel *The Razor's Edge* (1944) concerns a young American's search for spiritual fulfillment, with the protagonist based on Gerald Heard.

Maugham must be read into Auden's *Letters from Iceland* and *Letter to Lord Byron*. Auden tells us that Maugham's stories are being read on the Iceland trip. Now Byron has always been an idol for youth; but what is Maugham

W.S. Maugham

an idol of? In 1919, in *The Moon and Sixpence* Maugham writes into his novel's and his narrator's opening chapter the declaration that, where the post-war young are concerned, Maugham is "on the shelf," out of date; that he, the novel's author who also is its I-narrator, was out of step already among the pre-war modernists. The painter Charles Strickland, who is the novelist-narrator's subject, was not out of step with his time; in contrast, Maugham confesses, he himself might best be compared to the poet George Crabbe's survival into the era of the Romantics, who were the Stricklands and the modernists of their age. Given the confession, it is all the more wonderful that Maugham should be in Auden's Iceland, from which letters get sent to the Romantic modernist Byron, and not to out of date Maugham-Crabbe.

Maugham-Crabbe, yet another complex persona, enters the queer hyphen-spliced characters in this (*Letter to Lord Byron*) foray into literary history, and it is not surprising to notice that Maugham the narrator of Charles Strickland's tale becomes the artist's spokesman, his executive personality (and in effect, this is what Auden does in *Letter to Lord Byron*). In becoming that, almost against his will, in speaking for Strickland as well as about him, Maugham is perplexed by the contradictions that split personalities. "I'm reminded," he says of Strickland, "of those strange stories ... of another personality entering into a man and driving out the old one." The Maugham-narrator would seem to be an impervious foil to such changes of personality: always the same phlegmatic observer, he is all consistency, whereas Strickland is, indeed, incoherent, in his passionate likes and dislikes, and in his way of acting them out. Maugham-Crabbe undergoes a split: "an interest in the singularities of human nature" is "so absorbing that ... moral sense is powerless against it." The older generation falls into modernism. Strickland occasions the fall, but what encapsulates the fall is less the artist than his art. Strickland's painting of the seduced wife is discovered by the cuckold after his wife's suicide. The painting nullifies all the man's personal attachments: Strickland's victim, himself a painter, is "transported" by the painting "into a world in which the values were changed"; and he describes the painting as the birth of art's autonomy alongside Strickland's descent into multiple personality disorder — Strickland can only have painted this way by having made a new executive self of his own.

But the executive self finds resources in isolating flight from the world. Such a self can not have executive power unless it has pursued and experienced detachment. It goes off to an island, an appropriate place for art's radical self-sufficiency, just as an island was an Auden symbol for his mid 1930s poems. Given Strickland's flight, the I-narrator (hitherto an eye-witness) must become a researcher into the remainder of Strickland's life. The remainder resists, Maugham confesses, the narrative shape and coherence one associates with fiction. In fact, Maugham introduces the last third of his novel with the re-assertion that the text is biography, not fiction, and that Strickland resists even a biographer's requirements, which are less exacting than a novelist's, for making one's subject intelligible. One requirement for biography is context. Strickland goes to Tahiti, where as an artist-shaman he hides away and also makes autonomous his multiple personalities.

Maugham is a multiple personality in real life as well as in *The Moon and Sixpence*. Auden's favorite among the Maugham stories he read in Iceland is from Maugham's Ashenden volume, where Maugham makes spy fiction out of his own real life as a World War I secret agent, and where he is "His Excellency," which recounts the Eros-inspired double lives of two diplomats. One of the diplomats happens to be named Byring. Despite Byring's relevance to Auden, however, another Maugham production seems especially important to Auden's island/Iceland. This is Maugham's essay on El Greco, published in 1935 when Maugham was 61, in which Maugham debates the possibility of the painter El Greco's homosexuality. It's with this essay in mind that one hypothesizes Auden's alliance with Maugham.

The essay admits Maugham's love for El Greco. And he is one of the greatest painters because he isolated his art, and thereby freed it, from references both to the world and to religion. Although El Greco paints religious subjects, he has, Maugham maintains, no emotional attachment to them. His art's detachment, its self-referring character, is what makes it compelling. And its self-referential quality Maugham also thinks is a mark of El Greco's homosexuality. By virtue of sardonic detachment, his version of island/Iceland, El Greco dismisses the content of art in favor of its form; he endorses "the heresy," as Maugham calls it, "that subject is of no consequence." Much as Maugham is entranced by the heretic, Maugham objects to the heresy because he believes that El Greco's detachment and abstraction dissolve personality altogether. The dissolution in itself is not objectionable, for it is the threshold to the mysterium which multiple personality order, in all of its exponents, takes to heart. But in El Greco the dissolution of personality did not issue in the multiple personae that, despite grave difficulty, utter the sublime mystery underlying personhood and loan the mystery agency and liberty. Instead, El Greco's dissolution of personality issued in a corrosive skepticism towards agency and liberty, as well as towards art. Because of El Greco's detachment, art in his hands became beautiful but impotent, an empty formalism. And this means that El Greco's proto-modernism, homosexual and autonomy-inciting though it is, became a political liability rather than a strength. The post–Renaissance state found no challenge to its coercive power in art's investments in those potential accompaniments of formalism, inane flippancy and sardonic humor. Maugham finds that modernism's incarnation of El Greco's proto-modernism makes the same mistaken investments. And when modernist artists, as Maugham says, make "technical devices the end and aim of their endeavor," one gathers that artists follow a trajectory like T.E. Lawrence's. Their rebellious detachment from the state or religion becomes submission to them.

Maugham himself is having a cross-generational discussion about homosexuality and art. The El Greco essay reproduces and yet also criticizes the figure of Strickland the modernist, with whose character Maugham seems to fuse the gay El Greco. Undoubtedly Maugham himself has a conflict of feeling about previous — vastly previous — generations of gay utterance. He loves El Greco, but he loves alternative possibilities of expression more. There are sentences in Maugham's essay that wound homosexual self-love as much as does Auden's remark about Frederick Rolfe the "paranoid homosexual." Homosexuality is "abnormal," homosexual Maugham declares; and he declares as well that "it cannot be denied that the homosexual has a narrower outlook on the world than the normal man." For us now these are scarcely likeable assertions. But they might be plausible ones if their context is Maugham's intention to transform homosexual traditions, to bring them out of hermetic isolation and exclusiveness and into a state of worldly engagements. In the course of his cross-generational discussion, Maugham claims the cultural coming of age and the cultural aging of modernism and homosexuality, and claims even the aging of their conquest of autonomy. The motive for the claims is not self-censorship or a case of sleeping with the enemy; instead Maugham appears to be taking up — in the midst of the fascist era — a new political responsibility. In order to engage it, he seems to believe homosexuality and its artistic heritage must transform themselves.—ROBERT CASERIO

Mayer, Elizabeth

1884–1970, Auden's friend and co-translator of German texts. His lifelong correspondence to her has been an invaluable aid to scholars and biographers. She was a German refugee on a ship with her children headed to the U.S. to meet her husband William, a Jewish psychiatrist when she met Benjamin Britten's friend Peter Pears who later introduced her to Auden. She was 56, a lapsed Lutheran, and resembled Auden's mother to whom Auden was devoted as he would also be to Mayer. His first sign of affection was his dedicating "New Year Letter" to her, which is significant because the long poem was his effusive declaration of love and spiritual faith. Mayer encouraged Auden's Christianity, and in "New Year Letter," which is Auden's version of Goethe's Faust, Mayer becomes the Gretchen of Faust. (Auden's friend MacNeice would later translate Faust.) Auden, shortly after his mother died in 1941, would give Mayer a picture of himself as a baby in his mother's arms signed, "Elizabeth. I know my mother would be (and is) very happy to see who has taken her place." Auden would also consult Mayer regarding his verse, and her opinion mattered. They would later collaborate on translations of Goethe's Italian Journey (1962), and she would co-translate with Auden's friend Louise Bogan The Sorrows of Young Werther and Novella (1971), for which Auden translated the poems. In 1964 Auden's poem "Lines for Elizabeth Mayer" was for her eightieth birthday.

"The Maze" 1940

The harder we look through the maze of life, the less we find. We must be patient, empty our willful egos, and wait for grace to fill the heart. Auden sums up the quest of the mystic saying that the centre, while difficult to find, "Is known to my unconscious mind." Kierkegaard's point of view influenced this poem.

Mc- *see as if* Mac-

Medley, Robert

Robert Medley was another chum from public school and had been the first person to suggest to Auden he might try poetry. Back then, Auden had also an unrequited affection for Medley though they remained friends only. Later, through Medley, Auden would be introduced to Rupert Doone and the Group Theatre that would produce his plays. Medley was set and scenic director for the Group Theatre and would also make his mark as a painter.

In his autobiography, *Drawn from the Life*, is Medley's account of his school days with Auden: "At the time, Wystan and I had plenty to talk about. To summarize my attitudes to life at that time, I would say they consisted of a romantic and muddled mixture of William Morris' *Guild Socialism*, the social anarchy of Kropotkin's *Mutual Aid*, Shelley, and Blake's *Marriage of Heaven and Hell*. I had affirmed my resistance to organized religion when I refused confirmation. Walking with Wystan one afternoon towards the woods which lay about a mile and a half on the far side of the Sheringham Road, I made an attack on the Church and discovered to my surprise that Wystan was devout. An argument followed and to soften what I feared might become a serious breach, after a pause, I asked him if he wrote poetry, confessing by way of exchange, that I did. I was a little surprised that he had not tried and suggested he might do so."

One could conjecture of Medley's recollection — as Wystan the psychologist certainly would have — that Auden's religious fervor was, at this crucial moment, transferred to the poetic fervor. *Drawn from the Life* also has details, from Medley's viewpoint, of Auden, Rupert Doone, and the Group Theatre. Medley also contributed to *W.H. Auden: A Tribute*, published after the poet's death, and edited by Stephen Spender.

A Meeting by the River

1972; revised 1978. A play by Christopher Isherwood and Don Bachardy based on Isherwood's 1967 novel of the same name. *A Meeting by the River* focuses on Oliver, an upper-class Englishman who abandons his work with the Red Cross to become the disciple of an aging Hindu swami residing in Munich. When the swami, who profoundly influences Oliver, dies, Oliver believes the old man has chosen his exact moment of departure. Moved, Oliver travels to India to spread the swami's ashes in the Ganges,

staying on to continue studying Hindu precepts and, eventually, to take sannyasi (final monastic vows). Oliver's brother, Patrick, travels to Thailand on business, but makes a detour to India in hopes of persuading Oliver to abandon his plans. Despite the fact that he has a wife (Penelope) and two daughters, Patrick has recently embarked on a homosexual relationship with a young man named Tom. This situation is further complicated by Oliver's feelings for Penelope and the intrusions of an Auden-Generation Mother, a formidable presence who has concerns about Oliver's well-being. Manipulating Oliver in both subtle and obvious ways, Patrick attempts to shake his commitment to becoming a swami. He only succeeds briefly when he compels Oliver to recognize that within him is a powerful will and ambition counter to his Hindu beliefs, aspects of his persona that presumably must die if Oliver is to be reborn as a swami. Temporarily thrown by Patrick's assault, Oliver has a startling revelation while seated on his Hindu mentor's favorite bench; his resolve is restored and he takes his vows as Patrick decides to break off his relationship with Tom and return to his wife. With some humor about their individual dilemmas, the brothers move to a greater awareness of their connections and differences. A dramatic adaptation, written by Isherwood with collaborator Don Bachardy, was first produced at the Mark Taper Forum in Los Angeles, California, in 1972, receiving mildly positive reviews. Under producer Terry Allen Kramer and Harry Rigby, a subsequent production of *A Meeting by the River* tried out for a Broadway production at the University of Tennessee at Knoxville in 1979, under the direction of Albert Marre and with a cast including Simon Ward, Keith Baxter, Siobhan McKenna, and Sam Jaffe. The play, severely truncated by director Marre prior to Broadway, received predominantly negative reviews and closed after its initial performance. Isherwood and Bachardy later collaborated on an as-yet unproduced screenplay adaptation of *A Meeting by the River*.

A Meeting by the River logically proceeds from the plays Isherwood co-wrote with Auden in the mid 1930s for England's Group Theatre. The play version of *A Meeting by the River* provides interesting parallels in the recurring themes of both writers, as well as the progression of Isherwood's conceptions of modern man, The Truly Strong Man and The Truly Weak Man. The process of artistic collaboration between two men, seen first in the Auden-Isherwood plays and later in Isherwood's collaboration with Bachardy, is mirrored in the connections between two men prominent in the works themselves. Tied to each other in various ways by bloodlines, work, artistic collaboration, and sexuality, the complex intersections of the central male characters of *A Meeting by the River*, as well as those of their collaborating authors, are illuminating. All present a broadly conceived definition of brotherhood shown in various guises along difficult personal journeys toward spiritual fulfillment. Auden and Isherwood had been drawn to the theatre with the zeal of reformers of what they viewed as an exhausted medium. Firmly rejecting the popular commercial stage as well as the prevalent style and techniques of modern realistic drama, they looked instead toward inventing a lyrical, satiric dramatic style owing to Bertolt Brecht and Kurt Weill, but much more to their own original experimentation (demonstrating striking similarities with German expressionism and epic theatre). What truly connects Auden and Isherwood is their conception of the moral conundrums of the modern world, an increasingly technological society that invites a moral corruption resisted, with various degrees of success, by central characters who are humane rebels battling against this corruption and the outmoded and hypocritical values of the immediate past. This was a theme Isherwood was still examining in both the novelistic and dramatic treatments of *A Meeting by the River*, which is by far Isherwood's most interesting post–Auden dramatic achievement in that, like his work with Auden, it benefits from a collaboration. It is also interesting in that he chose to dramatize a novel that seems, at least on the surface, to be a decidedly non-dramatic source, and that the novel itself had not been especially well-received by critics. Some of the critical ambivalence toward Isherwood's later writings resulted from the inclusion of overtly homosexual characters and themes, but there was also a significant shift in his literary goals. Isherwood's writings became more intimately personal, less

overtly political, and, generally speaking, more delicate and spare in language, structure, and overall style. What Isherwood achieves in the novel, and what is carried through into the play, is a depiction of the social structures of two worlds, the space between them, and the emotions and drives of characters belonging to those worlds, but not completely encompassed by them, elements explored by Auden and Isherwood in their dramatic collaborations of nearly forty years earlier.

"Meiosis" 1933

Meiosis is the process that produces sperm and egg cells, and Auden here considers history and sex. The act of love (sex) is an attempt at mutual possession. Sperm when mating sheds half of its "family" (ghosts) and may thus, after its journey across the Northwest Passage, do better in the next generation it spawns. But will it be better? "Meiosis" should be read after "A Bride in the 30's." Mendelson notes: "In a friend's copy [Auden] wrote the name Nietzsche next to [the last] line, but whatever [Auden's] conscious source, he used the same structure and main verb that Dante used in the final line of a greater poem about love: '*L'amor che muove il sole e l'altre stelle.*' Dante's amor was both universal and personal at once, but Auden in 1933 was by no means prepared to accept a love so absolute and undivided..." (*Early Auden*).

Melville, Herman *see* "Herman Melville"

"Memorial for the City" 1949

(In memoriam Charles Williams, d. April 1945.) The poem begins with an epigram from Julian of Norwich: "In the self-same sense that our soul is made sensual, in the self-same point is the City of God ordained to him from without beginning." (The City of God is a Greek and Augustinian reference to the good city of Auden's imagination.) This poem in four stanzas contrasts naturalistic and Christian attitudes towards time. Natural time, really meaning man's devised artificial construct of time, is an enemy as it renders man unimportant. Christian time is the mystics' eternal now where the span of one life is not the strict, inclusive measure of time. When man sees himself as finite, he thinks only of the moment; if he embraces his being as a spirit that lived before and will live after his suitcase of a body that carries his spirit around, then he will think of the future and not just himself. Art and science must win out over nature. A city must be built unlike those of the corrupt Middle Ages that Luther protested against where man would be saved if he paid. In the Renaissance, art glorified man, but then science usurped man's divinity and made him an object of studied secularism. When a city is built on secularism alone it can only fail. Human timidity and stupidity must be overcome so that the spirit can return to build a City of God.

Mendelson, Edward

1946– , Auden named Mendelson his literary executor in 1971, acknowledging the Columbia graduate student's profound knowledge of Auden's life and art. Mendelson is now a professor at Columbia University in English and comparative literature and the leading Auden scholar in the world. He has begun the painstaking work of compiling Auden's collected work in definitive editions and thus far has published three on the plays, the libretti, and prose. He has also written the definitive studies of Auden's art: *Early Auden* (the British years), and *Later Auden* (American years). He is the president of the W.H. Auden Society, which publishes a newsletter.

"Merax & Mullin" 1955

In this poem the more blatant of two devils incites terrified souls to write nasty satires, while the less blatant devil has his victims fool themselves by denying impulses of hatred that they find too terrible to acknowledge.

Meredith, William

1919– , b. New York City, poet. U.S. Navy in World War II as a carrier pilot; served in the Aleutian Islands and Pacific Theater. *Love Letter from an Impossible Land* chosen for the Yale Series of Younger Poets Award by Librarian of Congress Archibald MacLeish who succeeded Stephen Vincent Benét and himself was succeeded by Auden. He continued to publish many volumes of verse, also taught, was a poetry editor, and befriended Auden. After Auden's death, Meredith and Monroe Spears became executors of Auden's estate, while Edward Mendelson became literary executor.

Merrill, James

1926–1995, American poet, novelist, and playwright, educated at Amherst College. His debut volume, *First Poems* (1951), was followed by *The Country of a Thousand Years of Peace* (1959), *Water Street* (1962), *Nights and Days* (1966), *The Fire Screen* (1969), *Braving the Elements* (1972), *Divine Comedies* (1976), *Mirabell: Books of Number* (1978), *Scripts for the Pageant* (1980), *Late Settings* (1985), *The Inner Room* (1988), and *A Scattering of Salts* (1995). Collected Poems appeared in 2001. Merrill also published two novels, *The Seraglio* (1957) and *The (Diblos) Notebook* (1965), in addition to plays, translations, a collection of interviews and essays (*Recitative*, 1986), and a late-life memoir *A Different Person* (1993). Merrill was one of a number of American poets — Anthony Hecht, John Hollander, Richard Howard, Karl Shapiro, and Richard Wilbur — deeply influenced by Auden, especially his post–World War II work characterized by decorum, urbanity, wit, and a masterful showcasing of traditional forms. Merrill's essays and interviews reveal a deep artistic affinity with Auden. Responding to an interview question about the older poet's influence on his work, Merrill said: "I read Auden by stages. I remember reading *The Sea and the Mirror* when I was in the army (just the place for that) and being dazzled by the range of forms, which meant most to me at that time. Certainly I was inspired to try some of these things myself" (Recitative). Indeed, much of Merrill's early and late poetry seems to revel cheerfully in traditional meters and forms; he also produced a number of sonnet sequences, including "The Broken Home," "Matinees,"

"Days of 1971," and "The Ring Cycle." Merrill's poems give the impression of being elegant and refined, but they are above all profoundly conscious of their form, often featuring traditional modes, complex structural patterns, in addition to (much more so than Auden) exploring artistic possibilities of free verse. Echoing Auden, he once observed that the use of form "at once frees and channels the unconscious" (Recitative).

Auden was an important though intimidating presence to many younger American poets throughout the fifties and sixties; Merrill's conflicted feelings of admiration and apprehension come through in his rare interactions with Auden reported in *A Different Person*. Throughout the 1960s Merrill was on much closer terms with Auden's companion Chester Kallman. Auden himself liked and admired Merrill's personality and viewed him as somebody with useful contacts in the U.S. publishing world. Auden was one of the judges who awarded Merrill his first National Book Award for *Nights and Days* in 1967, citing "his insistence on taking the kind of tough poetic chances which make the difference between aesthetic success and failure." In 1968 Merrill visited Kallman and Auden in their house in Kirschstetten, Austria. He was kept well-informed about the poet's final years through Kallman, who like Merrill, resided for a part of the year in Athens. As Kallman's close friend, Merrill was summoned in 1979 to make a deposition over the question of whether Kallman had intended to donate Auden's papers to the Berg Collection of the New York Public Library before his death. On October 18, 1983, Merrill and a number of other poets participated in a poetry reading in New York City commemorating the tenth anniversary of Auden's death, choosing to read from Part IV of *Letter to Lord Byron*, the most autobiographical section of the poem. By then, Merrill's poetry had made him Auden's heir in the eyes of numerous critics and fellow poets.

Merrill's relationship with Auden is noteworthy for another reason. In 1982 the poet published the complete edition of his 560-page epic *The Changing Light at Sandover*, an imaginative foray into the world of dead souls and otherworldly spirits, with themes ranging from metaphysics and apocalypse to homosexuality and opera. The trilogy offers Merrill an ideal opportunity to pay homage to Auden, by then a deceased mortal conversing via a Ouija board with Merrill and his companion David Jackson, but it also allows him to situate himself in regard to his exemplar's poetic legacy. Artistic affinity between the two poets is established on the pages of the epic, where Auden's wit and wisdom perfectly match Merrill's subtlety and sensitivity, while his civil or communal manner harmoniously supplements the younger poet's more personal or confessional style. Auden's status as a famous poet and public intellectual makes his presence in the trilogy justifiable, if not desirable. But while retaining his characteristic diction, "Wystan" undergoes several spiritual and philosophical transformations with respect to his views on poetry, art, the occult, science, knowledge, and religion. Thus, Merrill's creative construction of Auden's persona in the trilogy is a projection of what the older poet has always meant to him as a person and a writer; he is a necessary by-product of Merrill's reflections on his own art and career. "Wystan" is a literary model he simultaneously regrets and rejoices in never having lived up to, a poet he both admires and, in a misleadingly benign manner, continues to amend. Unburdened of his religious dogma, extolling the beauty of the younger poet's experiment even at the cost of its truthfulness, and, above all, eager to place artistic fable above historical fact — such is the portrait of Auden in *The Changing Light at Sandover*. — Piotr Gwiazda

Merwin, W.S.

1927– , William Stanley Merwin, American poet and translator, b. New York City. After graduating from Princeton in 1948, he traveled in Europe, studying romance languages. Merwin is noted for his restrained, spare, sometimes remote, often elegiac verse, which often focuses on nature and expresses an overwhelming sense of loss. Merwin was Auden's choice as Yale Younger Poet of 1952 for his volume *A Mask for Janus* (1952). Later volumes were *The Moving Target* (1963), *Lice* (1967), *The Carrier of Ladders* (1970; Pulitzer), *Opening the*

Hand (1983), *Selected Poems* (1988), *Travels* (1993), *Lament for the Makers* (1996), that includes a memorial poem for Auden, "Secrets," and *The River Sound* (1999). Merwin is also well known for his translations, among them *The Cid* (1959) and *The Life of Lazarillo de Tormes* (1962).

"Metaphor" 1966

This poem concerns not getting too outré with metaphors with the "nose" as an example, and finally listening to the "living word."

Miller, Charles

1930–1992, poet, novelist, and essayist. He was the author of a well-received memoir, *Auden: An American Friendship* (New York, 1983), an account that is centered on the months he spent as roommate and cook in Auden's house on Pontiac Trail, Ann Arbor, Michigan during the autumn and winter of 1941. He and Auden met when Auden came to lecture and read at the University during January 1940.

Milton, John

1608–74, English poet, b. London, one of the greatest poets of the English language.

His dislike of the increasing ritualism in the Church of England was the reason he later gave for not fulfilling his plans to become a minister. He wrote the masque *Comus* (1634) and *Lycidas* (1638), an elegy on the death of his friend Edward King. *Paradise Lost* tells the story of Satan's rebellion against God and the story of Adam and Eve in the Garden of Eden. Milton attempted to account for the evil in this world and, in his own words, to justify the ways of God to man. *Paradise Regained* (1671) describes how Christ, a greater individual than Adam, overcame the temptations of Satan. Milton also wrote numerous political and moral tracts. Disillusioned by the failure of his marriage, he started work on four controversial pamphlets (1643–45) upholding the morality of divorce for incompatibility. His *Areopagitica*

(1644) argues in favor of the freedom of the press.

To Auden, Milton was "the first poet in English literature whose attitude toward his art is neither professional like that of Ben Jonson nor amateur like that of Wyatt, but priestly or prophetic. Poetry to him was neither an amusing activity nor the job for which he happened to be qualified, but the most sacred of all human activities. To become a great poet was to become not only superior to other poets but superior to all other men" ("Introduction," *Poets of the English Language*, Vol. 3, 1950).

Mendelson in *Later Auden* observes that Auden's "In Memory of W.B. Yeats" (1939) is a response to both Yeats and to Milton's *Lycidas*, which is also an elegy. However, Auden also believed about Milton and Yeats that both dabbled too much in causes that took away from their creative gift. In 1970 Auden reread *Paradise Lost* and decided it was not Christian for its lack of sympathy, and earlier he noted that he thought it easier to read poets with whom he disagreed. In the poem "The Aliens" (1970), about insects, which he wrote concurrently with his rereading of *Paradise Lost*, Auden includes many phrases from Milton. (See also "The Duet.")

Minimum Working Hypothesis

The author Aldous Huxley composed this hypothesis by drawing on quotations from mystics throughout history. The four tenets of the hypothesis are as follows:

The phenomenal world of matter and of individualized consciousness—the world of things and animals and even gods—is the manifestation of a Divine Ground within which all partial realities have their being, and apart from which they would be non-existent.

Human beings are capable not merely of knowing about the Divine Ground by inference [intimating the Awe-sociations]; they can also realize its existence by a direct intuition [i.e., meditation, art] superior to discursive reasoning. This immediate knowledge unites the knower with that which is known.

Man possesses a double nature, a phenomenal ego and an eternal self, which is the inner man, the spirit, the spark of divinity within the soul. It is possible for a man, if he so desires, to identify himself with this spirit and therefore with the Divine Ground which is of the same or like nature with the spirit.

Man's life on earth has only one end and purpose: to identify himself with his eternal self and so come to unitive knowledge of the Divine Ground of all existence.

"Minnelied" 1967

This poem, to Kallman, makes him an idealized beloved, but is motivated by Auden's loneliness.

"Miss Gee" 1937

The ludicrous life of "Miss Gee" (to the melody of the song St. James' Infirmary) is an absurdist romp about a delusional virgin reminiscent of Mortmere, as it is a reaction to Auden's feelings of self-defeat after visiting the Spanish Civil War. He has her say "Does anyone care?" and this is the point. "Miss Gee" is a companion poem to "James Honeyman" and "Victor."

"Missing" *see* Poems

"A Misunderstanding" 1934

Here Auden takes the role, as Mendelson calls it, of "Indifferent Redeemer" and he is his own severest critic. He imagines being needed but is afraid to submit himself to the possible vulnerability that this entails; plus he fears letting people down and not getting their approval.

Mitchison, Naomi

1897– , British writer, b. Scotland, educated at Oxford, daughter of the biologist J.S. Haldane. She was active in local government in Scotland (1947–1976).

Very early in his career Auden met Mitchison and she had an impact on his verse and thinking that would influence the English Auden of the 1930s, and by extension via artistic evolution, the later Auden as well. Mitchison was one of Auden's contemporaries who helped to construct him as the representative of a younger generation of writers.

Mitchison had already established a reputation by the start of Auden's career. In 1920 she had published a play, *Barley, Honey and Wine*, set in the country of Marob, an imagined Scythian culture later to be the setting of one of her best known novels, *The Corn King* and *The Spring Queen*. In 1923 she published her first novel, *The Conquered*, set during the Roman conquest of Gaul.

Mitchison was also known as a political activist. In the twenties she published articles or stories in liberal and feminist journals concerned with the position of women. In 1931 her historical novel *The Corn King* and the *Spring Queen* was published to excellent reviews. Most reviewers did not pick up the feminist force of the novel, focusing on the King instead of the Queen. Her novel was exactly the type of fantasy-with-a-philosophy that Auden appreciated.

The novel uses Frazer (*Golden Bough*) and Marx's ideas of historical phases and social organization to explore a range of ways in which cultures have regarded and organized feminine and masculine power. This kind of quest was one in which Auden at this period was also interested. Indeed, many of Mitchison's interests were ones she and Auden could share — though without complete agreement.

Mitchison helped Auden early on in his career, and took an interest in him throughout his life. He, at least during the thirties, also took a close interest in Mitchison's writing, and they had some interesting exchanges of views. Naomi had a chance to review Auden's first volume of poetry, *Poems*, in *Weekend Review* in October 1930. The review is supportive of Auden and his generation.

The next thing that Mitchison was able to do for Auden (and he for her) was to invite him to contribute to an unusual children's book. Titled *An Outline for Boys and Girls and Their Parents*, this was intended to offer intelligent, approachable commentary on current cultural issues — social, scientific and artistic — for families of a left/liberal tendency. He would pen an essay on "Writing."

An Outline was brought out by Victor Gollancz, the leftist publisher, in 1932. Though clearly intended to reach the next generation before they had settled into unthinkingly conservative positions, it is unclear whether the contributors expected the reaction that the book received. A number of Anglican clergy, together with the headmasters of both Eton and Harrow, protested against the book in a letter sent to the major newspapers. Many liberal and left figures defended the book, Gollancz, George Bernard Shaw, Harold Laski, Rebecca West, C.E.M. Joad and, most particularly, the feminist Lady Rhondda.

The essay was the last formal publication on which Mitchison helped Auden. However, their correspondence at this time picks up interestingly on some of the joint interests and discussions that seem to inform the points at which their published writing touches.

Auden sometimes provided explanation for his poetry in letters to Naomi, including his "marginal notes" to *The Orators* in a letter of August 1931.

For his part, Auden made some comments about *The Corn King and the Spring Queen*: "Some of the scenes in the Prawn King and the String Queen were hotter than anything I've read. My dear, how do you get away with it?"

Mitchison and Auden lost touch in more ways than one after he went to the U.S. in 1939. Auden moved on almost as soon as he reached the U.S. from the kind of direct social responsibility that Mitchison had wanted him to embrace.

Nearly thirty years later, Mitchison wrote a piece about this period when she and Auden were in close contact, published in *Shenandoah* in 1967.—CHRISTOPHER HOPKINS

Moby Dick see *The Enchafèd Flood*

"The Model" 1942

This poem is about an "eighty-year-old

woman, sitting for a portrait, whose 'body ... exactly indicates her mind....' Being coherent in herself, she can make the world cohere around here" (Mendelson, Later Auden).

Montaigne, Michel

1533–92, French essayist, philosopher, His subject matter and style appealed to Charles Williams who quoted Montaigne in his book *The Descent of the Dove*, which Auden admired. It also inspired Auden to write much of his spiritually-searching verse of the 1940s. Auden quotes Montaigne for his epigram preceding *The Double Man*: "We are, I know not how, double in ourselves, so that what we believe we disbelieve, and cannot rid ourselves of what we condemn."

Montaigne was the son of a rich Catholic landowner and a mother of Spanish Jewish descent. From 1571 to 1580, in retirement, he wrote the first two books of his *Essais* (1580). The third book of *Essais* and extensive revisions and additions to the first two were published in 1588 and again, with more revisions, in 1595. The essays, which were trials or tests of his own judgment on a diversity of subjects, show the change in Montaigne's thinking as his examination of himself developed into a study of humankind and nature. The early essays reflect Montaigne's concern with pain and death. A middle period is characterized by Montaigne's motto *"Que sais-je?"* ("What do I know?"), which sums up his skeptical attitude toward all knowledge. This essay is an exposition on human fallibility. Montaigne's last essays reflect his acceptance of life as good and his conviction that humankind must discover their own nature in order to live with others in peace and dignity. Auden's brief, but telling poem "Montaigne," written in 1940, sums up Montaigne's skepticism as an important method of seeking truth. One must tear down the known to build up a new and better version of reality: "To doubt becomes a way of definition."

Moore, Marianne

1887–1972, American poet, b. St. Louis. Moore graduated Bryn Mawr College in 1909.

She spent most of her life in New York City, working first as a librarian and later as acting editor of the *Dial* (1925–29). Volumes of her verse include *Poems* (1921), *Observations* (1924), *What Are Years?* (1941), *Collected Poems* (1951; Pulitzer Prize), *O to Be a Dragon* (1959), and *Complete Poems* (1967). The translation *The Fables of La Fontaine* (1954) and the essays *Predilections* are two of her other notable works.

Auden's elegy, "In Memory of Sigmund Freud" (1939), adapts a meter that Moore employed, and "whose poetry he had known for some years but which he was only now coming to admire. Miss Moore herself lived in New York and whom Auden soon got to know, was described by him as 'one of the nicest people I have ever met'" (Carpenter, W.H. Auden).

That Auden admired Moore's verse and her person is evident in his 1962 essay "Marianne Moore." Moore's free verse is accentless and difficult, as is her content, but Auden's perseverance as a reader has made her one of his favorites. She has the qualities of Lewis Carroll's Alice: a distaste for noise, excessive fastidiousness, excessive love of order, and excessive precision. Her poems are overtly about animals. In this essay, Auden notes that in literature animals take on functions. 1) In beast fables, animal bodies have human consciousness to inform an audience as myths, or as satire, or as educative examples, or all three. 2) An animal simile is such that if an "A" behaves a certain way, "N" will act a certain way, e.g., "he fought like a lion." 3) An animal can be used as allegorical emblem: i.e., a badger is industrious. (A badger was the emblem of the Downs School and also the name of the school's magazine that Auden created for his students.) 4) Animals can imitate romantic encounters as reminders of human romantic encounters. 5) Animals can be objects of human affection, as for example pets with their personalization contrasted with and compared to man.

Moore is a naturalist, highlighting non-domestic animals, and like D.H. Lawrence, she is strongly metaphorical. Unlike Lawrence, she likes people, who to her are sacred animals. Moore's goodness shows through her poems.

Moore, Rosalie *see* Yale Series of Younger Poets

Moraes, Dom

1938, poet, b. Bombay, He studied at Oxford, and his first collection of poetry, *A Beginning* (1957), won the Hawthornden Prize. His autobiography is titled *My Father's Son* (1968). Moraes met Auden as an undergraduate at Oxford when Auden was lecturing there in 1956. In Moraes' autobiography, he reports that he then told Auden he was having trouble writing poetry. Auden replied, "Perhaps you ought to be in love." Moraes answered that he was. Auden countered, "Then it's the wrong person."

"The More Loving One" 1957

A lament for the fact that Auden loved Chester Kallman while Kallman did not reciprocate equally. Auden decided that "the more loving one should be me."

Mortmere *see* Isherwood, Christopher; *The Orators*

Mosley, Sir Oswald

1896–1980, British fascist leader. He organized (1932) the British Union of Fascists, based on the fascist parties of Germany and Italy. In 1936 he married Diana Guinness, sister of the writers Jessica and Nancy Mitford. Diana and another sister, Unity Freeman-Mitford, were friends of Hitler. Until after the outbreak of World War II, Mosley attacked workers and Jews. In 1940 he and his wife were captured but released in 1943. After the war Mosley tried to revive his movement, but failed.

Few remember today that Britain had a fairly large and vocal fascist party during the 1930s, which of course Auden's generation despised. One must understand that people like Mosley gave the Auden gang good reason to fear for their futures not only from Hitler but at home as well.

Mother Courage and Her Children *see* Brecht, Bertolt

"Mundans et Infans" 1942

(For Albert and Angelyn Stevens.) This poem concerns how a new baby affects not just the family but is symbolic of continuing previous paths of power and associations. Pindar's praise of athletic heroes is Auden's technique but the words chosen are those of contemporary dictators. Albert Steven was an English professor at Ann Arbor, Michigan, when Auden was there, and Auden wrote the poem when Angelyn was pregnant. The parents named the boy Wystan Auden Stevens. The poem also concerns Auden and Kallman.

Murray, Joan *see* Yale Series of Younger Poets

"Musée des Beaux Arts" 1938

Perhaps Auden's most anthologized poem. It is another rebuke to his own political poem "Spain" and a precursor to his withdrawal from activism that would follow Auden's arrival in America. He rejects some of his work of the previous three years with its grand exhortations ("Spain," *The Ascent of F6, On the Frontier*) and offers a cold truth that, rather than being dramatic, is numbing. It signifies as well what Aldous Huxley called Wholly Truthful Art where the mundane is equal to the magnificent and that there is always much more of the mundane than the magnificent. Auden agreed. High style does not transform events from what they really are, or the fact that some care and most don't. Life goes on. In the poem, motivated by Brueghel's painting *Icarus*, Icarus, his wax-fastened wings shorn because he had the hubris to fly too close to the sun, falls into the sea while farmers, ships, workers, children do not even notice or, worse, don't care. It is not important because it is not happening to them and they are self-absorbed in their own lives, not the lives of others, and no one can make them be aware if they choose not to be.

"Music Is International" 1947

Columbia University's Phi Beta Kappa poem for the year. The thought behind music's worldly reach is that, perhaps, music is the most flexible of the arts and relies less on pre-knowledge than any other artistic medium, and certainly before literature, which depends on one's ability to know and understand a language. Music becomes Auden's metaphor for all art but also a symbol of that mystical knowledge that transcends language, and that is the knowledge of faith, compassion, and the Vision of Agape. Art is one of the mediums that can lead to the transcendent urge that can then lead to the Vision of Eros and then Agape. Yet, while art can be white magic that influences with no intent to harm, one must also know that art can be black magic — or propaganda — that deceives. Auden says that from the great composers tyrants learned to erase reason by playing on emotions. He is here thinking of Hitler and Wagner. Auden admired the composer but not what Hitler used his music for.

Mysticism

In 1941 Auden told Stephen Spender that the highest vocation was the "mystical life because [it is] the most difficult, exhausting, and dangerous." Later Auden would often see artistic pursuit as a form of mystical contemplation. Auden had a mystical experience on "A Summer Night" in 1933 and wrote a poem about it. By his arrival in America in 1939, this experience strongly influenced his re-conversion to Christianity, one that sought little dogma but more of an intuitive self-discovering of an intellectual spirituality. While Auden was disappointed that Christopher Isherwood left him in New York to see Gerald Heard in California, it can be noted that Isherwood became a devoted follower of Vedanta, an Eastern philosophy derived from ancient Hindu religious scriptures (The Bhagavad-Gita, the Upanishads, etc.) which rely on mysticism as their basis. Consequently, Auden matched Isherwood's fervor but chose to find a western mysticism to counter his friend's eastern mysticism. For both men, the inner life and search for meaning were paramount. This search drew correlations between the spiritual search and the artistic vocation.

Auden said "ignorance is impiety"; conversely, an artist's highbrow understanding is piety of the first order. On this, Auden continued, "One of the principal functions of poetry—of all the arts ... is the preservation and renewal of natural piety toward every kind of created excellence, toward the great creatures like sun, moon, and earth on which our lives depend, toward the brave warrior, the wise man, the beautiful woman. Sometimes poetry regards the excellence of its subjects as self-derived, at other times as an outward and visible sign of an invisible uncreated God, but in either case it is with the outward, concrete and visible that it is concerned" ("Foreword" in Daniel Hoffman, *An Armada of Thirty Whales*).

Auden sought to recreate in poetry the feelings of awe aroused in people when encountering nature and beauty. He also himself believed there was another form of awe that flows from the stirrings of romantic love, and before he states this cause, to prepare us, he explains the difference between physical and spiritual beauty. For physical beauty, he said:

Moral approval is not involved. It is perfectly possible ... to say: "Elizabeth has a beautiful figure, but she is a monster."

If, on the other hand, I say: "Elizabeth has a beautiful ... expression," ... I am speaking of something which is personal.... Nature has nothing to do with it. This kind of beauty is always associated with the notion of moral goodness. And it is this kind of beauty which arouses in the beholder feelings [not of admiration or lust], but of personal love. [This love is] intended to lead the lover towards the love of the uncreated [unmediated] source of all beauty [or the awe that such beauty evokes] ("Introduction" to *Shakespeare: The Sonnets*).

In his introduction to *Shakespeare: The Sonnets*, Auden discusses this other kind of love that romantic love leads to. He explains what the bard was really writing about to that mysterious person (W.H.) who has never been positively identified. "The subject was, indeed, love, but not of just a romantic, or even sexual love, but mystical love—known as the Vision of Eros, which is concerned with a single person, who is revealed to the subject as being of infinite sacred importance.... It can, it seems, be experienced before puberty. If it occurs later, though the subject is aware of its erotic nature, his own desire is always subordinate to the sacredness of

the beloved person.... Before anything else the lover desires the happiness of the beloved.... When [the Vision of Eros] is genuine, I do not think it makes any sense to apply to it terms like heterosexual or homosexual. Such terms can only be legitimately applied to the profane erotic experiences with which we are all familiar, to lust, for example, an interest in another solely as a sexual object, and that combination of sexual desire and philia, affection based on mutual interests, values, and shared experiences which is the securest basis for a happy marriage.

That, in the Vision of Eros, the erotic is the medium, not the cause, is proved, I think, by the fact, on which we all agree, that it cannot long survive an actual sexual relationship."

Auden also in this Introduction defines how one can determine if he has had the mystical Vision of Eros: a) the experience is a genuine revelation, not a delusion; (b) the erotic mode of the vision prefigures a kind of love in which the sexual element is transformed and transcended; (c) he who has once seen the glory of the Uncreated revealed indirectly in the glory of a creature [beloved one] can henceforth never be fully satisfied with anything less than a direct encounter with the former.

For Auden art and romantic love are rivers to the ocean from which all mystical Awe really derives, the ocean of mystical consciousness. Awe, however it chooses to manifest itself, intimates the unified unconscious of the psychic Eden (see Audience). Artists and lovers are attempting to feel the vicarious God-Awe correlative; consequently, they are seeking to do unconsciously what the mystics are trying to do deliberately—which is to un-separate themselves and re-unify with the all of mankind, the all of the universe.

Auden further interprets mystical experience by telling us how a person can identify that one has taken place. Auden again does so in his introduction to *Shakespeare: The Sonnets*. Auden believed that Shakespeare's principal motivation in writing the sonnets, "the primary experience—complicated as it became later—out of which the sonnets to the friend spring—was a mystical one." Hence, Auden then followed by explaining what "mystical experience" means:

All experiences, which may be called mystical, have certain characteristics in common.

1) The experience is "given." That is to say, it cannot be induced or prolonged by an effort of will, though the openness of any individual to receive it is partly determined by his age, his psychological make-up, and his cultural milieu.

2) Whatever the contents of the experience, the subject is absolutely convinced that it is a revelation of reality. When it is over, he does not say, as one says when one awakes from a dream: "Now I am awake and conscious of the real world." He says, rather: "For a while the veil was lifted and a reality revealed which in my 'normal' state is hidden from me."

3) With whatever the vision is concerned, things, human beings, or God, they are experienced as numinous, clothed in glory, charged with an intense being-thereness.

4) Confronted by the vision, the attention of the subject, in awe, joy, dread, is absolutely absorbed in contemplation and, while the vision lasts, his self, its desires and needs, are completely forgotten.

Further, there are four different types of mystic visions: The Vision of Dame Kind is the mystical state catalyzed by an awesome experience found in nature, which induces a state of oneness with nature; the aforementioned Vision of Eros is the mystical state aroused by the awesome experience inspired by love for another individual. By extension, if it is possible, through the Vision of Eros, to feel "mystical" about one person, then, as the Vision of Agape, one can feel mystical about not just the one, but the many. Auden recounts this incident as personal evidence:

One fine summer night in June 1933 I was sitting on a lawn after dinner with three colleagues, two women and one man. We liked each other well enough but we were certainly not intimate friends, nor had any of us a sexual interest in another. Incidentally, we had not drunk any alcohol. We were talking quite casually about everyday matters when, quite suddenly and unexpectedly, something happened. I felt myself invaded with a power which, though I consented to it, was irresistible and certainly not mine. For the first time in my life I knew exactly — because, thanks to the power, I was doing it — what it means to love one's neighbor as oneself. I was also certain, though

my conversation continued to be perfectly ordinary, that my three colleagues were having the same experience. (In the case of one of them, I was later able to confirm this.) My personal feelings towards them were unchanged — they were still colleagues, not intimate friends — but I felt their existence as themselves to be of infinite value and rejoiced in it.

I recalled with shame the many occasions on which I had been spiteful, snobbish, selfish, but the immediate joy was greater than the shame, for I knew that, so long as I was possessed by this spirit, it would be literally impossible for me deliberately to injure another human being ["Introduction," *The Protestant Mystics*].

Auden wrote about this experience many years later; however, he did write a poem about his experience at the time, "A Summer Night." In this poem Auden describes — but does not name — the mystical vision of Agape, the transcendent love for all existence. Shortly after this mystical "Summer Night," Auden, duly inspired, wrote this in a review of the *Book of Talbot*: the "first criterion of success in any human activity, the necessary preliminary, whether to scientific discovery or to artistic vision, is intensity of attention or, less pompously, love."

Auden recounted this Vision of Agape, and, it would seem that "A Summer Night" did influence the future spiritual direction of Auden's Christianity. Of the experience, he later said, "among the various factors which several years later brought me back to the Christian faith in which I had been brought up, the memory of this experience and asking myself what it could mean was one of the most crucial…" ("Introduction," *The Protestant Mystics*).

After one achieves the Vision of Agape, the fourth vision is the Vision of God directly, which is the rarest, and beyond possible expression even analogously. This vision is felt; and there are no words that will suffice to remotely intimate the feeling. Mystics of all persuasions have said and would ultimately say, there's nothing to be said about it.

Aldous Huxley, much influenced by Gerald Heard as Auden was, also pursued mysticism in the 1940s. In 1944 Huxley published an anthology, *The Perennial Philosophy*, in which he compiled quotations from mystics throughout history, showing that despite separations of time and space, there was a consistent pattern of thought concerning mysticism. He distilled these thoughts to form four tenets that summarize mystical philosophy and called this a "Minimum Working Hypothesis," which reflected on the nature of a "Divine Ground of all existence."

Auden, in his own way, also sought a divine ground of all existence through an existential Christianity (Paul Tillich referred to a Ground of Being), and through his art as philosophical extensions of his search for a transcendent ideology. In 1956 he would read a book by Owen Barfield, *Saving the Appearances*, that would give him a further understanding that the One and the Many, are not distinct, but, indeed, inseparable, as mysticism has always asserted. (See also Christianity; Heard, Gerald.)

"The Mythical Sex" 1947

Auden wrote this essay when he was with Rhoda Jaffee, and it is "a casual-seeming prose piece he wrote ... about the impersonal myths of Infernal Venus and Celestial Venus, which mask the personal reality of beautiful women" (Mendelson, *Later Auden*).

Mythmaking

In their efforts to combine the saga with the pseudo-saga of the British Public School, Isherwood and Auden had two concerns regarding their interpretation of psychology in relation to art: 1) the mythological aspects of the saga reflect the past and show how that past inevitably becomes the antecedent influences that dominate the present; 2) psyches in the present are conflicted with an inner duality that is attempting to resist the influence of the past consciously while succumbing to that influence subconsciously.

Nabokov, Nicolas

1903–1978, b. Russia, composer, cousin to novelist Vladimir Nabokov. He went to Paris where he met ballet director/conductor Sergei Diaghilev, and later to the U.S.A. He taught music at different institutions and was active after World War II as an advisor to the American military government in Germany where he first met Auden. Nabokov, when he was secretary general of the Congress of Cultural Freedom, asked Auden in 1951 to speak for the congress in India. Auden accepted which allowed him to visit his brother John Auden and his family. Nabokov arranged for the first performances of Stravinsky's opera of *The Rake's Progress*, with libretto by Auden-Kallman, in Venice. In 1969 Lincoln Kirstein suggested to Nabokov that he and Auden-Kallman should do their own opera, which resulted in Shakespeare's *Love's Labour's Lost* that premiered in Brussels in 1973.

"Natural Linguistics" 1969

(For Peter Salus.) Another poem in Auden's last phase of addressing nature rather than people, this poem considers the lexicon of animal; mineral, and vegetable, and is in the manner of Goethe.

"Nature, History, and Poetry" 1950

This essay followed the poem "One Circumlocution" and is something of an explanation of it. Auden notes that a poem's verbal order "Is an attempt to present an analogy to that paradisal state [see also Eden] in which Freedom and Law, System and Order are united in harmony ... An analogy, not an imitation; the harmony is possible and verbal only. The effect of beauty ... is good to the degree that, through its analogies, the goodness of created existence, the historical fall into unfreedom and disorder, and the possibility of regaining Paradise through repentance and forgiveness are recognized. Its effect is evil to the degree that beauty is taken, not as analogous to, but identical with goodness, so that the artist regards himself or is regarded by others as God, the pleasure of beauty taken for joy of Paradise, and the conclusion drawn that, since all is well in the work of art, all is well in history. But all is not well there."

Needham, Joseph

1900–1995, scientist. In the 1930s Needham was a coming scientist just as Auden was the coming poet. In his 1942 collection of essays written from 1932, he chose the title *Time the Refreshing River*, which is a line from Auden's poem "Spain" (1937). In the May 1932 issue of *Scrutiny* Needham reviewed Aldous Huxley's *Brave New World* and Auden also had a review "Private Pleasure."

Negroes see Grierson, John

New Country see *New Signatures*

New School for Social Research

Located in Lower Manhattan. Auden taught classes here in the 1940s.

New Signatures 1932

"[In 1932 *New Signatures* was] published by the Hogarth Press [of Virginia and Leonard Woolf]. This [Michael Roberts] followed a year later with a second volume, containing prose [including Isherwood's] as well as poetry, called *New Country*. These two anthologies revealed the existence of a new, for the most part socially conscious, group of young writers.... These writers wrote with a near-unanimity, surprising when one considers that most of them were strangers to one another, of a society coming to an end and of revolutionary change" (Stephen Spender, *World Within World*).

The title of *New Signatures* came from a line of a poem by Cecil Day Lewis. What seemed to join the poets together was the strength of Michael Roberts' introduction, which claimed a uniformity of (leftist) purpose and activism that was not quite so true in actuality, but the British literary world took it as fact.

New Signatures, title page of first edition.

The poets were Auden, Spender, Day Lewis, Julian Bell, Richard Eberhart, William Empson, John Lehman, William Plomer, and A.S.J. Tessimond. The critical acceptance of this volume led to *New Country* in 1933, which featured prose and poetry by, among others, Auden, Day Lewis, Spender, Plomer, Lehman, Roberts, and Rex Warner. (See also Roberts, Michael.)

New Verse

Poetry journal created by Geoffrey Grigson 1905–1985. Samuel Hynes: "In the six years of its publishing life—from January 1933 to January 1939—it published more good poems by young poets, and more unfavourable reviews, than any other English journal. *New Verse* did not exactly speak for the [Auden] generation—and it was too individualistic for that—but it spoke to the generation, and so both recorded the changing consciousness of the decade and helped to change it by the judgments it made. [Geoffrey] Grigson was an editor of independent mind, great intelligence, and strict literary values, who insisted on the

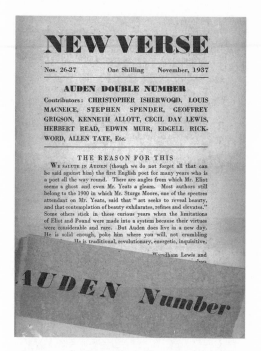

New Verse, **cover of 1937 tribute issue to Auden.**

naked distinction between good art and bad art...." (*The Auden Generation*). And it was Auden that Grigson acknowledged was the poetic leader of the decade. The November 1937 issue was an "Auden Double Number," devoted entirely to Auden, with his admirers contributing articles and praise. Grigson wrote on the cover, under the title, "The Reason for This: ... We salute in Auden (though we do not forget all that can be said against him) the first English poet for many years who is a poet all the way round. There are angles from which Mr. Eliot seems a ghost and Mr. Yeats a gleam.... But Mr. Auden does live in a new day. He is solid enough, poke him where you will, not crumbling like fudge. He is traditional, revolutionary, energetic, inquisitive, critical and intelligent.... There are plenty of writers who do recognize Auden's broad power of raising ordinary speech into strong and strange incantation, and see no reason for waiting to praise and criticise Auden until he has been dead a hundred years." Why wait, indeed? There are articles and tributes from Isherwood, Spender, MacNeice, Grigson, Kenneth Allott, Edwin Muir, George Barker, Frederic Prokosch, David Gascoyne, Dylan Thomas,

Berthold Viertel, Day Lewis, Bernard Spencer, Charles Madge, Herbert Read, Ezra Pound, John Masefield, Graham Greene, and Sir Hugh Walpole.

New Writing see Lehmann, John

"A New Year Greeting" 1969

In this poem Auden speaks to the microorganisms on his skin. He speculates about how these microorganisms might imagine the world outside of Auden and his skin.

"New Year Letter" 1940

"New Year Letter" is Auden's first long poem written in America and is included in the 1940 American volume *The Double Man* (the English title of the volume was *New Year Letter*). This reflects Auden's break from Europe and his re-emerging Christianity that at this time was very much motivated by the writings of Kierkegaard, a nineteenth century Christian polemicist who was a rebellious, solitary Christian who presciently posed questions about the coming influence of the media on the Public. In philosophical terms, Kierkegaard saw the break from the past and into modernity and this is a theme of the poem: a rejection of modernism for integration with a pre-romantic (Augustan) past. Auden uses rhymed couplets to signify the reference to *Another Time*, a second volume of verse also published in 1940. In addition to Kierkegaard, Paul Tillich's demonic is factored in as those powers which act through us whether we know it or not or like it or not. And it will be artists that will have some notion of the demonic as art itself is a manifestation of the powers.

"New Year Letter" sits before the imaginary tribunal of Rimbaud whose silent presence requires Auden to justify if his own writing is worthier than silence. This is an Auden who refuted the "low dishonest decade" of the 1930s in "September 1, 1939" and was considering if the role of a poet should or should not include social activism. Indeed, herein he rebukes his "sermons" of the 1930s that include

"September 1, 1939" and "Spain." The poem is dedicated to his friend Elizabeth Mayer (who reminded Auden of his mother), and she is an exemplar of the selfless good and charity that reconciles existence when all else fails. *The Double Man* is Kierkegaard's sense of the man who thinks universally but exists alone within his own thoughts, which result in the enduring conflict of the duality of public and private spheres. In addition to the influence of Kierkegaard, Auden had been very moved by Charles Williams' study *The Descent of the Dove: A History of the Holy Spirit in the Church*, from which Auden incorporated the theme of *Freedom and Necessity* as necessary opposites created to further an evolving spiritual consciousness. Indeed, he quotes lines from the book near the long poem's finale. Freedom comes from choices. Necessity makes the choices more difficult in the face of contingent exigencies and expediency. Williams also considered the idea of the Double Man. In *Descent* Williams quotes from Montaigne: "we are, I know not how, double in ourselves, so that we believe what we disbelieve, and cannot rid ourselves of what we condemn." Auden chose this as his epigraph for *The Double Man*, and it signifies the conflict of the inner man who is influenced by the collective subjectivity in his outer world while he argues with that society in his inner world. Which will he choose?

Another influence is Goethe's Faust, particularly the aged Faust who has learned from his faults and wants to build the Just City. Auden also wishes in "New Year Letter" to build, not just a just city, but St. Augustine's City of God.

In this city the image of a clock, previously authoritarian in "The Witnesses," is now more benign, a watcher rather than a teller. Nature passively endures chaos. Art is also far apart, as is nature; art is a conscience, a reflector of time, and not an actor influencing time. This idea reflects Gerald Heard's evolving consciousness where history is not what it seems, but merely a byproduct of psychic evolution, which is, instead of man's material residue, the real purpose of existence. Consequently, what seems evil may still produce good on a psychic level. (For example, from the tragedy of September 11, 2001, came a deluge of heroism and goodness.)

The "machine" of modern society has turned the individual into a faceless cog in the urban-industrial-capitalist engine. The ego chases greed as an erroneous substitute for the real need: love. The individual is a Kafka anti-hero, isolated, anonymous, a faceless member of the faceless public, a public that can anonymously be shaped by media into forming opinions for which they are not held responsible as identifiable human beings. This anti-hero can be exceptional or average; it doesn't matter in relation, as his anonymity makes him invisible in either case.

The vast landscape of existence is held up by two Atlases, one inner, one outer, one private, one public. Very often the landscape reflects the human nature it frames as either lush and smart or stagnant and rotten with shoddy thinking. World War II is indirectly linked to the falsely idealized reverberations of Romanticism that engendered a too optimistic trust in the good will of men that failed to counter fascism.

Where is the answer to evil to be found? If only every single "one" could make a quest to spiritual consciousness, which, in fact, as per Heard, Williams, Aldous Huxley, and the exponents of the mystical Perennial Philosophy believe, is already man's destiny, if only one would look inside himself after shedding the outer flux of life's hurricane to find the inner calm that waits only to be discovered.

This work is too complex for a short summary, and it is, indeed, followed by over 90 pages of copious notes referring to the sources of Auden's Christianity, which are invaluable; so is Mendelson's analysis in *Later Auden*.

New York Pro Musica

Auden in the 1950s was invigorated by his work with this early music group, led by a young labor activist named Noah Greenberg until Greenberg's death in 1966. Auden and Kallman worked with Greenberg on *An Elizabethan Song Book* (1955). Auden wrote the verse narrative for the Pro Musica's production of the medieval music drama *The Play of Daniel*, and in 1958 he joined in preparations for its first performance. (See also *The Play of Daniel*.)

New York Public Library *see* Archives

Newton, Caroline

1893–1975. Newton wished to be Auden's patron shortly after Auden's arrival in America, and he accepted money from her in this regard, for which he would give her original manuscripts. Auden may have been motivated to take this payment in order to meet the increasing expenses resulting from his support of Chester Kallman, and one could speculate that Kallman, who happily lived off of Auden, may have encouraged Auden to do to Newton what Kallman did to Auden. After Newton, Auden never again sold manuscripts, as he was ashamed of having done so, but gave them to friends to show his affection for them. Newton is the "huge sad lady" in Auden's poem " The Duet" (1947).

Nicolson, Sir Harold

1886–1968, English biographer, historian, and diplomat, b. Tehran, Iran. Educated at Oxford, he entered the foreign office in 1909, and, until his resignation 20 years later, he represented the British government in various parts of the world. His work at the Paris Peace Conference (1919) prompted the study *Peacemaking, 1919* (1933) and stimulated an interest in diplomacy that is reflected in *Diplomacy* (1939) and *The Evolution of Diplomatic Method* (1954, 3d ed. 1963). He served in the House of Commons from 1935 to 1945 and was knighted in 1953. Among the subjects of his biographies are Paul Verlaine (1921), Tennyson (1923), Byron (1924), Swinburne (1926), Curzon (1934), Dwight Morrow (1935), King George V (1953), and Sainte-Beuve (1957). Other works include *The Congress of Vienna* (1946), *Good Behaviour* (1956), *The Age of Reason* (1961), and *Kings, Courts, and Monarchy* (1962). He was married to the novelist Vita Sackville-West.

Auden knew Nicolson in England. Auden thought enough of his work on Tennyson to quote Nicolson at length in his introduction to a selection from Tennyson. Harold Nicolson notes the subject of an uncompleted Auden

poem in his diary entry of 4 August 1933: "The idea," Nicolson writes, "is Heard as Virgil guiding him through modern life" (*Diaries*).

Niebuhr, Reinhold and Ursula

Reinhold Niebuhr, 1892–1971, American religious and social thinker, b. Wright City, Mo. In 1928 he began teaching at Union Theological Seminary in New York City where he stayed until 1960. In the early 1930s he became a political activist and a Socialist. After World War II, he changed from a socialist to a conservative.

Auden met Niebuhr and his wife Ursula shortly after he arrived in America and introduced him to many at the Union Theological Seminary, including Paul Tillich who, even more so than Niebuhr himself, would influence Auden's Christianity, although Mendelson observes that in the early to mid 1940s "Auden's political and ethical positions were indistinguishable from Niebuhr's" (*Later Auden*).

Nietzsche, Friedrich

1844–1900, German philosopher, b. Röcken, Prussia. The son of a clergyman, Nietzsche rejected Western bourgeois civilization and believed Christianity to be decadent. He also believed a compassionate superman was needed to save civilization from the herd instinct and unscrupulous rulers. Nietzsche's thought was very influential but was misinterpreted by Hilter and Nazism. Among his works are *The Birth of Tragedy* (1872, tr. 1910); *Thus Spake Zarathustra* (1883–91, tr. 1909, 1930), and *Beyond Good and Evil* (1886, tr. 1907).

Indeed, early Auden would find in Nietzsche and D.H. Lawrence the concept of the exceptional man, and the term pure in heart man, derived more directly from Homer Lane, also had its basis in the superman. After being in Berlin and seeing the effect of Hitler on the "herd of inferior humanity," Auden understood how both Nietzsche and Lawrence could be misinterpreted and their ideas turned into a danger. Even a man who starts out "pure in heart" may become corrupted by the power he attains and the machinations required to keep that power. This conflict would take artistic form in Auden's *The Orators* (1932), with its absurdist depiction of a hero and hero worship, but reach its full explication in the Auden-Isherwood play *The Ascent of F6* (see Plays with Isherwood). (See also "Meiosis"; Wagner, Richard.)

Night Mail *see* Grierson, John

"1929" *see* *Poems*

"No Change of Place" *see* *Poems*

"No, Plato, No" 1973

Auden considers in his old age with his body slowly failing if it would be more fun to be a disembodied spirit who need not worry any longer about bodily functions.

"Nones" *see* *Horae Canonicae*

Nones 1951

Dedicated to Reinhold and Ursula Niebuhr, this volume has poems written from c. 1948 to 1951, and includes *Horae Canonicae*.

Northwest Passage

A term derived by Christopher Isherwood that "was a private key to a certain group of responses; all needless to say, related to the idea of 'The Test.' More rationally, it symbolized, in my mind, the career of the neurotic hero, The Truly Weak Man — antithesis of 'the Truly Strong Man'" (*Lions and Shadows*). The Truly Weak man who is not pure in heart allows his ego to take over his rational thinking and he egotistically seeks approval by deliberately facing Tests: mountain climbing, sports, riding a motorcycle at high speed — all of which fails to satisfy the greater underlying, subconscious need, which is to be liked and loved for one's private and true self, rather than one's vainglorious show-off self. (See also The Auden Generation.)

"A Note on Order" 1941

This essay is another Auden search for absolutes from this period of 1940–41. R.G. Collingwood is a starting point that Auden bolsters with Alfred North Whitehead's *Process and Reality* (1929).

"Notes on the Comic" 1952

Auden's reference point here is Ronald Firbank. Comedy is the relief from feared tragedy that is not ultimately culminated. Affectionate criticism is comic; hate is not. "All those I love," says Auden, "can make me laugh." Types of comic contradiction: 1) Inanimate becomes animate to a passive human such as an inverted umbrella. 2) Inorganic vs. organic, such as a slip on a banana peel. 3) Male vs. female, where lovers are unique while sex is not. A farce is in bad taste because serious emotion does not offer a counterpoint to the humor. 4) Lovers vs. the citizens they encounter in a social context. 5) Irony, such as Falstaff's speech on honor. To Auden, this poignantly comic speech exemplifies the best kind of comedy.

"The Novelist" 1938

The novelist in question is Auden's best friend Christopher Isherwood. He, like Auden, needs to grow out of their egoistic boyish gifts into the figure like the Roman poets (i.e. Horace) who contributed to an adult sense of community. This poem is a warning against the trap of self-serving solipsism and a contrast to the silence of the poet Rimbaud in the poem "Rimbaud" who renounced poetry for action. There is also here an early intimation of a wish for Christian atonement, or as Gerald Heard called it, "at-one-ment," as a reconciliation of the collective Self through suffering, which would be emphasized in Auden's Christianity after Auden's arrival in America.

Nursery Library

The earliest Auden was a child nurtured by doting, upper-middle class parents who were socially progressive and encouraged their son to read copiously of marvels and tales. This nurturing led to a precocity of daring invention that would manifest itself later as Auden the poet/dramatist/essayist. The adult Auden clung to childhood, saying in old age that being doted on a as a child had the effect of having him believe "that in any gathering, I was the youngest person present. It was not that I imagined myself younger in years than I actually was.... I simply thought of others as older" ("Aging," *A Certain World*). Auden, near the end of his life, credited the beginning of his life with giving him the fantastical imagination that dominated all of his life in between. In Auden's 1970 anthology, *A Certain World*: a Commonplace book, he has a section, "Nursery Library," in which he lists the favorites among his childhood reading:

Beatrix Potter	All her books
Hans C. Andersen	The Snow Queen
Morris and	
Magnuson	Icelandic Stories
Lewis Carroll	The two Alice books
George	
MacDonald	The Princess and the Goblin
Jules Verne	The Child of the Cavern, Journey to the Center of the Earth
Rider Haggard	King's Solomon's Mines, She
Dean Farrar	Eric, or Little by Little
Ballantyne	The Cruise of the Cahelot
Conan Doyle	The Sherlock Holmes Stories

"Nursery Rhyme" 1947

This poem is about a past as fantasy that then gives in to an inflexible present that is not so much fun. Auden based the somewhat villanelle form on a medieval Portuguese poem he received from Theodore Spencer.

"O What Is That Sound" 1932

A rebel leaves his lover to fight for a cause;

the threat of revolution is not here romanticized, but depicted as a danger. The poem ends with a betrayal.

"Objects" 1956

Neutral nature just observes; thoughtful humans observe and express, which is the difference between knowledge and understanding.

"Ode to Diaencephalon" *see Thank You Fog*

"Ode to Gaea" 1954

This poem follows "Bucolics," and the earth here is not quite so loving as in those poems. Nature is neither friend nor foe and man fends for himself within it.

"Ode to Terminus" 1968

The Roman god Terminus is the god of vocation. Terminus evokes the same idea of coherence and individuality that Auden had speculated on in 1932, when he wrote a poem to the "Lords of Limit."

"The Old Man's Road" 1955

The "old man" is God. How does one find God? The way or path of life across "the Great Schism" is not to be found by logic or in churches but through intuition, the intuition of the mystic.

Old Norse and Old English Literature

Early Writings: With Iceland's loss of political independence (1261–64) came a decline in literature, although the linguistic tradition continued and the old writings were still venerated. In the thirteenth and fourteenth centuries, the sagas of antiquity flourished; many were based on Eddic poems. Chivalric romances appeared c. 1300, emphasizing classical and ecclesiastical themes. Many foreign works were translated. Old Norse works were copied and compiled, and new religious poems were written in the old meters. The fourteenth century saw the development of the rímur, metrically ingenious narrative poetry based on the sagas; it was popular until the nineteenth century and was revived in the twentieth.

Auden's father imbued in the child a love for Icelandic literature and these sagas would influence Auden for the rest of his life. In 1928 he and Isherwood would see the resemblance between Icelandic sagas (that Auden introduced Isherwood to) and the pseudo-sagas of their British Public School. Isherwood writes in *Lions and Shadows*, "These warriors, with their feuds, their practical jokes, their dark threats conveyed in puns and riddles and deliberate understatements: they seemed so familiar — where had I met them before? Yes, I recognized them now: they were the boys at our preparatory school. Weston [Auden] was pleased with the idea: we discussed it a good deal, wondering which of our school fellows best corresponded to the saga characters. In time, the school-saga world became for us a kind of Mortmere — a Mortmere founded upon our preparatory-school lives, just as the original Mortmere had been founded upon my life with Chalmers at Cambridge." For Isherwood, Edward Upward, and Auden, the profound influence of their pubescent and adolescent prep and public school years remained deleterious as regarded their conceptions of real life. The crossing of the saga with the Old School was an imaginative leap, but Isherwood and Auden were recognizing the perpetual continuum in connecting the ancient Icelandic sagas to the contemporary Old School saga. As contemporary tellers, they would "mythify" particular aspects of the Old School by identifying those aspects within the school context that would be universally recognizable in any context. As Isherwood said, the school boys were the same as the saga warriors.

With this realization that the Icelandic sagas had just been ancient realities that were turned into myths, Isherwood understood that myths were just previous realities extrapolated

and aggrandized. He would no longer need to write about the mentality of the Old School in the more rarified metaphors of Mortmere; now he could attempt to depict it directly: "I actually tried the experiment of writing a school story in what was a kind of hybrid language composed of saga phraseology and schoolboy slang. And soon after this, Weston produced a short verse play in which the two worlds are so confused that it is almost impossible to say whether the characters are epic heroes or members of a school O.T.C. [Officer Training Corps]" (LS). The story was "Gems of Belgian Architecture." Auden's play was an earlier version of what became *Paid on Both Sides*. Both were written in the obscurantist secret code of their exclusive gang. The Isherwood-Auden gang continued where the Isherwood-Upward gang left off.

There was no need to pretend that the Old School was something else as Isherwood and Upward had done with Mortmere. The "feuds" and "dark threats" of the sagas were understood to be no different than the feuds and dark threats of their experiences at school. Thereafter, Auden would retain his interest in the quest and saga as themes in his work, and the style of the Icelandic epics was always a factor directly or indirectly suffusing a context or subtext of his work. In 1936 he traveled to Iceland to see the land of (maybe) his ancestors and this trip became the Auden-MacNeice book *Letters from Iceland* that contained Auden's epic *Letter to Lord Byron*, which is Auden's quest and saga of his role in art, life, and history. The later Auden would co-translate the ancient Icelandic sagas (*The Elder Edda*, and *Völuspá = The Song of the Sybil*), and also verse by contemporary Norse authors (Lagerkvist, Ekeloff). (See also "The World of the Sagas.")

"On Sunday Walks" *see Poems*

On the Frontier see Plays with Isherwood

"On This Island" 1935

This poem illustrates a theory of perception and its ethical consequences. The island is a place that one either escapes from, as in earlier poems, or now is a place to escape to.

Sex without love is bad and selfish; love — with or without sex — is good and unselfish and leads to social responsibility. The poem's lines fall lightly as passive impressions of choiceless awareness for which nature asks no response from man. Man, however, unlike nature, cannot be viewed as just another neutral extension of nature; his responsibility through the choices he makes is required. *On This Island* was also the American title for the collection *Look, Stranger.* (See also *Look, Stranger.*)

"One Circumlocution" 1949

Mendelson: "Where Caliban [in *The Sea and the Mirror*] sees the human condition as 'drabness and sham,' estranged from the absolute, the poems Auden now wrote, especially 'One Circumlocution,' accept drabness and shame and rename them ordinariness and play, states not of estrangement but of inadequacy and need, and open to forgiveness.... Auden placed 'One Circumlocution' immediately before 'Horae Canonicae' when he arranged his *Collected Shorter Poems 1927–1957*. It earns its position as gatekeeper through its extraordinary richness of theme and allusion" (*Later Auden*). The style came from William Empson, some of the ideas from Martin Heidegger. (See also Play and Work; "Nature, History and Poetry.")

"Open Letter to Knut Hamsun" 1940

Hamsun was a Norwegian novelist who won the Nobel Prize in 1920. Auden, in his role as the artist who should not be an activist and take sides, raked Hamsun for writings that indulged and supported the Nazi victors of his homeland.

The Orators 1932

"What do you think of England, this country of ours where no one is well?" — W.H. AUDEN

The Orators has always been considered Auden's most inscrutable and challenging work. On a first read, it is; and, yes, it is inscrutable for much of a text-only reading. Yet, it is not so puzzling if one knows the Auden-Isherwood schema that *The Orators* is based on. There are keys, and once the keys are known, the logic — even in his madcap opus — is apparent.

The Orators was published in 1932 and was Auden's follow-up to the critical success of Poems two years earlier. If the volume *Poems* was thought to be obscure, much of *The Orators* seemed impenetrable. The first edition's dust jacket text obfuscates admirably: "Of W.H. Auden's first volume of poems the most discerning readers remarked that the author was often very 'obscure,' but that he was unquestionably a poet, and one of the few poets of first-rate ability who have so far appeared to voice the post-war generation, a generation which has its own problems and its profound difficulties. *The Orators* is not a collection, but a single work with one theme and purpose, partly in prose and partly in verse, in which the author continues his exploration of new form and rhythm. It will not disappoint those who have been excited by the unfamiliar metric and the violent imagination of the previous book." This is the entire description. No further word on what the "one theme" and its "purpose" might be. Apparently, Faber & Faber's publicist wasn't taking any chances. Even Auden admitted to *The Orators'* density in a preface to the 1966 reissue:

As a rule, when I re-read something I wrote when I was younger, I can think myself back into the frame of mind in which I wrote it. *The Orators*, though, defeats me. My name seems a pseudonym for someone else, someone talented but near the border of sanity, who might well, in a year or two, become a Nazi.

The literary influences I do remember more or less. [Mendelson, in *Early Auden*, cites Baudelaire and D.H. Lawrence, among others.]

The central theme seems to be Hero-Worship, and we all know what that can lead to politically ... my unconscious motive ... was therapeutic, to exorcise certain tendencies in myself by allowing them to run riot in phantasy.... I realize that it is precisely the schoolboy atmosphere and diction which act as a moral criticism of the rather ugly emotions and ideas they are employed to express.

Auden continues to say that by treating serious matters in a juvenile way, this "makes it impossible to take them seriously." He notes that at the end of *The Orators* "in one of the Odes I express all of the sentiments with which his followers hailed the advent of Hitler, but these are rendered, I hope, innocuous by the fact that the Fuhrer so hailed [in the ode] is a new-born baby and the son of a friend [Rex Warner]."

Auden's self-criticism may have been warranted. When *The Orators* was written there was a great deal of Mortmere in it; yet, few readers knew Isherwood's name and virtually none had ever heard of Mortmere. One key to understanding *The Orators* is to see it as a new Mortmere story written with a more conscious understanding of the Isherwood-Auden schema that the Isherwood-Upward originals did not have. Edward Mendelson observes in *Early Auden* that Ode IV of *The Orators* lists characters from Mortmere as an in-joke for Isherwood's benefit. More than just names from Mortmere can be found in *The Orators*; its over-the-top outrageousness matches Isherwood's stories just as does the anger and frustration behind the satire. Subtitled "An English Study," the satire and anger are directed at the British past and the traditions that Auden and Isherwood rejected. As in Mortmere, the British Public School is a metaphor for Britain and the principal target of Auden's wrath. Nonetheless, even with this correlation to Mortmere, there is much in *The Orators* that remains obscure including excess as Auden cut a great deal from the 1966 version.

The dedication is to Stephen Spender:

Private faces in public places
Are wiser and nicer
Than public faces in private places.

On an immediate level, this alludes to Isherwood, Auden, and Spender's experiences in Berlin's boy bars. More deeply, it goes back to the Auden-Day Lewis Introduction of *Oxford Poetry 1927*, and the interaction of "private spheres" with "public chaos." A public face in a private place is a mask worn even during intimacy and

signifies the Truly Weak Man who is not comfortable with his inner self. A private face in a public place belongs to the Truly Strong Man whose inner Self (with a Vedantic capital "S") is his only Self, which he manifests equally in public or private. Auden said the theme of *The Orators* is Hero-Worship. It is, but not as praise; it is a warning that those who wish to be heroes by design at whatever cost (a Hitler), and those who need a hero to follow, are Truly Weak. Auden said, in a letter to Naomi Mitchison, "In a sense the work is my memorial to D.H. Lawrence; i.e. the theme is the failure of the romantic conception of personality…. The four parts … are stages in the development of the hero who never appears at all." Auden continues:

Thus Part I. Introduction to influence.
Part 2. Personally involved with hero. Crisis.
Part 3. Intellectual reconstruction of hero's teaching. The cerebral life.
Part 4. The effect of the hero's failure on the emotional life.

The Orators is about how "no secular saviour can equal the hopes of his youthful followers." (In 1937 Auden and Isherwood would say this very directly in *The Ascent of F6*.) Auden was acting upon his own experiences on three counts: he was witness to hero-worship at his British Public School; he observed the cult of personality as it evolved with Hitler in Germany; and John Layard, for whom he'd had such great enthusiasm, later showed up at Auden's door with a bullet wound from a suicide attempt. (Indeed a Layard anthropological paper about "Flying Tricksters" is one of the sources for *The Orators*.)

Auden's Prologue ("Adolescence"), like the rest of the volume, is cryptic without a primer. Yet it succinctly introduces the Isherwood-Auden schema once a reader has been primed. An unnamed stranger views the landscape and is reminded of his "mother's figure." With "mapping pens" he traces "family names" as he charts an expedition to some frontier. He hears subliminally: "Dear boy, be brave…" which is a call that he should face his Test. "And yet this prophet" when he returns from defending his country is greeted with "Coward, Coward," and the "giantess," the mother figure, "cries deceiver."

The mother figure is tied to the land along with the family names that represent the past. The past must be defended and preserved. This is a Test for the hero-son who is urged on to be brave. By succumbing to the pressure to confront a Test, the son only proves himself to be Truly Weak and is called a coward. Further injury is added by his own mother who calls him a deceiver for pretending to be a hero. The Prologue proclaims the Isherwood-Auden schema as the theme. What follows is the Mortmereish elucidation of the theme.

Book One is called "The Initiates." Part One of Book One is titled "Address for a Prize Day." The address is by an ancient Other to school boys who are being prepared for Empire-Saving with his cant and rant reminding them of the war: "What does it mean? What does it mean? Not what does it mean to them, there, then. What does it mean to us here now? Why are we here? What are we going to do?" The address continues with warnings for the hearties to be alert for subversive aesthetes (such as Isherwood, Upward, Auden, and Spender). The aesthetes are "those who have been guilty in their life of excessive love towards themselves or their neighbours, those guilty of defective love towards God and those guilty of perverted love" (see Dante). For the ancient Other, "excessive love" in any form that is not directed at the school and state is nonconformist and distracts one from blind allegiance to the school and state. The lovers of themselves are scorned because they are not joiners or game-players, preferring solitude, nature, and the arts. In order to help them, the ancient Other exhorts the hearties to go for a walk alone in a wood with one and subtly say: "I suppose you realise you are fingering the levers that control eternity." The excessive lovers of their neighbors are suffering from the fact that "They need love" and try too hard to get it. The defective lovers are compulsive-obsessives who are "often collectors." The ancient Other says they need to be kept busy. "Hit them in the face if necessary. If they hit back you will know they are saved." "Last and worse, the perverted lovers. So convincing at first, so little apparent cause for anxiety. A slight proneness to influenza…. They've lost their nerve." Then the ancient Other describes the hated

British Public School honor system in action: "Draw up a list of rotters and slackers, of proscribed persons under headings like this. Committees for municipal improvement…. All these have got to die without issue." In other words, non-conformists like Auden are doomed.

"The Initiates" represents the Mortmereish patriotic brainwashing that most of the hearties were susceptible to, which the aesthetes rejected, automatically making them suspect to The Others. In the second part of "The Initiates," titled, "Argument," there are three sections: (I) the brainwashed are ready to succumb to the cult of the leader, known only as "Him." Here, one recalls Isherwood's Mortmere tale of "The World War" as well as *Paid on Both Sides* and the poems from Auden's first volume. Of the allusions to his own poems, one might think Auden is making fun of himself and his reputed obscurity in this section. Images include: "talk of generals," "interrogation of villagers," "execution of a spy," "a tale of sexual prowess," "establishment of a torpedo base," "the mine with obsolete machinery." (II) The Leader's followers issue a litany of rhapsodic chants, each of which is punctuated by the name of a known public or fictional figure: "From all nervous excitement and follies of the will; from the postponed guilt and deferred pain; from the oppression of noon and from the terror in the night, O Bulldog Drummond deliver us." Sherlock Holmes and Hercule Poirot are also named. (Detective stories were Auden's favorite leisure reading.) His followers associate Him with other heroes, and mythicize Him into a saga figure. (III) The leader, Him, is betrayed and killed leaving behind a confused body of followers without a head. His followers use His memory as a cohering force to retain their fledgling identity. Him becomes even more mythicized combining the heroic and bizarre: "His ability to smell a wet knife at a distance of half a mile. His refusal to wear anything but silk next to his skin." The worship of Him and His past gives His followers a way to remain intact as an identifiable entity; it also prevents them, who are really school boys, from growing up.

Part III is a "Statement" that opens with a self-aggrandizing list of what the followers attributes are: "One charms by thickness of wrist; one by variety of positions; one has a beautiful skin, one a fascinating smell." These would seem to be allusions to the boys in Berlin. "One jumps out of windows for profit.... one makes leather instruments of torture for titled aristocrats." The list goes on for good or ill and seems to be an inventory of all possible personality types Auden can remember or imagine. Mendelson observes, "The response to the emotional vacancy left by the hero's absence is to construct a visionary orthodoxy. Like all orthodoxies it is largely an adaptation of various traditions of wisdom, many of them used in ways unimaginable to their originators" (*Early Auden*). The past is reconstituted to fit the needs of the present in ways that are not only unimaginable, but also unrecognizable. The past perverted in this way is no longer history but propaganda. Auden parades the endless types to say that while "life is many," life is also an inevitable cycle of these types and their behaviors repeated over and over. For example, "The soldier shall say 'It is a fine day for hurting.'" Auden then delves into the quasi-mystical (with a poke at Yeats and Lawrence): "Sun is on right, moon on left, powers to earth. The action of light on dark is to cause it to contract." What does this mean? Like much that precedes it this is a cryptic pronouncement implying some kind of eternal inevitability that governs the cycle of regenerated types. It is portentous but not to be taken too seriously, just as Auden warned that none of *The Orators* should be. Nonetheless, the metaphysical quality intimated by Auden was very serious to him in other contexts, if not necessarily this one.

The fourth and last part of Book I is "Letter to a Wound." This letter is a self-satire of the kind of narcissistic martyrdom that Isherwood, Auden, and Spender recognized in themselves and their peers. The wound is not explained, but the wound has become the speaker's preoccupation — dangerously so, like a child's imaginary friend who has begun to supersede external reality and rationality. Auden here mocks the overweening self-introspection that his generation was prone to in their new age of psychoanalysis. Auden, by writing to the wound satirically, shows that art is an escape into a secondary world from the pain in the primary world. The irony of the satire is that the primary pain itself becomes

the secondary world of the narcissistic martyr. The narcissist's private sphere personifies the wound and talks to it. By doing so he withdraws himself from public chaos and into private fantasy. Subsequently, the divided mind bifurcates the border between public and private until the private sphere is reality and the public sphere seems fantasy. Of the wound Auden writes: "Who'll ever guess what it is? Once I carved on a seat in the park 'We have sat here. You'd better not.'" This hints vaguely at what only the gang knew for sure: Auden's wound had been a rectal fissure that required surgery and a prolonged healing period. Of his carving on the park bench — which symbolizes an unconscious cry for approval — he says to the wound: "Now I see that all that sort of thing is juvenile and silly, merely a reaction against insecurity and shame." This statement is not just about a wound, but it is an apologia for all reactions, physical or mental, caused by the narcissistic angst of Auden's generation.

Book Two is "Journal of an Airman." While Book One was about the gang mentality of a group of followers and their focus on Him and the aftermath of Him, the airman is alone — a solitary Him in the making. He is above the din, seeing with the hawk vision of the cypher-witness who, at the right moment, will assert his identity and swoop suddenly to lead his troops. This potentiality, however, raises three questions for the airman: Who are the troops? Who are the enemy? And is there a difference? Mendelson notes, "the airman begins alone, worries over the crucial problem — 'group organisation,' slowly acknowledges his reliance on an ancestor, and finally accepts the undifferentiated unity of surrender and death" (*Early Auden*). This summary sounds quite serious — and it is; however, this parable of serious intent is in no way serious in method. The airman's journal is about the Isherwood-Auden schema and Auden is still combining saga, the Old School, and Mortmere.

The journal seems the work of a precocious school boy fantasizing about himself as a hero while showing off his intellect. Just as Mortmere was, Auden's airman fantasy, however outrageous, is an escape from either pain, tedium, or both. This is not evident from a text-only reading. The seriousness behind this satiric parable requires a good deal of non-text knowledge of Auden (and Isherwood) in order to understand it. Auden said as he was writing it: "The flying symbolism is fairly obvious. The chief strands are [the airman's] uncle (Heredity-Matrilineal descent and initiations), belief in a universal conspiracy (the secret society mind), kleptomania (the worm in the root)." The "dead uncle" was the black sheep of the airman's family because he was homosexual. He is based on Isherwood's Uncle Henry, still quite alive. The homosexuality is implied only. The airman discovers that he and his uncle are of the same homosexual tribe and his reliance on the memory of his uncle's aggrandized image becomes an inspiration for the nephew's heroic aspirations.

The journal opens with aphorisms and charts that are quasi-philosophical and pseudo-scientific. For example: "It is a sure sign of a busybody if he talks of *laissez-faire*." Auden declares that "The airman is the agent of central awareness," and as such, he must observe and analyze himself, his troops, and the enemy before he can take any action. Among the airman's observations there are staples of the Isherwood-Auden schema such as "ancestor worship," "signs of a mixed character ... the two-faced," "enemy propaganda," and "ghost stories." The airman learns that the real enemy exists within his own divided mind. Later, after a dream, the airman writes, "Why the words in my dream under Uncle's picture, 'I HAVE CROSSED IT.'" The dream's cryptic message is that the martyred uncle, in death, has crossed the border, braved the metaphysical frontier, and found the answers that can't be found in life. The airman doesn't fully comprehend this as yet, but the dream does spur a self-realization: "My whole life has been mistaken, progressively more and more complicated, instead of finally simple. My incredible blindness, with all the facts staring me in the face, not to have realised these elementary truths...." In appreciation of this realization, the airman gives credit to the dream, believing his uncle was sending him a message. "To my uncle, perpetual gratitude and love for this crowning mercy. For myself absolute humility." The airman's outlandish journal and journey end. He and Auden have come to the quite sane understanding that salvation comes from within.

The airman's journey, High Camp as it is, portrays the rite of passage from the mask-wearing, youthful precocity and rebellion that is Truly Weak, to the introspective maskless knowledge of the Self that is Truly Strong. The airman began as two Lawrences: T.E. and D.H. The former is the hero who, Truly Weak, confronts Tests, and the latter is the glorifier of life worship which emphasizes "blood" instead of spirit, which is also Truly Weak. By the end of his journal, the airman has merged with spirit. Auden finds salvation for the airman (and himself) within the serious interior of his outwardly satiric parable. Serious or not, Auden did not neglect his gang.

The airman mentions "the essay club and Stephen, [Spender]," and Isherwood is well-represented with the allusions to Uncle Henry and the names of his Mortmere characters in one of the concluding odes. Another Ode is for Rex Warner's son. John Layard is mentioned as well. Mendelson believes that Auden added the odes as a somewhat more serious — and clearer — postscript for the themes that preceded them. For the reader in 1932, the tenor of *The Orators'* reckless abandon superseded its obscurity and this tenor would be imitated during the decade. The imitators were indirectly flattering the Mortmere stories, which were unknown to all but perhaps a few of them. (Other than Upward and Auden, it is unclear who else may have heard of Mortmere.)

Among the imitators would be Isherwood and Auden themselves in collaboration on their three plays in 1935, 1936, and 1938. However, less than a year later in 1933, the very first imitator of *The Orators* would be the emulative Day Lewis in his *The Magnetic Mountain*, which is a deliberate homage, dedicated to Auden. In 1932 another important publication was the anthology *New Signatures*, which championed the activist poet. One of the new poets who attracted the most attention was Stephen Spender whose first volume of poems would be published the next year. (See also Lawrence, D.H.; Layard, John; Ciceronian Rhetoric; Owen, Wilfred.)

"Orpheus" 1937

This poem is very short but loaded with implications. Written shortly after Auden wrote

"Spain," it is deliberately obscure as it signified Auden's confusion over his role as an activist, one he was not comfortable with. In this poem, unlike life, there are no challenges and no answers as Auden has pulled back from the world, which is frustrating him. Does poetry share the song of the world — that is, participate in events — or just detachedly observe (see "Musée des Beaux Arts"). Auden knows there is a division within community, the body with its sensual and aristocratic mind against conscious authority, and instinct vs. willfulness. Auden rebukes his art as he infers that whatever one's song, or poetry, or hopes, one cannot have them and act upon them equally.

Orwell, George

1903–50, pseud. of Eric Arthur Blair, British novelist and essayist, b. India. Orwell is best known for *Animal Farm* and *Nineteen Eighty-Four*. After attending Eton, where Aldous Huxley was one of his teachers, he served (1922–27) with the British police in Burma and hated his role as an oppressor. He returned to Europe in 1927, living pennilessly in Paris and later in London. In 1936 he fought in the Spanish Civil War with the Republicans and was wounded. His earlier writings —*Down and Out in Paris and London* (1933), *Burmese Days* (1934), *The Road to Wigan Pier* (1937), and *Homage to Catalonia* (1938) — are autobiographical.

Orwell's works deal very much with the sociopolitical issues of his time. *Animal Farm* (1946) is a fable about the failure of Communism, and *Nineteen Eighty-Four* (1949) is a novel about totalitarian dehumanization. Orwell's other novels include *A Clergyman's Daughter* (1935), *Keep the Aspidistra Flying* (1936), and *Coming Up for Air* (1940). Orwell also wrote many literary essays. His volumes of essays include "Dickens, Dali and Others" (1946), "Shooting an Elephant" (1950), and the *Collected Essays, Journalism and Letters of George Orwell* (4 vol., 1968).

The principal importance of Orwell to Auden was Orwell's criticism of the poem "Spain" and this was very important indeed. After Orwell died Auden befriended his second wife, Sonia, through the Sterns. (See "Spain.")

The Others

When Christopher Isherwood was at Repton's preparatory school and then Cambridge with Edward Upward, they considered themselves a clan of two against The Others, and these were the dons, clergy, politicians, Auden-Generation mothers, relatives, hearties and just about anyone who represented the bourgeois traditions of British life that they rebelled against. Later, Auden would join for a clan-of-three, and the three would scathingly attack, in both conversation and in their writing, this enemy they steadfastly erected mental barriers against.

"Our Hunting Fathers" 1934

This poem is about the life force trying to move upward rather than downward, working out the beast (a Tennysonian, nineteenth century term for the ego), toward a more unified consciousness and exploring the intricate ways of guilt contrasted by human love and animal innocence. There is a dark view of the way life is really lived, abandoning the vision of Eros to err blindly after our own confused devices and desires. Because the hunters hunted for sport (confusing love with ego) the result is only isolation and conceit for a past that is no longer useful. Paradox: from a loss that can't be satisfied, isolation can learn to free itself to become the unified Self of collective consciousness. The last two lines of the poem refer to Lenin and at this time Auden mentioned both Lenin and T.E. Lawrence, in a review of Liddell Hart's Lawrence biography, as exemplars who combined action with reason. In this same review Auden refers to the Auden-Isherwood schema of the Truly Weak and Truly Strong Man.

"Our Time" 1939

As with other poems written in the latter half of 1939, Auden is concerned with the construct of time. What is time really? A Human-designed artificial device to measure man's responsibilities; hence, time is a burden that tells one where and when he must account for himself. For the mystic time is an eternal now, no past, no future, no regrets no apprehension. Indeed, "Time, however loud its chimes or deep" doesn't really have any effect on nature, including man in nature.

An Outline for Boys and Girls and Their Parents see Mitchison, Naomi

Owen, Wilfred

1893–1918, English poet, b. Shropshire. He fought in World War I and was killed in France on Nov. 4, 1918, one week before armistice. Owen's verse details the horrible tragedy of war. Nine of these poems are the basis of the text of Benjamin Britten's *War Requiem* (1962). Owen had worked on poems while living in France between 1913 and 1918, but he never published them. While on sick leave from the front in a Scottish hospital, he met the poet Siegfried Sassoon. Sassoon encouraged him to publish his work in magazines. He took Sassoon's advice, but he had to return to the front before his work was actually published. Two years after his death Sassoon arranged for the publication of 24 poems (1920). A 1931 edition included Owen's draft preface to his poems, in which he writes an axiom that became words that Auden would live by: "My subject is war, and the pity of war.... All a poet can do today is warn. That is why the true poets must be truthful."

Owen's poems clearly depicted the horror of World War I and in the 1920s he became a heroic martyr to the T.S. Eliot-Aldous Huxley generation as well as one to the Auden Generation that attended school in the 1920s and then became artists in the 1930s. In Auden's earliest verse he began using Owen's slant rhymes with same first letters such as right/rate, wall/well. In *The Orators* Auden's line for the airman, "Hands in perfect order," reflects an Owen letter just before he was killed in which he said that his "nerves are in perfect order."

"Oxford" 1937

This poem evokes Oxford as a place of stagnant vanity and dons who reek of the past.

Oxford and the Group Movement see "The Group Movement and the Middle Class"

Oxford Book of Light Verse 1938

(Dedicated to E.R. Dodds, whose wife, A.E. Dodds, helped put the volume together.) Auden wrote the introduction for this anthology. He observes that an artist's three wishes are to make, to perceive, and to communicate what he perceives. Each era has a standard number of artists/geniuses. Peaks/valleys of poetry depend on externals (society), not internals (artists themselves). A) When a poet's interests are similar to his audience, he is not self-conscious and his language will meet them half way while they do the rest. B) If a poet is not akin to his audience, he will be self-conscious and write for himself or a specialized group.

The first case, A, writes "light" verse such as songs that are to be read as "real," even if they are humorous nonsense — all of which can be serious or not. Until the Elizabethans, all poetry was light as society was united by religion, tradition, and conformity, which the poet reflected. With social upheaval, poetry became "heavy" with language reflecting nonconformity. In the seventeenth century Milton was the first British eccentric for making myth out of his personal experience and not myths out of others' experiences. *The Restoration* renewed stability, and poets such as Dryden returned to poetic conformity — albeit reflecting a leisured class — in order to please the audience. *Romanticism* returned to rebellion derived from a societal turning away from "the manor" to urban industry, which led to the "fall of the community," where a "rentier" class became the reading public to whom artists, now without patrons, must "please" in order to live. (This gave rise to escapist art.) Poets became "highbrow" as the subject matter of poetry could no longer describe a standardized lifestyle, which no longer existed, but had became internalized for each individual. The psyche is man's last commonality. A poet is no longer just an entertainer, but a prophet who is "to know more and more about less and less." Romantics: Byron (aristocrat) and Burns (peasant from community) were exceptions. Byron's satires required vernacular and created a new kind of "light," appealing to the unconscious need for a bond in the form of a parent/child relationship since the bond to community was gone. Conclusion: "A poetry which is at the same time light and adult can only be written in a society both integrated and free."

Oxford Poetry, 1927

Auden, Cecil Day Lewis, Warner, Louis MacNeice, and Stephen Spender were at Oxford in 1927. That year, *Oxford Poetry, 1927* appeared with a jointly written Preface by Auden and Day Lewis that was considered the declaration of independence of the coming 1930s poets from their predecessors. The Preface acknowledges the era's New World of psychoanalysis and its impact on the poet:

A tripartite problem remains, and may be stated thus: (a) The psychological conflict between self as subject and self as object, which is patent in the self-consciousness and emotional stultification resultant from the attempt to synchronize within the mind the synthesis and the analysis of experience. Such appears to be the prime development of this century, our experiment in "the emergent evolution of mind." Emotion is no longer necessarily to be analysed by "recollection in tranquility": it is to be prehended [sic] emotionally and intellectually at once. And this is of most importance to the poet: for it is his mind that must bear the brunt of the conflict and may be the first to realize the new harmony which would imply the success of this synchronization.

The duality of subject and object, private and public, inner and outer, would be the key to the poet's New World, one that gives homage to Freud in science and Eliot in verse. By stating that emotion "be prehended ... intellectually at once," Auden and Day Lewis were declaring that the poet should be an active participant, recorder, transcriber, and interpreter of existing circumstances. The poet as activist was a crucial aspect of the Auden Generation and this aspect is exemplified by a well-known quote from the Auden-Day Lewis introduction: "All genuine poetry is in a sense the formation of private spheres out of public chaos."

This process is also one of self-realization. One determines to what degree one is Truly Weak, even while trying to be Truly Strong.

Paid on Both Sides 1930

This verse play was dedicated to C. Day Lewis. According to Mendelson, "Auden wrote in his 1929 journal, 'The Tyranny of the Dead one cannot react against.' *Paid on Both Sides* is a study in that tyranny'" (*Early Auden*). For Auden, with Isherwood's encouragement (see Old Norse and Old English Literature), the early and later versions of the play were part of their study and interest in the predicament of their generation.

Mendelson believes the play "is an autobiographical study also. [Auden, in] annotating a friend's copy of the play in the 1940s, called it 'A parable of English Middle Class (professional) family life 1907–1929'" (Auden's year of birth and the play's date of completion). "Parable" is the key word and another byword for the 1930s. The play is narrated by a cypher-witness and is autobiographical only to those who recognize that it is a secret code about the British Public School. Nothing in it is about Auden as could be found in his biographical file; everything is about Auden (and Isherwood) as could be found in a psychological profile. Mendelson notes: "*Paid on Both Sides* is subtitled 'A Charade,' and a charade implies a solution. However opaque the manner of the play, its story is simple. It is a tragedy of revenge. Two mill-owning families have been feuding for generations. The son of one family, John Nower, and the daughter of the other, Anne Shaw, fall in love. A truce is declared on the occasion of their engagement. But on their wedding day one of the Shaws, urged on by his mother, murders Nower, avenging the Shaw brother whom Nower had earlier killed.... The play ... fluctuates from schoolboy slang to alliterative Old English pastiche; all murders are reported in the rhythms of Old English verse ... both in his alliterative metres and his direct quotations from *Beowulf,* 'The Wanderer,' [and] 'Wulf and Eadwacer'" (*Early Auden*). The clipped "telegraphese" diction of fragmented sentences also comes from the work of poet Laura Riding.

The use of the old style for the murders may have signified the pastiche aspect of the play, particularly the early version, which is a Mortmere-like satire in a bare-bones depiction that is stripped to the psychological essentials of the Isherwood-Auden schema: us against them, saving face, faux allegiance, unreasonable peer pressure, and stultifying alienation. The early version "emphasizes only the matter of the inherited past and what might be called the social genetics of 'habit.'" The ideas and habits of the "Middle Class" and the Old School are emphasized by Auden's careful descriptions of the characters' costumes and props: dinner jackets, trench coats, homburgs, sportsman's guns, field glasses. The play's "announcer" is in "The uniform of a cinema commissionaire, [and has] a megaphone." The members of the chorus are deliberately depicted as hearties in "rugger [rugby] things. The leader wears a scrum cap." In the early version, there are also more extensive stage directions that signify satirical intentions: "Someone does a cartwheel across the stage." The prop list and directions are largely left out of the later version, which increases the latter's obscurantism for the reader or viewer; without them, the particulars of Britain and the Old School give way to a more ambiguous and starkly serious universal portrayal of human nature. Although the subtitle, "A Charade," implies a solution, there isn't one except in the sense that through recognition of the events depicted one might learn how to avoid their cyclical repetition. In terms of the Isherwood schema one chooses not to be Truly Weak by continuing the killing cycle but chooses to be Truly Strong and start a new cycle of peace. Much of the Truly Weak and Truly Strong theme in the play — early or late versions — is subliminal. Later the theme would be more pronounced for the Isherwood-Auden plays in collaboration.

There are three sources for *Paid on Both Sides*: The first is from Old Norse and Old English literature. The play's title is taken from *Beowulf,* line 1305, adapted from John R. Clark Hall's 1901 prose translation: "That was no good exchange — that they should pay on both sides with the lives of friends." *Beowulf,* however, also provides a possible source for the revenge plot at the wedding of John Nower and Anne Shaw that concludes the charade. This episode closely parallels the account of the blood feud and its effects at the wedding of Ingeld in *Beowulf,* lines 2017–2067. The ambush of Red Shaw in revenge for the killing of John Nower's father resembles the *Anglo-Saxon Chronicle* for 755. In this episode Cyneheard discovers that Cynewulf, who has killed his brother, is going to visit a woman in Merantune, accompanied by a few followers. In *Paid on Both Sides* Red Shaw "goes to Brandon Walls today, visits a woman," with "a few" followers. He is similarly ambushed by John Nower in a revenge attack.

Papers *see* Archives and Papers

Parable-Art

In Samuel Hynes's important book *The Auden Generation*, he coined the term "parable-art" as a theme of the 1930s, and Hynes took his cue from Auden who wrote: "You cannot tell people what to do, you can only tell them parables; and that is what art really is, particular stories of particular people and experience, from which each according to his own immediate and peculiar needs may draw his own conclusions" ("Psychology and Art Today" 1935).

"Partition" 1966

This poem is about the 1947 partition of India into India and Pakistan from the view of the Briton who implemented it without thought that human beings were to be affected, and like "Rois Faineants" concerns the difference between private and public personas.

Pascal, Blaise

1623–62, French scientist and religious philosopher. Pascal in 1654 experienced what he called a conversion and thereafter turned to religion. Pascal's religious writings were posthumously published as *Pensées de M. Pascal sur la religion et sur quelques autres sujets* (1670). For a modern edition see *Thoughts: An Apology for Christianity* (tr. 1955). In the *Pensées* Pascal states his belief in the inadequacy of reason to solve man's difficulties or to satisfy his hopes. He preached instead the final necessity of mystic faith for true understanding of the universe and its meaning to man.

In 1956 Auden recalled that when he was younger that "writers did and do exist who, if not always, perhaps, completely orthodox, are effective Christian apologists, capable of showing the meaning and relevance of Christian dogmas to secular thought and action, but I never heard of them. I sometimes wonder, for example, what would have happened if, when I was at school or university, a godparent or friend had given me the works of Kierkegaard.... The only theological writer I knew of at the time whom I found readable and disturbing to my complacency was Pascal.... Today I find a certain element of fake in his writings, a kind of romantic indulgence in unhappiness not so far removed from *The Sorrows of Young Werther* [Goethe], which may have attracted me at the time; but at least he did not talk like a parson and he prevented me from banishing God from my mind when I should very much have preferred to do so" (*The Canterbury Pilgrims*). Auden's conflicted view of Pascal, which seems to say that he was better than reading nothing, is reflected in his poem "Pascal" in 1939, just before Auden moved onto Kierkegaard and others wholeheartedly.

Mendelson: "The poem uses Pascal as a mask to disguise a parabolic autobiography.... Auden could not convince himself of his own parable." The first part reflects Pascal's "curse of childhood isolation and the saving blessing of an adult vision," that Auden also claims for himself although his childhood was not so severe. In the second part Pascal has his vision of Christ that converts him, and Auden pretends this is also similar. "But 'Pascal' has the same evasiveness found in other complacent prophecies that he later abandoned, like 'Spain' and 'September 1, 1939'" (*Later Auden*). The trouble is that Auden did not believe his own prophecies and thought he had resorted to Black Magic, that is, propaganda, bereft of the crucial sincerity that he believed was the poet's only truth and his obligation to convey.

Pastoral *see The Age of Anxiety*

Paul Bunyan see Britten, Benjamin

"Paysage Moralisé" 1933

This poem was written before "A Summer Night" and does not reflect that subsequent change in Auden's vision. Auden compares a "rotting harvest" caused by flood with the rot in human nature and he hopes to rebuild both the desolated landscape and human spirit after the flood. Islands are an escape from a society-caused selfish isolation; valleys are passiveness; mountains are the effort to change; cities represent society; water is a drink of belief. These ideas would be developed in Auden's "Bucolics."

Pears, Sir Peter

1910–86, English tenor. Pears studied at the Royal College of Music and became a member of the Sadler's Wells Opera and the English Opera Group. In 1948 he made his Covent Garden debut. He worked closely with Benjamin Britten. Together they made a number of international tours, presenting works by Britten and other English composers. Pears sang many premieres of Britten operas, including *Peter Grimes, Billy Budd, Gloriana*, and *The Turn of the Screw*. In 1974 he made his Metropolitan Opera debut singing Aschenbach in Britten's opera *Death in Venice*, based on the novella by Thomas Mann. He was knighted in 1978. Britten first befriended Auden in Britain and after meeting Pears they briefly lived with

Auden in the early 1940s in a Brooklyn house rented by George Davis and shared with Carson McCullers, Gypsy Rose Lee, Louis MacNeice, Paul and Jane Bowles, and Erika and Klaus Mann.

Pearson, Norman Holmes *see* Poets of the English Language

"A Permanent Way" 1954

On a train ride, Auden considers a somewhat anti-existential celebration of the virtues of the less harmful dogmas as permanent ways, which leave one without the responsibility of choice but free to dream.

Perse, St.-John

1887–1975, Pseud. of Alexis Léger, French poet and diplomat, b. West Indies. Léger was against appeasing the Nazis. He came to the United States in 1940. Encouraged by André Gide, he published his first verse in 1909. His symbolic *Éloges* (tr. 1944) followed in 1911, then *Amitié du Prince* (1921) and *Anabase* (1924, tr. by T.S. Eliot, 1930). His work has been translated by Auden, Eliot, and MacLeish. Léger was awarded the 1960 Nobel Prize in Literature, and Auden translated his acceptance speech into English. In the 1966 reissue of *The Orators* Auden would credit Perse as one of his influences for that work.

"The Philosophy of a Lunatic" 1951

Auden: "The Christian conception of a unique revelation in history is as compatible with Jung as it is with Marx, with cyclical theories of time as with doctrines of the Wave of the future.... One cannot, for instance, identify the cult of the Earth Mother with the cult of the Madonna; the former is a dynamo [see "Making, Knowing, and Judging"] in disguise, the falsely personal image of the impersonal

forces of nature; the latter, through her actual personal historical existence on earth, has become the type and pledge of the redemption of the natural order."

"The Platonic Blow" 1948

Auden's pornographic poem, which he circulated privately until 1965 when it was, without his permission, published — in an erotic magazine. Auden disavowed it at first, but later would sometimes disavow his disavowal. The poem was a satirical counter to "In Praise of Limestone," which celebrated the boy in a more spiritual manner.

Play and Work

The poet, driven by empathy and sympathy, needs to see, hear, and tell, to explain, justify, and immortalize himself so as to intimate through Awe-sociations the intuitive yearning for the ultimate reality residing in the collective unconscious. Thus he chooses to explore more than just the merely utilitarian use of language; he wants, in Auden's nomenclature, to be a player of games, not just a worker. In life, work is a necessity for survival; play is a gratuitous desire or wish to be fulfilled, which one's psyche may depend on, but not one's physical existence. When an individual's work is also his play, it is a sign to the wise that God exists. For Auden,

> ...The writing of art is gratuitous, i.e. play.... Natural Man hates nature, and the only act which can really satisfy him is the acte gratuite. His ego resents every desire of his natural self for food, sex, pleasure, logical coherence, because desires are given, not chosen, and his ego seeks constantly to assert its autonomy by doing something of which the requiredness is not given.
>
> In addition to wanting to feel free, man wants to feel important.... The rules of a game give it importance by making it difficult to play, a test of skill. In this, however, they betray that their importance is really frivolous, because it means that they are only important to those who have the physical or mental gifts to play them, and that is a matter of chance....

The only serious possession of men is not their gifts but what they all possess equally, independent of fortune, namely their will, in other words, their love, and the only serious matter is what they love, themselves, or God and their neighbor....

The gulf between frivolity and seriousness is so infinite that all talk about children's games being preparation for adult life is misleading twaddle....

If the Fall made man conscious of the difference between good and evil, then the Incarnation made him conscious of the difference between seriousness and frivolity.... Before that, one might say that only children, i.e. those in whom consciousness of good and evil was not yet fully developed, could play games. The adult had to take frivolity seriously, i.e. turn games into magic, and in consequence could never wholeheartedly enjoy them because necessarily he was always anxious as to whether the magic would work this time....

Obviously then, for Auden, frivolity is very serious, but, then again, not to be taken too seriously.

For Auden, poetry is childlike frivolity, gratuitous play, a cosmic word game, and the ultimate mystic crossword puzzle.

The Play of Daniel 1959

This sacred medieval play, written in verse narration, resembled grand opera, and the production became an international success. It was often performed in churches, with the narrator, costumed as a monk, reading from the pulpit. Auden played the narrator in performances at an Oxford church in 1960. (See also New York Pro Musica.)

"A Playboy of the Western World" see Wilde, Oscar

Plays with Isherwood

In 1928 Auden tried his hand at a play, first called The Reformatory, then, in collaboration with Isherwood it became The Enemies

of a Bishop, or Die When I Say. Both versions were meant as private fun, and not for performance, and they include in-jokes, as well as the philosophy of Homer Lane. Nothing came of the play except that Auden knew that Isherwood could be a substantial partner in writing one, but Auden did add a statement of his dramatic method: "Dramatic action is ritual. 'Real' action is directed towards the satisfaction of an instinctive need of the actor [here inferred as acting on or off stage] who passes thereby from a state of excitement to a state of rest. Ritual is directed towards the stimulation of the spectator who passes thereby from a state of indifference to a state of acute awareness."

In 1933 Auden had written the play The Dance of Death (and in the play's program Auden wrote more on the drama) for Rupert Doone and the Group Theatre and this newly emerging company wanted more from Auden who was the icon of the avant-garde. Auden began writing a new play based on two previous attempts called The Fronny and The Chase. He discussed it with Isherwood, who made substantive suggestions. Auden decided that Isherwood should get credit and co-write the play with him. There was some resistance from Doone as well as from T.S. Eliot at Faber & Faber. Auden would not yield. The result was The Dog Beneath the Skin. "Dogskin," as they called it, is a satirical farce like The Dance of Death.

The quest saga would be the parable form that Isherwood and Auden would implement for the three plays that they would write in collaboration. The questors, whether satirical as in Dogskin or serious as in The Ascent of F6 and On the Frontier, would venture into the public chaos on a metaphorical search for inner peace in the private sphere. The plays were explicitly political, tacitly metaphysical. The villains are Truly Weak; the heroes are Truly Strong. In fact, they are also one and the same.

The Dog Beneath the Skin evolved from an earlier, unpublished and unproduced play of Auden's called The Chase. Dogskin would be a parable of current events using humor to satirize the serious issues "beneath the skin" of the farce. (The two former players of "The Waste Land Game" got their title from the line "the skull beneath the skin" from Eliot's "Whispers

FIRST PRODUCTION OF THIS PLAY

THE DOG BENEATH THE SKIN

in the early autumn of 1935

to be produced by Rupert Doone.

by THE GROUP THEATRE

(London effort to establish independent theatre movement)

Directors:
Tyrone Guthrie
Rupert Doone

Masks by Robert Medley
Music by Herbert Murrill

■ INFORMATION
from the Organiser
The Group Theatre
9 Great Newport St
London W.C.2

FULL MEMBERSHIP ONE GUINEA A YEAR

Promotion sheet for the first production of the play *The Dog Beneath the Skin*.

of Immortality.") *Dogskin* owes much to Gilbert and Sullivan, Thornton Wilder, and Brecht's plays *Threepenny Opera* and *The Rise and Fall of the City of Mahogonny*. (Isherwood would later translate lyrics for the former, and Auden with Chester Kallman would translate all of the latter.) *Dogskin* became a Mortmere story with absurd content barely masking rebellious intentions. Mendelson notes in Early Auden: "The pattern introduced beneath the wanderings of the hero amounts to a parabolic lesson in history. This takes the form of a progress from innocence, in both the hero and his native village, to experience (see Blake, William), of two opposed kinds: the revolutionary awakened in the hero and the reactionary hysteria that emerges in the village" (*Early Auden*). Auden and Isherwood had made their own progress from innocence to experience as witnesses to the Nazi terror in Berlin.

The play's hero, Alan Norman, is selected by his village to search for a missing heir whose return might bring some stability back to the town. Alan is sent off with pomp and circumstance across the border and into unknown frontiers where he has burlesque adventures. Norman sets out with the village's favorite "dog" as a companion. Alan returns home with the heir Francis who in fact had disguised himself as the "dog" years before, and had been in the village all along. Alan and Francis find that their village has become a fascist enclave with the concomitant fear and paranoia this entails. Throughout the play a Chorus comments on the action in the didactic mode. In the play's prologue, the chorus (with Auden's appropriations from Anthony Collett's 1935 book *The Changing Face of England*) invokes the idyllic and pastoral British past and compares it to the Depression present.

The town's vicar, another ancient Other as in Isherwood's *The Memorial* and Auden's *The Orators*, exhorts the village to select a questor who will preserve the past by bringing back the "missing" heir, Sir Francis Crewe. Alan is sent off as the hero-saviour with jingoistic fervor. His search includes the usual Isherwood-Auden staples of spies and secret agents. The play has left-leaning implications that capitalists are bad while socialists and Communists are good. A visit to a red light district includes a stop at the Cosy Corner, the name taken from the boy bar Isherwood and Auden had frequented in Berlin. In addition to the red light foray, Norman and the "dog," named Francis after the subject of their search, meet among others two journalists, a king, a crooked financier, a surgeon and his students in a medical school, and the inmates of a lunatic asylum who are led by "The Voice of the Leader." This leader spouts rabid fascist nonsense. After the asylum, they go to Paradise Park. Norman asks a poet he meets in the park if he knows the missing heir. The poet, pointing to his head, answers: "Here. Everything's here. You're here. He's here. This park's here. This tree's here. If I shut my eyes they all disappear." The poet reminds the audience of the ephemeral nature of the search and the illusory status of the human condition, which the poet attempts to reflect in the "here" of his imagination. After Norman and the dog take a nap in the park, the Chorus states: "Dear sleep, the secretary of that strange club / Where all are members upon one condition, / That they forget their own importance...." Whether in dreams or in life, only when the ego is suspended are people truly equal.

The satire belies the serious undertone of the Isherwood-Auden schema. There is little difference between the various groups encountered. The lunatics are no more paranoid than normal people are. Negative behaviors are a result of living in a capitalist world that produces inevitably deleterious conditions. These conditions are perpetuated by a devotion to the past that ignores current crises such as the Depression and fascism. As postulated by the park poet, reality is in the eye of the beholder. Nothing exists outside each mind's uniquely self-designed perception. This individual perception is distorted by the cultural compulsives or the collective subjectivity of societal attitudes and pervasive propaganda. These attitudes are the obstacles Alan encounters on his quest (Test) over the Northwest Passage. Norman learns, just as Auden's airman learned in *The Orators*, that solutions are not to be found externally. Answers must be found within.

In a long monologue the "dog" confesses to what the audience already knows, that he is Francis. He explains that he had taken on his dog disguise to "sever all ties with the past." Masked, he had observed the foibles of human nature as a spy amidst the subjects of his study: From this view he learned that all were playing at "charades" of self-deception and wearing their public masks in both public and in private. (People acted and spoke in front of a "dog" as they never would have in front of people.) He learned that people form masks because they are overwrought with neuroses and psychoses that make them easy prey to outside influences. Echoing the Paradise Park poet, Francis says, "Too many ideas in their heads! To them I'm an idea, you're an idea, everything's an idea." These archetypal ideas, once pure, are now tainted by societal influences that have "subjectivized" them so that they have come to supersede the reality of immediate experience. After this quasi-metaphysical lecture to the audience, the dog also confesses to Alan that he is indeed Francis.

Alan and Francis (as himself) return to their village for the last scene. The Chorus precedes the final scene by saying: "Do not speak of a change of heart, meaning five hundred a year and a room of one's own, / As if that were all that is necessary. In these islands alone, there are some forty-seven million hearts." Bourgeois comfort and complacency are not enough to bridge the gaps created by separate egos who should otherwise strive for an ego-less undifferentiated unity. Each of the forty-seven million hearts is another island within the islands; each wears a mask as a shield to conceal vulnerability, but while these shields try to prevent pain, they also deny love from access. The Chorus continues with a reiteration of the Isherwood-Auden schema:

Man divided always and restless always: afraid and unable to forgive: / Unable to forgive his parents. / An isolated bundle of nerve and desire, suffering alone, / Seeing others only in reference to himself: as a long-lost mother or his ideal self at sixteen. / Dreaming of continuous sexual enjoyment or perpetual applause. Some turn to … solutions of sickness or crime: some to the … sport of the moment. / Some to good works, to a mechanical ritual of giving. / Some have adopted [a] system of beliefs or a political programme, others have escaped to ascetic mountains. / Or taken refuge … among the boys on the bar stools, on the small uncritical islands. / Men will profess devotion to anything; to God, to humanity, to Truth, to Beauty: but their first thought on meeting is 'Beware!' / They put their trust in Reason or feelings of the Blood but will not trust a stranger with half-a-crown.

(The "feelings of the Blood" refers to the obsolete "life-worship" of D.H. Lawrence, once an Auden favorite but now considered by Auden as a false hope.) After this litany of the Truly Weak, the Chorus suggests that the only hope for each individual is a transformation from within. This is followed by a transcendent merging into the undifferentiated unity that is engendered by the mystical vision of Agape: Norman and Francis return to the village only to find that it has succumbed to fascist influences. The vicar makes a long speech of patriotic cant warning of what will happen if the enemy succeeds: What the vicar imagines sounds as if Isherwood and Auden had read Aldous Huxley's 1932 novel, *Brave New World*:

"No family love. Sons would inform against their fathers, cheerfully send them to the execution cellars. No romance. Even the peasant must beget that standard child under laboratory conditions. Motherhood would be by licence. Truth and Beauty would be proscribed as dangerously obstructive. No books, no art, no music." A villager who lost both her sons in a previous war, responds that this cant will get more children killed.

Francis, having revealed himself, tells them: "I've had a dog's-eye view of you for the last ten years.... I was horrified and fascinated by you all." He continues with a scathing evaluation that amounts to Isherwood speaking for himself. (Isherwood wrote the prose passages.) "I thought such obscene, cruel, hypocritical, mean, vulgar creatures have never existed before.... As a dog, I learnt with what a mixture of fear, bullying, and condescending kindness you treat those whom you consider your inferiors, but on whom you are dependent for your pleasures." The play ends with Francis declaring he will join the Anti-Others of the world to spread the truth about The Others. He departs with his first recruits including Alan, and the Chorus concludes with a paraphrase of the Communist dictum "To each his need: from each his power."

The Dog Beneath the Skin turns the Isherwood-Auden schema into a blend of parable and didacticism. The themes that dominated their individual works coalesce in collaboration: the duality of private and public, inner and outer, is broadly manifested by Francis as "dog" and then Francis as rebel. Norman's quest is a Test beyond the borders and over the Northwest Passage. Nothing is learned from this quest except the realization that external quests and Tests are for the Truly Weak. Realization is circular, not linear. One must return to his inner self. Before the quest, Francis had been in the village all along just as the answers to society's problems are hidden in each individual all along if one turns inward to seek them. *Dogskin*, even though staged by the Group Theater as a burlesque aiming for political laughs, is another metaphysical exercise signifying Isherwood and Auden's call for a change of heart. This change is sought by the sensitive man who wishes to become Truly Strong. With

Dogskin as a warm-up, Isherwood and Auden's next play would explore the same themes more seriously and the metaphysical intentions would be front and center.

In *The Ascent of F6* the hero/anti-hero Michael Ransom would represent what Isherwood and Auden had learned in their lives and through their work over the previous ten years. Ransom, would be the symbolic star of his decade and the anti-hero role model for the future. (For this play, see also Thornton Wilder.)

Michael Ransom's very name carries with it the implication of a man held hostage. Ransom is a captive of the past who becomes a victim of it when that past inflicts its inexorable will on him through The Others. In *Dogskin* the burlesque still had one foot in the pseudo-fascism of the British Public School with the other foot stepping towards the new school of real-world fascism. *The Ascent of F6* has both feet firmly rooted in current history, and the Old School is no longer a source of satire in light of these events. Isherwood and Auden felt an urgency about current events that demanded tangible responses in the more public forum of the theatre. In his 1934 essay on T.E. Lawrence, Auden explicitly stated the dichotomy of the Truly Weak and Truly Strong Man. Until then this dichotomy had only been expressed through tacit parables. *In The Ascent of F6* the Truly Weak and Truly Strong Man are defined explicitly and T.E. Lawrence is the role model for both.

The listing of the play's characters "in order of their appearance" begins with "Michael Forsyth Ransom" followed by "Sir James Ransom (his twin brother)." The twinship is a metaphor. They are actually two halves of the same person. The play begins with Michael Ransom's existential monologue that is inspired by Ransom having just read in Dante that men "were not formed to live like brutes, but to follow virtue and knowledge." Ransom, a weary cynic, says of Dante, "a crook speaking to crooks." Then after calling Dante an aristocratic Other, Ransom asks, "who was Dante to speak of virtue and knowledge?" (Auden will also quote from Dante's Canto XXVI of the *Inferno* where Ulysses listens to false advice and leads his men to doom, a foreshadowing for Ransom in the play.) Ransom questions if, to

Dante, "virtue and knowledge" really meant a quest for power. Ransom secretly despises the world of his own upper class: "the generals and industrial captains: justifying every baseness [of their] schoolboy lives." (Ransom has retreated into the solitude (and Tests) of mountain-climbing.

Ransom speaks bitterly that it would be better to be dead or ignorant than be caught in the "web of guilt that prisons every upright person ... oh happy the foetus that miscarries and the frozen idiot that cannot cry 'mama!'" Ransom may be an aesthete who was tormented by hearties. He may also be an aesthete who disguised himself as a hearty and suffers the guilt of having conformed instead of being his true Self. Ransom is a cynic; he is Francis Crewe without the satire. From the hero's disappointment with life, the anti-hero is born.

The scene shifts to a typical middle-class British couple at home and describes their middle-class routine as one of stultifying, spirit-killing ennui. They are listening to the wireless. Mr. A: "I'm sick of the news. All you can hear is politics...." Mrs. A: "They will ask for our children and kill them; sympathise deeply and ask for some more." Mr. A: There is "Nothing to make us proud of our race.... Nothing to take us out of ourselves. Out of the oppression of this city.... Give us something to live for. We have waited too long." This middle-class couple will appear frequently as a contrast to the behind-the-scenes manipulations of The Others. Mr. And Mrs. A represent the anonymous public who know only what they are fed by a manipulated media.

The next scene emphasizes the contrast of Mr. and Mrs. A with The Others by shifting to, as per the stage directions, "Sir James Ransom's room at the Colonial office. On the wall ... hangs a large boldly-printed map showing British Sudoland and Ostnian Sudoland. The frontier between the two colonies is formed by a chain of mountains: one peak, prominently marked F6, is ringed with a red circle." Sir James, the evil twin, speaks as a stereotypical Other about the Sudoland problem. This British colony, with socialist Ostnia's influence, has been yanking at its colonial chains. The Others denounce Socialism and Lord Stagmantle proudly boasts: "We were out to smash the

Labour Government ... and, by God, we did." The "by God" is a hint of a church-sanctioned imperialist hypocrisy. James forms a plan to inflame public opinion into wanting to keep Sudoland for the British: An expedition will scale the previously insurmountable mountain, F6. Propaganda will arouse British pride and the public will wish to defend their prize, F6, and this means retaining control of British Sudoland at all costs. F6 is also known as the "Haunted Mountain," and Lady Isabel recalls that it is reputedly protected by a "guardian demon." The General retorts that this is a "fairy-tale." James, however, always the politician, responds: "A fairy-tale is significant according to the number of people who believe in it...." He is suggesting that propaganda can manufacture nefarious "fairytales" to suit a hungry public starved for self-serving news. James tells The Others that he will recruit his bother, the famous climber, to lead the expedition. Next the audience watches Mr. And Mrs. A listen to the first wave of propaganda on the wireless: "The haunted mountain [is] inhabited only by monks [who] practise a mysterious cult ... and there are wonderful tales of their mystical and psychic powers." Isherwood and Auden foreshadow the metaphysical messages to come later in the play.

In Scene III we return to Michael Ransom and meet his climbing fellows: the Doctor, Lamp, Shawcross (Lawrence's adopted name was Shaw), and Gunn. Ransom is the magnetic leader; Shawcross and Gunn are his devoted followers. Gunn is a jokester, conniver and compulsive Test-seeker. Shawcross is a fawning worshipper. (The name of Shawcross has meaning in that Shaw was the second name that T.E. Lawrence feigned when he re-enlisted into the R.A.F. anonymously as a "common" soldier, after having been the fabled Lawrence of Arabia; later he took the name of Ross.) Gunn is a court-jester worshipper, appealing through humor. Shawcross is judgmental of Gunn and a snitch when Gunn is caught in some petty connivance. Shawcross and Gunn are still living as honor system schoolboys in the British Public School mentality; they are the younger boys trying to please the older leader of the senior class. Shawcross and Gunn are Truly Weak. Ransom understands this undercurrent and is suitably patient with each. Still, recalling his opening monologue, he himself has his own undercurrent of stark cynicism towards his fellow men.

The Others, led by James, visit Michael and his gang to persuade Michael to surmount F6. James tries flattery on Michael: "In all humility I say it — my brother is a great man." Michael sees through this, recalling their childhood when James would whine and wheedle for what he wanted. He tells James to cut the subterfuge and get to the point. James starts off: "In the name of His Majesty's Government, I have come to make you an important proposition —," Michael does not want to hear it and interrupts, "Which I unconditionally refuse." The invocation of king and country is enough to repel him. "I know your propositions James: they are exceedingly convincing. They contain certain reservations. They are concerned with prestige, tactics, money, and the privately prearranged meanings of familiar words. I will have nothing to do with any of them. Keep to your world. I will keep to mine." The Others and the opposing Anti-Other are clearly in conflict, with The Others manipulating their world through a secret code of "familiar words." James tempts Michael the mountain-climber by telling him that the goal is F6. Michael questions: "What does your world have to do with F6? Since boyhood, in dreams … F6 is my fate…. But not now, not like this." Lady Isabel tries to manipulate him by shamelessly impugning his manhood: "I see it in your eyes, you are afraid." She confronts Michael with a Test. He does not succumb to the bait. "I am afraid of a great many things…. But of nothing which you in your worst nightmares could ever imagine." This alludes to his angst in the opening monologue. Ransom realizes that he has inner demons spurred by some hidden guilt. He also realizes that in his efforts to be Truly Strong and refuse this Test, he knows that he is, like anyone else, also Truly Weak because otherwise he would feel no temptation. Speaking of temptation, The Others pull out their ace. There is a knock on the door. James says: "Here is somebody who may be able to persuade you…."

Ransom [with a cry of dismay] Mother!

Mother [advancing to Ransom] Michael, I am so proud —

Ransom [recoiling] You too! No, it isn't impossible! Your shadow adds to theirs, a trick of the light.

His mother — an archetypal Auden Generation mother — knows no bounds for laying on guilt and shame. Michael tells her that when he and his brother were boys she neglected him in favor of James of whom he was jealous; hence, his guilt and retreat into solitude. She invokes the memory of their father saying that James was like him: "he cannot live an hour without applause…. But you, you were to be truly strong who must be kept from all that could infect or weaken; it was for you I steeled my love deliberately and hid it. Do you think it was easy to shut you out? But I won. You were to be unlike your father and brother, you were to have the power to stand alone…. There was a mother who crucified herself to save her favorite son from weakness." On this pathetic note Michael gives in.

His mother, in her twisted effort to make Michael Truly Strong, succeeded superficially, but left him with a core of vulnerability as seen in the bitterness of his opening meditation in Act One. The past lurks always in the psyche to disturb the present. The great irony is that his mother, who claims she withheld her love to make him strong so he could "stand alone," won't let him. Mrs. Ransom gives back the love she withheld, but since this is only a ploy to make him Truly Weak and accept this Test, she contradicts herself. Here, more so than in Isherwood's first two novels that dealt with the Truly Weak and Truly Strong theme subliminally, the requirements of the stage demanded a stark directness that enunciated the themes succinctly and viscerally.

After having succeeded in their entrapment, The Others leave, and Ransom has a dream (or nightmare) that punctuates his own particular mother-son conundrum: Michael hears his mother tell him she will be with him always, right to the top of the mountain. Her son's tormented voice is heard "Far off, frightened, It's the demon, mother!" The line is deliberately ambiguous as it could refer to the mountain-as-demon or the mother-as-demon.

Act Two begins "in a monastery on the Great Glacier." Shawcross tells Michael that Gunn "steals." Michael laughs, calling a Gunn an essentially harmless "magpie." Ransom also notes to Shawcross that he hasn't changed much since he was captain at school, meaning that he epitomizes the Old School's faults. Shawcross fawns some more while still slipping in his derision of Gunn whom he refers to as being fearful of F6. Michael tells him it is the fear that pushes Gunn: "being frightened is his chief pleasure in life." Shawcross knows that only two climbers can actually reach the summit of F6 and begins his campaign to be chosen. He jealousy calls Gunn a "neurotic." Shawcross and Gunn are Truly Weak, only differing in approach. Shawcross needs approval from his hero Ransom to validate himself. He endures Tests for Ransom's sake. (As Auden previously said concerning *The Orators*, "no secular saviour can equal the hopes of his youthful followers.") Gunn needs Tests for his own sake.

Gunn wonders if the monks communicate by "telepathy" in some secret code known only to themselves. The monks unnerve Gunn because his instinct tells him that they understand that his compulsion to live dangerously is a weakness. The monks have a magic crystal into which one can glimpse his future if not necessarily realize what that future means. The reflections are also omens of death.

Alone, the monastery's Abbot and Ransom philosophize. (Mendelson sees the Abbot as A.E. Housman; Izzo sees him as Yeats or Eliot. Yet, while Mendelson sees the Abbot's talk as a "whiff of parody," Izzo sees it in the tone of Auden's "A Summer Night." Of this latter view Isherwood wrote: "When we collaborate, I have to keep a sharp eye on him — or down flop the characters on their knees.") This dialogue signifies Isherwood and Auden's shift away from the distracting public chaos and into private spheres where the only true salvation can be found. Ransom reveals to the Abbot that when it had been his turn to look into the crystal he saw the "ragged denizens" crying out for help and wonders if their cry was for him to save them. The Abbot tells him "Only God is great," implying that if fate chooses him to be a saviour, so be it, but he cannot put this burden on himself if he is doing so as a com-

pensation for some secret guilt. The Abbot warns Michael not to let his Western sensibility discount the idea of a Demon on the mountain, telling him that the peasants, unencumbered with the veneer of civilization, "see it more clearly than you or I. For it is a picture of truth. The Demon is real. Only his ministry and his visitation are unique for every nature. To the complicated and sensitive like yourself … his disguises are more subtle…. I understand your temptation. You wish to conquer the Demon and then to save mankind." The Abbot continues:

> Nothing is revealed [in the crystal] but what we have hidden from ourselves…. Your temptation … is written in your face. You could ask the world to follow you and it would serve you with blind obedience; for most men long to be delivered from the terror of thinking and feeling for themselves…. And you would do them much good. Because men desire evil, they must be governed by those who understand the corruption of their hearts…. but woe to the governors, for by the very operation of their duty, however excellent, they themselves are destroyed. For you can only rule men by appealing to their fear and lust; government requires the exercise of the human will: and the human will is from the Demon.

And the Demon (the ego) is a metaphor for the neuroses and psychoses that result from the conflict of trying to shake off the shackles of the past. Ransom asks the Abbot what choice does he have but to climb the mountain. The Abbot answers: "There is an alternative, Mr. Ransom; and I offer it to you…. The complete abnegation of the will." Ransom asks what this means, but they are interrupted before the Abbot can explain.

In the mystic's purview the "abnegation of the will" is the eradication of the willful ego's lower-case self in favor of Vedanta's transcendent upper case Self. Auden's "Summer Night" vision of Agape encouraged the possibility of this mystical viewpoint. But can any ruler abnegate his will? Isherwood and Auden understood that even the well-meaning man becomes corrupted by the process of ruling. Hero-worship entails that a hero fill the needs of the

Truly Weak. The amorphous public will objectify the hero and give him an image that no man can possibly live up to. The hero feels compelled to try and match their image of him. A Truly Strong Man, if asked to be a leader, would wish to maintain his private face in public places, but he would find that this private face may not be the face his public expects or wants. The Truly Weak Man who becomes a leader does not have this problem; his mask is always in place to fit the vision others have of him and indeed need of him.

After he and the Abbot are interrupted, Ransom wonders: "Is it too late for me.... There was a choice once ... I made it wrong, and if I choose again now, I must choose for myself alone, not for these others." He implores some greater power to help him: "Save us from the destructive element of our will, for all we do is evil." The term, "destructive element" came from the title of Stephen Spender's 1935 book of literary criticism.

Spender asserted that the technique in the middle to late novels of Henry James was a prelude to literary modernism. Spender said that James used interior monologues to tacitly express beliefs in absentia through stating unbelief, or that by having the characters reject certain ideas, readers inferred new ideas antithetically. Further, Spender analyzed James, Yeats, Eliot, and D.H. Lawrence as exemplars of "unbelief" from which the astute reader should connote new beliefs. Spender declared that there must be a "tearing-down" of the old before there can be a "building-up" of the new. In *F6* Isherwood and Auden convey their understanding of this process, having spent ten years tearing down the influences of the past. The building-up of new beliefs must have some underlying metaphysical basis so one can act in the world as a Truly Strong Man uninfluenced and unimpeded by the needs of the individual ego. To know this is to know also that the public will resist the ideals behind such a theory. Further, what are the beliefs that will supplant the unbelief?: socialism? Communism? mysticism? These are only words if the private face cannot find its balance in the public chaos. In 1937 Isherwood and Auden were not yet certain of the answers, but they knew enough to pose the questions.

As they climb a skull is found, and like Hamlet, Ransom speaks to it. Hamlet is Ransom's literary role model; both are internally conflicted concerning their mothers and driven by forces they cannot control or fully understand. As with Hamlet, Ransom's angst will supply ample blood sacrifices. In *F6* the first to die is Edward Lamp from an avalanche. Ransom says of Lamp: "The first victim to my pride." Back in England Lamp is lionized by the media as the newest martyr for the cult of the dead.

Ransom decides that Gunn, not Shawcross, will go with him to the summit. Ransom tells the doctor that Shawcross can't deal with the Test because he is a nervous wreck and the climb is too psychotically connected with his self-esteem. This makes him a risk. (It took one to know one.) Ransom informs Shawcross who does not take the decision well. Shawcross, unable to bear what he considers to be his failure, jumps to his death. Shawcross saw in his hero Ransom what his lack of self-esteem prevented him from seeing in himself. No actual hero can live up to such a follower's ego-derived vicarious need.

In the next scene Gunn dies of exhaustion as he and Michael are just short of reaching the summit. Ransom thinks that this is Gunn's good luck for he has achieved the release of death that "extricates you now from the most cunning trap of all," which is life.

Ransom goes on, nears the summit, and collapses. At the summit he sees a veiled, but as yet, unidentifiable figure. The Chorus is in the background wearing the monks' cowled robes. They recite: "When shall the deliverer come to destroy this dragon?" After a fanfare of trumpets, James Ransom appears as the Dragon. He spews propaganda. Michael rises and steps into the circle of light around the dragon. James signals and life-size chessmen appear. Their ensuing debate is a matter of gamesmanship. All of the play's characters encircle the twin brothers. The middle-class couple grumble about their dull lives. The General tells them that they have it easy compared to the brave climbers. Maybe so, but in Wholly Truthful art one's egocentric everyday life goes on. Mr. And Mrs. A can only suffer for themselves; they cannot feel what the climbers felt or what another feels. For Mr. and Mrs. A, as for any individual, one's own existence is paramount. Another's suffering may be apprehended intellectually, but it is an abstraction viscerally, even to one who is well meaning and tries to empathize. One's intellect cannot live in another's body. (Later Auden would use this theme in the poem "Musée des Beaux Arts.") Of course, the rich Others find it easy to chastise others not so rich. Lord Stagmantle shallowly asserts that money isn't everything: "I know there are far too many people who have too little. It's a damned shame, but there it is."

Mrs. A asks, "Why were we born?" She does so in despairing ennui, not as a philosophical inquiry. James misinterprets her meaning and sarcastically mimics Michael's scholarly bent by responding with ad hoc nonsense about the "immensity of the universe" in which the life of the individual has no importance but to pass the torch, die, and be forgotten. Michael protests that this is a twisted paraphrase of how he truly feels. His thoughts were distorted just as a controlled media manipulates propaganda. James taunts him, repeating what Michael said to him in Act One: "Keep to your world. I will keep to mine." The chess game commences. Michael wins. James falls dead and is eulogized by The Others who continue their patriotic cant and accuse Michael of murder.

The Abbot appears in a judge's wig and robe. Michael cries out that he is innocent and that the Demon gave the sign for his brother's death. The Abbot calls as witnesses the victims of Michael Ransom's pride. Shawcross appears and implicates the former subject of his hero-worship. Gunn and Lamp follow and are also of no help to their friend. The Abbot asks Michael if he wishes to appeal to the all-seeing crystal. The Abbot looks into it and tells Ransom that the Demon was not the temptation. Ransom realizes his pride was the temptation. He is found guilty to a chorus of: "Die for England! All lights are extinguished below; only the [veiled] Figure and Ransom remain illuminated. Ransom turns to the Figure, whose draperies fall away, revealing Mrs. Ransom as a young mother."

Then, darkness hides the stage. The sun rises; the stage is empty, except for the body of Ransom at the summit. He has been dead or near death all along. The preceding scene was an illusion, or perhaps the dream vision of one dying. After his death, Ransom is praised by The Others as, indeed, having died for England. James says: "He had many sides to his character and I doubt if anyone knew the whole man. I as his brother certainly did not. He had an almost feminine sensibility which, if it had not been allied to great qualities of soul and will-power and a first class intelligence, might easily have become neurotic—" James did not know him. What he said of his brother is true, but a misinterpretation reversing the real meaning. If his brother was "neurotic," it was not due to a "feminine sensibility" (or sensitivity). This sensibility had more likely ameliorated his mental illness instead of worsening it; that is, at least until he had given in to the temptation of his masculine side, which led him to charge up F6. Had his feminine sensibility been stronger, he might not have let his manly pride push him to accept the mission that killed him and his friends. His past, in the symbolic form of his young mother, overcame the common sense of his sensitive, feminine side.

Ransom failed because he gave in to the public chaos instead of listening to his private sphere. His inner Self had an intuition for mysticism as revealed in his conversation with the Abbot. The Abbot had told him that the secret to his salvation would be in the "abnegation of the will," but Ransom could not resist his ego and he succumbed to the temptations of worldliness that his mother represented. Isherwood and Auden created a character who was the defining figure for their generation. Michael Ransom was an aspiring Truly Strong Man who was overwhelmed by Truly Weak temptation. He was a realistic anti-heroic hero; his divided, angst-filled being had a conscience. Ransom cared—too much! Had he cared less and not been so vulnerable, he might have ignored the appeals of The Others and acted more in self-preservation. Ransom was the sensitive man who had an intuition that it is in the world of the spirit where answers might be found. His intuition, however, became clouded by his ego.

For Isherwood and Auden, Michael Ransom's quest represented their own quest. Ransom was their last hope for the 1930s. Metaphorically, his failure would signify the futility that would overcome their iconoclastic generation when it was unable to prevent World War II. This generation, with all its activism, had not been able to save the world. When the decade ended, all that was left for them to do was to try and save themselves by somehow turning inward.

The success of *The Dog Beneath the Skin* and *The Ascent of F6* were responded to in the usual manner of the 1930s: they were imitated. The imitations all shared the Isherwood-Auden theme of a conflicted man trying to reconcile his private sphere in public chaos by maturing from Truly Weak to Truly Strong. Day Lewis, in 1936, wrote the play *Noah and the Waters*, a didactic parable leaning more heavily on the didactic. Noah is an anti-hero conflicted about saving the world and whom to save. In 1937 Louis MacNeice's satire *Out of the Picture* has a sensitive artist as anti-hero conflicted over the integrity of his art versus the bourgeois world he is a member of. Also in 1937 Spender's *Trial of a Judge* features a conflicted anti-hero who has to choose between truth and political expediency. All these plays gave homage to Francis Crewe and Michael Ransom. (*Note*: A chorus from an unfinished film *Negroes* is used in F6.)

The last Auden-Isherwood play was *On the Frontier* (1938), a production backed by economist John Maynard Keynes. The play has two plots, a satire of a munitions manufacturer who tries to agitate near-war conditions to keep him rich but to stop just short of war. The second is of two families, one in each of the "near-war" nations with a "Romeo and Juliet" theme of "star-crossed lovers." Here Auden and Isherwood were, by their own accounts, heavily didactic and, in fact, a bit worn out, so that this play has neither the humor of *The Dog Beneath the Skin* nor the palpable psychodrama of *The Ascent of F6*. Moreover, current events were taking a turn for the worse with the Spanish Civil War looking like a defeat by the fascists and Hitler making imperialistic inroads that would soon become World War II. The play's anti-war message and the dialogue that was now falsely optimistic could not and did not appeal to reviewers or audiences, and the play did not succeed.

Plomer, William

1903–1973, b. South Africa, British poet, novelist. Plomer knew John Lehmann

who introduced him to Stephen Spender who led him to Isherwood and Auden. Plomer charmed them with his stories of South Africa and Japan where he had spent a good deal of his youth. His novel *Turbott Wolfe*, 1925, was an indictment of South Africa's treatment of the native inhabitants. The book was well received and Plomer followed this with short stories in 1927, *I Speak of Africa*. He would later astutely examine Japan's national character in 1931's *Sado*.

John Lehmann on Plomer: "What struck me at once about the rather burly figure with the deep voice who came into my office was the shrewdly observant look behind the spectacles, the sensitive mouth and humour that would leap into the whole expression of his face. I found his delight in anything eccentric or fantastic, the continuous bubble of crazy commentary that he would keep up in responsive company, completely irresistible. Like so many people of lively personality, he seemed to create his own surroundings" (*The Whispering Gallery*).

After meeting Plomer himself, Isherwood described him in a letter to Edward Upward. "He is a big man with big round glasses and the look of a benign muscular owl. His descriptions of people were witty and exact; once, he called someone an 'art lout.' He seemed to take everything lightly. Then, beneath the malice and fun, you became aware of an extraordinary strength—a strength that lent itself to others.... You were also aware that his fun was that of a person who was capable of intense private suffering. Therefore it should never seem trivial under any circumstances. He would have been wonderful in a lifeboat with the survivors of a shipwreck" (*Christopher and His Kind*).

Poe, Edgar Allan

1809–49, American poet, short-story writer, and critic, b. Boston. He is acknowledged as one of the most original writers in American literature. His tales and poems convey the mysterious, dreamlike, and often macabre forces that pervaded his sensibility. He is also considered the father of the modern detective story.

Auden introduced and selected a 1950 anthology of Poe's works titled *Poe: Selected Prose*,

Poetry, and Eureka. Says Auden, "What every author hopes to achieve from posterity is justice." Conversely, an author fears being known only for fragments, or he fears becoming a limited cult figure. The first is unjust because even if the fragments are his best work, readers cannot truly judge him overall; the second is embarrassing because no author believes he is that good. Poe is in both categories.

In Poe's tales, the characters are not humans who would actually exist as both natural and historical beings with free choice of their own. In his stories, there are two groups of characters, distinguished by two states of mind. The first group represents states of willful being in the imposition of the willful ego trying to control reality, in which there are extremes without shading, and "operatic" illusions by intention. (At this time Auden was writing his first libretto, *The Rake's Progress*). The second group represents the relation of the will to environment as reversed; the hero is not trying to get control but is passive. Things are done to him rather than by him. The first group has no history because characters refuse to change; the second group has no history because characters can't change, they can only experience.

In Group 1 the missing historical individual coincides with the history of science where individuality is subservient to facts and numbers. These characters are caught up in an urban-industrial evolution created by historical forces that make these characters less capable of self-initiative and more prone to being caught up in the fate of the anonymous mass.

Poe's tales influenced Dostoyevski (the working of the perverse mind), Conan Doyle, H.G. Wells, Jules Verne, and others.

Auden considers Poe's poems experiments; they could have used more "lab time" to reach their full potential, but Poe was too absorbed in the tragedy of his life to devote this time. The poems are florid rushes of raw ability.

Although Poe's philosophical work, *Eureka*, is presently neglected, Auden feels that the thoughts it expresses on science and the origins and destiny of the universe are intuitively correct. Written near the end of his life, Eureka combines Poe's obsessions: one ego compelled to merge with another, and a passion for logic, explanation, and resolution.

When Auden turns to Poe's critical writings he takes the moment to define a critic as a polemicist who must balance a defense of tradition while praising novelty derived from contradiction. A first rate critic is only as good as the work he reviews. Poe railed against long poems of philosophical pretense in favor of evocations of mind enacted through craft, which is what Auden also championed.

Poems 1930

In October 1929 *Transitional Poem* was published and C. Day Lewis introduced Auden's innovative ideas in a traditional manner. This partially prepared a similar audience for the arrival of Auden's non-traditional poems in May 1930. Auden's poems reject the past as indicated by their content, but Auden also rejects traditional poetic technique with a new diction. This is what set him apart from his poetic predecessors including Day Lewis. Auden's justifiably famous obscurity in these poems becomes less obscure in light of the Isherwood-Auden schema. (The poems also benefit enormously from Edward Mendelson's study, *Early Auden*.) Auden's poems are written in the secret code of a game directed at the intimates and non-squares who were part of their gang. Before they were published, the poems had been written, as Auden said, "to amuse my friends," and were read by Isherwood and then a selected few Anti-Others such as Day Lewis and Spender. The poems have a purpose: to be coded passwords into the Isherwood-Auden cosmology. According to Mendelson: "The poems were taken as fragments of an activist allegory whose key, although hidden, really did exist. Auden's readers while agreeing on this view were divided into two camps: those who complained that the key was a private myth or private joke reserved for a coterie of cronies and insiders, and those who felt they were the insiders, by virtue of membership in Auden's generation, and proceeded to fill the gaps in his broken pattern with their own political and psychological enthusiasms."

Political enthusiasms included socialism and Marxism (and for the misinterpreters, fascism). Psychological and metaphysical enthusiasms were

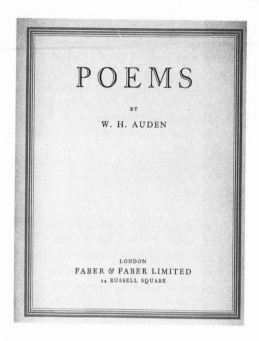

Poems, by W.H. Auden.

Freud, Jung, Yeats's version of Vedanta, and Gerald Heard, who was Auden's friend and influenced him with his theories of an "evolving consciousness." Heard postulated in numerous books that history is a sequence of "inevitable phases of a single evolutionary process — evolution being carried on now in the mind as it was once carried on in the body" (*The Emergence of Man*). Heard's theme of an evolving consciousness can be found in Auden's poems. The questor in them is a cypher-witness seeking The Northwest Passage by facing tests, crossing borders and exploring frontiers that are symbols of his divided mind. He is conflicted within himself because he is separated from his real need, which is, Mendelson observes, "submergence in the undifferentiated sea," of the World Mind's collective consciousness. (In Vedanta the ocean is the metaphorical symbol for an undifferentiated consciousness into which individual drops of water representing separated egos merge, signifying mystical transcendence into one ocean of cosmic unity.) Auden said previously "Life is one whole thing made up of smaller whole things ... always groups.... The whole cannot exist without the part, nor the part without the whole" ("Writing" *Outline*). Much of Auden's thought in

1929 was influenced by Heard's theories, which, though Auden thought them new, were actually quite old. Heard would learn when he came to America with Aldous Huxley in 1937 that his theories had been explained by Vedantic cosmology 2,500 years before.

Consequently, in 1930, Auden's early poems, as influenced by Heard, correlated to Vedanta even though at the time neither Auden nor Heard realized it. Mendelson says of Auden "the question he asked in his first poems was not What should I do now? But of what whole can I be part?" Auden was looking for some kind of psychic integration for himself in particular, for his highbrow group in general, and for everyone universally. For the most part, however, his supporters and imitators asked just the first part of the question: "What should I do now?" They interpreted Auden's poems with their martial images as a call to action. This was a call he hadn't actually intended; yet, he didn't mind being thought of as responsible for it. When Isherwood and Auden went to America in 1939, Isherwood followed Heard to California to learn about "this thing," which Heard realized was the basis of his previous theories. "This thing" was Vedanta. Auden stayed in New York and never accepted Isherwood and Heard's Vedanta philosophy even though Auden had been heading in the same direction. Auden stopped short of rejecting Christianity as Isherwood and Heard had done; instead he returned to the High Anglicanism of his childhood but did so while writing about his own unique brand of mysticism that was derived from a quasi–Kierkegaardian existentialism and Christian mysticism. At bottom there is little difference between Vedanta and Auden's hybrid mysticism. Each reflects the Perennial Philosophy (see Mysticism), which means they're both derived from the original Vedas, the basis of all the world's spiritual systems. At this point, one can say that in 1930 both Isherwood and Auden where unconsciously seeking the mysticism that they would later find and were on the path that would ultimately get them there.

In 1930, however, their conscious paths were still uncertain. Auden's poems were more like random darts thrown at a large but not entirely charted map. For Auden there were still many areas that were labeled "waiting to be explored." This map was filled in to some extent by preexisting ideas and the language that represented these ideas. Auden understood that language can teach or deceive depending on how it is used or misused. Consequently, Auden's early poems are minimalist in the use of language, forsaking standard syntax to strip them down to the words-as-symbols with the barest embellishment, which was influenced by the work of Laura Riding. Language always represents the past because it can only exist as a reactionary medium to what has come before. If existing language is the chronicle of a rejected past, then conventional language needs to be rejected and remade also (see Language).

Kierkegaard said, and Auden repeated, "Life is learned backwards, but must be lived forwards." In 1930 Auden might have interpreted this aphorism to mean: even though one learns from the past, one must abandon it in order to move forward. Later, he would interpret it as: life is a perpetual continuum; what was is integral to what is and to what will be. The past is integral to the present and future and all three are undifferentiated in the mystical sense; they are only falsely observed as separate entities by the ego's misinterpretation. For Auden the latter interpretation would come later. In 1930 the former interpretation was the only one that seemed relevant: the past was rejected, and the future is now.

Auden and Isherwood's mind's-eye border is the metaphor that draws the line between past and future; the frontier beyond the border is the no man's land or the Northwest Passage that one needs to cross in order to escape from the past and move forward. Over time, Mendelson notes, "the idea of the border slowly generated its antithesis: the idea of an undifferentiated unity beyond the border...." This unity can also be seen as a mystical unity where there are no borders at all.

In the 1930s few readers of Auden's *Poems* saw them as metaphysical. What many readers embraced from them was that the future was right now and for themselves to make. These poems were written before the stock market crash but not published until eight months after when the effects were taking hold; the poems seemed to be abstract warnings that had anticipated the crisis and were now metaphorically

referring to it. Featuring the British Public School symbolism of "spies," "secret agents," "firms," "leaders," "borders," and "frontiers," the poems were interpreted as parables for class animosities, political animosities, and international animosities. The world had become a scary place, a place where paranoia was justified. The fascist paranoia of the Old School had graduated to the world at large and Auden's poems, which are the Old School "mythified" into saga, reflect this world. Auden's critical acclaim made him a leader by default. He had intended his poems for a small circle of friends; that circle grew to encompass the entire decade.

In Auden's *Poems* the play *Paid on Both Sides* is reprinted, having been in the *Criterion* two months earlier. The poems follow the play in the volume. Consequently, the feud, war, and ancestral curse symbology in the play, which is somewhat less obscure than the poems, precede the poems and give readers more of a frame of reference for the poems themselves. For the complete interpretation of the poems, Mendelson is the guide to whom all are indebted. Herein, however, are examples pertinent to the Isherwood-Auden schema.

The original volume is dedicated to Christopher Isherwood with four lines about honoring the man who stands up vertically in public but truly valuing the man who is at peace when he is horizontal. This epigram is about the public man (vertical) and the private man (horizontal). The private man can only achieve inner peace through the releases of sex, dreams, and death, which are "horizontally" considered to be metaphysically equal. The "vertical man" is the conscious man as he exists in society; his public face can be honored, but it is only from his private face that he can truly be known and valued.

In Auden's early poems he began a lifelong quest for a metaphysical balance in the otherwise divided mind. Within the mind the degree of conflict between public and private, inner and outer, love and fear, is determined by how much one needs to escape from his public face through daytime fantasy or nighttime dreams. The degree of corresponding withdrawal that one makes from everyday existence is in proportion to the pain one feels while living in that existence. While one's public face may appear convivial and adjusted, this face may only be the mask of one role — the gregarious glad-hander — that is a disguise for a frustrated, maladjusted private face. Fantasy and dreams are the psychological means by which the private face relieves the internal pressures caused by the wearing of a public mask. The wearer of the mask is always reminded by the proverbial "Watcher-in-Spanish" that this mask is insincere and a denial of private truth. (Isherwood and Auden hid their homosexuality, which was not only subject to moral censure by The Others but also subject to a criminal penalty that could incur jail time.) If the outlet of fantasy and dreams is not satisfactory, or one does not accept fantasy and dreams, but rejects them, one will not be able to reconcile public and private spheres and will withdraw unhappily from life. One can withdraw under the guise of daydreams or one can withdraw into dreams at night. One hopes for a change in the spirit and structure of existence; in fact, one cries out for this renewal in order to begin a new life. If one does not listen to his inner self, and lets the poison persist, then, he becomes "a *cypher* with codified conduct and a vacant vessel for a heart." (Italics in Auden's poems are this author's.) The "codified conduct" is the conformist conduct of The Others. As a "cypher" one can appear to publicly conform to this code as one role while privately yearning to fulfill a sublimated inner role such as "Isherwood-the-artist." The public face may be admired, but it hides a private emptiness as exemplified in a poem about a rich Other who appears to be suave and accomplished as he steps in and out of limousines while deftly wearing his cape. He would seem to be a figure to be envied by the poor, but, in fact, he is only acting. In truth, he is not a heroic figure; instead, he is "poised between shocking falls on razor-edge" and his apparent sense of clever balance is an act. (Long before Auden and Maugham the "razor-edge" metaphor was used in the Upanishads. Maugham's book was a result of his spending a good deal of time with Isherwood and Heard in the early 1940s.) This poem could have been interpreted by socialists and Communists as representing the false face of capitalism. (If so, they would have also liked this line from another poem about "proletariat against police.")

This figure who is wearing a mask recalls Robinson's "Richard Cory" as well as Isherwood's alienated cypher-witness. This figure needs the release of fantasy and dreams to console him in his hatred for the public role he disdains. If there is no solace from fantasy or dreams, the only other consolation that could substitute for or complement inner fantasy would come from meeting a sympathetic friend or lover. This is not easy. Finding a commiserating friend is hard, seeking a lover who helps more than hurts is even harder and that often is still "of no use." There is "no use" because the "I" and "you" do not speak the same language. Written in January 1929, this poem reflects the Berlin aftermath of the boy bars and the nightly mating ritual. There is also the impenetrable isolation between individuals separated from each other and from undifferentiated unity as well. There is also the problem of miscommunication. Language, foreign or otherwise, is a barrier. Language is a "feat of translation" as Auden would later call it between "another I" and "another you" where the ego, in collaboration with the mouth's duplicity, often obfuscates both truth and unity. Still, even while understanding that there is a divide between the "two," the future hope will be that the "two" can learn to communicate with each other and then this "two" will teach another "two" and form the small group. Re-education of consciousness starts with "twos and twos" who form a group, and then group to group there can be change.

The "two" can become one through love if the psychological barriers of the past can be overcome. The selfish ego is symptomatic of the Truly Weak Man. Abnegation of the selfish ego is how one becomes selfless and Truly Strong. In another poem Auden says that an ambitious love is a barrier to true love for it is ego-generated. Ambition by its nature separates and finds it hard to say yes instead of no, and no hurts; no denies love and causes the anxiety that leads to "The tightening jaw." An ego-bound ambitious love cannot succeed because the ego divides the mind and sets up barriers to protect itself from its own vulnerable sensitivity. To shed the ego while still remaining sensitive requires one to forsake the fear of failure and allow love to overcome the barriers that the ego sets up in self-defense. The Layard-Lane ideal states that inhibition is the underlying cause of fear. To be free of inhibition is to be free of fear. In 1929 and 1930 Isherwood and Auden sometimes blurred Layard-Lane to confuse love and promiscuity. Auden's poems acknowledge this confusion but still express hope that sex might lead to love. Yet, it is so hard to make a commitment to another while one also fears rejection. One always invades, but never explores, "For this is hate and this is fear." For Auden, to invade is sex alone; to explore is to seek love if one can overcome fear. The ego fears rejection more than it needs love and will set up Watchers-in-Spanish that guard against the weakness of giving in to love. Auden calls them "Sentries against *inner* and *outer*." What is their plan? Will they bring war or peace? Can they be bribed by the ego, which will attempt to look noble but instead will give in to the lies made by a duplicitous mouth. Then what strategy of betrayal will the ego pursue?

These sentries, posted by the ego's fear, prevent a raid on the emotions that might be love, but the sentries also lock out the enduring peace that could come if true love were let in. Betrayal of the private sphere that wants love will come from one's own ego-generated defense mechanisms. The mouth collaborates with the ego and speaks through a public mask of insincerity. The ego tells the deceitful mouth to lie in order to conform to the codified conduct of The Others, but the person behind the ego then suffers for denying the true voice of his inner self. The Weak many succumb to the code and lie; the Strong do not.

Human nature reflexively juxtaposes one's self with other selves to determine where one stands in relation to his public and private faces. Auden thinks of a master he once hated that has died of cancer, and a friend who has attempted to explain his own failings. One always compares one's self to other selves, some of whom are worth emulating. Auden notes the "...Absence of fear in Gerhart Meyer ... the *truly strong man*." Auden explicitly states that there are Weak and Strong, which is to be expected and recognized without making judgments about persons in either camp. This does not mean one should ignore or be fooled by the faults of the Weak; yet, one can still be wary of

human nature in general but still love people in particular. The Truly Strong Man does not judge the Truly Weak Man, but tries to help him. The Weak can learn from the example of the Strong. This is a precept of The Bhagavad-Gita. The "friend" who failed could have been Isherwood at medical school, or Layard who had attempted suicide, or both.

Auden also implies that a new race might be needed to develop the traits of The Truly Strong for the future. Foreigners going to new countries will intermarry to create a new race, and then there will also be a new language so that the soul can "Be *weaned* at last to independent delight." The allusion to Berlin is evident along with the need to create a new language to replace the old language that represents the past.

Auden's *Poems* aroused his generation who read into them a sociopolitical activism instead of the psychological and metaphysical activism he had intended for them. His peers made him famous, even if many of them had no clear idea — or created their own idea — of what he was talking about. Auden accepted their approval and even swayed over to their activism during the mid 1930s. Still, the early poems were not sociopolitical battle cries, but psycho-metaphysical parables about the evolution of consciousness. With Isherwood's influence Auden incorporated into his metaphysical questing, The Test, The Northwest Passage, and The Truly Weak and Truly Strong Man. Below are individual poems from the volume.

"Taller Today": Calm after a sexual storm and after "the adversary put too easy questions / On Lonely roads."

"Missing": About the First heroes "Who died beyond the border" while searching for a new life.

"The Watershed": Mendelson believes this poem signaled Auden's new maturity that began his career in earnest. There is a distant figure, a stranger in a lean, barren country that will not communicate with him. He is directionless, yet unaffected, in a limbo that is neither past nor future.

"The Secret Agent" follows "The Watershed" and is more ominous; an inner "spy" must thwart sexual urges by a conscious will. The landscape is dry and foreboding. The stranger is now a spy, and not just isolated and trapped; yet, despite nostalgia, he cannot go home to the group who should help him because they will ignore him instead as a traitor. (See also Heard, Gerald.)

"No Change of Place": Border now takes on an aspect of a safe barrier and not just a no man's land.

"This Loved One": In Berlin with Auden, the first boy that Isherwood made sounds at (he could not speak German yet) was Bubi (baby). Isherwood imbued him with a romantic aura that fit the Homer Lane version of the Truly Strong Man: "In addition to being able to play the German Boy and the blond, Bubi had a role which he created for himself; he was the Wanderer, the Lost Boy, homeless, penniless, dreamily passive yet tough, careless of danger, indifferent to hardship, roaming the earth. Bubi's vulnerability, combined with his tough independence, was powerfully attractive and at the same time teasing. You longed to protect him, but he didn't need you. Or did he? You longed to help him but he didn't need help. Or did he? Wystan [Auden] wasn't at all impressed by Bubi's performance as the Wanderer. Yet, largely to please Christopher, he wrote a beautiful poem about Bubi, 'This Loved One'" (*Christopher and His Kind*).

Later, Isherwood, like Auden, became less infatuated with Bubi's performance. Auden's poem is indicative of his friendship with Isherwood and the mutual influence one had on the other. This influence involved the still developing Isherwood-Auden schema that the poem reflects. Auden begins, "Before this loved one" were many other lovers of the moment who at those particular moments were each the special one. Before them was ancestry and history that haunt like ghosts to influence the present and create the vulnerability that requires the crossing of frontiers (Berlin) to overcome. If read without a context, pretext, or subtext this poem can be obscure to the non-initiated or non-members of the gang. The ghosts of the past, of families and history, hinder the search for love in the present and future. Solace can only be found at the frontier, or no-man's land. For the pioneer Berlin had no past or tradition. The penetration into the frontier becomes the quest of an aspiring Truly Strong Man who recognizes the ways in which he is Truly Weak and

strives to overcome his weaknesses. "This Loved One" is a romantic representation of Auden and Isherwood's "mythified" view of their world.

"Easy Knowledge": The stranger does not know how to get away nor where he is in order to get away. He is conflicted by the Duality of a "divided face."

"Between Adventure" means the line or border, and the confusion about which way one must go next. This is a dangerous crossing from isolation to possible fulfillment. Sex is easy; love is harder.

"Family Ghosts": A lover speaks to a lover about an inability to love that is caused by ancestral ghosts who have created mental images and expectations that can't be met.

"The Questioner Who Sits So Sly": The title comes from Blake. The anonymous, faceless secret agent meets more of the anonymous and faceless in a land of the diseased and perverted (like Dante's Purgatory). He is on his own, rejecting the past, but still in an unsatisfying present and a future unknown. There is in this poem a mention of an "invalid" who is actually the father of Auden's student Peter Benenson. Peter's mother, through Auden, commissioned Isherwood to translate Baudelaire's *Journaux Intimes.*

"Venus Will now Say a Few Words": is addressed by some elite force to the prevalent bourgeois mentality running through the British middle class and explains why this class will be eclipsed and replaced by another form of society. The bourgeois while they play tennis — a symbol of their milieu — have no idea that their existence is illusory and that they are not in control, as they would like to believe. Evolution's power, in the form of the path towards Gerald Heard's unified consciousness, will supplant them.

"1929" is in four sections and is also known by the first line, "It is Easter as I Walked Out In the Public Gardens." Overall, "1929" promotes a new division through Auden's use of biological and evolutionary metaphors; yet, it attacks old divisions with religious metaphors. Part I believes that new love needs the death of the past by a weaning away from the past; that is, a weaning away from the nostalgia for the past that blocks the future. Reflecting Berlin, the boys Auden met contrasted with the street riots he witnessed; he talks about an "absence of fear" in the "truly strong man" who can end the self-conscious "I" for an unconscious "we" and will not turn back to the old ways.

Part II measures Auden's role as a foreigner in the new frontier (Berlin) who sees detachedly as if from the great height of the hawk's vision (Hardy); this signifies the early meetings with "boys" in the Cosy Corner when Auden's inadequate German created a distancing effect as if he were looking at what he saw through a window, seeing, but not understanding, causing a disruption of the social personality he knew in England and requiring a new persona in Berlin. He refers to the battles in the streets that heighten tension, socially and sexually. In this new frontier, he is a new baby going through birth trauma to escape one consciousness and enter into another. A romantic search unifies a perceiving mind to gain a moment's peace and self-forgiveness for the old ways in the old body.

Part III seems to evoke a sense of drowning in a new, yet still divided consciousness that leans toward home, the past, and also away from home, the future. In this part Auden moves away from a solitary consciousness to a dream world of possibility to be found in a unified consciousness, and he hopes that this will lead to a global transformation. The dream is a preparation for the death of the old ways.

Part IV begins that "It is time for the destruction of error." The real war is not in the superficial public masks found in society but in the individual minds that are divided between public faces and private faces. Love, not sex, is the way, to be found with a dying of the old self so that a new Self of a unified consciousness can begin a new life.

"On Sunday Walks" concerns the duality of the divided condition where the bourgeois façade tries to live up to a heritage that was true once but is now an illusion. The mask wearers idealize past ancestors who become a cross to bear in trying to live up to as the mask wearers are faced with constant reminders of the past all around them.

"This Lunar Beauty": a fantasy written as if by a child and composed after Auden began teaching at Larchfield Academy. This fantasy

counters a grimmer reality than that posed in "1929." A child's golden age is one of innocence as a child is free from the adult conflicts that come from searching for love while finding sorrow. Blake's *Songs of Innocence and Experience* factor in this poem. The diction comes from Laura Riding.

"The Question" begins: "To ask the hard question is simple," and this becomes an invocatory evocation of the subconscious. Can memory of the real, visceral past ("fish, sheep") help create a real meeting of minds in the present, even one begun as a sexual meeting? Can it go further, back to a spontaneity unhindered by conditioning? Awaking from this reverie, there is a repetition of human frailty, and Auden wonders if we can get past this old role of adherence to the past to begin new relationships without societal burdens.

"Consider": Society represses natural — and better — instincts as Auden looks down from afar "as the hawk sees it" (Hardy) on sociopolitical themes that attack the financiers after the Wall Street crash. Social classes are isolated from each other, and each individual is isolated from a truer inner life. This is a final warning of the psychological illness that will bring down society.

"The Wanderer" wears an Old Norse mask in depicting half-concealed, half-naturalized recollections from Old English sources. (The first line "Doom is dark and deeper than any sea dingle" is from an Old English prose work "Sawles Warde.") There is a sense of loss and social/psychological isolation. The message is that the past/present never changes without changes from within.

"Half Way" seems to be inspired by the Isherwood-Upward lunacy of Mortmere. (See also Heard, Gerald.)

Poems of Freedom 1938

Introducing this anthology Auden wrote that poets are not social reformers, nor neurotic escapists. Escape is inevitable and is the reaction to social reformers by readers who seek "truth" from poets and are disappointed when they learn that poets turn out to be — other than their gift for poetry — as ordinary as their readers. The difference is that poets say what the public already thinks (whether they realize it or not) since a poem is a record/reflection of society. In this book, the poems reflect oppression in society. Artists: if they know and say too much (that is, intimate they are reformers), then "the neighbors start talking."

"The Poet and the City" 1962

According to this essay, all workers (who were once craftsmen) have been reduced to laborers. Only artists remain personally responsible and self-initiating. Their audience seeks to escape its condition and humdrum existence by basking in the reflected glow of the artist's art. For a person to self-describe as a "poet" invites skepticism even if the poet is a successful one, as verse has lost its utilitarian value as a mnemonic. The public thinks artists do not seem to labor at their work and that artists are either parasites or dilettantes. Gratuitous creation of art is no longer sacred if it is divorced from utility. Education is limited to that which society considers important. Medieval poets were recorders and trained; modern poets are left to their own devices. (Here Auden inserts his day dream college for Bards.)

How does a poet both write and live without patrons? Why is artistic vocation difficult? 1) loss of belief in the eternity of the physical universe; art will not outlast existence, 2) loss of belief in the significance of sensory world; faith no longer intertwines with sensory phenomena, 3) loss of belief in norms, things change. Will a new audience like poems 20 years hence; the poet may think, "why should I bother?" 4) loss of public realm as stage for personal, revelatory deeds. Public life is impersonal, unsatisfying; from this anonymous life the poet loses his source of ideas. Only his introspection is personalized and gives him something to write about. There are no heroes anymore; scientists are heroes, but their subject matter is not so appealing to the public as an artist's angst is.

To whom can a poet appeal? 1) Crowd/mob is active, 2) public is an abstracted media creation, passive, a void, faceless. The public does not buy highbrow or real art but prefers pop culture lowbrow pseudo-art dictated by a consumer nation motivated to buy by advertising.

A poet/artist is a guerilla warrior of the intermittent.

If society were like a good poem it could come about in a Huxleyan *Brave New World*: conformity without soul or without the inspiration of divergent politics and party issues. Poets are personal; the public is impersonal. Poets write about singularity; the masses (public) consume commonality. The poet is on the side of revolution making him and his audience the minority. "Today there is only one genuine world-wide revolutionary cause, racial equality. If an African American gives his life for the cause of racial inequality, his death is meaningful to him.... What is utterly absurd, is that people should be deprived everyday of their liberty and their lives, and the human race may quite possibly destroy itself over what is really a matter of practical policy like asking whether, given its particular historical circumstances, the health of a community is likely to be better secured by Private Practice or by Socialized Medicine." This essay, to some degree, was inspired by the life of John Howard Griffin.

"A Poet of the Actual" 1972

Auden's review of *Anthony Trollope* by James Pope Hennessy.

"The Poet of the Encirclement" *see* Kipling, Rudyard

"Poetry and Freedom" 1948

Inspired by the work of Eugen Rosenstock-Huessy, Auden in this essay examines four revolutions and their heroes: the papal revolution, the Reformation, and the French Revolution. The fourth is the modern era, and the hero is the "naked, anonymous, numbered figure."

Poets of the English Language 1950

(Five volumes, ed. by Auden and Norman Holmes Pearson, a professor at Yale whom

Auden met through Elizabeth Mayer, with Auden writing the introductions to each volume.) Vol. I. Langland to Spenser, Vol. II. Marlowe to Marvell, Vol. III Milton to Goldsmith, Vol. IV. Blake to Poe, Vol. V. Tennyson to Yeats. Auden's introductions are typically unique with his views superseding any general academic overview, which is of little interest to him. In fact, in these introductions Auden's Christianity and his version of Christian history — via Kierkegaard, Tillich, de Rougemont, and others — are emphasized.

"Poets, Poetry, and Taste" *see* Audience

The Poet's Tongue 1935

An anthology of poems for schoolchildren edited and selected by Auden and John Garrett with an Introduction by Auden. Auden writes his line that poetry is memorable speech and that it is better heard than read and that the "test of a poet is the frequency and diversity of the occasions on which we remember the poetry." Poetry cannot be put on a pedestal so that it is remote and distant. It can be light or heavy to appeal to all audiences. (See also Audience.)

Pope, Alexander

1688–1744, English poet. Pope was born in London of Roman Catholic parents. During his later childhood he was afflicted by Pott's disease. He never grew taller than 4 ft 6 in. In his early years he won the attention of William Wycherley and the poet-critic William Walsh, among others. Before he was 17 Pope was admitted to London society and encouraged as a prodigy. The shortest lived of his friendships was with Joseph Addison and his coterie, who eventually insidiously attacked Pope's Tory leanings. His attachment to the Tory party was strengthened by his warm friendship with Swift and his involvement with the Scriblerus Club.

Pope's poetry basically falls into three periods. The first includes the early descriptive poetry; the *Pastorals* (1709); *Windsor Forest*

(1713); the *Essay on Criticism* (1711), outlining critical tastes and standards; *The Rape of the Lock* (1714), a mock-heroic poem ridiculing the fashionable world of his day. Pope's second period includes his translations of Homer, written in heroic couplets. In the last period of his career Pope turned to writing satires and moral poems. These include *The Dunciad* (1728–43), a satire on dunces and literary hacks; *Imitations of Horace* (1733–38), satirizing social follies and political corruption; *An Essay on Man* (1734), a poetic summary of current philosophical speculation; *Moral Essays* (1731–35); and the *Epistle to Arbuthnot* (1735), a defense in poetry of his life and his work.

At Oxford Auden, contrary to literary fashion (and he liked being contrary), read Pope, about whom he would say, "At his best there are few poets who can rival his fusion of vision and language" (*From Anne to Victoria*, ed. by Dobree (1937). In 1932's "In the Year of my Youth" (uncollected, but see Mendelson, *Early Auden*), which is much inspired by Gerald Heard, Auden takes Pope's style from *The Rape of the Lock*, and particularly from the section of Belinda's toilette. In 1938 Auden chose selections from Pope for his *Oxford Book of Light Verse* (in a section along with Byron). His 1969 review of Peter Quennell's book on Alexander Pope is titled "A Civilized Voice," which signifies Auden's regard for Pope's style and grace, even under fire.

"Port and Nuts with the Eliots" 1949

A humorous review of T.S. Eliot's *Notes on a Definition of Culture* that concerns the psyche's tyranny. The mind's household is a trinity metaphorically comprised of the archdeacon, the crazy grandmother, and the bewildered guest. The fun belies a more serious Auden view of the spiritual trinity.

The Portable Greek Reader 1948

An anthology of classical Greek literature introduced and selected by Auden. The introduction becomes a venue for Auden to enunciate personal views, as was his design in all of his essays. Mendelson: "The introduction emphases the strangeness of the classical Greeks from the perspective of the twentieth century, but it makes most of its points through analogies that collapse centuries of change. He appended to it a 'Chronology Outline of Classical Greek Civilization,' laid out in two columns, one with dates of births and deaths, the other with dates of 'events.' ...This was a clear renunciation of the nonhistorical alphabetical arrangement he had used for two earlier collections, the school anthology, *The Poet's Tongue* in 1935 and his own *Collected Poetry* in 1945" (*Later Auden*).

Katherine Anne Porter at the book introduction party for her novel *The Ship of Fools*.

Porter, Katherine Anne

1890–1980, American author, b. Indian Creek, Tex. Her first book of stories, Flowering Judas (1930), received critical recognition and was followed by *Pale Horse, Pale Rider* (1939) and *The Leaning Tower* (1944). A collection of her essays and occasional pieces appeared under the title *The Days Before* (1952). Her first long novel, *Ship of Fools*, was published in 1962 and takes place on a German ship shortly before Hitler's rise to power.

Auden met Porter through her very good friend Glenway Wescott. In 1939 Auden and Kallman stayed with Porter for two days in

Texas and she would write in a letter to James Stern about Auden's "faith that mankind was good." The fervor of love for Kallman, on what Auden considered their honeymoon, no doubt encouraged his feeling.

"Portrait of a Whig" *see* Smith, Sydney

Potter, Beatrix

1866–1943, English author and illustrator. She published her first animal stories in *The Tale of Peter Rabbit* (1902) and *The Tailor of Gloucester* (1903), and over a period of 30 years published 21 more books. Potter's stories, although fantasy, depict animals in an intelligent, unsentimental, and humorous manner. The books are enhanced by her drawings and watercolor paintings. She was a favorite of Auden and Isherwood with Auden listing her in his list of books for his nursery library in *A Certain World*.

Pound, Ezra

1885–1972, American poet, critic, and translator, b. Hailey, Ida. His poetry received attention in England, where he also led the imagists movement. Pound encouraged many young writers, including T.S. Eliot and James Joyce. In the early 1920s he moved to Paris, where he became associated with Gertrude Stein and Ernest Hemingway. By 1925 he settled in Italy, and, finding fault with England and America, broadcast fascist and anti–Semitic propaganda to the United States for the Italians during World War II. He was indicted for treason and brought to the United States for trial and from 1946 to 1958 was confined to St. Elizabeth's mental hospital in Washington. After his release he returned to Italy, where he remained until his death at the age of 87. Pound's major works are "Homage to Sextus Propertius" (1918), *Hugh Selwyn Mauberley* (1920), and the *Cantos* (1925–60).

Pound advocated a new poetic language and the earliest Auden agreed. T.S. Eliot discovered

Auden, and it was Pound who edited Eliot's *The Waste Land* (1922) into the landmark debut of "modernism" it became; hence, Pound was known by Auden and was an influence on all modernists. Mendelson notes that "*Hugh Selwyn Mauberley* [and] *The Waste Land* ... depend for their effect on contrasts between ancient form and modern chaos" (*Early Auden*). Auden, to some degree, did the same in *Paid on Both Sides, Poems* (1930), *The Orators, Letter to Lord Byron*, his Horatian odes begun in the late 1930s, and his verse in general thereafter. Mendelson, in *Later Auden*, said that he believes that in "New Year Letter" (1940), "Auden wrote the poem that Ezra Pound, after much self-advertisement, had failed to write in *The Cantos*."

In 1946 Bennett Cerf, the chief of Random House, Auden's American publisher, said that he was going to exclude Pound from any anthologies because he was a traitor. Auden protested that banning his poems over political considerations rather than artistic considerations was censorship no different than fascism and that he would drop Random House if Pound were excluded. Cerf changed his mind.

Powell, Anthony *see* America

"Precious Five" 1950

This poem refers to the five senses that an artist employs as his tools. This is an homage to both existence and the muse that inspires the artist to mirror existence.

"The Price" 1936

The Price refers to the various psychological ransoms one must pay in order to get on with life. It was written while Auden and Isherwood were writing *The Ascent of F6* with its protagonist, Michael Ransom, and the play's mountain-climbing theme as a metaphor for current events as well as a showcase of the Auden-Isherwood schema of ghosts, The Others, quests, and The Truly Weak and Truly Strong Man. "The Price" speaks of the man who tries to please the ghosts of the past only

to find that this isolates his present from progress,. An image of a "pit of terror" is the converse of the mountain peak F6 but both pit and peak signify that there is no place else to go.

"Prime" *see Horae Canonicae*

"The Prince's Dog" 1962

An essay on Falstaff as a character of comic opera. Falstaff is an obtuse chorus of one; in and outside the play he "asides" to the audience, seeking approval. He is a contrast to Shakespeare's ideal ruler who is moral, just, strong, compelling, and inspires loyalty to and from subjects who see him as legitimate. This is not Richard II in which a tyranny of one is less unjust than a tyranny of many. Falstaff functions to prove Hal has become a ruler by the new king's rejection of him. Falstaff's fatness is a sexual relation to womb. Fat drunks wean on a bottle, rejected by mother and Eden. A drunk disturbs us because we could be him. Falstaff disturbs us because he could be England. The act of forgiveness is tacit; hence, it does not play on stage without sounding false. Law does not forgive; it punishes. Only people forgive. Falstaff is untalented, unmotivated, unworldly. Hal is talented, motivated, and worldly. Falstaff's only talent is comic joy, and he radiates happiness until Hal, who radiates power, rejects him. (See also "Balaam and his Ass.")

"Private Pleasure" 1932

Reviews of books on education. "education is a dope to allay irritation" and keep the poor amused; it segregates "your sort," that is, the pseudo-liberals who offer a carrot. The powers that be remain exactly where they are.

Private vs. Public

"Private faces in public places
"Are wiser and nicer
"Than public faces in private places."

(Dedication to Stephen Spender in *The Orators*.)

One who wears his public mask in both public and private is a Truly Weak Man; one who wears his private, that is, only face in both public and private is a Truly Strong Man.

"Problems of Education" 1932

Review of a book by Bertrand Russell. "This book is excellent propaganda. Does Russell ever contemplate the possibility that intellectual curiosity is neurotic, a compensation for those who are isolated from the social group, sexually starved, and physically weak." Russell hates what cannot be explained by science: sex and religion. Russell ignores man's duality of passion/power vs. cerebral/gentle. A liberal education works for the latter, not the former. The individual is only nurtured through passionate relationships; hence, the importance of the family as a model of good relations.

"Profile" 1965-66

Autobiographical haiku during a period starting in 1964 when Auden, who swore off autobiography, was indulging in it nonetheless. (See also Shakespeare; Kallman, Chester; "It Seemed to Us"; *A Certain World*.)

The Prolific and the Devourer 1939

Though it would not be published until nearly a decade after his death, *The Prolific and the Devourer* provides the most significant and extended documentation of Auden's return to Christianity. Auden takes his title from a passage in William Blake's *The Marriage of Heaven and Hell* in which Blake refers to "two classes of men" who are "always upon earth" and always enemies. He begins with a quote from Blake that asserts the perpetual opposition of these two figures, and their mutual interdependence: "Whoever tries to reconcile them seeks to destroy existence." In the course of what his pen

sees, Auden seldom refers to Blake's formulation. At one point he does directly associate the Prolific with the Artist and the Devourer with the Politician, yet here too he is interested primarily in their "complementary" qualities:

> The Prolific and the Devourer: the Artist and the Politician. Let them realize that they are enemies, i.e., that each has a vision of the world which must remain incomprehensible to the other. But let them also realize that they are both necessary and complementary, and further, that there are good and bad politicians, good and bad artists, and that the good must learn to recognize and to respect the good.

Even in this passage, Auden's main concern is not Blake. Rather, he is more concerned with reconceptualizing his own vocation as a poet in terms that are, from the start, less political — and then increasingly theological.

Most notably, Auden's account of Blake's Devourer directly anticipates his encounter with Tillich's "demonic," especially the kind of self-inflation — the "absolute claim for a relative reality" — that Tillich considers one of the demonic's most persistent features: "To the Devourer it seems as if the producer was in his chains but it is not so, he only takes portions of existence and fancies it the whole." Central to Auden's crisis of vocation, in fact, is his fear that the writer, like the politician, might be particularly susceptible to this temptation: "The Dictator who says 'My People': the Writer who says 'My Public.'" For Auden, it was not a new problem. In earlier works like *The Orators* and in the poem that begins "Here on the cropped grass of the narrow ridge I stand," he had considered the seductions and perils of the writer's profession in the modern world. As a poet who had been highly acclaimed since the early stages of his career — and thus highly "public" — he had come to understand that public proclamations are always at risk of becoming the language of demagogues.

Now, more than ever before, Auden needed to understand the destructive forces of history — that is, the power of Blake's Devourer — in terms more compelling and explanatory than "collective lying." Even though he maintained his long-standing suspicion about any human claim to universal truth, he needed to believe in a divine law. The result was a combination of faith and skepticism that he would soon find echoed in Tillich's theology. In *The Prolific and the Devourer*, Auden wrote,

> Human law rests upon Force and Belief, belief in its rightness. The Way rests upon Faith and Scepticism. Faith that the divine law exists, and that our knowledge of it can improve; and scepticism that our knowledge of these laws can never be perfect.

Particularly in the powerful elegies he wrote in this period, Auden was able to generate compelling poetry not so much out of any particular theological explanation for modern destruction as out of his sense of the need for such an explanation.—BRIAN CONNIFF

The structure and style of *The Prolific and the Devourer* came from Pascal's *Pensées* and St. Augustine's *Confessions*, which in the 1960s Auden's Oxford friend Rex Warner would translate into contemporary English. (See also Jesus.)

"Prologue at Sixty" 1967

Auden wrote this for his birthday, and it is optimistic. He considers the role of language as a means to the end of crossing divides and overcoming alienation.

"Prologue: The Birth of Architecture" *see About the House*

"The Prophets" 1939

This poem was written a month after Auden met Chester Kallman, the love of his life. He believes that the prophets are always with us but that they do not speak to us until we are ready to hear them.

"The Protestant Mystics" 1964

Anne Fremantle's *The Protestant Mystics* featured an introduction by Auden, in which

the poet observed that human society is always institutionalized, governed not by intuition but by authority based on faith in that authority. All religion begins with homage to the past referentially to account for present belief. "Stimulus to intelligence is doubt…. [but] to doubt for the sake of doubting, to differ for the sake of being different is pride." Dogma is derived to exclude heresy more so than to define or convert. Dogma changes as needed. Debate without an audience will limit the ego and be more sincere. Adam is spiritual, not physical. So is sin; hence, choice is involved. Sharing experiences enables one to add to the Catholic's we believe still, the protestant's I believe again. (See also Mysticism.)

"Psychology and Art Today" *see* Freud, Sigmund

"Psychology and Criticism" 1936

Review of *In Defense of Shelley* by Herbert Read. The only way to truly defend or attack a poet is to quote him. Read suggests "ontogenetic criticism" of the artist's psyche and socio-economics. He rejects T.S. Eliot's ethical/theological criticism: "This is interesting, but does not explain why Mr. Read admires Shelley and Mr. Eliot does not." Auden agrees with Eliot. Read asserts ontogenetic makes no moral judgments, which is impossible. For Auden, Shelley is too abstract, thus unreal: "I cannot believe that an artist can be any good who is not more than a bit of a reporting journalist" and to whom the subject is not paramount rather than his own self-edification.

The Public and Propaganda

Kierkegaard believed the anonymous Public was the bastard-child of the Industrial Revolution, universal education, and mass media. This Public can be influenced by the media but cannot be held accountable for any resulting behaviors that these media appeals might provoke. The Public is comprised of individuals who can be manipulated in general but need not be responsible for anything in particular because they are not identifiable as specific human beings. Media can influence an anonymous Public to take sides on an issue; yet, these unidentifiable individuals can remove themselves from subsequent results by fading into their anonymity as a so-called silent majority. In effect, by reading and hearing the news in private, one can be moved to love or hate another person or group without the personal scrutiny or judgment that might involve the conscience. Anonymity can be irresponsible. The anonymous Public becomes the proverbial "They" that authority figures can invoke to praise conformists and chastise non-conformists. This concept of a Kierkegaardian Public is crucial in understanding the rise of propaganda in the 1930s. How did this Public and its anonymity come about?

In the agrarian and small town culture before the Industrial Revolution, anonymity was less prevalent, and thus the concept of an impersonal Public not as applicable. The anonymous Public emerged from the depersonalized, industrialized city-state where mass production necessitated regimentation among workers. This regimentation required a universal, basic education that allowed workers to function in their roles as cogs in the mechanized city. These workers would then consume the goods they read about in advertising and perpetuate their own existences in a slavish cycle. Universally, if minimally educated, this easily influenced Public consumes media and not necessarily with great discernment. As Auden said in *Letter to Lord Byron* (1937), "Our age is highly educated / There is no lie our children cannot read." It was one thing for the mass producers to influence the Public to become mass consumers through advertising, but it became something quite nefarious when tyrants used the media to influence the Public to be mass followers through propaganda.

Søren Kierkegaard, a nineteenth century existential Christian polemicist, said: "The public is a concept which could not have occurred in antiquity because the people en masse, *in corpare*, took part in any situation which arose and were responsible for the actions of the individual, and, moreover, the individual was personally present and had to submit at once to applause or disapproval....

Only when the sense of association in society is no longer strong enough to give life to concrete realities is the press able to create that abstraction 'the public,' consisting of unreal individuals who can never be united in an actual situation or organization — and yet are held together as a whole.... A public is everything and nothing, the most dangerous of all powers and the most insignificant" (Auden, W.H., ed., *The Living Thoughts of Kierkegaard*).

"The Public vs. the Late W.B. Yeats" *see* Yeats, W.B.

Pure-in-Heart *see* Berlin; Lane, Homer

"Purely Subjective" 1943

A lengthy, contemplative essay on religion where Auden "attempts to evade ... subjective anxiety by denying subjectivity itself" (Mendelson, *Later Auden*). Indeed, Auden wrote this when he was first writing *The Age of Anxiety*.

The Queen's Masque 1940

The Queen's Masque, a tale of charm rewarded, by "Bojo, the Homo," was written for a performance in Ann Arbor, Michigan on 7 January 1943, for the twenty-second birthday of Chester Kallman. Auden was not able to be there, but "Kallman's Klever Kompanions" made up the cast at the University of Michigan. The masque is in a manuscript of ten sheets, and is now in the formidable Auden archive at the New York Public Library's Berg Collection.

A duo, Mabel and Ella, enter, prepare for Queen Anastasia's birthday, and talk about the affection she wins. A ghost performs a German cabaret song. Another Ghost goes to his knees and does a parody of the Monks' chant in *The Ascent of F6*. A Litany forms a typical Auden-like list of enemies for Anastasia, and a Grand Chorus invites the players to end the illusion of the masque and begin the more riotous phases of the party.

Quest

From Auden's earliest work to the very last in verse, drama, libretti, and essays, the idea of the quest is of great importance. The quest, while often acted out externally, is really a search for inner truth. (See also "The Quest"; "The Quest Hero.")

"The Quest" 1940

This twenty-stanza poem is an important measure of Auden's arrival in America, where he hoped to escape the past and seek knowledge unhindered by an ancestral curse.

Certainly, the quest is for knowledge, and knowledge steeped in the poet's return to a unique version of Auden's Christianity, which in "The Quest" is much influenced by Kierkegaard. The quest motif itself has been with Auden since his earliest *Poems* (1930), when the seeker was often silent and a cypher, and in *The Orators* (1932), when the airman learns that truth is not out there, but in here, meaning the heart, and in the plays with Isherwood where the seekers, an Alan Norman (*The Dog Beneath the Skin*) and Michael Ransom (*The Ascent of F6*), dared cross the Northwest Passage only to end up back where they started (Alan) or dead (Ransom) because they gave in to temptation to go on false quests that originated outside instead of true quests that are motivated from within. The poem's sonnets are on the order of "In Time of War" in *Journey to a War*, but, as Mendelson notes, while they are partly modeled on "In Time of War" Auden also saw it as a corrective to the former. "The earlier sequence was largely composed in generalities and collectives." In "The Quest" the generalities are now particulars, with Auden giving credit to each person as unique, rather than the symbolic archetypes of the "War" sonnets.

I. A mission as in the earlier poetry with an individual singled out to leave his comfortable, if dulling life, for a terrifying responsibility. A "door" awaits that he must open signifying the Freudian divide between conscious and unconscious troubles.

II. Preparations are made for the trip to guard against self-love and seek unselfish love.

III. The seeker faces a crossroads, aware that this journey, seemingly arduous from an external view, should take no time at all from an inner perspective.

IV. The seeker understands that he is now also a pilgrim seeking spiritual truth.

V, VI, VII, VIII. The seeker enters cities where temptations await. Sonnets VI, VII, VIII, offer three temptations which would seduce exceptional individuals, those with special, divinely inspired gifts, into egoism and isolation.

IX. He reaches the tower, a symbol for achievement, and there is a Kierkegaardian consideration of the exceptional vs. the average person. Danger: is the ivory tower one of isolation for the genius who avoids commitment to belief? Freud: is genius a compensation for emotional or physical defects?

X. The presumptuous, vain and very average hero-seekers are Truly Weak, and while they may seem well-adjusted, if boring, are doomed to either fail or abandon the quest.

XI. Auden expresses the egoism of the average man's parents — "the pressure of their fond ambition," as they ask him for more than he is capable of giving.

XII. Is it the seeker's vocation to suffer, as would a Kafka-esque worldly ironist? The seeker is "incredulous" when the official taking names adds his to "Those whose request to suffer was refused." A self-imposed martyrdom is just another variation of egotistic vanity.

XIII. The failures of past seekers are not all in vain if new seekers can learn from their mistakes, as even lunatics may hide some useful truth in their nonsense.

XIV. Auden notes here that as one learns one must also be willing to hear the "Fresh addenda" added to the knowledge of "the Way."

XV. Sometimes the lucky seeker will succeed but luck is not to be depended on, nor is it a substitute for a belief in Grace.

XVI. The true hero — the Kierkegaardian Knight of Faith — has humility.

XVII. The humble man knows better than to think that by seeking God, he becomes God-like. God is no mirror in which one will see himself.

XVIII. Forsake temptation, give up memories of the past if they are burdens, and seek the eternal now from "pure cold water."

XIX. The waters of the wells represent human longing for belief, which sometimes is truth, but more often self-delusion.

XX. The garden of truth is reached where "all journeys die" and desires and burdens are removed. Here, seekers "felt their centre of volition lifted." Here, the focus of their will is no longer on their egotistical selves, but they now understand and become the collective Self of a unified consciousness as per Gerald Heard.

"The Quest Hero" 1961

In Auden's essay "The Quest Hero," he says, "The Quest is one of the oldest, hardiest, and most popular of literary genres.... the persistent appeal of the Quest as a literary form is due to its validity as a symbolic description of our subjective personal experience of existence as historical." Auden then gives six elements that are integrally systemic to the typical Quest story:

1. A precious Object and/or person to be found and possessed or married.

2. A long journey to find it, for its whereabouts are not originally known to seekers.

3. A hero. The precious object cannot be found by anybody, but only by one person who possesses the right qualities of breeding or character.

4. A Test or series of Tests by which the unworthy are screened out, and the hero revealed.

5. The Guardians of the Object who must be overcome before it can be won. They may be simply a further test of the hero's *arete*, or they may be malignant in themselves.

6. The Helpers who with their knowledge and magical powers assist the hero and but for which he would never succeed.

"Does not each of these elements correspond to an aspect of our subjective experience of life?"

Then Auden goes on to answer his own question by relating these elements to conditions universally prevalent in the human psyche. In summary: 1) man in various ways or "quests" seeks happiness in some ideal or substitute: art, theology, romantic love, hero worship, state worship; 2) time is a process of irreversible change which is the metaphorical quest journey; 3) each person is unique, a new Adam, who, like Adam, will be tested; 4) man understands, consciously or unconsciously, the duality of contradictory forces within him of which he must judge what is either good or evil "and either yield to desire or resist it."

Often the quest is not only to the benefit of the questor, but ultimately a benefit to his society: i.e., Arthur becomes King and establishes the Knights of the Round Table, itself a symbol of circularity or time without beginning or end.

There are two types of quest hero: "One resembles the hero of the epic; his superior *arete* is manifest to all. Jason is instantly recognizable as the kind of man who can win the Golden Fleece. The other type, so common in fairy tales, is the hero whose *arete* is concealed.... [The] least likely to succeed turns out to be the hero when his manifest betters have failed." The hero benefits from outside help through magic means and he gets it, not for outward bravado, but for his humble virtues shown by his good will towards others. Within the two types of Quest hero are numerous variations, just as, for Auden, there are variants of the Quest story such as the detective novel, the adventure story, Moby Dick, and Kafka's novels. Within each type, Auden's six elements prevail in many configurations. Some are timeless dream states which are imaginary and others have recognizable socio-historical settings. Auden turns now to an example of the former, which creates its own complex socio-historical context such as Tolkien's *Lord of the Rings*. Tolkien's world is imaginary, but this world is consistent within itself with its own history, which appeals to the modern reader "who has been exposed to the realistic novel and scientific research."

A dream world may be full of inexplicable gaps and logical inconsistencies; an imaginary world may not, for it is a world of law, not of wish. Its laws may be different from those which may govern our own, but they must be as intelligible and inviolable. Its history may be unusual but it must not contradict our notion of what history is, an interplay of Fate, Choice, and Chance. Lastly, it must not violate our moral experience....

Good and evil are to be incarnated in individuals and societies [so that] we must be convinced that the evil side is what every man would acknowledge as evil.

Conversely, every sane man should also recognize what is good. In Tolkien's world, the internal logic is bolstered by the author's extensively layered construction of the "imagined" societies and their histories. Auden praises Tolkien's ability to maintain not just an internal logic that readers, notwithstanding the overall complexity of this imaginary world, see and identify within the imaginary world that retains Auden's six quest elements. Auden says, "If there is any Quest Tale which, while primarily concerned with the subjective life of the individual person as all such stories must be, and manages to do more justice to our experience of socio-historic realities than *Lord of the Rings*, I should be glad to hear of it."

"The Question" *see Poems*

"The Questioner Who Sits So Sly" *see Poems*

Raby, F.J.E. *see* "Under Sirius"

The Rake's Progress 1951

In 1947, at the suggestion of his very good friend Aldous Huxley, the composer Igor Stravinsky asked Auden to write a libretto for an opera based on Hogarth's series of engravings, *The Rake's Progress*. Auden wrote three long poems during the 1940s — *For the Time Being*, *The Sea and the Mirror*, and *The Age of Anxiety* — that were dramatic in nature if not quite verse plays. With this experience, he was reasonably well prepared to write the libretto to a major opera for a composer of Stravinsky's stature.

Stravinsky and Auden met in California to work out the structure. They prefaced Hogarth's eight scenes with a pastoral vignette, in which the devil intrudes in the guise of a ser-

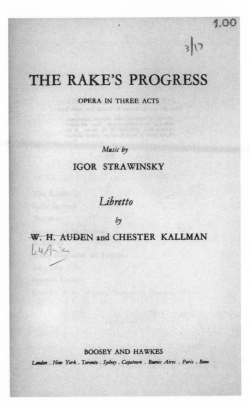

The Rake's Progress, first edition of the libretto.

pent and tempts the Rake (who is a new Adam) just as the devil tempted the first Adam. Auden followed the eight scenes with an epilogue, a moral summary of the previous action that borrows from Mozart's Don Giovanni. After returning to New York, Auden asked Chester Kallman to work with him — an appropriate choice since it was Kallman who had originally been the opera fan who introduced Auden to opera.

In *The Rake's Progress* Auden and Kallman turned Hogarth's morality fable into a philosophical and religious parable. Tom Rakewell gives in to three temptations that represent three philosophical errors. The first is a childish egoism based on Rakewell's trust in nature. The second is a metaphysical acte gratuite that causes him to marry Baba the Turk precisely because he doesn't want to or have to. The third is the belief that an evil world can be cured by material change — which he imagines can be brought about by a machine that he is foolish enough to believe can turn stones into bread.

Each of these errors has Rakewell believing he can elude time's responsibilities. He pursues a world where time is changeable, irrelevant, or unreal, the unreality represented by the stone-into-bread machine that the Rake believes promises instant riches. Anne Trulove, left by Rakewell, uses Kierkegaard's religious nomenclature when she vows to always offer Rakewell the opportunity to return; to counter Anne, Nick Shadow (the Jungian name adopted by the devil when he becomes Rakewell's servant) invokes Kierkegaard when he teaches Rakewell to fear repetition as a bad omen and to believe that no return is possible. (Kierkegaard praised repetition, calling it a recollection that looks forward, and declared that the true repetition is eternity.) In the end, Rakewell remembers his love for Anne and tries to reclaim his life by calling on love to return. This call is answered when he hears a miraculous repetition of her vow. He can then defeat the devil by repeating his recollection. In the card game he plays with the devil for his soul, he names the Queen of Hearts a second time after seeing the devil throw away the card when Rakewell named it the first time. Repetition cannot reverse time. Anne's love can save Rakewell from death, but his previous acts allow the devil to condemn him to madness.

The opera premiered in Venice in September 1951. It was a great success, and more productions were staged in Europe and America. (See also Stravinsky, Igor.)

Read, Herbert *see* **Shelley, Percy Bysshe**

"The Real World" *see* **White Magic and Black Magic**

Red Ribbon on a White Horse 1950

In his introduction to this novel by Anna Yesierska, Auden describes the difference between desire and fantasy: desire can be remotely possible but its disappointment is material in nature; fantasy is impossibly remote and its-disappointment is despair that's spiritual in nature.

Yesierska, in the early 1900s, recounts her leaving a Polish ghetto to live in the Lower East Side of Manhattan. She writes: "Poverty here [in America], relatively, is filled with shame as the objects of contempt are to suffer hazing which their position deserves — 'better to die there [Poland] than live here.'" She becomes a writer so that "By writing out what I don't know and can't understand, it would stop hurting me." On to Hollywood: culture shock and fear freezes her writing; competition kills art. She returns east and works for the Work Projects Association. In the depression the Arts Project of WPA gave recognition to artists as like minds united by art and poverty.

"Reflections in a Forest" 1957

This poem contrasts the stability of trees with the vagaries of human deceit, which itself Auden defends as a necessary by-product of the evolution of consciousness. (See also "Bucolics.")

The Reformatory *see* **Plays with Isherwood**

"Review of *T.E. Lawrence* by Liddell Hart" *see* **Essays**

"Reviews: Education" 1933

In this essay Auden gives a definition of a highbrow (see *Aesthetes and Hearties*). Moreover, Auden writes that the collapse of previous standards of education coincides with a perfection of mass communication. A revolution is inevitable, hopefully by a critical Highbrow minority rather than merely the loudest voice. Children must be taught to detect and deter bogus propaganda. Mass media causes a "leveling" in society as the society/public become able to read but most do not read well and follow the herd. Auden's view of the public and propaganda intimates his future interest in Kierkegaard.

Rich, Adrienne

1929– , American poet, b. Baltimore, graduated from Radcliffe in 1951. Since the 1970s her volumes of verse have increasingly reflected feminist and lesbian themes. Among her volumes of poetry are *A Change of World* (1951), which was Auden's choice that year for the Yale Younger Poets Series. Her prose reflections on the function of poetry are contained in *What Is Found There: Notebooks on Poetry and Politics* (1993).

Richards, I.A.

1893–1979, born Ivor Armstrong Richards, Cambridge. English critic, poet, and teacher who was influential in developing a way of reading poetry. In 1939 he went to Harvard, where he finished his career.

In 1935 Isherwood and Auden's friend Stephen Spender published a book of literary criticism, *The Destructive Element*, with ideas he shared with his friends. As Samuel Hynes writes in *The Auden Generation*, "The 'destructive element' of the title is the phrase from Conrad's *Lord Jim*, but that is not Spender's immediate source. As he explains in the introduction, he took the phrase, and the argument of which it is part, from Richards' *Science and Poetry*, and specifically from that influential footnote on *The Waste Land*. Richards had said of Eliot that 'by effecting a complete severance between his poetry and all beliefs, and this without any weakening of the poetry, he has realised what might otherwise have remained largely a speculative possibility, and has shown the way to the only solution of these difficulties. 'In the destructive element immerse. That is the way.'"

The effect is that by a method of unbelief, that is, by nihilism of outlook that reflects the modern world, one must by the absence of belief consider what beliefs can fill the void. The term "destructive element" would become part of a line in the Isherwood-Auden play *The Ascent of F6* to signify a nod to Spender and also to Richards. (See also Spender, Sir Stephen; Plays with Isherwood [*The Ascent of F6*].)

"The Riddle" 1939

This poem was written shortly after meeting Chester Kallman whom Auden thought would be the love of his life. The poem is a contrast to "As He Is," which concerned the faithlessness of love and the falsity of history. In "The Riddle" Auden looks to history for some kind of resolution and hopes the riddle will find the end of sorrow in the present in a personal love that, at last, is not faithless. This was not to be.

Riding, Laura

1901–1991, Laura Riding Jackson, b. Laura Reichenthal, New York City. In 1925 she went to England and wrote some twenty books of poetry, criticism, and fiction. She also wrote, in collaboration with Robert Graves, *A Survey of Modernist Poetry and a Pamphlet Against Anthologies*. In 1939 she returned to the United States, and married Schuyler B. Jackson, with whom she co-wrote, in 1941, *Rational Meaning: A New Foundation for the Definition of Words*. In 1991, she was awarded the Bollingen Prize for her lifetime contribution to poetry.

Early in his career Auden wrote some of his poems in direct imitation of Riding's poetic voice. Laura Riding's 1928 volume *Love as Love, Death as Death* echoes the diction of Emily Dickinson and the meters of John Skelton. An adolescent Auden admired Dickinson and Skelton. Through Riding, he saw how they could be fit into his own work. "This Lunar Beauty" and six or so other poems from 1929–1930 show the Riding influence. Auden's short verse play *Paid on Both Sides* (1930) is another primary example of the influence of Riding's telegraphic diction of clipped sentence fragments. After *Poems* (1930), and, to some degree, *The Orators*, Auden replaced Riding's style with a more verbally discursive and relatively normal syntactic approach.

Rilke, Rainer Maria

1875–1926, German poet, b. Prague, married briefly at the turn of the century. Rilke chose a vagabond existence among other writers; in 1899–1900 his travels to Russia influenced him. In Paris the sculptor Rodin introduced Rilke to the craftsman's idea of creativity, which Auden would take up from the 1950s, which asserted that the artist was a maker, a craftsman who worked at his art rather than waiting for an inspired muse. After going to Italy and North Africa, Rilke returned to Paris (1913), but World War I returned him to Germany, where the war and ill health interfered with his work. After 1919 he lived in Switzerland. His death from a blood disease was hastened by the prick of a rose thorn, an irony not lost on future poets.

Rilke's first book of poetry, *Leben und Lieder* [Life and Songs], appeared in 1894, but not until *Stories of God* (1904) did his mysticism mature. His visits to Russia inspired Poems from the *Book of Hours* (1905), with which he found fame in his consideration of God as an evolutionary being, an idea central to the philosophy of Gerald Heard, who in turn was a major influence on Auden. Rilke's own favorite verse, his *Duino Elegies* (1923), which are written in a telegraphic, clipped style (as were Auden's early poems), contain Rilke's most positive praise of human existence.

Rilke was sensitive and introspective. The Vision of Eros, where the erotic can become a source of spiritual love between men and women, is a frequent subject for Rilke and also became an Auden theme. Rilke's verse was often mystical and prophetic, as Auden's would be in many, if not all, cases; Rilke used symbolism in poetry that is medieval in diction, just as Auden would imitate Old Norse and Old English literature. And like Auden, Rilke sought goodness and transcendence while also seeing death as a poetic theme.

Rilke's voice — and his predilection for similes — appears in Auden's work in the late 1930s. A particular example is Auden's Sonnet XXIII of "In Time of War" in *Journey to a War* (1939). Auden did have some conflicting feelings about Rilke; he admired the poet but was less enthusiastic about Rilke's detachment from worldly problems. After his arrival in America in 1939, Auden reviewed a new translation of Rilke and, as he often did in essays, gave his own take on matters of concern to him, including Rilke's growing status in English verse: "It is … no accident that as international crisis becomes … more acute, the poet to whom writers are increasingly drawn should be the one who felt it was pride and presumption to interfere with the lives of others (for each is unique and the apparent misfortunes of each may be his very way of salvation)" ("Rilke in English," *The New Republic*, 6 September 1939).

Writing this review more or less concurrently with *The Prolific and the Devourer*, Auden at this time was asserting his new view that the writer must be very careful about his role as an activist. Auden did not believe in a poet's complete detachment from the world since the world is where a poet finds his subjects, but he was very circumspect and reticent about the degree to which a poet might be active in the world without causing more harm than good.

For Auden, by 1949 Rilke had lost some of his allure; Auden wrote in an essay that Rilke's influence had made "some of my poems too schöngeistig, too much Poetry with a capital 'P.'" ("How Can I Tell What I Think Until I See What I Say"—the title is a line from E.M. Forster).

Rimbaud, Arthur

1854–1891, Jean-Nicolas-Arthur Rimbaud, French poet. Rimbaud's poetic career was brief and extraordinary, as was his life. Born into a bourgeois family in Charleville (Alsace), near the Belgian border, Rimbaud quickly distinguished himself as a scholar in local schools. Encouraged by his teachers, especially Georges Izambard, he read widely in contemporary poetry, wrote conventional verse of freshness, lyric purity, and idealism, and yearned for an intellectual life wider than his immediate life could provide. He twice ran away to Paris during the months when the Franco-Prussian war was at its height. On the second occasion, he had a transformative experience, probably homosexual that changed his outlook and writing. The result was work of astonishing power,

Arthur Rimbaud

breaking with old forms, mixing idealism, spirituality, and visionary qualities with images of bitter revulsion and contempt, in a new poetic language studded with scientific and cabalistic terms, obscenity and even nonsense words. French poetry would never be the same. He also developed a new poetic theory in which poets were to be "Vates," or "seers," and the true poet was lifted out of the personal: "*Je est un autre*," Rimbaud declared in his "Lettre du Voyant." He was seventeen.

In 1871 he wrote to the man who would figure most prominently in his artistic life, the poet Paul Verlaine, arriving to see this lyrical, emotionally susceptible, dissipated, already famous poet with "Le Bateau Ivre" ("The Drunk Boat"), one of the masterpieces of French symbolism, in hand. Verlaine introduced Rimbaud into literary cafes, but Rimbaud was beyond self-congratulatory bohemianism.

A period of sustained creativity for both Rimbaud and Verlaine followed over the next several years, during which some of Rimbaud's masterpieces ("Le Poète de Sept Ans," "Memoire," and the prose later published as *Illuminations*) were composed. His relations with Verlaine broke up the latter's marriage as the two of them, impoverished, wandered from Paris to London to Brussels in a tumultuous relationship

in which opium and absinthe played a large role. Rimbaud gained dominance over the weaker Verlaine, who in despair shot Rimbaud. With Verlaine imprisoned for this act, Rimbaud returned to Alsace, where he probably finished the only book he (self-) published in his life, the chaotic and coruscating *Une Saison en Enfer* (*A Season in Hell*). Less than ten copies changed hands in Rimbaud's lifetime.

One further meeting with Verlaine showed the futility of this relationship, and after 1875 it is doubtful that Rimbaud wrote any more imaginative literature. When poetry failed to bring him the spiritual satisfactions for which he thirsted, Rimbaud gave it up and became by turns an explorer, a gunrunner, and an ivory and gold trader. In 1886 Verlaine published Rimbaud's prose poems, *Illuminations*, which created a sensation, as did the other verse of Rimbaud's Verlaine put out. Rimbaud, however, kept to himself in Abyssinia. In 1891 his health declined; a grotesquely swollen knee was either the symptom of a carcinoma or tertiary syphilis. Brought back to France to recover his health, he died in a hospital in Marseille, where his sister recorded that on his deathbed he reported the same ecstatic visions as were in his poetry of two decades previous.

Rimbaud is one of the few French writers, with Baudelaire and Valéry, to influence Auden. He is seen clearly in three places. Perhaps the most important is in *The Orators* (1932). *Une Saison en Enfer* is a model behind that book: its chaos, its experimentation, its ambiguous resolution (does the airman go over to the enemy or commit suicide?), its forays into the personal ("Letter to a Wound"), its attitude toward homosexuality ("new glosses on the noun amor" or a sign of weakness?), its mixture of prose and poetry, its insistent undermining of its own premises. John Fuller reports of a letter in the Colby College library in which Auden identifies the airman's quest as possibly like Rimbaud's: both sought wholeness and integration. (In *Une Saison en Enfer*, Rimbaud sought "posséder la vérité dans une âme et un corps.")

There are obvious connections of poetry and homosexuality between the two men, but more essentially the disparity between Rimbaud's yearning for purity and the sordidness of the physical world make him a figure with whom Auden could identify. In the sonnet that Auden wrote in late 1938, Rimbaud is seen as one whose poetic expression (like Auden's own) grew out of adversity. The cold bursts the pipes or "rhetorician's lie"; however, unlike Auden, Rimbaud tragically and ironically could not find "integrity" sufficient and embarked on a new, futile quest for a truth that the sordid world around him ("lying men") would reject anyhow.

Rimbaud the poet makes an appearance in Auden's next work, "New Year Letter," as one of the supreme appraisers. This is, naturally, the "young" Rimbaud, not the "negotiant." Muttering a line from *Une Saison en Enfer*, Rimbaud both supports Blake and possibly serves as a foil to him, as his later career represents the life of a man of action, and poetry makes "nothing happen").

Auden saw Rimbaud's abandonment of poetry as a key aesthetic event for the twentieth century; the placing of poetry in the context of human life, which Rimbaud dealt with by simply rejecting poetry, was something that preoccupied Auden. In "The Dyer's Hand," Auden writes that "The Rimbaud Myth, the tale of a great poet who ceases writing, not because, like Coleridge, he has nothing more to say, but because he chooses to stop, may not be true, I am pretty sure it is not, but as a myth it haunts the artistic conscience of this century" ("Making Knowing and Judging.") Auden continued to write, as most true writers do, but Rimbaud remained intriguing as one who rejected poetry for a life of action. Ultimately, Auden sought to reconcile the world of aesthetics and the world outside them by using religion as mediator to inspire, order, and judge. —ROGER LATHBURY

The Rise and Fall of the City of Mahogonny see Brecht, Bertolt

"River Profile" 1966

This poem "is the greatest poem of his last years, and one of the greatest and strangest poems of its century. Its rapid, stately, and encyclopedic allegory compresses into twelve Sapphic stanzas

the course of a river and the course of a life" (Mendelson, *Later Auden*). The river moves from north (birth and youth) to south (aging and decline), but finally to resurrection.

Robbins, Jerome *see The Age of Anxiety*

"Robert Frost" *see* Frost, Robert

Roberts, Michael

1902–1948. Michael Roberts was a poet in his own right, but also an extremely influential editor of poetry and spokesman for the new — and newly political — poetry of the nineteen thirties. He is better remembered as an editor and spokesman than as a poet, but these roles should be considered together, along with his work as a cultural critic. Like John Lehman and Cyril Connolly, he helped focus and publish the work of contemporaries, and has an important place in the literary politics and cultural history of the nineteen thirties. Indeed, he was himself a cultural historian in many respects, keen, as were several contemporaries, on locating poetry and literary culture within a wider vision of society. His major publications were, as an editor, *New Signatures* (1932), *New Country* (1933) and *The Faber Book of Modern Verse* (1936); as a spokesman for the "new verse" and a cultural critic, *A Critique of Poetry* (1934), and *The Modern Mind* (1936); and as a poet, *Poems* (1936) and *Orion Marches* (1939).—CHRISTOPHER HOPKINS

The Rocking Horse Winner 1941

Auden and James Stern adapted for radio this 1926 short story by D.H. Lawrence. It was performed on CBS radio on 6 April 1941.

"Rois Fainéants" 1968

This poem is about the trap of the child kings of France who were ruled by others, and like "Partition" concerns the difference between private and public personas.

Rolfe, Frederick

1860–1913, English novelist, also known as Baron Corvo. After trying to become a priest, Rolfe painted and taught before he began to write under the name Baron Corvo. His most famous work is the novel *Hadrian the Seventh* (1904), which chronicles the life of Arthur Rose, who, although rejected for the priesthood, eventually becomes pope Hadrian the Seventh, and this novel was dramatized by Peter Luke in 1967 and successfully produced in London and New York. Rolfe's bizarre, abusive, and erudite personality is revealed in his *The Desire and Pursuit of the Whole* (1934), which tells of his final sordid years in Venice.

"Rolfe, Frederick (Baron Corvo)" 1961

Introduction to *The Desire and Pursuit of the Whole*. Rolfe's genuine style conceals him deliberately but reveals him by his choices for evasion. This book is a vision of a paranoid homosexual that weaves nightmare and daydream, "a person who surrenders himself so completely to a daydream without acknowledging its absurdity is bound to make his life in the world a nightmare." Who is Crabbe's (the Rolfe surrogate's) "other half"? A seventeen-year-old boy—a servant by choice not by fate, finding in the service of his master, "perfect freedom." A paranoid believes he is too extraordinarily unique to be just means but is an end; his worst insult is to be ignored. A "normal person" knows that "we make use of each other with mutual consent," and love (Vision of Eros) is a hopeful product that may lead to the Vision of Agape. A paranoid is one-sided and a bore. This is a grim story relieved by Crabbe's love for Venice, which was for him the "Great Good Place" built by men for their mothers: beauty, tradition, grace, ease.

It is easy to mistake and underestimate Auden's important relation to one preeminent queer eccentric in the older generation, Fred-

erick Rolfe, who belongs among the grandfathers of Auden's cultural time. Auden has an impulse to resist Rolfe; and the resistance can look like Auden's phobic compromising of his own group label. A crabby foreword Auden wrote in 1953 for a re-issue of *The Desire and Pursuit of the Whole* (1909) intensifies one's unease. Auden's foreword stresses the unpleasant character of Rolfe's protagonist, Nicholas Crabbe, and the likeness of Crabbe to the real-life Rolfe, who for Auden epitomizes "a homosexual paranoid." The phrase is unsettling: how narrow or how broad a specification is it? Does Auden want us to read Rolfe because it would purge us — even us homosexuals — of paranoia; or would reading him renew invidious reductions of homosexuality to a clinical condition? *The Desire and Pursuit of the Whole* manages to represent, against the odds of cultural censorship, male-male romance of the greatest intensity; so why is Auden edgy about this gloss on Amor in the eccentric generation he was celebrating in the mid 1930s? One answer is that the paranoid style stands in Auden's mind for elitist, neo-aristocratic ideas of heroism, and consequently for anti-democratic practices in love and politics. In his foreword Auden is not charmed by Rolfe's characterization of the male lovers in the novel, because one of the lovers is only the soothing submissive subordinate of the demanding, and paranoid, heresiarch Crabbe. Yet Auden does pay his respects to Rolfe; so why? Auden recommends Rolfe's creative ability to turn watery Venice, an island city, into a utopia, "The Great Good Place ... the perfect embodiment of ... beauty, tradition, grace and ease." In 1953 Rolfe's Venice perhaps resonates with Auden's memory of his own island journey to a Good Place two decades earlier. But to understand Auden's dialogue and differences with Rolfe still more answers are necessary. Rolfe belongs undoubtedly to the context in which *Letters from Iceland* was gestated. *The Desire and Pursuit of the Whole* was posthumously first published in 1935. In the preceding year appeared A.J.A. Symons' brilliant *The Quest for Corvo: An Experiment in Biography*.

It is from Symons that Auden derives the diagnosis of Rolfe as a homosexual paranoid. It also is notable that Symons' diagnosis, on which

Auden's foreword relies, is subtle and generous; and a similar generous diagnosis (albeit more euphemistic about Rolfe's sexuality) would have been read by Auden a decade earlier. In 1925 D.H. Lawrence (whose work was consumed by young Auden) introduced a re-issue of Rolfe's greatest success, the novel *Hadrian the Seventh* (1904). If we judge solely from Auden's reaction to the paranoid protagonist of the Venetian novel, we might think that the Great Good Place is successfully imagined there only despite Rolfe and Crabbe's elitist and suspicious projections. But Crabbe is another version of the earlier novel's Hadrian, who also is aristocratic, homosexual, and paranoid, and who is the vehicle of another utopian imagination (a radically renewed and unworldly Catholic Church). Side by side the homoeroticized figures of Crabbe and Hadrian suggest a creative tie between exceedingly isolated (hence paranoia-prone) singular individuals and utopian places. Moreover, because Hadrian is a pope, and because the character of Crabbe combines homosexual desire with priestly asceticism, what is continually refigured and kept vivid in Rolfe's work is homosexual shamanism. This shamanism has a compelling political as well as aesthetic interest for Auden. It signifies another layer of intergenerational exchanges and differences among gay modernists.—ROBERT CASERIO

"Roman Wall Blues" *see* "Twelve Songs"

Romanticism

Auden for the most part was anti–Romantic, although he revered Blake, admired Byron, liked Keats's letters, but only for the sides of these writers that were down to earth rather than faux grandiloquent and optimistic; hence, Auden had no use for Shelley whatsoever. Auden believed that the Romantics presented the world as needing only some love to put it right, while suffering for their art in search of love. Auden believed in love also but preferred a more concrete approach to love that made egotistical self-created suffering a silly notion that becomes obviated in

a Christian context rather than in a self-martyring mode that did little to account for suffering and injustice in the real world, however seemingly elusive and inexplicable the world remained. For the Romantics, this missing "inexplicable" was a "blessed" pain, as its melancholia was thought to be soil for the elusive muse. The Moderns, belabored more by the Freudian revolution, cannot enjoy their pain because the credit for it is no longer attributable to the notion of Romantic muse, but more to the mundane neuroses and psychoses they have not chosen, but have contracted like the mumps. Auden gives credence to neither the Romantics' muse nor to the psychology that artists create as a reaction to the sublimation of mental illness. (Does this mean that if the illness goes away, the artist stops creating?) Although dreadful experiences may provide materials for art, to seek them for their own sake as muse/motivation is the narcissism of martyrdom.

Nonetheless, modern artists do not so easily give up on the old ways; consequently, many suffer just as much in their modern, maladjusted angst as did their predecessors in their muse.

"Romeo and Juliet" 1958

In this introduction to an edition of the play, Auden discusses how poetic speeches encapsulate Shakespeare's own thought at the time of his writing Romeo & Juliet.

Friar Laurence represents the earth, which is nature's mother but can also be nature's tomb. Auden sees an analogy between natural and moral order. Disease is physical, sin is spiritual. Individual egos confront and resist the common good for their own ends; the common good can be achieved only by the egoistic "I" giving way to the less selfish, more cooperative "we." Romeo and Juliet is a tragedy of a city that is not "of God"—it is not ruled by spiritual cooperation, and all of its citizens are responsible for its ills.

Mercutio talks of dreams and how each person has his own, but these dreams go unfulfilled. What is harmless in sleep as dreams is not harmless awake if the impulses of the dreams are enacted in reality. Evil, in the form of anger, arises when man in his waking reality is faced with rejections of his dream perceptions. This is a problem more of the upper class than of workers who know a more harsh reality and understand the difference between the fantasy and reality. Another difference is how each class deals with reality. The upper class, with little or no work to be done, asks, "How can I show off?" The workers ask, in reference to their daily duties, "What ought I to do?"

Other characters: Escalus is God's secular representative in the city. He is supposed to impartially see that sinners obey the law, but he is too lenient and does not deter trouble. Benvolio, Tybalt, and Mercutio are one-dimensional embodiments of contrasted states — Reason vs. Belligerence. They show what is wrong in the city, which ignores reason and condones the bully who thinks life is a game. With the slaying of Tybalt it is shown that the city lacks a central authority, the absence of which engenders clan loyalty so that revenge becomes a social requirement. Capulet demonstrates that justice is shallow; he exemplifies melancholic passivity but reacts to his wife's pressure with feeble attempts at assertion. The friar is God's spiritual representative who, when interfering in the temporal, creates havoc. The nurse defends her sex, damns men, and is dogmatic in asserting that passion is illusory. Her advice to Juliet is that the girl serve herself first. She is not a good influence on Juliet. The apothecary who makes the poison symbolizes that the city is not perfect or egalitarian; power corrupts the Capulets and Montagues, and poverty tempts the apothecary to make the poison.

Language: The commoners in the play speak prose, while the upper class speaks the verse of "young gentlemen." The exception is when the young gentlemen indulge in horseplay, during which they also speak in prose and in effect set the servants a bad example, instead of a noble example. Romeo and Juliet offers a variety of verse styles and metaphors; the metaphors are all straightforward, with themes such as night is good, day is bad; hot weather means dark blood; impassive natural law opposes willful humanity.

Fate, choice, and chance: The Greeks lean toward fate as the determinant of tragedy and beyond the control of the characters; the Elizabethans lean to the characters' choices as their downfall. In Romeo & Juliet, the tragedy entails both fate and choice. Fated events occur, but it is the choices made in response to these events that lead to tragedy. In Romeo and Juliet, the factors of fate in the form of random chance are 1) the guest list, which Romeo sees; 2) his love for Juliet at first sight; 3) Mercutio's death; and 4) the friar being detained from his meeting, which causes the tragic turn of events that follow.

The deaths of Romeo and Juliet are suicides in the manner of the Greeks and Romans, but their suicides are not Christian, because to slay oneself is an indifference to God. The Elizabethan audience was Christian, and they would have asked, "Was there repentance?" Their answer would be no. Ultimately, Romeo and Juliet's love was too selfish and too tragic because their love was an impulsive act of unreasoned idolatry rather than a love nurtured by time.

Rosenstock-Huessy, Eugen

1888–1973, b. Berlin. Born a Jew, at age 17 Rosenstock-Huessy joined the Protestant faith; this conversion became central to his work. Rosenstock-Huessy was aware that World War I was an historical watershed. In 1931, he published the first of his major works: *The European Revolutions and the Character of the Nations*, which depicted one thousand years of European history created in five different European national "revolutions" that collectively came to an end with World War I. In 1933, Germany fell to the Nazis, and Rosenstock-Huessy left for America. He wrote more books, and his *Out of Revolution* (1938) influenced Auden with its view of history. Auden became a fan and read everything that Rosenstock-Huessy wrote thereafter, with particular interest in *The Christian Future* (1946). Auden was captivated by Rosenstock-Huessy's vision of a series of unique culminating events that would lead to the Second Coming. The last verse in *The Age of Anxiety*, "His World to Come," comes from passages in *The Christian Future*.

Runner 1962

A short film produced by the National Film Board of Canada about a seventeen-year-old long-distance runner, Bruce Kidd. Auden wrote a commentary to footage of Kidd running. Auden wrote to Lincoln Kirstein of his work, "I am rather pleased — a mixture of Pindar and Beowulf."

Russell, Bertrand

1872–1970, b. England, philosopher, social critic, writer. Nobel Prize for Literature in 1950. Russell was the subject of an Auden review of his book *Education and Social Order* (see "Problems of Education").

Bertrand Russell

Russell, George *see* AE

"A Russian Aesthete" 1970

Auden's review of *Against the Current* by Konstantin Leontiev.

"The Sabbath" 1959

A cheerful version of Armageddon where natural creatures rejoice over man's ruin so they can get their space back; but then man reappears, and is simultaneously more evil and God-like than ever.

Sacks, Oliver

1933– , American neurologist and author, b. London. Educated at Oxford. In 1960 he immigrated to the United States. Sacks' approach is to treat patients holistically in both body and mind. His books — among them *Awakenings* (1973), which became a film with Robin Williams as Sacks and Robert DeNiro as his patient; *The Man Who Mistook His Wife for a Hat* (1985); *An Anthropologist on Mars* (1995); and *The Island of the Colorblind* (1997) — describe case histories of people with neurological and perceptual disorders. Auden met Sacks in 1971 through Orlan Fox, before Sacks became famous for his book *Awakenings*, which Auden read in manuscript. That book concerned Sacks' treatment of patients with sleeping sickness. Auden, the son of a doctor, enjoyed Sacks for his humor and his ability to talk about his work contemplatively, the way scientist Loren Eiseley did. In 1971 Auden reviewed Sacks' book *Migraine* with the review's title "The Megrims," the British colloquial term for migraine.

Sacred and Profane *see* "Making, Knowing, Judging"; Secondary Worlds

St. Augustine

St. Augustine's writings greatly influenced very early Christianity; his *Confessions* (c. 400) is a profound Christian autobiography. *The City of God* (after 412) defends Christianity against critics. Augustine regarded all history as God's creation of two mystical cities, one of God and one of the devil, and that the choice of which to belong to is up to each person. St. Augustine believed in original sin and the fall of humanity. His writings praise the idea of grace.

In 1939 Auden's *The Prolific and the Devourer* took its style from Pascal and Augustine's *Confessions*, with Auden's reading of the latter a prelude to his re-conversion to Auden's Christianity. (In the 1960s Auden's Oxford friend Rex Warner would translate the *Confessions* into contemporary English.) In 1940s "New Year Letter" Auden would quote St. Augustine in the poem and in the poem's notes. When Auden reviewed theologian Reinhold Niebuhr's *The Nature and Destiny of Man* in 1941, he praised his friend's book and called him Augustinian in his emphasis on the personal experience of God and grace. In *For the Time Being* (1944), Auden paraphrases St. Augustine's line from the *Confessions*, "I would rather have been deprived of my friend than of my grief," in a speech by Prospero to Ariel, and then Simeon alludes to Augustine's term *fantastica fornicato* "as the imagination's 'promiscuous fornication with her own images'" (Mendelson, *Later Auden*). In Auden's poem "Memorial to the City" of 1949, and dedicated to Charles Williams, he refers to St. Augustine's just City of God, a prevalent Auden theme. St. Augustine stayed with Auden right through his almost autobiography of 1970, *A Certain World*, where Auden thinks enough of him to give him the last word: "What the poet has to convey is not 'self-expression,' but a view of reality common to all, seen from a unique perspective, which it is his duty as well as his pleasure to share with others. To small truths as well as great, St. Augustine's words apply.... 'The truth is neither mine nor his nor another's; but belongs to all of us whom Thou callest to partake of it, warning us terribly, not to account it private to ourselves, lest we be deprived of it.'"

St. Edmund's School

Situated at Hinehead, Surrey, England, St. Edmund's was Isherwood and Auden's preparatory school (see also Dodo Minor; British Public Schools). When Auden was in his first year, Christopher Isherwood was in his last. They met here and would meet again when Auden was at Oxford where their recollections of St. Edmund's were treated with a humor that belied the seriousness of how much they hated

this typical British Public School, which lead to their concocting a mythified version in Isherwood's "Gems of Belgian Architecture" and Auden's *Paid on Both Sides*.

Sandburg, Carl

1878–1967, American poet and biographer, b. Galesburg, Ill. He married Lillian Steichen, sister of the photographer Edward Steichen, in 1908. Sandburg became famous with the appearances of *Chicago Poems* (1916), *Cornhuskers* (1918), *Smoke and Steel* (1920), and *Slabs of the Sunburnt West* (1922). His later verse includes *Good Morning, America* (1928), *The People, Yes* (1936), *Complete Poems* (1950; Pulitzer Prize), *Harvest Poems*, 1910–1960 (1960), and *Honey and Salt* (1963). His verse is written without regard for conventional meter and form, in language both simple and noble. Sandburg completed a six-volume biography of Abraham Lincoln (1926–39).

Auden appreciated Sandburg's "thoughts of the wise man in the speech of the common people" (see *Yeats, Auden on Writing*), and his use of urban-industrial images, which are featured in Auden's early verse. Auden read Sandburg's *Lincoln*, and this may have influenced Auden's mythmaking in *Paul Bunyan*. In a review of *Lincoln* Auden wrote that geniuses "are conscious of how little depends on their free will and how much they are vehicles for powers they can never fully understand but to which they can listen" ("The Double Focus: Sandberg's *Lincoln*" *Common Sense*, March 1940). These powers — or Paul Tillich's demonic — were now empowering Auden's ideas. In Aldous Huxley's essay "The Subject Matter of Poetry" (see Huxley, Aldous), when he says that a poet has a right to use the word "bohunk," the poet is Sandburg.

Sartre, Jean-Paul

1905–80, French philosopher, playwright, and novelist. Influenced by German philosophy, particularly that of Martin Heidegger, Sartre was a leading exponent of twentieth century existentialism. Auden's oblique interest in

Sartre came from Sartre's interest in Heidegger, and the fact that Sartre wrote a study of Baudelaire.

Sassoon, Siegfried

1886–1967, English poet and novelist. An officer in World War I, he expressed his hatred of war in realistic verse. His part fiction, part-autobiographical trilogy—*Memoirs of a Fox-Hunting Man* (1928), *Memoirs of an Infantry Officer* (1930), *Sherston's Progress* (1936)—was collected as *The Memoirs of George Sherston* (1937). Sassoon also wrote several autobiographical works—*The Old Century and Seven More Years* (1938), *The Weald of Youth* (1942), and *Siegfried's Journey* (1945).

Sassoon was a hero to the Eliot-Huxley (1920s) and Auden (1930s) generations for his denunciations of World War I and the British upper classes that he believed fomented it. While Auden did not admire Sassoon's verse as much as he did Wilfred Owen's, it was Sassoon who knew Owen and arranged for the publication of the martyred fellow soldier's poems, an effort by Sassoon that Auden did admire.

"Schoolchildren" 1937

This poem is a reaction to both Auden's visit to Spain during the Spanish Civil War and his writing of "Spain," the poem. It also refutes an earlier poem, "This Lunar Beauty," which was more rapturous about schoolchildren. In this case, beneath a child's beauty, the sex itch lurks to damn the future.

Scrutiny see Leavis, F.R.

The Sea and the Mirror 1944

"By writing *The Sea and the Mirror* as a series of monologues for fictional characters borrowed from Shakespeare, Auden could write autobiographically in a deeper and more comprehensive way…" (Mendelson, *Later Auden*).

(Dedicated to James and Tania Stern.) The title comes from Shakespeare who said art was a "mirror held up to nature." In Shakespeare's *The Tempest*, Prospero lives with his daughter Miranda on a deserted island. On the surface, he appears to be a benevolent leader doing his best to protect and care for the inhabitants of the island, especially for Miranda. On closer inspection, however, Prospero plays God, controlling and creating each individual to fit the mold he desires. He takes advantage of his authority over the people and situations he encounters while wearing a facade of integrity and compassion to disguise his wily intentions and to retain love and respect.

In Act I of the play, Prospero finally tells Miranda the woeful story of how she and he arrived on the island. From the beginning, Prospero plays his subjects and his sympathetic audience as pawns in his game of manipulation. He explains that twelve years ago he was the Duke of Milan, but being enthralled with his studies, he left most of the governmental responsibilities to his brother Antonio. Antonio, hungry to be "Absolute Milan" himself, proceeded to betray him with the help of King Alonso of Naples. When Miranda asks why they were not killed, Prospero sighs, "Dear, they durst not, / so dear the love my people bore me." From the beginning, Prospero portrays himself as a distinguished scholar and beloved leader unjustly victimized by his power-hungry brother. Who would suspect such a humble man of being psychologically manipulative? Prospero succeeds in deceiving many with this credible guise.

Auden's long poem derived from *The Tempest* is a definition of relations between the mirror of art and the sea of reality, and the role of the spirit and faith as regards both. Indeed, he said the poem was about the Christian conception of art.

Preface: Considers the limits of art and art's difference from life beginning with audience psychology: art moves us but does not affect the will; and while art may be "unreal," the "real" world is also illusory.

I. Prospero to Ariel: Bids adieu to imagination; renounces the aesthetic for the religious (see Kierkegaard, Søren). Art has no privileges; art is escape, magic, and a denial of reality that can mask truth and numb pain. Art (magic) tempts Antonio to treason and demand's Caliban's devotion. Other characters have been hunted until they found themselves rejects, in traps of youth — and here Auden considers the difference between play and work — but now they can accept the egoless life for a life of faith.

II. The Supporting cast, sotto voce: Antonio is wicked, usurping his brother (Auden in a letter to Isherwood called him Iago-Antonio); he is an unchanged ironist who scoffs at others' changes. His revenge is to prevent Prospero's return to innocence. Ferdinand is reverent to Miranda whom he loves. Stephano is a drunken butler and contrast to Ferdinand. Gonzalo is the good old man of the island; he encourages pomposity and magic. To leave the island is to reassert reality, which is to be avoided. Alonso, seeking balance (and echoing Whitehead's terms of triviality and vagueness), speaks of Ferdinand's unprincely behavior and much more: The sea is flesh and senses potentiality and subjectivity; the desert is the mind, abstract thoughts that tempt one to ignore human limitations. The sea and the desert can find balance only if the desert dries lust, and the sea dissolves pride. The sea nor desert recognizes nor cares about "nobility." This is a warning against pride and a reminder of mortality. To succumb to the temptations of pride is to become like all "the unjust kings." Yet, there is difficulty in holding to a middle "way." One must not have regrets but learn to be better. Sebastian had tried to kill Alonso but was prevented by Ariel and now rejoices in his defeat and exposure: "It is defeat that gives proof we are alive." Miranda: speaks with fairytale imagery and the need to reflect on life; she is limited, vulnerable as she is reminded about Prospero's misgivings over how she and Ferdinand would cope in the real, that is, non-island world.

III. Caliban to the Audience is written as a prose pastiche of the late style of Henry James, which has ideas imbedded in its circuitous verbosity. Paul Tillich's concept of the demonic informs Caliban's speech in *The Sea and the Mirror*, in which primitive energy and anarchic impulse are nearly — but not quite — concealed by the refined prose of James. Here Auden debates art and life as illusion vs. reality, and this style, removed from reality by its own technique, frames the argument.

Caliban speaks to the audience and to Shakespeare, the author of *The Tempest*. The audience wishes to keep the distinction of art and life; art's intrusion into life is an insult to reality because it is an obstacle to the audience's escape through art by reminding them of the real world. *Juxtapositions* of Caliban/Ariel, Sea/Desert, Alonso/Ferdinand, deed/sensation, word/abstraction, are an attempt to recover the lost Eden of childhood. If the realms of art and reality are confused, this can lead to dire consequences. A message to prospective poets is the topic of the poet as citizen in the world. What effect does the poetry have on the poet? If the poet finds public success, will seduction follow that tempts the poet to compromise in order to please the audience instead of pleasing himself by making sincere art? If he becomes addicted to applause, will he be enslaved to compromise?

What does the audience want from art? Transcendence. To where? If one would realize the religious, mystical nature underlying reality, then art becomes a medium to the spiritual that guides one to, but does not substitute for, a true spiritual quest to return to the childhood sense of Eden to be found in adult faith. Caliban is like Hermes, an individualist; Ariel is like Apollo, a manager. Caliban would like to be a Cupid to the world and offer love and frivolity; yet, there must be a balance so that when the noise of frivolity becomes the ennui of reality, Ariel, the manager can balance the swaying scale.

Caliban returns to the plight of the artist and real life vs. the divine. The artist cannot represent both the divine and the truth, which in fact is the condition of human estrangement from truth. The mirror that divides the individual from himself, and the proscenium that divides audience from the stage — and metaphorically, all art — signify the gap. The artist must be aware of "fooling" people into thinking art is a bridge to the "other," that is, the spirit, if these people will mistakenly substitute art for a sense of pseudo-spirit instead of finding the true spirit through genuine faith.

Postscript: Ariel speaks to Caliban: Ariel equals inhuman perfection, and Caliban, human imperfection; Ariel would prefer to be Caliban. Auden said to Isherwood, "it's OK to say that Ariel is Chester [Kallman], but Chester is also Caliban ... Ariel is Caliban seen in the mirror." (See also *The Enchafèd Flood*.)

Secondary Worlds

For Auden, the desire for truth seeks dual paths to the same goal. "Present in every human being are two desires, a desire to know the truth about the Primary world, the given world outside ourselves in which we are born, live, love, hate, and die, and the desire to make new secondary worlds of our own or, if we cannot make them ourselves, to share in the secondary worlds of those who can" ("The World of the Sagas"). All human beings want to partake of a secondary world to temporarily (or permanently, for an autistic) relieve themselves of the everyday routine of the primary world. In simple daydreams, everyone imagines being the smart one, or the heroic one, or the one who saves the day and is loved and approved of by all.

For children of all ages imaginative myth-making is more pronounced in a context when there is a greater need to escape everyday reality. W.H. Auden, at age sixty-three, looked back at his childhood to explain a thought process that not only pertained to his own artistry, but to any artist.

> Between the ages of six and twelve I spent a great many of my waking hours in the fabrication of a private secondary sacred world the elements of which were (a) a limestone landscape, and (b) an industry — lead mining. It is no doubt psychologically significant that my sacred world was autistic, that is to say, I had no wish to share it with others.
>
> From this activity, I learned certain principles which I was later to find applied to all artistic fabrication. Firstly, whatever elements it may include, the initial impulse to create a secondary world is a feeling of awe surrounded by encounters in the primary world, with sacred beings or events. Though every work of art is a secondary world, such a world cannot be constructed exnihilo but is a selection and recombination of the contents of the primary world. I was free to select this and reject that, on one condition, that both were real objects in the primary world, physical im-

possibilities and magic means were forbidden. At this point I realized it was my moral duty to sacrifice aesthetic preference to reality or truth. When I began writing poetry, I found that the same obligation was binding. A poet must never make a statement simply because it sounds exciting; he must also believe it to be true. This does not mean that one can only appreciate a poet whose beliefs coincide with his own. It does mean that one must be convinced that the poet really believes what he says, however odd that belief may seem to oneself [*A Certain World*].

Auden asserts that an artistic secondary world will have no meaning if it is created from a realm that a reader cannot recognize as a possible truth. The need for a secondary world as a form of autistic escapism is a fact of human nature that children discover early. Fantasy as escapism is normal — on a temporary basis. Everyone, child or adult, wishes for temporary escapes from the everyday world. The more troublesome that everyday world is, the longer one spends in a secondary world, and the more complex the secondary world becomes. Majorities of people to some degree straddle both worlds, sometimes blurring the primary and secondary worlds into each other; it is the degree that one becomes absorbed in a secondary world, not the nature of the secondary world, that determines the fine lines between neuroses, psychoses, and insanity. (A severe autistic withdraws permanently into a secondary world; for him, there is no blurring of primary and secondary worlds because there is no primary world to the extent that what is meant by primary can be accessed and understood by the many, while the autistic's primary world is only understood by himself.)

For relatively normal children of any generation, fantasy escapes into secondary worlds are standard, and these escapes are elementary training for the subsequent coping mechanisms that children will need when they become adults. Human beings sometimes require themselves to be somewhere else physically or metaphysically. Very often that somewhere else is self-constructed within the inner world of the mind and not otherwise present in the outer world of the body. For the most part the average person keeps this secondary world to himself. Conversely, the artist is a person who usually chooses to make his secondary world available for public consumption.

The artist is prolonging his childhood with the sanction of others who give their approval to him because he is willing to share his creations with them. The artist gets to play his game of art and continue his child-like fantasizing, which is what all adults really wish to do in various vicarious ways. For non-artists one of these ways is through the artist's art. Non-artists love the artist because they can participate in his secondary world secondarily. The adult who is a child-like artist is viewed by his audience as a benefactor. The artist is a metaphorical child playing at a game and by extension his audience gets to play the game too. For the artist and the audience this play in a secondary world is a means to forget the work in the primary world. According to Auden, the impulse to create a work of art is felt when, in certain persons the passive awe provoked by sacred beings or events is transformed into a desire to express that awe in a rite of worship or homage, and to be homage, this rite must be beautiful. In poetry the rite is verbal, it pays homage by naming. "[A] child looks [at the moon] and for him this is a sacred encounter. In his mind "moon" is not a name of a sacred object but one of its most important properties and, therefore, numinous...."

"It is from the sacred encounters of his imagination that a poet's impulse to write a poem arises.... Every poem he writes involves the whole past.... But the encounter... must be suffered by a poet before he can write a genuine poem ... every poem is rooted in imaginative awe. ... [T]here is only one thing that all poetry must do; it must praise all it can for being and for happening" ("Making, Knowing, Judging").

Secondary Worlds 1968

A collection of essays, dedicated to Valerie Eliot, based on the commemorative T.S. Eliot lectures at the University of Kent in Canterbury. (See "The Martyr as Dramatic Hero"; "The World of the Sagas"; "Words and the Word.")

"The Secret Agent" see Poems

The Selected Writings of Sydney Smith see Smith, Sydney

"September 1, 1939" 1939

This poem was written in the manner of Yeats's "Easter 1916" as an attempt by Auden to emulate that poem's public outcry. "September 1, 1939" (written to account for the start of World War II) has been quoted frequently—particularly the line "We must love one another or die"—in the aftermath of the events of 11 September 2001. While a case is made that the poem fits that tragedy, there is an irony because Auden, a few years after writing the poem, deemed it to have lacked sincerity because he had written it for effect; he then banned it from future collections as he also did "Spain." Yet, it now seems to have the effect of being overwhelmingly appropriate and sounds more than sincere to readers who judge the words for themselves independent of the author who wrote them because, for the most part, they do not know of Auden's ban on these words. Mendelson, as Auden's literary executor, has respected the poet's wish to ban the poem from collections, but Mendelson, the Auden scholar, feels no restraint to discuss and quote the poem in Later Auden, which he does expansively. It is a "poem that begins in a drumbeat catalogue of despair and ends by soaring into affirmation...." For Auden it was the "soaring affirmation" part that later troubled him, as he didn't believe it when he wrote it. The poem contains the famous line about the 1930s having been "a low dishonest decade" because the Auden generation had failed to stop, with their words, the troubled events that led to World War II. Consequently, the Auden who soared at the end of "September 1, 1939" realized that he had been dishonest again. Yet, these words of affirmation resonate strongly since 9/11/01 so that 28 years after his death, Auden's self-described dishonesty seems true to readers who are now, following the tragedy, comforted by his words. While the irony of Auden's ban is profound the comfort is real; and while he would have acknowledged the irony, it is just as likely that he would not have quarreled with the comfort that he was able to give.

In 1964 Lyndon Johnson's campaign ran a now infamous commercial of a little girl threatened by nuclear destruction in which Auden's poem was paraphrased. This incident contributed to his ban.

Yet, E.M. Forster noted, "Because he once wrote 'We must love one another or die,' he can command me to follow him." (See also "First Things First.")

The Seven Deadly Sins see Brecht, Bertolt

"Sext" *see Horae Canonicae*

Shakespeare, William

In the truest sense of the word "pure," [Shakespeare] is the purest poet who ever lived; that is to say, he explored all of life through a single medium, that of language.

—Auden, "The Dyer's Hand," *The Nation*, 1939

1564–1616, English dramatist and poet, b. Stratford-on-Avon. He is considered the greatest playwright and literary influence in any language. He influenced all literature, artists and audiences, in every medium. Auden is included in the legacy and he gave Shakespeare his due in art, essays, and lectures.

His first plays in the 1590s are believed to be the three parts of *Henry VI*; *Richard III* is related to these plays as the final part of a first tetralogy of historical plays. Following these are *The Comedy of Errors, Titus Andronicus, The Taming of the Shrew, The Two Gentlemen of Verona, Love's Labour's Lost*, and *Romeo and Juliet* (for which Auden would write an introduction). Next Shakespeare wrote *Richard II, A Midsummer Night's Dream, King John, The Merchant of Venice*, Parts I and II of *Henry IV, Much Ado About Nothing, Henry V, Julius Caesar, As You Like It*, and *Twelfth Night*. The two parts of *Henry IV* feature Falstaff, who Auden writes about in the essay "The Prince's Dog."

Shakespeare's tragedies and the philosophical plays began in 1600 with *Hamlet*. He then wrote *The Merry Wives of Windsor*, which was written in response to Queen Elizabeth's request for another play with Falstaff, *Troilus and Cressida, All's Well That Ends Well, Measure for Measure, Othello, King Lear, Macbeth, Antony and Cleopatra, Coriolanus*, and *Timon of Athens*.

Othello (see "Joker in the Pack"), *Lear*, and *Macbeth* are contrasts of good and evil. *Coriolanus* and *Antony and Cleopatra* involve the study of politics, social history, and psychology.

The remaining four plays — *Pericles, Cymbeline, The Winter's Tale*, and *The Tempest*, from which Auden derived his long poem *The Sea and the Mirror* (with the subtitle A Commentary on Shakespeare's *The Tempest*) — are tragicomedies. They feature characters of tragic potential, but resemble comedy in that their conclusions have pleasing resolutions achieved through magic, with all its divine, humanistic, and artistic implications, which is why they appealed to Auden.

His characters are neither wholly good nor wholly evil, and it is their flawed, anti-heroic nature that makes them eternally compelling.

Shakespeare's poetry began with two narrative poems, *Venus and Adonis* (1593) and *The Rape of Lucrece* (1594). A love elegy, *The Phoenix and the Turtle*, was published in 1601, from which Auden takes the "Lords of Limit" phrase in his poems "A Happy New Year" (1932, unpublished but discussed in Mendelson's *Early Auden*) and "The Watchers" (1932). Shakespeare's sonnets are his most important nondramatic poetry, and Auden wrote an introduction to them in 1960. They were first published in 1609, although it is agreed that the poems were written sometime in the 1590s. The first 126 of the 154 sonnets are addressed to a young man whose identity has long intrigued scholars. The publisher wrote a dedication to the first edition that claimed "W.H." had inspired the sonnets. The dark lady of sonnets 127–152 has never been identified. The sonnets are noted for themes of beauty, youthful beauty ravaged by time, and the ability of love and art to transcend time and even death.

Auden admired Shakespeare for his art, but also for a sense that Shakespeare was a craftsman who didn't take his artistic gift or himself too seriously. At Oxford Auden read Shakespeare; later he recalled that at the time, Shakespeare's economy of the carefully "picked word" influenced him away from temptations to bombast.

In Auden and Isherwood's 1937 play *The Ascent of F6*, the protagonist, Michael Ransom, talks to a skull, as Hamlet does.

Auden biographer Humphrey Carpenter considers that when Auden wrote his 1960 introduction to the sonnets, his description of Shakespeare's "W.H." may also have described Auden's early and then later years with Chester Kallman. Said Auden, "He has selected someone at a stage of possibility. He wants to make an image so that the person will not be a dream but rather someone he knows as well as he knows his own interest. He wishes the other to have a free will yet his free will is to be the same as [his own]." As was his habit when writing introductions, reviews, and other criticism, Auden uses this introduction as a takeoff point for other ideas beyond the ostensible subject. In this case, Auden, besides discussing the sonnets, and his relation to Kallman, gives his views on Auden's mysticism.

The basis for Auden's introduction was a series of lectures he gave in 1946 at the New School for Social Research in lower Manhattan. (These lectures were published in 2000.) He talked about the plays in the order of their writing and did not hesitate to criticize them. Students enjoyed the lectures because Auden related the plays to their lives.

In 1957 at Oxford, Auden spoke about the use of music in Shakespeare.

Auden's work contained many allusions to Shakespeare. He took the title *The Dyer's Hand* from Shakespeare's Sonnet CXI, "My nature is subdu'd / To what it works in, like the dyer's hand." He would use the title three times: for a book review of Shakespeare in 1939, for a long essay in the *Anchor Review* in 1957, and for a collection of essays in 1962. With Kallman, Auden wrote a libretto for Nicolas Nabokov's opera *Love's Labour's Lost*. The line "The great quell" in Auden's "Nones" is spoken by Lady Macbeth when she plans to kill Duncan. ("The great quell" is the metaphorical noise and furor that may hide crime behind its tumult but is never loud enough to hide the crime from a guilty conscience.) The poem "Prime" alludes to

Henry IV with Shakespeare as pun-maker with the phrase "we owe god a death / debt...." In the poem "Plains" (from Bucolics) Auden's picture of "abominable desolation" alludes to the rapist's guilt in Shakespeare's Lucrece and evokes the idea that Auden's folly is the product of his own chaotic loves. "Down There," a poem in the sequence "Thanksgiving for a Habitat," is about a cellar, but Auden equates this cellar with ideas of danger that are directly from *Richard III*. In the poem "Forty Years On" (1968), one sees that Auden expresses himself best when he is Shakespeare in disguise. (The same idea is present in "Caliban to the Audience" from *The Sea and the Mirror* [194].) In this poem, an old Autolycus recalls *The Winter's Tale*, which Auden equates to his own world.

"Shakespeare: The Sonnets" *see* Kallman, Chester; Mysticism; Shakespeare, William

Shaw, George Bernard

1856–1950, Irish playwright and critic. The lengthy prefaces to Shaw's plays reveal the ideas behind the plays. In 1925 he was awarded the Nobel Prize in Literature.

Auden wrote an essay about Shaw, "Fabian Figaro" (1942). That is, on one level the essay was about Shaw, but as was his habit, Auden used the essay's ostensible subject as a forum for his personal views on another subject, in this case religion. A writer, says Auden, is great when he is both relevant in his time and also relevant for posterity. Shaw is both. Shaw's concerns were religion and politics, but Auden believed that Shaw omitted love from these concerns. According to Auden, Shaw was raised by unaffectionate parents as a Unitarian. For Auden, Unitarians see God as did the Greek philosophers, with God as a first cause but then an absentee landlord of the universe with the church as bailiff. After the church's rule, the original spiritual intuition of the holy word made flesh was imprisoned either in the rigid church organization of the Catholic Church or in the boy scouts of the Protestant Church.

Hence, individual spiritual intuition gave way to dogmatic teaching to willing followers. True Christian faith was abandoned to forms of propagandized politics and religion that were palatable to the "haves." The bohemian "have-nots" (artists and intellectuals) attacked the views of the "haves" and the suffering that resulted from the haves' institutions and policies. For artists and intellectuals, suffering is not a cause of genius but its guardian angel, compelling the use of talent to find freedom. Shaw with his artistic gift sought, in lieu of sex or money, the Good Life, and this goal almost turned him into a stoic without balance and almost into an apologist for fascism. For the worship of necessity and history Shaw substituted heroes such as Hercules and Prometheus who usurped their creator, God, which Shaw also sought to do; however, Auden notes, it is easy to be a hero on a private income as Shaw was. Shaw saved himself from his ego with a self-effacing humor. He never sought to be more than an artist. Says Auden, "Whatever pleasure and profit one derives from a work of art depends on what one brings to it."

Shelley, Percy Bysshe

1792–1822, English poet. He is considered one of the greatest English poets of the Romantic period, but not by Auden, who thought him floridly superfluous. Matthew Arnold labeled him an ineffectual angel with which Auden agreed. (From this remark by Arnold the American poet-novelist Elinor Wylie — who loved Shelley — wrote her 1926 novel, *The Orphan Angel*, with Shelley as the protagonist.) Shelley said that the poet could legislate the betterment of the world, which the American Auden could not abide for its egotistical self-importance that would lead a poet to write for effect rather than with sincerity, an Auden byword. Auden reviewed Herbert Read's *In Defence of Shelley*, and wrote that he thought the "bulk of Shelley's work, with the exception of a few short pieces, empty and unsympathetic." Auden continues in this review to make his case that a poet should be a "bit of a reporting journalist," and that Shelley was all abstraction without detail.

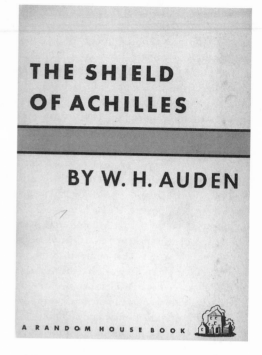

The Shield of Achilles, cover of first edition.

"The Shield of Achilles" 1952

In "The Shield of Achilles," a parable to modernity, the goddess Thetis comes to realize, when she takes her son to the underworld to receive a new shield from Hephaestos, that the "Iron-hearted man-slaying Achilles" is no more noble than a "ragged urchin," wandering about a vacant lot, throwing stones at birds. Girls are assaulted and knifed but who cares other than those who weep for them. (This is an echo of "Musée des Beaux Arts.") This poem is, in fact, about an ego-absorbed, vainglorious Truly Weak Man, a figure developed in the late 1920s by Auden and Isherwood and a precursor to the image of Tillich's demonic man. The Truly Weak Man's opposite is the Truly Strong Man who aspires to abnegate his will and merge into the collective good of Gerald Heard's evolving consciousness.

The poem's elegant interplay of ballad and rime royal stanzas, and its narrative "frame" of classical myth, eventually reveal a "modern condition" of extreme brutality and compassionlessness. Again and again, in its most compelling expressions, the poetics of Auden's

Christianity depend upon this particular theological understanding of humanity: whatever seems most cultivated, or most civilized, or most courageous, is likely to mask the demonic as these are all expressions of willfulness. The poem also symbolizes art and the human condition in a mock-heroic pose. This shows his audience, not the city but plains of modern life where dictators order multitudes. (In Auden's "Bucolics," the "Plains" are soulless and evil.) Barbed wire replaces ritual pieties where a cruel crucifixion is reenacted as juvenile sociopathy.—BRIAN CONNIFF

"A Shock" 1971

This poem is about Auden's being frisked for a weapon at the Vienna airport and his amazement, as he imagined he looked the least likely to be carrying one.

"A Short Ode to a Philologist" 1962

This poem was for J.R.R. Tolkien's retirement.

"A Short Ode to the Cuckoo" *see Thank You Fog*

Simmons, A.T.W. *see Thank You Fog*

Sincerity

Auden: "Sincerity in the proper sense of the word, meaning authenticity ... ought to be, a writer's chief preoccupation. Some writers confuse authenticity, which they ought always to aim at, with originality, which they never should bother about. There is a certain kind of person so dominated by the desire to be loved for himself alone that he has constantly to test those around him by tiresome behavior; what he says and does must be admired, not because

it is intrinsically admirable, but because it is his remark, his act. Does this not explain a lot of avant-garde art?" ("Poets, Poetry, and Taste").

"Sincerity is like sleep. Normally one should assume that, of course, one will be sincere, and not give the question a second thought. Most writers, however, suffer occasionally from bouts of insincerity as men do from bouts of insomnia. The remedy in both cases is often quite simple: in the case of the latter, to change one's diet, in the case of the former, to change one's company" ("Writing," *The Dyer's Hand*).

Auden's quick-test of a poet's sincerity was to ask: "'Why do you write poetry?' If the young man answers: 'I have important things I want to say,' then he is not a poet. If he answers, 'I like hanging around with words listening to what they say,' then maybe he is going to be a poet." To which Auden added, "a poet is before anything else, a person who is passionately in love with language" ("Squares and Oblongs").

Sino-Japanese War *see Journey to a War*

Sitwell, Edith and Sacheverell

1887–1964. The Sitwells are one of the most well-known literary families of the twentieth century. In addition to Edith, its members included Sir Osbert Sitwell, 1892–1969, English author, and Sir Sacheverell Sitwell, 1897–1988, English art critic. (It was Sacheverell who initially encouraged Auden to send his poems to Eliot.) All three Sitwells were interested in music, art, and literature. Dame Edith Sitwell was famous for her wit and her peculiar appearance. Among her important critical works are *Poetry and Criticism* (1925), *Aspects of Modern Poetry* (1934), and *A Poet's Notebook* (1943), a collection of aphorisms on the art of poetry that predates Auden's *Viking Book of Aphorisms*. Other prose works include *Alexander Pope* (1930); *The English Eccentrics* (1933); *I Live under a Black Sun* (1937), a novel about Jonathan Swift; and *Fanfare for Elizabeth* (1946) and *The Queens and the Hive* (1962). She was made dame of the British Empire in 1954.

At Oxford Auden dismissed all of the Sitwells in total, a rejection which may have been due in part due to the family's undeniable ties to the extreme of aristocratic Others, as the name went back 600 years and their features were decidedly Plantaganet. In 1932 he had tea with Edith, one of the darlings of the 1920s, who was not so keen on her seat being usurped by this darling of the 1930s. She had dismissed Auden's poetry when his *Poems* appeared in 1930. The tea was cordial and Auden reported that she was like one of his aunts. Both would return to Christianity, and this would foster a change in their mutual estimations. Later she approved of Auden's verse. They became friends and exchanged books; they also complained to each other about "fans."

Skelton, John

1460–1529, English poet and humanist. Many of his works are written in verse forms he himself devised, called Skeltonics. They consist of short lines and insistent rhymes, sometimes repeated through several sets of couplets; they also employ alliteration.

Skelton's "Skeltonics" became an influence on Auden's early poems with their clipped telegraphese style that was also influenced by Laura Riding. In 1932 Auden reviewed a new edition of Skelton for Eliot's *Criterion*. In 1935 Auden wrote an essay on Skelton for *The Great Tudors*, ed. Katherine Garvin. In the mid 1930s Auden was still willing to admire Skelton, and poets in general, for his role in shaping society. This would change after Auden's arrival in America.

Slick but Not Streamlined see John, Betjeman

Smedley, Agnes

1892–1950. While not often associated with the writers of proletarian literature of the 1920s and 1930s, Smedley published in the *Masses*, the *Nation*, *Modern Review*, and other leftist periodicals of the period. Moreover, in her novel *Daughter of Earth* (1929), she utilized Marxian, Freudian, and feminist insights and was rediscovered in the 1970s by a new generation of readers and writers. The novel was published anew in 1973 and in 1987 by the City University of New York's Feminist Press, as was a compilation of tracts from her several books in the volume *Portraits of Chinese Women in Revolution* (1976). In fact, her activism for China and her record of its history in the 1930s are Smedley's enduring legacies.

Auden and Isherwood met Smedley in 1938 during their *Journey to a War* in China. Isherwood wrote: "It is impossible not to like her and respect her, so grim and sour and passionate, so mercilessly critical of everyone, herself included — as she sits before the fire, huddled together, as if all suffering, all injustice of the world were torturing her bones like rheumatism. She has just suffered a great personal disaster. Her notes and photographs, taken during her latest visit to the Eighth Route Army, have all disappeared in the Chinese post. 'There's plenty of people,' she commented, darkly, 'who didn't want them to arrive....' Towards the end of our interview she appeared to soften a little. Auden's untidiness pleased her, I think. 'After all,' one could see her reflecting, 'they're [Auden and Isherwood] probably quite harmless.' 'Do you always,' she asked ironically, 'throw your coats on the floor?' Before we left she wrote us an introduction to the Hankow office of the Eighth Route Army."

Smith, Sydney

1771–1845, English clergyman, writer, and wit, ordained in the Church of England in 1794. He went as a tutor to Edinburgh in 1798, and with others founded the Edinburgh Review in 1802. The periodical was successful due in large part to his efforts. He moved to London in 1803, lectured on moral philosophy at the Royal Institution, and became a well-known figure in literary society. He was a defender of the oppressed. His wit has been compared to that of Swift and to Voltaire. This wit combined with spiritual devotion appealed to Auden, who would select and introduce *The

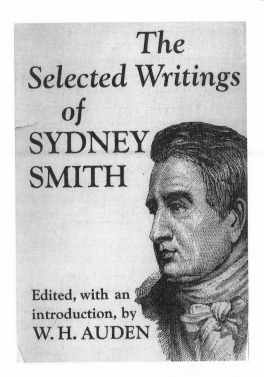

Selected Writings of Sydney Smith, cover of first edition.

Selected Writings of Sydney Smith (1956), with "Portrait of a Whig" which follows.

In his introduction to that volume, Auden wrote that Smith's wit was a counter to melancholia. He was a pragmatic intellectual, concrete rather than spectacular; he attacked intolerance and the clergy's dependence on Tory (aristocratic) patronage. He succeeded with luck and charm but not sycophancy. Even after he was made canon of prestigious St. Paul's, he maintained his rural parish where he had championed the poor farmers and workers. Smith was a polemical writer who could write for the "average educated man" as well as the "unlettered rustic and child." He was "lucid, well-informed, fair, diverse," poetic or plain as needed, always humorous, a perfect Whig with a liberal mentality that originated from his religious activism, but this activism was based in an institutional pragmatism that advocated organic change, not revolution, even though he believed even the king was not above natural and religious law. Auden then defines Smith's English liberalism of a limited sovereignty: 1) individuals are unique. Imposed uniformity is

tyranny; a flexible framework is best (beliefs prevent anarchy). 2) Conformity of outward behavior, not private belief; this is the individual's responsibility. 3) Violent change is as injurious as inertia. 4) Utopians are a menace; reform must be sensible. Auden compares Smith to Kierkegaard's Knight of Faith, a high compliment.

"The Song" 1956

The rebellious bird sings, as does the independent poet.

"Song of the Beggars" *see* "Twelve Songs"

"Spain" 1937

"Spain" is the best poem that Auden wished he had never written. He revised it in 1939 for the volume *Another Time*; kept it in his *Collected Poems* of 1944; regretted it; and banned the poem from any future collections beginning with *Selected Poems* in 1957. "Spain" is brilliant poetry, so why did Auden disavow it? He realized that regardless of his original good intentions, his sincere support of the anti-fascist loyalists in the Spanish Civil War, and his masterful artistry, he had written propaganda. Auden had the same feeling about "Spain" as he would have for his one and only political speech: "I just felt so covered with dirt afterwards." An argument has been made that Auden was too hard on himself. At the time George Orwell believed Auden deserved to be hard on himself. Orwell's criticism may have been a catalyst for Auden's self-criticism. Orwell's criticism concerned the end of the poem.

The opening of "Spain" is structured to signify Auden's idea of inclusive time as a perpetual continuum. He begins with alternations of "Yesterday" and "Today" then a focus on "Today" followed by alternations of "Tomorrow" and "Today." The past is the present is the future. The themes elucidated within this structure represent a concise version of the same themes in *Letter to Lord Byron* and *Look, Stranger*: the influence of history for good or ill, public and private spheres, responsibility for one's inner life. The first six stanzas summarize the history of the world. The last three of these six stanzas begin with "Yesterday" followed by a succinct capsule of a historical epoch, and each ends with "but — today the struggle." On the visceral level "the struggle" is the Spanish Civil War as the symbol of anti-fascism. The more subtle implication is the struggle of man attempting to place himself in the current context by asking of the past that it explain the present. Auden talks about history as that which operates and organizes, calling it "Time the refreshing River."

"Time the refreshing river" is the time that heals all wounds. This line is sonorously appealing and a wonderful image. Scientist Joseph Needham, a great admirer of Auden, would use this line as the title for a book of essays in 1943. However, Auden's intention for this line is not quite so positive. Time, as a river, is a linear view of time. Man tends to favor the past and postpone changes needed in the present until faced with dilemmas that those changes might have prevented, in this case, the advent of fascism. Auden moves away from the man-devised illusion of linear time and toward a sense of time, as the mystic understands it. A succinct definition of mystical time comes from Thornton Wilder: "It is only in appearance that time is a river. It is a vast landscape and it is the eye of the beholder that moves" (*The Eighth Day*). Time has no divisions; yesterday, today, and tomorrow are seen as one picture. This picture may be too large for the eye to encompass in a single glance, but it is still one image, not many divided.

Nonetheless, in 1937, today is today, and there is a crisis to be overcome. How will it be done? Who will find Justice? Auden's protagonist says that he will even if that means death. Spain is personified as he who must stand up and take responsibility for this crucial juncture in history, even if that means "he" must be sacrificed. This point in time has arrived due to past influences that confuse present minds. The past has become the present. Auden then contrasts today with the expectation that tomorrow will still come just as the "today" of the poem

is yesterday's tomorrow. He lists items both magnificent and mundane because in Huxley's Wholly Truthful art the magnificent and mundane arrive in tandem. After a litany of "tomorrows" Auden's first point is that, yes, tomorrow will be better than today, but his second point is that tomorrow will forget the past and not learn from it. If so, the past will repeat itself. Then Auden says again that for today there is only struggle. The possibility of death by conflict is great as well as the guilt that comes with causing deaths that are inevitable. These deaths will be determined by the use of power and propaganda. Nature will be ashamed to witness such deaths, but expediency requires that murder be done. All that will be left to the vanquished victims is a history that "May say alas but cannot help or pardon."

Auden's conclusion is that history, as an abstract monolith, doesn't give a damn. "In Spain's final words," Mendelson believes, "Auden indicates how deeply he abhors the idea of history in his own poem. What purposive history cannot give is pardon, a word that carries special force in Auden's vocabulary. Pardon has nothing to do with vague notions of courteous tolerance; it is the means by which one who is isolated by guilt or circumstance may be restored to wholeness and community. Other needs are vital — hunger and love — but as Auden implied before in 1934 [in his review of *The Book of Talbot*], it is 'our greater need, forgiveness, that matters most.' With all its powers, History cannot help or pardon; and the sense of the final two lines of Spain is that history cannot help or pardon the defeated, those whose need for pardon is greatest of all" (*Early Auden*).

History did not pardon the victims of the Spanish Civil War. In 1938, George Orwell, who fought in Spain, did not pardon Auden for writing about war in the abstract: "Mr. Auden can write about 'the acceptance of guilt for the necessary murder' because he has never committed a murder, perhaps never had one of his friends murdered, possibly never even seen a murdered man's corpse."

Auden apparently agreed. In his Foreword to *Collected Shorter Poems*, 1966, he writes:

A dishonest poem is one which expresses, no

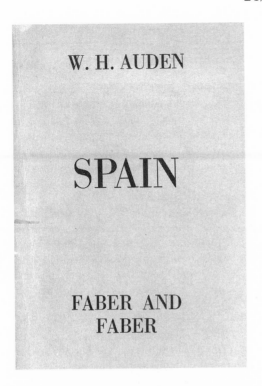

Spain, **cover of first edition.**

matter how well, feelings or beliefs which its author never felt or entertained…. I once wrote:

> History to the defeated
> May say alas but cannot help or pardon.

To say this is to equate goodness with success. It would have been bad enough if I had ever held this wicked doctrine, but that I should have stated it simply because it sounded rhetorically effective is quite inexcusable.

In art as in life, bad manners, not to be confused with a deliberate intention to cause offence, are the consequence of an over-concern with one's own ego and a lack of consideration (and knowledge of) others. Readers, like friends, must not be shouted at with brash familiarity. Youth may be forgiven when it is brash or noisy, but this does not mean brashness and noise are virtues.

On one hand, Auden was being too hard on himself. Mendelson believes that all of "Spain" expresses the dilemma faced by Auden and his generation: "By speaking for the Republic, he accepted a degree of complicity in the actions done in its name…. Other poets of the Spanish war had no trouble ignoring this uncomfortable truth; Auden insisted on facing it. Divided between the moral revulsion and what he felt to be his public obligations, he chose, almost despairingly, the 'conscious acceptance of guilt'" (*Early Auden*).

On the other hand, although Auden accepted his complicity in the fact that others had killed or been killed, he had not volunteered to fight. Ultimately, Auden had used art for propaganda or in his nomenclature "black magic." He had gone against his intuition and allowed the public sphere to motivate his ego into writing a poem that his private sphere couldn't accept. In Auden's perception, he had not been pure-in-heart; consequently, he had been Truly Weak. Perhaps as an atonement, in 1939 Auden would make a *Journey to a War* with Isherwood. (See also Caudwell, Christopher.)

Spanish Civil War

Auden's experiences in the Spanish Civil War (1936–9) are extremely difficult to reconstruct, but they continue to attract interest because they led him to write one of his most enigmatic and controversial poems. The Spanish interlude also marked, and arguably occasioned, Auden's break with the Marxist left and his gradual return to Auden's Christianity.

The Spanish Civil War began on 18 July 1936 as a nationalist army rebellion, backed by traditionalist forces within Spanish society, against the left-wing secularism of the Second Republic's Popular Front government. The outbreak of war also triggered a social revolution led by political forces to the left of the Madrid government. For three years, Spain was a vortex of all the principal contending ideologies in Europe: liberalism, socialism, Communism, fascism, anarchism, and Trotskyism. Consequently, thousands of international volunteers flowed into Spain, mainly to the Republican side. When Germany and Italy intervened on the side of General Franco's nationalists, and Soviet Russia backed the Madrid government, the Civil War assumed center stage in the deteriorating international situation. The conflict ended with the victory of the nationalist forces in 1939.

In Britain, the Spanish Civil War was the cause célèbre of the literary left, many of whose leading lights gave their support to the Popular Front—a broad and informal coalition of anti-fascist political forces. Although there were major literary figures on the right, this was what F.R. Leavis called the "Red Decade" in British literature. Auden, Stephen Spender, Cecil Day Lewis, Edward Upward, and Christopher Isherwood all expressed some degree of Communist sympathy, and Louis MacNeice was the only Audenite consistently skeptical about the prevailing intellectual climate of Marxism. In 1937, a survey of writers' views on Spain was published as *Writers Takes Sides on the Spanish War*, and Auden was one of the 127 (out of 149) respondents declaring themselves for the Republic.

Galvanized by support for the Spanish political experiment, by revulsion at the reactionary politics of the nationalists (epitomized by the murder of Spanish poet and playwright Federico Garcia Lorca), and by Byronic precedents of "warrior-poets," a number of literary figures volunteered to fight in the Republican cause. Many of them produced literary dispatches from the war. Others returned to fictionalize their experiences, or to write memoirs. And some lost their lives, including Ralph Fox, John Cornford, Christopher Caudwell, Charles Donnelly, and Julian Bell.

Auden was in Iceland with MacNeice when he first learned of the Franco rebellion. Around Christmas 1936 he told Isherwood that he intended to volunteer in Spain, preferably as an ambulance driver, but possibly as a soldier. His departure for Spain on 11 January 1937 was widely celebrated in the left-wing press. But the venture was a disappointment, not least to Auden himself. He neither fought, nor drove an ambulance. He never reached Madrid, and his time seems to have been spent in Valencia and Barcelona. He did, however, make a number of propaganda broadcasts on behalf of the Republican government.

Auden's subsequent refusal to discuss his Spanish experiences has left the way clear to his critics, who have represented his contribution as comic and ineffectual. The Communist journalist Claud Cockburn depicted Auden as a quixotic buffoon adrift in a situation beyond his comprehension. In a December 1937 *Spectator* article, Graham Greene, though himself sympathetic to the Republican cause, drew humorous parallels between the 1930s poet-volunteers and Tennyson's inglorious dabbling in Spanish liberal politics a century earlier. Others have made much of Auden's arrest by the Republican authorities for public urination.

Auden's frustration at his failure to contribute effectively to the Republican cause was compounded by his disillusionment with the cause itself. His one dispatch from the war, "Impressions of Valencia," published in the *New Statesman* on 30 January 1937, was unequivocally pro–Republican but written before he encountered the phenomena that were to induce his reevaluation. Auden later recalled that his discomfort at anti-clericalism in Barcelona confirmed that religion had never really lost its importance for him. He also criticized the British left for acknowledging neither the infighting on the Republican side nor the Soviet Union's manipulation of the war in its own ideological and strategic interests.

Nonetheless, upon his return to Britain, Auden continued to speak and write on behalf of the Spanish Republicans. His poem "Spain" was written between January and April 1937. Faber and Faber published it in May 1937, and its proceeds went to the Spanish Medical Aid Committee. Despite its vagaries and equivocations, "Spain" was a propaganda success and was read at many pro–Republican rallies. Yet it also drew criticism from across the political spectrum, and Auden himself was to regret and repudiate some of its content. He would later rewrite some lines, delete others, and eventually exclude the poem from collections of his work.

The ongoing controversy over "Spain" arises in two principal areas. The first is the ethics of killing. A reference to the necessity of murder provoked fierce condemnation in the form of "Inside the Whale," George Orwell's 1940 essay in which he accused Auden of glibly supporting ideological and partisan violence. Auden would always protest that the attack had been unjust, though he had modified the offending lines when the poem was revised as "Spain 1937," two years after its original publication. The second controversy concerns the poem's philosophy of history. Critics have disagreed over dialectical and voluntarist readings of "Spain," but the more serious issue is the apparent Realpolitik and consequentialism of the final stanza. Auden, in excluding the revised poem from a 1944 collection, conceded that his words implied a historical judgment in which morality was equated with success.

The literary significance of "Spain" is simply that it is widely regarded as the best poem in the substantial corpus of Spanish Civil War poetry. Its biographical significance is that it records a transitional moment in Auden's life and illustrates important tensions between his 1930s Marxism and the liberalism and Anglicanism of his earlier life.—PETER C. GROSVENOR

Spears, Monroe

Spears wrote the first book-length study of Auden in 1963, *Poetry of W.H. Auden; the Disenchanted Island*, and in 1964 edited *Auden: a Collection of Critical Essays*. Spears and poet William Meredith are co-executors of Auden's estate, while Edward Mendelson is the literary executor.

Spencer, Theodore

1902–1949, writer and critic, particularly of the Elizabethan era. Auden corresponded with Spencer about their mutual interests. Spencer saw *The Age of Anxiety* in manuscript and offered his advice to the author.

Spender, Sir Stephen

"From 1931 onwards, in common with many other people, I felt hounded by external events."
—Spender

1909–95, English poet and critic, b. London. His early poetry—like that of W.H. Auden, C. Day Lewis, and Louis MacNeice—was inspired by social protest. His autobiography, *World Within World* (1951), describes the 1930s. A member of the political left wing during this time, he was one of those who expressed their disillusionment with communism

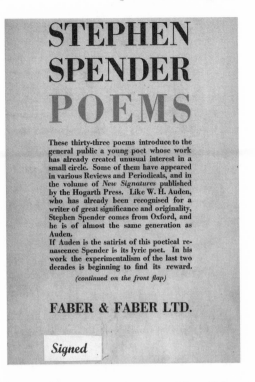

Poems by Stephen Spender, cover of first edition.

in the essay collection *The God That Failed* (1949). His verse is collected in such volumes as *Poems* (1933), *The Still Centre* (1939), *Poems of Dedication* (1946), *Collected Poems, 1928–1953* (1955), *Selected Poems* (1964), *The Generous Days* (1971), and *Collected Poems 1928–1985* (1986). *The Destructive Element* (1935), *The Creative Element* (1953), *The Making of a Poem* (1955), and *Love-Hate Relations* (1974) contain literary and social criticism. His other works include short stories *The Burning Cactus* (1935), the novel *The Backward Son* (1940), translations such as Schiller's *Mary Stuart* (1959), and sociological studies such as *The Year of the Young Rebels* (1969). He was co-editor of the magazines *Horizon* with Cyril Connolly (1939–41) and *Encounter* (1953–66). Spender was knighted in 1983.

In 1929 Isherwood met Spender (Stephen Savage in *Lions and Shadows*) through Auden who had shown Isherwood a story written by an Oxford undergraduate he had met. Both Isherwood and Auden thought the story quite good, as Isherwood wrote:

The story … described a young man's visit to the home of some male and female cousins. The young man is almost incredibly shy, gauche, tactless and generally neurotic; and his social shortcomings are exaggerated by contrast with the elegance, beauty and grace of his hosts. They appear to him as beings from another world; and his hopeless adoration of them fills him with self-hatred and despair. The cousins, on their side, are amused by the young man; they make fun of him, lightly, without malice; exposed to their unconsciously cruel mockery, he suffers tortures of humiliation — culminating in an extraordinary scene, in which, being unable to understand the simple mechanism of a folding card-table, he breaks down altogether and bursts into tears…. [*Lions and Shadows*].

Auden and Isherwood appreciated the protagonist, recognizable as an angst-driven victim of The Others. The neurotic cousin could have been Auden or Isherwood. "Having finished it," Isherwood said, "I agreed with Weston [Auden]: indeed the story was not quite like anything else I had ever read. You really cared about the problems of the blundering, tormented young man. The hero was so absorbingly interested in himself, in his own sensations and in everybody who came into contact with him that you couldn't help sharing his interest. In fact, the experience was so vivid as to be quite painful. You blushed for him, you squirmed at his every faux-pas; you wanted, simultaneously, to kick and protect and shake him" (*Lions and Shadows*). "The Cousins" would later appear in Spender's 1935 short story collection *The Burning Cactus*. Spender's story is psychologically autobiographical.

In 1929 Spender was quite abashed and honored to have Auden and Isherwood as friends, and just as insecure about keeping them as friends. Spender would purchase a hand press and print the first "volume" of Auden's poems, many of which ended up in the Faber & Faber first edition. Spender was the most politically active of the main trio, and wrote of strictly political matters in his book *Forward from Liberalism*; yet, he was not quite so active as C. Day Lewis or Edward Upward.

Spender did not go to America in 1939 and would never leave England permanently although he would make extended visits to teach at American universities. After Auden met Kallman, Spender was not so keen to see Auden and Kallman together but was happy to see Auden alone. As Auden got older and more of a curmudgeon Spender would write in his Journals that he had never seen anyone change so much from youth to old age and thought that he sometimes saw Auden out of respect for the past more than for the Auden of the present. He also regretted saying such things and remembered Auden's many kindnesses and generosity. Nonetheless, when Auden died, Spender was deeply affected and participated in arranging memorial events and edited *W.H. Auden: A Tribute*.

Spender's first books of poems and stories would not be published until 1933 and 1935 respectively. They were, however, written from 1927 forward while he was befriending Isherwood and Auden. Spender's themes are the Isherwood-Auden themes. Before his art was published, Spender was writing book reviews. In one of his earliest, written in 1930, one sees the practice of his generation to use the essay, even those on art, to express non-artistic views. In a Desmond MacCarthy book about famous people he has known (which Spender disliked in general because it was too much about The Others), Spender does admire the chapter on Henry James. (Spender regarded James highly, as did Auden at a time when James's reputation was in eclipse. Two years later Spender would contribute to a James revival and Spender's 1935 book *The Destructive Element* would proclaim James to have been the first modern writer.) Spender quotes MacCarthy who knew James personally. The choice of the quotation in the review tells as much about Spender — and his literary peers — as it does of Henry James:

It occurred after a luncheon party of which he had been, as they say, "the life." We happened to be drinking our coffee together while the rest of the party had moved on to the verandah. [James said] "What a charming picture they make…." In his attitude … I divined such a complete detachment, that I was startled into speaking out of myself: "I can't bear to look at life like that…. I want to be in everything. Perhaps that is why I can-

Stephen Spender

not write [fiction], it makes me feel absolutely alone." The effect of this confession on him was surprising…. "Yes, it is solitude. If it runs after you and catches you, well and good. But for heaven's sake, don't run after it. It is absolute solitude.

MacCarthy's sense of a "complete detachment" in James sounds like the cypher-witness (Auden-Isherwood) approach to writing, which is one of passive observation to be undertaken in an "absolute solitude." This does not mean physical solitude, but rather a solitude that reflects the inner detachment of the private sphere in order to observe the public chaos. More importantly, while the writer observes outwardly from within this sanctuary of inner solitude, he understands that each person observed in a public role also has an inner life that is separate from his outer life. (As regards the solitary observation of another's duality, James cited Hawthorne as the first modern writer.)

For Spender the conflict of an inner and outer life needs to be, if not always resolved, at least understood. Spender's art would also observe the conflict of inner and outer as reflected upon in solitude. Sometimes he would be the cypher-witness observing others; sometimes he

would be a more contemplative cypher-witness observing himself in order to learn from what he sees. In Spender's 1951 autobiography, appropriately titled *World Within World*, he looks back at his conception of the poet as it evolved for him in the late 1920s and through the 1930s: "The poet now became for me someone who rejects the preoccupations of the day, news, struggles for material gain, the machinery of society and even the apparatus for scholarship, by which men add stature to themselves, and who makes for himself a world out of timeless things, nature, and the beauty that he can create with his own imagination. He creates by virtue of the power that comes from the fullest realization of his own being. He does not add anything external to his personality: only that which will develop his inner life. However, my view of the poet was not solipsist. For I remember the thought striking me that to realize oneself to the fullest extent of one's powers means an entering into that which is beyond oneself."

The inner life became the governing principle of Spender's art and of the Auden generation. The inner life is not a retreat from the outer life; but command of the private sphere can come only when one no longer fears participating in the public chaos. This is a detachment from worldliness on a material level that allows one to be of the world but not in it. It is a Vedantic detachment that has often been misconstrued as indifference. The detachment aspired to by a Vedantist does not involve him cutting himself off from the world, but allows him to suffer less from the effects of the world. Inner calm allows one to have a greater participation in the world, not less, because one is no longer submitting the vulnerable ego for the world's approval. (Mysticism and art are similar means to the same end: transcendence.) In this state, Spender said, the poet was now a translator of the world which man projects around him through the actions of his will, back into language of the inner life of dreams and phantasy in which he has projected his materialistic external actuality." I believed now that everything which men make and invent is to some degree a symbol of an inner state of consciousness within them, as they are conditioned by their generation. Poetry was a use of language, which revealed external actuality as symbolic inner consciousness.... I began to realize that unpoetic-seeming things were material for poetry.... What excited me about the modern movement was the inclusion within new forms of material which seemed ugly, antipoetic and inhuman.... At Oxford I started writing poems containing references to gasworks, factories and slums. I understood the significance beneath the affectation of Auden saying that the most beautiful walk in Oxford was that along the canal, past the gas-works, and that the poet must go dressed like 'Mr. Everyman'" (*World Within World*).

Spender's "Mr. Everyman" acknowledged that simplicity and reality — or Huxley's Wholly-Truthful art — were the keys to the new poetry: "It was as though the twentieth-century writer had extended the range of his material, but in doing so had made the external world an object of interior sensibility. He had cast away the husk of its outwardness in attempting to digest it in his mind, and he had often become sick in the process. The hero of this literature was inevitably the *exceptionally sensitive person* [this author's italics], that is to say he who was most capable of receiving a wide range of impressions, most conscious of himself as a reviewer of impressions, and most likely to make use of his impressions as a means of cultivating himself rather than of acting upon the world" (*World Within World*).

The "sensitive person" who would "become sick in the process" of digesting the world was the anti-hero who underwent the trials of maturing from Truly Weak to Truly Strong. The writers of the 1930s did not create the Truly Strong and sensitive person; he had appeared already in the works of authors they admired such as James. They did, however, define this person as a model to be written about in their art and emulated in actuality. Auden's airman from *The Orators* (1932) learned little from the external world until he understood that his inner world was one connected to an undifferentiated unity. The authors of the 1930s would not only display sensitivity, but would, through parable-art and didactic essays, analyze the psychology of what "sensitive" meant. Could the sensitive man prevail over his weaknesses in order to become Truly Strong or would he re-

main "sick" and Truly Weak from the excess of the world and succumb to that excess? The implications of this view are metaphysical, but Isherwood, Auden, and Spender were not yet ready to make the leap into the spiritual. That would come later.

Spender's early poems reflect the view of poetry that he ascribed to them in 1951. In them, public issues and private feelings are intertwined with the ambiguity that a sensitive person (or highbrow) feels when struggling with his environment, especially an environment as tumultuous as the 1930s. The conflicts of inner and outer, public and private, hero and anti-hero, Truly Weak and Truly Strong, are reflected in Spender's poems. His first volume begins with very private poems and gradually turns to more public poems. Spender's poems, whether public or private, whether comments on the external world or introspection upon his internal self, are always about his perceptions. The world Spender depicts, inner or outer, is his world. Spender's self-portraits are a declaration of autonomy from his two best friends. Auden and Isherwood at this time were still writing as objective witnesses using the third person to imply a detachment that was not the case in actuality. Spender does not hesitate to be subjective and take blame or credit. The first person "I" is the definitive part of his repertoire.

The opening poems of the volume have been called the "Marston" poems. "Marston" is the male object of Spender's unrequited affection and is based on a real acquaintance. Spender recounts actual incidents with Marston. Isherwood and Auden, even when portraying themselves, did so most often in the third person, which obfuscates personal responsibility. Spender is not so cagey. He talks about the body being real which enemies can attack (the anxieties created by the ego); conversely, any positive gesture by the person whom one cares for can inspire new lines of poetry, which, in fact are written because Spender is afraid to say what he feels to the object of his desire. Instead he and his object walk the rolling hills, and "And this climbing was a monumental sign of country peace."

By the next day, however, doubt overcomes peace, and the emptiness of his room

"All splintered in my head and cried for you." Later there is a return to peace that includes Auden-esque urban-industrial images stimulated by a mere accidental touching of hands that triggers enough electricity to "give a city power, or drive a train."

More images from Auden country are also represented with images of soldiers, boundaries, rebels, mutinies, cigarettes, prisoners, bombs, machines, and that Auden staple, "gasworks."

Spender's "I" is not necessarily an egotistical "I" but a self trying to find its way among other selves. He says an 'I' can never be truly great as too much "I" is a measure of the ego's insecurity. Within the self are more than one "I." There is the "I" that eats, the "I" that loves, or gets angry, or excretes, or tries to make friends or find a lover. Yet each "I" can never be at peace if "I" can only think of "I." When the ego is abnegated then "all those other 'I's' … long for 'We dying.'"

The egotistical "I" is Truly Weak; the "I" who can also say "We" learns how to seek unity instead of separation and is Truly Strong. The ego is also an obstacle to love: "Ambition is my death…." Spender wonders how the temptation of materialism could ever obscure "The palpable and obvious love of man for man" (SP 48).

There is another poem that intimates that the child is father to the man, and that the unhappy child is father to a Truly Weak Man. Spender as a child hears his parents arguing in the next room, which causes him to weep: "I am your son and from bad dreams arise." This depicts a very personal past. The collective haunted past also pervades other poems. One escape route from the forbidding past or equally forbidding present is the creation of secondary worlds: "This writing is my only wings away." There is also sympathy for the unemployed who hang out on street corners: "I'm haunted by their emptiness."

Then there is recognition of Germany's new order and its victims. Spender writes that these real tests are rather more serious than schoolboy sports. Swimming and climbing are the Tests of the Truly Weak. In the New World of fascist threats these Tests are rendered foolish as understood by the Truly Strong Man. Compared to fascist oppression, swimming and climbing are not Tests, but games.

Two poems are particularly lucid on the theme of The Truly Weak and Truly Strong Man. In "What I expected," Spender states that he thought Tests — climbing, etc. — would make him strong; but he learns that these Tests were weakening his will instead of fortifying it. He realizes that pointless Tests of daring are for the Truly Weak when compared to the stoic suffering of the poor. Conversely, in the second poem, titled "I think continually of those who are Truly Great," Spender recognizes the Truly Strong whose only ambition is to sing of the joy found in the human spirit. The will of the Truly Strong should never allow the noise of the material world to drown out the call of the spirit, and when the Truly Strong complete their journey into spirit, they will leave, "the vivid air signed with their honor."

Spender's *Poems* continue the shift that Auden began to allude to in *The Orators*. Man will not find salvation in hero-worship, state-worship, or self-worship that is ego-generated. Salvation will come when the egoless worship of the collective Vedantic Self asserts its detachment from the material world's "noise and fog" that impede "the flowering of the spirit." To find this path, man must open his mind to the whole world, and not just the sense world that satisfies the body only. To do so, one must be sensitive to his inner life in order to pass through a learning process that begins in ego-bound weakness and ends in ego-less strength. For Spender and the Auden generation, the anti-hero had arrived to stay for the rest of the century.

"Sportsmen: A Parable" 1938

This essay is about the loss of community and the unrequited desire for its return. The sportsmen are poets; the hunted are their poems. This essay concerns the history of poetry. It coincides closely with Auden's view of history in the introduction to *The Oxford Book of Light Verse*, but "Sportsmen" is less optimistic.

"Squares and Oblongs" 1948

An essay in *Poets at Work*. The poetic vocation comes from a desire to do something that is not required but is play as compared to work. Only our will to give Christian love is mandatory as it is also God's will — but how? People worry much more about what is legal or illegal rather than what is right and wrong and play "cops and robbers" instead of "saints and sinners." Work is responsibility; play is the rebellious refutation of work by doing something that is a choice not demanded by the need for survival. Art is one of these choices. Yet, there is a gulf between frivolity (play) and seriousness (work) that is much more profound than mere games and that no child's game can bridge, for when an adult plays a game, unlike a child, he is very aware of this gap and in a way that a child, not yet faced with responsibility, never need understand.

A poet loves (plays) with language, courts it, and metaphorically endures the courtship, marriage, and divorce, as he goes through phases of his development: i.e. imitation of others precedes one's own style and themes, after which the imitated are "divorced." "Free verse" is lazy. Poetry is a game of knowledge about emotions and hidden relationships. Excessive imagery (floridity) is compensation for inadequate feeling. The contemporary poet works alone. A society, like a poem, is a brave new world. (See also Audience; Play and Work; Yeats, W.B.)

Starkie, Enid

1903–1970. Starkie was an English literary critic and professor at Oxford who was an authority on twentieth-century French writers, writing biographies of two who were of particular interest to Auden — Rimbaud and Gide. In 1955 Starkie nominated Auden to follow C. Day Lewis as professor of poetry at Oxford. She led a faction that believed the post should go to a poet rather than a literary critic. Harold Nicolson was the choice of the "critic" faction, led by Maurice Bowra, including some who still resented that Auden left England and said so. Auden's supporters included E.R. Dodds, Nevill Coghill, and Lord David Cecil. Auden was elected for a term of four years. His first lecture was "Making, Knowing, Judging."

Gertrude Stein

Stein, Gertrude

1874–1946, American author and patron of the arts, b. Allegheny (now part of Pittsburgh), Pa. She influenced many literary and artistic figures. From 1903 until her death she spent most of her life in Paris. Stein's own innovative writing was marked by unconventional meanings, grammar, and syntax to evoke "moments of consciousness, independent of time and memory."

Early on as a student at Oxford, Auden thought Stein extraordinary with her unique view on the use of language, and Stein-like phrases and syntactical legerdemain appeared in some of his early poems. Shortly after, he would dismiss her, although he didn't abandon her outright. Stein (along with Eliot, Lawrence, St-John Perse, Yeats, Baudelaire, and who knows how many others) emerges as a parody in *The Orators*. Even to refute Stein, however, is to acknowledge that one will learn by not doing as she did. Indeed, many of Stein's admirers admired her work but never adopted her methods. Stein figures obliquely to Auden: "Cyril Connolly once asked Chester, whom he regarded as a parasite on Auden: 'How does it feel to be Alice B. Toklas to Gertrude Stein?'" (Carpenter, W.H. Auden). In 1941 Auden softened a bit when he reviewed Stein's *Ida*, and did so "In an affectionate parody of Stein's voice ('That is what Ida is. I like Ida')" (Mendelson, *Later Auden*).

Stern, James and Tania

James Stern, 1904–1993, writer, b. in Ireland. James settled in England in 1961 with his German-born wife Tania Stern. Auden and Isherwood praised Stern's writing during the late 1930s, and John Lehmann published him in *New Writing*. In 1934 he met Tania Kurella who left Germany in 1933. When they married in 1935 in London, Tania Kurella was given away by Freud's son Ernst, whom she had known since childhood. (The Sterns later were to translate together an important selection of Sigmund Freud's letters.) In 1937 they met Auden. In 1941 Stern collaborated with Auden on a radio version of D.H. Lawrence's *The Rocking Horse Winner*. In 1944 Auden dedicated *The Sea and the Mirror* to the Sterns. In 1945, Auden and James Stern were accepted for the newly formed United States Strategic Bombing Survey. During the mid 1940s, the Sterns and Auden shared ownership of a tarpaper shack on Fire Island, called Bective Poplars. In 1947 Auden had a cameo as "Merwyn" in Stern's novel *The Hidden Damage*. Stern contributed to Stephen Spender's *W.H. Auden: A Tribute* (1974).

Auden's letters to the Sterns are now in the Berg Collection at the New York Public Library. These letters provided Rupert Davenport-Hines with the impetus to write a new biography, *Auden*, in 1995.

Stewart, J.I.M.

John Innes Mackintosh Stewart, 1906–94, British writer and scholar at Oxford, b. near Edinburgh. Under his own name he wrote novels, short stories, and such critical studies as *Character and Motive in Shakespeare* (1949), *Rudyard Kipling* (1966), and *Thomas Hardy* (1971). As Michael Innes he wrote more than forty detective stories featuring John Appleby, a gentleman turned policeman. He knew Auden when both were undergraduates at Oxford. Later, when Stewart became Michael Innes, Auden, the mystery fan, became an Innes fan. Much later, when Auden returned to Oxford to live near the very end of his life, they renewed their acquaintance.

Stravinsky, Igor

1882–1971, Russian-American composer, Stravinsky helped to revolutionize modern music. Stravinsky's first distinctly original compositions—*The Firebird* (1910) and *Petrouchka* (1911)—were written for Diaghilev's *Ballets Russes in Paris.*

The ballet *The Rite of Spring* (1913), is a great influence on modern music. At the beginning of World War I, Stravinsky moved to Switzerland and composed several works based on Russian themes, including the ballet *The Wedding* (1923). Influenced by eighteenth century music, he wrote in an austere, neoclassical style in the dance-drama *The Soldier's Tale* (1918), the opera-oratorio *Oedipus Rex* (1927) (text by Jean Cocteau after Sophocles), and the choral composition *Symphony of Psalms* (1930).

Stravinsky became a French citizen in 1934, but five years later he moved to the United States and became an American citizen in 1945. Compositions of the 1940s include the *Ebony Concerto* (1946) for clarinet and swing band; the *Third Symphony* (1946) in three movements; the ballet *Orpheus* (1948); and a mass (1948) for voices and double wind quintet.

After composing the opera *The Rake's Progress* (1951), inspired by Hogarth's engravings, with libretto by Auden and Chester Kallman, Stravinsky turned to experiments with serial techniques in *Cantata* (1952) and in the chamber piece *Septet* (1953). He continued to compose in this way for the ballet *Agon* (1957) and in *Threni* (1958), for voices and orchestra. Lectures he gave at Harvard were published as *Poétique Musicale* (1942, tr. Poetics of Music, 1948).

Auden's 1971 essay "Craftsman, Artist, Genius" was a tribute to Stravinsky (reprinted as "A Tribute" in *Forewords and Afterwords*). (See also *The Rake's Progress.*)

"A Summer Night" 1933

This poem was written in August of 1933 after a summer night when Auden had a mystical revelation that would shape the rest of his life. The poem is about mystical unity and the totality of existence as the mystic sees it; like the mystic, however, one must go through stages of reconciliation from the particular to the universal, from the secular to the spiritual, before one can sense the totality that each step leads to.

Stanza 1 introduces the scene. In Stanza 2 he says, "Lucky this point," to signify the unearthly confluence of time and nature, more unwilled than willed. In 3 he senses that things are both hidden and exposed in a circle that is unbroken in the spirit that he and his companions are feeling. Throughout stanzas 1–8 the effect of a new Garden of Eden is evoked. In 4 Auden is free from any fear of life or death, and he feels only love. In 5 he gives his sense of both looking out at the universe and having the universe look back. Stanza 6 notes that the divergence of directions seems to have merged in a transcendental unity observed by the moon. In 7 the moon sees all existence at once and as one entity, and private faces become public by dropping their masks as their fears and vulnerability are set aside. In 8 he says this secure feeling should be recalled in the future when one fears letting love in. Stanza 9 observes that with this feeling noted in stanza 8 one does not know or recall that there is pain in the world. Stanzas 9–16 evoke a New Jerusalem that can be possible if all can experience this feeling of transcendental unity. Stanza 10 recognizes the division of the cloistered few and the wretched many. Stanza 11 hopes that this inner world will find life in an outer revolution. Stanza 12 knows that one could trade all materiality for such a feeling. Stanza 13 recognizes that the dam of consciousness that now protects them must and will give way to let normal life "flood" them again. In 14 when the Leviathan (the normal world) is struck down, one can build a new city with a collective love (echoes Stanza 4). In 15 the old life will drown

and the flood will give rise to a new order; private and public love will become one. In 16 the word love is never spoken, as if saying it would lose the feeling of it, which is much more important than saying it without meaning it. (See also Mysticism.)

Sympathy

Auden: "A universal art can only be the product of a community united in sympathy, sense of worth, and aspiration; and it is improbable that the artist can do his best work except in such a community." The most lasting, meaningful exchange between artist and audience is when it is based on a genuine sympathy and not faux sympathy, which is not about the artist but about manipulation of the audience by the artist as the end in itself. This is why Auden also said, "There is only one general rule and that is sincerity, which is easy to say, but impossible to obey perfectly" ("Poets, Poetry, and Taste").

"T the Great" *see* "Makers of History"

The Table Talk of W.H. Auden 1991

Alan Ansen met Auden in 1946 while taking the poet's Shakespeare class at the New School in Manhattan and offered to help Auden as secretary, to which Auden agreed only if he could pay Ansen. In 1947 Auden commissioned Ansen to create a table of events that is included in the Auden-edited *The Portable Greek Reader*, and later to do the same for the five volume *Poets of the English Language*, co-edited with Norman Holmes Pearson. Ansen and Auden became friends and Ansen was Auden's audience for a variety of observations that Ansen recorded. "Between November 1946 and April 1948 ... Ansen filled four bound composition books and eighty closely typed sheets (now in the Auden Archives, New York Public Library) as he dashed down what he remembered Auden saying. *The Table Talk of W.H. Auden* has been quarried from those pages" (N. Jenkins, "Fore-word" to *Table Talk*...). The book was published in 1990 and edited by Nicholas Jenkins with an introduction by poet Richard Howard. Auden's "table-talk" (after E.M. Forster's writing technique in a phrase coined by Edward Upward) is a delightful and fascinating display of Auden relatively unguarded while he ranges from people, to poetry, to events, and himself.

"Talking to Dogs" *see Thank You Fog*

"Talking to Mice" *see Thank You Fog*

"Taller Today" *see Poems*

Tao *see* "Many Happy Returns"

Telling

Auden: "The first half of art is perceiving. The artist is the person who stands outside and looks, stands even outside himself and looks at his daydreams.

"The second half of art is telling. If you asked any artist why he works ... he would say, "to make money and to amuse my friends" ("Poets, Poetry, and Taste").

"Behind the work of the creative artist there are three principal wishes: the wish to make something; the wish to perceive something either in the external world of sense or the internal world of feeling; the wish to communicate these perceptions to others" (*Oxford Book of Light Verse*).

"Tennyson" *see* Tennyson, Alfred

Tennyson, Alfred

1809–92, English poet, representative of the Victorian era. At Cambridge, Tennyson wrote *Timbuctoo* (1829) and *Poems, Chiefly Lyrical* (1830), and began his close friendship with Arthur Hallam. His volume *Poems* (1832) included some of his best known work. In 1833 he grieved the sudden death of Hallam. Tennyson's next published work, *Poems* (1842), was evidence of his philosophic doubts and his wish for a sustaining belief. *Princess* (1847) was followed in 1850 by *In Memoriam*, which records Tennyson's years of doubt and despair after Hallam's death. That same year he was appointed poet laureate. Occasional poems, including *Ode on the Death of the Duke of Wellington* (1852) and *The Charge of the Light Brigade* (1855), were part of his duties. The first group of *Idylls of the King* appeared in 1859; it was expanded in 1869 and 1872, and Tennyson added the final poem in 1885. He arranged the 12 poems chronologically in 1888 to chronicle King Arthur. He was a popular and a critical success, and was revered by the public.

Auden remembered his father reading *In Memoriam* to him when he was a child and this influence remained with the poet Auden, which, indeed, was augmented by his father's opinion that Tennyson was a model in his role as a poet for his age, a model that his son might emulate. Auden did not see Tennyson as his role model and he was not quite sure of where he placed Tennyson in his overall poet's hierarchy. In 1944 Auden introduced ("Tennyson") and chose *A Selection from the Poems of Alfred, Lord Tennyson*, in which Auden, while giving Tennyson credit as the English poet with "the finest ear," also said of him that he was "undoubtedly the stupidest" English poet as well. An uproar ensued from Tennysonians who wondered why Auden bothered doing the book if he disliked Tennyson so much. Auden answered, in effect, that he wouldn't have done the book if he didn't like Tennyson and seemed to believe that "stupidest" applied to one aspect of Tennyson — his role as a moralist trying to teach an ideal life in *Idylls of the King* — and he preferred the Tennyson of personal feeling of *In Memoriam*. Mendelson observes that during this period "Auden's prose continued ... to adjudicate between two ideas of the artist, the autonomous romantic hero and the responsible moral educator" (*Later Auden*).

"Terce" *see Horae Canonicae*

The Test *see* Auden's Generation

Thank You Fog 1974

This was Auden's last volume of poems, written 1969–1973 and published posthumously. Auden biographer Edward Mendelson observes that the poems here, as well as others written just before this volume, "are spoken to — not, as before, spoken about — silent objects, persons absent or dead, and the untalkative species" As examples Mendelson offers "A New Year Greeting" (1969), written to the microorganisms in Auden's own body; "Talking to Dogs" (1970); "Talking to Mice" and "Short Ode to the Cuckoo" (1971); "A Lullaby" (1972), addressed to himself going to sleep; "A Curse," speaking to the automobile; "Ode to Diencephalon," addressing the region of the brain that controls automatic responses; "Address to the Beasts.'" There are more poems of this kind and poems to proverbial persons but to no one exactly, as if Auden were talking to himself for lack of anyone else, which often was the case. One could say that these last poems do indeed signify a voice without an audience, forced to converse with animals, inanimate objects, and imaginary anonymous no ones. On the more positive side one might say that Auden's addresses to disembodied or natural or proverbial persons brings him back full circle to one of his earliest teenage influences: the mystical poems of AE.

"A Thanksgiving" 1969

This poem thanked all of the poets who had influenced Auden.

"Thanksgiving for a Habitat" *see About the House*

"Their Lonely Betters" 1950

Contrast between the human and the natural begun in *Nones* and later expanded in *Homage to Clio*. The natural world does not have a voice that concerns itself with the past or future as humans do.

"There Will Be No Peace" 1956

Modern paranoia as symbol of alienation, isolation.

"They" 1939

The proverbial They in a vicious cycle of opposites clashing; the good becomes evil becomes good becomes evil depending only on the eye of the beholder. One man's evil is another man's crusade, and the Public will follow with herd intoxication. Auden makes a reference to the "crooked" (gay) who are afraid to be "straight," which refers to himself. When the poem first appeared, Auden followed it with an epigram from Dante's *Purgatorio* about "they" who are condemned for the sin of envy.

"This Loved One" *see Poems*

"This Lunar Beauty" *see Poems*

Thomas, Dylan

1914–53, Welsh poet, b. Swansea. His *Eighteen Poems*, published in 1934, made him famous, and was followed by *Twenty-five Poems* (1936), *The Map of Love* (1939), *The World I Breathe* (1939), *Deaths and Entrances* (1946), and *In Country Sleep* and *Other Poems* (1952). His published prose is collected in *Portrait of the Artist as a Young Dog* (1940), *Adventures in the Skin Trade* (1955), and *Quite Early One Morning* (1955). In addition he wrote for the radio *A Child's Christmas in Wales* (1954), and his dramatic work, *Under Milk Wood* (1954), which records life in a small Welsh town. Thomas drank heavily. His third tour of the United States ended in his death. The autobiography of Thomas's wife, Caitlin Thomas, *Leftover Life to Kill* (1957), and the account of the Thomases' tours by J.M. Brinnin, *Dylan Thomas in America* (1955), describes his last years.

Thomas's copy of Auden's *Poems* (1930) is well read and patched with tape. (It is now at the University of Texas, Austin.) In the 1937 special Auden issue of New Verse, Thomas wrote, "I think [Auden] is a wide and deep poet ... and as potentially productive of greatness...." For Thomas's last illness Auden "sat with him in hospital, when he was in an oxygen tent, and, following his death, was a signatory to a public letter appealing for funds to pay the funeral expenses and medical bills, and keep Thomas's family from poverty" (Carpenter, *W.H. Auden*).

Thomas, Edward

1878–1917, English poet. He began his literary career writing essays, travel books, and critical studies. His friendship with Robert Frost, which began in 1912, turned him to writing poetry, primarily on nature themes. His first volume of verse, *Six Poems* (1916), mostly pastoral verse, was published shortly before he was killed in World War I.

Thompson, John

1906–65. A British psychoanalyst Auden befriended at Swarthmore who was the model for Malin in *The Age of Anxiety*. Thompson was also a close friend of Dorothy Day.

Threepenny Opera see Brecht, Bertolt

"Through the Looking-Glass" 1934

In this poem the mirror metaphor signifies division and refers to Lewis Carroll's Alice books as an illusion. Auden's boyhood security is lost but has not yet been replaced by maturity. This was written six months after "A Summer Night," but the love of that poem is still missing. A "glowing hearth" signifies a wish for domestic bliss with a partner. Lost between the child's security and early-adulthood insecurity, there is no satisfaction, and the mind projects fantasies that obstruct a search for true love. These fantasies are a yearning for childhood that only a new "character" in the fantasies — a real lover — can provide; yet, one cannot turn fantasy into idolatry (sex), and it would be better to be chaste if one could resist temptation. The ego blocks maturity, as it is easier to be immature as it entails less responsibility for one's actions, but immaturity also obstructs true love. The ego is pleased with the safety of its own isolation, but displeased that the ego, by its unwillingness to suffer, will not take the risk of finding true love that would bring comfort instead. The ghosts of "mother and father" both inhabit and inhibit the psyche from moving forward.

Tillich, Paul

1886–1965, American philosopher and theologian, b. Germany. He taught theology until he was dismissed in 1933 because of his opposition to the Nazi regime. In the same year, at the invitation of Reinhold Niebuhr, he went to the United States and joined the faculty of Union Theological Seminary. In 1954 he became a professor at Harvard; in 1962 he became a professor of theology at the University of Chicago. His theological system embraced the concept of "the Protestant Principle," according to which every Yes must have its corresponding No, and no human truth is ultimate. Faith, to Tillich, was "ultimate concern," and God was "the God above God," the "Ground of Being" (see Mysticism for the Divine Ground of Huxley's Minimum Working Hypothesis), or "Being-Itself." New Being, rather than "salvation," should be the human goal. Tillich incorporated depth psychology and existentialist philosophy into his system and considered them essential elaborations of Christian doctrine. He aimed at a correlation of the questions arising out of the human condition and the divine answers drawn from the symbolism of Christian revelation. The great questions, in his classification, dealt with being, existence, and life. His writings include *The Interpretation of History* (1936), *The Protestant Era* (1948), *The Shaking of the Foundations* (1948), *Systematic Theology* (3 vol., 1951–63), *The Courage to Be* (1952), *Love, Power, and Justice* (1954), *Biblical Religion and the Search for Ultimate Reality* (1955), *The New Being* (1955), *Dynamics of Faith* (1957), *Christianity and the Encounter of the World Religions* (1963), *My Search for Absolutes* (1967), *My Travel Diary: 1936*, ed. by J.C. Brauer (1970), and *A History of Christian Thought*, ed. by C.E. Braaten (1972). (See also Christianity.)

Tolkien, J.R.R.

1892–1973, British novelist. A fantasy writer, John Ronald Reuel Tolkien wrote *The Hobbit* (1937), adapted from stories he told his children. His characters reappear in *The Lord of the Rings* (1954–55), a trilogy in which he details the life, history, and cosmology of the mythological Middle Earth, and for which he invented several languages, most notably Elvish. He was also a respected medieval scholar. Auden was one of the first to recognize — and publicize — the merit of Tolkien's fiction, and the elaborate Secondary Worlds that Tolkien created were in line with much of the reading Auden enjoyed as child, adolescent, and adult.

In 1962 Auden wrote "A Short Ode to a Philologist" for Tolkien's retirement. In the spring of 1966, popular interest in the writings of J.R.R. Tolkien was at its height. Much to his annoyance, the aging Oxford philologist had become a cult figure among the young. Mushroom-eating, costumed, Middle Earth-inspired "Tolkien Societies" had sprung up everywhere. And just at that time W.H. Auden stopped writing a booklet he had contracted to write, a critical appraisal of Tolkien's work. He stopped work because Tolkien himself insisted that he stop. And the main factor that deprived the world of a sustained 48 pages of Auden on Tolkien, it now seems certain, was a single sentence spoken by Auden. Ironically, it was the

year of the publication of Auden's *About the House*, and the doomed sentence was, of all things, a sentence about J.R.R. Tolkien's house.

He had published review essays on Tolkien's works as they appeared, was in fact one of the first reviewers to recommend these books as major achievements of historical imagination. A few months after the contract was signed, Auden said that he could not finish the book. Professor Tolkien (who was always referred to under his academic title by Auden, a former student) had asked him not to, and that was that. The somewhat puzzling rift between these men from February through April of 1966 was not so much about Auden's credentials as about that comment he had made, or was reported to have made, about Tolkien's house. The Eerdmans' office, trying to put things back on track, kept bumping into what was called "the house thing." Tolkien's stern letter to Auden, now in print in *The Letters of J.R.R. Tolkien*, makes a vague reference to "reports" that had displeased Tolkien about Auden's visit to a meeting of a Tolkien Society in Brooklyn. The "press reports" turned out to be reports in the London papers of an off-handed little item in the *New Yorker* about a meeting of the Tolkien Society in Brooklyn to which Auden, arriving late, addressed a few remarks. What was briefly quoted said really nothing about Tolkien's "views" or biography or "opinions." Auden was reported to have said (*New Yorker*, January 15, 1966) that Professor Tolkien "lives in a hideous house — I can't tell you how awful it is — with hideous pictures on the walls." That this was the offending piece, and that it was the major irritant in Tolkien's outcry against the projected book, was made clear in Tolkien's second letter about Auden (April 8th):

> Judging by Mr. Auden's remarks as reported in the New Yorker, "The Elvish Mode," I do not think his discussion would have been either valuable or under-standing, unless he had been willing to consult me personally: a distraction for which … I have no time at present.

We had no idea whether Auden knew that Tolkien had seen the insulting remark. We had no evidence that Auden himself had seen what the *New Yorker* alleged he had said. But Auden did not respond. What he had said that night at the Library of Congress was still true. The book was well along, but, Auden said, "if Professor Tolkien does not wish it to be written, it shall not be written."—ROD JELLEMA

Toller, Ernst

1893–1939, German dramatist and poet of the expressionist school. He was imprisoned (1919–24) for participating in the Communist Bavarian revolution. In 1932 he left Germany, and in 1936 he went to New York City, where he later committed suicide. His plays of social protest include *Transfiguration* (1919); *Man and the Masses* (1920); *The Machine-Wreckers* (1922), based on the Luddite riots, *Brokenbow* (1924), and *Pastor Hall* (tr. 1939), about Martin Niemöller. *Swallow Book* (1923), a collection of lyric verse, and *Letters from Prison* (1935), an account of his imprisonment, appeared together in English translation as *Look Through the Bars* (1937).

Auden highly regarded Toller. The most telling example is one of his best poems, "In Memory of Ernst Toller." Forced to leave Germany, Toller spent more than two years in England, where he acquired a considerable reputation for his plays and anti-fascist speeches. During this period his work appeared in English translation, accompanied by good reviews. Many of his personal appearances drew large and enthusiastic crowds. At the same time Paul Tillich was beginning to establish himself in the United States, Toller became a powerful symbol of German opposition in exile.

Auden met Toller briefly in 1936, when he and Isherwood were living in Portugal and writing *The Ascent of F6*. Seventeen years later, Isherwood remembered Toller talking through dinner like a general "entertaining his troops" and "building up their morale on the night before a desperate battle" (*Exhumations*).

[T]hroughout supper it was he who did most of the talking — and I was glad, like the others, merely to sit and listen; to follow with amused, willing admiration, his every gesture and word. He was all that I had hoped for — more brilliant, more convincing than his books, more daring than his most epic deeds.

It was easy enough to see him on that cinema platform, years ago, when he told the workers: "You must occupy the factories. You must resist." I could picture him at the magnificent moment of defeat, crying out to his judges: "You can silence me. You can never silence history." I watched him pace his cell, five years long, in the mountain fortress, aloof and dangerous as the untamed tiger [E].

It was probably at this same meeting that Auden agreed to translate songs from Toller's play *No More Peace!* a month later at London's Gate Theatre. This play has many similarities with Auden's dramatic work of the mid 1930s, especially *The Ascent of F6*. Toller's title mocks the familiar slogan of the pacifist movement, "No More War," which Toller had endorsed in his youth but had later come to view as inadequate in the face of fascist expansion. Three years later, reading Niebuhr and considering his return to Christianity, Auden would employ a nearly identical logic in his own rejection of pacifism.

Toller's later lyric drama shares a leftist stance and stylized irreverence with much of the literature, "high" and "low," that had shaped Auden's thinking about poetry since the late 1920s, when he first visited Berlin after graduating from Oxford. Like Brecht's drama, popular German cabaret songs, Erika Mann's musical satires, Edward Upward and Christopher Isherwood's *Mortmere* stories, and Isherwood's early fiction, Toller's later work satirizes bourgeois complacency and political oppression in a manner that is often manic, sometimes brilliant, and occasionally merely adolescent. When Auden "adapted" the songs from *No More Peace!* for the English translation, he dealt loosely with Toller's text, applying his own light verse style and some of his familiar preoccupations.

When Toller visited Republican Spain in 1938, his status in Auden's circles could only have risen further. After moving to New York later that year, Toller spent the last few months of his life organizing and seeking support for a Spanish relief plan intended to provide food to civilians on both sides of the lines.

Though Toller's compassion and personal commitment were truly impressive — very near the end of his life, he would still confide to friends, "I can never forget the faces of those starving Spanish children"— many of those who knew him best also considered him difficult and egocentric. In more recent terminology, he was pretty clearly manic-depressive.

Nonetheless, it was not hard for Auden to see Toller as a victim of political and historical circumstances. Suddenly Toller seemed to have outlived his time and place. In May of 1939, as Auden was beginning *The Prolific and the Devourer*, Toller hanged himself. Auden saw in Toller's suicide much of the artistic and ideological foundation of his own past now brought to destruction, somehow persuaded to destroy itself, as he stood idly by in the nervous new world, trying to find a way to rebuild his own life and beliefs.

Largely because Auden was now inclined toward this tragic sense of history, the elegiac mode came easily to him. On a personal level, "In Memory of Ernst Toller" is a lament, in the face of the "European crisis," for the conception of the engaged intellectual life Auden had famously tried to cultivate in the early and mid 1930s— a conception which, ironically, Toller came to represent just as Auden was preparing to abandon it. In this particular sense, "In Memory of Ernst Toller" is a precursor to Prospero's farewell to Ariel in *The Sea and the Mirror*, another of Auden's elegies to his own poetic past and another of his greatest poems. "In Memory of Ernst Toller" should also be considered as part of the series of elegies— including those for W.B. Yeats, Sigmund Freud, and Henry James— that Auden wrote through this transitional period of his career. Viewed collectively, these poems address his current condition through what he would call, decades later in "Thanksgiving for a Habitat," "the companionship of our good dead." (Together, they constitute one of Auden's most remarkable accomplishments: a transformation of a conventional elegiac tension— between the private experience of loss and the public expression of mourning— into a moving commentary on the social condition of the creative intellectual in a world that seems increasingly dependent on collective thought and raw political power.)

"In Memory of Ernst Toller" is also a crucial poem in the development of Auden's career,

because in it he tries to confront the demonic at a point in his life when he is nearly ready to commit himself to Christian faith and practice. The elegy begins as an effort to find a voice that can express emotions of grief, ask for forgiveness, and still demand the kind of public moral judgment for which Toller had come to be known. As such, the poem is a moving testimony not so much to Toller's life as to Auden's belief that his culture is in need of a richly symbolic, even ritualistic, poetic language.

Five months after Auden's arrival in America, he still imagines his "New World" as an atmosphere of undeniable, almost oppressive brilliance. Yet it has no voice of judgment. The bright light of America's possibilities— its "shining neutral summer"— is not enough to banish the "shadows" surrounding the grave of the wounded and self-destructive exile.

Again, Auden looks back, briefly, to some of the preoccupations of his earlier career. Not long ago, he would have found the forces that drove Toller to suicide in a repressed childhood memory or an oppressive social order. In this poem, he still recognizes that such forces take their toll on human lives, but he assigns them a secondary role. The audacious self-assurance that had characterized his earliest poetry gives way to a tone that is genuinely searching.

By turning some of the most fundamental assertions of his earlier system of thought into a series of questions, Auden suggests that his familiar approaches will no longer suffice— not even his famous fusion of Marx and Freud, with its conflation of psychological repression and political oppression, with its amplification of psychosomatic illness into a cultural death wish. The ideas most responsible for giving his earlier poems their characteristic and disturbing "modernity" now seem inadequate to combat the forces that have driven Toller to his destruction.

At the same time, Auden has abandoned the "clinical detachment" so often praised by his early critics— or as he himself had recently put it, "the surgeon's idea of pain." He has arrived at a more reverent sensibility.

Auden no longer even imagines that he might reasonably view a man like Toller merely as a psychological case study or a as product of historical circumstances. Existence itself— not just artistic production or political action but the very act of being in the world — depends upon belief.

The poem's most striking feature is the passive construction of the penultimate sentence: "We are lived by powers." Later that year, Auden would repeat this formulation, and elaborate on it, in a review of Walter de la Mare's *Behold the Dreamer*. In doing so, he would indicate the sources of the Toller elegy in Tillich's conception of the demonic:

> We are confronted today by the spectacle, not of a utilitarian rationalism that dismisses all that cannot be expressed in prose and statistics as childish stuff, but rather by an ecstatic and morbid abdication of the free-willing and individual before the collective and daemonic. We have become obscene night worshippers who, having discovered that we cannot live exactly as we will, deny the possibility of willing anything and are content masochistically to be lived, a betrayal that betrays not only us but our daemon itself ("Jacob and the Angel").

In this essay, Auden proposes an alternative to the kind of passive suffering that overcame Toller at the end of his life. The alternative is not an escape from suffering. Rather, it is an acceptance, by conscious choice, of a kind of suffering that is more personal and more meaningful: "After a labyrinth of false moves and losses, you come at last to the place that you know is for you, unfortunately — the place you must learn to suffer."

Here is the answer that Auden anticipated at the start of "In Memory of Ernst Toller," when he called upon Toller's memory, lest the shadows gathered around Toller's grave "should learn without suffering how to forgive." In one of his essays on Kierkegaard, Auden would propose the same answer to the twin temptations of "demonic defiance" and "demonic despair":

> For, while ultimately the Christian message is the good news: "Glory to God in the highest and on earth peace, good-will towards men —" "Come unto me all that travail and are heavy laden and I will refresh you"; it is proximately to man's self-love the worst possible news — "Take up thy cross and follow me."

This acceptance of suffering only makes sense if one believes that one's suffering is an inescapable consequence of bearing the cross — that is, as Auden suggests with the final line break of "In Memory of Ernst Toller," that "existence is believing." Even though the language of "In Memory of Ernst Toller" is never specifically religious, the poem concludes with a powerful statement of one of the central concerns of Auden's later career: his growing need for a community of faith — the "we" of the poem's closing lines — to confront the demonic forces, the "powers we pretend to understand," that will live our lives if we let them.

"In Memory of Ernst Toller" is one of the greatest of Auden's poems that no one seems to read. Like Auden's other great elegies of this period — and like several of his other poems of the period, including "Voltaire at Ferney," "Rimbaud," and "Pascal" — it considers the figure of the intellectual struggling to articulate a system of belief commensurate to the horrors — as Tillich would say, the "demonry" — of the twentieth century. To put it another way, these poems are a response to the problem posed by Auden's "New Year Letter," his conscious farewell to the "low dishonest decade of the 1930s. — BRIAN CONNIFF

"To-Night at Seven-Thirty" *see* **About the House**

"The Truest Poetry Is the Most Feigning" 1953

This poem is a defense of exaggeration (lying) with Dante as the example and the title from Shakespeare.

Truly Strong and Truly Weak Man *see* The Auden Generation

Turville-Petre, Francis

British aristocrat and archaeologist. In 1929 Auden met him in Berlin and introduced him to Isherwood who would meet his companion Heinz at Turville-Petre's home in 1932. Francis owned his own tiny island in Greece. Isherwood and Heinz stayed there for four months in 1933 to avoid Heinz's conscription in the German army. In Berlin's boy bars, Turville-Petre was known as *Der Franni* and this inspired the character of the lost heir in Auden's play *The Fronny* and the Auden-Isherwood play *The Dog Beneath the Skin*. He is also "Ambrose" in Isherwood's *Down There on a Visit*.

"Twelve Songs" 1935–1937

I. "Song of the Beggars": Here are traces of Auden's redeemer fantasies that begin with exaggerations of everyone's desires with "six beggared cripples"— the phrase will become a stanza-closing refrain — that ask a statue for the material goods that they see the rich have. There is an implication that all people are crippled and beggars.

II. and III. These poems indicate an anti-political mood for Auden and a return to love poems.

IV. Superiority of love counterpointed by conflict between the lovers.

V. A contrast between creaturely necessity and human freedom. The creatures follow instinct without thought. Man initiates by instinct until thought begins to circumscribe his actions. Thought, however, can also lead to anxiety so one must distinguish thoughts based in reality from those based in fantasy.

VI. "Autumn Song": Caught in between the irresolution of two worlds — the past and future. The past is painful but where will the future lead?

VII. This poem is a "commentary" on Auden's bringing out Benjamin Britten's awareness that Britten was gay.

XIII. "There is always another story, there is more than meets the eye."

IX. Today this poem is known as "Funeral Blues" after it was recited and popularized in the film *Four Weddings and a Funeral*. While rather sad in the film, Auden wrote this and other songs in this sequence to be sung by Hedli Anderson, a cabaret performer who was the wife of Auden's Oxford classmate, friend, and Iceland companion Louis MacNeice who collaborated with Auden on *Letters from Iceland*.

X. An over-effusive love poem to "Johnny" that is not meant too seriously.

XI. "Roman Wall Blues" is a satirical lament.

XII. Auden grapples with his ignorance of true love — "Some say love's a little boy"— because its occurrence is so rare, and the fact that he must learn to be more tolerant of imperfection and change.

"Under Sirius" 1949

This poem, autobiographical, is about a secularist who regrets mundane choices. Auden borrows from two books by F.J.E. Raby: *A History of Christian Latin Poetry from the Beginnings to the Close of the Middle Ages* (1927), and *A History of Secular Latin Poetry in the Middle Ages* (1934).

"Under Which Lyre" 1946

This poem is subtitled "A Reactionary Tract for the Times" and is a post–World War II poem, and Auden's fullest attack on mass collectivism, uniformity, conformity, and the herd-intoxicated public willing to submit to the collective subjectivity created for them by societal dogma and mass media dictation. It is "reactionary" because Auden the Christian sees how lack of faith becomes a lack of grace and compassion by the alienated, unknown many for the people who are in need. Auden contrasts Apollo and Hermes, with the former as the bureaucratic prigs who impersonally micromanage the world while the latter is the unruly individualists — the aesthetes, intellectuals and artists without whom the world would slip away completely into Aldous Huxley's *Brave New World* of totalitarianism by pacification. Auden says, "Truth is replaced by useful knowledge" and prefers the first to the second for the "useful," as in strictly utilitarian, is knowledge calculated from indifference. Inner Truth becomes difference and sees the public as individuals again. Auden wrote "Under Which

Lyre" as Harvard's Phi Beta Kappa poem for the year.

"The Unknown Citizen" 1939

This is a poem about describing the "average" man as a statistic and as the man who goes about his business without fanfare; but the poem also asks "Was he free? Was he happy?" Auden facetiously concludes that the question is absurd because if anything was amiss, the statisticians representing the managers would have let us know. The "poem appears to be a neat uncomplicated satire on the corporate state in which freedom and happiness are equated to conformity" (Mendelson, *Later Auden*).

"Unpredictable but Providential" 1972

(For Loren Eiseley.) Auden wrote E.R. Dodds that he wanted to try a Lucretian poem (*De rerum natura*). "Overturning Auden's old ideas about nature as the realm of cyclical, involuntary behavior, the poem reimagines it as the realm of freedom, experimentation, 'irritable' relations between the self and not self" (Mendelson, *Later Auden*). Auden makes a case here that nature is not as inevitable as scientists would have us believe; after all, man had no physical capability to survive compared to great beasts but did so, and here he is going back to Gerald Heard's idea of "foetilization"— the ability to either adapt to changes in the environment in order to survive or move to a new environment.

"Up There" *see About the House*

Upward, Edward

1903– . Teacher, novelist, and school friend of Isherwood's at Repton's Public School and then Cambridge where they were the gang of two against The Others. He is also "Allen

Chalmers" in Isherwood's *All the Conspirators* and *Lions and Shadows*. Upward also befriended Auden who noted that he owed as much to Upward as Isherwood for the ideas he appropriated from Isherwood. This meant Mortmere — the town of weird stories Upward and Isherwood created that became a direct influence on early Auden, particularly *The Orators*. Another Upward influence on Auden was the short story "Sunday" that Auden read in 1932. The story is Upward's fictional account of his own conversion to Marxism.

US 1967

The film was made in 1967-68 for showing at the United States Pavilion at HemisFair '68, an international exposition held in San Antonio, Texas. The film was a documentary of American History with narration written by Auden and music by David Amram.

Valéry, Paul

1871–1945. A poet, essayist, and aphorist, Valéry was influenced by Stéphane Mallarmé and Rainer Maria Rilke. He was a close friend of André Gide. Valéry's poetry dealt with the conflict between the possibilities of intellect and the reality of life. *The Idol of Intellect* described a static state of pure reason set apart from emotion and the demands of the world, the struggle between the possible and impossible in man's life, and the conflict in human life between the desire for contemplation and the will to action. All of the printed writings of Paul Valéry have been collected by the *Bollingen Series*, a subset press of Pantheon Books. They are currently being reprinted in paperback. The books are as follows: *Poems, Prose Poems, Plays, Dialogues, Idee Fixe, Monsieur Teste, The Art of Poetry, Leonardo, Poe, Mallarme, Masters and Friends, History and Politics, Occasions, Degas, Manet, Morisot, Aesthetics, Analects, Moi.*

By 1937 Auden was reading Valéry and said of him later in a 1969 essay, "Whenever I feel in danger of becoming un homme serieux [a too serious man], it is on Valéry, un homme d'esprit [a man of spirit], if there ever was one, more often than any other poet, I believe, that I call for aid" ("Valéry: L'Homme d' Esprit"). Auden, in reference to his predilection for textual revisions of his poems, liked to quote Valéry, that "A poem is never finished, only abandoned." According to Mendelson, Auden told a lecture audience in 1950 that Valéry's notebooks had inspired the subject of his poem "Prime" in the sequence "Horae Canonicae." Valéry the aphorist has numerous entries in the Auden-Kroneberger *Viking Book of Aphorisms* and Auden's *A Certain World.*

Van Gogh, Vincent

1853–90, postimpressionist painter, b. the Netherlands. Only one of Van Gogh's paintings was sold while he lived. The majority of the works he is remembered for were painted in a 29 month period that ended in suicide. Vincent had one constant ally and support, his younger brother Théo, to whom he wrote revealing letters detailing his conflicts and aspirations. Auden, certainly sympathetic to the plight of the troubled artist, would edit and write a foreword to a selection of these letters, *Van Gogh, a Self-Portrait* (1961).

Auden: "In most cases, to go through a man's correspondence and make the proper selection for publication would be easy. One would merely have to pick out the few letters that were interesting and discard the many which were dull or unintelligible to the general reader without elaborate editorial notes. But there is scarcely one letter by Van Gogh which I, who am certainly no expert, do not find fascinating.... 'What,' I asked myself, 'is the single most important fact about Van Gogh?'—That he painted pictures. I have therefore, confined my selection to those of his letters which contain references upon the art of painting and the problems of being a painter, and have only included letters concerned with his personal relations, to his father and his brother.... Van Gogh was an extraordinary character."

Van Vechten, Carl

1880–1964, novelist, critic, photographer,

VanGogh: A Self Portrait, **cover of first edition.**

and early editor of Gertrude Stein. He was a supporter of the Harlem Renaissance. He photographed Auden and Isherwood in 1939 in New York City. The photos are now in the Carl Van Vechten American Collection at the Library of Congress.

Vedanta

Vedanta is the mystical derivation of Hindu philosophy that Christopher Isherwood became devoted to after he left Auden in New York City and went to California in 1939. Auden then counterpointed his friend with his own blend of a Christian-based form of Auden's mysticism. Vedanta is derived from the later Upanishads known as the Vedas.

Vedanta encourages the individual towards a self-realization that comes from within in a method that Aldous Huxley summed up in his Minimum Working Hypothesis, which he first stated in his introduction to the Isherwood-Prabhavananda translation of the Bhagavad-Gita in 1944.

"Venus Will Now Say a Few Words" *see Poems*

"A Very Inquisitive Old Party" 1968

This essay is a review of a reprint of *London Labour and the London Poor*, by Henry Mayhew.

"Vespers" *see Horae Canonicae*

"Victor" 1937

With the madcap ranting of a religious maniac (to the melody "Frankie and Johnny") on the order of *Mortmere* and *The Orators*, this is a reaction to Auden's visit to the Spanish Civil War and a companion poem to "Miss Gee" and "James Honeyman."

Visions *see* Mysticism

"Vocation and Society" 1945

From a lecture at Swarthmore. Auden: "...to acknowledge vocation is, like marriage, to take a vow, to live henceforth by grace of the Absurd, to love for better or for worse, for richer or for poorer, in sickness and in health, until death do us part. No one can hope to have a vocation, in fact, if he makes a private reservation that, should circumstances alter, he can get divorced ... without passion [society] must inevitably dissolve into an amorphous distraction called the General Public." This "public" is Kierkegaard's public.

Voltaire

1694–1778, French philosopher and author, Voltaire personifies the Enlightenment. Many of W.H. Auden's liberal humanist views and distrust of bureaucrats were similar to Vol-

taire's and thus the latter engendered admiration and emulation in the former.

Voltaire acquired an independent fortune through speculation, and he was often noted for his generosity. In 1726 a young nobleman resenting a witticism made at his expense by Voltaire, had Voltaire beaten. Far from obtaining justice, Voltaire was imprisoned in the Bastille through the influence of the noble's family, and he was released only upon his promise to go to England. For the rest of his life he asserted himself in struggling against judicial arbitrariness. Voltaire purchased (1758) an estate, Ferney, where he lived in unofficial exile until shortly before his death. He managed his estate, taking an active interest in improving the condition of his tenants. In 1778, his 84th year, Voltaire attended the first performance of his tragedy *Irène*, in Paris. His reception was enormous, but the emotion was too much for him and he died in Paris soon afterward. To a friend he gave the following written declaration: "I die adoring God, loving my friends, not hating my enemies, and detesting persecution."

In his philosophy, based on skepticism and rationalism, he was indebted to Locke as well as to Montaigne. Despite Voltaire's passion for clarity and reason, he frequently contradicted himself, as would Auden. Also like Auden he would maintain on the one hand that man's nature was as unchangeable as that of animals and would express elsewhere his belief in progress and the gradual humanization of society through the action of the arts, sciences, and commerce. In politics he advocated reform but, also like Auden, he had a horror of the ignorance and potential fanaticism of people and the violence of revolution.

In Auden's 1939 poem "Voltaire at Ferney," Voltaire is in exile, cultivating his garden, while remembering the great fights against injustice and the power that would rob France of decency. He is in exile but not done yet; he will fight again. As he contemplates, the last line, in an echo of "Musée des Beaux Arts," states that while he tended to his flowers "The uncomplaining stars composed their lucid song." One works, plays, fights, while nature continues on as always.

Auden wrote again about Voltaire, in the 1939 essay "A Great Democrat: Voltaire." His legend, said Auden, obscures his writing. Democracy is a state of mind and has 3 enemies: 1) Pascal: mystic pessimism which believes man has no free will, 2) Rousseau: mystic optimism of romantic who believes in an absolute free will, 3) mystic certaintist who believes man can know absolute good and final truth. Pascal's view of original sin denied man any free will, rendering interrelations as useless extremes except as certainty defined by the Catholic Church. Rousseau: certainly will emerge from free will uncorrupted by society. Voltaire: moderation/balance — men are not all bad (Pascal) or all good (Rousseau) but they need guidance, not absolute certainty.

"Voltaire at Ferney" *see* Voltaire

Völuspá: The Song of the Sybil

Translated by Paul B. Taylor and Auden with the Icelandic text edited by Peter H. Salus and Paul B. Taylor, 1968. (*See also* Old Norse and Old English Literature.)

Vozsnesensky, Andrei

1933– , Russian poet, b. Moscow. He became a close friend and protégé of novelist Boris Pasternak. After publishing his first poems in 1958, Voznesensky became popular. In 1963 the government limited his writing. Gradually his poetry appeared again, but his dramatic work, though not political in content, had to be withdrawn (1970), and he was placed under close surveillance in 1971. Auden would always take note of an artist who was prevented from telling the truth. In 1967 Auden would write a foreword to and translate some of the poems in Vosnesensky's *Antiworlds*.

W.H. Auden: A Tribute

The volume was published in 1975 after Auden's death in 1973 and was edited by Stephen Spender. Contributors included Spender, Edward Mendelson, Geoffrey Grigson, John Auden (brother), Robert Medley, John Betjeman, Gabriel Carritt with Rex Warner, William Coldstream, Cyril Connolly, Christopher Isherwood, Anne Fremantle, Golo Mann, Ursula Niebuhr (wife of Reinhold Niebuhr), James Stern, Lincoln Kirstein, Nicolas Nabokov, Robert Craft, Louis Kronenberger, Orlan Fox, Hannah Arendt, Oliver Sacks, John Hollander, Chester Kallman, Joseph Brodsky, and Cecil Beaton.

Wagner, Richard

1813–83, German composer, b. Leipzig. Wagner began composing at 17. In 1843 Wagner was made musical director of the Dresden Theater. His opera *Der Fliegende Holländer* (1841) was based on Heine's version of the legend of the Flying Dutchman, a phantom ship, and the idea is developed in *Tannhäuser* (1843–44) all with the theme, as in later works, of redemption by love. In *Lohengrin*, Wagner is more interested in his characters as symbols than as actual characters in a drama. Wagner participated in the Revolution of 1848, fled Dresden, and with the help of Franz Liszt escaped to Switzerland, where he stayed eight years. There he wrote essays, including *Oper und Drama* (1851), in which he began to articulate aesthetic principles that would guide his subsequent work.

Der Ring des Nibelungen (1853–74) is his tetralogy based on the Nibelungenlied. In 1857, having completed the composition of the first two works of the cycle, *Das Rheingold* (1853–54) and *Die Walküre* (1854–56), and two acts of *Siegfried* (1856–69), Wagner laid the Ring aside without hope of ever seeing it performed and composed. He then composed *Tristan und Isolde* (1857–59) and *Die Meistersinger von Nürnberg* (1862–67), his only comic opera. In 1874 he completed the third act of Siegfried and all of *Götterdämmerung*, the last work of the *Ring* cycle, and returned to Germany. He was able to build a theater, Das Festspielhaus, adequate for the proper performance of his works, in which the complete *Ring* was presented in 1876. *Parsifal* (1877–82) was his last work.

Wagner's operas represent the fullest of German romanticism. His ideas influenced the work of later composers. Adapting German mythology, Wagner applied intensity to produce what he termed a complete artwork.

Chester Kallman introduced Auden to opera in general and Wagner in particular right after they first met. They attended the *Ring* at the Metropolitan Opera in New York after which Auden called Wagner "the greatest and the most typical modern artist, the forerunner, and in many ways the creator, of both the highbrow and the lowbrow tastes of our time" ("Mimesis and Allegory" 1940). This, in effect, meant that Wagner could appeal to everyone. Wagner's words from *Siegfried* would find their way into "New Year Letter" (1940), along with allusions to numerous other Auden heroes. Auden's admiration for Wagner was not limited to music: "...the story of Wagner is absolutely fascinating, and it would be even if he had never written a note." Auden wrote this in his essay about Wagner in which the title says a great deal, describing Wagner as "The Greatest of the Monsters." (This was a 1969 book review in the *New Yorker* of Robert Gutman's *Richard Wagner, The Man, His Mind and His Music*.)

There is some irony in Stravinsky's choice of Auden to write a libretto for *The Rake's Progress* as the composer's intent was to score an opera that was anti–Wagner. In Auden's poem "Ascension Day 1964," according to Mendelson, "Auden chooses the temptress from Parsifal as his specific figure for the spirit of denial who laughs at the crucifixion and is doomed to loneliness thereafter, a reminder of the Wagnerian enthusiasm he had learned from Kallman" (*Later Auden*), and a reminder of Auden's own cross to bear in loving Kallman, which may have been the point of the poem as Auden was getting older and he chose Wagner's last opera to make his point. Auden's calling Wagner a "monster" was to say Wagner was larger than life and his genius compensated for his faults: "In his sexual life, he indulged in one affair after another.... Many artists have done the same, but they have not, as Wagner did in opera after opera, extolled the virtues of renunciation and chastity, just as in his prose phamplets, he preached vegetarianism while continuing to enjoy a French cuisine.... His taste in clothes and interior decoration were those of a drag queen." The last remark was probably unfair to drag queens but once again displayed Auden's ambivalence about homosexuality. Auden also states that the best interpreter of the "monster" was Nietzsche whom Auden quotes to prove Wagner's obsessiveness: "Someone always wants to be saved in his operas — this is his problem...." And of Wagner's heroines, Auden quotes Nietzsche saying, "Wagner's heroines ... once they have been divested of their heroic husks, are almost indistinguishable from Madame Bovary." One can read Auden's own predilections from his choice of quotations.

Waley, Arthur *see* "Many Happy Returns"

"A Walk After Dark" 1948

This poem conveys an ironic and pragmatic romanticism that prefers to think of "night" as "an Old People's Home" over "a shed for a faultless machine," and that pain exists because things that "needn't have happened did" anyway. Still the stars will shine nonetheless no matter what happens next.

"Walks" 1958

"Walks," one of the earliest of Auden's Kirchstetten poems, is a contrast between three types of walks or paths. There is the historically linear path of the straight "road from here to there"; even if one returns on this same path, the return trip "looks altogether new." The second walk is the focused, repetitive path of a circular walk taken for its own sake. The third path is the path of the heart that wishes for a safe barrier between its private self and the public world.

"The Wanderer" *see Poems*

Warner, Rex

1905–86, English author, b. Birmingham. Warner graduated from Oxford in 1928 where he had been a classmate and friend of C. Day Lewis who introduced him to Auden. A classical

The Wild Goose Chase, cover of first U.S. edition.

scholar noted for his translations from Greek and Latin, Warner taught in England, Egypt, and the United States. He was influenced by Kafka and early Auden — *Poems* (1930), and *The Orators* (1932), in which one of the concluding odes is addressed to Warner's newborn son. His early novels are expressionist allegories concerning abuses of power; they include *The Wild Goose Chase* (1937), *The Professor* (1938), and *The Aerodrome* (1941). His *Poems* (1937) was socially reflective of the 1930s. Warner also wrote several historical novels, including *The Young Caesar* (1958) and *Pericles the Athenian* (1963), and essays, such as *The Cult of Power* (1946) and *Men of Athens* (1973). He also immigrated to America but not until after World War II. Warner, as did Auden, rediscovered Christianity, and translated St. Augustine who had become an Auden favorite as well. Warner contributed to *W.H. Auden: A Tribute*, edited by Stephen Spender after Auden's death.

"The Watchers" 1932

This poem names the "Lords of Limit" who are from Shakespeare, and The Book of Revelations via D.H. Lawrence, and they signify comparably to the Watcher-in-Spanish, Isherwood's silent, cypher arbiter, who stands judge over the Auden gang as a reminder/ admonisher, administering judgment and, if necessary guilt, over the divided mind. The Lords of Limit, "training dark and light" and "left and right" oversee the conflicts that Auden previously considered hard divisions but now wishes to consolidate to make peace. The Lords prevent escape into distractions in order to save the mind for the future, in effect, saving the mind from itself.

"The Watershed" *see Poems*

Waugh, Evelyn

1903–66, English writer, satirist, educated at Oxford. Considered an archconservative by some critics, Waugh was a moralist who attacked society with scorn. He also attacked Auden and Isherwood with scorn when they went to America in 1939. (*See also* America.)

The Way to the Sea see Grierson, John

"Werther and Novella" *see* Goethe, Johann Wolfgang von

Wescott, Glenway

1901–1987, American novelist. b. Wisconsin, befriended Auden and Isherwood when they arrived in America. Wescott, in his published Journals, said that Auden's energy and vibrant enthusiasm reminded him of the poet Vachel Lindsay. In these journals there are additional remarks on Auden, such as: "What has New York amounted to this past winter, goodness knows. Lowbrow on the whole. Except for Auden and Isherwood; they raise the tone..." March 23, 1939.

West, Nathanael *see* "West's Disease"

"West's Disease" 1947

Ostensibly about the author Nathanael West, this essay also concerned Auden's tempestuous relationship with Chester Kallman. For Auden, a theatrical ego was really a sign of inner disorder. Auden writes, "The heroes of … West's novels cannot make their wishes issue in desires, and therefore live in a state of 'wishful despair.'" The sufferer from West's disease, Auden believed, is not selfish — because his wishes refer to nothing real. The sufferer has no designs on other persons or things — but he is "absolutely self-centered." The disease towards its end "reduces itself to a craving for violent physical pain — this craving, unfortunately, can be projected onto others — for only violent pain can put an end to wishing for something and produce the real wish of necessity, the cry Stop!" Auden is here referring to Kallman's predilection for "rough trade" or rough sex.

"What Is Culture?" 1940

This review signified Auden's return to writing about politics again. Here he would not accept the modern bias that morality was unimportant or illogical because it could not be proven empirically. These judgments are not based on reason but the same intuition that the mystic feels when intuiting God. In part this was Auden's answer to Hitler's victories in France and at Dunkirk. Auden and Isherwood at this time were enduring British criticism for not returning to England.

"What Ought We to Know?" 1962

In this essay Auden considers the meaning of "knowledge" in the Biblical sense — as in, "Adam knew Eve, his wife." He does not restrict intimacy to sex alone but speaks of a heightened intimacy where each of the partners knows the other better but also himself better.

White Magic and Black Magic

Auden: "Like the White Magic of poetry, Black Magic is concerned with enchantment. But while the poet is himself enchanted by the subjects and only wishes to share his enchantment with others, the Black Magician is perfectly cold. He has no enchantment to share with others, but uses enchantment as a means of securing domination over others and compelling them to do his will. He does not ask for a free response to his spell; he demands a tautological echo" ("The Real World," *New Republic*, December 9, 1967). White Magic is the artist's medium; Black magic is the propagandist's medium.

Black Magic is pejoratively meant to be negative manipulation of language and the public, i.e., propaganda. In this sense, for Auden, poetry is not magic; it should not be a tool for conversion of any kind: "The poet is capable of every form of conceit but that of the social worker: 'We are all here on earth to help others; what on earth the others are here for I don't know'" ("Squares and Oblongs," *Poets at Work*).

Whitehead, Alfred North

1861–1947, English mathematician and philosopher. He criticized traditional philosophy for failing to convey the essential interrelation of matter, space, and time. He invented a vocabulary to communicate his concept of reality, which he called the philosophy of organism. His philosophy applied to a concept of God as interdependent with the world and developing with it (see also Heard, Gerald). His works include *Process and Reality* (1929), which Auden read in 1941 when he was searching for some absolute reality, and Auden incorporated Whitehead's ideas and vocabulary (triviality, vagueness, order) into the essay "A Note on Order," and would keep this lexicon thereafter.

"Whitsunday in Kirchstetten" 1962

This poem concerns the question of how much one should conform to keep the peace rather than protest; that is, how far to bend without risk of breaking. Auden's example is his attendance at the Catholic Church in Kirchstetten while he retains his allegiance to the Anglican Church elsewhere. While the style is colloquial and the issue fairly tame, Auden infers the greater issues of conformity/nonconformity, joining/rebelling. His last line seeks the answer from God where he paraphrases from the Bible's Acts of John: "If thee when Grace dances, I should dance."

Who Am I? Whom Ought I to Become?

Every time one meets a person, a process of juxtaposition instinctively takes place. One juxtaposes himself with the other person. Every time one "meets" a poem, it is also like encountering an another person. Of this, Auden wrote,

> Reading a poem is an experience analogous to that of encountering a person. Just as one can think and speak separately of a person's physical appearance, his mind, and his character, so can one consider the formal aspects of a poem, its contents, and its spirit while knowing that in the latter case no less than in the former, these different aspects are not really separate but an indissoluble trinity-in-unity. We would rather that our friends were handsome than plain, intelligent than stupid, but in the last analysis it is on account of their character as persons that we accept or reject them ["Introduction," *A Change of World*, Adrienne Rich].

It is a person's character, his "isness" that we accept or reject. His appearance or material circumstances may attract attention, but those alone cannot retain it. Ultimately, we accept or reject a poem or a person's character by tacitly asking of the poem or person: "Who are you? What do you represent? What do you want to become?" These intuitive questions are explicit or implicit during human contacts and represent one person's reflexive comparing of himself to the other's "self." The automatic comparison-by-juxtaposition that these questions entail has an equally automatic flip side because by ask-

ing them, we are simultaneously asking ourselves, according to Auden: "Who am I? Whom ought I to become?" He then further defines these questions:

(1) Who am I? What is the difference between man and all other creatures? What relations are possible between them? What is man's status in the universe? What are the conditions of his existence, which he must accept as his fate which no wishing can alter?

(2) Whom ought I to become? What are the characteristics of the hero, the authentic man whom everybody should admire and try to become? Vice versa, what are the characteristics of the churl, the unauthentic man whom everybody should try to avoid becoming?

"We all seek answers to these questions which shall be universally valid under all circumstances, but the experiences to which we put them are always local both in time and place. What any poet has to say about man's status in nature, for example, depends in part on the landscape and climate he happens to live in and in part upon reactions to it of his personal temperament" ("Robert Frost"). (*See also* Language; "Writing"; Auden on "Writing")

Wholly Truthful Art *see* Huxley, Aldous

"Who's Who" 1934

A poem about T.E. Lawrence as myth written close in time to a book review of T.E. Lawrence. (*See also* Essays.)

Wilde, Oscar

1856–1900, Anglo-Irish poet, playwright, novelist, and essayist. Oscar Fingal O'Flahertie Wills Wilde, better known as Oscar Wilde, was perhaps the most celebrated literary figure of the late Victorian era, a wit who conquered the salons and stages of Europe and the Americas before the central tragedy of his life, two sensational trials for libel he brought against the Marquess of Queensberry. His suit back-fired when Wilde's homosexuality was revealed, leading to a major scandal and Wilde's subsequent imprisonment on sodomy charges. Wilde's health was broken by the brutality of his incarceration and, after his release, he spent his final years in poverty and ill health in France.

Wilde's earliest writings, lectures, and social successes established him as an aesthetic force before much of his work was widely known or acclaimed. His first play, *Vera: or The Nihilists* (1883), was a melodramatic work that found little favor in its initial New York production, while his second work, *The Duchess of Padua* (1891), was a blank-verse tragedy that similarly met with a generally apathetic response in its New York premiere. The great success of Wilde's novel *The Portrait of Dorian Gray* (1891) led to the completion of *Salomé*, a symbolist work in verse recounting the story of the killing of John the Baptist. Starring legendary actress Sarah Bernhardt, it was first produced in Paris in 1896 after the Lord Chamberlain's Office refused to license the work for production in London.

Wilde's first true theatrical triumph in London was *Lady Windermere's Fan* (1892), a traditionally constructed, well-made play in the comedy of manners vein focusing on attempts by the play's heroine to preserve her social reputation which has been compromised by the misplacing of a fan. This popular comedy encouraged Wilde to continue in a similar style in *A Woman of No Importance* (1893) and *An Ideal Husband* (1895), both of which firmly established Wilde's reputation as a peerless comic writer. If not a pioneer in terms of dramaturgical technique, Wilde's mastery of dialogue and characterization shapes a satiric view of human behavior revealed through his witty language and the juxtaposition of boldly conceived characters. His works depict the tyranny of the social conventions of his time and place. While late nineteenth century plays by George Bernard Shaw, Arthur Wing Pinero, and Henry Arthur Jones may have presented a more overt assault on Victorian mores, Wilde's more subtle subversions of the period's social constructions have provided enduring confections reflecting on the pretensions and illusions of humanity in universal terms.

Wilde's masterpiece, *The Importance of Being Earnest* (1895), perhaps the most produced British play of the 1890s, demonstrates the seemingly endless Wilde wit in probing and satirizing middle- and upper-class values. Following the play's triumph, the Marquess of Queensberry insulted Wilde by making public accusations of acts of sodomy between Wilde and Queensberry's son, Lord Alfred Douglas. Wilde's subsequent arrest and imprisonment abruptly ended his string of dramatic successes. George Alexander, producer of *The Importance of Being Earnest*, closed the production and for some years no one dared produce Wilde's plays in London. In prison, Wilde continued to write and planned several plays, but only completed *A Florentine Tragedy* (with the assistance of T. Sturge Moore), which was produced posthumously in 1906 in London. Ultimately, Wilde's plays, as well as his other writings, found popularity and critical acclaim and, over a hundred years after Wilde's death, his novels and poetry are widely read, his witticisms are a permanent part of the popular lexicon, and his plays are continually revived on stages and adapted in screen and television treatments.

Auden's connection to Oscar Wilde is largely ephemeral, but not without importance. The notoriety surrounding Wilde's sensational trial for gross indecency would certainly have given his poetry, novels, and dramatic works a tinge of the forbidden when Auden was a young man. As a young homosexual writer, Auden certainly regarded Wilde's honesty about his private life — and the personal tragedy it wrought — as both a model and a cautionary tale. Although Auden tended to live his life with a fair amount of openness about his sexuality, it was never thrown into the glare of the public spotlight as it was with Wilde. For most gay British writers, particularly those of Auden's generation, Wilde became something of a patron saint, and the increasing interest in Wilde's life and work in the past decade suggests that Wilde's image will remain an important one for the English homosexual artist and writer. In 1931, Auden spent months living at the Hôtel d'Alsace in Paris in the very room in which Wilde had died over thirty years earlier, during his last poverty-stricken years following completion of his prison sentence at Reading Gaol.

Auden reviewed a Wilde biography called *The Paradox of Oscar Wilde* by G. Woodcock, and published the critique in the *Partisan Review* (Vol. XVII, No. 4, April 1950, pp. 390–394). Titled "A Playboy of the Western World: St. Oscar, The Homintern Martyr," Auden's review offers harsh criticism of Wilde's literary accomplishments, but grudging admiration for Wilde's personal life. Auden writes that Wilde's "life is more honest than his writings; he was a phony prophet but a serious playboy," and he goes on to analyze Wilde as the homosexual writer:

> Wilde's life was epic; his work is not. The artist desires the approval of his work; Wilde sought the approval of himself with art as the reluctant means to this end. One who needs to be loved tests others with extreme behavior to prove he's loved in spite of himself. One who is gay seeks straight males in the test. At his trials his need became exhibitionistic, a display of truth, his truth, in order to be accepted for himself. His ruin was in wanting to be accepted by all words/worlds, as gay and straight.

Auden wrote further on the dilemma of the homosexual writer as specifically related to Oscar Wilde in "An Improbable Life." John Fuller finds Wildean elements in the failed Auden/Isherwood play *On the Frontier* (1938), and in a circa 1931 poem, "Uncle Henry (Isherwood's uncle). Auden also discussed Wilde, along with Charles Dickens, Ronald Firbank, and P.G. Wodehouse in an essay entitled "Dingley Dell & the Fleet," published in the collection *The Dyer's Hand and Other Essays* (New York: Random House, 1962), in which he explores notions of the myth of Eden. Richard Davenport-Hines found Wildean aspects in Auden's life, particularly in the "vivacity and sexual vagrancy" of Chester Kallman, Auden's on-and-off lover from the late 1940s. Auden is, of course, frequently grouped with other gay and bisexual English artists and writers seen by critics and scholars as part of a movement that inevitably began with Wilde.

Wilder, Thornton

1897–1975, American playwright and novelist, b. Madison, Wis. His technical innovations

changed modern theater. Wilder's second novel, *The Bridge of San Luis Rey* (1927), won a Pulitzer. Among his other novels are *The Cabala* (1926); *The Woman of Andros* (1930); *Heaven's My Destination*, (1934), the protagonist, George Brush, is based on Vachel Lindsay; *The Ides of March* (1948); *The Eighth Day* (1967); and *Theophilus North* (1973).

Although he had written one-act plays, which were published in *The Angel That Troubled the Waters* (1928) and *The Long Christmas Dinner* (1931) and included "Pullman Car Hiawatha," Wilder did not achieve critical recognition as a playwright until the production of *Our Town* (1938; Pulitzer). *The Skin of Our Teeth* (1942; Pulitzer) was inspired by James Joyce's *Finnegans Wake* (1939); it deals with the perpetual human struggle to survive. Wilder's other plays include *The Merchant of Yonkers* (1938), which was revised as *The Matchmaker* (1954) and adapted, by others, into the successful musical *Hello Dolly!* (1963); and *Plays for Bleecker Street* (1962), one-act plays from his projected "Seven Ages of Man" and "Seven Deadly Sins" cycles.

Wilder experimented with new ways of writing plays that were much influenced by Europeans such as Cocteau and André Obey. Harry Sidnell, in his book *Dances of Death: The Group Theatre of London in the Thirties*, cites Wilder's one-act play "Pullman Car Hiawatha" as an inspiration for the staging of Auden and Isherwood's play *The Dog Beneath the Skin*.

Williams, Charles

1895–1945. Williams was as much an influence on Auden in the late 1930s as Gerald Heard had been earlier in the decade. Williams was a devout Anglican, as Auden would later become. He was a writer of poetry, novels, and, of great theological importance to Auden, *The Descent of the Dove: The History of the Holy Spirit in the Church*. He was also an editor, teacher, and lecturer. Of him Auden wrote: "When I met Charles Williams I had read none of his books; our meetings were few and on business, yet I count them among my most unforgettable and precious experiences. I have met great and good men in whose presence one was conscious of one's own littleness; Charles Williams' effect on me and on others with whom I have spoken was quite different: in his company one felt twice as intelligent and infinitely nicer than, out of it, one knew oneself to be … more than anyone else I have ever known, he gave himself completely to the company he was in ("Introduction," *The Descent of the Dove*). Auden would later say he had met only two saints, Williams and Dorothy Day.

Williams, William Carlos

1883–1963, American poet, essayist, short story writer, and physician, b. Rutherford, N.J., He developed a verse that is close to speech. His many volumes of poetry include *Pictures from Brueghel, and Other Poems* (1963; Pulitzer Prize), and a five-volume, impressionistic, philosophical poem, *Paterson* (1946–58), in which he uses the experience of life in an American city to express his feelings on the responsibilities of the poet.

Auden did not admire Williams until he read a late poem "The Asphodel, That greeny flower," which he believed to be a great love poem. He then tried Williams' more colloquial technique in the poem "Encomium Balnei" in the sequence "Thanksgiving for a Habitat."

Wilson, Edmund

1895–1972, American critic and author, b. Red Bank, N.J. Wilson graduated from Princeton in 1916 where his classmates and friends had included F. Scott Fitzgerald and John Peale Bishop. From 1920 to 1921 he was managing editor of Vanity Fair, and he was later on the staffs of the *New Republic* (1926–31) and the *New Yorker* (1944–48). In the 1930s he was much interested in the theories of Freud and Marx, which are treated in many of his works. Among his major writings are *Axel's Castle* (1931), a study of symbolism and other imaginative literatures; *The Wound and the Bow* (1941); *The Shores of Light* (1952); and *Patriotic Gore* (1962). As a critic Wilson was concerned with the social, psychological, and political conditions that shape literary ideas.

Wilson was a loyal supporter of some and a terrible enemy to others, and from many accounts was a difficult, vindictive, envious critic who resented the artistic success that others received and he did not. He loved and promoted Thornton Wilder, but hated Wilder's friend Archibald MacLeish, whose career he tried his best to sabotage. Fortunately he also admired Auden, which is not the same as saying he liked Auden, although he may have. Since Wilson was sarcastic about everyone, it is hard to tell, although they did socialize on occasion.

In 1933 in a letter to poet Louise Bogan, who would later befriend Auden, Wilson told her she might be interested in Auden's *The Dance of Death* and *The Orators*. When he tells Bogan she should write the confession of a child of the century, he adds, "maybe Auden's Orators will give you a cue." In a 1937 letter Wilson suggests "W.H. might be the ideal person to translate Rimbaud." In 1947 Wilson wrote to Auden, who was a bit more famous than Wilson, especially as an artist, to say "— much as I usually approve of you — I have some very severe criticisms to make of certain of your recent activities," and goes on to list four items of rebuke, although he praises *The Age of Anxiety*, even while telling Auden that in it he stole from Joyce's *Finnegan's Wake* (which Auden did). This is ironic because in another letter to someone else he writes that Auden is incredibly tough about ignoring criticism. In 1954 he wrote that Auden's libretto for the *Rake's Progress* and Marianne Moore's translation of La Fontaine were the "two major literary mistakes of our time." Overall, however, in 1946 he called Auden "one of the top writers in English at the present time." In 1965 Auden dedicated *About the House* to Wilson and his wife Elena.

"Wish Game" 1959

Folk tales are not only for children, writes Auden in this essay; they are evolved from ritual and religion when ritual and religion need explain "how did something come to be?" Fairytales then evolve into literature, which the literary critic must judge of itself, not as questions of religion/history. The fairytale hero has special gifts and is an ideal man; he differs from the epic hero in that he is not genealogically predisposed, but a first generation Everyman. He is unknown prior to success and his innate goodness and kindness ensures his success, which is not ego-driven but selfless. The difference between wish and desire: a wish is safe; desire is dangerous. Fairy tales have rules and resolutions that must be obeyed.

"The Witnesses" 1934

Here Auden sees that there is a limit to what a formal and "normal" education can teach. At this time he was now a public school teacher and this idea had greater relevance. Hence, this poem has the point of view of a student's dilemma. The Others bar progress of the young by filling their brains with that which isolates and destroys. What is to be done but seek the Northwest Passage to a better place. The image of the town clock signifies authority, denial, and fear. The Others decide on the knowledge to be given as only that knowledge which will perpetuate a society that perpetuates themselves. One must be aware of who The Others are and watch out for their manipulations. (See discussion of The Watcher in Spanish under Isherwood, Christopher.)

Woolf, Virginia

1882–1941, English experimental novelist and essayist. In 1912, she married Leonard Woolf, a critic who also wrote about economics, with whom she started Hogarth Press in 1917. Their home became a gathering place for artists, critics, and writers known as the Bloomsbury group. Woolf's early works, *The Voyage Out* (1915) and *Night and Day* (1919), were conventional, but her innovations began in *Jacob's Room* (1922), *Mrs. Dalloway* (1925), *To the Lighthouse* (1927), and *The Waves* (1931). Other experimental novels are *Orlando* (1928), *The Years* (1937), and *Between the Acts* (1941). Her essays are included in *The Common Reader* (1925), *The Second Common Reader* (1933), *The Death of the Moth and Other Essays* (1942), and *The Moment and Other Essays* (1948). *A Room of One's Own* (1929) and *Three Guineas* (1938)

Virginia Woolf

are feminist writings. Some of her short stories from *Monday or Tuesday* (1921) appear with others in *A Haunted House* (1944). Virginia Woolf suffered mental breakdowns in 1895 and 1915; she drowned herself in 1941.

Auden was Auden because of the bursts of literary modernism that became the 1920s. All literature in the 1930s either accepted or refuted the 1920s but could not ignore it. Woolf's work in the nature of consciousness and her tragic life of the mind that she feared so much that she ended it, found Auden's sympathy. In Auden's 1959 introduction to poet Phyllis McGinley's *Times Three*, he asked, "What does the poetry men write owe to the influence of women, whether as mothers, sisters, and wives, or as women authors whom they admire?" He then listed Woolf as one of his examples.

Auden wrote two essays titled "Squares and Oblongs." The title was derived from a favorite passage from *The Waves*. "There is a square and there is an oblong. The players take the square and place it along the oblong. They place it very accurately; they make a perfect dwelling-place. Very little is left outside. The structure is now visible; what is inchoate is here stated; we are not so various or so mean; we have made oblongs and stood them upon squares. This is our triumph; this is our consolation." Auden saw here the great, but very rewarding, struggle that can come from the effort to reconcile opposites in life and art.

In 1954, Auden reviewed Woolf's *A Writer's Diary* in an essay titled "A Consciousness of Reality."

"A Worcestershire Lad" 1972

Auden's review of *The Letters of A.E. Houseman*, ed. Henry Mass.

"Words" 1956

The relation between language and our fate compares to knights upon the quest for truth.

"Words and the Word" 1968

In this essay Auden writes that man is both a member and an individual influenced within and without to the degree that society's collective subjectivity allows or disallows. Language follows accordingly: Names — functional/symbolic/influential. Auden: "We respond and obey before we summon and command." Knowing names makes people/things more real: You-feeling is attribution, I-feeling is responsibility. Every dialog is a feat of interpretive translation. Individuals: He/she does not lie, but a person's words may lie and since we initially ALL believe, a lie subverts humanity's trust in both people and language. Intimate language differs from social, but today the art of social conversation is lost, rendering all conversation as pseudo-intimate, ultimately banal, and false. The flood of books etc., to the masses makes them easily consumable as mind candy, but immemorable, thus, adding to the general dumbing-down and cultural illiteracy. With less ability to discern, readers are subject to the manipulation of language as advertising or worse, propaganda.

Poetry is unique in that it is not consumed by mass readers, but digested by choice; it is unique and speaks uniquely to each reader who, if not inclined to think, would otherwise read pabulum. Poetry is for persons who are analogy makers by instinct. A work of art has both permanence (longevity) and nowness (identifiable era).

Art: study of personal and chosen. Science: study of impersonal and necessity.

Man lives not by bread alone but for the word of God and God is the person to whom we speak/pray. We can hear God and we can come to God by choice, not fear. God is the word; words are not God. What God is cannot be described in words but only by intuition. Still poets try: "one might say that for truth the word silence is the least inadequate metaphor, and words can only bear witness to silence as shadows bear witness to light."

Christian poet is a recorder of what bears witnessing, but he is not a proselytizer by design; that aspect is residual. Ergo: the poet/artist cannot affect history only capture it and allow us subsequently to have "communion with the dead," without which "fully human life is impossible."

Wordsworth, William

1770–1850. One of the great English poets, he was a leader of the Romantic Movement in England. The spirit of the French Revolution had strongly influenced Wordsworth, and he returned (1792) to England imbued with the principles of Rousseau and republicanism. Wordsworth became the intimate friend of Samuel Taylor Coleridge and, probably under his influence, a student of David Hartley's empiricist philosophy. Together the two poets wrote *Lyrical Ballads* (1798), in which they sought to use the language of ordinary people in poetry; it included Wordsworth's poem "Tintern Abbey." The work introduced Romanticism into England and became a manifesto for Romantic poets. A second edition of the *Lyrical Ballads* (1800) included a critical essay outlining Wordsworth's poetic principles, in particular his ideas about poetic diction and meter. *The Prelude*, his long autobiographical poem, was completed in 1805, though it was not published until after his death. His next collection, *Poems in Two Volumes* (1807), included the well-known "Ode to Duty," "Intimations of Immortality," and a number of famous sonnets. In 1843 he was named poet laureate.

Wordsworth was one of Auden's earliest models for his teenage verse. In a 1929 journal entry Auden writes that the "progress of man" includes "Wordworthian nature –worship…." Mendelson writes of this period that Auden's "theory of perception is virtually the same as Wordsworth's. His memories of past sensations give rise to feelings in the present" (*Later Auden*). Mendelson also observes that on the one hand in Auden's early (and late) verse he "denounced Wordsworthian nature-worship, but he also adopts a thoroughly Wordsworthian worship of a child ["This Lunar Beauty"]. It is a Wordsworthian technique also to compare the beautiful to a dream." In 1938 Auden, while writing about Byron, would say, "For Byron was not really odd like Wordsworth; his experiences were those of the ordinary man" implying that Wordsworth was not ordinary (*Fifteen Poets*). Of Auden's 1940 "New Year Letter" Mendelson notes that it is a "modern epic of an international and psychological kind introduced by Goethe's *Faust* and Wordsworth's *The Prelude*" (*Later Auden*). In lectures that became Auden's 1949 *The Enchafèd Flood*, Auden borrows from Wordsworth's fifth book of *The Prelude* the symbolism of the stone and the shell. In the spring of 1973 he considered doing his own autobiographical *Prelude* but had only a sketch when he died that October.

Work, Carnival, Prayer

The third century theologian Irenaeus was the first to interpret the meaning of the body of Christ, and he gave Auden the impetus for his definitions. Work: the creative father. Carnival: the incarnate son. Prayer: the gift of tongues that marked the descent of the spirit. (*See also* "Epistle to a Godson.")

"The World of the Sagas" 1968

Auden refers to Tolkien in this essay, describing a primary world as the world that describes truth as a historian would, with apparent objectivity, as contrasted to a secondary world of the imagination within each individual or created by an artist.

The historian, while thinking he is objective, interprets "truth" through language, which is an analogy of facts rather than an imitation of facts. The historian chooses the words he will use in order to describe facts as he sees them, but his word choices are personal and they become a subjective interpretation of history that will be read be a reader who also subjectively interprets the words he reads. Hence, subjectivity is inevitable, and the truth of history is in the eye of the beholder.

While the historian may think he is objective when he isn't, the Artist knows he is subjectively distorting and that his spirit creates secondary worlds to counter dissatisfaction with the primary world in order to escape life, death, and limitations. This creation temporarily makes the artist feel omnipotent, omniscient, and in control rather than just an object of outside forces. He is able to escape from the strictly plausible to venture into the implausible.

With a saga an artist combines history, myth and poetry, but in a manner that recreates history and myth to give the artist some degree of control over the already known. In Homer's sagas the historical aspects sound like fiction to please a reader's preconception of heroic formulae, but Homer's poetic style predominates to heighten the mythical aspects.

Conversely, in Icelandic (Old Norse) literature the historian predominates and writes fiction that sounds historical by using a more journalistic rather than a poetic style. These realistic narratives and characters have ambiguities, which allow surprises. Icelanders were individual adventurers and aristocrats, choosing not to bow before a king. They were individualistic and independent in a rural democracy with no class distinctions or hierarchy of betters. This equality fostered realism. Their language was precise and consistent (i.e., not divided between court speech and vulgar speech). In a small, closed, homogeneous society, the writers can presume an audience knows the events and can focus more on characters' psyches via monologues and dialogues in verse with "prose gloss" added later to update subsequent generations.

Worsley, T.C.

British writer and teacher, in 1938 he

collaborated with Auden on a Hogarth Press pamphlet, *Education: Today and Tomorrow*.

Wright, Basil *see* Grierson, John

Wright, James *see* Yale Series of Younger Poets

"Writing" 1932

In this essay Auden sets out to give a complete theory not just of literature, but of writing in a wider sense. This theory is rooted in ideas about language, beginning with speech and moving through the following headings: Speech, Meaning, Language and Words, Inflection, Writing, Spoken and Written Language, Verse Forms, Different Kinds of Writing, Why people Write Books, How People Write Books, Why People Read Books, Books and Life.

Auden's attitude to language here shows signs of an interest in primitivism, anthropology and cultural phases. Language was, he argues, at first essentially expressive. It showed:

The feelings of the speaker; feelings about something happening to him (the prick of the pin), or attitudes towards other things in the world (the other hungry dog; the darling baby), or ... as a help to doing something of his own kind (pulling the boat in).

The last kind of co-operative expression is privileged by Auden: other animals can use the other two kinds of expression, but "the last is peculiar to the most highly organized." Auden argues from a variety of scientific examples that connection and co-operation are the world's natural state:

Nucleus and cell, cell and organ, organs and the human individual, individual and family, nation and world, always groups linked up with larger groups, each group unique, different from others, but without meaning except in its connections with the others.

(This sentence comes more or less directly from Gerald Heard's ideas.) However, humanity has fallen from this world of connections, with the growth of consciousness: "man became self-conscious; he began to feel, I am I, and you are not I; we are shut inside ourselves and apart from each other." Language grew as a "bridge over the gulf," a way of recovering wholeness. Some language is imitative (through onomatopoeia, for example), but most, says Auden, is not, a disconnectedness which paradoxically makes language work more authentically: "in fact, most of the power of words comes from their not being like what they stand for" (quoted in Mendelson, *English Auden*). By not corresponding simply to a single entity, language has more resonance — a space and applicability that the imagination must work on.

Writing develops from speech eventually, again motivated by "man's growing sense of personal loneliness, of the need for group communication." However, speech and writing are distinguished by different perceptions of loneliness:

while speech begins with the feeling of separateness in space, of I-here-in-this-chair and you-there-in that-chair, writing begins from the sense of separateness in time, of "I'm here today, but I shall be dead to-morrow, and you will be active in my place and how can I speak to you?"

This new mode of communication leads in due course to the recording of oral forms such as stories and also to the invention of new forms, particularly of record keeping and genres designed for more abstract kinds of knowledge. Printing leads to the wider dissemination of all kinds of written material, with, says Auden, mixed effects. He claims that vocabulary increases with print culture, so that language choices become more complex, resulting in poorer language use:

Education in the use of language becomes more and more necessary. At present nobody gets such an education. The speech of a peasant is generally better i.e. more vivid, better able to say what he wants to say, than the speech of the average University graduate.... It is not the language which is to blame, but our skill in using it.

Poetry is partly an antidote to this, as it restores

authenticity — particularly emotional effect — which has a collective impact on readers or hearers:

> When a poet is writing verse, the feeling, as it were, excites the words and makes them fall into a definite group, going through definite dancing movements, just as feeling excites the different members of a crowd and makes them act together.

Reading, whether of poetry or prose, widens experience and thus overcomes isolation. However, reading can ironically become a substitute for experience, it is dangerous: "when we get frightened of real people and find books safer company; they are a rehearsal for living, not living itself. Swots and 'bookish' people have stage fright." The essay ends with a section on "Books and Life" which develops this point much further and into an analysis of culture and society which returns to Auden's ideas about language and isolation. In a healthy society, there is a good deal of "common interest." Great writing particularly arises in societies that have this common purpose:

> Homer, Dante, and Shakespeare.... There is something common to all three: the small size of the society and the unity of interests. Whenever a society is united ... it has a great outburst of writing.... Being made one, like the sailors pulling the rope, it has all the power.

This resembles in some respects a Marxist cultural analysis (of the kind which began to be developed by British leftists a little later into the decade, particularly after the Soviet Writers' Congress of 1934). It has something of the same concerns: how are culture and society related, and how can historical change help us to understand their relations? Though the term "ideology" is not used, perhaps the idea is that Homer, Dante and Shakespeare were able to express the concerns of their societies in ways that did authentically represent at least some of the interests of all classes in that culture.

Now, however, there is a social fragmentation that makes it difficult for writers to represent anything like social reality successfully. Indeed, there is an overproduction of writing which is a hysterical response to its own current ineffectiveness:

> But whenever society breaks up into classes, sects, townspeople and peasants, rich and poor, literature suffers. There is writing for the gentle and writing for the simple, for the highbrow and for the lowbrow; the latter gets cruder and coarse, the former more and more refined. And so, today, writing gets shut up in a circle of clever people writing about themselves for themselves, or ekes out an underworld existence, cheap and nasty. Talent does not die out, but it can't make itself understood. Since the underlying reason for writing is to bridge the gulf between one person and another, as the sense of loneliness increases, more and more books are written by more and more people, most of them with little or no talent. Forests are cut down, rivers of ink absorbed, but the lust to write is still unsatisfied. What is going to happen? If it were only a question of writing, it wouldn't matter; but it is an index of our health. It's not only our books, but our lives, that are going to pot.

In *Early Auden* Mendelson suggests that Auden's "complaint is political only in the broadest terms" and that "where the rest of the book advocates a practical communism, Auden's essay implies the fraternal visionary communism (or collective consciousness) he was imagining in some of his writings at this time." But, in fact, the idealism is not that unusual for thirties cultural analysis and nor are the broad and wide social perspectives of the piece. However, the interest in language is distinctive. Certainly, it is a serious and interesting essay expressed in very clear terms. — CHRISTOPHER HOPKINS (*See also* Heard, Gerald; Mitchison, Naomi; Writing, Auden on.)

Writing, Auden on

Auden: "To me writing is the enjoyment of the living" (1929 Journal).

Auden: "Of the many definitions of poetry, the simplest is still the best: 'memorable speech': That is to say, it must move our emotions, or excite our intellect, for only that which is moving or exciting is memorable, and the stimulus is the audible spoken word and cadence, to which in all its power of suggestion and incantation we must surrender, as we do when talking to an intimate friend" (Introduction to *The Poet's Tongue*).

The writer as poet/teacher is a role that for Auden, in part, is "a mixture of spy and gossip." The poet/teacher tells the listener/pupil news which amuses (in its literal meaning of "occupying pleasingly"), so that the listener will want to hear more in the future and reinvite the teller back. A poet who hopes to be listened to again learns that he must say something relevant and understandable, and even better, entertaining, if it is to please the listener and retain both his good will and a key to the cave door. According to Aldous Huxley, "Artists are eminently teachable and also eminently teachers. They receive from events much more than most men receive, and they can transmit what they received with particular penetrative force, which drives their communication deep into the reader's mind. One of our most ordinary reactions to a good piece of literary art is expressed in the formula: 'This is what I have always felt and thought, but have never been able to put clearly into words, even for myself'" ("Tragedy and the Whole Truth").

This is similar to Auden's remark that "the reaction one hopes for from a poem is that the reader will say, 'Of course, I've always known that, but I've never realized it before'" ("Interview with W.H. Auden," *Antaeus*, spring 1972). There must be a relevant connection in a poem that relates it to its readers. The poet either intimates to his audience something they already have at least a remote familiarity with, even if it is deeply subconscious, or he will lose them.

There have always been two views of the poet and his writing process. The poet is sometimes possessed, sometimes a diligent craftsperson and maker. Usually the process is not either/or, but combines both into an inspired maker. This may be somewhat contrary to what the public would like to believe, that art is a gift transmitted by a muse, and hence, is easy, leisurely play rather than work. Their envy is thus constituted: the public, through art, subconsciously wishes to have a peaceful moment, however fleeting, in their inner Eden that has

been intimated for them by the art's Awesociations. The effect provides temporary escape from their earth-bound existence. To carry this psychic correlation further, the public wishes to think that the cause of this transcendental moment, the art, certainly must have been derived by the artist from inspired play rather than work, which is what they themselves are trying to forget about and in no way be reminded of. All people wish their work could also be play and, through the artist's art, enjoy this possibility vicariously.

Auden continues to explain that even in a secondary world, one must constitute it from what can be referenced in the existing primary world. "Even the purest poem, in the French sense, is made up of words, which are not the poet's private property, but the communal creation of the linguistic group to which he belongs, so that the meaning can be looked up in the dictionary." Moreover, he said:

"I discovered that, this was a game.... No game can be played without rules. A secondary world must be as much as a world of law as the primary. I instinctively felt that I must impose two restrictions upon my freedom of fantasy. I was free to select this and reject that, on one condition, that both were real objects in the primary world.

"What the poet has to convey is not "self-expression," but a view of reality common to us all, seen from a unique perspective, which it is his duty, as well as his pleasure to share with others" ("Writing," *A Certain World*).

While it may be play for the artist to create art, it is rarely easy. Writing poetry is not something that is completed in an effortless trance. Art is inspiration, at least to get started; then, it is sustained by effort, care and perseverance as a craft, in the tradition of the craftsmen of another time. In fact, Auden preferred "...not the word 'poet' but the word that medieval people used, which was really a direct translation of the Greek: they [were] 'Makers,' like carpenters [making a] verbal object ... like a table ... [that's] intended to last" ("Interview with W.H. Auden," Antaeus). Poets were artists; long-ago craftsmen were artisans. Both groups took aesthetic pride in the outcome of their work.

For Auden, the sincere writer writes to

please himself while finding a universal message that can also please an audience: "Poetry is not concerned with telling people what to do, but with extending our knowledge of good and evil, perhaps making the necessity of action more urgent and its nature more clear, but only leading us to the point where it is possible for us to make a rational and moral choice" ("The Poet's Tongue"). (*See also* Heard, Gerald; Mitchison, Naomi; Writing.)

Wystan

Auden's first name was selected to reflect George Auden's interest in Old Norse and Old English literature and history. When George Auden attended Repton School in his youth he learned that the Derbyshire parish church was named after St. Wystan, a prince murdered in 849 after he protested the marriage of his uncle to his widowed mother. Wystan Auden noted the *Hamlet* correlation.

George's son Wystan loved his name.

Yale Series of Younger Poets

From 1947 to 1959 Auden was the editor of this series, which entailed selecting one poet a year and writing an introduction to the volume. He succeeded Stephen Vincent Benét, who died in 1943. The first work published under Auden was *Poems* by Joan Murray, a former student of Auden's, who died at age 25 and her book was posthumously published; next were the works of Robert Horan, Rosalie Moore, Adrienne Rich, W.S. Merwin, Edgar Bogardus, Daniel Hoffman, John Ashberry, James Wright, John Hollander, and William Dickey.

Yeats, William Butler

1865–1939, Irish poet and playwright, b. Dublin, son of the painter John Butler Yeats. Yeats was one of the major figures of modern poetry, and a leader of the Irish literary renaissance. He became fascinated by Irish legends and the occult. His first work, the drama *Mosada* (1886), reflects his concern with magic,

W.B. Yeats

but the long poems in *The Wanderings of Oisin* (1889) voiced the nationalism of the Young Ireland movement.

Yeats's verse from 1886 to about 1900 is influenced by mystical Irish mythology. He edited William Blake's works in 1893, and his own *Poems* were collected in 1895. In 1898, with Lady Augusta Gregory, George Moore, and Edward Martyn, he founded the *Irish Literary Theatre in Dublin*; their first production (1889) was Yeats's *The Countess Cathleen* (written 1889–92), and later his plays *The Hour Glass* (1904), *The Land of Heart's Desire* (1904), and *Deirdre* (1907). Yeats's fiction is collected in *The Celtic Twilight* (1893) and in the *Secret Rose* (1897).

In the verse of his middle and late years, a recurring theme is the polarity between extremes such as the physical and the spiritual, the real and the imagined, which he called "aintinomies" an idea based on Vedanta's reconciliation of opposites (see also Lewis, Cecil Day). Poems from this period include "The Second Coming," "The Tower," and "Sailing to Byzantium." Yeats's second period began with such volumes as *In the Seven Woods* (1903) and *The Green Helmet* and *Other Poems* (1910). In 1917 he married Georglie Hyde-Lees. His prose work *A Vision* (1937; privately printed 1926) is the basis of much of his poetry in *The Wild Swans at Coole* (1917) and *Four Plays for Dancers* (1921).

Yeats became a member (1922–28) of the Irish senate, and winner of the 1923 Nobel Prize in Literature. Some of his best verse was his last, as shown in *The Tower* (1928) and *Last Poems* (1940).

While Eliot's *The Waste Land* (1922) changed modern poetry and the poets who followed, Yeats still cast a long and influential shadow over Auden's generation. That Auden read Yeats early is indicated in his notebook of 1929 and this reading seems to have included verse and prose, art and theory. Yet, Shelley influenced Yeats, and Auden could not tolerate Shelley and saw some of Shelley's floridity and self-aggrandizement in Yeats. In the 1930s, Mendelson notes, Auden did not wish to look for happiness in Yeats's mystical (and fictional) "Byzantium," but in something more immediate and concrete — whatever that might be. However, by 1933 Auden wished to admire and emulate Yeats the activist, if not Yeats's style and symbolic choices. Yeats, via Lady Gregory via Aristotle, believed the poet should think like a wise man, but express himself like the common people. Auden agreed. Yet, as Mendelson writes of this period, "The more closely Auden followed Yeats's example, the more he contradicted his own beliefs.... When Auden tried to adapt Yeats's voice to a poetry that included both personal psychology and political history, but not as secondary expressions of a lunar cycle, he found himself inventing imaginary beings of his own," but not too well and not to his satisfaction" (*Early Auden*). By 1939, Auden had abandoned Yeats and written a number of poems that rejected mystical polemicism, including "In Memory of W.B. Yeats" (below). Nonetheless, after his conversion to Auden's Christianity, Auden would make a sea change again and also seek a Yeatsian Byzantium but instead call it "The Good Life" or "The City of God." In sum, the older Auden became, the more he became indulgent of artists with oversized egos that he called "monsters" as if they could not help themselves; this included Yeats, Ezra Pound, and Wagner, whom Auden believed may not have been the best human beings, but should never be denied their credit as artists. Auden wrote a poem and two essays about Yeats.

The poem, "In Memory of W.B. Yeats" (1939), shows that Auden admired William Butler Yeats in general but not absolutely. In this poem Auden evaluates Yeats and himself as two poets who struggle with how to use their gifts, which in Auden's Christianity come from God. Auden questions Yeats' later dissolution into pride and pomposity as a corruption of his gift, but feels that the later Yeats should not obscure the greatness of the earlier Yeats before he was corrupted. The poem begins with the observation that the most a poet can hope to achieve is that his verse be remembered, even if by a few. The poem ends, conversely, with Auden giving the poet credit for using language that can transform and elevate readers. While the poem's end constitutes Auden's final message, this poem still concerns Auden's late 1930s internal debate as to whether poetry can change anything in a socio-political world. (*See also* "The Duet.")

In the first of the essays, "The Public v. the Late William Butler Yeats" (1939), Auden writes that sincerity, sympathy, and passion are the keys to poetic expression. These attributes suit the poet as long as he keeps them in their proper perspective, which is to apply them to his poems for the intended purpose of saying what the poet genuinely feels, not what others might want to hear. As for passionate enthusiasm, Auden said bemusedly of the poetic muse in general, "All poets adore explosions, thunderstorms, tornadoes, conflagrations, ruins, scenes of spectacular carnage. The poetic imagination is therefore not at all a desirable quality in a chief of state" ("Squares and Oblongs"). Auden here alludes to his post-1939 conversion, in that a poet should not take an active role in politics and should confine his passion to his art. In "The Public v. the Late William Butler Yeats," Auden, in his eulogy to Yeats in the guise of a trial judging whether or not Yeats deserves to be remembered as a great poet, also states his own personal case for defining what the role of any poet should be in his society. After a thorough roasting of Yeats by the "prosecution" here speaks the counsel for the defense (Auden):

Take away the frills, and the argument of the prosecution is reduced to this: "A great poet must give the right answers to the problems which perplex his generation. The deceased gave the wrong answers. Therefore the deceased was not a great poet." We are tempted so to judge contemporary poets because we really do have problems which we really do want solved, and to blame them indiscriminately if they do not.

Auden does not suggest that an artist is not part of or should not react to society; he maintains that he is a recorder, a mirror, not a social worker. His role is not to give advice per se, but to share his passion from which readers might learn indirectly.

Poetic talent, in fact, is the power to make personal excitement socially available. Now when we turn to the deceased, we are confronted by the amazing spectacle of a man of great poetic talent, whose capacity for excitement not only remained with him until the end, but actually increased. The heroes and the fairies of the early work were an attempt to find through folk tradition the binding force for society; and the doctrine of Anima Mundi [world mind] found in the later poems is the same thing in a more developed form, which has left purely local peculiarities behind, in favour of something that the deceased hoped was universal; in other words, he was looking for a world religion... there is one field in which the poet is a man of action, the field of language, and it is precisely in this that the greatness of the deceased is most obviously shown. The diction of The Winding Stair is the diction of a just man, and it is for this reason that just men will always recognise the author as a master.

"Just men" will also recognize that any great poet, as was Yeats and his later predilection for the *Anima Mundi*, is actually a Perennial Philosophist, intimating Awe-sociations within the numinous and sacred territory of the Divine Ground.

"Yeats as an Example" (1948) is the second of the essays. Auden writes that a poet reading another poet is victim to judging a poem less by its actual merit and content, and more by what he can steal. Young poets overadmire those whom they feel kin to and will tend to imitate. After finding his way the young poet may reject those he has imitated with contempt. A poet's "duty to the present" is neither to copy nor deny the past, but resurrect it. Yeats should be judged by his approach to poetics and if his problems are the same or not the same as those of his audience. His cosmology, *A Vision*, is gone without a trace. Why was he attracted to the occult as those in California are? (Here Auden disparages Isherwood and Vedanta, which in large part was due to Auden resenting that Isherwood left for California, when, in fact, both sought and found the same "occultism" — really mysticism — but from different directions: Isherwood East, Auden West. Since all mysticism originated in the East, and then made its way West, Auden was not really so different at all.)

Auden then asks concerning Yeats; "What is the relationship of myth, belief, and poetry?" Yeats's conflict was one of reason vs. imagination, objective vs. subjective, universal vs. individual, with reason winning and artists becoming a vocal minority, zealous in their own defense. Now we know that science (reason) hasn't solved humanity's problems. There is good vs. evil, integration vs. alienation. An argument now seeks not empirical evidence but ulterior motives. The lack of real community has a public of alienated passive anarchists by disassociation. A poet may deny dogma but lives for myth, which is dogma aggrandized, in order to reach emotions. Yeats chose Celtic myths from his childhood, but as a modern cut off from tradition. He could only find coherence, not from the disassociated community, but from his intuition. Yeats's choices make him a major poet, one who developed over a body of work, a technique that is his own, evocative, but not imitative of tradition. He transformed the occasional poem into serious, personalized art, and released regular stanzas from iambic monotony. Yeats is both for his time and for posterity.

"You" 1960

The "you" addressed is the curse of sexual urges.

Bibliography

*Primary sources are grouped by type
and listed chronologically within their group.*

Primary Sources

POEMS

Poems. S.H. S[pender]., 1928. Auden's privately printed first book, of which only about 30 copies were made on a hand-press by his friend Stephen Spender and given to friends of the author. (Facsimile edition available from Books on Demand.)

Poems. Faber, 1930; 2nd edition, 1933. (The Random House edition, 1934, includes *The Orators* and *The Dance of Death*.)

The Orators. Faber, 1930; 2nd edition: 1934; 3rd edition, 1966. Random House, 1967.

On This Island. (British title: *Look, Stranger!*) Faber, 1936; reprint, 2001. Random House, 1937.

Spain. Faber, 1937. (Also in *Another Time*.)

Another Time. Faber and Random House, 1940.

The Double Man. (British title: *New Year Letter*.) Random House and Faber, 1941.

For the Time Being. Random House, 1944; Faber, 1945.

The Collected Poetry of W.H. Auden. Random House, 1945. (Includes new poems from 1941 to 1944.)

The Age of Anxiety. Random House, 1947. Faber, 1948.

Collected Shorter Poems, 1930–1944. Faber, 1950. (Similar to *The Collected Poetry,* above.)

Nones. Random House, 1951. Faber, 1952.

The Shield of Achilles. Random House and Faber, 1955.

Homage to Clio. Random House and Faber, 1960.

About the House. Random House, 1965, Faber, 1966.

Collected Shorter Poems 1927–1957. Faber, 1966. Random House, 1967.

Collected Longer Poems. Faber, 1968. Random House, 1969.

City Without Walls. Faber, 1969. Random House, 1970.

Epistle to a Godson. Faber and Random House, 1972.

Thank You, Fog. Faber and Random House, 1974.

Collected Poems. Faber and Random House, 1976.

PLAYS

The Dance of Death. Faber, 1933.

The Dog Beneath the Skin. With Christopher Isherwood. Faber and Random House, 1935.

The Ascent of F6. With Christopher Isherwood. Faber, 1936; 2nd edition: 1936. Random House, 1936.

285

On the Frontier. With Christopher Isherwood. Faber, 1938. Random House, 1939.

Collected Plays and Other Dramatic Writings. Princeton: Princeton University Press, 1989.

OPERA LIBRETTI

Paul Bunyan. Music by Benjamin Britten. 1941.

The Rake's Progress. With Chester Kallman. Music by Igor Stravinsky. 1951.

Elegy for Young Lovers. With Chester Kallman. Music by Hans Werner Henze. 1961.

Auden and Kallman translated Mozart's *The Magic Flute* (1956) and Don Giovanni (1961), and Goldoni's *Arcifanfaro, King of Fools*, as set by Dittersdorf (1962).

The Bassarids. With Chester Kallman. Music by Hans Werner Henze. 1966.

Collected Libretti and Other Dramatic Writings. Princeton University Press, 1993.

TRAVEL BOOKS
IN PROSE AND VERSE

Letters from Iceland. With Louis MacNeice. Faber and Random House, 1937; 2nd edition, Faber, 1967, Random House, 1969.

Journey to a War. With Christopher Isherwood. Faber and Random House, 1939; 2nd edition, Faber, 1973.

PROSE

The Enchafèd Flood. Random House, 1950. Faber, 1951.

The Dyer's Hand. Random House, 1962, Faber, 1963.

Secondary Worlds. Faber and Random House, 1969.

A Certain World: A Commonplace Book. Viking and Faber, 1970.

Forewords and Afterwords. Random House and Faber, 1973.

The Prolific and the Devourer. (Written in 1939.) Ecco Press, 1993.

Collected Prose, Volume I. Princeton University Press, 1996.

Lectures on Shakespeare. Reconstructed and edited by Arthur Kirsch. Princeton University Press and Faber, 2001.

Collected Prose, Volume I. Princeton University Press, 1998.

OTHER COLLECTED WORKS

The Map of All My Youth: Early Works, Friends and Influences. (Auden Studies, Vol. 1). Ed. Katherine Bucknell and Nicholas Jenkins. Oxford and New York: Oxford University Press, 1990.

The Language of Learning and the Language of Love: Uncollected Writing, New Interpretations. (Auden Studies, Vol. 2). Ed. Katherine Bucknell and Nicholas Jenkins. Oxford and New York: Oxford University Press, 1994.

In Solitude, for Company: W.H. Auden After 1940: Unpublished Prose and Recent Criticism. (Auden Studies, Vol. 3). Ed. Katherine Bucknell and Nicholas Jenkins. Oxford and New York: Oxford University Press, 1996.

Secondary Sources: Biography and Criticism

Bryant, Marsha. *Auden and Documentary in the 1930s*. Charlottesville: University Press of Virginia, 1997.

Carpenter, Humphrey. *W.H. Auden: A Biography*. London: George Allen & Unwin; Boston: Houghton Mifflin, 1981.

Davenport-Hines, Richard. *Auden*. London: Heinemann, 1995; New York: Pantheon, 1996.

Emig, Rainer. *W.H. Auden: Towards a Postmodern Poetics*. London: Macmillan, 1999.

Firchow, Peter Edgerly. *W.H. Auden: Contexts for Poetry*. Newark: University of Delaware Press, 2002.

Hall, Harriet. *Bill and Patience*. Lewes, Sussex: The Book Guild, 2000. A biography of Harriet Hall's parents, with extensive quotations from letters from Auden to Bill and Patience McElwee, whom he met at Oxford.

Hecht, Anthony. *The Hidden Law: The Poetry of W.H. Auden*. Cambridge, Mass.: Harvard University Press, 1993.

Hendon, Paul, ed. *The Poetry of W.H. Auden: A Reader's Guide to Essential Criticism*. Cambridge, England: Icon Books, April 2000. (An American edition will be published by Columbia University Press.)

Henze, Hans Werner. *Bohemian Fifths: An Autobiography*. London: Faber & Faber, 1998; Princeton: Princeton University Press, 1999.

(Includes many details about Henze's collaborations with Auden and Kallman.)

Izzo, David Garrett. *Aldous Huxley and W.H. Auden on Language*. W. Cornwall, Ct.: Locust Hill Press, 1998.

_____. *Christopher Isherwood: His Era, His Gang, and the Legacy of the Truly Strong Man*. (Columbia: South Carolina University Press, 2001.)

_____, ed. *Advocates and Activists 1919–1941: Men and Women Who Shaped the Period Between the Wars*. W. Cornwall, Ct.: Locust Hill Press, 2003. (Includes essays on John Grierson, Naomi Mitchison, and Michael Roberts.)

_____, ed. *W.H. Auden: A Legacy*. W. Cornwall, Ct.: Locust Hill Press, 2002. (Includes 27 essays on all aspects of Auden's life and work.)

Jacobs, Alan. *What Became of Wystan: Change and Continuity in Auden's Poetry*. Fayetteville: University of Arkansas Press, 1998.

Mendelson, Edward. *Early Auden*. London: Faber & Faber, 1999; New York: Straus, Farrar, & Giroux, 2000. (Revised paperback reprint of book first published in 1981.)

_____. *Later Auden*. New York: Farrar, Straus & Giroux, 1999; London: Faber & Faber, 1999.

Mitchell, Donald. *Britten and Auden in the Thirties: The Year 1936*. Woodbridge, Suffolk: Boydell, 2000 (reprint of 1981 edition).

Myers, Alan, and Robert Forsythe. *W.H. Auden: Pennine Poet*. Nenthead: North Pennines Heritage Trust, 1999. (Contains two papers: "W.H. Auden and the North" by Alan Myers, and "Auden's Pennine Names" by Robert Forsythe. The latter paper is an analysis of the place names from the area as used in Auden's work, with Ordnance Survey map references and a map showing many of the names.)

Page, Norman. *Auden and Isherwood: The Berlin Years*. London: Macmillan, October 1998; paperback, March 2002. New York: St. Martin's Press, October 1998; paperback, March 2000.

Smith, Stan. *W.H. Auden*. Plymouth: Northcote House, in association with the British Council, 1997 (Writers and Their Work). Distributed in the U.S. by the University Press of Mississippi.

Tabachnick, Stephen E. *Fiercer than Tigers: The Life and Works of Rex Warner*. East Lansing: Michigan State University Press, 2002. (The first biography of Warner, who was Auden's Oxford classmate and friend).

Wright, George T. *W.H. Auden*. Revised edition. Boston: Twayne, 1981.

Index